EIGHTH EDITION

TEACHING STRATEGIES FOR ETHNIC STUDIES

JAMES A. BANKS

University of Washington, Seattle

PEARSON

Boston • New York • San Francisco
Mexico City • Montreal • Toronto • London • Madrid • Munich • Paris
Hong Kong • Singapore • Tokyo • Cape Town • Sydney

KH

Series Editor: *Kelly Villella Canton*
Editorial Assistant: *Christine Pratt Swayne*
Marketing Manager: *Krista Clark*
Production Editor: *Gregory Erb*
Editorial Production Service: *Trinity Publishers Services*
Composition Buyer: *Linda Cox*
Manufacturing Buyer: *Linda Morris*
Electronic Composition: *Omegatype Typography, Inc.*
Cover Designer: *Kristina Mose-Libon*

For related titles and support materials, visit our online catalog at www.ablongman.com.

Between the time website information is gathered and then published, it is not unusual for some sites to have closed. Also, the transcription of URLs can result in typographical errors. The publisher would appreciate notification where these errors occur so that they may be corrected in subsequent editions.

ISBN-10: 0-205-59427-1
ISBN-13: 978-0-205-59427-6

Library of Congress Cataloging-in-Publication Data

Banks, James A.
    Teaching strategies for ethnic studies / James A. Banks.—8th ed.
        p. cm.
    Includes bibliographical references and index.
    ISBN 0-205-59427-1 (pbk.)
    1. Minorities—United States—Study and teaching.   2. Ethnicity—Study and teaching—United States.   3. Pluralism (Social sciences)—Study and teaching—United States.   4. Multiculturalism—Study and teaching—United States.
    5. United States—Ethnic relations—Study and teaching.   I. Title.
    E184.A1B24 2008
    305.8'0071073—dc22   2007038639

Printed in the United States of America

10 9 8 7 6 5 4 3 2   RRD-VA   12 11 10 09 08

10/10/10

To the memory of
Robert L. Banks (July 10, 1931–November 26, 1981)
my brother
who shared my dream for a better world
and to Cherry, Angela, and Patricia,
my family

THE AUTHOR

James A. Banks is Kerry and Linda Killinger Professor of Diversity Studies and director of the Center for Multicultural Education at the University of Washington, Seattle (http://depts.washington.edu/centerme/home.htm). He is a past president of the American Educational Research Association (AERA) and a past president of the National Council for the Social Studies (NCSS). Professor Banks is a specialist in social studies education and in multicultural education, and has written more than 100 articles and written or edited 20 books in these fields. His books include *Diversity and Citizenship Education: Global Perspectives; Cultural Diversity and Education: Foundations, Curriculum and Teaching; Educating Citizens in a Multicultural Society; and Race, Culture, and Education: The Selected Works of James A. Banks.* Professor Banks is the editor of the *Handbook of Research on Multicultural Education* (Jossey-Bass) and the "Multicultural Education Series" of books published by Teachers College Press, Columbia University.

Professor Banks holds honorary doctorates from six colleges and universities, including Bank Street College of Education, DePaul University, the University of Alaska, and Grinnell College. He received the UCLA Medal from the University of California, Los Angeles, in 2005, the university's highest honor. AERA honored Professor Banks with the Inaugural Social Justice Award in 2004 for a lifetime of research that advances social justice. Professor Banks has been a fellow at the Center for Advanced Study in the Behavioral Sciences at Stanford and is a member of the National Academy of Education. He was the Tisch Distinguished Visiting Professor at Teachers College, Columbia University, in fall 2007.

BRIEF CONTENTS

CONTENTS

▪ ▪ ▪ ▪ ▪ ▬▬▬▬▬▬▬▬▬▬▬▬▬▬▬▬▬▬▬▬▬▬▬▬▬▬▬

CHAPTER THREE
Key Concepts for the Multicultural Curriculum   55

CHAPTER FOUR
Planning the Multicultural Curriculum   89

PART II   THE FIRST AMERICANS AND AFRICAN AMERICANS: CONCEPTS AND STRATEGIES   117

CHAPTER FIVE

American Indians: Concepts, Strategies, and Materials   119

CHAPTER SIX

Native Hawai'ians:
Concepts, Strategies, and Materials   159

CHAPTER SEVEN

African Americans: Concepts, Strategies,
and Materials   187

PART III   EUROPEAN AMERICANS:
CONCEPTS AND STRATEGIES   231

CHAPTER EIGHT

European Ethnic Groups:
Concepts, Strategies, and Materials   233

SPANIARDS IN THE AMERICAS   235

CHAPTER NINE
Jewish Americans: Concepts, Strategies, and Materials   267

CHAPTER ELEVEN

Puerto Ricans in the United States: Concepts, Strategies, and Materials   337

CHAPTER TWELVE

Cuban Americans: Concepts, Strategies, and Materials   365

CHAPTER FOURTEEN

Arab Americans: Concepts, Strategies, and Materials   445

Appendixes

PREFACE

World and national events since the publication of the last edition of this book have illuminated the enduring significance of race, ethnicity, culture, and language diversity in Western nations such as Canada, the United Kingdom, France, Germany, and the United States. The growth of mainstream White populations is near zero in most of the Western developed nations, caused both by worldwide immigration and by a higher birthrate among ethnic and cultural minorities. This is also the situation in the United States, where most of the population growth is among ethnic, racial, and language minority population groups (U.S. Census Bureau, 2006).

In 2006—for the first time in U.S. history—ethnic minorities or people of color in the United States topped 100 million, becoming one-third of the nation's population of just above 300 million (Population Reference Bureau, 2007). In the thirty-year period between 1973 and 2004, the percentage of students of color in U.S. public schools increased from 22% to 43%. If current trends continue, students of color might equal or exceed the percentage of White students in U.S. public schools within one or two decades. Students of color already exceed the number of White students in six states: California, Hawaii, Louisiana, Mississippi, New Mexico, and Texas (Dillon, 2006). Religious diversity is also increasing in U.S. society and in its public schools. Islam is now the fastest-growing religion in the United States as well as in several European nations, such as France and the United Kingdom (Cesari, 2004).

As racial, ethnic, and language diversity remains significant and deepens in the United States and around the world, nation-states are faced with the challenge of implementing public and educational policies that will balance unity and diversity. Unity without diversity results in cultural repression and hegemony, as happened in the former Soviet Union and in China during the Cultural Revolution. Diversity without unity leads to Balkanization and the fracturing of the nation-state, as took place in Iraq after 2003 as sectarian conflict and violence threatened the construction of a nation in which all ethnic and religious groups felt included and identified. Diversity and unity should coexist in a delicate balance in a democratic, multicultural nation-state.

The U.S. Supreme Court's 2007 decision that ruled that the desegregation plans in Seattle (Wash.) and Louisville (Ky.) were unconstitutional indicates how difficult it is for nations to make policies that balance unity and diversity and promote justice and equality as perceived by different groups. The Court's majority argued that its decision promoted a color-blind and just society. Many Americans felt that this decision was regressive and might turn back the gains that resulted from the *Brown v. Board of Education of Topeka* decision in 1954, the Court's historic decision that declared school racial segregation unconstitutional.

This eighth edition of *Teaching Strategies for Ethnic Studies* is designed to help teachers conceptualize, develop, and implement a democratic multicultural curriculum that respects and honors diversity as well as promotes national unity within the context of democracy and social justice. To help practicing educators actualize these goals, this book describes America's democratic ideals and achievements as well as its conflicts, struggles, and failures to create a just society for all Americans. The historical overviews of the various ethnic groups make it clear that while people from across the world come to the United States in search of their dreams, there is still much work to be done to close the gap between America's democratic ideals and the realities for most of its citizens. A major tenet of this book is that a multicultural curriculum can help students acquire the knowledge, values, and skills needed to act to make the United States and the world more just and humane.

This eighth edition reflects current and emerging events, concepts, perspectives, knowledge, and issues in ethnic studies and multicultural education. In this edition, I have updated the 2000 population statistics that appeared in the last edition by using statistical data from the American Community Survey of the U.S. Census Bureau (http://www.census.gov/acs/www/). The American Community Survey is a new nationwide survey that updates population trends and developments between the decennial censuses.

The bibliographies have also been extensively revised, reflecting the large number of high-quality materials and resources that have been published since the last edition. The rich resources and publications that now exist in ethnic studies and multicultural education are evidence of the growth and maturity of these fields.

Most of the books annotated in this eighth edition were not included in the previous edition. Readers of this edition can refer to previous editions for older but nonetheless important titles. Each of the chapters on the ethnic groups has been updated with new information and census data from the American Community Survey. Appendix B, which consists of websites for teaching about ethnic and cultural diversity, has been updated by the deletion of sites that no longer exist and the addition of new sites. Appendix C, which describes visual media for teaching about U.S. ethnic groups, has also been updated to incorporate new materials and to delete those that are no longer available.

Teaching Strategies for Ethnic Studies is divided into five parts. Chapters 1 through 4 in Part I present rationales, goals, and key concepts for incorporating ethnic content into the mainstream curriculum. The main goal of the multicultural curriculum, as described in Part I, is to help students develop the ability to make reflective decisions so that they can—with thoughtful action—influence their personal, social, and civic worlds and help make them more democratic and just. At the end of each of these chapters are (1) a summary section, (2) references, and (3) an annotated bibliography.

Parts II through V contain chapters on the major ethnic groups in the United States. These chapters contain (1) chronologies of key events, (2) historical overviews of groups, (3) teaching strategies for illustrative key concepts, (4) references, (5) annotated bibliographies for teachers, and (6) annotated bibliographies for elementary and secondary school students.

Recommended grade levels are designated for the student resources in the student bibliographies. Although the bibliographies are selective, no book is appropriate for all purposes and settings. You should examine each book carefully before assigning it to your students. The annotations can help in this screening process.

The appendixes are designed to help you obtain information and materials for classroom use. Appendix A is a chronology of key events in the history of ethnic groups in the United States. Appendix B describes websites for teaching about ethnic diversity. Appendix C annotates visual media, including DVDs and videotapes, suitable for teacher education and for student use. Appendix D lists the Carter G. Woodson Award books, selected annually by the National Council for the Social Studies. Appendix E cites twenty classic and landmark books in ethnic literature.

ACKNOWLEDGMENTS

I am grateful to a number of colleagues and friends for their help in the preparation of this edition of *Teaching Strategies for Ethnic Studies*. Carlos F. Diaz contributed Chapters 6 (Native Hawai'ians) and 12 (Cuban Americans). Jeffrey A. S. Moniz updated the bibliographies in Chapter 6 and provided insightful and helpful comments on this chapter that enabled the author to strengthen it. Jerome L. Ruderman is the original author of Chapter 9 (Jewish Americans); Hallie Esbin Rosen revised this chapter for the seventh and eighth editions. Paula Hajar wrote Chapter 14 (Arab Americans). John P. Hopkins, a graduate student at the University of Washington, coauthored the revision of Chapter 5 on American Indians.

I owe a special thanks to Dennis Rudnick and Yuhshi Lee, research assistants at the Center for Multicultural Education at the University of Washington. Dennis worked extensively with the statistical data from the American Community Survey and on the new tables and figures in this edition. Yuhshi Lee helped with the American Community Survey data and with the tables and figures. Amber M. Graber, a graduate student at the University of Washington, updated Appendix B. Amber and Cherry A. McGee Banks helped me to update Appendix C.

Sam L. Sebesta, my colleague at the University of Washington, helped me to identify recently published books to insert into Chapter 4 as examples of excellent children's books that deal with race and ethnicity. He also annotated a group of books from which I selected specific books to highlight in the chapter.

I was able to complete this edition in a timely way because of the help I received from two individuals who annotated most of the books for students and teachers. I am greatly indebted to Lyn Miller-Lachmann, editor of *Multicultural Review,* for annotating most of the children's books that appear in the chapters of Parts III through V. She also annotated some of the books for teachers. Amber M. Graber also annotated some of the books for students and teachers.

Many thanks go to the reviewers of this edition for their valuable feedback: Patrick C. Coggins, Stetson University; Antoinette Miranda, The Ohio State University; Joyce Nichols, University of West Florida; and Susan Precht, Lee College.

I wish to acknowledge the editorial assistance given by John and Evelyn Ward of Trinity Publishers Services with this edition. I am grateful to Cherry A. McGee Banks—my intellectual and spiritual partner—for over three decades of encouragement, caring, and intellectual support. Our daughters, Angela and Patricia—who are young college professors—give us hope for the future.

James A. Banks

REFERENCES

Cesari, J. (2004). *When Islam and Democracy Meet: Muslims in Europe and the United States*. New York: Pelgrave Macmillan.

Dillon, S. (2006, August 27). In Schools across the U.S., the Melting Pot Overflows. *New York Times,* pp. A7, A16.

Population Reference Bureau Web Update. (2007, May 18). *U.S. Population: The New Generation Gap*. Sent to author via prbmembers@LISTSERV.PRB.ORG. Posted on website http://www.prb.org.

U.S. Census Bureau. (2006). *Statistical Abstract of the United States: 2006* (125th ed.). Washington, D.C.: U.S. Government Printing Office.

GOALS, CONCEPTS, AND INSTRUCTIONAL PLANNING

Part I of this book discusses the basic instructional problems in teaching ethnic content and integrating it into the curriculum. Chapter 1 reviews some of the major trends in teaching ethnic content and argues for a need to expand the definition of ethnic studies and to include content about a range of ethnic groups in the multicultural curriculum. The problem of formulating goals for the multicultural curriculum and the interdisciplinary, conceptual approach to teaching are discussed in Chapter 2, in which I state that the major goal of the multicultural curriculum should be to help students develop decision-making skills so that they can become effective change agents in society.

To help students develop effective decision-making skills, the multicultural curriculum must help them master higher-level concepts and generalizations. Chapter 3 discusses key concepts that can be used to organize a sound multicultural curriculum. In Chapter 4, the final chapter in Part I, I discuss practical ways to plan, organize, and teach multicultural units and lessons. The actual steps to follow in order to gain the needed content background, identify key concepts and generalizations, and choose ethnic content are discussed. Valuing strategies and social action projects are also discussed in Chapter 4.

··· ·· ·

CHAPTER ONE

THE MULTICULTURAL CURRICULUM
Rationale, Trends, and Goals

This chapter describes the nature and complexity of ethnic diversity in U.S. society. It also discusses emerging demographic trends, current developments in multicultural education in U.S. schools, and the goals of a multicultural curriculum. An important goal of the multicultural curriculum is to help students view events, concepts, issues, and problems from diverse cultural and ethnic perspectives.

THE PERSISTENCE OF ETHNICITY IN AMERICAN SOCIETY

Americans have always held tightly to the idea that ethnic cultures would melt or vanish. Consequently, a strong assimilationist idea has dominated U.S. society since the British gained control of most American institutions early in the nation's history. The assimilationist idea envisions a society in which ethnicity and race are not important identities. Group identities and affiliations would be based primarily on such variables as social class, politics, education, and other interests. The assimilationist idea that has deeply influenced U.S. life is symbolized by the melting pot concept that was celebrated in Zangwill's play *The Melting Pot*, staged in New York City in 1908.

Even though the strong assimilationist idea in U.S. society contributed greatly to the making of one nation out of diverse ethnic and immigrant groups, it has not eradicated ethnic and cultural differences and is not likely to do so in the future. Ethnic differences persist in U.S. society for several important reasons. Discrimination prevents many individuals and groups with particular ethnic, racial, cultural, religious, and language characteristics from attaining full structural inclusion in U.S. society (Bhatia & Ritchie, 2006; Cesari, 2004; Tatum, 2007). Ethnic cultures and communities often help individuals satisfy important human needs (Portes & Rumbaut, 2001). Ethnicity also persists because of continuing immigration to the United States (Suárez-Orozco & Páez, 2002; U.S. Department of Homeland Security, 2007).

Immigration to the United States has increased markedly since the Immigration Reform Act, enacted in 1965, became effective in 1968. Most new immigrants are coming from Spanish-speaking Latin American nations and from Asia rather than from Europe, the continent from which most immigrants to the United States came before 1960. Between 2000 and 2006, 73% of the legal immigrants to the United States came from nations in Asia and Latin America, 15.5% came from Europe, and just over 6% came from Africa (U.S. Department of Homeland Security, 2007). Most Asian immigrants came from China, the Philippines, India, Vietnam, and Korea. Mexico, Guatemala, El Salvador, Nicaragua, and nations in the Caribbean were the leading sources of immigrants from the Americas (U.S. Department of Homeland Security, 2007). Figure 1.1 shows the percentage of immigrants that arrived in the United States, by decade and region of origin, from 1950 to 2006.

The population of ethnic groups of color is increasing at a much faster rate than is the general population. In 2006, about one out of every three U.S. residents was part of a group other than single-race non-Hispanic White—according to national estimates by race, Hispanic origin, and age by the U.S. Census Bureau. In 2006, the U.S. minority population topped 100 million, becoming 33% of the total U.S. population of 300 million (Population Reference Bureau, 2007; U.S. Census Bureau, 2006). If current demographic trends continue, the minority population is expected to make up about 38.7% of the U.S. population by 2020 and about 50% by 2050 (U.S. Census Bureau, 2004a). Figure 1.2 shows the U.S. population by race and Hispanic origin in 2000 and the projected population in 2020 and 2050.

The U.S. Hispanic population increased much faster than the rest of the population and other ethnic groups between 2000 and 2004. The U.S. Hispanic population accounted for 14% of the population in 2004, but 49.2% of the four-year population increase (Haub, 2006). The White non-Hispanic population, generally considered to be the majority population at 67%, accounted for only 18.5% of the nation's population increase between 2000 and 2004 (Haub, 2006). The rapid growth in the Hispanic population during this period—and the much slower rate of growth in the African American population—caused the Hispanic population to become slightly larger than the African American population (see Table 1.1). The rapid growth in the Hispanic population resulted from several factors, including a high rate of immigration from Latin America, a higher birthrate than other U.S. population groups, and a much younger population compared to other groups. Table 1.1 shows the population of the major ethnic groups in the United States in 1990, 2000, and 2005.

Although frequently done in the popular media, it is misleading to view Hispanics or Latinos as a single ethnic or cultural group because they speak the same language (Suárez-Orozco & Páez, 2002). Extensive cultural, ethnic, and racial differences exist both among and within the various Hispanic groups, such as those from Mexico, Cuba, Puerto Rico, El Salvador, the Dominican Republic, Colombia, and Venezuela. Most Hispanics view themselves as Mexicans, Puerto Ricans, or Cubans rather than as Hispanics.

The Asian American population increased more than 38% between 1990 and 2004, from 7.4 to 11.9 million. In 2005, U.S. residents who said they were Asian or

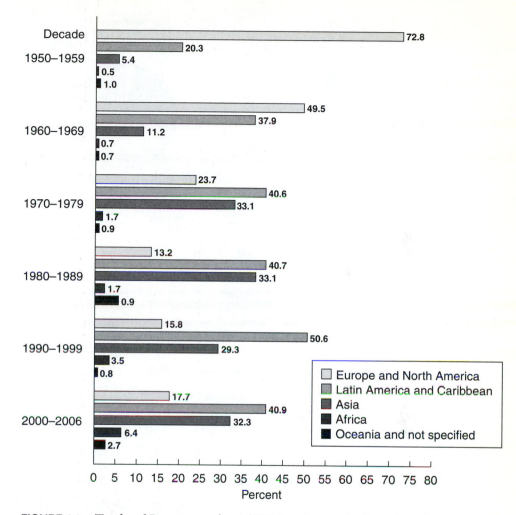

FIGURE 1.1   Total and Percentage of Legal U.S. Immigrants, by Decade and Region of Origin, 1950 to 2006

Source: U.S. Department of Homeland Security (2007), *Yearbook of Immigration Statistics: 2006,* table 2. Retrieved June 12, 2007, from http://www.dhs.gov/ximgtn/statistics/publications/LPR06.shtm.

Asian in combination with another race numbered 13.9 million, nearly 5% of the total population (U.S. Census Bureau, 2007a). By 2050, the Asian American population is projected to reach 33.4 million (U.S. Census Bureau, 2004b). Chinese Americans remain the largest group of Asian Americans and made up 23.4% (2,829,627) of Asian Americans in 2004. However, the Asian Indian population grew the most between 1990 and 2004, reaching 18.6% (2,245,239) of Asian Americans. Asian Indians have now surpassed Filipinos (17.8%, or 2,148,227) as the second largest Asian American group (U.S. Census Bureau, 2007a).

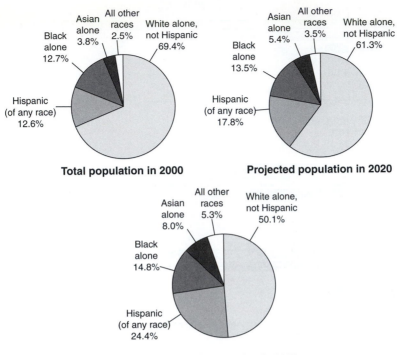

FIGURE 1.2   U.S. Population and Projected Population, 2000 to 2050

Source: U.S. Census Bureau (2004), "U.S. Interim Projections by Age, Sex, Race, and Hispanic Origin." Internet release date: March 18, 2004. Retrieved from http://www.census.gov/ipc/www/usinterimproj/.

The Demographic Imperative

The ethnic texture of the United States is changing substantially. The U.S. Census Bureau projects that ethnic minorities—including African Americans, American Indians and Alaska Natives, Asian and Pacific Islanders, and persons of Hispanic origin—will make up nearly 50% of the U.S. population by 2050 (U.S. Census Bureau, 2004a). The changing ethnic texture of the U.S. population has major implications for all of the nation's institutions, including schools, colleges, universities, and the workforce. These institutions must be restructured and transformed in order to meet the needs of the diverse groups who will work in and be served by them.

The demographic characteristics of the U.S. student population are also changing greatly. The percentage of White students in U.S. schools is gradually decreasing while the population of students of color is increasing. In 2004, 43% of public school students were students of color, an increase from 22% in 1972. In comparison, the percentage of public school students who were White decreased from 78% to 57% (U.S. Department of Education, 2006). The minority increase was largely

TABLE 1.1   Population of Ethnic Groups in the United States, 1990, 2000, and 2005

ETHNIC GROUP	1990 POPULATION	2000 POPULATION	2005 POPULATION
TOTAL	248,710,000	281,421,906	288,378,137
White Americans[a]	199,686,000	211,460,626	215,333,394
African Americans	29,986,060	34,658,190	34,962,569
Hispanics	22,354,000	35,305,818	41,870,703
Mexican Americans	13,496,000	20,640,711	26,781,547
Puerto Ricans	2,728,000	3,406,178	3,781,318
Cubans	1,044,000	1,241,685	1,461,574
Other Spanish Origin	5,086,000	10,017,244	9,846,265
Jewish Americans	5,981,000	6,000,000	6,452,030
American Indians	1,878,000	2,475,956[b]	2,357,544
Eskimos	57,000		51,577
Aleuts	24,000		13,557
Asians or Pacific Islanders	7,274,000	10,242,998[c]	12,471,815
Chinese Americans	1,645,000	2,432,585	2,797,966
Filipino Americans	1,407,000	1,850,314	2,282,872
Japanese Americans	848,000	796,700	833,761
Korean Americans	799,000	1,076,872	1,246,240
Asian Indians	815,000	1,678,765	2,319,222
Vietnamese, Americans	615,000	1,122,528	1,418,334
Native Hawai'ians and Pacific Islanders	211,000	140,652	397,030
Guamanians or Chamorros		58,240	76,062
Samoans		91,029	
Other Pacific Islanders		109,914	112,354

[a]This figure includes the 48% of Hispanics who classified themselves as White in the 2000 census.
[b]This figure for the 2000 census includes both American Indians and Alaskan Natives.
[c] This figure for the 2000 census includes Asian Americans only, not Pacific Islanders.

Sources: U.S. Census Bureau (2005), *2005 American Community Survey: Selected Population Profile.* Available online at http://factfinder.census.gov/servlet/IPCharIterationServlet?_ts=199301736409; D. Singer and L. Grossman (Eds.) (2006), *American Jewish Yearbook 2006.* Retrieved August 11, 2007, from http://www.jewishvirtuallibrary.org/jsource/US-Israel/usjewpop.html; U.S. Census Bureau (2001), *Profile of General Demographic Characteristics for the United States: 2000,* table DP-1. Available online at http://www.census.gov.

due to the growth in the proportion of Hispanic students. In 2004, Hispanic students represented 19% of public school enrollment, up from 6% in 1972. The proportion of African American and other students of color increased less during this period than the proportion of students who were Hispanic. African American students made up 16% of public school enrollment in 2004, compared with 15% in 1972. Hispanic enrollment surpassed African American enrollment for the first time in 2002. Asian/Pacific Islander (4%) and other minority groups (3%) made up 7% of public school enrollment in 2004, compared with 1% combined in 1972 (U.S. Department of Education, 2006).

The population of U.S. schools is coming increasingly from low-income families. The percentage of children in poverty increased from 16.2% in 1979 to 18.7% in 1998 (Terry, 2000). The overall poverty rate in the United States somewhat stabilized between 2000 and 2005. However, children under 18 still comprised a disproportionate percentage of people in poverty in 2005 (17.6%), compared to 18- to 64-year-olds (11.1%) and persons over the age of 65 (10.1%), and the overall poverty rate (12.6%) (Denavas-Walt, Proctor, & Lee, 2006).

American classrooms are experiencing the largest influx of immigrant students since the period from 1880 to 1924 (Matthews & Ewen, 2006). Most of these immigrants are coming from nations in Latin America and Asia. The children of immigrants—both foreign and U.S. born—are a growing percentage of the U.S. school population. The percentage of children in the U.S. school population who are children of immigrants tripled from 6% to 20% between 1970 and 2000. Their percentage will continue to expand, driven primarily by increases in the second generation. By 2015, children of immigrants are projected to make up 30% of the U.S. school population (Capps et al., 2004, p. 9).

A large but undetermined number of illegal or undocumented immigrants also enters the United States each year. In 2007, there were an estimated 12 million undocumented immigrants living in the United States ("Immigration Sabotage," 2007), which was one of the important causes of the polarized debate over the proposed immigration bill that took place in the Senate and House of Representatives during the spring and summer of 2007.

The influence of an increasingly ethnically diverse population on U.S. schools, colleges, and universities is, and will continue to be, enormous. In 2004, students of color comprised 43% of the student population (Dillon, 2006). In some of the nation's largest cities and metropolitan areas—such as Chicago, Los Angeles, Washington, D.C., New York, Seattle, and San Francisco—half or more of the public school students are students of color. Although students of color made of 43% of the total school population in 2004, they were distributed unevenly throughout the nation. In 2004, students of color were majorities in six states: California, Hawaii, Louisiana, Mississippi, New Mexico, and Texas (Dillon, 2006). Most teachers now in the classroom or in teacher educational programs are likely to have students from diverse racial, ethnic, cultural, and language groups in their classrooms during their careers. This is true for both inner-city and suburban teachers.

A major goal of multicultural education is to transform the challenges of racial, ethnic, cultural, and language diversity into educational and societal opportunities. To reach this goal, teachers will need to acquire new knowledge, skills, and attitudes. A major goal of this book is to help teachers to acquire the knowledge and skills needed to function effectively in multicultural classrooms and schools.

Diversity: An Opportunity and a Challenge

The cultural, ethnic, racial, and language diversity that the United States and other Western nations are experiencing is both an opportunity and a challenge to their schools, colleges, and universities. In addition to its racial, ethnic, and language diversity, the new immigration since 1968 has made the United States the "most religiously diverse nation on earth" (Eck, 2001). Buddhists, Hindus, Muslims, and Zoroastrians are now significant groups in the United States. The Council on American-Islamic Relations (2007) estimates that about 20,000 Americans convert to Islam each year. The new religious diversity within the United States poses new challenges to the nation's motto, *e pluribus unum*, and to the important phrase that begins the Constitution, "We, the people of the United States." "The people," as Eck insightfully points out, are not just Christian, but are religiously quite diverse. Consequently, when the issue of religion in the schools is raised, educators must ask, "Whose religion?" This important question seems to have eluded the many Americans who think of religion in the United States as primarily Christian.

When groups with different religions, cultures, and languages interact within a society, ethnocentrism and religious bigotry as well as other forms of institutionalized rejection and hostility usually occur. Ample examples of these forms of group hostility and rejection exist in every nation characterized by racial, cultural, and religious diversity (Banks, 2004; Eck, 2001; Fredrickson, 2002; Luchtenberg, 2004). In several nation-states throughout the world—including the United States, the United Kingdom, and Germany—the incidence of bigoted attacks on ethnic and cultural minorities increased during the late 1980s and early 1990s (Schierup, Hansen, & Castles, 2006; Solomos, 2003). Some observers link the increase in overt bigotry to the serious economic transformations that are occurring in Western nations.

Ethnic, cultural, language, and religious diversity is also an opportunity. It can enrich a society by providing novel ways to view events and situations, to solve problems, and to view our relationship with the environment and with other creatures. The exploitation of the environment is a serious problem in most developed nations, partly because of how Westerners have traditionally viewed their relationship with the earth. Traditional Indian cultures in North America viewed the earth as sacred and had deep reverence for other living creatures (Grim, 2001; Mann, 2005).

The challenge to Western societies and their schools is to try to shape a modernized, national culture that has selected aspects of traditional cultures coexisting in some kind of delicate balance with a modernized postindustrial society. In the past, in their singular quest for modernity and a technocratic society, the Western nation-states tried to eradicate traditional cultures and thus alienated individuals and groups from their first cultures and languages (Banks, 2004). This approach to shaping a unified nation-state has created alienation and has deprived individuals and groups of some of the most important ways in which people satisfy their needs for symbolic meaning and community. It has also resulted in the political and cultural oppression of some racial and ethnic groups within society and has consequently caused them to focus on their own particular needs and goals rather than on the overarching goals of the nation-state (Banks, 2004; Schierup, Hansen, & Castles, 2006).

Westernized nation-states will be able to create societies with overarching goals that are shared by diverse groups only when these groups feel that they have a real stake and place in their nation-states and that their states mirror their own concerns, values, and ethos (Kymlicka, 1995). A multicultural curriculum that reflects the cultures, values, and goals of the groups within a nation will contribute significantly to the development of a healthy nationalism and national identity.

THE COMPLEXITY OF ETHNICITY
IN AMERICAN SOCIETY

Ethnicity is an integral but complex part of American life. To acquire a sophisticated knowledge of the United States, students must master facts, concepts, generalizations, and theories related to the intricate, complex nature of race and ethnicity in American society. Although ethnicity is a significant part of American life, there is a national American culture and identity shared by all groups in the United States. This national culture resulted (and is resulting) from a series of multiple acculturations (Banks, 2006a). Diverse ethnic cultures—such as the Anglo-Saxon Protestant, African, Jewish, and Mexican cultures—influence each other. The national American culture and identity consist of cultural components that have become universalized and are shared by most people within the nation. These universalized cultural components are products of the ethnic cultures in the United States and the American experience.

While most Americans are members of cultural, ethnic, racial, and language communities, they share an overarching American identity. A goal of the multicultural education curriculum is to foster *unity within diversity* by helping all students to develop a thoughtful commitment to the overarching American identity that we all share while, at the same time, respecting as well as incorporating aspects of their cultural and community identities into the school culture and the curriculum (Banks et al., 2001).

In addition to the national American culture and identity, there are ethnic and other subsocieties and institutions in the United States whose characteristics have not been universalized or become part of the shared national culture. The Anglo-Saxon Protestant subsociety, like other ethnic subsocieties, has cultural elements that are not universalized or shared by other Americans. *Consequently, individual Americans are ethnic to the extent that they function within ethnic subsocieties and share their values, behavioral styles, and cultures.* An individual, however, may have a low level of ethnicity or psychological identification with his or her ethnic group or groups.

In Figure 1.3, the shaded area represents the American national culture shared by all ethnic and cultural groups. Circles A, B, C, and D represent ethnic subsocieties, such as the Anglo-Saxon Protestant, African American, Italian American, and Mexican American subsocieties. A major goal of the multicultural curriculum is to help students develop cross-cultural competency, which consists of the abilities, attitudes, and understandings students need to function effectively within the American national culture, within their own ethnic subsocieties, and within and across different ethnic subsocieties and cultures.

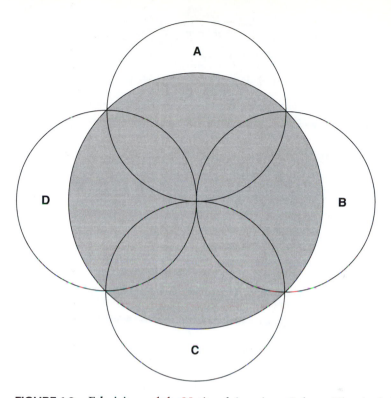

FIGURE 1.3   **Ethnicity and the National American Culture**   The shaded area represents the national American culture. Circles A, B, C, and D represent ethnic subcultures.

ETHNICITY AND INDIVIDUALS

Ethnicity becomes even more complex when we try to determine the ethnic group affiliations and identification of individuals. Many individuals in U.S. society not only perceive themselves as members of ethnic groups, but also are perceived as members of these groups by individuals outside their ethnic groups. This includes many, but not all, Americans who are Mexican, Polish, Jewish, or Vietnamese. The asterisks in the closed circles in Figure 1.4 represent individuals within these ethnic groups. However, these individuals also perceive themselves and are usually perceived by others to be American, as well as Mexican, Polish, Jewish, or Vietnamese, even though Mexican, for example, may be the first and most important identity for many Mexican Americans. Mexican Americans also share a broader American identity and the overarching idealized American values that cement the nation. Many Anglo-Saxon Protestants, such as those who are members of the Brahmin elite in Boston, also see themselves as members of a specific cultural group. Individuals represented by the asterisks in the closed circles in Figure 1.4 are clearly ethnic, from both inside and outside points of view.

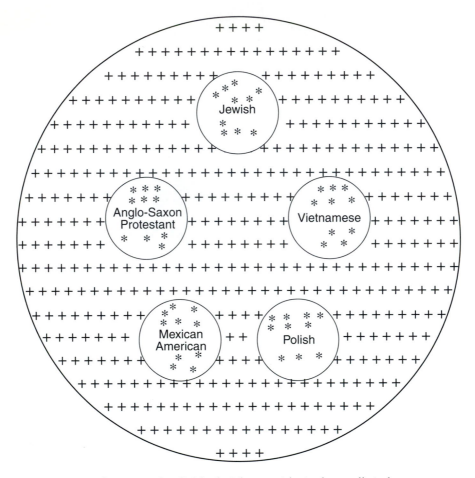

FIGURE 1.4   Ethnicity and Individuals   The asterisks in the small circles represent individuals who perceive themselves and who are perceived by other people to be members of clearly delineated ethnic groups. The plus signs [+] represent individuals who perceive themselves and are perceived by most other people to be merely *American.*

Other Americans are more difficult to characterize ethnically because of how they view themselves and how others view them. These individuals are represented by the plus signs in Figure 1.4. They perceive themselves only as American and do not consciously identify with a clearly defined ethnic group. This group of Americans includes many third- and fourth-generation Irish and Scandinavians as well as individuals with multiple European heritages. These individuals can best be described as *mainstream Americans,* from both a sociological and a psychological perspective. Culturally, however, mainstream Americans share many characteristics with Anglo-Saxon Protestants, because Anglo-Saxon Protestants have influenced the national culture more than any other American subgroup.

The increase of biracial marriages and births has made racial identification in the United States more complex (Lee & Edmonston, 2005; Root, 2001; Wallace, 2001; Wardle & Cruz-Janzen, 2004). Racial intermarriage increased from less than 1% of all married couples in 1970 to more than 5% of couples in 2000 (Lee & Edmonston, 2005). In 2006, 6.4% of all U.S. children lived in households headed by interracial married couples (Rice News Staff Reports, 2006). Interracial births have increased over the past three decades. In the early 1970s, 1.4% of infants were born to parents who reported different racial groups; by 1998, this percentage had increased to 4.3% (Parker & Madans, 2002).

In the American Community Survey of the U.S. Census in 2005, respondents were given the option of selecting one or more race categories to indicate racial identities; 2% of all respondents—or 5.5 million (5,557,184) people—reported two or more races (U.S. Census Bureau, 2007c). Figure 1.5 shows the percentage distribution of the population that selected two or more races, most of whom were younger people. The U.S. Census predicts that more people will choose the "two or more races" category in

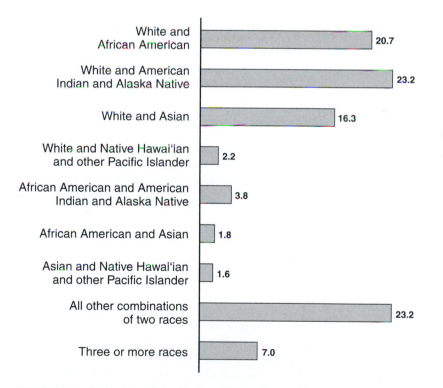

FIGURE 1.5   **Percentage Distribution of Population of Two or More Races**

Source: U.S. Census Bureau (2007), *2005 American Community Survey, Selected Population Profile.* Available online at http://factfinder.census.gov/servlet/IPCharIterationServlet?_lang=en&_ts=199640379208.

the future. Kenneth Prewitt, who was director of the 2000 census, believes that in 15 to 20 years about one-fourth of the population will identify themselves as multiracial (cited in Kent, Pollard, Haaga, & Mather, 2001, p. 33).

ETHNIC AND CULTURAL STUDIES: ASSUMPTIONS AND PRACTICES

Many educators realize the importance of race and ethnicity in U.S. society and the need to help students develop more sophisticated understandings of the diverse racial and ethnic groups that make up the United States and a greater acceptance of cultural differences. Educational institutions at all levels have made some attempts to include more information about ethnic groups in the social studies, language arts, and humanities curricula within the last three decades. However, some assumptions about ethnic studies and multicultural education have adversely affected the integration of ethnic content into the curriculum.

We need to examine and challenge these assumptions and related school practices and to formulate new assumptions and goals in order for the multicultural education movement to serve as a catalyst for curriculum reform and transformation. The greatest promise of multicultural education is that it will serve as a vehicle for general curriculum reform and transformation. If ethnic content is merely added to the traditional curriculum, which has many problems (Banks, 2006b), then efforts to modify the curriculum with ethnic content are likely to lead to a dead end. The total school curriculum should be transformed.

One pervasive assumption many educators embrace is that ethnic studies deals exclusively with groups of color, such as Asian Americans, American Indians, and African Americans. This assumption is widespread within the schools, and is often reflected in school programs. In many school ethnic studies units and lessons, little or no attention is devoted to the experiences of European American ethnic groups, such as Jewish Americans, Polish Americans, and Italian Americans. This narrow conceptualization of ethnic studies emerged out of the social forces that gave rise to the ethnic studies movement in the 1960s. To conceptualize ethnic studies exclusively as the study of people of color is inconsistent with how sociologists define *ethnicity* (Alba & Nee, 2003). Such a narrow view also prevents the development of broadly conceptualized comparative approaches to ethnic studies and multicultural education. Comparative approaches to ethnic studies and multicultural education are needed to help students understand fully the complex role of ethnicity in U.S. life and culture. Conceptualizing ethnic studies exclusively as the study of ethnic groups of color also promotes a "we-they" attitude among many White students and teachers. Many students think that ethnic studies is the study of them—"the Others"—whereas American studies is the study of "us." Many educators believe that ethnic studies has no place within an all-White classroom.

A related assumption that educators often make about ethnic studies is that only students who are members of a particular ethnic group should study that group's history and culture. Some ethnic studies units and lessons focus on one specific ethnic group, such as Puerto Ricans, African Americans, or American Indians. The ethnic group on which the units and lessons focus is usually either present or dominant in the local school population. Content related to diverse ethnic groups should be an integral part of the curriculum experienced by all students. *Ethnic modification of the total curriculum is essential.*

All students, regardless of their race, ethnicity, or social class, should study the cogent and complex roles of race, ethnicity, and cross-ethnic relationships and interactions in U.S. society and culture. Most Americans are socialized within ethnic or cultural enclaves and have low levels of cultural and ethnic literacy. Within their communities, people learn primarily about their own cultures and assume that their lifestyles are the legitimate ones and that other cultures are invalid, strange, and different. The school should help students to break out of their cultural enclaves and broaden their cultural perspectives. Students need to learn that there are cultural and ethnic alternatives within our society that they can freely embrace.

Many educators assume that ethnic studies is essentially additive in nature and that we can create a sound multicultural curriculum by leaving the present curriculum intact and adding ethnic heroes and heroines—such as Martin Luther King, Jr., Cesar Chávez, Sojourner Truth, Pocahontas, and Malinche—to the list of mainstream heroes and heroines who are already studied in most schools. Conceptualizing ethnic studies as essentially additive in nature is problematic for several reasons. In too many classrooms throughout the United States, teachers still emphasize the mastery of low-level facts and do not help students master higher levels of knowledge.

Modifying the school curriculum to include racial, ethnic, and cultural content provides a tremendous opportunity to reexamine the assumptions, purposes, and nature of the curriculum and to formulate a curriculum with new assumptions and goals. Merely adding low-level facts about ethnic content to a curriculum that is already bulging with discrete and isolated facts about mainstream American heroes will not result in significant curriculum reform. Isolated facts about Crispus Attucks and the Boston Massacre do not stimulate the intellect any more than do isolated facts about George Washington or Betsy Ross. To integrate ethnic content meaningfully into the total school curriculum, we must undertake more substantial curriculum reform. Adding facts about ethnic heroes and heroines and events of questionable historical significance is not sufficient. Transformation of the curriculum is essential.

An Expanded Definition of Ethnicity

Problems in teaching about ethnic groups result, in part, from the ways in which *ethnicity* and *ethnic group* in the United States are often conceptualized and defined by teachers and curriculum specialists. School practitioners often limit their conceptualization of an ethnic group to an ethnic group of color or to an ethnic minority group. Teachers and curriculum specialists must have a more accurate and inclusive definition of an *ethnic group* in order to integrate ethnic content into the curriculum in more meaningful ways.

What is an ethnic group? Individuals who constitute an ethnic group share a sense of group identification, a common set of values, political and economic interests, behavioral patterns, and other culture elements that differ from those of other groups within a society. Members of an ethnic group have a shared sense of peoplehood, culture, identity, and shared languages and dialects. Alba (1992) states that Max Weber's classic definition of an ethnic group is still the most useful definition. Weber (cited in Alba, 1992) defines an *ethnic group* as a group whose members "entertain a subjective belief in their common descent because of similarities of physical type or of customs or both, or because of memories of colonization and migration. It does not matter whether or not an objective blood relationship exists" (p. 16).

An individual is ethnic to the extent that he or she shares the values, behavioral patterns, cultural traits, and identification with a specific ethnic group. Many individuals have multiple ethnic group attachments; others consider themselves "American" rather than ethnic.

An individual's identity with his or her ethnic group varies significantly with period of life, economic and social status, and situations or settings. Ethnicity is very important for some Americans and of little or only symbolic importance to others. Groups based on other factors—such as religion, social class, region, sexual orientation, gender, or occupation—are more important to many individuals. As members of lower socioeconomic ethnic groups attain economic mobility, their social class interests often become more important to them than their ethnic affiliations.

In this book, ethnic studies is conceptualized broadly, as it is in the *Harvard Encyclopedia of American Ethnic Groups* (Thernstrom, Orlov, & Handlin, 1980). Information, materials, and strategies for teaching about White ethnic groups (such as Italian Americans and Jewish Americans) as well as about the experiences of ethnic groups of color (such as Mexican Americans, Puerto Ricans, and Asian Americans) are included. To conceptualize ethnic and cultural studies more narrowly will result in curricula that are too limited in scope and that will not help students understand fully both the similarities and differences in the experiences of the diverse groups in the United States.

The multicultural curriculum should enable students to derive valid generalizations and theories about the characteristics of ethnic, cultural, and religious groups and to learn how they are alike and different, in both their past and present experiences. Even though it is neither possible nor necessary for the curriculum of a particular school or district to include content about every ethnic group in the United States (there are more than 100), *each curriculum should focus on a range of groups that differ in their racial characteristics, cultural experiences, languages, histories, values, and current problems.* By studying a range of ethnic and cultural groups, students will be able to formulate valid comparative generalizations and theories about the nature of race, ethnicity, and culture in U.S. society. The curriculum can be transformed only when events, concepts, and issues are studied from the perspectives of a range of ethnic, cultural, and religious groups.

Ethnic Minority Groups/People of Color

Even though an ethnic group shares a common set of values, behavioral patterns, culture traits, and sense of peoplehood, an ethnic minority group can be distinguished from an ethnic group. An *ethnic minority group* has unique physical and/or cultural characteristics that enable people who belong to mainstream groups to identify its members easily and thus to treat them in a discriminatory way. Jewish Americans are an ethnic minority group with unique cultural and religious characteristics. African Americans are an ethnic minority group with both unique physical and cultural characteristics.

An ethnic minority group is usually a numerical minority and comprises only a small percentage of the national population. Ethnic minorities in the United States made up 33% of the national population of 300 million in 2006 (Population Reference Bureau, 2007). The non-White percentage of the U.S. population is growing at a much faster rate than the White population (U.S. Census Bureau, 2006). The U.S. Census projects that by 2050 ethnic groups of color will make up about 50% of the total U.S. population (U.S. Census Bureau, 2004a). The concept *minority* is becoming increasingly misleading and less useful in the United States as the population of people of color becomes closer to that of Whites.

In many school districts and in the schools of California, Hawaii, Louisiana, Mississippi, New Mexico, and Texas, students of color constitute majorities. In part for this reason, educators and social scientists are increasingly referring to such groups as African Americans, Hispanics, and Asian Americans as *people of color* rather than as *ethnic minorities*. Educators and social scientists are realizing that many terms and concepts used in the past do not accurately and sensitively describe the ethnic, racial, and cultural realities in the United States today. Although *people of color* is a contested term that some educators find perplexing, it is used often because a more helpful term has not yet been developed.

ETHNIC AND CULTURAL STUDIES: A PROCESS OF CURRICULUM REFORM

Ethnic and cultural content should not be studied only by ethnic groups of color or be limited to specialized courses. Rather, ethnic and cultural studies should be viewed as a process of curriculum reform and transformation that will result in the creation of a reformed curriculum based on new assumptions and perspectives. Such a transformed curriculum will help students gain novel views of the American experience and a new conception of what it means to be an American. Because the English immigrants assumed control of most economic, social, and political institutions early in U.S. national history, to *Americanize* has been interpreted to mean to *Anglicize*. During the height of nativism in the late 1800s and early 1900s, the English Americans defined *Americanization* as Anglicization (Bennett, 1988). This notion of Americanization is still widespread within U.S. society and schools today. Thus, when we think of American history and American literature, we tend to think of Anglo-American history and of literature written by Anglo-American authors.

Reconceptualizing American Society

Because the assumption that only what is Anglo-American is American is so deeply ingrained in curriculum materials and in the hearts and minds of many students and teachers, we cannot transform the curriculum by merely adding a unit or a lesson here and there about African American, Mexican American, or Italian American history or literature. Rather, we need to examine seriously the conception of American that is perpetuated in the curriculum and the basic canon, assumptions, and purposes that underlie the curriculum.

It is essential to reconceptualize and reenvision how we view American society and history in the school curriculum. We should view American history, literature, art, music, and culture from diverse ethnic and cultural perspectives rather than primarily or exclusively from the point of view of mainstream historians, writers, and artists. Most courses in the curriculum are taught primarily from mainstream perspectives (Sleeter, 2005). Often, ethnic and cultural content is added to the mainstream curriculum, which is left intact. Such courses, units, and lessons are contributions or an additive approach to curriculum reform (see Figure 1.6). Multicultural education, as a process of curriculum reform, can and often does proceed from the contributions and additive approaches to the transformative and social action approaches.

In courses, units, and activities based on contributions and additive approaches, ethnic content is additive to the major curriculum thrust, which remains mainstream oriented. Many school districts that have attempted ethnic modification of the curriculum have implemented contributions and additive curriculum changes and reforms. Courses on specific ethnic groups (such as African Americans and Mexican Americans) and special units on ethnic groups are examples of the contributions and additive approaches.

Approaches to Teaching Multicultural Content

The contributions approach to integration is the most frequently used approach. This approach is characterized by the addition of ethnic heroes into the curriculum. The heroes and heroines added to the curriculum are viewed from a mainstream-centric perspective and are also usually selected for inclusion into the curriculum using mainstream criteria. Consequently, ethnic heroes and heroines viewed positively by the mainstream society (such as Booker T. Washington, Marian Anderson, and Sacajawea) are most often chosen for study rather than are ethnic Americans who challenged the dominant class and social structure in society (such as W. E. B. Du Bois, Geronimo, and Angela Davis).

In the contributions approach, mainstream curriculum remains unchanged in terms of its basic structure, goals, and salient characteristics. This is the easiest

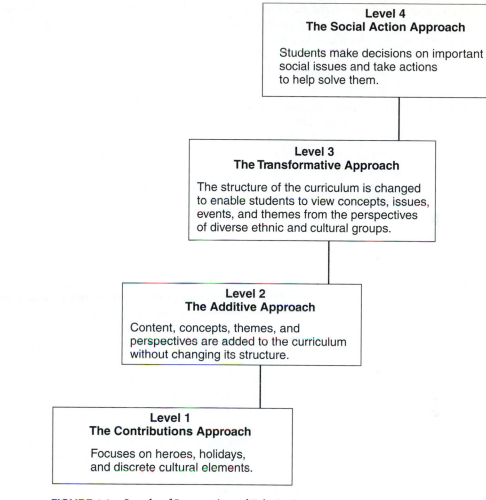

FIGURE 1.6   Levels of Integration of Ethnic Content

approach for teachers to integrate ethnic content into the curriculum. However, it has several serious limitations, including not helping students to attain a comprehensive view of the role of ethnic and cultural groups in U.S. society. Rather, they see ethnic issues and events primarily as an addition to the curriculum and thus as an appendage to the main story of the nation's development.

In an additive approach, content, concepts, themes, and perspectives are added to the curriculum without changing its basic structure, purpose, and characteristics. The content, concepts, and issues added to the curriculum are viewed primarily from mainstream perspectives. This approach is often accomplished by the addition of a book, unit, or course to the curriculum without changing it substantially. The additive approach allows the teacher to put ethnic content into the curriculum without restructuring it, which would take substantial time, effort, training, and rethinking of the curriculum and its purposes, nature, and goals.

The additive approach can be the first phase in a more radical curriculum reform effort designed to restructure the total curriculum and to integrate it with ethnic content, perspectives, and frames of reference. However, this approach shares several problems with the contributions approach. The most important shortcoming is that this approach usually results in the viewing of ethnic content from the perspectives of mainstream historians, writers, artists, and scientists because it does not involve a restructuring of the curriculum.

The transformative approach differs fundamentally from the contributions and additive approaches. This approach changes the basic assumptions of the curriculum and enables students to view concepts, issues, themes, and problems from several ethnic perspectives and points of view. The key curriculum issue involved in the transformation approach is not the addition of ethnic groups, heroes, heroines, and contributions, but instead the infusion of various perspectives, frames of reference, and content from different groups. These changes extend students' understandings of the nature, development, and complexity of the United States and the world.

Mainstream perspectives should be among many different perspectives taught in various content areas. Only by approaching the study of American society and culture in a transformative way will students obtain a holistic, rather than an ethnocentric, view of U.S. history and culture. A writer's or artist's experience and culture, including ethnic or community culture, cogently influences his or her works and views of the past and present. Feminists call this influence *positionality* (Code, 1991; Tetreault, 2007).

Positionality is used to describe how race, culture, social class, and gender—as well as other personal and cultural factors—influence how we view our society and the world. However, it would be simplistic to argue that there is one mainstream view of history, art, literature, or contemporary events, or one African American view. Wide differences in experiences and perceptions exist both within and across ethnic and cultural groups.

However, people who have experienced a historical event or social event, such as racial discrimination, slavery, or internment, often view the event very differently from people who have observed it from a distance. Accounts written by people who were enslaved or interned provide unique insights and perspectives on these events that cannot be provided by people who did not experience them.

A powerful account of slavery was chronicled by Olaudah Equiano, the son of an Ibo tribal leader who was one of 10 million to 12 million Africans captured and enslaved in the Americas (Johnson, Smith, & WGBH Series Research Team, 1998). The insights provided by Yoshiko Uchida (1982) in *Desert Exile,* which describes her experiences in a concentration camp during World War II, could not have been written by someone observing these events from the outside. However, those who viewed the internment from the outside can also provide unique and important perspectives. Hence, both insider and outsider perspectives (Merton, 1972) should be studied in a sound, critical multicultural curriculum.

Only by looking at events from many different perspectives can we fully understand the complex dimensions of American culture and society. Important goals of the multicultural curriculum are to broaden students' conceptions of what *American* means and to present them with new ways to view and interpret American society, literature, music, and art. Any goals that are less ambitious, while important, will not result in curriculum transformation or enable students to acquire a new conception of the United States and the world.

Table 1.2 contains a lesson that illustrates the transformative approach to teaching. In this lesson, students view Columbus's arrival in the Caribbean from the perspectives of both the Native people (the Arawaks or Taino) and Columbus.

The social action approach includes all of the elements of the transformative approach and adds components that require students to make decisions and take

TABLE 1.2   Teaching Multiple Perspectives: Christopher Columbus and the Arawaks

The students are presented with the following excerpts from Christopher Columbus's diary that describe his arrival in an Arawak Indian community in the Caribbean in 1492. These are some of the observations that Columbus makes about the Arawaks:

> They took all and gave all, such as they had, with good will, but it seemed to me that they were a people very lacking in everything. They all go naked as their mothers bore them, and the women also, although I saw only one very young girl.... They should be good servants and quick to learn, since I see that they very soon say all that is said to them, and I believe that they would easily be made Christians, for it appeared to me that they had no religious beliefs. Our Lord willing, at the time of my departure, I will bring back six of them to Your Highnesses, that they may learn to talk. I saw no beast of any kind in this island, except parrots.

The students are then encouraged to view Columbus's statement from the perspective of the Arawaks. The Arawaks had an oral culture and consequently left no written documents. However, archaeologist Fred Olsen (1974) studied Arawak artifacts and used what he learned from them to construct a day in the life of the Arawaks, which he describes in his book *On the Trail of the Arawaks*. The students are asked to read an excerpt from Olsen's account of a day in the life of the Arawaks and to respond to these questions:

1. Columbus wrote in his diary that he thought the Arawaks had no religious beliefs. You read about Arawak life in the report by Fred Olsen. Do you think Columbus was correct? Why?
2. Accounts written by people who took part in or witnessed (saw) a historical event are called primary sources. Can historians believe everything they read in a primary source? Explain.

Source: C. Jan (1930), *The Voyages of Christopher Columbus.* London: Argonaut Press.

TABLE 1.3   Student Action

After a unit on the civil rights movement of the 1960s and 1970s, a seventh-grade social studies class made this list of actions they could take to help reduce discrimination in their personal lives, school, and community:

1. Making a personal commitment to stop telling racist jokes.
2. Making a commitment to challenge our own racial and ethnic stereotypes either before or after we verbalize them.
3. Compiling an annotated list of books about ethnic groups that we will ask the librarian to order for our school library.
4. Asking the principal to order sets of photographs that show African Americans and other people of color who have jobs that represent a variety of careers. Asking the principal to encourage our teachers to display these photographs on their classroom walls.
5. Observing television programs to determine the extent to which people of color, such as African Americans and Asian Americans, are represented in such jobs as news anchors and hosts of programs. Writing to local and national television stations to express our concern if we discover that people of color are not represented in powerful and visible roles in news or other kinds of television programs.
6. Contacting a school in the inner-city to determine if there are joint activities and projects in which we and they might participate.
7. Asking the principal or the board of education in our school district to require our teachers to attend in-service staff development workshops that will help them learn ways in which to integrate content about ethnic and racial groups into our courses.
8. Sharing some of the facts that we have learned in this unit, such as that by the year 2050, one out of every two Americans will be a person of color, with our parents and discussing these facts with them.
9. Making a personal commitment to have a friend from another racial, ethnic, or religious group by the end of the year.
10. Making a personal commitment to read at least one book a year that deals with a racial, cultural, or ethnic group other than my own.
11. Do nothing; take no actions.

actions related to the concept, issue, or problem they have studied. Table 1.3 lists possible actions developed by a junior high school social studies class after studying a unit on the civil rights movements of the 1960s and 1970s.

The four approaches to the integration of ethnic content into the curriculum are often mixed and blended in actual teaching situations (see Figure 1.6). The move from the lower to the higher levels of ethnic content integration is likely to be gradual and cumulative. An important goal of teaching about racial, ethnic, and cultural diversity should be to empower students with the knowledge, skills, and attitudes they need to participate in civic action that will help transform our world and enhance the possibility for human survival.

MULTICULTURAL EDUCATION
AND GLOBAL EDUCATION

Students should also study world events, issues, and concepts from a transformative and cosmopolitan (Appiah, 2006) rather than a Eurocentric perspective (Banks, 2004; Luchtenberg, 2004). The world studies program in schools often uses a Eurocentric approach to examine problems, issues, and concepts. Events and issues are viewed primarily or exclusively from the perspectives of mainstream groups in European nations and cultures. There are many opportunities in the school curriculum to link multicultural education and global education, and to help students view international events, concepts, and issues from the perspectives of the ethnic and racial groups that live in the various nations of the world. Figure 1.7 illustrates how students can study a global event, problem, issue, or concept using a transformative approach.

It is important to link multicultural education and global education because they share several important goals and because the population of the United States is constantly being changed by the infusion of ethnic and immigrant groups from beyond its borders. The multicultural curriculum helps students better understand the lands and cultures from which these groups come.

When relating multicultural and global education, it is important for teachers to foster what Kymlicka (1995) calls *multicultural citizenship*. Multicultural citizenship education recognizes and legitimizes the right and need of citizens to maintain commitments to their ethnic and cultural communities as well as to the national civic culture. It also helps students develop a thoughtful global identification because cultural, national, and global identifications are interrelated (Banks, 2008). A healthy cultural identification is needed to develop a thoughtful and clarified commitment to the nation-state. A clarified and reflective national identification is needed to become thoughtful citizens of the global community. When students view issues and concepts globally, they can develop a cosmopolitan perspective. Cosmopolitans view themselves as citizens of the world who will make decisions and take actions in the global interests that will benefit humankind. Nussbaum (2002) states that cosmopolitans' "allegiance is to the worldwide community of human beings" (p. 4). Figure 1.8 shows the relationship between cultural, national, and global identifications.

Distinguishing Multicultural and Global Education

Although it is important to link multicultural and global education, it is essential that they not be confused and that one is not substituted for the other. Sometimes, teachers who have integrated a discussion of Mexico, Japan, and Nigeria into their lessons claim that these topics constitute multicultural education. They are confusing global with multicultural education. Multicultural education deals with ethnic, cultural, and gender groups within the United States (Banks & Banks, 2004). Global

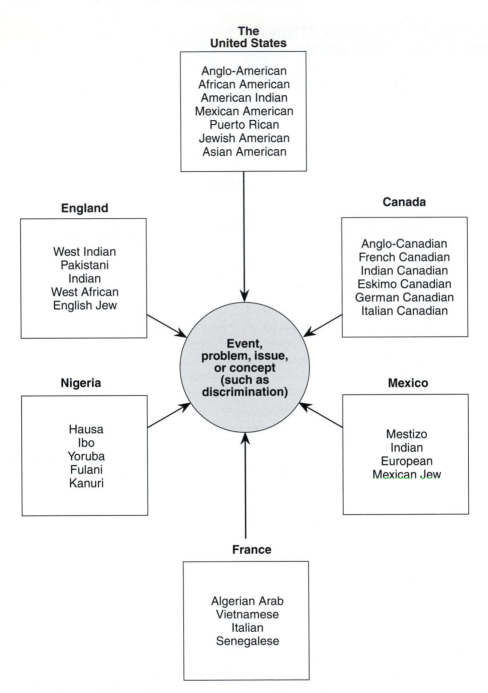

FIGURE 1.7   A Transformative Approach to Global Studies This figure illustrates how an event, problem, issue, or concept can be viewed from the perspectives of ethnic groups within several nations. A study of ethnic perspectives within other nations will help students gain a global framework for viewing and studying human events and problems.

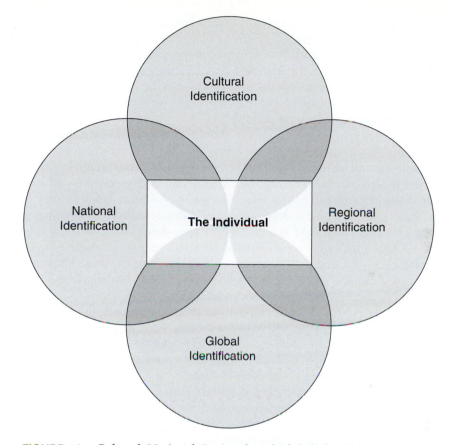

FIGURE 1.8   Cultural, National, Regional, and Global Identifications Multicultural citizenship education helps students to acquire a delicate balance of cultural, national, regional, and global identifications. These identifications are complex, interactive, and contextual.

Source: Copyright © 2007 by James A. Banks.

education deals with nations outside the United States and the interrelationships among nations (Banks et al., 2005; Noddings, 2005). Each type of education makes unique and important contributions to the knowledge of students.

THE GOALS OF THE MULTICULTURAL CURRICULUM

Concepts, content, and teaching strategies cannot be identified and selected until goals are clearly defined. The education of effective citizens in a diverse society is the key goal of multicultural education presented in this book. This goal requires that students develop decision-making and social action skills so they can take personal, social, and civic action to make the United States and the world more democratic and humane.

The multicultural curriculum should help students develop the ability to make reflective decisions on issues related to race, ethnicity, culture, and language and to take personal, social, and civic actions to help solve the racial and ethnic problems in our national and world societies. Effective solutions to the enormous ethnic and racial problems in our nation and world can be found only by an active and informed citizenry capable of making reflective personal and public decisions. Chapter 4 discusses decision making and its components in more detail.

The multicultural curriculum should also help students view historical and contemporary events from diverse ethnic and cultural perspectives, clarify their ethnic and cultural identities, and function effectively within their own cultural communities. Individuals must clarify their own ethnic and cultural identities before they can relate positively to people who belong to different racial and ethnic groups. Educators need to foster the development of self-acceptance but discourage ethnocentrism. Diversity and unity in a delicate balance should be fostered by the schools.

The multicultural curriculum should also help individuals develop cross-cultural competency—the ability to function within a range of cultures. Although individuals within a pluralistic society must learn to accept their own ethnic and cultural identities and become comfortable with them, they must also learn to function effectively within other cultures and to respond positively to individuals who belong to other ethnic, cultural, language, and religious groups. They also need to learn how to interact with and to resolve conflicts with people from diverse groups. The multicultural curriculum seeks to help individuals gain greater self-understanding by viewing themselves from the perspectives of other cultures.

Another important goal of the multicultural curriculum is to provide students with cultural and ethnic alternatives. Both the mainstream White Protestant and the Filipino American student should be provided with cultural and ethnic options in the school. Historically, the school curriculum has focused primarily on the cultures of Anglo-Saxon Protestants. In many schools the curriculum is primarily an extension of the homes, communities, and cultures of White mainstream students. It often does not present these students with cultural and ethnic alternatives, thereby denying them the richness of the music, literature, art, values, lifestyles, and perspectives that exist among such ethnic groups as Jews, Greeks, Puerto Ricans, and African Americans. Many behaviors and values within these ethnic groups can help mainstream White students to enrich their personal and public lives.

The multicultural curriculum should also try to reduce ethnic and cultural encapsulation and help students develop a better understanding and awareness of their own cultures. Individuals who only know, participate in, and see the world from their unique cultural and ethnic perspectives are denied important aspects of the human experience and are culturally and ethnically encapsulated. These individuals are unable to know and see their own cultures fully because of their cultural and ethnic blinders. The multicultural curriculum seeks to help individuals gain greater self-understanding by viewing themselves from the perspectives of other cultures.

The multicultural curriculum should also help students to expand their conceptions of what it means to be human, to accept the fact that ethnic minority cultures are functional and valid, and to realize that a culture can be evaluated only within a particular cultural context. Because cultures are made by people, there are many ways of being human. By studying this important generalization, students can develop an appreciation for the capacity of human beings to create a diversity of lifestyles and to adapt to a variety of social and physical environments.

Another important goal of the multicultural curriculum is to help students master essential reading, writing, and math skills. Multicultural content can help students master important skills in the content areas. Multicultural readings and data, if taught effectively, can be highly motivating and meaningful, especially when teachers help students to understand and grapple with the conflicts inherent within cross-cultural teaching and learning (Graff, 1992). Students are more likely to master skills when the teacher uses content that deals with significant human problems—such as race, culture, language, religion, and power—within our communities, nation, and world.

SUMMARY

The curriculum within the nation's schools, colleges, and universities should be transformed so that it will accurately reflect the racial, ethnic, cultural, language, and religious diversity within the United States. Schools, colleges, and universities are using various approaches to infuse multicultural content into the curriculum, including the contributions and additive approaches. Both of these approaches have important problems. To respond adequately to the diversity within the nation and the world, the curriculum should be transformed so that it can help students to develop the decision-making, social action, and cross-cultural skills needed for the twenty-first century.

REFLECTION AND ACTION ACTIVITIES

1. The melting pot concept does not accurately describe the nature of ethnicity in the United States. React to this position by stating whether you agree or disagree with it and why.
2. Make a list of the different ethnic, racial, cultural, religious, and language groups that constitute your ethnic heritage. Compare your list with similar lists made by other individuals in your class or workshop. What conclusions can you derive about culture and ethnicity in U.S. society by analyzing these data?
3. Study the results of the last national or local election. Note particularly the voting patterns of predominantly racial, ethnic, language, income, and religious groups. What generalizations can you make on the basis of these data? What are the limitations of your generalizations?
4. Interview a curriculum coordinator in one or two local school districts. Ask this individual to describe the school's efforts to implement multicultural education. If the school focuses on some ethnic, cultural, language, and religious groups and not on

others, ask for an explanation of this practice. How do your findings compare with the trends described in this chapter?

5. According to the author, what should be the goals of the multicultural curriculum? Write, in one sentence or more, what you think should be the goals of the multicultural curriculum. Compare your statement with the goals listed in this chapter. In what ways are your statement and the listed goals alike and different? Why? How are your assumptions about ethnic studies and ethnicity similar to and different from those of the author?

6. Divide into small discussion groups in your class or workshop. Appoint a group leader and a reporter for each group and discuss the following questions in your groups. When the small group discussions have ended, the class or workshop should reassemble. Reporters should give a brief summary of each group's discussion. The large group should then react both to the reports and to the following questions:

   a. Which of the approaches presented in Figure 1.6 best describes the curriculum in your school or in a school that you have attended or in which you have observed?

   b. Do you think it would be desirable to help your school (or a school that you have attended or in which you have observed) move from one approach to another (for example, from the contributions to the transformative approach)?

   c. What problems might you, as a teacher, encounter in trying to move the curriculum in your school (or a school that you have attended or in which you have observed) from one approach to another (for example, moving from contributions to transformative)?

   d. How might these problems best be overcome?

   e. What benefits might result for both you and the students if your school (or the school that you have attended or in which you have observed) changed from one approach to another?

7. Define each of the following concepts and terms and tell why each is important:

melting pot	contributions approach
ethnic group	additive approach
ethnic minority group	transformative approach
people of color	social action approach
multicultural citizenship	

REFERENCES

Alba, R. (1992). Ethnicity. In E. F. Borgatta & M. L. Borgatta (Eds.), *Encyclopedia of Sociology* (Vol. 2, pp. 575–584). New York: Macmillan.

Alba, R., & Nee, V. (2003). *Remaking the American Mainstream: Assimilation and Contemporary Immigration.* Cambridge, MA: Harvard University Press.

Appiah, K. A. (2006). *Cosmopolitanism.* New York: Norton.

Banks, J. A. (2006a). *Cultural Diversity and Education: Foundations, Curriculum, and Teaching* (5th ed.). Boston: Allyn and Bacon.

Banks, J. A. (2006b). *Race, Culture, and Education: The Selected Works of James A. Banks.* London and New York: Routledge.

Banks, J. A. (2008). *An Introduction to Multicultural Education* (4th ed.). Boston: Allyn and Bacon.

Banks, J. A. (Ed.). (2004). *Diversity and Citizenship Education: Global Perspectives*. San Francisco: Jossey-Bass.

Banks, J. A., & Banks, C. A. M. (Eds.). (2004). *Handbook of Research on Multicultural Education* (2nd ed.). San Francisco: Jossey-Bass.

Banks, J. A., Banks, C. A. M., Cortés, C. E., Hahn, C. L., et al. (2005). *Democracy and Diversity: Principles and Concepts for Educating Citizens in a Global Age*. Seattle: Center for Multicultural Education, University of Washington.

Banks, J. A., Cookson, P., Gay, G., Hawley, W. D., Irvine, J. I., Nieto, S., Schofield, J. W., & Stephan, W. G. (2001). *Diversity within Unity: Essential Principles for Teaching and Learning in a Multicultural Society*. Seattle: Center for Multicultural Education, University of Washington.

Bennett, D. H. (1988). *The Party of Fear: From Nativist Movements to the New Right in American History*. Chapel Hill: University of North Carolina Press.

Bhatia, T. K., & Ritchie, W. C. (Eds.). (2006). *The Handbook of Bilingualism*. Malden, MA: Blackwell.

Capps, R., Fix, M., Murray, J., Ost, J., Herwantoro, S., Zimmerman, W., & Passel, J. (2004). *Promise or Peril: Immigrants, LEP Students, and the No Child Left Behind Act*. Washington, DC: Urban Institute, Foundation for Child Development.

Cesari, J. (2004). *When Islam and Democracy Meet: Muslims in Europe and the United States*. New York: Pelgrave Macmillan.

Code, L. (1991). *What Can She Know? Feminist Theory and the Construction of Knowledge*. Ithaca, NY: Cornell University Press.

Council on American-Islamic Relations. (2007, June 9). Retrieved from http://www.cair-net.org.

Denavas-Walt, C., Proctor, B. D., & Lee, C. H. (2006). *Income, Poverty, and Health Insurance Coverage in the United States: 2005*. U.S. Census Bureau, Current Population Reports, P60-231. Washington, DC: U.S. Government Printing Office.

Dillon, S. (2006, August 27). In Schools across the U.S., the Melting Pot Overflows. *New York Times*, pp. A7, A16.

Eck, D. L. (2001). *A New Religious America: How a "Christian Country" Has Become the World's Most Religiously Diverse Nation*. New York: HarperSanFrancisco.

Frederickson, G. M. (2002). *Racism: A Short History*. Princeton, NJ: Princeton University Press.

Graff, G. (1992). *Beyond the Culture Wars: How Teaching the Conflicts Can Revitalize American Education*. New York: Norton.

Grim, J. (2001). *Indigenous Traditions and Ecology: The Interbeing of Cosmology and Community*. Cambridge, MA: Harvard University Press.

Haub, C. (2006). Hispanics Account for Almost One-Half of U.S. Population Growth. Population Reference Bureau. Retrieved January 11, 2007, from http://www.prb.org/Template.cfm?Section=PRB&template=/ContentManagement/ContentDisplay.cfm&ContentID=13604.

Immigration Sabotage. (2007, June 4). *New York Times* (editorial), p. A22.

Johnson, C., Smith, P., & the WGBH Series Research Team. (1998). *Africans in America: America's Journey through Slavery*. New York: Harcourt Brace.

Kent, M. M., Pollard, J. H., Haaga, J., & Mather, M. (2001, June). First Glimpses from the 2000 U.S. Census. *Population Bulletin, 56* (2), 3–39.

Kymlicka, W. (1995). *Multicultural Citizenship: A Liberal Theory of Minority Rights*. New York: Oxford University Press.

Lee, S. M., & Edmonston, B. (2005). New Marriages, New Families: U.S. Racial and Hispanic Intermarriage. *Population Bulletin, 60* (2), 1–36.

Luchtenberg, S. (Ed.). (2004). *Migration, Education, and Change*. London & New York: Routledge.

Mann, C. C. (2005). *1491: New Revelations of the Americas before Columbus*. New York: Knopf.

Matthews, H., & Ewen, D. (2006). *Reaching All Children? Understanding Early Care and Education Participation among Immigrant Families*. Retrieved June 20, 2007, from the Center for Law and Social Policy Center website: http://www.clasp.org/publications/child_care_immigrant.pdf.

Merton, R. K. (1972). Insiders and Outsiders: A Chapter in the Sociology of Knowledge. *American Journal of Sociology, 78* (1), 9–47.

Noddings, N. (Ed.). (2005). *Educating Citizens for Global Awareness*. New York: Teachers College Press.

Nussbaum, M. (2002). Patriotism and Cosmopolitanism. In J. Cohen (Ed.), *For Love of Country* (pp. 2–17). Boston: Beacon Press.

Parker, J. D., & Madans, J. H. (2002). The Correspondence between Interracial Births and Multiple-Race Reporting. *American Journal of Public Health, 92* (12), 1976–1981.

Population Reference Bureau Web Update. (2007, May 18). *U.S. Population: The New Generation Gap*. Sent to author via prbmembers@LISTSERV.PRB.ORG. Posted on website http://www.prb.org.

Portes, A., & Rumbaut, R. (2001). *Legacies: The Story of the Immigrant Second Generation*. Berkeley: University of California Press.

Rice News Staff Reports. (2006). Rice Study Shows More Interracial Children Question Their Identity. Retrieved January 9, 2007, from http://www.media.rice.edu/media/NewsBot.asp?MODE=VIEW&ID=8839&SnID=60986.

Root, M. P. P. (2001). *Love's Revolution: Interracial Marriage*. Philadelphia: Temple University Press.

Schierup, C., Hansen, P., & Castles, S. (2006). *Migration, Citizenship, and the European Welfare State*. Oxford, England: Oxford University Press.

Sleeter, C. A. (Ed.). (2005). *Un-Standardizinig Curriculum: Multicultural Teaching in the Standards-Based Classroom*. New York: Teachers College Press.

Solomos, J. (2003). *Race and Racism in Britain*. New York and London: Palgrave Macmillan.

Suárez-Orozco, M., & Páez, M. (Eds.). (2002). *Latinos: Remaking America*. Berkeley: University of California Press.

Tatum, D. (2007). *Can We Talk about Race? And Other Conversations in an Era of School Resegregation*. Boston: Beacon.

Terry, D. (2000, August 11). U.S. Child Poverty Rate Fell as Economy Grew, but Is above 1979 Level. *New York Times*, p. A10.

Tetreault, M. K. (2007). Classrooms for Diversity: Rethinking Curriculum and Pedagogy. In J. A. Banks & C. A. M. Banks (Eds.), *Multicultural Education: Issues and Perspectives* (6th ed., pp. 171–193). New York: Wiley.

Thernstrom, S., Orlov, A., & Handlin, O. (Eds.). (1980). *Harvard Encyclopedia of American Ethnic Groups*. Cambridge, MA: Harvard University Press.

Uchida, Y. (1982). *Desert Exile: The Uprooting of a Japanese-American Family*. Seattle: University of Washington Press.

U.S. Census Bureau. (2000). *Statistical Abstract of the United States* (120th ed.). Washington, DC: U.S. Government Printing Office.

U.S. Census Bureau. (2001). Available online at http://www.census.gov.

U.S. Census Bureau. (2004a). *U.S. Interim Projections by Age, Sex, Race, and Hispanic Origin*. Table 1a: Projected Population of the United States, by Race and Hispanic Origin: 2000 to 2050. Retrieved January 8, 2007, from http://www.census.gov/ipc/www/usinterimproj.

U.S. Census Bureau. (2004b). *U.S. Interim Projections by Age, Sex, Race, and Hispanic Origin*. Table 1b: Projected Population Change in the United States, by Race and Hispanic Origin: 2000 to 2050. Retrieved January 8, 2007, from http://www.census.gov/ipc/www/usinterimproj.

U.S. Census Bureau. (2006). *Nation's Population One-Third Minority*. Retrieved January 8, 2007, from http://www.census.gov/PressRelease/www/releases/archives/population/006808.html.

U.S. Census Bureau. (2007a). The American Community—Asians: 2004. *American Community Survey Reports*. Washington, DC: U.S. Department of Commerce, Economics and Statistics Administration, Author.

U.S. Census Bureau. (2007b*). 2005 American Community Survey: Selected Population Profile: Asian Alone or in Combination with One or More Other Races*. Retrieved June 25, 2007, from http://factfinder.census.gov/servlet/IPCharIterationServlet?_ts=200849058782.

U.S. Census Bureau. (2007c). *2005 American Community Survey, Selected Population Profile*. Available online at http://factfinder.census.gov/servlet/IPCharIterationServlet?_lang=en&_ts=199640379208.

U.S. Department of Education. (2006). *The Condition of Education 2006*. National Center for Education Statistics. NCES 2006-071. Washington, DC: U.S. Government Printing Office.

U.S. Department of Homeland Security. (2007). U.S. Legal Permanent Residents: 2006. *Annual Flow Report*. Washington, DC: Office of Immigration Statistics. Retrieved June 6, 2007, from http://www.dhs.gov/xlibrary/assets/statistics/publications/IS4496_LPRFlowReport_04vacce ssible.pdf.

Wallace, K. R. (2001). *Relative/Outsider: The Art and Politics of Identity among Mixed Heritage Students*. Westport, CT: Ablex.

Wardle, F., & Cruz-Janzen, M. I. (2004). *Meeting the Needs of Multiethnic and Multiracial Children in School*. Boston: Allyn and Bacon.

ANNOTATED BIBLIOGRAPHY

Banks, J. A. (2008). *An Introduction to Multicultural Education* (4th ed.). Boston: Allyn and Bacon.
This brief book introduces preservice and practicing educators to the major issues and concepts in multicultural education. It includes sample lessons, an evaluation checklist, and a bibliography.

Banks, J. A. (2006). *Cultural Diversity and Education: Foundations, Curriculum, and Teaching* (5th ed.). Boston: Allyn and Bacon.
This book discusses the historical, conceptual, and philosophical issues in multicultural education. It includes an important chapter on "Reducing Prejudice in Students: Theory, Research, and Strategies."

Banks, J. A., & Banks, C. A. M. (Eds.). (2004). *Handbook of Research on Multicultural Education* (2nd ed.). San Francisco: Jossey-Bass.
In 49 chapters and 1,088 pages, the leading scholars in multicultural education and related disciplines discuss the history, philosophy, practice, and future of the field. An important reference book for libraries and staff development collections.

Banks, J. A., & Banks, C. A. M. (Eds.). (2007). *Multicultural Education: Issues and Perspectives* (6th ed.). New York: Wiley.
A group of scholars in multicultural education discuss educational issues and strategies related to ethnicity, race, gender, social class, religion, and exceptionality in this introduction to multicultural education.

Banks, J. A., Cookson, P., Gay, G., Hawley, W. D., Irvine, J. I., Nieto, S., Schofield, J. W., & Stephan, W. G. (2001). *Diversity within Unity: Essential Principles for Teaching and Learning in a Multicultural Society*. Seattle: Center for Multicultural Education, University of Washington.
This publication describes twelve research-based principles that can be used to create school environments that reflect the diversity within U.S. society. It can be downloaded as a pdf file. Print copies can be ordered from the Center for Multicultural Education (website: http://depts.washington.edu/centerme/home.htm).

Bhatia, T. K., & Ritchie, W. C. (Eds.). (2006). *The Handbook of Bilingualism*. Malden, MA: Blackwell.
This book contains a gold mine of information about second language learning, not only in the United States but also within a number of nations and regions around the world. It is very comprehensive, consisting of 884 pages.

Bigelow, B., & Peterson, B. (Eds.). (1998). *Rethinking Columbus: The Next 500 Years*. Milwaukee: Rethinking Schools.
An excellent and thought-provoking selection of articles and documents that can be used to teach about Columbus using a transformative approach.

Loewen, J. W. (2005). *Sundown Towns: A Hidden Dimension of American Racism*. New York: New Press.

This interesting and informative book tells the sad and poignant story of the thousands of U.S. towns that excluded African Americans and other minority groups after sundown. It describes an important but untold part of American history.

Suárez-Orozco, C., & Suárez-Orozco, M. (2001). *Children of Immigration*. Cambridge, MA: Harvard University Press.

An excellently written, comprehensive, and informative book on children of immigrants by two of the foremost authorities on immigration and education in the United States.

Tatum, B. D. (2007). *Can We Talk? And Other Conversations in an Era of School Resegregation*. Boston: Beacon.

An interesting and highly readable book about race that is insightful, informative, and timely. Tatum is also author of *Why Are All the Black Kids Sitting Together in the Cafeteria?*

Waters, M. C., & Ueda, R. (Eds.). (2007). *The New Americans: A Guide to Immigration since 1965*. Cambridge, MA: Harvard University Press.

This comprehensive book includes a thoughtful and informative collection of chapters on many dimensions of the new immigrant groups that have settled in the United States since 1968. Some of the chapters focus on groups from specific regions and nations, such as West Africa, East Africa, Central America, China, and Cuba.

CHAPTER TWO

DEVELOPING A MULTICULTURAL CURRICULUM

The key goal of the multicultural curriculum should be to help students develop decision-making and citizen action skills. The decision-making process consists of several components, including knowledge, values, the synthesis of knowledge and values, and action designed to implement the decision made. However, the knowledge that comprises reflective decision making must have certain characteristics. It must be scientific, higher-level, conceptual, and interdisciplinary. Reflective decision makers must identify the sources of their values, determine how these values conflict, identify value alternatives, and choose freely from among the alternatives. They act only after identifying alternative courses of action, ordering them according to personal values, and expressing a willingness to accept the possible consequences of their actions.

This chapter focuses on the *knowledge components* of decision making. A presentation of the interdisciplinary conceptual approach is followed by a discussion of four categories of knowledge: *facts, concepts, generalizations,* and *theories.* You must be able to identify the categories of knowledge in order to structure interdisciplinary and conceptual lessons and units. Chapter 3 discusses concepts you can use to organize multicultural lessons and units. The valuing and social action components of the multicultural curriculum are discussed in Chapter 4. Key issues related to the selection and evaluation of multicultural teaching materials are also discussed in Chapter 4.

THE INTERDISCIPLINARY-CONCEPTUAL APPROACH

A decision-making curriculum is not only characterized by the sequential development of higher-level ideas, it is also *interdisciplinary.* In such a curriculum, concepts, when feasible and appropriate, are viewed from the perspectives of several disciplines and subject areas, such as the various social sciences, art, music, literature, physical education, communication, the physical and biological sciences, and mathematics.

It is necessary for students to view events and situations from the perspectives of several disciplines, because any one discipline gives only a partial understanding of issues and concepts related to ethnic and cultural diversity in society. Concepts such as *discrimination* and *ethnic diversity* are not merely sociological; they also have multiple dimensions, including economic, political, legal, cultural, and moral aspects. The values and experiences of people of color are reflected in their literature, art, music, drama, dance, communication styles, and foods. Dominant ethnic groups within a society also express issues related to ethnic diversity and respond to these issues in their artistic and cultural forms. Students must view concepts and issues related to ethnic groups from diverse disciplinary perspectives in order to gain a complete understanding of the experiences of the diverse cultural and ethnic groups in the United States and the world.

STUDYING CULTURE: AN EXAMPLE OF THE INTERDISCIPLINARY-CONCEPTUAL APPROACH

When students study a concept such as *culture,* they can gain a comprehensive understanding only by viewing ethnic cultures from the perspectives of the various social sciences and by examining the expressions of ethnic cultures in literature, music, drama, dance, art, communication, and foods. Content and insights from science and mathematics can also be incorporated into an interdisciplinary study of cultures. The next section discusses special issues involved in incorporating science and mathematics into the multicultural curriculum.

Concepts such as *culture* can be used to organize units and activities related to ethnicity that are interdisciplinary and cut across disciplinary lines. Other concepts, such as *cultural assimilation, acculturation,* and *values,* can also be analyzed and studied from an interdisciplinary perspective. However, it is neither possible nor desirable to teach each concept in the curriculum from the perspectives of all disciplines and curricular areas. Such an attempt would result in artificial relationships and superficial learnings by students.

There are many excellent opportunities within the curriculum for teaching concepts from an interdisciplinary perspective. Interdisciplinary teaching, however, requires the strong cooperation of teachers in the various content areas. Team teaching will often be necessary, especially at the high school level, to organize and implement interdisciplinary units and lessons. Table 2.1 contains key questions that students can pursue when they study cultures from an interdisciplinary perspective. Figure 2.1, on page 36, illustrates the process.

INCORPORATING ELEMENTS FROM SCIENCE AND MATHEMATICS INTO THE MULTICULTURAL CURRICULUM

Incorporating elements from science and mathematics into the multicultural curriculum is difficult for most teachers. Issues related to science and mathematics can be incorporated into the multicultural curriculum in at least three ways: (1) ways related to content; (2) ways related to concepts, paradigms, and perspectives; and (3) ways related to equity issues (Gutstein & Peterson, 2005; Lee & Luykx, 2007; Nasir & Cobb, 2007; Moses & Cobb, 2001).

TABLE 2.1   Studying Ethnic Cultures from an Interdisciplinary Perspective

DISCIPLINE OR CURRICULUM AREA	KEY OR FOCUS QUESTION
Social Studies	In what ways are the cultures of ethnic groups such as African Americans, Jewish Americans, and Mexican Americans similar and different? Why?
Reading and Literature	How do the fiction and other literary works by American ethnic authors reveal characteristics and components of their cultures?
Music	What does the music of an ethnic group reveal about its values, symbols, and culture?
Drama	What do plays written by ethnic authors reveal about their culture?
Physical Education	How do ethnic groups express their cultures, values, aspirations, and frustrations in their dances and creative movements?
Art	What does the art of an ethnic group reveal about its lifestyles, perceptions, values, history, and culture?
Communication (Language Arts)	How does the language of an ethnic group express and reflect its values and culture? What can we learn about an ethnic group by studying its symbols and communication styles, both verbal and nonverbal?
Home Economics	What do ethnic foods reveal about an ethnic group's values and culture? What can we learn about an ethnic culture by studying its foods?
Science	How do the physical characteristics of an ethnic group influence its interactions with other groups, intragroup relationships, and its total culture?
Mathematics	What is the relationship between the number system used within a society and its culture? What do the symbol systems within a culture reveal about it? Historically, what contributions have different ethnic groups made to our number system?

Some content related to science and mathematics can be incorporated into the multicultural curriculum. In science, the biological basis of skin color and the other physical characteristics of various racial groups can be studied. However, when the biological basis of race is studied, students should be helped to understand that race is largely a *socially constructed* concept or category even though scientists have attempted to formulate different racial categories (Gould, 1996; Harding, 1998; Roediger, 2005). Health issues and diseases related to various ethnic groups are other appropriate subjects for science in the multicultural curriculum.

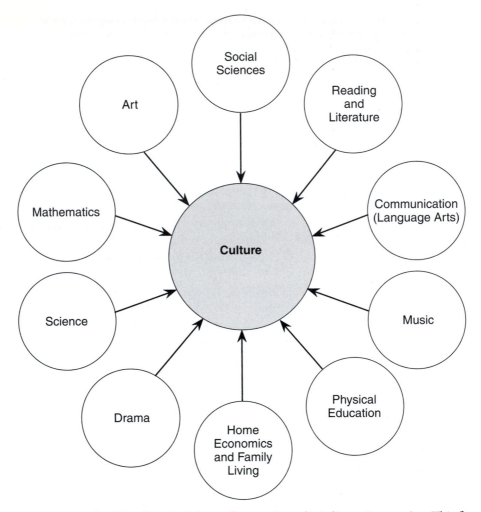

FIGURE 2.1   Studying Ethnic Cultures from an Interdisciplinary Perspective This figure illustrates how a concept such as *culture* can be viewed from the perspectives of a number of disciplines and areas. Any one discipline gives only a partial understanding of a concept, social problem, or issue. Thus, multicultural units and lessons should be interdisciplinary and cut across disciplinary lines.

The experience of various ethnic and cultural groups in science, in both past and contemporary society, is another appropriate study for science in the multicultural curriculum. The lives of African American scientists such as Daniel Hale Williams and Ernest E. Just should be examined in the scientific component of the multicultural curriculum. These individuals made significant contributions to science despite the blatant discrimination they experienced. Contemporary scientists from diverse groups should also be studied.

Content related to mathematics in the multicultural curriculum can highlight the role played by groups such as the Egyptians and Aztecs in the development of theory and practice in mathematics (Mason, 1962; Sertima, 1986). In the film *Stand and Deliver,* Mr. Escalante uses his knowledge of Aztec contributions to mathematics to motivate his Mexican American students to study calculus. Mr. Escalante reminds his students that their ancestors, the Aztecs, made significant mathematical breakthroughs. Students can also examine the experiences of mathematicians today from various cultural and racial groups.

Another important way to view science and mathematics in the multicultural curriculum is to examine the basic concepts, paradigms, and perspectives used in science and mathematics and the influence these paradigms, concepts, and perspectives have had and still have on various ethnic and cultural groups (Banks, 1995; Gould, 1996; Harding, 1998; Selden, 1999). This can be done more readily in science than in mathematics. Darwin's theory of evolution as well as other scientific theories— such as the genetic theory of intelligence—have historically been used, and are being used today, to support scientific racism (Gould, 1996; Herrnstein & Murray, 1994). Students can examine scientific racism from both a historical and a contemporary perspective (Banks, 1995).

Levins and Lewontin (1985), using a Marxist dialectic, argue that scientists act within a social context and from a philosophical perspective that is inherently political. Students can examine the Levins and Lewontin thesis and determine the extent to which it is applicable to their science textbooks and readings. Students can also study such questions as these: What major assumptions, concepts, and perspectives do scientists use today that are related to the experiences of ethnic groups? What major influence are these assumptions, concepts, and perspectives having on the experiences of ethnic groups? Students can also examine how applied mathematics is being used to influence societal issues and practices.

When examining how scientists have constructed ideas about the low IQs of African Americans and other ethnic groups historically and today, students can examine the arguments set forth by Herrnstein and Murray in *The Bell Curve* (1994) about the inferior intellectual abilities of Blacks and can discuss questions such as these: Why did Herrnstein and Murray create their theory? What groups in society benefit from it? What groups in society are hurt by it? Why are theories such as the one by Herrnstein and Murray created and popularized by the mass media when many scientists have serious doubts about them? Students can read critiques of the Herrnstein and Murray theory in *The Bell Curve Debate,* edited by Jacoby and Glauberman (1995), and in *The Bell Curve Wars,* edited by Fraser (1995).

A third, and perhaps the most important, way in which science and mathematics teachers can include multicultural content in their curricula is by examining equity issues in science and mathematics and by modifying their teaching techniques and expectations in order to enhance the academic achievement of students of color and of women. Researchers have indicated that students of color and female students often do not achieve as well as White males in higher-level mathematics and science courses (Nasir & Cobb, 2007).

Students of color and female students also take fewer high-level mathematics and science courses than do White males. Researchers have suggested that these situations result in part from low teacher expectations and from the teaching styles used in science and mathematics courses that are inconsistent with how many students of color and female students learn (Belenky, Clinchy, Goldberger, & Tarule, 1986; Cohen & Lotan, 1997). To make their teaching multicultural, science and mathematics teachers should encourage their students of color and their female students to enroll in higher-level courses, provide these students with support and encouragement, and modify their teaching techniques to make them more consistent with the learning styles of students of color and female students. Fullilove and Treisman (1990) have found that cooperative teaching and learning strategies can help students of color learn advanced calculus.

THE FORMS OF KNOWLEDGE

Above, I illustrated how a key concept such as culture can be viewed from diverse disciplinary perspectives. To identify and select key concepts such as culture, you must be familiar with the nature of knowledge and its various forms: *facts, concepts, generalizations,* and *theories.* A discussion of these major knowledge forms and the contribution that each can make to an interdisciplinary and conceptual multicultural curriculum follows.

Facts

Facts are low-level, specific, empirical statements about limited phenomena. Facts may be considered the lowest level of knowledge, and they have the least predictive capacity of all of the knowledge forms. In multicultural studies, as in all academic areas and disciplines, facts are the building blocks of knowledge. Students must master facts in order to learn higher levels of knowledge.

Examples of facts are:

- The Chinese immigrants who came to San Francisco in the 1800s established the *hui kuan.*
- More than 175,000 legal immigrants came to the United States from Mexico in 2004.
- Between 2001 and 2004, 578,000 legal immigrants from Europe settled in the United States.

A careful study of these facts about U.S. ethnic groups reveals several characteristics of factual statements. First, facts are *empirical* statements, or statements that can be tested with available data or data that can be obtained. By carefully studying and analyzing historical documents and statistical data, a social scientist can determine whether the Chinese immigrants who came to the United States in the 1800s actually established *hui kuan* societies. It is important to stress that factual statements are capable of verification or testing; however, many statements presented as facts, especially in multicultural studies, are, on closer scrutiny, normative or value statements that cannot be tested or can be tested only with great difficulty. An example of such a statement is "Indians were hostile." This statement is actually a misleading stereotype masquerading as a factual statement.

Because factual statements are limited in explaining causal relationships, students need to master higher levels of knowledge in addition to facts. Facts should not be the end goal of instruction because they are very limited. Many teachers end units by testing students primarily for their mastery of facts. Because facts in and of themselves do not encompass a large quantity of data, they have little transfer value, are quickly forgotten by students, and do not, if they are the end goal of instruction, help students to gain in-depth understandings of society.

However, to say that facts are limited in the contribution they can make to students' understanding of social events and problems is not to say that they are not important and that they do not have a proper role in instruction—quite the contrary. Factual statements are important in teaching. If you keep their limitations in mind and use them judiciously, they can contribute to student learning. Facts are the foundations of the higher levels of knowledge: concepts, generalizations, and theories. Without learning facts, as I later illustrate, students will not be able to master concepts and generalizations. However, you are justified in teaching facts only if they are used to help students develop higher forms of knowledge or to make decisions. Thus, for every fact you select for inclusion in the curriculum, you should have a concept, generalization, or theory in mind that the fact is intended to help students develop. Facts taught randomly and in isolation have little instructional value. Yet, they can become powerful instructional tools if they are carefully selected and taught.

Concepts

Concepts are words or phrases that enable us to categorize or classify a large class of observations and thus to reduce the complexity of our environment. In structure and function, concepts differ from facts, generalizations, and theories. Both facts and generalizations are empirical *statements;* a theory consists of a system of interrelated generalizations and principles. However, concepts are special constructs because they are necessary for the formulation of the other categories of knowledge and are contained in all facts, generalizations, and theories. Because concepts are contained in all other forms of knowledge, students cannot understand a fact, generalization, or theory unless the concepts contained within them are meaningful.

The following are some of the key concepts discussed in Chapter 3:

cultural assimilation	immigration
acculturation	power
race	values
culture	

Even though concepts are contained in all facts, generalizations, and theories, they are unique because they can also encompass a large range of facts and generalizations. A complete theory can be formulated about a single concept, such as cultural assimilation or discrimination. Some concepts are rather concrete, such as *street;* others are more abstract, such as *megalopolis.* Some concepts, such as *city,* are somewhere between these two extremes. We might call these kinds of concepts *intermediate-level* concepts. Thus, if we arrange these concepts into a hierarchy, it would look like this:

megalopolis
city
street

In this example, *megalopolis* is the highest-level concept because it consists of a region made up of several cities and their surrounding areas. *City* is the next-level concept because a city contains many streets. Of course, there are parallel concepts that are more concrete than *street.*

Concepts encompassing generalizations are often more abstract (or at a higher level) than are concepts that are contained in the generalizations encompassed. Also, the concepts contained in facts are often less abstract than those used to classify those facts. The same is true for theories. The example below illustrates how a higher-level concept, *immigration,* can be used to categorize a number of facts. The facts, of course, contain many concepts.

HIGHER-LEVEL CONCEPT
Immigration
Facts being categorized or grouped under concept:

- Between 1820 and 1979, 36,267,000 European immigrants came to the United States.
- There were 2,797,966 Chinese Americans living in the United States in 2005.
- There were 833,762 Japanese Americans living in the United States in 2005.
- Between 2001 and 2004, 261,900 people from India immigrated to the United States.

Higher-level concepts can also encompass or classify generalizations (see discussion below for definition of a generalization). In the next example, the concept *culture* is used to categorize a number of generalizations at varying levels of abstraction.

CONCEPT
Culture
Generalizations being categorized or grouped under concept:

- An ethnic minority group usually acquires some of the values, behaviors, and beliefs of the dominant ethnic groups within a society.

- Dominant ethnic groups usually acquire some of the cultural characteristics of ethnic minority groups.
- African Americans have made a number of contributions to American music.

In many cases, some concepts are clearly at a higher level than are others. For example, *city* is a higher-level concept than *street* because a city contains many streets. However, because a concept appears in a factual statement does not necessarily mean that it is a lower-level or concrete concept. Study this factual statement:

About 64,921 Chinese immigrants arrived in the United States in 2005.

This factual statement contains the higher-level concept *immigrant*. As previously illustrated, the concept *immigration* can be used to categorize a number of facts. The distinguishing characteristic of a higher-level concept is that it can categorize a number of facts and generalizations. This is true even though that same concept may sometimes appear within factual statements. By identifying higher-level concepts, you will be able to help students relate discrete facts and data to form generalizations about ethnicity, which they can apply when studying ethnic and cultural groups both within the United States and in other nations. Table 2.2 illustrates how key concepts can be used to do a comparative study of ethnic groups within the United States and in other nations.

Table 2.3 illustrates one strategy for teaching a concept. This strategy is called "Lesson Plan for Attaining a Concept." Try teaching this lesson to a group of students or to a group of your classmates or colleagues in your workshop. After teaching this lesson, respond to this question: What are the advantages of using a conceptual approach to teaching?

Generalizations

A generalization contains two or more concepts and states the relationship between them. Like empirical facts, generalizations are scientific statements that can be tested and verified with data. Generalizations are useful tools in instruction because they can be used to summarize a large mass of facts and to show the relationship between higher-level concepts that students have mastered. Like concepts, generalizations vary greatly in their level of inclusiveness. There are low-level generalizations, which are little more than summary statements, and there are high-level generalizations, which are universal in applicability. To illustrate levels of generalizations, we study one fact listed earlier in this chapter and state generalizations at various levels that encompass it.

FACT
The Chinese immigrants who came to San Francisco in the 1800s established the *hui kuan*.

Lower-level generalization:
Chinese immigrants in America established various forms of social organizations.

Intermediate-level generalization:
All groups that have immigrated to the United States have established social organizations.

TABLE 2.2 A Comparative Study of Ethnic Groups in Different Nations

KEY CONCEPTS AND RELATED KEY QUESTIONS	FILIPINO AMERICANS (USA)	BRITISH PAKISTANIS	FRENCH CANADIANS	NIGERIAN IBOS	MEXICAN INDIANS	FRENCH ALGERIANS
Origins Is the group native or did it migrate or immigrate to its current location? If an immigrant group, what caused the immigration?						
Discrimination Is the group experiencing discrimination? If so, what kinds? If not, why not?						
Culture What are the group's unique cultural and ethnic characteristics?						
Assimilation To what extent is the group assimilated both culturally and structurally?						
Economic Status Is the group facing economic problems or does it have a secure economic status?						
Education Are the group's youths experiencing problems in the schools? Why or why not?						
Power What role does the group play in the political system? Has it been able to organize and to exercise political power effectively?						
Ethnic Revitalization Is the group experiencing or has it experienced an ethnic revitalization movement? Explain.						

TABLE 2.3   Lesson Plan for Attaining a Concept

1. Write "Rite of Passage" on the board. Ask the students to repeat the words.
2. List these examples of rites of passage on the board and tell the students, "These are examples of rites of passage":

Marriage ceremony

Christening ceremony

Funeral

Vision quest among the Zuni Indians

Baptism

Bar Mitzvah

Bas Mitzvah

3. Ask the students to describe what these examples of the concept have in common. Put the list on the board.
4. Help the students to identify and state the critical attributes of "rite of passage."
5. Ask the students to write a definition of *rite of passage* using the list of key attributes that they formulated above. Their definitions should be a variation of this one: "Ceremonies that mark a critical transition in the life of an individual from one phase of the life cycle to another."[a]

Follow-up Activity: Ask the students to interview parents and other family members to find out what rites of passage have taken place in their families. Ask them to share at least one family rite of passage in which they have participated or observed. Ask the students: "What important functions do rites of passage play for individuals, families, and societies?"

[a]This definition is from G. A. Theodorson and A. G. Theodorson (1979), *A Modern Dictionary of Sociology*. New York: Barnes and Noble, p. 350.

> *Highest-level or universal generalization:*
> In all human societies, forms of social organizations are created to satisfy the needs of individuals and groups.

A study of these examples indicates that a generalization is a higher-level statement than a fact because a generalization encompasses a number of facts. The fact noted above tells us only that Chinese Americans established one kind of social organization, the *hui kuan*. The lower-level generalization in our example reveals that Chinese Americans established a variety of social organizations. Thus, the lower-level generalization encompasses not only the fact about the *hui kuan* but also the following facts:

- Chinese immigrants in America formed organizations called "clans."
- The Chinese Benevolent Association is a confederation of clans and secret societies.

- Secret societies emerged within Chinese communities in the United States.
- The Chinese secret societies provided help to Chinese Americans and obtained control of gambling in Chinese American communities.

The next generalization in the example—an intermediate-level generalization—encompasses facts not only about Chinese Americans but also about all immigrants and migrants in the United States. Thus, this generalization is at a higher level of abstraction because it encompasses more facts than the lower-level generalization. For example, the intermediate-level generalization, in addition to encompassing the facts about Chinese American organizations, encompasses the following facts:

- Puerto Ricans established the Puerto Rican Forum to help solve the problems of Puerto Rican migrants in New York City.
- Jewish Americans founded the Anti-Defamation League of B'nai B'rith to help mitigate anti-Semitism in the United States.
- In 1921, Spanish-speaking Americans formed the *Orden Hijos de America* (Order of the Sons of America) to train its members for U.S. citizenship.
- Japanese immigrants in America created the Japanese Association to provide services for its members.
- The National Urban League was founded in 1911 to help African American southern migrants adjust to city life.

The last generalization is the highest form of generalization possible because it encompasses all the other facts and generalizations above it and applies to all human societies in the past and present. Note that it does not contain a reference to any particular people, region, or culture. One way to determine whether a generalization is written at the highest possible level is to ascertain whether it is limited to a particular people, culture, or historical era. A generalization of wide applicability contains few or no exceptions and can be tested and verified, to varying degrees, within any human culture. The highest-level generalization in the example states that in every past and present human society one can find examples of social organizations. This generalization has been tested and verified by social scientists. Whether they studied a preliterate tribe in New Zealand or the cultures in medieval Europe, social scientists found types of social organizations such as the family and some kind of kinship system. It is true that the forms these organizations take vary greatly both within and between cultures, but nevertheless they exist.

It is necessary for you to be able to identify and write generalizations at various levels in order to incorporate ethnic content into the curriculum. During initial planning, you should identify generalizations of the highest order so that you can then select content samples from a variety of cultures to enable students to test them. If you start planning by identifying lower-level or intermediate-level generalizations, you will be greatly limited in the content that you can select to exemplify the generalizations. Consider, for example, that you select the generalization "Chinese immigrants in America established various forms of social organization." By selecting this lower-level generalization to organize instruction, you will not be able to help students derive generalizations related to the organizations that other ethnic groups—such as Anglo-Saxon Protestants, Mexican Americans, Jewish Americans, and Arab Americans—have formed in the United States.

You should begin planning by identifying high-level concepts and generalizations (called key or organizing generalizations in this book) and then should select lower-level concepts and generalizations related to the chosen content *samples*. This type of planning is necessary in order to help students develop higher-level statements, which is one of the ultimate goals of instruction. Chapter 4 discusses procedures you can use to identify high-level concepts and generalizations that can form the core of a sound multicultural curriculum.

We have noted that generalizations range from the concrete to those that are universal in application. A fact related to a Chinese American institution, the *hui kuan*, was chosen to illustrate how a single fact can be encompassed by generalizations at three different levels. The choice of three levels was an arbitrary decision; generalizations at fewer or more levels could have easily been written. For example, Hilda Taba has identified four levels (or orders, as she calls them) of generalizations (Taba, Durkin, Fraenkel, & McNaughton, 1971). Because generalizations exist at many different levels, it is not necessary for you to spend undue time trying to devise elaborate schemes for classifying levels of generalizations.

However, to plan effective units and lessons, you should know that generalizations exist at many different levels, that all generalizations are at a higher level than facts, and that the highest-order or highest-level generalizations should be identified during the initial stages of unit planning.

Earlier in this chapter, I said that a generalization is a statement capable of being tested or verified. This is true; but because human behavior is so complex, *generalizations in the social and behavioral sciences are always tentative statements and can never be proven to be 100% correct*. Almost always, social science generalizations will have some exceptions. Because social science generalizations tend to be tentative and nonconclusive, they often contain qualifying words.

Study this generalization: "When an ethnic minority group is oppressed and it sees no legitimate ways to alleviate its problems, rebellions will sometimes occur." The word *sometimes* qualifies this generalization, because in many situations an ethnic minority group may feel oppressed and see no legitimate ways to alleviate its problems yet ethnic rebellions may not occur. Japanese Americans, when they were forced to leave their homes during World War II and were sent to internment camps, did not resist or rebel as a group, although some individuals did resist internment. One social scientist has hypothesized that most Japanese Americans cooperated with the federal government because of the norms within their culture toward authority and because they did not believe that resistance would succeed (Kitano, 1976). On the other hand, many African Americans who felt oppressed in U.S. cities in the late 1960s violently rebelled. The particular times, the culture of a group, and the group's perceptions of its social and economic status greatly influence how it will respond to an oppressive situation. This example is used merely to illustrate that students should be taught how tentative social science conclusions and generalizations are and *should learn that social knowledge is constantly changing and is never absolute.*

Generalizations are important in instruction because they enable students to make predictions; the predictive capacity of generalizations varies directly with their degree of applicability and amount of empirical support. Generalizations that describe a large class of behaviors and that have been widely verified are the most useful for making predictions. We have called these types of generalizations *high-level* or *organizing generalizations.* Generalizations enable students not only to predict behavior with a fairly high degree of accuracy but also to solve problems in novel situations.

Theory

Theory is the highest form of knowledge and is the most useful for predicting human behavior. I stated that a *concept* is a word or phrase used to categorize or classify facts, data, and other forms of information and knowledge. A *generalization* is a statement that shows the relationship between two or more concepts that can be empirically verified. A review of the definitions of these terms is important because a theory consists of a number of interrelated generalizations. The generalizations within a theory constitute a deductive system and are logically interrelated. The generalizations contained within a theory are also *high-level* and *universal-type generalizations;* they are not low-level generalizations. A theory is called a *deductive* system because when several generalizations within a theory are stated, the concluding ones can be logically derived. In other words, when given some propositions within a theory, a conclusion can be derived from the stated generalizations. An empirical theory has the following characteristics:

- It consists of a set of interrelated lawlike propositions or generalizations that are testable.
- The propositions must show the relationship between variables or concepts that are clearly defined.
- The propositions must constitute a deductive system and be logically consistent: unknown principles must be derivable from known ones.
- The propositions must be a source of testable hypotheses.

The following example of a theory illustrates how the deductive process works. Gordon's (1964) theory of cultural and structural assimilation has heavily influenced the field of ethnic studies. Here are the four major generalizations within this theory:

1. With regard to *cultural behavior,* differences of social class are more important and decisive than are differences of ethnic group.
2. With regard to *social participation* in primary groups and primary relationships, people tend to confine these to their own social class segment within their own ethnic group, that is, the *ethclass.*

3. With a person of the same social class but of a different ethnic group, one shares behavioral similarities but not a sense of peoplehood.
4. With those of the same ethnic group but of a different social class one shares a sense of *peoplehood* but not behavioral similarities (pp. 52–53; emphases added).

Gordon's theory satisfies our criterion of a theory: *a system of high-level inter-related generalizations that constitute a deductive system.* In the first generalization in the theory, Gordon hypothesizes that in terms of cultural behavior, social class is more important than ethnicity. By cultural behavior, he means such things as the values a person holds, his or her speech patterns, and occupational aspirations.

This generalization suggests that an upper-class African American individual's clothing, values, and foods are likely to be more similar to those of an upper-class White than to those of a lower-class African American. The second generalization in the theory suggests that an upper-class Mexican American, while sharing cultural characteristics with White Anglo-Saxons, is more likely to participate in the private clubs and cliques of other upper-class Mexican Americans than in Anglo-Saxon private clubs and social cliques. The theory hypothesizes that even though upper-status individuals within different ethnic groups share similar values and behavior, their close, primary group relationships are largely confined to members within their ethnic groups of the same social class. This is also true for lower-class members of ethnic groups. Gordon presents much compelling evidence in his book to support the generalizations that comprise his theory.

Gordon's (1964) theory meets the criterion of a theory, because when given generalizations 1 and 2 of his theory (presented above), one can logically derive generalizations 3 and 4. To do so, however, it might be necessary to know how he defines two key concepts in his generalizations: *ethclass* and *sense of peoplehood.* He defines *ethclass* as the "subsociety created by the intersection of the vertical stratifications of ethnicity with the horizontal stratifications of social class" (pp. 52–53). Thus, lower-middle-class Vietnamese Americans constitute an ethclass. By *sense of peoplehood,* Gordon means "an individual's identification with a group that shares a common culture, religious beliefs, and values" (p. 23). He contends, for example, that African Americans in all social classes share an ethnic identification.

GRAND AND MIDDLE-RANGE THEORIES

Social science has few *grand theories.* Grand theories try to explain all of behavior. Freudian psychology is an example of a grand theory in social science. As Merton (1968) points out, most theories in social science are what he calls "theories of the middle range." Gordon's theory is middle range because it tries to explain only behavior related to cultural assimilation. Although Gordon's theory of assimilation has much explanatory power, it was created more than forty years ago; ethnic and race relations have changed in significant ways since Gordon first constructed his theory. Gordon's theory needs to be examined in light of new findings and studies in social science. Heath and McLaughlin (1993), for example, found that for many of the teenagers they studied, ethnicity or race was not their primary or most important identity. These youth often formed social groupings that cut across racial and ethnic lines.

Using Theories in Teaching

To help students fully understand the ethnic experience in the United States, you should, whenever possible, help them relate generalizations to a theoretical system. Generalizations have much more meaning when they are studied within a theoretical framework than when studied in isolation.

Because of their specialized structure and function, a complete theory can be structured around a single concept. Gordon's theory of *cultural and structural assimilation* is an example theory formed around the concept of assimilation. Cultural assimilation occurs when one ethnic group attains the values and behavior patterns of another ethnic group. Usually, the ethnic minority group attains the cultural characteristics of the dominant ethnic group. Structural assimilation occurs when one ethnic group participates in the primary groups, such as private clubs and social cliques, of another ethnic group (Gordon, 1964). Gordon concludes that, even though widespread cultural assimilation has taken place in U.S. society, little structural assimilation has occurred because ethnic groups within U.S. society, including dominant ethnic groups and people of color, participate mainly in the primary groups of their own ethnic communities. He maintains that our society has a high degree of cultural assimilation but is characterized by *structural pluralism*. Although Gordon's theory probably explains large classes of ethnic behavior in the United States, the research by Heath and McLaughlin (1993) indicates that his theory must be interpreted within the context of U.S. society in the twenty-first century.

AN EFFECTIVE MULTICULTURAL CURRICULUM

An effective multicultural curriculum helps students develop the ability to make reflective decisions on personal and public issues and to take successful social action. Integrating the curriculum with ethnic content can be viewed as a process of curriculum reform. During this process, the entire curriculum is transformed to enable students to view events, concepts, and issues from diverse ethnic and cultural perspectives.

The multicultural curriculum is broadly conceptualized and includes the study of a wide range of ethnic groups. These groups are studied using a comparative approach. The multicultural curriculum is also conceptual and interdisciplinary. Major concepts, when feasible and appropriate, are studied from the perspectives of disciplines such as the various social sciences, art, literature, communication, and the physical and biological sciences. Figure 2.2 summarizes these characteristics of an effective multicultural curriculum. Chapter 3 presents key concepts that can be used to plan and organize a multicultural curriculum.

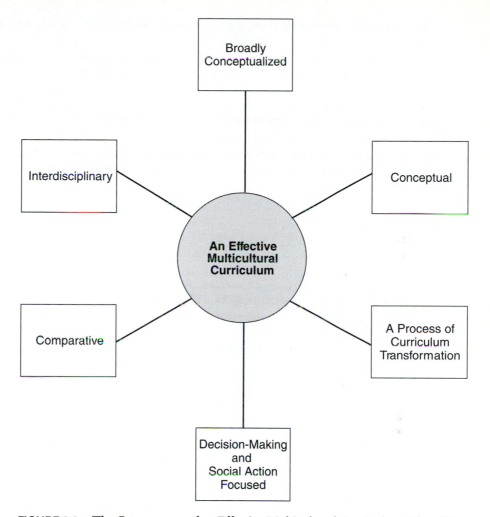

FIGURE 2.2   The Components of an Effective Multicultural Curriculum The effective multicultural curriculum must be conceptual, broadly conceptualized, interdisciplinary, comparative, decision-making and social action focused, and viewed as a process of curriculum transformation.

SUMMARY

The interdisciplinary-conceptual approach can best facilitate the integration of ethnic content into the curriculum and into the various subject areas. Using this approach, the teacher selects key concepts, such as culture, power, and discrimination, and then identifies content samples that can be used to help students attain these ideas. The interdisciplinary-conceptual approach allows the teacher to use content samples from several different disciplines and thus to teach in an interdisciplinary way.

When identifying concepts for a conceptual multicultural curriculum, you should make sure that a balanced approach is taken and that people of color are not depicted only or primarily as victims. Rather, they should be described as people who helped shape their own destinies, built ethnic institutions, and played major roles in attaining their civil rights. It is necessary to teach such concepts as prejudice, discrimination, and racism. However, it is also essential to teach such concepts as protest, empowerment, interracial cooperation, and ethnic institutions in order to portray a full and accurate view of the experiences of ethnic groups in the United States.

REFLECTION AND ACTION ACTIVITIES

1. Label each of the following a *fact, concept,* or *generalization* and justify each label:
   a. acculturation
   b. In every human society there is a conflict between unlimited wants and limited resources.
   c. assimilation
   d. In 1827 Vincente Guerrero became president of Mexico.
   e. Ethnic cultures, values, and behavior are undergoing constant change.
   f. On September 22, 1862, President Lincoln issued a statement that has been called the Preliminary Emancipation Proclamation.
   g. In 2000, Mexicans made up 58.5% of the Hispanic population in the United States.
   h. During the 1960s and 1970s, people of color strove less for cultural assimilation and more for cultural pluralism.
   i. cultural pluralism
   j. ethnic group

2. Here is a higher-level generalization: "Most foreigners who voluntarily immigrated to the United States were seeking better economic, political, and social opportunities." Examine several of the books on ethnic groups contained in the bibliographies in Parts II through V and write several factual statements and lower-level generalizations that this generalization will encompass.

3. Examine several of the books in the bibliographies in Parts II through V and find a number of factual statements and generalizations that the following concepts will encompass: cultural assimilation, structural assimilation, protest, discrimination.

4. Tell whether each of these statements is normative or empirical, and why:
   a. The American colonists should not have taken land away from the American Indians.
   b. Irresponsible African Americans rioted in many American cities in the 1960s.
   c. There were approximately 12 million illegal immigrants living in the United States in 2007.
   d. Japanese Americans should not have been sent to relocation camps in 1942.
   e. Many Puerto Ricans migrate to the United States mainland each year.
   f. Many Chinese Americans live in ghettos in U.S. cities.

5. What do you think should be the role of the following categories of knowledge in a sound multicultural curriculum? Why?
   a. facts
   b. concepts
   c. generalizations
   d. theories

6. Examine several books dealing with people of color (see the annotated bibliographies in Parts II through V of this book) and identify a theory related to ethnic groups. Can this theory be taught to a group of elementary or high school students? Why or why not? If you think it can be taught to a group of students, develop a plan for teaching it. If you are a classroom teacher or a student teacher, implement your teaching plan and evaluate its effectiveness.

7. Make a list of your close friends. Note their *ethnic, religious,* and *racial backgrounds.* Compare your list with similar lists made by other individuals in your class or workshop. What conclusions can you make about structural assimilation in U.S. society on the basis of the responses made by you and your classmates or fellow workshop participants?

8. If your parents are first- or second-generation U.S. immigrants, make a list of their values and lifestyles that are different from your own. If your parents are not first- or second-generation immigrants, interview individuals whose parents are and compare their values and lifestyles with those of their parents. What tentative generalizations can you make about cultural assimilation in U.S. society by studying these data?

9. Define each of the following terms and tell why each is important:

knowledge	ethclass
reflective decision	cultural assimilation
fact	structural assimilation
concept	intermediate-level generalization
generalization	high-level generalization
theory	high-level concept
normative statement	low-level concept
empirical statement	

REFERENCES

Banks, J. A. (1995). The Historical Reconstruction of Knowledge about Race: Implications for Transformative Teaching. *Educational Researcher, 24* (2), 15–25.

Belenky, M. F., Clinchy, B. M., Goldberger, N. R., & Tarule, J. M. (1986). *Women's Ways of Knowing: The Development of Self, Voice, and Mind.* New York: Basic Books.

Cohen, E. G., & Lotan, R. A. (Eds.). (1997). *Working for Equity in Heterogeneous Classrooms.* New York: Teachers College Press.

Fraser, S. (Ed.). (1995). *The Bell Curve Wars: Race, Intelligence and the Future of America.* New York: Basic Books.

Fullilove, R. E., & Treisman, P. U. (1990). Mathematics Achievement among African American Undergraduates at the University of California, Berkeley: An Evaluation of the Mathematics Workshop Program. *Journal of Negro Education, 59* (3), 463–490.

Gordon, M. M. (1964). *Assimilation in American Life*. New York: Oxford University Press.

Gould, S. J. (1996). *The Mismeasure of Man* (revised and expanded ed.). New York: Norton.

Gutstein, G., & Peterson, B. (2005). *Rethinking Mathematics: Teaching Social Justice by the Numbers*. Milwaukee: Rethinking Schools.

Harding, S. (1998). *Is Science Multicultural? Postcolonialisms, Feminisms, and Epistemologies*. Bloomington: Indiana University Press.

Heath, S. B., & McLaughlin, M. W. (Eds.). (1993). *Identity and Inner-City Youth: Beyond Ethnicity and Gender*. New York: Teachers College Press.

Herrnstein, R. J., & Murray, C. (1994). *The Bell Curve: Intelligence and Class Structure in American Life*. New York: Free Press.

Jacoby, R., & Glauberman, N. (Eds.). (1995). *The Bell Curve Debate: History, Documents, Opinions*. New York: Times Books.

Kitano, H. H. L. (1976). *Japanese Americans: The Evolution of a Subculture* (2nd ed.). Englewood Cliffs, NJ: Prentice-Hall.

Lee, O., & Luykx, A. (2007). Science Education and Student Diversity: Race/Ethnicity, Language, Culture, and Socioeconomic Status. In S. K. Abell & N. G. Lederman (Eds.), *Handbook of Research on Science Education* (pp. 171–197). Mahwah, NJ: Earlbaum.

Levins, R., & Lewontin, R. (1985). *The Dialectical Biologist*. Cambridge, MA: Harvard University Press.

Mason, S. F. (1962). *A History of the Sciences*. New York: Collier Books.

Merton, R. K. (1968). On Sociological Theories of the Middle Range. In R. K. Merton. *Social Theory and Social Structure* (enlarged ed., pp. 39–72). New York: Free Press.

Moses, R. P., & Cobb, C. E., Jr. (2001). *Radical Equations: Math Literacy and Civil Rights*. Boston: Beacon.

Nasir, N. S., & Cobb, P. (Eds.). (2007). *Improving Access to Mathematics: Diversity and Equity in the Classroom*. New York: Teachers College Press.

Olsen, F. (1974). *On the Trail of the Arawaks*. Norman: University of Oklahoma Press.

Roediger, D. R. (2005). *Working toward Whiteness: How America's Immigrants Became White*. New York: Basic Books.

Selden, S. (1999). *Inheriting Shame: The Story of Eugenics and Racism in America*. New York: Teachers College Press.

Sertima, I. V. (Ed.). (1986). *Blacks in Science: Ancient and Modern*. New Brunswick, NJ: Transaction Books.

Taba, H., Durkin, M. C., Fraenkel, J. R., & McNaughton, A. H. (1971). *A Teacher's Handbook for Elementary School Studies: An Inductive Approach* (2nd ed.). Reading, MA: Addison-Wesley.

ANNOTATED BIBLIOGRAPHY

Banks, J. A., Banks, C. A. M., Cortés, C. E., Hahn, C., et al. (2005). *Democracy and Diversity: Principles and Concepts for Educating Citizens in a Global Age*. Seattle: Center for Multicultural Education, University of Washington.

This informative publication contains principles and concepts for linking multicultural and global education. It can be downloaded from the Center for Multicultural Education website: http://depts.washington.edu/centerme/home.htm.

Banks, J. A., Au, K., Ball, A. F., Bell, P., et al. (2007). *Learning In and Out of School in Diverse Environments: Life-Long, Life-Wide, and Life-Deep*. Seattle: Center for Multicultural Education, University of Washington.

This brief publication contains researched-based principles that can be used by teachers to draw upon the language and cultural learning that students from diverse groups bring to school to enrich instruction and facilitate student learning. It also contains a useful checklist.

Gutstein, G., & Peterson, B. (2005). *Rethinking Mathematics: Teaching Social Justice by the Numbers*. Milwaukee: Rethinking Schools.

This books describes creative and engaging ways in which teachers can help students to develop knowledge and skills in math while also learning how to understand and develop a commitment to social justice.

Nasir, N. S., & Cobb, P. (Eds.). (2007). *Improving Access to Mathematics: Diversity and Equity in the Classroom*. New York: Teachers College Press.

This book contains helpful and thoughtful discussions of mathematical knowledge and power, teaching mathematics for social justice, and the ways in which math teachers can use the knowledge and experience of their students' families to enrich the teaching of math.

Sleeter, C. E. (2005). *Un-Standardizing Curriculum: Multicultural Teaching in the Standards-Based Classroom*. New York: Teachers College Press.

This helpful and informative book suggests creative ways in which teachers can prepare students to meet academic standards while also developing the knowledge and skills needed to act to make our nation and world more just and humane.

Valdes, G. (2001). *Learning and Not Learning English: Latino Students in American Schools*. New York: Teachers College Press.

This sensitive and informative ethnographic study describes some of the major issues and problems related to the experiences of the increasing number of U.S. students who learn English as a second language.

CHAPTER THREE

KEY CONCEPTS FOR THE MULTICULTURAL CURRICULUM

The multicultural curriculum should help students master higher levels of knowledge so that they can better understand race and ethnic relations and develop the skills and abilities needed to make reflective personal and public decisions. Sound multicultural lessons and units focus on higher-level concepts and generalizations and use facts primarily to help students master higher forms of knowledge and make decisions. Students must be able to make reflective decisions in order to take thoughtful personal, social, and civic action.

CRITERIA FOR SELECTING INTERDISCIPLINARY CONCEPTS

Within the various academic fields and disciplines is a wide range of concepts from which you might select when planning the multicultural curriculum. What criteria can you use when selecting concepts to organize multicultural units and lessons? First, you should consider whether the concept will help explain some significant aspect of the history, culture, and contemporary experiences of a range of ethnic groups in U.S. society. The experiences of ethnic groups in the United States have been characterized by a number of salient events, expressions, and themes, such as discrimination, protest and resistance, cultural assimilation, and acculturation. Consequently, these themes are highly appropriate organizing concepts for the multicultural curriculum.

Higher-level concepts that are capable of encompassing a wide range of data and information should also be selected for the multicultural curriculum. *Culture* is a more powerful concept than *language* because it can be used to organize and teach more information.

Concepts chosen for the multicultural curriculum should also be interdisciplinary. Interdisciplinary concepts are capable of encompassing facts, generalizations, and examples from several disciplines and areas. It is necessary to select interdisciplinary concepts because the curriculum should help students view and interpret events and situations from the perspectives of several disciplines. When students view events and situations from the perspective of a single discipline, they can acquire, at best, only a partial understanding of the event or situation they are studying.

When *social protest,* for example, is studied only from the perspective of political science, students learn that social protest occurs when alienated groups within a political system organize to push for political and social change. However, students need to study protest from other disciplinary perspectives to understand it fully (see Figure 3.1). During the civil rights movement of the 1960s, African Americans expressed protest not only in politics but also in their literature, songs, dances, art,

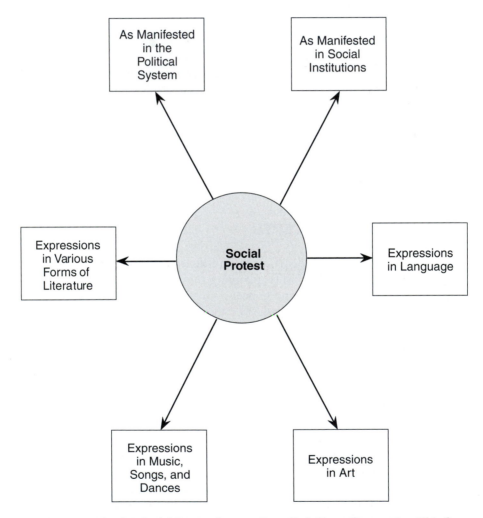

FIGURE 3.1   Viewing Social Protest from an Interdisciplinary Perspective This figure illustrates how a concept such as social protest must be viewed from diverse disciplinary perspectives in order for students to understand its total political, social, and artistic ramifications.

and language. Thus, students need to examine social protest in these forms of communication to fully understand Black protest in the 1960s.

Some concepts are important to the structure of a particular discipline but cannot function successfully in an interdisciplinary role. Rhythm, melody, harmony, and tone color are important concepts in music. Key concepts in art include form, line, and shape. Because these concepts are highly specific to their particular disciplines, they are not effective interdisciplinary concepts. However, both music and art, as well as dance and language, are forms of communication and culture. Music and art also have themes or convey central messages to the perceiver: so do a play, a dance, and many examples of human behavior. Consequently, communication, culture, and theme are effective interdisciplinary concepts because they can help students develop generalizations by studying examples drawn from the social sciences and the humanities.

When selecting organizing concepts for multicultural lessons, you should give some attention to the developmental level of your students. Young children can understand discrimination easier than they can understand institutionalized racism, in part because almost every child has been the victim of some kind of discrimination. He or she may have been the new child in the classroom, may be fat or thin, or may have had some other characteristic that other students singled out for ridicule. Young children can also understand discrimination more easily than institutionalized racism because discrimination is a more well-defined, less abstract, and less ambiguous concept than is institutionalized racism.

In the primary and middle school grades, you should focus on concepts that can be taught using concrete examples, such as similarities, differences, culture, race, discrimination, and ethnic group. A number of outstanding children's books, annotated in Parts II through V, are available that you can use successfully to teach these concepts. Open-ended stories and role-playing situations, many of which are described in Parts II through V, can make these concepts real and meaningful to young children.

Children's books are also a powerful tool for teaching concepts to students in the primary and intermediate grades. *Less than Half, More than Whole* by Kathleen Lacapa and Michael Lacapa (2001) is a well-crafted, well-written book that deals with racial identity. Tony realizes that he is neither a White like his friend Scott, nor 100% Indian like Will. *Rosa* by Niki Giovanni (2005), which describes the story of Rosa Parks and her refusal to give up her seat on a Montgomery bus, which led to the famous boycott, can be used to teach both discrimination and protest or resistance. The engaging photographs and simple but moving text in *Remember: The Journey to School Integration* by Toni Morrison (2004) is a powerful treatment of segregation and discrimination from the point of view of a child. *The Journal of Wong Ming-Chung: A Chinese Miner* by Lawrence Yep (2000) focuses on immigration. It tells the story of a ten-year-old boy who comes to California to help his uncle during the Gold Rush.

The students' previous experience with concepts and content related to race and ethnicity is an important consideration when selecting concepts for study. Concepts such as institutionalized racism, ethnic separatism, the ethnic revitalization movement, and colonialism are so complex and emotional that they are often inappropriate for students who are studying race and ethnicity for the first time. More concrete and less controversial concepts are appropriate for such students. A student who is not familiar with such basic concepts as ethnic group, ethnic minority group, people of color, discrimination, and prejudice will have a difficult time understanding and appreciating abstract concepts such as institutionalized racism and ethnic separatism. These concepts should be studied only after students have mastered the basic concepts in ethnic studies.

INTERDISCIPLINARY CONCEPTS

Concepts drawn from various behavioral science disciplines that can be used effectively to organize interdisciplinary units and lessons are discussed below. The social and behavioral sciences are a rich source of interdisciplinary concepts, because behavioral scientists study a wide range of human behavior. Art, music, dance, foods, language, and literature are expressions of concepts studied by behavioral scientists. Table 3.1 summarizes the major concepts discussed in this chapter. Table 3.2

TABLE 3.1   Key Concepts

Culture, Ethnicity, and Related Concepts	Culture
	Ethnic group
	Ethnic minority group
	Stages of ethnicity
	Ethnic diversity
	Cultural assimilation
	Acculturation
	Community culture
Socialization and Related Concepts	Socialization
	Prejudice
	Discrimination
	Race
	Racism
	Ethnocentrism
	Values
Intercultural Communication and Related Concepts	Communication
	Intercultural communication
	Perception
	Historical bias
Power and Related Concepts	Power
	Social protest and resistance
Movement of Ethnic Groups	Migration
	Immigration

Note: This table contains a list of high-level concepts that can be used to develop units and lessons that draw content, examples, and information from several disciplines. These concepts are defined and illustrated in this chapter.

TABLE 3.2 An Interdisciplinary Study of Ethnic Groups

KEY CONCEPTS AND RELATED QUESTIONS	AMERICAN INDIANS	MEXICAN AMERICANS	AFRICAN AMERICANS	JEWISH AMERICANS	FILIPINO AMERICANS	PUERTO RICANS
Culture What ethnic cultural elements are present in the group's culture today? How is the group's culture reflected in its music, literature, and art?						
Ethnic Enclave To what extent are members of the group concentrated within particular geographical regions?						
Racism and Discrimination To what extent is the group a victim of racism or other forms of discrimination?						
Communication To what extent do members of the group encounter problems when communicating with other ethnic groups?						
Self-Concept How have the group's societal experiences affected the self-concepts of its members?						
Power To what extent does the group exercise power within the ethnic community? Within the economic system? Within the larger society?						

Note: This table illustrates how a data retrieval chart organized around key concepts can be used by the teacher to plan and implement a comparative study of ethnic groups.

illustrates how key concepts such as those in the following discussion can be used to plan and implement a comparative study of ethnic groups. Table 3.3 describes nine key concepts that can be used to organize a focused study of an ethnic group in the United States.

Culture, Ethnicity, and Related Concepts

Culture. *Culture* is the key concept in cultural anthropology. It is an essential concept in ethnic studies because an ethnic group is a type of cultural group. Culture consists of the behavior patterns, symbols, institutions, values, and other human-made components of society. It is the unique achievement of a human group that distinguishes it from other groups. Even though cultures are in many ways similar, a particular culture constitutes a unique whole.

There is tremendous debate and controversy within anthropology about the meaning of culture. Some anthropologists do not consider tools and other artifacts examples of culture and believe that the meaning and interpretation of these elements are what constitute culture. Bullivant (1993) defines *culture* as a program for survival; Geertz (cited in Kuper, 1999) defines it as "an ordered system of meaning and symbols" (p. 98).

The U.S. culture is composed of many smaller groups. These microcultural groups share many characteristics with the national culture but have some distinguishing characteristics that set them apart from other groups. Thus, it is possible to describe the U.S. culture, as well as the various microcultures that constitute it (for example, the Appalachian culture, Southern culture, or gay culture).

Ethnic Group and Ethnic Minority Group.   Ethnic groups are types of microcultural groups within the United States that have unique characteristics that set them apart from other cultural groups. Many microcultural groups are voluntary groups, but an ethnic group is usually an involuntary group, although individual identification with the group may be optional. An ethnic group has a historic origin and a shared heritage and tradition. The origins of the group preceded the creation of the nation-state or were external to the nation-state. An ethnic group also has an ancestral tradition, and its members share a sense of peoplehood and an interdependence of fate. It has some value orientations, behavioral patterns, and interests—often political and economic—that differ from those of other groups within society. Ethnic groups tend to have an influence, often substantial, on the lives of their members. Anglo-Saxon Protestants, Italian Americans, and Irish Americans are examples of ethnic groups.

An *ethnic minority group* is an ethnic group with several distinguishing characteristics. Although an ethnic minority group, like an ethnic group, shares a common culture, a historic tradition, and a sense of peoplehood, it also has unique physical and/or cultural characteristics that enable individuals who belong to other ethnic groups to identify its members easily, often for discriminatory purposes. Ethnic

TABLE 3.3   Organizing Concepts for a Focused Study of an Ethnic Group

The experience of each ethnic group in the United States can be viewed and compared using a few key concepts and themes. Below are nine concepts that can be used to study the experiences of an ethnic group.

ORIGINS AND IMMIGRATION
It is important to examine the origins and immigration pattern of an ethnic group in the United States.

SHARED CULTURE, VALUES, AND SYMBOLS
Most ethnic groups in the United States have unique cultures and values that resulted from an interaction of their original culture with the host culture in the United States, from ethnic institutions created partly as a response to discrimination, and from their social class position.

ETHNIC IDENTITY AND SENSE OF PEOPLEHOOD
A shared sense of peoplehood and ethnic identity is one of the most important characteristics of an ethnic group in the United States. This shared sense of identity results from a common history and current experiences.

PERSPECTIVES, WORLDVIEWS, AND FRAMES OF REFERENCE
Members of the same ethnic group often view reality in a similar way and differently from other groups within a society. This results largely from their shared sense of peoplehood and identity described above.

ETHNIC INSTITUTIONS AND SELF-DETERMINATION
Many ethnic institutions were formed by ethnic groups in the United States in response to discrimination and segregation. Many of these institutions continue to exist today because they help ethnic groups to satisfy unique social, cultural, and educational needs.

DEMOGRAPHIC, SOCIAL, POLITICAL, AND ECONOMIC STATUS
When studying a U.S. ethnic group, its current demographic, social, political, and economic status needs to be determined. The economic and educational status of an ethnic group can change. New immigration can change the demographic and economic profile of an ethnic group.

PREJUDICE, DISCRIMINATION, AND RACISM
Prejudice, discrimination, and racism have been major themes and issues in the history and contemporary experiences of U.S. ethnic groups, particularly those of color.

INTRAETHNIC DIVERSITY
Even though ethnic groups share a culture, values, a sense of identity, and a common history, there are tremendous differences within ethnic groups. These important differences must always be kept in mind when ethnic groups are studied, or new stereotypes and misconceptions may arise.

ASSIMILATION AND ACCULTURATION
The experiences of ethnic groups in the United States have been and still are characterized by widespread cultural assimilation on the part of ethnic minority groups and ethnic minority cultures. The influence of ethnic minority cultures on the mainstream culture should be examined as should the assimilation of minority groups into the mainstream culture.

minority groups also tend to be a numerical minority and to exercise minimal political and economic power. Vietnamese Americans are an ethnic minority group with unique physical and cultural characteristics. Non-White ethnic minority groups, such as Vietnamese Americans and African Americans, are often called *people of color.* Jewish Americans, another ethnic minority group, are distinguished on the basis of their religious and cultural characteristics.

Culture, ethnic group, ethnic minority group, and people of color are essential concepts for the multicultural curriculum and should be introduced in the primary grades. You can introduce the concept of culture by showing the students a menorah, an engagement ring, and the numeral 5. By asking the students what these objects have in common, and by class discussion and the use of more examples, you can help your students formulate a definition of culture. When introducing the concept of culture, you should emphasize the meanings that artifacts and cultural elements have to individuals and groups and how they use and interpret them.

After students have studied culture, they can then be introduced to the concept of microcultural group. The concepts of *ethnic group* and, later, *ethnic minority group* can be introduced using appropriate examples. When you introduce *ethnic group,* you should help students understand that individuals are members of many different groups, such as religious, kinship, and economic groups, and that an ethnic group is only one of the many groups to which individuals belong.

A person's attachment to and identity with these various groups varies with the individual, the times in one's life, and the situations and settings in which one finds oneself. Depending on experiences, social class, and many other variables, ethnicity may be important to an individual or it may be unimportant. Students should be helped to understand that just because they think an individual is a member of a particular ethnic group, this does not mean that the individual has a strong identity with his or her ethnic group or that ethnicity is important in his or her life. Ethnicity is rather unimportant in the lives of many highly assimilated and upper-status members of ethnic groups but tends to be a cogent factor in the lives of many lower-class ethnic individuals.

The Stages of Cultural Identity: A Typology

We often assume that ethnic groups are monolithic and have homogeneous needs and characteristics. Rarely is sufficient attention given to the enormous differences within ethnic groups. We also tend to see ethnic groups as static and unchanging. *However, ethnic groups within modernized democratic societies are highly diverse, complex, and changing entities.* I have developed a typology that attempts to describe some of the differences that exist between individual members of ethnic and cultural groups. This typology assumes that individual members of ethnic and cultural groups are at different stages of development and that these stages can be identified and described.

The typology is an ideal-type construct in the Weberian sense and constitutes a set of hypotheses based on the existing and emerging theory and research and on my observations and study of ethnic and cultural behavior (Banks, 2006). The typology is presented here because it can be used as a departure point for classroom discussions of race, ethnicity, and culture. However, *its tentative and hypothetical nature should be emphasized in class discussions.*

Stage 1: Cultural Psychological Captivity

During this stage, individuals have internalized negative ideologies and beliefs about their ethnic or cultural group that are institutionalized within the society. Consequently, Stage 1 individuals exemplify cultural self-rejection and low self-esteem. These individuals are ashamed of their cultural group and identity during this stage and may respond in a number of ways, including avoiding situations that lead to contact with other cultural groups or striving aggressively to become highly culturally assimilated.

Stage 2: Cultural Encapsulation

Stage 2 is characterized by cultural encapsulation and cultural exclusiveness, including voluntary separatism. Individuals in this stage participate primarily within their own cultural community and believe that their cultural group is superior to that of others. Many Stage 2 individuals, such as many Anglo-Saxon Protestants, have internalized the dominant societal myths about the superiority of their group and the innate inferiority of other groups and races. Many individuals who are socialized within all-White suburban communities and who live highly ethnocentric and encapsulated lives may be described as Stage 2 individuals. Alice Miel (with Kiester, 1967) describes these kinds of individuals in *The Short-changed Children of Suburbia.*

Stage 3: Cultural Identity Clarification

At this stage, individuals are able to clarify personal attitudes and cultural identity, reduce intrapsychic conflict, and develop positive attitudes toward their cultural group. Individuals have learned to accept self, thus developing the characteristics needed to accept and respond more positively to outside cultural groups. Self-acceptance is a requisite for accepting and responding positively to other people.

Stage 4: Biculturalism

Individuals within this stage have a healthy sense of cultural identity and the psychological characteristics and skills needed to participate in their own culture as well as in an outside cultural group. Such individuals also have a strong desire to function effectively in two cultural communities. We may describe such individuals as *bicultural.*

Stage 5: Multiculturalism and Reflective Nationalism

Stage 5 describes the idealized goal for citizenship identity within a culturally diverse nation. Individuals at this stage are able to function, at least at minimal levels, within several cultural communities and to understand, appreciate, and share the values, symbols, and institutions of several cultures. Such multicultural perspectives and feelings, I hypothesize, help these individuals live more enriched and fulfilling lives and formulate more creative and novel solutions to personal and public problems.

Stage 6: Globalism and Global Competency

Individuals within Stage 6 have clarified, reflective, and positive cultural, national, and global identifications and the knowledge, skills, attitudes, and abilities needed to function in different cultural communities within their own nation as well as in cultures within other nations. These individuals have the ideal delicate balance of cultural, national, and global identifications, commitments, literacy, and behaviors. They have internalized the universalistic ethical values and principles of humankind and have the skills, competencies, and commitments needed to act on these values.

Individuals within Stage 6 also have cosmopolitan values, perspectives, skills, and behaviors. *Cosmopolitanism* is defined as openness and broad open-mindedness that transcends one's own group—whether defined by family, locality, religion, ethnicity, or nationality. Cosmopolitans view themselves as citizens of the world. Nussbaum (2002) writes: "Their allegiance is to the worldwide community of human beings" (p. 4). She points out, however, that "to be a citizen of the world one does not need to give up local identifications, which can be a source of great richness in life" (p. 9). Appiah (2006), another proponent of cosmopolitanism, also does not see a conflict between "local partialities and universal morality—between being a part of the place you were and a part of a broader human community" (p. xviii).

Characteristics of the Typology.   The stages of cultural identity typology is an ideal-type construct and should be viewed as dynamic and multidimensional rather than as static and unilinear. The characteristics within the stages exist on a continuum. Thus, within Stage 1, individuals are more or less culturally psychologically captive; some individuals are more culturally psychologically captive than others.

The division between the stages is blurred rather than sharp. Thus, a continuum exists between as well as within the stages. The culturally encapsulated individual (Stage 2) does not suddenly attain clarification and acceptance of personal cultural identity (Stage 3). This process is gradual and developmental. Also, the stages should not be viewed as strictly sequential and unilinear. I am hypothesizing that some individuals may never experience a particular stage. I also hypothesize that once an individual experiences a particular stage, that person is likely to experience the stages above it sequentially and developmentally. However, individuals may experience the stages upward, downward, or in a zigzag pattern. Under certain conditions, for example, the bicultural (Stage 4) individual may become multicultural (Stage 5); under new conditions the same individual may again become bicultural

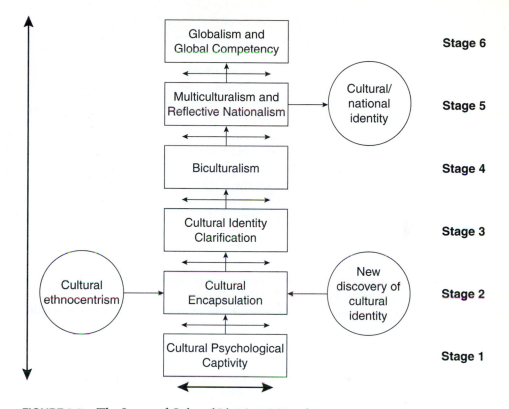

FIGURE 3.2   The Stages of Cultural Identity: A Typology

(Stage 4), culturally identified (Stage 3), and culturally encapsulated (Stage 2). For example, many individual members of northern White ethnic groups became increasingly more culturally encapsulated as busing for school desegregation gained momentum in northern cities such as Boston during the 1970s.

Figure 3.2 illustrates the dynamic and multidimensional characteristics of the development of cultural identity among individuals. Note especially the arrowed lines, which indicate that continua exist both horizontally and vertically.

Ethnic Diversity

Students should learn that there are many different ethnic cultures in our society, and that these differences are not likely to vanish. Events cause them to emerge in each new generation. This concept is the antithesis of the melting pot theory. When studying about ethnic differences in the United States, students should be helped to understand that, even though we have not experienced a true melting pot, most ethnic groups have acquired many mainstream American cultural characteristics. The mainstream culture has also incorporated many components of ethnic minority cultures, such as African American music. This process is still taking place. Consequently, both ethnic cultures and the mainstream culture are being transformed as they interact.

Many ethnic individuals are bicultural; that is, they usually acquire traits of mainstream American culture but also retain many of their ethnic characteristics. Even though the more upwardly mobile members of ethnic groups tend to be less ethnic than are lower-class members, this generalization is nevertheless valid. A highly acculturated Chinese American, for example, will often marry another Chinese person, eat Chinese foods, and belong to Chinese social organizations. Many ethnic youths attend public schools during the day and a language or ethnic school after regular school hours or on the weekend. Most African Americans who obtain college degrees speak standard English on their jobs and in other settings where it is appropriate to conform to the dominant society's norm. However, when socializing with less assimilated relatives and friends, they often use many words and phrases that linguists call Black English or Ebonics (Alim & Baugh, 2007). Upwardly mobile Mexican Americans will eat "Anglo-Saxon steak" at fancy Anglo restaurants with their Anglo friends, but they often drive to Spanish-speaking neighborhoods to eat foods such as enchiladas and chiles rellenos.

In other words, ethnic individuals acquire those mainstream cultural characteristics necessary for them to survive and attain social and economic mobility in the wider society but often retain many elements of their ethnic cultures. The more upwardly mobile an individual is, the more likely he or she is to acquire mainstream cultural traits. The acquisition of mainstream Anglo-American speech, behavior, and values is necessary for upward mobility in the United States, because mainstream Americans control entry to most social, economic, and political institutions.

When studying about ethnic differences, students should learn that cultural differences exist within as well as between various ethnic groups. Too many Americans think of groups of color as monolithic, and they find it difficult to understand why conflict exists within these groups. *It is very important for students to study about the differences that exist within ethnic groups, which are called intraethnic differences.* When many mainstream Americans are introduced to an African American or an Asian American, certain stereotypic images often emerge. They often assume that all African Americans know something about the Black inner-city community because of their personal experiences and can tell them how the Black community feels about interracial marriage or interracial adoptions. Many mainstream individuals assume that all Asian Americans are stoic, shy, and have a high scientific aptitude.

It is true that we can associate certain general characteristics with the various American ethnic groups. However, within these groups, individuals embrace these characteristics to varying degrees. Some deliberately attempt to reject them. When we meet an individual and know only that he or she is a Mexican American, there are but a few conclusive statements we can accurately make about that person.

Mexican Americans, like Asian Americans and African Americans, are a highly diverse group. Some Mexican Americans strongly identify with their ethnic group, support bilingual education, and try to make sure that their children learn Spanish and become bilingual. Others, especially those in the upper classes, tend to identify more strongly with their Spanish heritage. Such individuals are more likely to prefer the term *Latin American* or *Spanish American* to *Mexican American* and to reject their Indian heritage. Some Mexican Americans consider themselves Spanish, even though their biological traits may be identical to others who consider themselves Chicanos or Mexican Americans. According to the 2000 Census (U.S. Census Bureau, 2001), 48% of Latinos classified themselves as White.

The tremendous differences that exist within various ethnic groups often make it difficult for many mainstream Americans to understand why many Japanese Americans are anti-Korean, why the nisei (first-generation Japanese American) often express disappointment about the values and lifestyles of the sansei (second generation), or why some upwardly mobile Mexican Americans disdain Mexican migrant workers. Intragroup differences and conflict exist within dominant ethnic groups as well as within minority groups. While mainstream Americans may understand why a German American corporation president might disdain a German American dishwasher, they may not understand how an upper-class African American can wonder about what life is like in the Black inner city. Class differences within the African American community are deepening as the income gap between those who are very poor (the so-called underclass) and upwardly mobile Blacks increases. The U.S. Census categorized about 20% of African Americans as middle class in 2005 (U.S. Census Bureau, 2006).

Cultural Assimilation

When a member of an ethnic minority group acquires the behavior patterns, lifestyles, values, and language of the mainstream culture, we say that she or he has become culturally assimilated. *Cultural assimilation* is the process by which an individual or group acquires the cultural traits of a different ethnic or cultural group. Because the dominant group controls most of the social, economic, and political institutions in a society, members of dominant ethnic minority groups must acquire its cultural characteristics to move up the social and economic ladder. When studying this concept, it is important for students to learn that although people of color may become totally assimilated culturally (i.e., in cultural characteristics they may become indistinguishable from Anglo-Saxon Protestants), they will still be victims of discrimination and racism because of their different physical characteristics.

A widespread misconception is that Mexican Americans and African Americans experience discrimination because they often have meager educations and live in inner-city communities. Even though it is true that many Mexican Americans and African Americans are members of the lower socioeconomic classes and that all lower-class individuals are treated differently than middle- and upper-class people, it is also true that Mexican Americans and African Americans with high educational levels and incomes frequently experience discrimination because of their physical characteristics. Because American racism is based largely on skin color, no degree of cultural assimilation eliminates it. A number of popular books describe the racism experienced by middle-class African Americans (Cose, 1993; Feagin & Sikes, 1994).

Some discussion of forced assimilation and cultural genocide should take place when students study cultural assimilation. Assimilation often occurs when a minority group "voluntarily" acquires the behavior patterns and lifestyles of the dominant group in order to attain social mobility and occupational success. I use the word *voluntarily* here reluctantly, because without some degree of cultural assimilation a group that is very different culturally may not be able to survive in a particular culture. However, in the history of the United States, some forms of cultural assimilation that took place were totally nonvoluntary and might be called *forced* assimilation because the cultures of certain groups were deliberately destroyed (cultural genocide). These groups were forced to acquire the language, lifestyles, and values of the dominant culture.

Individuals and groups who refused to accept the dominant culture were sometimes the victims of severe punishments, including death. The cultures of African groups were deliberately destroyed by the slave masters. This cultural destruction began on the slave ships. Historians have documented that systematic and deliberate attempts were made to destroy Indian cultures (Brizan, 1998; Wilson, 1997). These efforts were highly successful. Many of the cultural elements of these groups now exist only in the pages of history and sometimes not even there, because their artifacts were often destroyed before they could be recorded.

Acculturation.   When an Anglo-Saxon Protestant eats chow mein and a Chinese American sees a Shakespearean play, we say that acculturation is occurring because two different ethnic groups are exchanging cultural elements and complexes. Although the exchange of cultural traits is widespread within U.S. society, we often think only of the cultural traits that ethnic minorities acquire from dominant ethnic groups; we hear little about the cultural traits that dominant groups have acquired from ethnic minorities. Because this is the case, you should highlight the ethnic minority cultural traits that have been acquired by mainstream Americans.

Students should study the contributions that African Americans have made to American music, especially through their spirituals, blues, and jazz (DjeDje & Meadows, 1998). American cultural traits of Indian origin are rarely mentioned in schoolbooks. Indian contributions to American culture include the selection of sites for many American cities, as well as dress styles, tobacco, foods, and values related to the veneration and preservation of the earth. In two important books, Weatherford (1988, 1991) describes the contributions Native Americans made to the world (*Indian Givers*) and to the United States (*Native Roots*).

All American ethnic groups, including people of color, have contributed material elements (such as foods and fashions), as well as nonmaterial traits (such as values and norms), to mainstream American culture. Students can use a data retrieval chart similar to the one illustrated in Table 3.2 to record examples of contributions that various groups have made to American life. This type of chart is a convenient tool for studying cultural contributions as well as other aspects of ethnic group life in the United States.

Community Culture. Most Americans grow up in communities in which ethnic and cultural values, lifestyles, language patterns, and behavior patterns differ from those of many other groups. This is as true for Puerto Ricans who grow up in East Harlem as it is for Anglo-Saxon Protestants who are raised in wealthy suburban neighborhoods such as Mercer Island, Washington, and Forest Park, Illinois. We usually do not think that middle-class or wealthy White suburbs have a unique culture because the culture within them constitutes the dominant one in the United States. However, Miel (with Kiester, 1967) in *The Shortchanged Children of Suburbia,* and Henry (1963, 1971), in *Culture against Man* and *Pathways to Madness,* describe some of the unique cultural traits of middle-class mainstream U.S. communities.

Because most Americans grow up in ethnic or cultural enclaves, they are *culturally encapsulated.* Ethnic minority groups, in order to attain social and economic mobility, are usually forced out of their ethnic encapsulation. However, mainstream Americans, who control entry to most social, economic, and political institutions, often spend their entire lives within their own unique cultural communities. The cultures of other groups remain foreign, nonhuman, and exotic to them. These groups are viewed as "the Other." African Americans who grow up in small southern rural communities often think that everyone eats sweet potato pie, chitterlings, and hog head and black-eyed peas to celebrate New Year's Day. Without this kind of New Year's meal, bad luck will be imminent. When these African Americans migrate to northern and western cities and begin to participate in social institutions that have other norms and values, they discover, sometimes abruptly, that their world is not the entire world, and that not only do many people not eat sweet potato pie, but they have serious questions about people who eat hog intestines.

A sound multicultural curriculum should help all students—from both majority and minority groups—to break out of their cultural and ethnic enclaves and learn that there are many ways to live and survive and that, because an individual has a different lifestyle, he or she is not inferior or superior. Many youths of color tend to devalue their ethnic cultures when they begin to participate in the mainstream society. Mainstream students should learn that there are different ways of living that are as legitimate and functional as their own. I am not suggesting that the school should attempt to force different lifestyles on students. However, the school should help release students from cultural and ethnic encapsulation so that they can learn to appreciate cultural differences and thus learn how to live with people who speak a different dialect or language, eat different foods, and value things they may not value. We can learn to respect and appreciate different cultures without choosing to participate in them. Participation should be an individual decision, but cultural understanding and empathy for other people should be fostered by the school.

Socialization and Related Concepts

Socialization.   *Socialization* describes the process by which people become human. Sociologists who use socialization as their central concept assume that, even though people are born with the physical capacities to become human, they are capable of becoming many things. People can acquire the characteristics of other animals if they grow up with them and not with other human beings. Sociologists assume that people acquire human characteristics only by interacting with the human group. The group makes use of norms and sanctions to ensure that the individual acquires the attitudes, values, and behavior patterns it deems appropriate.

Socialization and related concepts, such as values and norms, are important in multicultural education because they provide useful insights that help us understand how individuals acquire prejudices and ethnocentric values and how people learn to discriminate against other groups. Socialization theory teaches us that children are not born with racial antipathies. Children learn these attitudes from the adults in their environment early in life (Stephan & Stephan, 2004; Van Ausdale & Feagin, 2001).

Modern sociological research and theory dispel old notions, such as the racial and cultural difference theory, which held that individuals have an instinctive fear and dislike of people who are physically and culturally different from them. The theory that explains prejudice as emerging from a traumatic experience has also been discredited. Negative attitudes toward certain ethnic groups are institutionalized within our society. Children acquire them by interacting with "significant others" in their environment and reading books in school, watching television, and going to their places of worship (Stephan & Stephan, 2004; Van Ausdale & Feagin, 2001). Most institutions within our society, including the schools, reinforce and teach negative lessons about America's ethnic groups of color. Students need to understand the relationship between socialization, prejudice, racism, and discrimination.

Prejudice and Discrimination.   *Prejudice* is a set of rigid and unfavorable attitudes toward a particular group or groups that are formed in disregard of facts. Prejudiced individuals respond to perceived members of these groups on the basis of preconceptions, tending to disregard behavior or personal characteristics that are inconsistent with their biases. Individuals who are anti-Semitic will argue that Jews are loud and rudely aggressive no matter how many Jews they meet who do not have these characteristics. Prejudiced people see the world with blinders on and refuse to perceive people, incidents, and groups that do not reinforce their negative attitudes and stereotypes.

Although prejudice and discrimination are highly related and are usually associated, they are different concepts, though often confused. Prejudice is a set of *attitudes,* whereas *discrimination* consists of differential *behavior* directed toward a stigmatized group. Discrimination exists when individuals are treated differentially because they belong to a particular social category or group.

Merton's typology (1949) can be used with students in the middle, upper, and high school grades to help them better understand discrimination. This typology makes it clear that a prejudiced individual will not necessarily discriminate and that an individual who is not prejudiced may discriminate. Merton's typology clarifies the extent to which discrimination is contextual, situational, and related to the social settings in which individuals function. Merton identifies four types of persons:

> *Type I: The unprejudiced nondiscriminator, or all-weather liberal.* This individual believes in racial equality and acts on his or her beliefs.
>
> *Type II: The unprejudiced discriminator, or fair-weather liberal.* This is a person of expediency. She or he does not have personal prejudices but will discriminate when it is easier or more profitable to do so.
>
> *Type III: The prejudiced nondiscriminator, or fair-weather illiberal.* This person does not believe in racial equality but does not discriminate because of laws or external factors that negatively sanction racial discrimination.
>
> *Type IV: The prejudiced discriminator, or the all-weather illiberal.* This is the bigot who is not ashamed of her or his attitudes and who acts on prejudices and beliefs.

When using Merton's typology with students, point out that it is an *ideal type conceptualization.* This means that no actual individual is a pure example of any of Merton's four types. Rather, the typology can be used to think of and to classify individuals who approach one of the types. Students can also use Merton's typology to describe individuals they encounter in readings, media presentations, or social settings. They can use the typology to analyze and think about their own behavior and attitudes toward other racial and ethnic groups.

Race.   Physical anthropologists attempt to divide the human species into subgroups on the basis of biological traits and characteristics. They use the concept of *race* to differentiate among the various human subgroups. However, anthropologists have had considerable difficulty trying to structure valid racial categories because of the wide variety of traits and characteristics that human groups share, the extensive mixture among groups, and the racial categories they have formulated are socially constructed (Mukhopadhyay, Henze, & Moses, 2007). Consequently, the schemes they have developed for classifying human races vary greatly in number and in characteristics.

Montagu (1997), who calls race "man's most dangerous myth" and "one of the most tragic" (p. 41), seriously questions the validity of the concept of race and believes it has been a highly destructive factor in the history of humankind. He writes: "The myth of race refers not to the fact that physically distinguishable populations exist, but rather to the belief that races are populations or peoples whose physical differences are innately linked with significant differences in mental capacities, and that these innate hierarchical differences are measurable by the cultural achievements of such populations, as well as by standardized intelligence (IQ) tests" (p. 44).

In most societies, *the social significance of race is much more important than the presumed physical differences among groups.* The social definitions of race also reveal the arbitrariness of the concept and why it might well be humankind's most dangerous and tragic myth. In the United States, any individual with any acknowledged Black African blood is classified as Black, regardless of that person's phenotype (Davis, 1991). Some of these individuals, of course, look completely Caucasian and classify themselves as White. The majority of them accept the racial category imposed on them by society. We have no reliable statistics of how many such individuals "pass" as White.

Jacobson calls races "invented categories" (1998, p. 4). Omi and Winant (1994) state that the "determination of racial categories is an intensely political process" (p. 3). Their theory of racial formation "emphasizes the social nature of race, the absence of any essential racial characteristics, the historical flexibility of racial meanings and categories and the irreducible political aspects of racial dynamics" (p. 4).

In early Mexico, the Spaniards invented so many concepts and terms for different types of racial mixtures that the cumbersome system of racial classification eventually became so complex and dysfunctional that it died of its own weight (Hunt & Walker, 1974). Partly as a result, the attitudes toward differences in skin color and in physical characteristics are considerably more flexible in Latin America than they are in the United States. In Puerto Rican society today, for example, individuals with a wide range of skin colors are regarded as White. Other variables, such as socioeconomic status, income, education, and hair texture, are important in determining an individual's racial designation (Flores, 1993). In Mexico, the rural Indian can become a Mestizo by moving from the village to the city, becoming assimilated into the dominant Mestizo culture, and learning to speak Spanish (van den Berghe, 1978). By exploring the complex ramifications of the social meaning of race both in the United States and in other nations, students will be able to gain a better understanding of both its arbitrariness and political implications.

Racism   Racism is closely related to the idea of race. *Racism* is a belief that human groups can be validly grouped on the basis of their biological traits and that these identifiable groups inherit certain mental, personality, and cultural characteristics that determine their behavior. A corollary belief is that some biological groups, such as Caucasians, have superior mental and behavioral traits and that others, such as African Americans and Indians, are mentally and culturally inferior. Van den Berghe (1978) defines racism as "any set of beliefs that organic, genetically transmitted differences (whether real or imagined) between human groups are intrinsically associated with the presence or the absence of certain socially relevant abilities or characteristics, hence that such differences are a legitimate basis of invidious distinctions between groups socially defined as races" (p. 11).

Racism is not merely a set of beliefs but is practiced when a group has the power to enforce laws, institutions, and norms based on its beliefs that oppress and dehumanize another group. Gay (1973) stresses the behavioral aspects of racism: "It is an extension of an attitude into an action. Although the focus of attention is on *behavior,* attitudes are of crucial importance for they are the motivating forces which determine the nature of the actions one takes" (p. 30). In a racist society, political, economic, and social systems reflect and perpetuate racism; thus, racism is institutionalized.

Even though ethnocentrism is found in all human societies, racism is not. The kind of racism that exists in the modern world is a rather recent historical development. In the ancient world, different groups and peoples were often the victims of oppression or were enslaved. However, discrimination was rarely done on the basis of racial characteristics. Rather, it was usually based on religious, cultural, political, and social class differences. Social scientists have noted that, with few exceptions, racism as we know it today was not practiced up through the seventeenth century (Montagu, 1997). According to van den Berghe (1978), however, racism "has been independently discovered and rediscovered by various peoples at various times in history" (p. 21). He notes that it was not until the nineteenth century that racism became an elaborate ideology distinguishable from ethnocentrism. Racism developed in the modern world to justify the exploitation and enslavement of aboriginal peoples by Europeans when they began their explorations into Africa, the Caribbean, and the Americas (Davis, 2006).

The European explorers and slave owners were Christians who needed an ideology to justify slavery when it was attacked. They needed an ideology they could view as consistent with both their religious beliefs and their economic institutions. The arguments they structured eventually blossomed into an elaborate racist ideology. According to van den Berghe (1978): "Racism was congruent with prevailing forms of capitalist exploitation, notably with slavery in the [Americas] and incipient colonial expansion in Africa. There is no question that the desire to rationalize exploitation of non-European peoples fostered the elaboration of a complex ideology of paternalism and racism" (p. 17).

When students study racism, they can try to determine the extent to which it is institutionalized within U.S. society, such as in the mass media or within schools and churches, and how racism is manifested in employment and in housing. The students can also discuss whether they are unconscious participants within an institutionalized racist system and what they might be able to do to change the system. Gay (1973) has distinguished *individual, cultural,* and *institutionalized* racism. Fruitful activities for students are to attempt to formulate working definitions for each of these concepts and to identify examples of them (Feagin & Vera, 1995).

Ethnocentrism.   Most ethnic groups within a society tend to think that their culture is superior to the culture of other groups. This is especially true of the most powerful and dominant groups. In U.S. society, Anglo-Saxon Protestants are the dominant group. Many of them believe that their culture is superior to the cultures of other groups and define *culture* as those aspects of *their* culture that they value highly, such as European classical music and paintings by the European masters.

Students must understand *ethnocentrism* to comprehend fully the complex dimensions of American racism and the separatist movements that have emerged within ethnic minority groups. Although some minority persons, because of their socialization, tend to have low self-concepts and value the mainstream culture over their own, ethnocentrism among people of color escalated in the late 1960s. Some African Americans, Mexican Americans, and Asian Americans extolled the virtues of their cultures and demanded separatism and independent institutions. It may be that some degree of ethnocentrism is necessary for a group to attain cohesion and a strong identity and that separatism is, as Sizemore (1972) has suggested, a necessary step toward inclusion within the larger society. However, you can ask students this question: How much cultural and political separatism can a society experience and remain cohesive? If this question is raised, several related ones should also be posed: If a society needs some common goals in order to survive, what groups within it should determine these goals? How might we change our society so that each ethnic group can influence policy that shapes common societal goals? At present, dominant groups determine most societal goals and the means to attain them. However, ethnic groups of color made it clear during the 1960s and 1970s that they will not accept this kind of power arrangement without protest and conflict. These kinds of questions and problems, related to ethnocentrism, should constitute a vital part of the multicultural curriculum.

Values.   Those elements within a culture to which individuals and groups attach a high worth are called *values*. Within a social system are values that influence the group's feelings toward foods, human life, behavior patterns, and attitudes toward people who belong to outgroups. Sociologists have studied how values develop within societies and how they are inculcated by individuals in a community. Values, like attitudes and beliefs, are learned from the groups in which the individual is socialized; we are not born with a set of values and do not derive them independently. Groups use norms and sanctions to inculcate individuals with the pervasive values within their culture or microculture.

Even though there are some common values embraced by most U.S. communities (such as a respect for the lives of those regarded as human beings and loyalty toward national symbols such as the U.S. flag and the Constitution), these shared values are often defined and perceived differently within various ethnic microcultures or they take diverse forms. Other values are important in some ethnic communities and largely absent in others.

The nisei usually endorse many traditional Japanese values, including personal control, the samurai ethic, a high respect for authority, the achievement ethic, and a strong sense of family obligation (Tamura, 1994). Family obligation in traditional Japanese cultures was often considered more important than personal freedom. Although many of the nisei values have eroded among the sansei because the sansei in the United States are highly culturally assimilated, important vestiges of these values remain in Japanese communities today, especially among the aged. Some of these values, such as a high respect for authority and a strong sense of family obligation, conflict with mainstream American values. In mainstream U.S. society, authority is often challenged. It is rarely concentrated in one family member. Mainstream Americans also tend to be highly individualistic rather than group oriented.

Values in ethnic minority communities are often different from those in mainstream U.S. society. In the traditional Puerto Rican family, daughters were highly protected, and the father was the undisputed head of the family. The family was also a highly interdependent unit. Uncles, aunts, and other relatives were often considered integral parts of the family unit. This type of extended family was also common among African Americans in the Deep South. As African Americans and Puerto Ricans become more urbanized and more heavily represented in the middle classes, these aspects of their cultures diminish. However, the extended family is still a part of these ethnic cultures. Puerto Rican girls in New York City often do not have the same freedom to come and go with boys as do their Anglo-American peers.

When American Indians are studied in school, students are often introduced to certain stereotypic components of their cultures, such as tipis, baskets, canoes, or moccasins. These physical elements were parts of the cultures of certain American Indian groups, but they were by no means the most essential parts of them. Thus, students gain a superficial view of Indian cultures when they study only tangible cultural elements. *The essence of a culture can be understood only by studying its central values and their relationships to the daily lives of the people.*

The Indian view of people and their relationship to the universe must be studied to understand Indian values toward people and nature. Indian groups tended to look on the universe as a whole, with every object having a sacred life; to separate people from nature was antithetical to the Great Spirit, for to the Great Spirit all was life.

Values and related lifestyles of ethnic communities are what constitute their essence, not stereotypic components (such as chow mein, basket weaving, sombreros, or soul food). These values and related behavioral characteristics and perspectives should be emphasized in the curriculum, not exotic cultural elements whose major outcome is the reinforcement of stereotypes. I am not suggesting that tangible cultural elements should not be studied, but rather that they should not be emphasized. Even though the study of ethnic values should constitute a large part of the multicultural curriculum, it is important to realize that the values of all of America's ethnic groups are slowly changing, especially in urban areas. People of color are becoming urbanized at a faster rate than are mainstream Americans. It is also important to remember that highly assimilated and higher-status members of ethnic minority groups may share few, if any, characteristics with their more humble brothers and sisters. Despite these caveats, *ethnic values are an integral part of life in the United States and add strength and diversity to the national culture.* This significant message should be communicated to students in all grades.

Intercultural Communication and Related Concepts

Communication.   Social science literature is replete with definitions of *communication*. Common to these many definitions are behavior and symbols perceived and interpreted by another individual. When an individual communicates, he or she uses symbols that are interpreted by the perceiver. Successful communication occurs when both the sender and receiver of the symbols interpret them in a similar way. Communication is unsuccessful when the sender and receiver of the symbols interpret them differently.

Individuals who are socialized within the same culture or microculture are more likely to have shared meanings of symbols than are individuals who are socialized within different microcultures, cultures, and nations. The wider the differences in cultures or microcultures among individuals, the more ineffective communication is likely to be. A middle-class Australian is less likely to interpret correctly the symbols made by a lower-class African American than is a middle-class mainstream American.

Intercultural Communication.   In response to increased communication among nations and world cultures (caused in part by new technological developments and a heightened interest in ethnic minorities in the United States), the field of *intercultural communication* was developed. This field draws concepts and generalizations from various disciplines and studies the variables involved in communication across cultures. The field is also known as cross-cultural communication, interethnic communication, and transracial communication. Lustig and Koester (1993) define *intercultural communication* as "a symbolic, interpretive, transactional, contextual process in which people from different cultures create shared meanings" (p. 51). Communication often fails across cultures because the message producer and the receiver have few shared symbols and have been socialized within environments in which the same symbols are interpreted differently.

Intercultural communication is an important concept in multicultural studies. It helps explain many of the conflicts and misunderstandings that often occur among ethnic groups in the United States. During the 1960s, many African Americans interpreted Black power symbols positively and viewed them as symbols of racial pride and political efficacy (Joseph, 2006). Whites often viewed Black power negatively and considered it threatening and a form of Black racism. A national survey conducted by the Pew Research Center (2003) in 2002 indicated that 82% of non-Whites but only 49% of Whites expressed support for racial preferences for minorities in affirmative action programs.

Cross-cultural communication can be improved when individuals from different cultures begin to interpret symbols in similar ways and when they have a strong desire to communicate effectively. When teaching about intercultural communication, you can identify many examples of barriers to effective communication across ethnic boundaries on radio and television news programs and in local and national newspapers and magazines. The class can use role-playing and discussion techniques to explore ways in which cross-ethnic and cross-racial communication can be improved.

Perception.   Social scientists define *perception* as the "complex process by which people select, organize, and interpret sensory stimulation into a meaningful and coherent picture of the world" (Berelson & Steiner, 1964, p. 88). This concept helps us better understand the factors that influence how individuals come to know and interpret their physical and social environments. Many factors influence how people view their world. Social and cultural factors are cogent variables. In our society, race, ethnic group membership, and social class often influence how people see and interpret events, situations, and social issues. An African American civil rights leader and a mainstream U.S. corporation president are likely to view the high unemployment rate among African American youths quite differently.

Cultural, ethnic, and racial variables affect the perception of historians, writers, and artists, as well as laypeople. Culture and ethnicity may have a cogent influence on a particular historian, writer, or artist, or practically no influence. Individuals' identification with their cultural or ethnic group will highly influence whether their work is affected by culture or ethnicity. Ethnicity tends to be a strong factor in people's lives in a society characterized by inequality and high levels of ethnic discrimination; it tends to be a less important factor in a society in which the various ethnic groups experience social and economic equality. The United States is highly stratified along racial, social class, and ethnic lines. Consequently, culture, ethnicity, and race are cogent factors that often influence members of both dominant and minority groups, including the members of these groups who are historians, writers, and artists.

Historically, American history and literature written by mainstream Americans have been mainstream-centric and have interpreted events and situations primarily from mainstream perspectives (Phillips, 1918/1966). Often, minority group cultures were not regarded as worthy of inclusion in literature anthologies, American history textbooks, or music and art textbooks. Within the last four decades, many mainstream American historians and writers have attempted to include more information about ethnic groups in their works. However, often their interpretations of the experiences of other ethnic groups are mainstream-centric, although more benignly so than in the past. Since the 1970s, more historical, sociological, and artistic works by people of color have been produced (Acuña, 2007; Andrews, Foster, & Harris, 1997; Alim & Baugh, 2007; Takaki, 1998). Many of the perspectives presented in these works are refreshing and add a vital component to our academic, artistic, literary, and social worlds.

Historical Bias.   The social, cultural, and ethnic variables that influence how historians perceive their data result in *historical bias*. Historians' views of the past are influenced by their culture, personal biases, purposes for writing, availability of data, and the times in which they live and write (Appleby, Hunt, & Jacob, 1994). Because historians can never totally reconstruct past events and are unable to report all the data they uncover about particular events, they must use some criteria to determine which aspects of an event to report. Historians must also interpret historical events. History cannot be written without presenting interpretations and points of view. Because this is the case, it is important for you to teach students about the biases in all historical writing and how to recognize and analyze them.

It is especially important for you to teach students how to analyze historical materials that are related to America's ethnic groups of color. Prior to the 1970s, most histories of minority groups were written by mainstream historians. They often wrote histories of ethnic minorities that legitimized the dominant social and economic structure and that often depicted minorities negatively (Phillips, 1918/1966). Mainstream American writers and social scientists often perpetuated myths and stereotypes about ethnic minorities to explain why they "deserved" the low status in society to which they were most often assigned. Many of the stereotypes and myths that were constructed in early historical and social science research are still widespread within U.S. society, as for example: African Americans were enslaved because they were uncivilized and lazy; slavery would not only civilize them, but would also deliver their souls to God; Indians were savages who had to be civilized by Whites in order to survive; Japanese Americans were a threat to national survival during World War II and thus had to be confined to relocation camps for national security. Some mainstream historians and social scientists are gatekeepers of the status quo; they generate research legitimizing the myths and stereotypes that dominant groups create about powerless groups to justify their status (Herrnstein & Murray, 1994; Jensen, 1969; Tucker, 1994).

Throughout human society, history has been written by the victors and not by the vanquished. Thus, most students in our schools study histories of American Indians and African Americans that were written by American mainstream historians who most often had little empathy or understanding of those cultures. Because this is the case, you should help students view the experiences of ethnic minority groups from their perspectives. I am not suggesting that the histories of ethnic minorities written by mainstream writers should be banned from the schools. However, the study of America must also be seen through the eyes of the vanquished, because students now study it primarily from the viewpoints of the victors. Even though both views can add to our understanding of the American experience, we must stress other viewpoints because mainstream views of American history are so widespread within our schools and the larger society. Only by trying to see this nation from the viewpoints of marginalized peoples will we be able to understand fully its complexity.

Histories and social science accounts written by ethnic minority writers, like the writings of dominant groups, reflect particular points of view and biases. However, students need to study these writings seriously in order to gain a "balanced" perspective on U.S. life and history.

Power and Related Concepts

Power.   The ethnic experience within the United States cannot be understood without considering the role that the struggle for power among competing ethnic groups has played in shaping American history. History and contemporary social science teach us that in every past and present culture, individuals have had, and still have, widely unequal opportunities to share fully in the reward systems and benefits of their society. The basis for unequal distribution of rewards is determined by elitist groups in which power is centered. Most decisions made by people in power, including economic policy, are made to enhance, legitimize, and reinforce their power. Powerful groups not only make laws, but they also determine which traits and characteristics are necessary for full societal participation. They determine necessary traits on the basis of the similarity of such traits to their own values, physical characteristics, lifestyles, and behavior. At various periods in history, powerful groups have used celibacy, gender, ethnicity, race, and religion, as well as many other variables, to determine which individuals and groups would be given or denied opportunities for social mobility and full societal participation.

In colonial America, male Anglo-Saxon Protestants with property controlled most social, political, economic, and military institutions. These were the men who wrote the Declaration of Independence and the United States Constitution (Wilkins, 2001). They excluded from full participation in decision making people, such as African Americans and American Indians, who were different from themselves. Our founding fathers had a deep suspicion of and contempt for individuals who were culturally and racially different. They invented and perpetuated stereotypes and myths about excluded groups to justify their oppression (Wilkins, 2001). The United States, like all other nations, is still controlled by powerful groups who deny some individuals opportunities to participate in society on the basis of how similar such individuals are to themselves.

Money and power in the United States are highly concentrated; the gap between the rich and the poor continues to widen. The top earning 1% of the U.S. population received 17% of all income in 2004; the bottom 90% received slightly less than 58% of all income. The distribution of wealth is even more unequal than the income distribution. Over 34% of all net worth was held by the top 1% of the population in 2004, while less than 29% was held by the bottom 90% (Economic Policy Institute, 2006).

When studying about power relationships in American society, students can be asked to hypothesize about how we can make the United States an open society and thus more consistent with its democratic national ideology. Students can define an open society as one in which rewards and opportunities are not necessarily evenly distributed but are distributed on the basis of the knowledge and skills that each person, regardless of ethnic characteristics, can contribute to the fulfillment of the needs of society. Students should be asked to discuss which of their hypotheses are most sound and how actions based on them might be implemented and to state their limitations.

Social Protest and Resistance.   Throughout U.S. history, movements have emerged within ethnic communities to protest social conditions, political policies, and economic practices that were considered unjust and unconstitutional. The types of protest have varied widely, from the actions of individual Japanese Americans to resist the internment during World War II to the race riots that occurred in U.S. cities in the 1960s. Groups tend to resort to extreme methods of protest, such as riots and rebellions, when they feel that the political system is oppressive, that there are no legitimate channels for the alleviation of their grievances, that there is some cause for hope, or that their protest movement might succeed. When studying about social protest, it is important for students to understand that such movements occur only when oppressed people feel that there is a cause for hope. For example, students can derive this generalization when studying the Black protest movements of the 1960s (Joseph, 2006). This movement emerged partly because prior policies aimed at reducing discrimination had occurred. These included the desegregation of the armed forces by President Harry S. Truman, the laws that desegregated many southern state universities, and the historic *Brown* v. *Board of Education* Supreme Court decision in 1954, which legally outlawed *de jure* school segregation. These events were necessary precedents to the Black civil rights movement of the 1960s.

Many people think that the ethnic protests of the 1960s were the first of their kind in U.S. history. Even though it is true that ethnic protests reached their zenith during these years, ethnic groups have protested discrimination and racism throughout U.S. history. Black protest actually began on the slave ships on the journeys from West Africa to the Americas. Slave uprisings and mutinies often occurred on these ships (Davis, 2006). Many slaves also committed suicide by throwing themselves into the Atlantic rather than acquiesce to bondage. Protest by African Americans continued during and after slavery. Slave uprisings, led by such individuals as Denmark Vesey, Gabriel Prosser, and Nat Turner, sometimes resulted in the mass murder of Whites (Aptheker, 1943/1987; Genovese, 1979).

Near the turn of the century, Black organizations emerged to fight systematically for civil rights, including the National Association for the Advancement of Colored People (NAACP) and the National Urban League. Other ethnic groups have also continually fought for their rights. Organizations such as the Anti-Defamation League of B'nai B'rith, the Japanese American Citizenship League, the League of United Latin-American Citizens, and the Puerto Rican Forum were organized to work for the civil rights of various ethnic groups in a systematic way. Oppression of any human group is likely to lead to organized protest and resistance. Such protest and resistance have emerged within all of America's ethnic minority groups, although the forms and styles of that protest have reflected the unique cultural values, lifestyles, and histories of the particular groups.

The Movement of Ethnic Groups

Migration and Immigration.   When individuals or groups move within a nation in which they are natives or citizens, we say that they are *migrants*. Individuals or groups who settle in a foreign country are called *immigrants*. Thus, migration describes the movement of individuals and groups within a nation, and immigration describes the settlement of people in a foreign nation. These two concepts must be studied in the multicultural curriculum, because all groups that comprise the United States, except for a few (such as American Indians, Eskimos, Aleuts, and Native Hawai'ians), immigrated to this land from a foreign nation or migrated from Puerto Rico. We call Puerto Ricans migrants rather than immigrants because they became U.S. citizens with the passage of the congressional Jones Act of 1917. Archeological theories and evidence indicate that some American Indians immigrated to the Americas from Asia via the Bering Strait. Although this evidence is strongly endorsed by some anthropologists, it is inconclusive. Many American Indians believe that they were created in the Americas by the Great Spirit.

When studying these two concepts, students can formulate hypotheses about why very large numbers of immigrants entered the United States in the nineteenth century. Between 1820 and 1930, about 38 million immigrants came to the United States, most of them from Europe. Students might hypothesize that many individuals and groups came to the United States to avoid religious and political persecution and to improve their economic conditions. When studying statistics on immigration to the United States, students can be asked to note the countries from which most immigrants came and to explain why. For example, between 1820 and 1979, 6,985,000 German immigrants entered the United States. During the same period, only 3,038,000 immigrants came from the entire continent of Asia, and 36,267,000 came from the rest of Europe. Only 142,000 came from Africa. An investigation into why many more immigrants came from Europe than from Asia and Africa will lead students to discover that our immigration policies, until they were reformed in 1965, were designed to keep this nation largely White and to keep out non-Whites.

A study of immigration to the United States since the Immigration Reform Act of 1965 reveals that the source of immigration to the United States has changed substantially since that time (see Table 3.4). Over 70% of the legal immigrants to the United States between 1950 and 1969 were from Europe and North America. Europeans and North Americans comprised only 17.7% of immigrants to the United States between 2000 and 2006 (see Figure 1.1, page 5) (U.S. Department of Homeland Security, 2005). Table 3.4 shows immigrants to the United States, by country of birth, 1981 to 2005.

During their study of the immigration and migration of ethnic groups, students can profitably compare and contrast the reasons why various groups immigrated and the kinds of experiences they had in their new country. The special case of African immigrants to the United States should be highlighted. This group differed from all the other immigrant groups because their immigration was forced. They were also the only group enslaved on their arrival in the Americas. All the other groups of immigrants voluntarily came to the Americas, although many were escaping abject poverty, religious persecution, and political repression. Many of the early immigrants to the Americas were indentured servants who had few rights. However, most White indentured servants were eventually able to obtain their freedom.

When studying about the southern and eastern European immigrants to the United States, students can note how each group experienced discrimination and lived in urban ghettos, and how many of them eventually became culturally assimilated, attained social mobility, and moved to the suburbs of cities such as New York, Boston, and Chicago. Groups like Italians and Poles discriminated against African Americans and Mexican Americans when these groups started migrating to large cities after the two world wars.

European immigrant groups, especially the southern and eastern ones, were often the victims of discrimination and racist ideologies, but the racism they experienced never reached the proportions it did in the South against African Americans or

TABLE 3.4 Immigrants by Country of Birth, 1981 to 2005 (in thousands)

COUNTRY OF BIRTH	1981–1990 TOTAL	1991–2000 TOTAL	2001–2004 TOTAL	2005
All countries	7,256.0	9,080.5	3,779.7	1,112.4
Europe[a]	705.6	1,309.1	581.6	176.6
Albania	(NA)	26.2	15.3	5.9
Armenia	(X)	b26.6	6.7	2.6
Belarus	(X)	b28.9	9.9	3.5
Bosnia and Herzegovina	(X)	b38.8	65.6	14.1
Bulgaria	(NA)	23.1	16.1	5.6
France	23.1	27.4	14.3	4.4
Germany	70.1	67.6	30.8	9.3
Ireland	32.8	58.9	5.4	2.1
Italy	32.9	22.5	9.7	3.1
Poland	97.4	a169.5	49.3	15.4
Portugal	40.0	22.7	4.8	1.1
Romania	38.9	57.5	19.7	7.1
Russia	(X)	b127.8	72.4	18.1
Serbia and Montenegro[c,d]	19.2	25.8	22.9	5.2
Soviet Union[c]	84.0	103.8	7.1	2.9
Ukraine	(X)	b141.0	67.9	22.8
United Kingdom	142.1	135.6	59.0	19.8

COUNTRY OF BIRTH	1981–1990 TOTAL	1991–2000 TOTAL	2001–2004 TOTAL	2005
Syria	20.6	26.1	10.1	2.8
Taiwan	(e)	106.3	37.8	9.2
Thailand	64.4	48.4	15.8	5.5
Turkey	20.9	26.3	13.5	4.6
Vietnam	401.4	420.8	122.6	32.8
Africa[a]	192.3	382.5	228.9	85.1
Egypt	31.4	46.7	18.9	7.9
Ethiopia	27.2	49.3	27.6	10.6
Ghana	14.9	35.6	18.0	6.5
Nigeria	35.3	67.2	33.6	10.6
Somalia	(NA)	20.1	13.9	5.8
South Africa	15.7	22.6	13.5	4.5
Oceania	(NA)	47.9	21.9	6.5
North America[a]	3,125.0	3,910.1	1,401.0	345.6
Canada	119.2	137.2	68.0	21.9
Mexico	1,653.3	2,205.5	715.4	161.4
Cuba	159.2	178.7	85.4	36.3
Dominican Republic	251.8	340.8	100.4	27.5
Haiti	140.2	181.7	73.7	14.5

Country			
Asia[a]	2,817.4	2,890.2	1,267.2	400.1
Bangladesh	15.2	66.0	25.3	11.5
Cambodia	116.6	18.5	11.1	4.0
China	[c]388.8	424.4	213.4	70.0
Hong Kong	63.0	74.0	21.9	3.7
India	261.9	383.0	261.2	84.7
Iran	154.8	112.5	41.0	13.9
Iraq	19.6	40.7	16.1	4.1
Israel	36.3	31.9	14.5	5.8
Japan	43.2	61.4	31.5	8.8
Jordan[f]	32.6	39.7	14.9	3.7
Korea	338.8	171.1	73.4	26.6
Laos	145.6	43.5	4.7	1.2
Lebanon	41.6	43.4	15.3	4.3
Pakistan	61.3	124.5	51.6	14.9
Phillipines	495.3	505.3	207.1	60.7
Jamaica	213.8	173.4	57.9	18.3
Trinidad and Tobago	39.5	63.2	21.9	6.6
El Salvador	214.6	217.3	120.2	21.4
Guatemala	87.9	103.0	63.0	16.8
Honduras	49.5	66.7	23.2	7.0
Nicaragua	44.1	94.6	38.4	3.3
Panama	29.0	24.0	6.1	1.8
South America[a]	455.9	539.3	269.7	103.1
Argentina	25.7	24.3	14.9	7.1
Brazil	23.7	52.2	35.8	16.7
Colombia	124.4	130.8	69.0	25.6
Ecuador	56.0	76.3	35.9	11.6
Guyana	95.4	73.8	31.4	9.3
Peru	64.4	105.6	44.2	15.7
Venezuela	17.9	29.9	20.6	10.6

Note: Years are fiscal years ending Sept. 30. Number of immigrants by country prior to 1996 are unrevised. NA = Not available; X = Not applicable. [a]Includes countries not shown separately. [b]Prior to 1992. [c]Covers years 1992–2000. [d]Prior to 1992, data include independent republics; beginning in 1992, data are for unknown republic only. [d]Yugoslvaia (unknown republic) prior to February 7, 2003. [e]Data for Taiwan included with China. [f]Prior to 2003, includes Palestine; beginning in 2003. Palestine included in Unknown.

Source: U.S. Department of Homeland Security, Office of Immigration Statistics (2005), *Yearbook of Immigration Statistics, 2005.* Available online at http://uscis/gov/graphics/shared/statistics/yearbook/index.htm.

on the West Coast when Asian immigrants started arriving there in the 1800s. It is important for students to realize that, even though certain classes of European immigrants, such as lunatics, convicts, and idiots, were prevented from entering the United States in the 1800s, the first national group that was totally excluded from the United States was non-White. The Chinese Exclusion Act of 1882 completely stopped Chinese immigration to the United States for several decades. In the 1920s, the number of southern and eastern European immigrants entering the United States was reduced to a trickle because discrimination against them became intense and widespread. Non-White groups were virtually excluded from the United States. Only groups from northern and western Europe were favored by the "national origins" quota system that was enacted by Congress in 1921 and tightened in 1924. The quota was based on the percentage of residents of a particular nationality in the United States in 1920.

The McCarran Act of 1952 relaxed some of the earlier restrictions but made the national origin parts of the law even more severe. Significant immigration reform did not occur until the Immigration Act of 1965, which amended the Immigration and Nationality Act of 1952. This act became effective in 1968. The 1965 act removed the national origin quotas and liberalized U.S. immigration policy. A consequence of the civil rights movement led by African Americans, the 1965 act dramatically changed the ethnic and racial makeup of the United States. One important consequence of this act, which led to the large number of people who are now immigrating to the United States from Asian and Latin American nations, is that the U.S. Census projects that people of color will be about half of the U.S. population by 2050.

SUMMARY

This chapter has discussed a number of high-level concepts that can be used effectively to organize and teach multicultural units and lessons. I suggested that key concepts selected for the multicultural curriculum should be able to function successfully in an interdisciplinary role, should help explain some significant aspects of the cultures and experiences of ethnic groups, and should be able to encompass a wide range of data and information. When choosing concepts for the multicultural curriculum, you should also consider your students' developmental levels and their prior experiences with content related to race, ethnicity, and culture. Chapter 4 discusses ways in which the multicultural curriculum can be planned and organized.

REFLECTION AND ACTION ACTIVITIES

1. Identify a racial, ethnic, or religious problem in your community, such as a controversy over affirmative action, the question of open housing, or discrimination directed against a particular religious or ethnic group, such as Arab Americans after

the September 11, 2001, bombing of the World Trade Center in New York City and the Pentagon in Washington, D.C. List concepts and generalizations from several disciplines that might help students understand the problem. What strategies and materials would you use to teach the problem to students?

2. State the advantages of interdisciplinary multicultural lessons and units. What problems might you encounter in trying to structure these kinds of lessons and units? How might you resolve them?

3. Examine several of the books dealing with specific ethnic groups listed in the bibliographies of this book. Identify and list cultural traits that are unique to different ethnic communities. What is the origin of these cultural traits? Why do they continue to exist? Are they unique to particular ethnic groups or merely associated with lower-class status or a certain region? Explain your responses.

4. After reading a book on each of the major ethnic groups, make a list of the types of cultural and physical differences existing within them. Explain why these differences emerged and why they still exist.

5. Make a list of the major occupations in which most American Indians, Mexican Americans, Asian Americans, Puerto Rican Americans, and African Americans work (see U.S. Census Bureau online at http://www.census.gov.)

    Note the percentages of each group working in the major occupations identified. Carefully study the data you have gathered. What generalizations and conclusions can you make about the occupational status of ethnic groups of color in U.S. society? What factors explain their occupational status?

6. Using a map of your city or community, pinpoint the regions in which the various ethnic groups live, using different-colored markers to represent each major racial or ethnic group. What conclusions and generalizations can you make about where different racial or ethnic groups are concentrated in your community? What factors explain their location patterns?

7. Locate several conflicting accounts of slavery or the U.S.-Mexican War and develop an inquiry lesson to teach students how personal biases influence the writing of history.

8. Study the treatments of the major ethnic groups in your basal social studies, language arts, or other textbooks. What conclusions can you make? What materials and strategies can you use to extend textbook treatments of ethnic groups? How?

9. List examples of racial and ethnic discrimination you have seen and/or experienced. Why did the discrimination occur? How might this type of discrimination be reduced? How did you respond to it? Explain.

10. Watch several television programs during the week that have ethnic minority characters. Also study the treatment of ethnic groups such as African Americans and Mexican Americans in a newspaper or news magazine for a one-week period. Write a three- to five-page paper summarizing your observations about the treatment of ethnic minorities on television and in the printed sources you examined. Did you find any examples of racism? Explain.

    A helpful book for this activity is Carlos E. Cortés (2000), *The Children Are Watching: How the Media Teach about Diversity.*

11. Try to think of several examples of problems that result from communicating across different ethnic cultures. Develop and write a lesson plan for teaching the concept of intercultural communication to students.

12. Define each of the following terms and tell why each is important:

high-level concept   ethnic group

interdisciplinary   socialization

conceptual curriculum   intercultural communication

microculture

REFERENCES

Acuña, R. F. (2007). *Occupied America: A History of Chicanos* (6th ed.). New York: Pearson Longman.

Alim, H. S., & Baugh, J. (Eds.). (2007). *Talkin Black Talk: Language, Education, and Social Change.* New York: Teachers College Press.

Andrews, W. L., Foster, F. S., & Harris, T. (Eds.). (1997). *The Oxford Companion to African American Literature.* New York: Oxford University Press.

Appiah, K. A. (2006). *Cosmopolitanism: Ethnics in a World of Strangers.* New York: Norton.

Appleby, J., Hunt, L., & Jacob, M. (1994). *Telling the Truth about History.* New York: Norton.

Aptheker, H. (1943/1987). *American Negro Slave Revolts.* New York: International.

Banks, J. A. (2006). *Cultural Diversity and Education: Foundations, Curriculum and Teaching* (5th ed.). Boston: Allyn and Bacon.

Berelson, B., & Steiner, G. A. (1964). *Human Behavior: An Inventory of Scientific Findings.* New York: Harcourt, Brace and World.

Brizan, G. (1998). *Grenada: Island of Conflict.* London: Macmillan Education.

Bullivant, B. M. (1993). Culture: Its Nature and Meaning for Educators. In J. A. Banks & C. A. M. Banks (Eds.), *Multicultural Education: Issues and Perspectives* (pp. 29–47). Boston: Allyn and Bacon.

Cortés, C. E. (2000). *The Children Are Watching: How the Media Teach about Diversity.* New York: Teachers College Press.

Cose, E. (1993). *The Rage of a Privileged Class.* New York: HarperCollins.

Davis, D. B. (2006). *Inhuman Bondage: The Rise and Fall of Slavery in the New World.* New York: Oxford University Press.

Davis, F. J. (1991). *Who Is Black? One Nation's Definition.* University Park: Pennsylvania State University Press.

DjeDje, J. C., & Meadows, E. S. (Eds.). (1998). *California Soul: Music of African Americans in the West.* Berkeley: University of California Press.

Economic Policy Institute. (2006). Wealth Flows to the Wealthiest as the Percentage of Americans Who Own Stock Falls: Growing Share of Households Face Inadequate Retirement Income; Personal Debt Reaches New High. Retrieved January 25, 2007, from http://www.epinet.org/newsroom/releases/2006/08/SWApr-wealth-200608-final.pdf.

Feagin, J. R., & Sikes, M. P. (1994). *Living with Racism: The Black Middle-Class Experience.* Boston: Beacon Press.

Feagin, J. R., & Vera, H. (1995). *White Racism: The Basics.* New York: Routledge.

Flores, J. (1993). *Divided Borders: Essays on Puerto Rican Identity.* Houston: Arte Público Press.

Gay, G. (1973). Racism in America: Imperatives for Teaching Ethnic Studies. In J. A. Banks (Ed.), *Teaching Ethnic Studies: Concepts and Strategies* (pp. 27–49). Washington, DC: National Council for the Social Studies.

Genovese, E. D. (1979). *From Rebellion to Revolution: Afro-American Slave Revolts in the Making of the Modern World.* Baton Rouge: Louisiana State University Press.

Giovanni, N. (2005). *Rosa.* Illustrated by B. Collier. New York: Holt.

Henry, J. (1963). *Culture against Man.* New York: Vintage Books.

Henry, J. (1971). *Pathways to Madness*. New York: Random House.

Herrnstein, R. J., & Murray, C. (1994). *The Bell Curve: Intelligence and Class Structure in American Life*. New York: Free Press.

Hunt, C. L., & Walker, L. (1974). *Ethnic Dynamics: Patterns of Intergroup Relations in Various Societies*. Homewood, IL: Dorsey Press.

Jacobson, M. F. (1998). *Whiteness of a Different Color: European Immigrants and the Alchemy of Race*. Cambridge, MA: Harvard University Press.

Jensen, A. R. (1969, Winter). How Much Can We Boost IQ and Scholastic Achievement? *Harvard Educational Review, 39*, 1–123.

Joseph, P. E. (2006). *Waiting 'Til the Midnight Hour: A Narrative of Black Power in America*. New York: Holt.

Kuper, A. (1999). *Culture: The Anthropologist's Account*. Cambridge, MA: Harvard University Press.

Lacapa, K., & Lacapa, M. (2001). *Less than Half, More than Whole*. Illustrated by Michael Lacapa. Chapel Hill, NC: Storytellers Publishing.

Lustig, M. W., & Koester, J. (1993). *Intercultural Competence across Cultures*. New York: HarperCollins.

Merton, R. K. (1949). Discrimination and the American Creed. In R. M. MacIver (Ed.), *Discrimination and National Welfare* (pp. 99–126). New York: Harper & Row.

Miel, A., with Kiester, E., Jr. (1967). *The Shortchanged Children of Suburbia*. New York: American Jewish Committee.

Montagu, A. (1997). *Man's Most Dangerous Myth: The Fallacy of Race* (6th ed.). Walnut Creek, CA: AltaMira Press.

Morrison, T. (2004). *Remember: The Journey to School Integration*. Boston: Houghton Mifflin.

Mukhopadhyay, C. C., Henze, R., & Moses, Y. T. (Eds.). (2007). *How Real Is Race: A Sourcebook on Race, Culture, and Biology*. Lanham, MD: Rowman & Littlefield.

Nussbaum, M. (2002). Patriotism and Cosmopolitanism. In J. Cohen (Ed.), *For Love of Country* (pp. 2–17). Boston: Beacon Press.

Omi, M., & Winant, H. (1994). *Racial Formation in the United States: From the 1960s to the 1990s* (2nd ed.). New York: Routledge and Kegan Paul.

Pew Research Center. (2003). Conflicted Views of Affirmative Action. Washington, DC: The Pew Research Center for the People and the Press. Retrieved June 27, 2007, from http://people-press.org/reports/display.php3?ReportID=184.

Phillips, U. B. (1918/1966). *American Negro Slavery*. Baton Rouge: Louisiana State University Press.

Sizemore, B. A. (1972, January). Is There a Case for Separate Schools? *Phi Delta Kappan, 53*, 281–284.

Stephan, W., & Stephan, C. W. (2004). Intergroup Relations in Multicultural Education Programs. In J. A. Banks & C. A. M. Banks (Eds.), *Handbook of Research on Multicultural Education* (2nd ed., pp. 782–798). San Francisco: Jossey-Bass.

Takaki, R. (1998). *A Larger Memory: A History of Our Diversity, with Voices*. New York: Little, Brown.

Tamura, E. H. (1994). *Americanization, Acculturation, and Ethnic Identity*. Urbana: University of Illinois Press.

Tucker, W. H. (1994). *The Science and Politics of Racial Research*. Urbana: University of Illinois Press.

U.S. Census Bureau. (2001). [Online]. Available at http://www.census.gov.

U.S. Census Bureau. (2006). *Current Population Survey, Annual Social and Economic Supplement*. PINC-01: Selected Characteristics of People 15 Years and Over by Total Money Income in 2005, Work Experience in 2005, Race, Hispanic Origin, and Sex. Washington, DC: Author.

U.S. Department of Homeland Security. (2005). *Yearbook of Immigration Statistics: 2005*, table 2. Washington, DC: Author.

Van Ausdale, D., & Feagin, J. R. (2001). *The First R: How Children Learn Race and Racism*. Lanham, MD: Rowman & Littlefield.

van den Berghe, P. L. (1978). *Race and Racism: A Comparative Perspective* (2nd ed.). New York: Wiley.

Weatherford, J. (1988). *Indian Givers: How the Indians of the Americas Transformed the World.* New York: Fawcett Columbine.

Weatherford, J. (1991). *Native Roots: How the Indians Enriched America.* New York: Fawcett Columbine.

Wilkins, R. (2001). *Jefferson's Pillow: The Founding Fathers and the Dilemma of Black Patriotism.* Boston: Beacon Press.

Wilson, S. M. (Ed.). (1997). *The Indigenous People of the Carribbean.* Gainesville: University Press of Florida.

Yep, L. (2000). *The Journal of Wong Ming-Chung: A Chinese Miner.* New York: Scholastic.

ANNOTATED BIBLIOGRAPHY

Lahiri, J. (2003). *The Namesake.* Boston: Houghton Mifflin.
This novel about an Indian immigrant family in the United States powerfully illuminates concepts such as ethnic identity, assimilation, and the problems faced by children of the first generation of immigrants as they try to become Americans and yet maintain roots in their immigrant culture. *The Namesake* is now a major motion picture.

Lewis, A. E. (2004). *Race in the Schoolyard: Negotiating the Color Line in Classrooms and Communities.* New Brunswick, NJ: Rutgers University Press.
This informative sociological study of race in two multiracial schools and one predominantly White suburban schools reveals the ways in which race is a powerful factor in school life.

Mukhopadhyay, C. C., Henze, R., & Moses, Y. T. (Eds.). (2007). *How Real Is Race: A Sourcebook on Race, Culture, and Biology.* Lanham, MD: Rowman & Littlefield.
This helpful and informative sourcebook will help teachers and teacher educators to design and implement teaching strategies that will enable students to understand how race is socially constructed.

Pollock, M. (2004). *Colormute: Race Talk Dilemmas in an American School.* Princeton, NJ: Princeton University Press.
This book, which was the recipient of an American Educational Research Association (AERA) Best Book of the Year Award, is an ethnographic study of race talk in a California high school. It is an informative and perceptive book.

Roediger, D. R. (2005). *Working toward Whiteness: How America's Immigrants Became White: The Strange Journey from Ellis Island to the Suburbs.* New York: Basic Books.
This important book, which is a study of race as a social construction, describes how U.S. ethnic groups, such as Jewish Americans, Italian Americans, and Polish Americans, did not become part of White America until the 1920s and 1930s.

CHAPTER FOUR

PLANNING THE MULTICULTURAL CURRICULUM

The multicultural curriculum should help students develop the ability to make reflective personal and public decisions. A curriculum focused on decision making must be conceptual and interdisciplinary and based on higher levels of knowledge. The preceding chapter, "Key Concepts for the Multicultural Curriculum," presents criteria and examples of concepts that you can use to organize multicultural units and lessons.

This chapter discusses ways to organize a decision-making curriculum after you have selected appropriate concepts and content. It also presents other components of an effective multicultural curriculum, including valuing and personal, social, and civic action. Steps you can take to select and evaluate instructional materials are also discussed.

IDENTIFYING KEY CONCEPTS AND ORGANIZING GENERALIZATIONS

When planning multicultural lessons and units that have a comparative approach and focus, you or a curriculum committee should start by identifying key concepts. These concepts should be higher-level ones that can encompass numerous facts and lower-level generalizations. They should have the power to organize a great deal of information and to explain significant aspects of the experiences and histories of ethnic groups. These concepts should also be able to function successfully in an interdisciplinary role.

After you or a curriculum committee has selected key concepts from several disciplines, at least one organizing generalization related to each concept should be identified. Each organizing generalization should be a higher-level statement that explains some aspects of human behavior in all cultures, times, and places. It should not contain references to any particular culture or group but should be a universal type of statement capable of being scientifically tested. Table 4.1 presents a list of key concepts and related organizing generalizations that can be used to plan a multicultural conceptual curriculum incorporating the experiences of a range of ethnic and cultural groups.

TABLE 4.1   Key Concepts and Organizing Generalizations for a Multicultural Curriculum

KEY CONCEPT	ORGANIZING GENERALIZATION
Acculturation	Whenever ethnic groups have extended contact, exchange of cultural traits occurs between minority and majority groups, as well as between different ethnic groups.
Intercultural Communication	Individuals and groups socialized within different ethnic cultures are often unable to communicate effectively because they interpret the meanings of symbols differently. Ineffective communication frequently results in conflict between ethnic groups.
Perception	In a society stratified along racial and ethnic group lines, ethnicity and race tend to influence cogently how individuals see and interpret events, situations, and public issues.
Racism	Powerful groups that hold racist beliefs usually structure institutions, laws, and norms that reflect their beliefs and oppress the victims of racism.
Power	Within an ethnically stratified society, individuals and power groups struggle for power and influence. Power struggles often lead to social change.
Immigration–migration	In all cultures, individuals and groups have moved to seek better economic, political, and social opportunities. However, movement of individuals and groups has been both voluntary and forced.

IDENTIFYING INTERMEDIATE-LEVEL GENERALIZATIONS

After an organizing (universal-type) generalization is identified for each key concept chosen, an intermediate-level generalization that relates to each organizing generalization should be formulated. An intermediate-level generalization applies to a nation, to regions within a nation, or to groups comprising a particular culture. Table 4.2 presents an intermediate-level generalization for *immigration–migration*, a key concept listed in Table 4.1. In an actual curriculum, intermediate-level generalizations would be identified for each organizing generalization selected and shown in Table 4.1. However, the example in Table 4.2 is limited to save space.

DETERMINING WHICH ETHNIC GROUPS TO STUDY

Selecting a Range of Groups

When an intermediate-level generalization has been identified for each key concept, you must decide which ethnic groups will be selected for study. A range of groups should be included in comparative multicultural units and lessons in order to teach significant concepts related to U.S. ethnic groups and to illustrate both the differences

TABLE 4.2   Generalizations Related to Immigration–Migration

KEY CONCEPT
Immigration–migration

ORGANIZING GENERALIZATION
In all societies, individuals and groups have moved to seek better economic, political, and social opportunities. However, movement of individuals and groups has been both voluntary and forced.

INTERMEDIATE-LEVEL GENERALIZATION
Most individuals and groups who immigrated to the United States and who migrated within it were seeking better economic, political, or social opportunities. However, movement of individuals and groups to and within the United States has been both voluntary and forced.

LOW-LEVEL GENERALIZATIONS
Indians: Most movements of Indians within the United States were caused by forced migration and genocide.

Mexican Americans: Mexicans who immigrated to the United States came primarily to improve their economic condition by working as migrant laborers in the western and southwestern states.

European Americans: Most southern and eastern Europeans who immigrated to the United States came primarily to improve their economic status.

African Americans: Large numbers of Blacks migrated to northern and western cities in the early 1900s to escape lynchings and economic and political discrimination in the South.

Asian Americans: Most Asian immigrants who came to the United States in the 1800s expected to improve their economic conditions and return to Asia. During World War II, Japanese Americans were forced to move from their homes to federal internment camps.

Puerto Ricans: Puerto Ricans usually come to the U.S. mainland seeking better jobs; they sometimes return to the island of Puerto Rico because of American racism and personal disillusionment experienced on the mainland.

Indochinese Americans: Most Indochinese Americans, unlike most American immigrant groups, came to the United States because of political developments in their native lands.

and the similarities in their experiences, cultures, and histories. Groups that differ in racial characteristics, levels of assimilation, social class status, and in the periods and circumstances of immigration to or migration within the United States should also be studied in the multicultural curriculum.

Units that include ethnic groups that have been successful educationally and economically, such as Jewish Americans and Japanese Americans, and those that still face massive social and economic problems, such as American Indians and Mexican Americans, can illustrate the enormous range in the experiences of ethnic groups in the United States. However, when ethnic groups such as Jewish Americans and Japanese Americans are studied, you should help students understand that although Jewish

Americans and Japanese Americans have experienced tremendous educational and social mobility, members of these groups are often victims of discrimination and sometimes face identity problems related to their ethnicity (Goldstein, 2006; Ichioka, 2006). Thus, these groups share some characteristics with lower-status ethnic groups such as American Indians, African Americans, and Mexican Americans.

Studying ethnic groups such as Chinese immigrants and Cuban Americans can illustrate the differences and similarities of two ethnic groups who came in large numbers to the United States at different points in history and for different reasons. The first Chinese immigrants came to the United States in the 1800s hoping to get rich quickly and return to their homeland. Most of the Cubans who settled in the United States between 1959 and 1970 came to escape a communist form of government (Olson & Olson, 1995). African Americans provide an interesting contrast to these groups. They were the only ethnic group that was forced to come to America and who came in chains (Davis, 2006).

The experiences of Jewish Americans in the United States have also been unique. Jews comprise a White ethnic, cultural, and religious group that has experienced high levels of educational and economic mobility but still retains significant aspects of their ethnic culture and identity (Brodkin, 1998). In 2000, about 52% of Jews still married within their own ethnic group (see Chapter 9). Usually, White ethnic groups become mainstream Americans when they attain high levels of educational and economic mobility (Alba & Nee, 2003). American Indians, Eskimos, Aleuts, and Native Hawai'ians differ from most other ethnic groups because they can claim America as their native land. Indochinese Americans can be studied to illustrate the problems faced by ethnic groups displaced by a modern war and relocated in an alien and highly industrialized society.

Studying Groups That Illustrate Key Concepts.   No single multicultural curriculum can include a study of each American ethnic group. The number is much too large to be manageable. There are more than 100 ethnic groups in the United States (Vecoli, Galens, Sheets, & Young, 1995). In addition to the groups of color that have, since the 1960s, urged educators to include more information about their histories and cultures in the curriculum, some White ethnic groups—such as Italian, Jewish, and Polish Americans—are also urging teachers to include the study of their experiences and histories in the school curriculum. Arab Americans and Muslims—growing and important populations within the United States (Haddad & Esposito, 2000; McCarus, 1994)—also deserve attention in the school curriculum. Teachers need to help counteract the pernicious stereotypes about Arabs and Muslims that are institutionalized within the United States and other Western societies (Cesari, 2004; Bayoumi & Rubin, 2000).

A major goal of the multicultural curriculum is to help students master key concepts that will help them make better decisions and become more effective citizens in a pluralistic democratic society. *Thus, the focus should be on helping students master key concepts that highlight major themes in the experiences of racial, ethnic, language, and cultural groups in the United States.* Within a conceptual curriculum, which particular groups are selected for study becomes a secondary, though important, consideration. The experiences of the groups selected for study should be the best examples of particular concepts.

It is essential that students master certain concepts—such as *race, racism, prejudice,* and *discrimination*—if they are to gain a full understanding of U.S. society and history. Racism has been a decisive force in the United States since its beginning and is still a major force in the United States today (Feagin, 2001; Tatum, 2007). Consequently, students must study this concept in a sound multicultural curriculum. When studying racism, students will need to examine the histories and contemporary experiences of ethnic groups of color such as African Americans, American Indians, Mexican Americans, and Asian Americans. Racism emerged to justify the enslavement of African Americans and was later developed into a full-blown ideology used to defend the exploration and exploitation of America and its native peoples (Davis, 2006).

Racism is still a major problem in U.S. society. A study of various ethnic groups that are victimized by institutionalized racism will help students develop a better understanding of this complex problem and the ability to reason about it thoughtfully. The different forms of prejudice and discrimination that exist in U.S. society also merit serious study by students in all grades, kindergarten through the university level. Research by Glock, Wutnow, Piliavin, and Spencer (1975) indicates that students who are more cognitively sophisticated and who can reason more logically about prejudice are likely to express fewer prejudices than are less cognitively sophisticated students. Gabelko and Michaelis (1981), influenced by the Glock et al. findings, developed a handbook of activities to help students reason more logically about prejudice and thus to reduce it.

A study of the experiences of Jews in the United States can facilitate an examination of the forms of prejudice and discrimination in contemporary U.S. society. Research indicates that anti-Semitism is still a problem in American society (Brodkin, 1998) that warrants open examination by students within democratic classrooms.

Concepts such as *cultural assimilation* and *structural assimilation* are also important in the multicultural curriculum. A study of groups of color, such as African Americans and Filipino Americans, can illustrate how some members of these groups have become *culturally* assimilated but have been denied *structural* assimilation, or the ability to participate freely in most U.S. institutions, because of their physical characteristics. However, the study of White ethnic groups, such as Irish Americans and German Americans, can illustrate how these groups have attained high levels of cultural and structural assimilation (Ignatiev, 1995). Often, members of these groups are indistinguishable from other mainstream Americans (Alba & Nee, 2003).

When studying cultural and structural assimilation, students can also examine such groups as Polish Americans and Italian Americans. By studying these groups, students can see how some White ethnic groups are experiencing particular levels of cultural and structural assimilation but still retain many ethnic institutions. Individuals within these ethnic groups often participate in ethnic communities and institutions, especially in cities with large White ethnic group populations, such as Chicago, Detroit, and New York City (Bukowczyk, 2006).

Other factors will also influence which ethnic groups you or the curriculum committee selects for study, including your interests and academic background and the ethnic groups represented in your class, school, and local community. However, units and lessons should not be limited to a study of local ethnic groups. Puerto Rican students should have the opportunity to study their own ethnic culture. They also need to learn about other ethnic cultures in order to understand more fully their own ethnic culture and the total human experience. Learning only about one's own culture is encapsulating and restricting. As Edward T. Hall has perceptively stated, "The future depends on [humankind's] transcending the limits of individual cultures" (Hall, 1977, p. 2).

IDENTIFYING LOW-LEVEL GENERALIZATIONS

When key concepts and organizing generalizations have been selected and the ethnic groups to be studied have been identified, low-level generalizations related to each ethnic group should be stated. Identifying a low-level generalization for each group will ensure that specific information about each group will be included in the teaching units and lessons that will be developed later. Table 4.2 presents low-level generalizations related to seven major ethnic groups and to the key concept *immigration–migration*.

Organizing generalizations are universal statements that omit references to specific peoples, cultures, and places. Intermediate-level generalizations refer to a particular nation, to regions within a nation, and to a particular culture. Low-level generalizations differ from both organizing and intermediate-level generalizations in that they apply to specific groups or microcultures within a culture and a nation.

CONCEPTS AND GENERALIZATIONS IN THE MULTICULTURAL CURRICULUM

To help you plan the multicultural curriculum, I have identified five key concepts related to ethnic groups and related intermediate-level generalizations. To save space, related organizing generalizations are not stated. However, these can be inferred from the generalizations given. For example, the first concept is *conflict*. The related organizing generalization, which encompasses the two statements below it, is: *Throughout history, conflict has arisen between and among groups in all societies.* Although organizing generalizations are not given below, they are important because they enable you to incorporate content from other nations for comparative purposes and to help students appreciate the power of high-level ideas. Table 4.3 shows how the students can use a data retrieval chart to make a comparative study of the key

TABLE 4.3 Using Selected Key Concepts for a Comparative Study of American Ethnic Groups

KEY CONCEPTS	AMERICAN INDIANS	MEXICAN AMERICANS	AFRICAN AMERICANS	JEWISH AMERICANS	VIETNAMESE AMERICANS	PUERTO RICANS	CUBAN AMERICANS
Conflict Within group: With other groups:							
Cultural Diversity Within group:							
Values Unique: Shared with others:							
Social Protest Types used: Results of:							
Immigration–Migration Reasons for: When: Results of:							
Assimilation Cultural: Structural:							

concepts below, as well as *immigration–migration* (which is in Table 4.2). Note that the words and phrases in capital letters are concepts; the statements that follow them are related generalizations.

CONFLICT

Conflict exists among different generations and subgroups within ethnic minority groups. These conflicts are especially evident in values, goals, and methods of protest.

CULTURAL DIVERSITY

There is wide diversity among and within various ethnic groups. The extent of group identification by members of ethnic groups varies greatly and is influenced by many factors, such as skin color, social class, and personal experiences.

VALUES

Many values within ethnic minority communities differ from those of mainstream Americans, even though their values are changing, especially as people of color become more culturally assimilated.

SOCIAL PROTEST

At various times in history, movements within ethnic minority groups emerge to develop more pride in their groups, shape new identities, gain political power and control of institutions, and shatter stereotypes. The intensity, scope, and type of movements have varied widely from group to group and have been influenced by the unique histories, values, cultures, and lifestyles of ethnic groups.

ASSIMILATION

As ethnic groups become more assimilated and attain higher socioeconomic status, they tend to abandon certain elements of their traditional cultures. However, they sometimes reclaim aspects of their cultural heritage once they are secure in middle- or upper-class status. This assimilation usually occurs in the third generation.

TEACHING STRATEGIES AND MATERIALS

Once you or the curriculum committee has identified the key concepts and generalizations that can serve as a framework for a multicultural curriculum or unit and has stated lower-level generalizations related to the experiences of ethnic groups in the United States, you (or the committee) can then identify the materials and teaching strategies necessary to help students derive the concepts and their related generalizations. A wide variety of teaching strategies, content, and materials can be used to teach ethnic content, many of which are described in the chapters on ethnic groups in this book (Chapters 5 through 14).

The sample generalization about immigration–migration in Table 4.2 can be effectively taught using content related to the forced westward migration of the Cherokee, which occurred in 1838 and 1839. This poignant migration is often called "The Trail of Tears."

Simulation and role-playing, as well as other strategies described in Parts II through V, can be used to teach effectively about immigration and other key concepts identified in this chapter. The six key concepts and organizing generalizations presented in Table 4.1 can be taught at every level within a spiral conceptual curriculum and developed at increasing levels of complexity with different content samples. At each level, K–12 materials related to a range of ethnic groups should be used as content samples to teach students key social science concepts and generalizations. Figure 4.1 illustrates how six key concepts can be spiraled within a conceptual

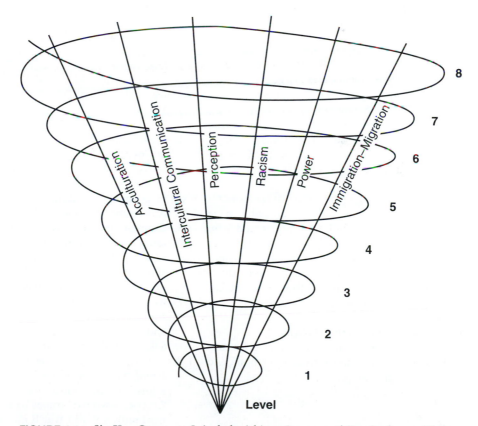

FIGURE 4.1   Six Key Concepts Spiraled within a Conceptual Curriculum at Eight Different Levels This diagram illustrates how information related to America's ethnic groups can be organized around key concepts and taught at successive levels at increasing degrees of complexity.

curriculum at eight different levels. This same curriculum design, of course, can be used in a K–12 program, an 8–12 curriculum, or with any level.

Planning Lessons

To ensure that every lower-level generalization identified in the initial stages of planning is adequately developed within a unit, the teacher can divide a sheet of paper in half and list the key concepts and the organizing, intermediate-level, and lower-level generalizations on one side of it and the strategies and materials needed to teach these ideas on the other side. An example is provided in Table 4.4.

Table 4.4   Key Ideas and Teaching Strategies

KEY IDEAS	ACTIVITIES
KEY CONCEPT Immigration–Migration **ORGANIZING GENERALIZATION** In all cultures, individuals and groups have moved to different regions in order to seek better economic, political, and social opportunities. However, movement of individuals and groups has been both voluntary and forced. **INTERMEDIATE-LEVEL GENERALIZATION** Most individual and groups who have immigrated to the United States and who have migrated within it were seeking better economic, political, and social opportunities. However, movement of individuals and groups within the United States has been both voluntary and forced. **LOWER-LEVEL GENERALIZATION** During World War II, Japanese Americans were forced to move from their homes to internment camps.	1. Reading aloud selections from Takashima, *A Child in Prison Camp.* 2. Discussing how Shichan, Yuki, and Mother felt when David and Father were taken away. 3. Viewing and discussing the drawings in *A Child in Prison Camp.* 4. Viewing and discussing the photographs in Conrat and Conrat, *Executive Order 9066: The Internment of 110,000 Japanese Americans.* 5. Hypothesizing about why Japanese Americans were interned. 6. Comparing textbook accounts of the internment with accounts in *Executive Order 9066* and *Within the Barbed Wire Fence: A Japanese Man's Account of His Internment,* by Takeo U. Nakano. 7. Reading selections from the novel *Journey to Topaz,* by Yoshiko Uchida, and discussing the experiences of the Sakane family during internment. 8. Viewing and discussing the videotape *Family Gathering* (New York: New Day Films). In this videotape, a Japanese American woman comes to terms with her family's World War II internment. 9. Summarizing and generalizing about the forced migration (internment) of Japanese Americans during World War II.

THE VALUE COMPONENT OF THE MULTICULTURAL CURRICULUM

Although higher-level scientific knowledge is necessary for reflective decision making on ethnic and racial problems, it is not sufficient. To make reflective decisions, citizens must also identify and clarify their values and relate them to the knowledge they have derived through the process of inquiry. Values education today is often referred to as *character education* (Damon, 2002). However, to be consistent with the notion of values education in this book, character education must enable students to think critically about values and to make value choices freely. A didactic approach to character education will not enable students to undertake the kind of value analysis that is essential for reflective decision making and action.

Because many ethnic and racial problems within our society are rooted in value conflicts, the school should play a significant role in helping students identify and clarify their values and make moral choices reflectively. Although the school has a tremendous responsibility to help students make moral choices thoughtfully, teachers often fail to help students deal with moral issues reflectively.

Some teachers treat value problems like the invisible person; they deny their existence. They assume that if students know all the "facts," they can resolve value problems. Such teachers may be said to practice the cult of false objectivity. Other teachers use an evasion strategy: when value problems arise in the classroom, they try to change the subject to a safer topic. A frequently used approach to value education in the elementary and high school is the inculcation of values considered "right" by adults or the indoctrination of these values. Such values as honesty, justice, truth, freedom, equality, and love (as defined by teachers) are taught with legendary heroes and heroines, stories, rituals, and patriotic songs. This approach to value education—which is the way that character education is conceptualized by some educators—is unsound and inconsistent with a democratic classroom and society.

The school should promote democratic values such as human dignity, justice, and equality. However, these values cannot be taught in a didactic fashion. Didactic approaches to moral education are unsound because they fail to help students learn a process for handling value conflicts and dilemmas. Often, individuals must choose between two equally "good" values, such as freedom and equality. In a democratic pluralistic nation such as the United States, values such as freedom and equality are often interpreted differently by different individuals and groups. The values themselves are also often in conflict.

During the mid 1990s, many African Americans, Mexican Americans, American Indians, and women argued that affirmative action programs were necessary for them to attain equal employment opportunities because of past discrimination (Anderson, 2005). White males often opposed affirmative action and felt that it denied them equality and justice. In 1995, Governor Pete Wilson of California became a visible and influential leader in an anti-affirmative action movement that resulted in the end of affirmative action in the state's colleges and universities

(Orfield, 2001). In two rulings on June 23, 2003, the Supreme Court upheld the University of Michigan Law School's affirmative action policy in *Grutter* v. *Bollinger*. However, in *Gratz* v. *Bollinger,* the Court ruled unconstitutional the Michigan undergraduate admissions policy, which awarded twenty points for African American, Hispanics, and Native Americans. Affirmative action is a highly contentious issue because of the different ways that various interest groups view and interpret it (Perry, 2007).

Because of the different ways in which various ethnic and racial groups often interpret the same values, such as justice, equality, and freedom, and because of the conflicts inherent in these values, teaching students in a didactic manner that they should value honesty, freedom, or justice is ineffective. Rather, students should be taught a *process* for identifying value conflicts, analyzing them, and resolving value conflicts and dilemmas.

Students should also be helped to make reflective moral choices and learn how to justify their moral decisions. All values are not equally valid. Some values, such as inequality, racism, and oppression, are clearly inconsistent with human dignity and other American creed values that are set forth in the basic legal and constitutional documents of the United States. Although standards that guide a person's life must be freely chosen from alternatives after thoughtful consideration of their consequences, students who choose or hold values that conflict with human dignity and other American creed values should be helped to see how their values conflict with democratic values and ideologies.

Students should also be helped to understand and predict the possible consequences of the values they embrace. The major goal of moral education should be *to help students develop a process for identifying value conflicts, resolving them, and rationally choosing and defending their moral choices*. This is the only approach to value education that is consistent with democratic teaching and learning. Serious value problems arise in the classroom when ethnic groups are studied. Students of color often have important value questions about their ethnic cultures, their identities, and effective strategies to use to effect social and political change. Public issues such as poverty, affirmative action, and discrimination in housing and employment pose controversial and complex moral dilemmas.

APPROACHES TO MORAL EDUCATION

A number of models, approaches, and theories related to value education have been developed that you can use to organize and teach value inquiry lessons. These include the public issues approach developed by Oliver and Shaver (1966) and Newmann (1970), the values clarification approach conceptualized by Simon, Harmin, and Raths (1991), and the cognitive-developmental approach developed by Lawrence Kohlberg (1975). The next section presents a brief summary of the cognitive-developmental approach developed by Kohlberg and a value inquiry model that I have developed.

The Cognitive-Developmental Approach to Moral Education

Kohlberg (1975) hypothesized that an individual's ability to reason morally develops sequentially in a series of definite stages and that these stages are found in all nations and cultures. He identified three levels of moral development: (1) the *preconventional*, (2) the *conventional*, and (3) the *postconventional*. Each level has two stages. The six stages constitute a hierarchy: each higher stage is a more sophisticated and more rational form of moral reasoning (see Table 4.5).

TABLE 4.5   A Summary of Kohlberg's Stages of Moral Development

LEVEL 1: PRECONVENTIONAL
At this level an individual's moral reasoning results from the consequences of actions (punishment, reward, exchange of favors) and from the physical power of those in positions of authority.

Stage 1:   Decisions result from a blind obedience to power, an attempt to avoid punishment, or an attempt to seek rewards.

Stage 2:   Decisions result from a desire to satisfy one's own needs and occasionally the needs of others. Individuals view reciprocity as a matter of "You scratch my back and I'll scratch yours." Reasoning involves little consideration of loyalty, gratitude, or justice.

LEVEL 2: CONVENTIONAL
At this level an individual's moral reasoning involves consideration of the interest of others (family and peers) and a desire to maintain, respect, support, and justify the existing social order.

Stage 3:   Decisions result from a desire to please and help others and receive their approval in return. Behavior is frequently judged by intention—"He means well" becomes important for the first time.

Stage 4:   Decisions result from a desire to maintain the existing authority, rules, and social order. Right behavior consists of doing one's duty.

LEVEL 3: POSTCONVENTIONAL
At this level an individual's moral reasoning incorporates moral values and principles that have validity and application beyond the authority of groups. Moral reasoning becomes more comprehensive and reflects universal principles.

Stage 5:   Decisions result from recognition of an individual's rights within a society that has a social contract. As a result the individual's reasoning emphasizes the "legal point of view," but with an emphasis on the possibility of changing laws.

Stage 6:   Decisions result from an obligation to universal ethical principles that apply to all [human-]kind. The universal principles of justice, reciprocity, and equality of human rights, and respect for the dignity of human beings as individuals serve as a basis for individual reasoning.

Source: R. E. Galbraith and T. M. Jones (1975), An Application of Kohlberg's Theory of Moral Development to the Social Studies Classroom, *Social Education, 39*, p. 17. Copyright 1975 by National Council for the Social Studies. Reprinted by permission.

The theory assumes that an individual's stage of moral development can be determined and that moral education must be based on the student's stage of moral reasoning. A major goal of moral education, according to Kohlberg, is to stimulate students by using moral dilemmas to move to the next higher stage of moral development.

Kohlberg (1975) believed that students cannot understand levels of moral reasoning that are more than one stage higher than their own. However, instruction below a student's stage of moral development will not stimulate her to think at the next higher stage. Kohlberg's research indicated that when students are engaged in discussions about moral dilemmas in which they are required to reason at one stage above their current stage, moral development and growth occur. Two basic assumptions of Kohlberg's theory are that an individual must proceed through the stages sequentially and that none can be skipped.

The theory assumes that there is an indirect relationship between chronological age and level of moral development. Very young children, according to the theory, tend to reason at the lower levels. As individuals grow older, they tend to reason at the higher levels. However, Kohlberg found that most individuals he studied were not able to reason beyond Stage 4. Kohlberg used open-ended stories that present moral dilemmas and discussion related to the dilemmas to stimulate students to think at higher stages of moral development. The nature and quality of the subsequent discussion are an extremely important part of this teaching strategy. Kohlberg used stories similar to "What Should the Johnsons Do?"

WHAT SHOULD THE JOHNSONS DO?

Mr. and Mrs. Johnson, a middle-class African American professional couple, live in a racially mixed neighborhood in a large midwestern city. Their daughter Susan, who is in her first year of high school, is attending Einstein High School, a predominantly White magnet school that specializes in science. Because Susan wants to be a physician, she and her parents decided that she should attend Einstein High rather the more racially mixed high school in her neighborhood.

Susan's experiences at Einstein have been mixed. The science curriculum is excellent. However, almost no attention is given to the history and culture of ethnic groups in any of the subject areas. Susan feels racially isolated and has only been able to make a few friends. Several teachers as well as students have made comments to her that suggest that they believe she is one of the low-income students who has been bused to Einstein from the inner city to achieve racial integration.

Question
Should the Johnsons leave Susan at Einstein High School?

A VALUE INQUIRY MODEL

I have developed a value inquiry model (presented in detail in Banks, 2006) that you can use to help students to identify value conflicts, examine them reflectively, and choose and defend their moral choices. The model is reprinted below (in list form), along with a sample lesson illustrating how it can be used when discussing value problems related to race and ethnicity.

- Defining and recognizing value problems: observation-discrimination.
- Describing value-relevant behavior: description-discrimination
- Naming values exemplified by behavior described: identification-description, hypothesizing
- Determining conflicting values in behavior described: identification-analysis
- Hypothesizing about sources of values analyzed: hypothesizing (citing data to support hypotheses)
- Naming alternative values to those exemplified by behavior observed: recalling
- Hypothesizing about the possible consequences of the values analyzed: predicting, comparing, contrasting
- Declaring value preference: choosing
- Stating reasons, sources, and possible consequences of value choice: justifying, hypothesizing, predicting

Value Inquiry Lessons: Examples

For value inquiry lessons, you can use case studies clipped from the daily newspaper, such as incidents related to racial profiling, housing discrimination, and ethnic and racial incidents at school. Ethnic literature and open-ended stories are excellent resources for value inquiry. On the next page I include an open-ended story, "Seed of Distrust," to show an example of a value inquiry lesson. Photographs, role-playing activities, and case studies related to ethnic events can also be used effectively.

An Open-Ended Story.   Open-ended stories present problem situations. If carefully chosen or written, they are excellent tools for stimulating class discussions of issues related to race and ethnicity as well as other human relations problems. After reading an open-ended story to the class, you can have the students identify the problems within it, the values of the characters, the courses of action they might take to resolve the problems, and the possible consequences of the proposed solutions. The students can also act out or role-play solutions to the problems.

Role-Playing in the Curriculum, by Fannie R. Shaftel and George Shaftel (1982), includes several open-ended stories that deal with intergroup problems. The story reprinted below is from this book. Questions that can be used with the story are also provided.

■ ■ ■ ■ ■

SEED OF DISTRUST

Betty was all excited when she ran into the apartment. "Mother, will you iron my green dress tonight?"

"I was planning to do it Saturday night, honey, so you'd have it for Sunday School."

"But I'll need it!"

"What's the rush?"

"Nora's invited me to a party tomorrow after school."

"Oh. I see," her mother said slowly, as if thinking hard. "Nora's the little girl on the second floor?"

"Yes. She's real nice."

Betty's sister Lucy, who was a sophomore in high school, asked, "Does her mother know?"

"Know what?" Betty asked.

"Nora's White. Isn't she?"

"Sure!"

"Does her mother know she's invited you?"

"Of course! I m–mean. I guess so."

"Does her mother know you're Black?" [Or Mexican, or Puerto Rican, etc.]

"Sure!"

"You mean you think so?"

"Y–Yes," Betty stammered.

"Better make sure," Lucy said, and turned back to the math she was studying.

"I'll iron your dress, honey," Betty's mother said reassuringly. "You'll look real nice."

"Uh-huh," Betty said dully. "Thanks, Mom."

And then, next day, after lunch, the thing happened—Nora met Betty in the hall, outside the fifth-grade room.

"Betty. I've been hunting for you," Nora said urgently. "Listen. My Aunt Dorothy phoned last night. She's arriving today for a visit. My grandma's coming over to see her, and mother's making a dinner for the whole family, cousins and all. You see? We've got to postpone my party. Until next week, maybe. I'll let you know!"

Betty looked at her, blank-faced.

"Don't bother," Betty said. "Don't bother at all." And Betty turned and walked away, her back very straight. For an instant Nora just stood and stared. Then she ran. She caught Betty's arm and stopped her.

"Betty, what's the matter? Why're you talking like that?" (pp. 383–384)

(Copyright © 1982 by Prentice-Hall. Reprinted by permission of Fannie Shaftel and George Shaftel.)

Questions

1. What is the main problem in this story?
2. What do you think of these characters: Betty, Lucy, Nora? Why? What kinds of things and people do you think are important to each of them? Why?
3. Do you think that Lucy should have asked Betty if Nora's mother knew that she was an African American? Why or why not?

4. Do you think Nora told the truth about the family dinner? Why or why not?
5. What are some courses of action that Betty can take? What should Betty do? Why?
6. What would you do if you were Betty? Why?
7. What might be the consequences of your action? Why?

PROVIDING OPPORTUNITIES FOR PERSONAL, SOCIAL, AND CIVIC ACTION

People of color in all regions of the United States are victims of institutionalized racism, poverty, and political powerlessness. When you identify concepts and generalizations, you should select those that will help students make decisions and take personal, social, or civic actions that reduce prejudice and discrimination in their personal lives, in the school, and, when possible, in the other social settings in which they function. Primary grade students cannot take actions that will reduce discrimination in the larger society. However, they can make a commitment to not tell or laugh at racist jokes; to play with and make friends with students from other racial, ethnic, and religious groups; and to read books that describe children from other racial, ethnic, and religious groups. Middle, upper-grade, and high school students can also take personal and social actions within the school community to improve race and ethnic relations (Lewis, 1998).

Teachers must play an active role in getting students to undertake personal and social action to improve race relations in their personal lives and in the institutions in which they function. To improve race relations in the classroom, you can structure interracial work and study groups, making sure that students of color have equal status roles in these groups (Cohen, 1994). Research has indicated that when students from different races and social classes have equal status within interracial work and study groups, these groups can improve interracial attitudes and help students of color increase their academic achievement (Slavin, 2001). A number of researchers, such as Slavin (2001) and Cohen (1994), have published works that will enable you to structure cooperative groups that will help students develop more positive intergroup and interracial attitudes. If you structure groups within the classroom that improve students' interracial and ethnic attitudes, the students will be more likely to take actions in their personal lives outside of the classroom that will make their lives more interracial and multicultural.

After they have mastered higher-level knowledge related to racial and ethnic problems and have clarified their values, you can ask your students to list *possible actions* they can take to help improve race relations in their personal lives, in the school, and in the other institutions in which they function. Also ask them to list the *possible consequences* of each action they identify. Students should participate in action activities and projects only after they have studied the issues related to the action from the perspectives of the social sciences and humanities, analyzed and clarified their values regarding them, identified the possible consequences of their actions, and expressed a willingness to accept them.

Figure 4.2 is a graphic you can use when asking students to list possible actions and consequences they can take when planning action and participation projects and activities.

MULTICULTURAL RESOURCES FOR INSTRUCTION

Finding Student Resources

Hundreds of children's books are published each year. Consequently, you will find it necessary to rely on bibliographies periodically published by professional and ethnic organizations to locate the most recent books. Some of the best bibliographies that list books on ethnic groups are published by public and private organizations, such as state departments of education, school systems, civil rights organizations, public libraries, and professional organizations.

Periodicals.   One of the most comprehensive periodic publications that contains critical reviews of children's books dealing with ethnic groups is *Multicultural Review,* published quarterly by Goldman Group, located in Tampa, Florida. *Multicultural Review* contains feature articles as well as reviews of videotapes and other audiovisual materials. *Multicultural Perspectives,* a quarterly publication of the National Association for Multicultural Education, includes a column, "Guide to New Resources," that periodically includes a discussion of materials for students, including films, videotapes, and books. Most of the materials included in the column are for teachers and other professionals. *Teaching Tolerance,* a magazine published twice a year by the Southern Poverty Law Center, is distributed to teachers without charge. This magazine also has a website (www.TeachingTolerance.org), which has helpful ideas for teaching about diversity as well as books and other materials for use with students. The National Women's History Project in Windsor, California, publishes a periodic *Women's History Catalog,* which includes some excellent materials on women of color for students and teachers.

Rethinking Schools, an excellent and informative periodic publication targeted for a teacher audience, contains perceptive and serious reviews of both student and teaching materials related to diversity. Rethinking Schools is located in Milwaukee, Wisconsin. Its website address is www.Rethinkingschools.org.

Resources on Groups of Color.   Several publishers specialize in books on ethnic groups of color. Asian American Curriculum Project (AACP), in San Mateo, California, markets books and materials on Asian Americans. It publishes a comprehensive catalog periodically and has a useful website (www.AsianAmericanBooks.com). Arte Publico Press at the University of Houston (www.arte.uh.edu) specializes in books on Latinos. Publishers that specialize in multiethnic books include Children's Book Press (San Francisco) (www.childrensbookpress.org), Lee and Low Books (New York City) (www.leeandlow.com), The New Press (New York City) (www.thenewpress.com),

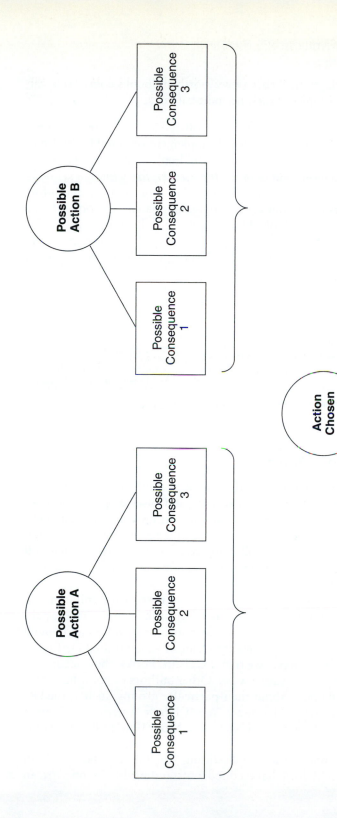

FIGURE 4.2 Possible Actions and Consequences

and Northland Publishing (Flagstaff, Ariz.) (www.northlandbooks.com). You can check their websites and obtain copies of their periodic catalogs.

Reviews of Children's Books.   *Social Education,* the official journal of the National Council for the Social Studies, publishes an annual supplement on notable children's books. Periodic publications that contain reviews of children's books are: *The Booklist* (American Library Association), *Bulletin of the Center for Children's Books* (Johns Hopkins University Press for the Graduate School of Librarianship and Information Science at the University of Illinois, Urbana-Champaign), *School Library Journal* (R. R. Bowker), and *Horn Book* (Horn Book, Inc., Boston, Mass.). *The Language Arts,* published by the National Council of Teachers of English, occasionally publishes articles that discuss children's books. The NCTE periodically issues special publications on books dealing with ethnic groups.

Magazines and newspapers, such as *Ebony* and the *New York Times,* also publish book lists and reviews of children's books periodically. Browsing in the children's section of local bookstores in large cities can lead to the discovery of a gold mine of recent children's books. The salesperson in charge of children's books is usually willing and able to help the browsing teacher or school librarian.

A book-length work that includes valuable annotations and information on children's books about diverse ethnic groups is *The New Press Guide to Multicultural Resources for Young Readers,* edited by Daphne Muse (1997). This comprehensive guide, which includes an index, consists of 688 pages.

Evaluating and Selecting Materials

Some of the books and other materials on ethnic groups published each year are insensitive, inaccurate, and written from mainstream and insensitive perspectives and points of view. Nevertheless, good materials on each group are published annually. Identifying them requires a considerable amount of time and careful evaluation and selection. The books discussed in the following pages suggest criteria that will help teachers, curriculum specialists, and librarians evaluate and select ethnic studies resources for classroom and library use.

One useful way to select excellent books on ethnic themes for children and young adults is to examine carefully the new works of authors who have established reputations for writing sensitive and excellent books for children and young adults. African American authors, such as Walter Dean Myers, Mildred D. Taylor, and Carole Boston Weatherford, have written excellent books that accurately depict African American culture in sensitive ways. Other authors of color have also written sensitive and powerful books about their particular groups, such as the late Yoshiko Uchida (Japanese American), Laurence Yep (Chinese American), Virginia Driving Hawk Sneve (American Indian), and Nicholasa Mohr (Puerto Rican). Some writers who are not members of the ethnic groups they write about have also established excellent reputations for writing and editing outstanding books. Both Dorothy Sterling and Milton Meltzer have edited outstanding books on African Americans.

Consider the following guidelines when selecting instructional materials.

1. *Books and other materials should accurately portray the perspectives, attitudes, and feelings of ethnic groups.* Certain values, aspirations, and viewpoints are prevalent in American ethnic communities. Books should honestly and accurately reflect these perspectives and feelings, both through characters and in the interpretations of events and situations. One of the best ways to ensure that books describe the perspectives of ethnic groups is to use books written by them. In *The Magic Paintbrush,* Lawrence Yep (2000b) describes how eight-year-old Steve turns to art to cope with the death of his parents and the destruction of his home in a fire. Walter Dean Myers's (2007) *Harlem Summer* is a skillfully written and poignant coming-of-age story of 16-year-old Mark Purvis. *Moses: When Harriet Tubman Led Her People to Freedom* by Carole Boston Weatherford (2006)—with powerful illustrations by Kadir Nelson—is a striking, engaging, and informative book.

2. *Fictional works should have strong ethnic characters.* Many books have characters of color who are subservient, weak, and ignorant. Robin and Mr. Tsow are strong characters in *Angelfish* by Lawrence Yep (2001). Robin, who is half Chinese, discovers that Mr. Tsow's cruel behavior is a consequence of his being a victim of the Chinese Cultural Revolution. Strong Chinese Americans are also in Yep's other books, such as *Child of the Owl* (1977) and *Dragon's Gates* (1993).

3. *Books should describe settings and experiences with which all students can identify and yet should accurately reflect ethnic cultures and lifestyles.* Farah, a Muslim immigrant child, finds how difficult it is to be the new child in school in *One Green Apple* by Eve Bunting (2006). *The Moon Lady* by Amy Tan (1992), *Finding the Greenstone* by Alice Walker (1991), *Drylongso* by Virginia Hamilton (1992), and *The Patchwork Quilt* by Valerie Flournoy (1985) each describe authentic ethnic cultures within the context of universal stories with which all children can identity.

4. *The protagonists in books with ethnic themes should have ethnic characteristics but face conflicts and problems that are universal.* The characters in *Dragon's Gate* by Laurence Yep (1993), *The Best Bad Thing* by Yoshiko Uchida (1985), and *The Road to Memphis* by Mildred D. Taylor (1990) have authentic ethnic characteristics and values yet describe universal human problems.

5. *The illustrations in books should be accurate, ethnically sensitive, and technically well done.* Many books have beautiful photographs or drawings that are inaccurate. Excellent and powerful illustrations or photographs are in these titles: *The Middle Passage: White Ships/Black Cargo* by Tom Feelings (1995); *Remember: The Journey to School Integration* by Toni Morrison (2004); and *Lift Ev'ry Voice and Sing—the African American National Anthem* by James Weldon Johnson (1995), illustrated by Spivey Gilchrist.

6. *Ethnic materials should not contain racist concepts, clichés, phrases, or words.* Many books contain words, phrases, and statements that have negative connotations, even though these books might have many other strengths. Books on Eskimos sometimes present them as carefree, happy people who have no serious human problems.

Some books on Indians either state or imply that all Indians lived in tipis, were hostile to European settlers, and were savages. Words such as *savage, squaw, hostile, primitive,* and *uncivilized* can alert you to a possibly insensitive book or resource, although their use in a book does not necessarily mean that it is insensitive. An author might use these words for the sake of historical accuracy, to depict the language of bigots, or other justifiable reasons. The teacher or librarian must judge the use of words and phrases within the total context of the book or resource. Nevertheless, you should watch for these kinds of words when evaluating instructional materials. You should also be sensitive to stereotypes of ethnic groups that are subtle. Subtle ethnic stereotypes are more frequent in books today than are blatant ones.

7. *Factual materials should be historically accurate.* Books that present inaccurate information about ethnic groups confuse students and reinforce stereotypes. They can also be the source of misconceptions and stereotypes. Examples of accurate informational books about ethnic groups are *The Middle Passage: White Ships/Black Cargo* by Tom Feelings (1995); *Stubborn Twig: Three Generations in the Life of a Japanese American Family* by Lauren Kessler (1994); *The Chinese American Family Album* by Dorothy Hoobler and Thomas Hoobler (1994); and *The Voice That Challenged a Nation: Marian Anderson and the Struggle for Equal Rights* by Russell Freedman (2004).

8. *Multiethnic resources and basal textbooks should discuss major events and documents related to ethnic history.* Events such as the removal of Indians to Indian Territory in the 1800s and the large migrations of Puerto Ricans to the U.S. mainland that began in the 1920s should be included in every comprehensive U.S. history textbook. Key legal documents such as the Treaty of Guadalupe Hidalgo (1848) and the Chinese Exclusion Act of 1882 should be included. To be able to determine which key events and documents should be included in basic factual sources, you will need to read at least one general book and a comprehensive chapter on each of the major ethnic groups.

In addition to the guidelines suggested above, you should determine the age level for which a particular book might be appropriate. Both interest and reading level should be considered. Some books are excellent for adult reading but are inappropriate for school use; others are fine for older readers but inappropriate for young children. The type of classroom situation should also be considered when selecting multicultural materials. A particular book might be appropriate for use with some classrooms but not with others. You should bear in mind whether your class is, for example, all African American, all American Indian, all Asian, all White, or ethnically integrated. You should also consider how you will use each resource. Some books are excellent for basic information but will not give students a feeling for the ethnic group. Other books have excellent illustrations but poor and distorted texts. Some excellent books, such as *Angelfish* by Laurence Yep (2001) and *In Nueva York* by Nicholasa Mohr (1977), are not appropriate for all students, all purposes, and in all kinds of settings. You should exercise sound judgment, sensitivity, integrity, and insight when selecting and evaluating multicultural materials for class use. In the final analysis, only you can determine which materials can best help to achieve your teaching goals.

SUMMARY

This chapter has described the steps you need to take to structure a multicultural curriculum focused on decision making. These steps include (1) the identification of key concepts and generalizations, (2) the formulation of intermediate-level generalizations, and (3) the identification of lower-level generalizations related to the ethnic groups selected for study. Once these steps are completed, you can then proceed to structure lessons and gather materials. When formulating lessons, you should make sure that lessons include value inquiry exercises as well as social action and participation activities when these are appropriate. Examples of value inquiry lessons and social participation activities were discussed.

Prior to implementing a multicultural curriculum, you should plan a reading program that includes (1) one or two general books on ethnic groups in the United States and (2) at least one survey book or comprehensive chapter on each of the major ethnic groups. Recommended books in both categories are in the bibliography of this chapter. The selection and evaluation of student materials is a challenging task. Guidelines and resources for completing this task were given.

REFLECTION AND ACTION ACTIVITIES

Respond to the following ethnic literacy test and discuss your responses, giving reasons for them, with your classmates or colleagues. Determine your ethnic literacy score by comparing your responses with the answers given at the end of the test. How might you use this test with your students to stimulate research and discussion? What sources might they use to check their responses? Administer this test, in part or whole, to your class. Adapt it to your students' reading and grade levels. How well did they do on the test? Why?

Ethnic Literacy Test

Directions: Indicate whether each of the following statements is true or false by placing a T or F in front of it.

1. The U.S. Census projects that people of color will make up about 50% of the United States population by 2050.
2. The first Chinese immigrants who came to the United States worked on the railroads.
3. In 2005, the population of African Americans in the United States exceeded the national population in Canada as well as that of Australia.
4. Puerto Ricans on the island of Puerto Rico became U.S. citizens in 1920.
5. In 2000, Mexican Americans made up 59% of the Hispanics in the United States.
6. Between 1820 and 1930, 15 million immigrants came to the United States.
7. White Anglo-Saxon Protestants are the most powerful ethnic group in the United States.

8. Rosh Hashanah, which in Hebrew means "end of year," is a Jewish holiday that comes early in the fall.
9. While most Arabs are Muslims, Arabs make up no more than 20% of the Muslims in the world.
10. The first law to limit immigration to the United States was passed in 1882 to restrict the number of African immigrants.
11. Puerto Ricans in New York City tend to identify strongly with African Americans in that city.
12. In the 2005 American Community Survey of the U.S. Census, about 5.5 million people, or 2% of the population, identified with two or more racial groups.
13. Most African Americans came from the eastern parts of Africa.
14. The internment of the Japanese Americans during World War II was opposed by President Franklin D. Roosevelt.
15. The 2000 U.S. Census indicated that the Hispanic population slightly exceeded the African American population.
16. Between 1990 and 2000, the Chinese population increased more than any other group of Asian Americans.
17. Congress passed a Removal Act that authorized the removal of Indians from the east to west of the Mississippi in 1830.
18. A Japanese settlement was established in California as early as 1869.
19. The United States acquired a large part of Mexico's territory under the terms of the Treaty of Guadalupe Hidalgo in 1848.
20. Agriculture dominates the economy of the island of Puerto Rico.
21. The first Africans to arrive in North America came on a Dutch ship that landed at Jamestown, Virginia, in 1619.
22. Whites made up about 72% of the U.S. population in 2000.
23. *Paper sons* is a custom that is associated with Chinese Americans.
24. There were fewer than two million American Indians, Eskimos, and Aleuts in the United States in 2000.
25. Some of the bloodiest riots involving African Americans and Whites occurred in the early 1900s.
26. Between 1991 and 2004, over 600,000 immigrants came to the United States from Africa.
27. The United States acquired the island of Puerto Rico from Spain in 1898.
28. There are only 438 Japanese surnames.
29. Chinese immigrants to the United States became distinguished for their outstanding work on truck farms.
30. The 2000 U.S. Census indicated that 11.4% of Latinos were Central, South, and Dominican Americans, which was larger than the percentage of Puerto Ricans.
31. A third-generation Japanese American is called a *sansei*.
32. About 56,800 Iraqis immigrated to the United States between 1991 and 2004.
33. About 64% of Native Americans lived outside tribal areas in 2000.
34. Most Chinese immigrants to the United States came from western China.
35. Eleven Italian Americans were lynched in New Orleans in 1892.
36. Nativism directed against southern and eastern European immigrants was intense when the Statue of Liberty was dedicated in 1886.
37. In 2000, there were more than three million Cubans living in the United States.

38. Approximately 255,500 Haitians immigrated to the United States between 1991 and 2004.

Answers to Ethnic Literacy Test

1. T   2. F   3. T   4. F   5. T   6. F   7. T   8. F   9. T   10. F
11. F   12. T   13. F   14. F   15. T   16. F   17. T   18. T   19. T   20. F
21. T   22. T   23. T   24. F   25. T   26. T   27. T   28. F   29. F   30. T
31. T   32. T   33. T   34. F   35. T   36. T   37. T   38. T

REFERENCES

Alba, R., & Nee, V. (2003). *Remaking the American Mainstream: Assimilation and Contemporary Immigration.* Cambridge, MA: Harvard University Press.

Anderson, T. H. (2005). *The Pursuit of Fairness: A History of Affirmative Action.* New York: Oxford University Press.

Banks, J. A. (2006). *Race, Culture, and Education: The Selected Works of James A. Banks.* London and New York.

Bayoumi, M., & Rubin, A. (Eds.). (2000). *The Edward Said Reader.* New York: Vintage Books.

Brodkin, K. (1998). *How Jews Became White Folks and What That Says about Race in America.* New Brunswick, NJ: Rutgers University Press.

Bukowczyk, J. J. (2006). *Polish Americans and Their History: Community, Culture, and Politics.* Pittsburgh: University of Pittsburgh Press.

Bunting, E. (2006). *One Green Apple.* New York: Clarion Books.

Cesari, J. (2004). *When Islam and Democracy Meet: Muslims in Europe and the United States.* New York: Palgrave Macmillan.

Cohen, E. G. (1994). *Designing Groupwork: Strategies for the Heterogeneous Classroom* (2nd ed.). New York: Teachers College Press.

Damon, W. (2002). *Bringing in a New Era of Character Education.* Stanford, CA: Hoover Institution Press.

Davis, D. B. (2006). *Inhuman Bondage: The Rise and Fall of Slavery in the New World.* New York: Oxford University Press.

Feagin, J. R. (2001). *Racist America: Roots, Current Realities, and Future Reparations.* New York: Routledge.

Feelings, T. (1995). *The Middle Passage: White Ships/Black Cargo.* Illustrated by the author. New York: Dial Books.

Flournoy, V. (1985). *The Patchwork Quilt.* Illustrated by J. Pinkney. New York: Dial.

Freedman, R. (2004). *The Voice That Challenged a Nation: Marian Anderson and the Struggle for Equal Rights.* New York: Clarion Books.

Gabelko, N. H., & Michaelis, J. U. (1981). *Reducing Adolescent Prejudice: A Handbook.* New York: Teachers College Press.

Glock, C. Y., Wutnow, R., Piliavin, J. A., & Spencer, M. (1975). *Adolescent Prejudice.* New York: Harper and Row.

Goldstein, E. (2006). *The Price of Whiteness: Jews, Race, and American Identity.* Princeton, NJ: Princeton University Press.

Haddad, Y. Y., & Esposito, J. L. (Eds.). (2000). *Muslims on the Americanization Path.* New York: Oxford University Press.

Hall, E. T. (1977). *Beyond Culture.* Garden City, NY: Doubleday.

Hamilton, V. (1992). *Drylongso.* Illustrated by J. Pinkney. New York: Harcourt.

Hoobler, D., & Hoobler, T. (1994). *The Chinese American Family Album*. New York: Oxford University Press.

Ichioka, Y. (2006). *Before Internment: Essays in Prewar Japanese-American History*. Edited by G. H. Chang & E. Azuma. Stanford, CA: Stanford University Press.

Ignatiev, N. (1995). *How the Irish Became White*. New York: Routledge.

Johnson, J. W. (1995). *Lift Ev'ry Voice and Sing*. Illustrated by J. S. Gilchrist. New York: Scholastic.

Kessler, L. (1994). *Stubborn Twig: Three Generations in the Life of a Japanese American Family*. New York: Dutton.

Kohlberg, L. (1975, October). Moral Education for a Society in Moral Transition. *Educational Leadership, 33,* 46–54.

Lewis, B. A. (1998). *The Kids' Guide to Social Action: How to Solve the Social Problems You Choose—And Turn Creative Thinking into Positive Action* (updated ed.). Minneapolis: Free Spirit.

McCarus, E. (Ed.). (1994). *The Development of Arab-American Identity*. Ann Arbor: University of Michigan Press.

Mohr, N. (1977). *In Neuva York*. New York: Dial.

Morrison, T. (2004). *Remember: The Journey to School Integration*. Boston: Houghton Mifflin.

Muse, D. (Ed.). (1997). *The New Press Guide to Multicultural Resources for Young Readers*. New York: New Press.

Myers, W. D. (2007). *Harlem Summer*. New York: Scholastic.

Newmann, F. N., with Oliver, D. W. (1970). *Clarifying Public Controversy: An Approach to Teaching Social Studies*. Boston: Little, Brown.

Oliver, D., & Shaver, J. P. (1966). *Teaching Public Issues in the High School*. Boston: Houghton Mifflin.

Olson, J. S., & Olson, J. E. (1995). *Cuban Americans*. New York: Twayne.

Orfield, G. (Ed.). (2001). *Diversity Challenged: Evidence on the Impact of Affirmative Action*. Cambridge, MA: Harvard Education Publishing Group.

Perry, B. A. (2007). *The Michigan Affirmative Action Cases*. Lawrence: University Press of Kansas.

Rodriguez, C. (1991). *Puerto Ricans Born in the U.S.A.* (rev. ed.). Boulder, CO: Westview.

Shaftel, F. R., & Shaftel, G. (1982). *Role-Playing in the Curriculum* (2nd ed.). Englewood Cliffs, NJ: Prentice-Hall.

Simon, S. B., Harmin, M., & Raths, L. E. (1991). *Values and Teaching: Working with Values in the Classroom* (rev. ed.). Columbus, OH: Merrill.

Slavin, R. E. (2001). Cooperative Learning and Intergroup Relations. In J. A. Banks & C. A. M. Banks (Eds.), *Handbook of Research on Multicultural Education* (pp. 628–634). San Francisco: Jossey-Bass.

Tan, A. (1992). *The Moon Lady*. Illustrated by G. Schields. New York: Macmillan.

Tatum, B. D. (2007). *Can We Talk about Race? And Other Conversations in an Era of School Resegregation*. Boston: Beacon.

Taylor, M. (1990). *The Road to Memphis*. New York: Puffin (Penguin).

Thernstrom, S., Orlov, A., & Handlin, O. (Eds.). (1980). *Harvard Encyclopedia of American Ethnic Groups*. Cambridge, MA: Harvard University Press.

Totten, H. L., & Brown, R. W. (1994). *Culturally Diverse Library Collections for Children*. New York: Neal-Schuman.

Uchida, Y. (1985). *The Best Bad Thing*. New York: Atheneum.

Vecoli, R. J., Galens, J., Sheets, A. J., & Young, R. V. (Eds.). (1995). *Gale Encyclopedia of Multicultural America* (2nd ed.). Farmington Hills, MI: Gale Group.

Walker, A. (1991). *Finding the Greenstone*. New York: Harcourt.

Weatherford, C. B. (2006). *Moses: When Harriet Tubman Led Her People to Freedom*. Illustrated by K. Nelson. New York: Hyperion.

Yep, L. (1993). *Dragon's Gate*. New York: HarperTrophy.

Yep, L. (1977*). Child of the Owl*. New York: Harper & Row.

Yep, L. (2000a). *The Journal of Wong Ming-Chung: A Chinese Miner.* New York: Scholastic.
Yep, L. (2000b). *The Magic Paintbrush.* Illustrated by S. Wang. New York: HarperCollins.
Yep, L. (2001). *Angelfish.* New York: Putnam.

BIBLIOGRAPHY

Multiethnic References

Daniels, R. (2002). *Coming to America: A History of Immigration and Ethnicity in American Life* (2nd ed.). New York: HarperCollins.
Roediger, D. R. (2005). *Working toward Whiteness: How America's Immigrants Became White.* New York: Basic Books.
Waters, M. C., & Ueda, R. (Eds.). (2007). *The New Americans: A Guide to Immigration since 1965.* Cambridge, MA: Harvard University Press.
Zolberg, A. R. (2006). *A Nation by Design: Immigration Policy in the Fashioning of America.* Cambridge, MA: Harvard University Press.

African Americans

Franklin, J. H., & Moss, A. A., Jr. (2000). *From Slavery to Freedom: A History of Black Americans* (8th ed.). New York: Knopf.
Hine, D. C., Hine, W. C., & Harrold, S. (2006). *The African American Odyssey* (3rd ed., combined volume). Upper Saddle River, NJ: Prentice-Hall.
Painter, N. I. (2006). *Creating Black Americans: African-American History and Its Meanings, 1619 to the Present.* New York: Oxford University Press.

American Indians

Deloria, P. J. (2004). *Indians in Unexpected Places.* Lawrence: University Press of Kansas.
Garroutte, E. M. (2003). *Real Indians: Identity and the Survival of Native America.* Berkeley, CA: University of California Press.
LaDuke, W. (2005). *Recovering the Sacred: The Power of Naming and Claiming.* Cambridge, MA: South End Press.
Tate, M. L. (2006). *Indians and Emigrants: Encounters on the Overland Trails.* Norman: University of Oklahoma Press.

Arab Americans

Haddad, Y. Y. (2004). *Not Quite American? The Shaping of Arab and Muslim Identity in the United States.* Waco, TX: Baylor University Press.
Naff, A. (1987). *Becoming American: The Early Arab Immigrant Experience.* Carbondale: Southern Illinois University Press.
Suleiman, M. (Ed.). (1999). *Arabs in America: Building a New Future.* Philadelphia: Temple University Press.

Asian Americans

Ancheta, A. N. (2006). *Race, Rights, and the Asian American Experience.* New Brunswick, NJ: Rutgers University Press.
Danico, M. Y., & Ng, F. (2004). *Asian American Issues.* Westport, CT: Greenwood Press.
Lien, P., Conway, M., & Wong, J. (2004). *The Politics of Asian Americans: Diversity and Community.* New York: Routledge.
Okihiro, G. Y. (2001). *The Columbia Guide to Asian American History.* New York: Columbia University Press.
Takaki, R. (1998). *Strangers from a Different Shore: A History of Asian Americans* (rev. ed.). Boston: Little, Brown.

Hispanic Americans

Acuña, R. F. (2007). *Occupied America: A History of* Chicanos (6th ed.). New York: Pearson/ Longman.

Garcia, J. E., & De Geiff, P. (2000). *Hispanics/Latinos in the United States: Ethnicity, Race, and Rights.* New York: Routledge.

González, A. (2002). *Mexican Americans and the U.S. Economy: Quest for Buenos Dias.* Tucson: University of Arizona Press.

Olson, J. S., & Olson, J. E. (1995). *Cuban Americans.* New York: Twayne.

Portes, A., & Rumbaut, R. G. (2001). *Legacies: The Story of the Immigrant Second Generation.* Berkeley: University of California Press.

Suárez-Orozco, M., & Páez, M. M. (Eds.). (2002). *Latinos: Remaking America.* Berkeley: University of California Press.

European Americans

Amore, B. (2006). *An Italian American Odyssey: Lifeline-Filo della Vita: Through Ellis Island and Beyond.* Translated by F. Bagnolini. New York: Center for Migration Studies.

Barton, H. A. (2007). *The Old Country and the New: Essays on Swedes in America.* Carbondale: Southern Illinois University Press.

Bukowczyk, J. J. (2006). *Polish Americans and Their History: Community, Culture, and Politics.* Pittsburgh: University of Pittsburgh Press.

Guglielmo, J., & Salerno, S. (2003). *Are Italians White? How Race Is Made in America.* New York: Routledge.

Houghton, G. (2004). *Ellis Island: A Primary Source History of an Immigrant's Arrival in America.* New York: Rosen.

Jewish Americans

Feinstein, E., (Ed.). (2007). *Jews and Judaism in the 21st Century: Human Responsibility, the Presence of God, and the Future of the Covenant.* Woodstock, VT: Jewish Lights Publishing.

Goldstein, E. (2006). *The Price of Whiteness—Jews, Race, and American Identity.* Princeton, NJ: Princeton University Press.

Howe, I. (2005). *World of Our Fathers: The Journey of the East European Jews to America and the Life They Found and Made.* New York: New York University Press.

THE FIRST AMERICANS AND AFRICAN AMERICANS

Concepts and Strategies

Part II consists of content, concepts, teaching strategies, and materials for teaching about American Indians, Native Hawai'ians, and African Americans. Although different in many ways, these groups share some important experiences. American Indians and Native Hawai'ians are native to the land that is now the United States. African Americans were one of the first groups to come to America from a distant land. They were the only group to come in chains. Each of these groups has deep roots in America.

According to 2005 U.S. Census reports, American Indians and Native Hawai'ians are two of the nation's smallest ethnic groups: 2,357,544 (which includes Native Alaskans) and 397,030, respectively. African Americans have been in the past the nation's largest ethnic minority group, with 34,962,569, or about 12.1% of the nation's population. Collectively, the population of the various Hispanic ethnic groups, at 41,870,703, exceeded the population of African Americans in 2005.

Despite the tremendous differences in the sizes of the populations of African Americans, Indians, and Native Hawai'ians, the experiences of these groups have often been characterized by common concepts and themes, such as racism, discrimination, protest, and resistance. A study of these three ethnic groups will help students better understand the long journey toward freedom in the United States and might also help them renew their commitment to justice and equality.

CHAPTER FIVE

AMERICAN INDIANS
Concepts, Strategies, and Materials

The earth was created by the assistance of the sun, and it should be left as it was. The earth and myself are of one mind.

—Chief Joseph, Nez Perce

Popular images about American Indians and Eskimos are widespread and often stereotypic, contributing to students' misunderstandings of Indian and Eskimo cultures. Older western movies shown on television contribute greatly to the stereotypic image of American Indians within U.S. society. Statements made in schools by educators, such as "Sit like an Indian," also contribute to the perpetuation of Indian stereotypes. Even though popular books today do not include the blatant stereotypes of the "hostile" Indian often found in books in the past, they usually present history from a Western-centric point of view and perspective. Popular books often call the Americas *the New World,* implying (if not stating) that Columbus "discovered" America, and describe the migration of European Americans from the eastern to the western part of the United States as "The Westward Movement."

These approaches to the study of American history and culture are Eurocentric and mainstream-centric because they imply that American civilization did not exist until the Europeans first arrived in the late fifteenth century. They consequently deny the existence of the Native American cultures and civilizations that had existed in the Americas for centuries before the Europeans came.

Archaeologists estimate that human beings have lived in the Americas for at least 40,000 years. These peoples had established complex civilizations before the Europeans arrived in the fifteenth century. These cultures included elaborate irrigation works and massive artificial mounds crowned with temples. The Olmec in Mexico, the Chavin in Peru, and the civilizations of the Teotihuacan, the Maya, the Toltecs, and

The revision of this chapter was coauthored by **John P. Hopkins,** director, Office of Intercultural Initiatives, Saint Martin's University, Lacy, WA, and doctoral student, University of Washington, Seattle. The annotated bibliographies were prepared by **Lyn Miller-Lachmann,** editor, *MultiCultural Review.*

the Aztecs were important American civilizations before the Europeans arrived in the Americas (*Hammond Past Worlds,* 1988).

A major goal of American Indian curriculum content should be to help students to view the development of the Americas—and of U.S. society in particular—from the point of view of the Native Americans. For example, the movement of the European Americans from the eastern to the western part of the United States was not, from the Indian point of view, a westward movement. The Lakota Sioux did not consider their homeland the West but the center of the universe. Students should be helped to understand key events, concepts, and issues from different ethnic and cultural perspectives. "The Westward Movement" had very different meanings for the migrating European Americans and for the Indians whose homelands were being invaded. To Indian people, it could more appropriately be called "An Age of Doom" or "The Great Invasion" rather than "The Westward Movement." By helping students to view concepts, events, and issues from diverse cultural and ethnic perspectives, we can help them become critical thinkers and more compassionate citizens of the nation-state. Content about American Indians can contribute greatly to these important and generic educational goals.

EARLY LIFE IN THE AMERICAS

When the European explorers arrived in the Western Hemisphere in 1492, it was populated by many different cultures and groups that became collectively known as "Indians" to Europeans. Columbus thought that he had reached India when he landed in San Salvador in 1492. This misnaming of the aboriginal peoples of the Americas by the Europeans foreshadowed the misunderstandings, distrust, and hostility that later developed between the two groups.

The early history of American Indians is still somewhat of a mystery to scientists. Archaeologists are trying to unravel their early history by digging up fossils that give clues to early human life in the Americas. Occasionally, landmark archaeological discoveries are made, enabling scientists to learn more about early people in the Western Hemisphere. In 1927, near Folsom, New Mexico, scientists found embedded between the ribs of a Pleistocene bison a stone spear point that early Americans used for hunting. This finding proved that humans were in the Americas when Ice Age animals roamed freely on this continent. Similar points were found at an archaeological dig near Clovis, New Mexico, in 1932. Scientists were able to date the points to 9200 B.C. by using the carbon-14 method (Ceram, 1971). An excavation in Monte Verde in southern Chile provided strong evidence that humans settled in the Americas approximately 1,000 years prior to the date determined in the Clovis excavation (Thomas, 2000). These two excavations have led to debate among anthropologists about when early humans first appeared on the American continent. Such scientific debate often occurs when new findings or theories challenge existing ones.

AMERICAN INDIANS: HISTORICAL PERSPECTIVE

Important Dates	Events
1513	Juan Ponce de León landed on the Florida peninsula while en route from Puerto Rico. The relationship between Europeans and North American Indians began.
1565	The Spaniards established the St. Augustine colony in Florida, the first settlement organized by Europeans in present-day United States.
1637	Connecticut colonists killed more than 500 Indians when the Pequot tribe tried to stop the colonists from invading their territory. This event is known as the Pequot War.
1675–1676	King Philip, a Wampanoag chief, led a coalition of Indian troops that nearly defeated the English colonists. However, his forces were eventually beaten and his body dismembered by the colonists.
1680	The Pueblos rebelled against the Spaniards and drove them from Pueblo territory. Many Spaniards were killed during the uprising.
1754–1763	The French and Indian War occurred. It was one of a series of wars in which the French and the British struggled for control of the eastern part of North America. Each nation vied for Indian support.
1784	A group of Indians suffered a crushing defeat at Fallen Timbers in Ohio on August 20. In 1795, they were forced to sign a treaty that ceded large segments of their lands in the Northwest Territory to Whites.
1812	The War of 1812, a war between the United States and Britain, caused deep factions among the Indian tribes because of their different allegiances. The Indian allies of the British were severely punished by the United States when the war ended.
1824	The Bureau of Indian Affairs was established in the War Department.
1830	Congress passed a Removal Act that authorized the removal of Indians from east to west of the Mississippi and stated conditions under which removal could be legally undertaken.
1831	The Supreme Court recognized Indian tribes as "domestic dependent nations" within the United States. In an 1832 decision, the Court declared that such nations had a right to self-government.
1838–1839	The Cherokee were forcefully removed from Georgia to Indian Territory in present-day Oklahoma. Their poignant journey westward is recalled as the "Trail of Tears."
1864	The Colorado militia killed nearly 300 Cheyenne in a surprise attack at Sand Creek, after the Cheyenne leaders had negotiated an armistice. This incident is known as the Sand Creek Massacre.
1871	A congressional act prohibited the making of further treaties with Indian tribes.

Important Dates	Events
1876	Sioux tribes, under the leadership of Sitting Bull, wiped out Custer's Seventh Cavalry at Little Big Horn. This was one of the last victories for Indian tribes.
1881	Helen Hunt Jackson's *A Century of Dishonor* was published. It was the first influential book to dramatize the plight of Indian peoples in the United States.
1886	The brave Apache warrior Geronimo surrendered to U.S. forces in September. His surrender marked the defeat of the southwest tribes.
1887	Congress passed the Dawes Severalty Act, which was designed partially to terminate the Indians' special relationship with the U.S. government. It proved to be disastrous for Indians.
1890	Three hundred Sioux were killed at Wounded Knee Creek in South Dakota.
1924	The Snyder Act made American Indians citizens of the United States.
1928	The Meriam Survey recommended major changes in federal policy related to Indian affairs. Many of its recommendations were implemented in subsequent years.
1934	The Wheeler-Howard Act made it possible for Indians to reestablish aspects of their traditional cultures, including tribal lands and governments.
1944	The National Congress of American Indians was organized by Indians.
1946	The Indian Claims Commission was established to hear cases related to possible compensations due Indians for loss of land and property.
1948	Indians were granted the right to vote in New Mexico and Arizona.
1954	Congressional acts terminated the relationship between the federal government and several Indian tribes, including the Klamath tribe in Oregon, the Menominee of Wisconsin, and the California Indians.
1969	*Custer Died for Your Sins: An Indian Manifesto* by Vine DeLoria, Jr., was published. This book represented a significant point in the Indian civil rights movement. N. Scott Momaday won the Pulitzer Prize for *House Made of Dawn.*
1970	President Richard M. Nixon made a statement advocating Indian self-determination.
1972	Congress restored the Menominee tribe of Wisconsin to federal trust status.
1973	Members of the American Indian movement and other Indians occupied Wounded Knee, South Dakota, to dramatize the Indians' condition in the United States.
1975	The Indian Self-Determination Act recognized the autonomy of Indian tribes and their special relationship with the federal government.
1978	The Indian Freedom of Religion Act was passed. This act granted Indians the right to practice their religious beliefs.

Important Dates	Events
1979	The Supreme Court upheld the fishing rights claims of the Indian tribes of Washington state.
1980	The Passamaquoddy and Penobscot tribes of Maine received a settlement of their land claims after a long and difficult legal battle.
1989	Native American tribal groups were successful in convincing the Smithsonian Institution to develop a policy that will allow it to return the remains of their ancestors to them. Native American tribes felt that the remains of their ancestors were being desecrated by the Smithsonian as well as by other museums.
1990	The Native American Graves Protection and Repatriation Act was enacted. It requires federal agencies to return human remains and other objects to tribes that request them.
1991	Native Americans were honored by the renaming of the Custer Battlefield to the Little Bighorn National Monument.
2000	The U.S. Census revealed that the American Indian and Alaska Native population was 2,475,956, or 0.9% of the U.S. population.
2002	There were thirty-two tribally controlled colleges and universities serving an estimated 25,000 students in the United States.
2004	The National Museum of the American Indian opened to the public on the National Mall of Washington, D.C. An estimated 25,000 representatives from Native America were present, from Canada to South America.
2006	The Native American Language Preservation Act was enacted to help preserve and foster language fluency among Native American students.

The Origins of American Indians

We do not know exactly when people first came to the Americas. Archaeologists have ruled out the possibility that human beings evolved in the Western Hemisphere, because no fossils of pre–Homo sapiens have been found on the American continent (Josephy, 1991). No remains of the closest cousins of human beings, the great apes, have been found in the Americas either. Archaeologists believe that the ancestors of American Indians originally came from Asia over the Bering Strait, which today is the body of water separating Siberia and Alaska. The Bering Strait theory holds that at various times in prehistory, this water receded and a landmass, called Beringia, bridged present-day Siberia and Alaska. The early ancestors of the Native Americans, according to this theory, walked across this stretch of land while hunting animals and plants to eat.

Many Indian groups believe that they were created by the Great Spirit in the Americas. The Lakota scholar Vine Deloria, Jr. (1995) was critical of the Bering Strait theory, arguing that it contradicts the oral traditions of many American Indians and is not an adequate scientific explanation of their origins. Deloria cited the scant physical evidence supporting the theory and pointed to the extreme conditions that would have been present during the period in which Paleo-Indians would have crossed the Bering Strait, such as rugged terrain, impassable mountains, and frozen tundra.

Today some scientists are rethinking aspects of the Bering Strait theory. Some now think that humans arrived in the Americas 15,000, 20,000, or even 30,000 years ago (Parfit & Garrett, 2000). Other scientists suggest that ancestors of the Indians came to America by boat, instead of by walking across Beringia. Research from various linguists and molecular biologists supports the dating of human origins in the Americas between 30,000 and 40,000 years ago. This would place migration much earlier than indicated by the Bering Strait theory (Thomas, 2000).

The Indian Population before the Europeans Came

There is as much controversy about the size of the Indian population when the Europeans arrived in the Americas in the fifteenth century as there is about when the Indians crossed Beringia to reach the Americas. The population estimates vary greatly. In 1924, Rivet (cited in Stuart, 1987) estimated the Western Hemisphere population to have been 40 to 50 million and the North American population to have been 2 to 3.5 million when the Europeans arrived in 1492. In 1928, Mooney (cited in Stuart, 1987) estimated the Indian North American pre-Columbian population to be about 1.2 million. In 1939, Kroeber estimated the Western Hemisphere population to be 8.4 million and the North American continent population to be 0.9 million (Stuart, 1987).

In the 1960s and 1970s, researchers such as Dobyns (1976) and Denevan (1976) seriously challenged the estimates by Mooney (1928) and Kroeber (1934) and made much higher estimates. Dobyns believes that the Americas were heavily populated when the Europeans arrived. In 1966, Dobyns estimated that the Western Hemisphere population at contact was 90 million and that the North American population was 9.8 million (Stuart, 1987). Dobyns and Denevan estimate that the population north of the Rio Grande was at least 10 million when the Europeans first came to the Americas.

The Diversity of Indian Cultures

Although the word *Indian* often connotes a stereotypic image in the popular mind, Indian peoples are quite diverse, both physically and culturally. Their skin color, height, hair texture, and facial features vary greatly, as do their cultures and behaviors.

It is not possible to determine exactly how many languages were spoken in the Americas before the Europeans came or to determine how many people spoke each language. Two frequently accepted estimates of the number of languages spoken are 1,800 and more than 2,000 (Harris & Levey, 1975). Anthropologists have tried, with great difficulty, to categorize Indian languages into six major language families.

How Indians survived also varied widely. Some groups, like the tribes of the subarctic, did not practice agriculture but obtained food by fishing and hunting. Other communities, such as the complex cultures of the southwest Indians, survived by farming.

Political institutions in Indian cultures were also quite diverse. Highly sophisticated confederations were common among the northeast tribes, such as the Creek Confederacy and the League of the Iroquois. These confederations contrasted strikingly with political life within the California tribes. These tribes usually had no formal political institutions but were organized into small family units headed by men who had group responsibilities but little authority over others. Warring and raiding were important aspects of the Apache culture. However, the Hopi, who called themselves "the peaceful ones," were one of the most tranquil peoples on earth. Social class had little meaning among the southwest tribes, but it was extremely important in the northwest Pacific Coast cultures.

Food, hunting methods, house types, clothing, tools, and religious ceremonies also varied greatly among and within various American Indian cultural groups (Hunt, 1999). An example of ceremonial differences would be how the potlatch of the northwest coastal tribes differed from the sun dance of the Plains tribes. Potlatches were a time for clans to distribute wealth to poorer clans; sun dances were re-creation ceremonies, or world renewal rites (Johnson, 2000). Many non-Natives believe that American Indians represent one unified cultural group. However, differences in language, geography, and culture preclude any one representation of Indian cultures.

Similarities in Indian Cultures

Although American Indian cultures are highly diverse, they are similar in many ways. Some similar characteristics, especially those related to core values, make up "Indianness," or what is uniquely "Indian." Indian cultures were and are based on a deep spirituality that greatly influences all aspects of life. Because Indians see people existing within a spiritual world that includes all other living things, they see themselves living in harmony with all beings on earth. They view the universe as a harmonious whole, with every object and being having a sacred life. To separate human beings from nature is antithetical to the Great Spirit, for to the Great Spirit, all is life.

Tewa scholar Gregory Cajete (2000) offers a systematic presentation of a distinctively indigenous worldview. Based on a wide variety of Native traditions, Native American philosophy is an integration of the rational, spiritual, and emotional elements of human experience. This philosophy is centered on the human interaction with the world, connecting individuals and communities directly to the natural landscape, and mediated by cultural practices that teach the people their proper relationship to the earth. The fundamental belief within an indigenous worldview is that everything in life is connected and animated and that our role as human beings is to maintain our connection and relationship to the world in a harmonious manner.

The tribes of the northwest Pacific Coast believed in many spirits. They sought the protection of these spirits through various ceremonies and rituals. American Indians often called on the help of the spirits in their daily lives. Shamans, who played a key role in many Indian religions, helped individuals gain contact with the spiritual world. The southwest tribes had a rich and elaborate year-round sequence of ceremonials, including songs, dances, and poetry. The Hopi performed dances to bring rain. The Apaches engaged in special dances and ceremonies to gain the support of the spirits before undertaking raids or going into war. Many Indian groups often sought contact with the spirits by going on a vision quest. Spiritual beliefs and ceremonies permeate every aspect of Indian life (Stripes, 2001).

American Indians had a deep respect and reverence for the earth and for all other living things. They believed that people must not harm the earth and should regard it as sacred. Osage scholar George Tinker (cited in Tinker et al., 2003) remarks that early Native Americans did not worship the earth as a goddess, as many European Americans believed, but rather recognized the earth as a living being and relative, usually referring to it as "mother" or "grandmother." The earth was considered a living person, deserving of respect and gratitude for the life it gives. Many Indian religious leaders were often shocked by the ways in which the White people's agriculture defiled the Mother Earth. Forbes (1973) has summarized these beliefs:

> The Earth our Mother is holy and should be treated as such . . . ALL forms of life are our brothers and sisters and have to be respected. Life itself is a holy, sacred experience . . . we must live our lives as a religion, that is, with constant concern for spiritual relationships and values . . . we must live lives that bring forth both physical and spiritual "beauty." All life has the potentiality of bringing forth Beauty and Harmony, but [humans] in particular [have] also the ability to bring forth ugliness and disharmony. (pp. 208–209)

In their literature and speeches, American Indians often bemoaned how the Whites destroyed and defiled the earth, as in this passage by a Winto elder (cited in McLuhan, 1971):

> The White people plow up the ground, pull down the trees, kill everything. The tree says, "Don't. I am sore. Don't hurt me." But they chop it down and cut it up. The spirit of the land hates them. They blast our trees and stir it up to its depths. How can the spirit of the earth like the White man? Everywhere the White man has touched it, it is sore. (p. 15)

The Indians' conception of the earth and their relationship to the land differed greatly from that of the Europeans and was a source of conflict among the cultures. The Indians believed that people could use the earth as long as they treated it with respect, but they could not sell it any more than they could sell the air or the sea. Lakota philosopher Robert Bunge (1994) describes how Western and Native American conceptions of the land were significantly different. Whereas Westerners viewed the land as dead matter, a commodity to be sold, parceled, and owned, Native Americans viewed land as sentient, imbued with intelligence and personality. Owning, selling, or parceling land would be similar to owning, selling, or parceling a person. When, in exchange for gifts, American Indians gave Europeans permission to use their lands, many did not realize that from a European viewpoint they were also giving up their own rights to use the lands. The Europeans regarded the earth as a commodity that could be broken into parts and owned by individuals. To the American Indian, the earth was sacred and consequently could never be owned by human beings.

Indian people also had a deep respect for the rights and dignity of the individual. Decisions in Indian councils and confederacies were usually based on group consensus. Deliberations were often long and decisions of governing bodies slow because consensus had to be attained. The Creek Confederacy reached all of its decisions by consensus. However, each nation within the confederacy maintained its autonomy and was not bound to a decision with which it did not agree. The Europeans learned a great deal from the American Indians about representative government and the rights and dignity of the individual, which they incorporated into the major constitutional documents on which U.S. democracy is based.

Leaders of groups within the subarctic tribes had little authority over their followers. This was characteristic of Indian societies. Leaders were rarely deified as they were in Europe, the Middle East, and Asia. There were few hierarchical political organizations in the Americas. Leaders often had to earn the respect of others by becoming outstanding warriors, acquiring a special ability to communicate with the spirits, or learning to perform some other service the community needed and valued. Communities were usually democratic, with no kings or other kinds of rulers. However, there were important exceptions to these generalizations. The Inca Empire of Peru was one of the most totalitarian states that ever existed in human history.

Because of their feudalistic background, the Europeans looked for kings among the Indians and assumed that Indian chiefs had absolute authority over their tribes. The European settlers created tremendous problems by imposing their conceptions of the nation-state on Indian societies. They made treaties with chiefs and assumed that they were binding on their tribes. They did not understand that the chief's authority was usually limited by the tribal council. He had little power that the tribe did not grant him. This cultural difference between the Europeans and Indian groups haunted their relationships for centuries.

Early Contact with Europeans

The Indians' earliest contacts with the Europeans were usually friendly and generally involved trade. The French, English, and Dutch exchanged European goods and tools for furs. This exchange of goods was initially beneficial for both groups. The furs greatly increased the Europeans' wealth; the European goods and tools made life easier for the Indians. Eventually, the Indians began to consider the European goods as necessities rather than luxuries. What had begun as a mutually beneficial trade relationship was destined to cause disaster for the Indians.

Early contact also brought a host of epidemic diseases that would reshape the lives of Indians forever. According to historians, epidemics of smallpox, influenza, and measles ravaged entire villages within the first decades of encountering the Spanish. Approximately 75% of the indigenous populations in central Mexico and several islands in the Caribbean were decimated by diseases brought to the Americas by the Europeans (Nichols, 2003).

Indians acquired rum, guns, gunpowder, horses, and other goods from the Europeans. Tribes that wanted European goods but had depleted the supply of fur-producing animals on their lands began to invade the territories of other tribes to obtain furs for trade. These invasions led to skirmishes and eventually to wars. European goods made intertribal warring more likely and possible. It was easy for the tribes that had European guns and gunpowder to defeat tribes lacking these supplies. Thus, the Europeans, through trade and other schemes (discussed later), initiated divide-and-conquer tactics among the Indian tribes in New England. Indian wars, raids, and attacks were greatly intensified by the presence of the Europeans.

The League of the Iroquois began an aggressive campaign to gain a monopoly of the European trade and to dominate competing tribes. The league had eliminated hundreds of Hurons and forced those remaining into captivity in 1649. The Iroquois were feared by tribes throughout New England. They eventually dominated the Delawares, the Nanticokes, and other groups of Algonkian-speaking tribes by 1680. The league became so powerful that the British regarded it as a power to be reckoned with.

Indian and European Wars

From about 1540 to the 1790s, no one power was dominant in the Indian territory that had been invaded by the Europeans in the Northeast. The Swedes and the Dutch had been driven from the area before 1700, and the French, Spanish, and English struggled for control of the region. The Indians also tried to maintain their power. The power struggle became more intricate and intense when the British colonies entered the contest. Until the American Revolution, the Indians were unable to tell which of the European nations, if any, would become the dominant power. The Indians probably thought that a balance of power, in which they would be a major participant, would eventually be established in the region.

The European wars and struggles for power deeply influenced Indian policy and political institutions. In each war with European people, the Indians had to decide which group, if any, they would support. Each of the powers competed for Indian alliance and support. Although the Indians often tried to maintain a policy of neutrality, this became increasingly difficult as the European nations aggressively vied for Indian support. The Creeks and the Cherokees fought on the side of the French, against the British, in the French and Indian War. The French were defeated, and their Indian allies were severely punished by the British for helping the enemy. The Indians were also weakened by their severe losses during the war.

The European wars caused deep factionalism within the Indian tribes and confederations. In the War of 1812, the various tribes became deeply divided over whether they should support the United States or the British. The treaties ending the American Revolution and the War of 1812 stunned and angered Britain's Indian allies. Neither treaty acknowledged the decisive roles the Indians had played in these wars. After the American Revolution, the British granted the colonists lands that were occupied by their Indian allies. The British had pitted Indian tribes against each other and then ignored these allies' interests when the fighting stopped. In time, the Indians began to see the futility of becoming involved in the European wars and became increasingly committed to a policy of neutrality. Alexander McGillivray, the Creek diplomat, used the Europeans' tactics and, by astutely negotiating, pitted the colonists against the Spaniards.

The Decline of the League of the Iroquois

The League of the Iroquois was seriously affected by the European wars and was eventually destroyed by the factionalism caused by the wars. The league, the French, and the British were the three major powers in the Northeast in the first decades of the 1700s. Factionalism developed within the league over the positions it should take in the European wars. One of the nations, the Senecas, fought on the side of the French in the French and Indian War. The other nations supported the British. Even greater disunity developed within the league when the American Revolution began. Some of the nations supported the British; others were sympathetic to the colonists. Internal splits developed within several of the nations over this issue. The colonists looted and burned Iroquois villages after the Revolution and flaunted their newly gained power.

The fate of the Iroquois was later experienced by other tribes. The Iroquois had warred against other Indian tribes in order to obtain furs to trade and had fought as allies in the European wars. Their confederation was later destroyed because of splits caused by the European wars. The Indian nations did not realize that they had a common fate in the Northeast, and that the future of one Indian nation was tied to the future of all Indian tribes. Culturally and politically, the Indians were separate and distinct groups. However, the Whites saw them as a group that had to be pushed west of the Mississippi and ultimately conquered or destroyed.

Treaties and Indian Removal

The relationship between Indians and European settlers had developed into a pattern by the time of the American Revolution. The initial contact usually involved trade, whereby Indians acquired tools and firearms and the Europeans obtained furs. These initial events usually pitted Indian tribes against each other as they competed for the European trade and for the lands containing fur-producing animals. When the furs had been depleted, the Europeans began an aggressive drive to obtain the lands the Indians occupied. The Indians often formed confederations and alliances to push back the European invaders or extended the functions of existing confederations. Ironically, however, the Indians' involvement in the White people's wars usually disrupted these confederations. Indians adamantly resisted the attempts by the Whites to displace them. They fought defensive wars, such as the King Philip's War in 1675 and the Black Hawk War in 1832. Indian uprisings also occurred, such as the Sioux uprising in 1862 and the Little Crow uprising in 1863.

Despite the Indians' aggressive and bold resistance, the Europeans were destined to win the struggle. The Whites retaliated with shocking massacres, such as at Sand Creek in 1864, with biological warfare, and with massive wars in which men, women, and children were killed and often dismembered and scalped. After Indian resistance was crushed, the Whites legitimized the taking of Indian lands by convincing the Indian leaders to sign treaties. Indian chiefs were frequently offered gifts or other bribes to sign treaties. Once an Indian group had signed a treaty, the Whites schemed to remove them from their land. Often the Indians were forced west of the Mississippi into Indian Territory (present-day Oklahoma), land the Whites considered uninhabitable. If only a few Indians remained after the conquest, they were often absorbed by local tribes or forced onto reservations. Between 1778 and 1868, 373 treaties were signed between the United States government and American Indian nations. Congress officially ended treaty making in 1871, stipulating that the legality of prior treaties would always be upheld (Rosier, 2003).

This cycle was repeated many times as White settlers pushed westward. When Whites went farther west, Indians were forced to sign new treaties granting Whites the lands that earlier treaties had assured them. Some Indian groups, like the Winnebagos, were forced to move as many as six times during a period of thirty years. Not long after the Lakota signed the Fort Laramie treaty of 1868—which secured their presence in the Black Hills, the center of Lakota cultural and religious life—gold was discovered in the Black Hills. When the Lakota retaliated against White encroachment, the United States Army was dispatched to defend the settlers' interests, an action that led directly to the Battle of Little Bighorn in 1876, one of the greatest victories for Native peoples (Nichols, 2003). No aspects of U.S. history are more poignant than the accounts of the making and breaking of Indian treaties by Whites and the forced removal of Indians across the United States. This prediction by a Cherokee newspaper describing how Whites would obtain Indian land in Texas highlights how treaties were often made (cited in Hagan, 1961):

> A Commissioner will be sent down to negotiate, with a pocket full of money and his mouth full of lies. Some chiefs he will bribe, some he will flatter, and some he will make drunk: and the result will be something that will be called a treaty. (p. 99)

THE WESTWARD JOURNEYS

Some Indian tribes, realizing the futility of resistance, moved westward without force. Others bitterly resisted removal and were forcibly removed by military troops. Though all suffered greatly, generally, the tribes that had to be removed at gunpoint suffered the most. The Winnebagos, who offered little resistance, were shifted from place to place between 1829 and 1866. About half of them perished during their perpetual sojourn. The Seminoles, who signed a removal treaty in 1832, violently resisted removal. Hostilities began in 1835 and continued for seven years. The United States lost nearly 1,500 men and spent more than $50 million in its attempts to crush the Seminoles' resistance. Most of the Seminoles were eventually forced to move to Indian Territory. However, several hundred remained in the Florida Everglades, where their descendants live today.

The Georgians began an aggressive drive to remove the Cherokees from their homeland when gold was discovered on Cherokee land in 1829. The Cherokees initiated a court battle against removal. In 1832, the Supreme Court ruled that the Cherokees had a right to remain on their land. However, this ruling by the high court did not halt the determined efforts of the Georgians and President Andrew Jackson to remove the Cherokees. Harassed and pressured, part of the tribe finally signed a removal treaty in 1835. Even though only a minority of the tribe's leaders signed the treaty, the Cherokees were forced to move to Indian Territory. During the long march from Georgia to Oklahoma in 1838 and 1839, almost one-fourth of the Cherokees died from starvation, disease, and the perils of the journey. Their long westward journey is recalled as the "Trail of Tears." The Creeks were forced to sign a treaty in 1832, which gave the Whites rights to their lands east of the Mississippi. Nearly half of the Creeks perished during the migration to and during their early years in the West.

Like the White people's wars, removal caused deep factions within the various Indian tribes and nations. Some leaders felt that it was in their best interests to cooperate with the White authorities; others believed that removal should be resisted until the bitter end. These splits within the tribes intensified when the Indians arrived in the West and hastened the disintegration of their institutions that had begun before removal.

In retrospect, it is clear that Indian people either had to relocate or be exterminated. The federal government legitimized Indian removal with the Removal Act of 1830. This act legalized Indian removal and specified the conditions under which Indians could be removed legally. The act provided funds for removal and authorized an exchange of lands for displaced Indians. The act stipulated that the tribe's consent must be obtained, but this made little difference in the actual removal of Indians. Local officials continued to use any possible tactics to convince Indians to sign treaties and to move westward.

Indians in the West

Much tension developed in the western territories when the eastern tribes reached their destinations. Many of the eastern tribes were forced to settle in territories occupied by the Plains Indians. The Plains tribes had acquired the White people's guns and horses and were fierce fighters when the eastern tribes began to settle in their territories. When competition for the buffalo became acute, they fought and raided the eastern tribes. The U.S. government failed to provide the eastern tribes military protection as it had promised when they were forced to settle in the West.

The conquest and displacement of tribes that took place in the East later occurred west of the Mississippi. However, the conquest of the Plains tribes and other western tribes took place in a shorter period of time. The powerful Sioux nations of the northern plains were defeated and forced onto reservations within twenty-seven years. The Comanche of the southern plains had been conquered by the White settlers by 1873. Spicer (1969) comments, "The other plains tribes presented about the same picture as the Comanche or the Sioux: a twenty- or twenty-five-year period of intensive warfare both with other tribes and the Americans, a period of unsettled and sometimes desperate conditions as they were forced on reservations and finally unhappy acceptance of the new way" (p. 87).

When the United States acquired most of the territory that now comprises the Southwest from Mexico in 1848 (see Chapter 10 on Mexican Americans), the southwestern tribes quickly learned that their new conquerors were enemies, not friends. The Spaniards had never completely conquered the southwestern tribes; these tribes had retained a great deal of their culture and many of their institutions. Indians such as the Pueblos and the Pimas had hoped that the United States would protect them from the Navajos and the Apaches. However, the government's goals were to conquer all of the tribes and to place them on reservations. The California gold rush of 1849 hastened the defeat of the western tribes. A congressional act in 1871 that prohibited further treaties indicated that Indian resistance had been broken and that the Indians were now considered a conquered and defeated people. The act declared that in the future, "no Indian nation or tribe within the United States shall be acknowledged or recognized as an independent nation, tribe, or power" (cited in Josephy, 1991, pp. 339–340). This act represented a major change in federal policy in Indian affairs and reversed the policy declared by the Supreme Court in 1831. The Court had ruled in 1831 that the "Cherokees and other Indians were dependent domestic nations . . . definable political entities within the United States" (Spicer, 1969, p. 66). The 1871 congressional act closed an important chapter in Indian history. When he surrendered in 1877, Chief Joseph of the Nez Perce said, "Hear me, my chiefs, I am tired; my heart is sick and sad. From where the sun now stands, I will fight no more forever."

Messianic Movements: The Utopian Quests

Indians had been conquered by the late 1880s, and vigorous efforts to eradicate their cultures, values, and ways of life were already under way. Many were forced to live on reservations that were operated by superintendents and government agents who ruled the Indians with an iron hand and stifled all their efforts for self-initiative. Confined to reservations (some of which were fenced), many were forced to farm, which they considered women's work. In their desperation, Indians turned to religious prophets who promised a return to the traditional ways and the extermination of Whites and their lifestyles. Messianic leaders who heralded the end of White domination emerged within many of the eastern and western tribes.

As early as the 1760s, a prophet arose among the Delawares. He urged his followers to reject European goods and return to their old way of life. Tenskwatawa, a

Shawnee, experienced a revelation in 1805 that told him that White Americans would be destroyed by a natural catastrophe. Tenskwatawa and his brother, Tecumseh, taught the Shawnees to hold firm to their lands and refuse to relinquish them to the Whites. Handsome Lake began preaching among the Senecas around 1800 after the League of the Iroquois had been broken up. He urged the Senecas to remain neutral in the White people's wars, not to indulge in the White vices, and to live by his moral code. Handsome Lake became important to those Senecas who were trying to resist cultural domination by the Whites.

As Whites began to conquer Indian tribes in the West, prophets who envisioned a utopian future emerged among the western tribes. In 1855, a prophet called Smohalla began preaching among the Wanapum Indians in the Oregon Territory. Like the eastern prophets, Smohalla preached that the White people would be eliminated and that their way of life was detrimental. He believed that the way the White people farmed harmed Mother Earth. In 1881, John Slocum, a Squaxin Indian in the Pacific Northwest, was "apparently" dead and revived at his own wake. Slocum believed he had died and journeyed to heaven only to be denied entry due to his sinful life. He was instructed to return to earth and tell others of his experience. A short time later, when Slocum again was nearing death, his wife, being distraught, began shaking uncontrollably while praying over her husband's body. Miraculously, Slocum healed, and shaking was considered the primary reason for his recovery. Shaker Indian religion, while varying across Native traditions, is characterized by intense shaking during prayer, which is considered to have healing effects (Lehnhoff, 1982; Gill & Sullivan, 1992).

A Paiute prophet named Wovoka began having visions in 1885. He preached that a natural catastrophe would destroy White people and that the Indians' ancestors would return. The White authorities became alarmed about Wovoka's religion and its ritualistic "Ghost Dance." It spread rapidly among the Great Plains Indians and eventually reached the Lakota on the Pine Ridge Reservation in South Dakota. A frightened Indian agent called soldiers to the reservation in 1890. When a misunderstanding arose between the soldiers and Big Foot followers, the soldiers killed 300 Sioux at Wounded Knee Creek. This incident shocked the nation and wiped out the Ghost Dance among most Indian tribes.

AMERICAN INDIANS AND FEDERAL POLICY

When the Indians had been thoroughly subjugated and placed on reservations, White authorities began efforts to "civilize" them, which meant to make them as much like Whites as possible. The goal of federal policy was to assimilate the Indians quickly into the mainstream society. No attempt was made to give them a choice or to encourage them to retain elements of their cultures. Efforts were made to make Indians farmers and to give their children White people's education. Indian children were sent to boarding schools far away from home reservations so that the authority of their parents would be undermined (Lomawaima, 1994; Lomawaima & McCarty, 2006).

In 1879, Richard Henry Pratt founded the Carlisle Indian School. Pratt's famous saying, "kill the Indian to save the man," spurred a flurry of federally funded boarding schools that replaced many of the government-supported mission schools (Szasz, 1999). Pratt's military approach to educating Indian children was based on the presumption that the environment shapes the individual: if Indian children were taught the dominant values of American society—far removed from their "savage" ways—then their transition into mainstream society would be successful. Children from many tribes across the country were sent to off-reservation boarding schools. Chemawa Indian School in Oregon was first established in 1880 and still educates many Alaska Native and American Indian students today. The schools were a dismal failure. The quality of the teachers and the curricula was very poor. When Indian children left them, they were frequently unable to function well either in their ethnic communities or within the mainstream society. What the schools tried to teach had almost no relevance to life on the reservations. In addition, the schools also failed to teach Indian children the White people's culture.

Policymakers felt that they had to break up the Indians' communally held tribal lands and make individual allotments to family heads in order to make Indians independent and successful farmers. That this would violate Indian cultures and traditions was not a major concern. In 1887, Congress passed the Dawes Severalty Act. Designed to make Indians independent and to terminate their special relationship with the federal government, the act was destined to have the opposite effect. The act authorized the president to break up tribal lands and to make individual allotments to family heads. Each family head was to receive 160 acres; minors received 80 acres each. "Surplus" land was to be sold on the open market. The government was to hold the land in trust for twenty-five years. Citizenship was to be granted to family heads when they received their allotments. Many tribes adamantly opposed the act from the beginning.

The Dawes Act also established the "blood quanta" criterion to determine American Indian identity. In order for allotments of land to be disseminated, the federal government had to determine who was Indian. Government officials designated "full-blood" status to less assimilated individuals and "mixed-blood" status to those considered closer to Whites (Grande, 2004). The blood quanta criterion still serves today as the primary means by which most tribes and the Bureau of Indian Affairs legally define American Indians.

The results of the act were disastrous for Indians. Many Whites bought or leased lands from Indians at outrageously low prices or obtained land from them in extralegal ways. Some Whites persuaded their Indian friends to will them their lands. Indians who made such wills often turned up mysteriously dead shortly after finalizing the will. A 1906 congressional act gave the federal government more authority to supervise the administration of the Dawes Act. However, schemes for obtaining the Indian land developed more rapidly than government policies to safeguard it. Many Indians became poverty stricken during the period in which the act was in effect. Indians lost about 90 million out of a total of 138 million acres of land between 1887 and 1932.

It was clear by the late 1920s that the Dawes Act had failed. It had not only resulted in the loss of millions of acres of tribal land but had also increased, rather than decreased, the role of the federal government in Indian affairs. The Meriam Report, published in 1928, recommended major reforms in federal Indian policy, including the abandonment of the allotment plan and the consolidation of Indian land for use by the tribes. John Collier, who became commissioner of Indian affairs in 1933, believed that tribal land should be reestablished, as well as Indian government and other aspects of Indian culture. In 1934, Congress passed an act sanctioning the new federal policy. Termination had failed; the government would now take a more active role in Indian affairs and urge Indians to reestablish aspects of their cultures. The Wheeler-Howard Act of 1934 brought a halt to the allotment of Indian lands, made it possible for tribes to acquire additional lands, and granted American Indians the right to local government based on their traditional cultures.

By the 1950s, advocates for the termination of the federal government's role in Indian tribal affairs were again dominant in the nation's capital. In 1953, the federal government stated its intent in House Concurrent Resolution 108 to abolish the federal role in tribal affairs and to treat Indians the same as other Americans. During the 1950s, Congress passed several laws that gave the states additional responsibilities for Indian affairs. A 1954 termination bill ended the relationship between the federal government and the Klamath tribe in Oregon. The tribe and its reservation were abolished. However, the termination was disastrous for the Klamaths, because they had not achieved economic independence when it began. The Menominee Reservation in Wisconsin was also terminated during the 1950s.

SELF-DETERMINATION AND THE CHALLENGE TO TERMINATION

Most Indians are strongly committed to their tribal groups and to the continuation of their special legal relationship with the federal government. They feel that only in this way can they, a relatively small group, acquire their political rights and justice. Quechua scholar Sandy Grande (2004) offers a vision of self-determination for indigenous people by arguing for the ongoing survival of a nation-people. Nation-people are indigenous groups unified by a common purpose based on the shared historical struggles for sovereignty. Sovereignty entails supporting the nation-people's continued existence against colonialism. Indian peoples are unified by a common purpose based on historical struggles for survival and identity. As a nation-people, American Indians strive to maintain their traditional life ways while negotiating their place within the broader political discourse.

Because Indians believe that they are too few to exercise significant political power, most Indian leaders remained strongly committed to self-determination and against termination during the period of the 1950s and 1960s, when the termination policy was pursued by the federal government. However, termination received a severe blow when President Richard Nixon stated his Indian policy in 1970 (cited in Spicer, 1980):

> Self-determination among the Indian people can and must be encouraged without the threat of eventual termination. This is the only way that self-determination can effectively be fostered. This, then, must be the goal of any new national policy toward the Indian people: to strengthen the Indians' sense of autonomy without threatening the sense of community. We must assure the Indian that he can assume control of his own life without being separated involuntarily from the tribal group. And we must make it clear that Indians can become independent of federal control without being cut off from federal concern and federal support. (p. 120)

The challenge to termination and the support of Indian self-determination continued throughout the 1970s. According to the U.S. Commission on Civil Rights (1981), "The executive branch repudiated the policy of termination and successive administrations adopted a policy of Indian self-determination—a policy favoring Indian control over decision-making and promoting tribal interest" (p. 180). In 1975, the Indian Self-Determination Act made it clear that Indians could "control their relationships both among themselves and with non-Indian governments, organizations, and persons." The 1978 Indian Child Welfare Act provides for tribal jurisdiction and Indian community involvement in the adoption and foster placement of Indian children.

FISHING RIGHTS AND LAND CLAIMS

Tremendous controversies developed during the 1970s over both Indian fishing rights in the state of Washington and the land claims of Indian tribes in the states that originally made up the thirteen colonies. The fishing rights controversy arose because of treaties signed by the federal government and Indians in the Washington Territory in the 1850s. The Indians gave up vast land claims in return for specific federal promises. One was a recognition of Indian fishing rights. The Indians were promised that they "could continue to fish where they always had fished, exclusively on reservation and in common with the citizens of the territory at the Indians' usual and accustomed grounds and stations off reservation" (U.S. Commission on Civil Rights, 1981, p. 180).

As the supply of fish grew smaller, the state of Washington began to regulate fishing in a way that favored non-Indian fishing and violated the Indians' treaty promises. Some Indians were jailed for fishing in ways that violated state law. However, these Indians felt that their fishing was legal because of the terms of the nineteenth-century treaties. When the Indians took their cases to the courts, they won major legal victories. In 1974, Judge George Boldt ruled in a federal district court that the Indians had separate rights to a significant share of the fish and that the state should protect their rights and not interfere with them. The Boldt decision evoked a storm of controversy among the non-Indians of Washington state and led to personal attacks on Judge Boldt.

The non-Indian fishermen strongly rejected the Boldt decision and worked to get the case to the Supreme Court. They hoped that the high court would reverse the Boldt decision. The Supreme Court ruled on the controversial case on July 2, 1979, and upheld the decision made by Judge Boldt.

In 1790, the U.S. Congress enacted the Indian Trade and Intercourse Act, also known as the Nonintercourse Act of 1790. This act, which is still in effect, requires the federal government to supervise the transfer of Indian lands to non-Indians in states that formerly made up the original thirteen colonies. This act was designed to maintain friendly relationships between Whites and Indians. Most of the land in these states was transferred from Indians to non-Indians without the required federal supervision. During the 1970s, a number of eastern Indian tribes went to court to claim that their lands had been transferred illegally and to demand redress and compensation for the illegal transfer of their lands.

The Passamaquoddy and Penobscot tribes of Maine took legal actions to regain more than 10 million acres of land in the state of Maine. Their claim made up one-half of the state and included land inhabited by 350,000 non-Indians. This property was valued at $25 million. After a long and difficult battle, these tribes received a settlement of their claim in 1980.

Other tribes that have made land claims, with varying results, include the Oneidas in New York state, the Mashpee tribe in Massachusetts, the Schaghiticoke tribe in Connecticut, and the Narrangansetts in Rhode Island. The Narragansetts made their claim in 1976 and received a settlement in 1978 in which Congress provided funds to establish an 1,800-acre settlement.

Maintaining and accessing sacred sites is another important issue for Native American communities. These places are deemed holy and serve as the basis for a community's spiritual and religious existence (Deloria, 1973). The Lakota believe that the Black Hills are Paha Sapa, "the heart of everything that is." Currently, Devil's Tower, a sacred site in northeastern Wyoming near the Black Hills in South Dakota, is a popular site for rock climbers, who believe that it should be accessible to the public because it is a national park. When park officials created a volunteer "no climbing policy" during the month of June, the height of the Lakota's religious ceremonies, several climbers filed lawsuits, maintaining their right to climb Devil's Tower anytime during the year.

AMERICAN INDIANS TODAY

The Indian Population

Once known as the "vanishing Americans," the American Indian population has increased at every census count since 1940. The Indian population in 1940 was 345,000. The first complete census of American Indians was conducted in 1860.

There were 44,021 Indians counted that year. The biggest increase in the Indian population since 1860 occurred between the 1970 and the 1980 censuses. The Indian population increased by over 42% during that ten-year period, from 827,255 to 1,420,400 (Gibson & Jung, 2002). A number of factors other than the increase in the number of births over deaths may have accounted for this dramatic increase in the Indian population. These factors may have included improvements in the way the U.S. Census Bureau counted people since 1980, the wider use of self-identification to obtain information about ethnic group membership, and the greater tendency for people to identify as Indian in 1980 than in 1970 (Ogunwole, 2006). In 2000, the American Indian and Alaskan Native population was 2,475,956 (U.S. Census Bureau, 2001). In 2005, the U.S. Census estimated that the American Indian and Alaska Native population, including those of more than one race, was 4.4 million (U.S. Census Bureau, 2005).

The 2000 U.S. Census identified 558 American Indian tribes and bands. These tribes and bands vary greatly in size. About 16% of all Indians are identified as Cherokee; about 12% are identified as Navajo; and 6% each as Chippewa and Sioux. Figure 5.1 shows the ten largest American Indian tribes in 2005 and their populations. The four states with the largest Indian populations in 2000 were California (324,938), Oklahoma (262,931), Arizona (252,270), and New Mexico (171,507) (U.S. Census Bureau, 2001).

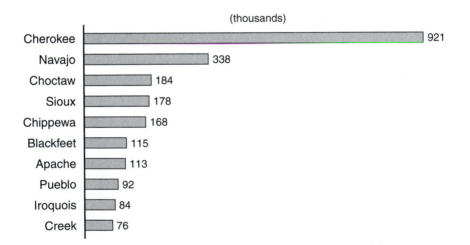

FIGURE 5.1   Ten Largest Indian Tribes, 2005

Source: U.S. Census Bureau (2007), *American Community Survey, 2005: Selected Population Profiles.* [Data set]. Retrieved June 13, 2007, from http://factfinder.census.gov/servlet/IPCharIterationServlet?_ts=199817016031.

Indians in Urban Communities

American Indians have become increasingly urbanized since the 1950 census. In 1950, about 56,000 Indians, or 16% of the total population, lived in urban areas and cities. That number increased to 146,000, or 28% of the population, in 1960. In 1980, about 49% of Indians lived in urban areas (Snipp, 1991), a 4% increase from 1970. In 2000, 33.5% of American Indians, Eskimos, and Aleuts lived on reservations and trust lands; 2.4% lived on tribal jurisdiction statistical areas; and most (64.1%) lived in other parts of the United States (see Figure 5.2). About 60% lived in urban areas in 1990. In 2001, nearly two-thirds of Indians lived in cities and towns off reservations (Edwards, 2001).

Even though about two-thirds of American Indians lived off reservations in 2001, many reports, statistical sources, and other kinds of informational sources focus on the minority of Indians who live on reservations. Detailed studies of urban Indians are scarce. Wax (1971) includes a chapter, "Indians in the Cities," in his dated but informative book, *Indian Americans: Unity and Diversity.* After a general discussion of Indians in cities, Wax discusses several case studies of urban Indian communities, including the Sioux in Rapid City, South Dakota, the Tuscarora (a branch of the Iroquois) in New York state, and the Indians in Minneapolis.

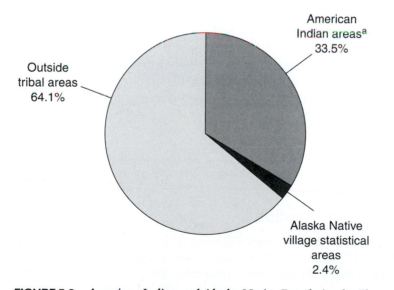

FIGURE 5.2   American Indian and Alaska Native Population by Place of Residence, 2000

[a] Includes federal reservation and/or off-reservation trust lands (20.9%), Oklahoma tribal statistical areas (9.3%), tribal-designated statistical areas (0.1%), state reservations (0.04%), and state-designated American Indian statistical areas (3.2%).

Source: S. U. Ogunwule (2006), American Indians and Alaska Natives in the United States, figure 10. *Census 2000 Special Reports, 28,* p. 14.

Wax (1971), as well as other authors, such as Sorkin (1978) and Bolt (1987), point out that many Indians have a difficult time adjusting to life in urban communities. Often cut off from families and reservation benefits, they have trouble getting jobs, health and medical care, and good schooling for their children. Reservation Indians who migrate to urban areas tend to settle in towns and cities near reservations (such as in Gallup, New Mexico, Rapid City, South Dakota, and Ponca City, Oklahoma) and to maintain contacts with their kin on the reservation.

When teaching about Indians in the cities, you should not gloss over the enormous problems that urban Indians often have. You also should remember that there is tremendous diversity within Indian urban communities. White, in a study summarized by Wax (1971), identified three social classes among Indians in his study of the Indians in Rapid City, South Dakota. He called one group "middle-class mobiles." These individuals constituted what White called "the mixed-blood elite." They were upwardly mobile and not highly identified with the full-blood Indians who lived on the reservation. He called another group "upper-middle-class White Indians." These individuals were descendants of upwardly mobile mixed-blood families. They occasionally identified with a female Indian ancestor. The final group of urban Indians that White identified were lower-class, rural, and reservation Indians who faced tremendous problems in the urban environment.

In a revealing and interesting study of Indians living in an urban community in a Great Lakes area city, Jackson (2001) found that the people she studied were trying to reconnect with their Indian pasts. To assimilate into White society, their parents had denied their Indian heritages and not revealed them to their children. Jackson described these children as having "holes in their hearts" because of the pain they experienced from being cut off from their Indian heritages. Jackson stated that urban Indians, who tend to be dispersed rather than concentrated in cities, form Indian organizations that cut across tribal lines. In *Genocide of the Mind* (Moore, 2003), the stories of contemporary Indians from many walks of life are captured beautifully. As one scholar notes, urban Indians "need to tell new stories about growing up and living urban lives" (p. 79). Many Natives today want to recapture and reclaim a contemporary Indian identity in spite of stereotypical and racist conceptions of American Indians in popular media.

Indians Face the Future

American Indians are in a unique demographic, cultural, legal, and historical situation. In 2000, Indians and Alaskan Natives numbered 2,475,956. Indians are increasing, rather than vanishing, Americans. Because of their relatively small population in a nation that numbers more than 300 million people, they are never likely to be a powerful political force. However, they have treaty rights to land and a special relationship with the federal government that no other ethnic group has. Consequently, they are able to exercise considerable power in the courts, although when they do so, as with fishing rights and land claims, they often evoke considerable hostility among non-Indians.

Many Native communities today recognize the need to salvage their languages and revitalize their cultures. Tremendous efforts are being made to teach young children the language and traditions, particularly since only a few elders in most tribal communities are fluent in their tribal languages.

By most measures, Indians are one of the nation's poorest and least educated ethnic groups. Yet they own lands that contain rich resources that are of enormous value to this nation (Dorris, 1981). The challenge that Indians face today is how to marshal their legal claims and resources in ways that will help them to attain the full benefits of U.S. citizenship. New reports have come out on the impact of Indian gaming, which has increased economic and political stature for Native communities. In 2006, Indian gaming garnered $25 billion among 387 tribal facilities in 28 states (Werner, 2007). Revenue from gaming and other enterprises has allowed tribes to reinvest in infrastructure, such as schools, housing, and healthcare, as well as cultural revitalization and language preservation programs (Rosier, 2003).

TEACHING STRATEGIES

To illustrate how content related to Indians can be used to integrate the curriculum, examples of strategies are identified for teaching the following concepts at the grade levels indicated: *cultural traditions* (primary grades), *cultural diversity and similarity* (intermediate and upper grades), and *federal policy* (high school grades).

Primary Grades

Concept

Cultural traditions

Generalization: Cultural traditions, such as potlatches, help us to remember and celebrate our past, to express caring and kindness, and to fulfill obligations and expectations.

1. Ask the students to list some of the ways that we show kindness and caring to family members and to friends. Responses might include: (1) with warm and cordial greetings such as "good morning and "good-bye"; (2) saying "thank you" and "excuse me," helping family members with chores; and (3) helping a friend who is in trouble. Write their responses on the board or butcher paper.
2. Tell the children that we have special days that we celebrate. On these special days, we give gifts to family members and friends to show kindness and caring, to fulfill expectations, and to satisfy obligations. Ask the children to name some of the special days on which we give or receive gifts. Responses might include birthdays, Valentine's Day, weddings, Christmas, and Chanukah. List their responses on the board or butcher paper.
3. Ask the children to name the people to whom we usually give or from whom we usually receive gifts on these special days. Responses will probably include family members and friends. List their responses on the board or butcher paper.
4. Ask the children: "Why do we usually give or receive gifts on these special days to family members and friends and not to strangers or to people we do not know?" By using questions and discussion, help the students to develop and state the idea that

"gift giving is a way of continuing our cultural traditions and expressing caring and kindness for family members and friends and of fulfilling obligations and expectations."

5. Tell the students that some American Indian and Eskimo groups have special occasions for giving gifts, namely, potlatches. Explain that *potlatch* is from the Indian word *pat shotl,* which means "giving" (Tucker, 1995). Read or phrase in your own words the description of potlatch that Mark Tucker, a Yup'ik Eskimo from Emmonak, Alaska, wrote in 1990:

> At a potlatch, one village invites another village to watch some dancing and to accept gifts. Alaska native villages have sponsored this kind of potlatch as far back as anyone can remember. The Indians of the Northwest Coast also hold potlatches to celebrate the completion of a new totem pole or to celebrate the building of a new house by members of the clan. [Explain what a totem pole is to the students and show them pictures of some. Excellent photographs of totem poles are in Bruggmann & Gerber (1987), *Indians of the Northwest Coast.*]
>
> Once a child attains a certain age, the parents and grandparents prepare a "first dance" [like a debut] for that child. The mother and grandmothers make such gifts as yarn gloves, socks, mittens, hot plate holders, and aprons. The father and grandfathers make things like spears, spear throwers, harpoons, ice picks, fish traps and ulus.
>
> When the child is ready to dance, his family hands out these gifts to the family of the person whose name was handed down to the child. It is a Yup'ik custom that a newborn child is named after the last elder in the village to die. After the potlatch, the child is allowed to dance as many songs as he or she wants at any social event (pp. 193–194).

6. Summarize the lesson by pointing out how the traditions of giving gifts within mainstream U.S. society are in some ways similar to traditions within American Indian and Eskimo groups to show caring and kindness and to fulfill obligations and expectations. Stress these similarities so that the students will understand the ways in which gift giving is a tradition shared by human groups. Potlatches are also unique and different in many ways from giving traditions within mainstream society. In later grades, students can learn about other unique characteristics of the potlatch, such as its relationship to social status and its spiritual aspects.

Intermediate and Upper Grades

Concept

Cultural diversity and similarity

Generalization: Indian cultures used both different and similar means as other cultures to satisfy common human needs and wants.

1. Ask the students to name some things they think all human beings need in order to survive and satisfy human wants. Their responses will probably include "food," "a place to live in," and "clothing." Probing questions might be necessary to bring out that other human needs include the need to explain unknown phenomena in the universe, for government, and for self-esteem.

2. List the student responses on the board and, with the class, group them into specific categories, such as food, shelter, clothing, government, family, religion, and economy.

3. Ask the students to name some institutions and means used in our society to meet the needs they have identified and categorized. Write their responses, in abbreviated form, on the board. Tell the class that in this unit they will be studying how four earlier cultures in North America satisfied these same human needs in ways different from the ways in which we usually satisfy them today.

4. Before introducing the four cultures, develop with the class key questions related to each category. The students will use the questions as guides when studying the four cultures. Examples are as follows:

  a. Food
    (1) What kinds of foods did the people eat?
    (2) Were they primarily hunters and gatherers or farmers?
    (3) How was the food usually prepared? By whom?
  b. Government
    (1) Who or what group made major decisions and laws?
    (2) How were major decision makers chosen?
    (3) How were rules and laws enforced?
  c. Economy
    (1) What goods and services were produced?
    (2) How were they produced? By whom? For whom?
    (3) How were goods and services exchanged? Was some form of money used? Was barter used?

5. The students should record the key questions in their notebooks. They will use them as guides when examining the four cultures.

6. Introduce the four cultures the class will study. When selecting four Indian cultures for the unit, try to select cultures (1) that have both similarities and differences that the students will be able to see clearly, and (2) for which you have adequate and high-quality student books and resources. To ensure cultural diversity, select the four groups from four different geographical areas, such as the Southeast, the Northwest, the Southwest, and California. This unit could be taught with as few as two groups. Although generalizations are more powerful when they are developed from a larger content sample, it is difficult for elementary students to study more than four cultures in one unit. In our example, we have chosen the Iroquois (Northeast), the Haida (Northwest), the Hopi (Southwest), and the Pomo (California). These four groups clearly illustrate both the similarities and diversity that existed within Indian cultures.

7. Ask the students to construct a data retrieval chart (similar to the one illustrated in Table 5.1) that includes (1) the categories and key questions they identified earlier, and (2) the names of the four groups. As they read and discuss each group, they should complete the blank spaces in the chart. When the chart is completed, ask the students key questions that will enable them to formulate this generalization: *Indian cultures used both different and similar means to satisfy common human needs and wants.* Excellent sources for factual information about various Indian tribes are Hoxie (1996), *Encyclopedia of North American Indians,* and Hunt (1999), *Illustrated Atlas of Native American History.*

8. Show the students the videotape *Weave of Time: The Story of a Navajo Family, 1938–1986.* This videotape shows four generations of change in one Navajo family

TABLE 5.1   Data Retrieval Chart for Comparing and Contrasting Four Cultures

CATEGORIES AND RELATED QUESTIONS	IROQUOIS	HAIDA	HOPI	POMO
Food (Questions)				
Shelter (Questions)				
Clothing (Questions)				
Government (Questions)				
Family (Questions)				
Religion (Questions)				
Economy (Questions)				

over a period of nearly fifty years. Ask the students to compare the changes over the four generations in the Navajo family with changes over the generations in their own families.

Valuing Activity

Speeches and selections that highlight traditional Indian values can inspire reflective value discussion and reasoning among students. Rich and powerful Indian speeches and statements are found in *Great Documents in American Indian History,* edited by Wayne Moquin with Charles Van Doren (1973), and *Touch the Earth: A Self-Portrait of Indian Existence,* edited by T. C. McLuhan (1971). The following statement was made by Chief Standing Bear (1933), a Sioux born in 1868. You can read this statement to the class and/or project it using a PowerPoint presentation. Ask the questions that follow the selection and discuss them with the class. Encourage the students to give reasons for their responses and to rationally defend their moral choices.

The Lakota Was a True Naturalist—a Lover of Nature

He loved the earth and all things of the earth, the attachment growing with age. The old people came literally to love the soil and they sat or reclined on the ground with a feeling of being close to a mothering power. It was good for the skin to touch the earth and the old people liked to remove their moccasins and walk with bare feet on the sacred earth.

Their [tipis] were built upon the earth and their altars were made of earth. The birds that flew in the air came to rest upon the earth and it was the final abiding place of all things that lived and grew. The soil was soothing, strengthening, cleansing, and healing.

That is why the old Indian still sits upon the earth instead of propping himself up and away from its life-giving forces. For him, to sit or lie upon the ground is to be able to think more deeply and to feel more keenly; he can see more clearly into the mysteries of life and come closer in kinship to other lives about him. Kinship with all creatures of the earth, sky, and water was a real and active principle. For the animal and bird world there existed a brotherly feeling that kept the Lakota safe among them and so close did some of the Lakotas come to their feathered and furred friends that in true brotherhood they spoke a common tongue. The old Lakota was wise. He knew that a man's heart away from nature becomes hard; he knew that lack of respect for growing, living things soon led to lack of respect for humans too. So he kept his youth close to its softening influence. (pp. 192–197)

Questions

1. What are the main values of the Lakota (tribal name for the Sioux) that are revealed in this statement by Chief Standing Bear?

2. In what ways might these values of the Lakota have conflicted with the values of the Europeans who settled in North America?

3. What problems do you think developed between the Lakota and the Europeans because of their value differences? Why?

4. How do traditional Lakota values, as revealed in the statement by Chief Standing Bear, conflict with many modern-day American values?

5. Do you think it is possible for individuals who endorse traditional Lakota values, such as those revealed in Chief Standing Bear's statement, to function successfully within a highly modernized nation such as the United States? Why or why not? What conflicts might such individuals experience? How might they resolve them?

6. Do you think that traditional Lakota values, as revealed in the chief's statement, could help strengthen a modernized nation such as the United States? Why or why not? If so, in what ways?

7. Which of the traditional Lakota values revealed in Chief Standing Bear's statement do you personally endorse? Which do you reject? Are you willing to act on those that you endorse? Why or why not?

8. When did you last act on the values in the statement that you endorse? When do you plan to act on them again?

High School Grades

Concept

Federal policy

Generalization: Most federal policy on Indian affairs was made without Indian input and usually sought Indian assimilation and the termination of federal-tribal relationships.

1. To gain an understanding of the legal relationship that Indian tribes have with the federal government, the students should examine some of the Indian treaties made

between the United States government and Indian tribes. These treaties were usually made when Indian tribes were forced to cede their territories and to relocate on reservations. They were granted reservation land in exchange for their land. Several such treaties are reprinted in Chapter 2 of *Of Utmost Good Faith,* edited by Vine Deloria, Jr. (1971).

2. Shortly after Indians had been conquered and forced onto reservations in the late 1800s, efforts were begun by the federal government to terminate its special relationship with the tribes, to force them to give up most aspects of their cultures, and to force assimilation into the dominant culture. These goals of federal policy were implemented in the Dawes Severalty Act of 1887. Ask the students to research the arguments, both pro and con, that preceded the passage of the act.

   a. Although many White liberals favored the passage of the act, most Indian tribes opposed it. When the bill was being debated in Congress, representatives of the Five Civilized Tribes sent a strong message to Congress opposing its passage. Ask the class to read and discuss this statement, which is reprinted in *Of Utmost Good Faith* (Deloria, 1971).

   b. White allies of Indians strongly supported the passage of a bill, such as the Dawes Act, that would break up tribal lands and allot them to individual household heads. They felt that such a bill would enable Indians to assimilate into the dominant culture. In 1884, the Indian Rights Association of Philadelphia, whose members were White friends of the Indian, issued a pamphlet strongly advocating the passage of an allotment bill. Ask the students to read and discuss excerpts from this pamphlet, reprinted in *The Indian and the White Man* (Washburn, 1964). The class should then compare the statement sent to Congress by the Five Civilized Tribes with the excerpt from the pamphlet. They should discuss the merits and weaknesses of the two positions.

3. Ask several students to role-play a debate between those who favored the Dawes Act and those who opposed it.

4. Ask the students to research these questions: "What effects did the Dawes Severalty Act have on Indian people?" "On White society?" "How do you think Indian life might be different today if the bill had failed in Congress?" "Why?" Two books, *The Indian Heritage of America* (Josephy, 1991) and *A Short History of the Indian in the United States* (Spicer, 1969), contain good discussions of the disastrous effects of the act on Indian tribes.

5. Because of the loss of millions of acres of tribal lands and the severe poverty of Indians, it was clear by the 1920s that the Dawes Act had been a colossal failure. John Collier, who became commissioner of Indian affairs in 1933, outlined a new federal policy for Indians. Ask the students to read and discuss his statement, "A New Deal for the Red Men" (in Washburn, 1964), and the Wheeler-Howard Act (in Deloria, 1971), the federal act of 1934 that embodied the new federal policy.

6. Ask the class to research the effects the Wheeler-Howard Act has had on Indian life and on the larger society. They can share their research findings by using role-playing, debates, or group discussion techniques.

7. Heated arguments for the termination of the federal-tribal relationship surfaced again in the 1950s. Ask the class to prepare research reports on these topics:

   a. The origins of the House Concurrent Resolution 108 (83rd Congress, 1st session), passed on August 1, 1953, which called for the termination of the federal role in Indian affairs.

    b. How termination policy affected these tribes and the conditions of the termination policy in each case:

      (1) the Klamaths of Oregon

      (2) the Menominees of Wisconsin

      (3) the Alabamas and the Coushattas in the South

8. Ask the class to study the various debates on termination that took place in the 1960s and 1970s between Indians and federal officials. An interesting argument against termination by an Indian is that of Earl Old Person (Blackfoot). See "Testimony against Proposed Congressional Legislation, 1966," reprinted in *Great Documents in American Indian History* (Moquin & Van Doren, 1973).

9. To conclude this unit, ask the students to divide into three groups and pretend that they are three different reservation tribes that have legal relationships with the federal government. Each tribe must unanimously decide, in the Indian tradition, whether they will terminate or maintain their legal relationship with the federal government. When the role-playing is over, the class should reassemble and discuss the decisions of each tribe and the process and arguments they experienced in reaching them.

REFERENCES

Bolt, C. (1987). *American Indian Policy and American Reform: Case Studies of the Campaign to Assimilate the American Indians.* London: Allen and Unwin.

Bruggmann, M., & Gerber, M. (1987). *Indians of the Northwest Coast.* New York: Facts on File.

Bunge, R. (1994). *Native American World Views: An American Philosophy before Pragmatism.* Grand Forks: University of South Dakota.

Cajete, G. (2000). *Native Science: Natural Laws of Interdependence.* Santa Fe, NM: Clear Light.

Ceram, C. W. (1971). *The First Americans: A Story of North American Archaeology.* New York: Mentor Books.

Chief Luther Standing Bear. (1933). *Land of the Spotted Eagle.* Boston: Houghton Mifflin.

Deloria, V., Jr. (Ed.). (1971). *Of Utmost Good Faith.* San Francisco: Straight Arrow Books.

Deloria, V., Jr. (1995). *Red Earth, White Lies: Native Americans and the Myth of Scientific Fact.* New York: Scribner.

Denevan, W. M. (1976). *The Native Population of the Americas in 1492.* Madison: University of Wisconsin Press.

Dobyns, H. F. (1976). *Native American Demography: A Critical Bibliography.* Bloomington: Indiana University Press.

Dorris, M. A. (1981, Spring). The Grass Still Grows, the Rivers Still Flow: Contemporary Native Americans. *Daedalus 110,* 43–69.

Edwards, B. (2001, January 31). *Morning Edition with Bob Edwards: Who Is Indian?* Available online at: http://www.npr.org/programs/morning/010131.cfoa.html.

Forbes, J. D. (1973). Teaching Native American Values and Cultures. In J. A. Banks (Ed.). *Teaching Ethnic Studies: Concepts and Strategies* (pp. 201–225). Washington, DC: National Council for the Social Studies.

Gibson, C., & Jung, K. (2002). *Historical Census Statistics on Population Totals by Race, 1790 to 1990, and by Hispanic Origin, 1970 to 1990, for the United States, Regions, Divisions, and States.* Population Division: Working Paper No. 56. Washington, DC: U.S. Census Bureau.

Gill, S. D., & Sullivan, I. F. (1992). *Dictionary of Native American Mythology.* New York: Oxford University Press.

Grande, S. (2004). *Red Pedagogy: Native American Social and Political Thought.* Boulder, CO: Rowman & Littlefield.

Hagan, W. T. (1961). *American Indians*. Chicago: University of Chicago Press.

Hammond Past Worlds: The Times Atlas of Archaeology. (1988). Maplewood, NJ: Hammond.

Harris, W. H., & Levey, J. S. (Eds.). (1975). *The New Columbia Encyclopaedia*. New York: Columbia University Press.

Hoxie, F. E. (Ed.). (1996). *Encyclopedia of North American Indians*. Boston: Houghton Mifflin.

Hunt, S. (Ed.). (1999). *Illustrated Atlas of Native American History*. Edison, NJ: Chartwell.

Jackson, D. D. (2001). "This Hole in Our Heart": The Urban-Raised Generation and the Legacy of Silence. In Susan Lobo & Kurt Peters (Eds.), *American Indians and the Urban Experience* (pp. 189–206). Walnut Creek, CA: Altamira Press.

Johnson, M. (2000). *Encyclopedia of Native Tribes of North America*. New York, NY: Random House.

Josephy, A. M., Jr. (1991). *The Indian Heritage of America* (enlarged ed.). Boston: Houghton Mifflin.

Kroeber, A. L. (1934). Native American Population. *American Anthropologist, 36,* 1–25.

Lehnhoff, P. (1982). Indian Shaker Religion. *American Indian Quarterly, 6* (3/4), 283–290.

Lomawaima, K. T. (1994). *They Called It Prairie Light: The Story of Chilocco Indian School*. Lincoln: University of Nebraska Press.

Lomawaima, K. T., & McCarty, T. L. (2006). *"To Remain an Indian": Lessons in Democracy from a Century of Native American Education*. New York: Teachers College Press.

McLuhan, T. C. (Ed.). (1971). *Touch the Earth: A Self-Portrait of Indian Existence*. New York: Pocket Books.

Mooney, J. M. (1928). *The Aboriginal Population of America North of Mexico*. In J. R. Swanton (Ed.), *Smithsonian Miscellaneous Collections* (vol. 80, no. 7). Washington, DC.

Moore, M. (Ed.). (2003). *Genocide of the Mind: New Native American Writing*. New York: Thunders Mountain Press/Nation Books.

Moquin, W., with Van Doren, C. (Eds.). (1973). *Great Documents in American Indian History*. New York: Praeger.

Nichols, R. L. (2003). *American Indians in U.S. History*. Norman: University of Oklahoma Press.

Ogunwole, S. U. (2006). *We the People: American Indians and Native Alaskans in the United States: Census 2000 Special Reports*. Washington, DC: U.S. Department of Commerce, Economics and Statistics Administration.

Parfit, M., & Garrett, K. (2000). The Dawan of Hamans: Hunt for the First Americans. *National Geographic, 198* (6), 40–67.

Rosier, P. (2003). *Native American Issues*. Westport, CT: Greenwood Publishing Group.

Snipp, C. M. (1991). *American Indians: The First of This Land*. New York: Russell Sage Foundation.

Sorkin, A. L. (1978). *The Urban American Indians*. Lexington, MA: D. C. Heath.

Spicer, E. H. (1969). *A Short History of the Indians in the United States*. New York: Van Nostrand Reinhold.

Spicer, E. H. (1980). American Indians: Federal Policy Toward. In S. Thernstrom, A. Orlov, & O. Handlin (Eds.), *Harvard Encyclopedia of American Ethnic Groups* (pp. 114–122). Cambridge, MA: Harvard University Press.

Stripes, J. (2001). Native Americans: An Overview. In G. T Kurian, M. Orvell, J. E. Butler, & J. Mechling (Eds.), *Encylopedia of American Studies* (vol. 3, pp. 197–204). New York: Grolier Educational.

Stuart, P. (1987). *Nations within a Nation: Historical Statistics of American Indians*. New York: Greenwood Press.

Szasz, M. C. (1999). *Education and the American Indian: The Road to Self-Determination since 1928*. Albuquerque: University of New Mexico Press.

Thomas, D. H. (2000). *Skull Wars: Kennewick Man, Archeology, and the Battle for Native American Identity*. New York: Basic Books.

Tinker, G. E., Noley, H., & Kidwell, C. S. (2003). *A Native American Theology*. Maryknoll, NY: Orbis Books.

Tucker, M. (1995). Contemporary Potlatches. In A. Hirschfelder (Ed.), *Native Heritage: Personal Accounts by American Indians 1790 to the Present* (pp. 193–194). New York: Macmillan.

U.S. Census Bureau. (1993, September). *We, the First Americans*. Washington, DC: U.S. Government Printing Office.

U.S. Census Bureau. (2000). *Statistical Abstract of the United States*. Washington, DC: U.S. Government Printing Office.

U.S. Census Bureau. (2001). Available online at http://www.census.gov.

U.S. Census Bureau. (2005). *American Community Survey, 2005*. [Data profile highlights]. Washington, DC: U.S. Government Printing Office.

U.S. Commission on Civil Rights. (1981). *Indian Tribes: A Continuing Quest for Survival*. Washington, DC: Author.

Washburn, W. E. (Ed.). (1964). *The Indian and the White Man*. New York: Doubleday.

Wax, M. L. (1971). *Indian Americans: Unity and Diversity*. Englewood Cliffs, NJ: Prentice-Hall.

Werner, E. (2007). Tribal Casinos Report Record Earnings of $25 Billion in 2006. [Electronic version]. *Indian Country Today*. Retrieved July 6, 2007, from http://www.indiancountry.com/content.cfm?id=1096415164.

The World Atlas of Archaeology. (1985). New York: Portland House.

ANNOTATED BIBLIOGRAPHY

Books for Teachers

Especially Recommended

Beardslee, L. (2004). *Rachel's Children*. Walnut Creek, CA: AltaMira Press.
> Through a combination of interviews, narrative, and theatrical script reflective of the Ojibwa storytelling style, Beardslee details the life of a family held together by the spirit, courage, persistence, and traditional teachings of a woman confronting poverty and racism in rural Michigan.

Bruchac, J. (2005). *At the End of Ridge Road*. Minneapolis: Milkweed Editions.
> The noted storyteller and author of books for children reflects on his life, the circularity of life, and the importance of a life that is peaceful and environmentally sustainable.

Cajete, G. (2003) *Native Science: Natural Laws of Interdependence*. Santa Fe, NM: Clear Light.
> This text provides a systematic presentation of Native American science and philosophy based upon multiple traditions within Native America.

Deloria, V., & Wildcat, D. (2001). *Power and Place: Indian Education in America*. Golden, CO: Fulcrum Resource.
> This text offers an American Indian perspective on educational issues and addresses the topic of self-determination for Native communities.

Community History Project. (Ed.). (2003). *Urban Voices: The Bay Area Indian Community*. Tucson: University of Arizona Press.
> This slender but rich volume is an oral history of an urban Indian community from the 1950s to the present. Contributors describe the culture shock of moving from reservation to city, the creation of intertribal organizations, the impact of civil rights and protest movements beginning in the 1960s, and the nineteen-month occupation of Alcatraz Island from 1969 to 1971.

Conley, R. J. (2005). *The Cherokee Nation: A History*. Albuquerque: University of New Mexico Press.
> The Cherokee author tells the story of his people with affection, humor, and optimism. Extensive notes, primary documents, photos of Cherokee leaders, and biographical sketches add educational value to this book. Conley is also the author of the well-regarded *Cherokee*

Medicine Man: The Life and Work of a Modern-Day Healer (University of Oklahoma Press, 2005).

Garroutte, E. M. (2003). *Real Indians: Identity and the Survival of Native America*. Berkeley: University of California Press.
This text describes the various ways in which Native Americans are defined within American society and offers a distinctive approach for Native American scholarship.

Grande, S. (2004). *Red Pedagogy: Native American Social and Political Thought*. Boulder, CO: Rowman & Littlefield.
This text criticizes the dominant paradigms addressing American Indian education and presents a way for indigenous communities to remain distinct while participating within mainstream educational issues.

Jones, G. W., & Moomaw, S. (2002). *Lessons from Turtle Island: Native Curriculum in Early Childhood Classrooms*. St. Paul, MN: Redleaf.
This resource guide will help teachers of young children to avoid stereotyped books and activities, to locate authentic age-appropriate materials, and to develop alternative lesson plans and activities. The authors provide selection guidelines and explore five themes—children, homes, families, communities, and the environment—with a focus on art, music, and cooking as well as literacy and mathematical skills.

Katanski, A. V. (2005). *Learning to Write "Indian": The Boarding School Experience and American Indian Literature*. Norman: University of Oklahoma Press.
A critical resource, this guide explores the impact of the boarding school experience on American Indian literature from the late nineteenth century to the present.

Mann, C. C. (2005). *1491: New Revelations of the Americas before Columbus*. New York: Knopf.
In contrast to stereotypical views that the Americas were nearly uninhabited wilderness before European settlement, the author documents the existence of numerous large and complex societies, describes how Native peoples managed their natural surroundings, and addresses the devastating impact of European diseases on the indigenous population.

Molin, P. (2006). *American Indian Themes in Young Adult Literature*. Lanham, MD: Scarecrow Press.
The author examines contemporary and historical fiction and nonfiction for teens, with a critical eye for the portrayal of American Indian characters, histories, cultures, and settings; she also takes standard review sources to task for praising seriously flawed books.

Moore, M. (Ed.). (2003). *Genocide of the Mind: New Native American Writing*. New York: Thunders Mountain Press/Nation Books.
This collection of essays and poetry explores the perspectives of urban Indians as they criticize stereotypes of Native Americans in contemporary society and challenge the myth that American Indians are a vanishing people.

Reyhner, J., & Eder, J. (2004). *American Indian Education: A History*. Norman: University of Oklahoma Press.
The well-known authorities on American Indian education describe how Indian parents and communities gained control of their education, beginning with resistance to the nefarious boarding schools.

Seale, D., & Slapin, B. (Eds.). (2005). *A Broken Flute: The Native Experience in Books for Children*. Walnut Creek, CA: AltaMira Press.
This collection, winner of the 2006 Before Columbus Foundation American Book Award, features personal essays by American Indian authors, teachers, scholars, mothers, and storytellers as well as topical bibliographies and critical essays. Copublished with the highly respected American Indian resource center Oyate (www.oyate.org), this reference title is the first source for those seeking to use books about American Indians in the classroom.

Waters, A. (Ed). (2004). *American Indian Thought: Philosophical Essays*. Malden, MA: Blackwell. One of the first of its kind, this text brings together a collection of philosophical essays written exclusively by American Indian scholars.

Other Books

Anderson, G. C. (2006). *The Conquest of Texas: Ethnic Cleansing in the Promised Land, 1820–1875*. Norman: University of Oklahoma Press. The genocidal acts of the Texas Rangers against the Indian population of the region is the subject of this well-documented study.

Bailey, G., & Swan, D. C. (2004). *Art of the Osage*. Seattle: University of Washington Press. One of a growing literature on Native arts, this book is distinguished by its readable, insightful writing and its appealing presentation of Osage beadwork and ribbonwork.

Benes, R. C. (2004). *Native American Picture Books of Change: The Art of Historic Children's Editions*. Foreword by Gloria Emerson. Santa Fe: Museum of New Mexico Press. Benes examines the bilingual picture books featuring American Indian illustrators that were produced by the Bureau of Indian Affairs (BIA) from the 1920s through the 1940s. She offers an insightful analysis of the aesthetics of these books, while Diné scholar Emerson examines the politics of the BIA, the residential schools, and efforts to preserve indigenous languages.

Bright, W. (2004). *Native American Placenames of the United States*. Norman: University of Oklahoma Press. A unique linguistic reference source, this book traces the language, history, and cultural context for hundreds of placenames throughout the United States.

Calloway, C. G. (2003). *One Vast Winter Count: The Native American West before Lewis and Clark*. Lincoln: University of Nebraska Press. This detailed and comprehensive history combines Native American creation stories with traditional narrative to describe the rise and fall of a myriad of indigenous cultures from the distant past to the early nineteenth century.

Deloria, P. J. (2004). *Indians in Unexpected Places*. Lawrence: University Press of Kansas. The Lakota historian addresses white popular cultural stereotypes of Indians from the late nineteenth century to the present.

Deloria, V., Jr. (2006). *The World We Used to Live In: Remembering the Powers of the Medicine Men*. Golden, CO: Fulcrum. First-person accounts by medicine men and those who have witnessed their work explore the value of traditional healing practices in a secular, materialistic society. See also *Spirit and Reason: The Vine Deloria, Jr., Reader* (Fulcrum, 1999), a comprehensive anthology of essays by this respected Native educator and writer who died in 2005.

Ellis, C., Lassiter, L. E., & Dunham, G. H. (Eds.). (2006). *Powwow*. Lincoln: University of Nebraska Press. The editors offer a comprehensive look at this important modern ceremony, with essays on the significance of the powwow, the performances themselves, and the way that powwows have adapted to changes in the larger society.

Glancy, D. (2002). *American Gypsy: Six Native American Plays*. Norman: University of Oklahoma Press. Ranging from dramatic monologues to two-character dialogues to complex dramas with multiple characters, this collection explores Cherokee mythology, history, Christianity, and personal crises of divorce, violence, and illness. A concluding essay by the Cherokee playwright and poet explains her aesthetic and worldview.

Glatthaar, J.T., & Martin, J. K. (2006). *Forgotten Allies: The Oneida Indians and the American Revolution*. New York: Farrar, Straus & Giroux.

This narrative history of the eighteenth-century Oneida includes insights into the myths and cultural practices of this Nation, which sought to maintain its autonomy by negotiating with the conflicting parties—rebellious colonists and British forces—for its support.

Glover, V. (2004). *Keeping Heart on the Pine Ridge: Family Ties, Warrior Culture, Commodity Foods, Rez Dogs, and the Sacred.* Summertown, TN: Book Publishing/Native Voices.
Through humorous and poignant vignettes, the author, a resident of the Pine Ridge Lakota Reservation, provides a glimpse into everyday life on a large reservation today.

Iverson, P. (2002). *Diné: A History of the Navajos.* Albuquerque: University of New Mexico Press.
The author combines archival research, traditional histories, interviews, and personal observations to provide a comprehensive narrative history. Those looking for primary sources should see Iverson's companion volume *For Our Navajo People: Diné Letters, Speeches, and Petitions, 1900–1960* (University of New Mexico Press, 2002).

Jonaitis, A. (2006). *Art of the Northwest Coast.* Seattle: University of Washington Press.
The author illustrates the vibrancy and diversity of Northwest Coast art, beginning with the precontact period and ending with the present. The book focuses on how indigenous art has changed and adapted to different living conditions and the emergence of a market for the art.

Karson, J. (Ed.). (2007). *Wiyaxaykt/Wiyaakaa'awn/As Days Go By: Our History, Our Land, Our People—The Cayuse, Umatilla, and Walla Walla.* Seattle: University of Washington Press.
A collection of essays describes the history, culture, arts, oral traditions, and ways of life, past and present, of three Northwest Coast nations from the perspectives of members of these nations.

LaDuke, W. (2005). *Recovering the Sacred: The Power of Naming and Claiming.* Cambridge, MA: South End Press.
The highly acclaimed Native environmental activist describes struggles over land use and the ways in which indigenous groups throughout North America try to preserve their ways of life.

Marshall, J., III. (2004). *The Journey of Crazy Horse: A Lakota History.* New York: Viking.
Marshall offers a richly textured portrait of the Lakota leader and introduces readers to the history and culture of his people.

Mercredi, M. (2006). *Morningstar: A Warrior's Spirit.* Regina, Saskatchewan: Coteau Books.
The author of the acclaimed children's book *Fort Chipewayan Homecoming* (Lerner, 1997) tells her own story of overcoming poverty, abuse, and alcoholism through the support of her community and her love for her son.

Paper, J. (2006). *Native North American Religious Traditions: Dancing for Life.* Westport, CN: Greenwood/Praeger.
This book provides an overview of contemporary American Indian spiritual traditions divided geographically—the Great Lakes and Northeast, Southeast and Southwest, Plains and Northwest Coast—along with an account of Christianity's impact on Native American theology.

Porter, J., & Roemer, K. M. (Eds.). (2005). *The Cambridge Companion to Native American Literature.* New York: Cambridge University Press.
Despite some unevenness, the seventeen essays in this collection offer insight into the historical, cultural, and genre contexts of American Indian literature and in-depth treatments of the works of N. Scott Momaday, James Welch, Simon Ortiz, Leslie Marmon Silko, Gerald Vizenor, Louise Erdrich, Joy Harjo, and Sherman Alexie.

Power, S. (2002). *Roofwalker.* Minneapolis: Milkweed Editions.
The twelve short stories in this collection explore intergenerational ties, Sioux culture and history, and the lives of Indian women in cities, on the reservation, and at elite universities.

Roberts, D. (2004). *The Pueblo Revolt: The Secret Rebellion That Drove the Spaniards Out of the Southwest.* New York: Simon & Schuster.
This is a well-researched and well-written account of the 1680 revolt against the Spanish that ushered in a decade of Pueblo independence in present-day New Mexico.

Smith-Morris, C. (2006). *Diabetes among the Pima: Stories of Survival.* Tucson: University of Arizona Press.
The author, an anthropologist, examines the intersection of chronic disease and cultural change through historical narrative, interviews with Pima women, and an analysis of diabetes education programs on the reservation.

Swann, B. (Ed.). (2006). *Algonquian Spirit: Contemporary Translations of the Algonquian Literatures of North America.* Lincoln: University of Nebraska Press.
This comprehensive anthology documents the voices of the Native peoples of the Northeast, including songs, folktales, and personal stories. The nations of the western half of the United States appear more prominently in Swann's earlier volume, *Voices from Four Directions: Contemporary Translations of the Native Literatures of North America* (University of Nebraska Press, 2004).

Tate, M. L. (2006). *Indians and Emigrants: Encounters on the Overland Trails.* Norman: University of Oklahoma Press.
A fast-paced and enlightening read, this book describes encounters between Indians and White settlers between 1840 and 1870, detailing acts of friendship as well as sources of conflict.

Warren, N. H., & Tiller, V. E. V. (2006). *The Jicarilla Apache: A Portrait.* Illustrated with photos by Nancy Hunter Warren. Albuquerque: University of New Mexico Press.
This collection of black-and-white photographs taken over a fifteen-year period, paired with Jicarilla Apache writer Tiller's text, depicts the culture and daily lives of a small tribe in northern New Mexico that shares linguistic and cultural characteristics with the Apache, the Navajo, and the Pueblo people.

Williams, R. A., Jr. (2006). *Like a Loaded Weapon: The Rehnquist Court, Indian Rights, and the Legal History of Racism in America.* Minneapolis: University of Minnesota Press.
Though the focus is on recent Supreme Court decisions, the author explores the history of Indian rights from the eighteenth century and the racist precedent that earlier decisions created.

Wilson, D. (2006). *Spirit Car: Journey to a Dakota Past.* St. Paul, MN: Borealis Press.
The author's genealogical search for her Dakota ancestors uncovers a history of oppression and endurance, including poverty, dislocation, land loss, and forced assimilation in boarding schools.

Books for Students

(Note: The following designations are used throughout this book: **Primary,** grades 1–3; **Intermediate,** 4–6; **Middle School,** 7–8; **High School,** 9–12.)

Alexie, S. (2007). *Flight.* New York: Grove Press.
A fifteen-year-old orphan escapes his latest foster home, and with the help of a gun, embarks on a series of time travel adventures in this satiric novel by the author of *The Lone Ranger and Tonto Fistfight in Heaven* (Atlantic Monthly, 1993). (High School)

Armstrong, J. (2005). *Dancing with the Cranes.* Illustrated by Ron Hall. Penticton, BC: Theytus.
An Indian girl learns from her mother about the circle of life after the death of the child's beloved grandmother. (Primary)

Beardslee, L. (2003). *Lies to Live By.* Illustrated by the author. East Lansing: Michigan State University Press.

Drawing on her Anishinaabe (Ojibwe) traditions, the author offers forty-four original stories full of beauty and wisdom along with black-and-white artwork. (High School)

Bruchac, J. (2006). *Geronimo*. New York: Scholastic.
This book is a well-written and often humorous biography of the Apache leader, as told by his adopted grandson. (Middle School)

Bruchac, J. (2001). *Skeleton Man*. New York: HarperCollins.
A contemporary Mohawk preteen relies on traditional teachings to survive when her parents disappear mysteriously and she is placed in the custody of an abusive man claiming to be her great-uncle. A sequel to this horror classic, *The Return of Skeleton Man*, was published in 2006. (Intermediate/Middle School)

Bruchac, J. (2002). *The Winter People*. New York: Dial.
Set in an Abenaki village during the French and Indian War, this novel follows a fourteen-year-old Abenaki boy as he sets off to rescue his mother and sisters, who have been captured by British soldiers. (Middle School)

Bruchac, J., & Bruchac, J. (2003). *Turtle's Race with Beaver*. Illustrated by Jose Aruego and Ariane Dewey. New York: Dial.
Joseph Bruchac and son James present a Seneca story in which Beaver overruns and enlarges Turtle's pond but refuses to share with his neighbor. A race between the two teaches Beaver an important lesson. (Primary)

Bruchac, M. M. (2005). *Malian's Song*. Illustrated by William Maughan. Middlebury: Vermont Folklife Center.
A young Abenaki girl from the mid-eighteenth century describes the night that the British raided and burned her village. Soft and beautiful illustrations accurately depict the clothing and lives of the Abenaki people of that era. (Primary)

Campbell, N. L. (2005). *Shi-shi-etko*. Illustrated by Kim LaFave. Toronto: Groundwood.
A young girl going off to an Indian boarding school says goodbye to all the people, animals, and things in her community that she loves. (Primary)

Carlson, L. M. (Ed.). (2005). *Moccasin Thunder: American Indian Stories for Today*. New York: HarperCollins.
Established and emerging American Indian writers offer ten short stories about identity, family connections, traditional values in modern times, and making the right choices. (Middle/High School)

Carvell, M. (2005). *Sweetgrass Basket*. New York: Dutton.
At the turn of the twentieth century, a father sends two Mohawk sisters to the Carlisle Indian School after their mother's death. In alternating first-person chapters, told in free verse, the sisters recount the abuse they suffer and the close bond between them that helps them to survive. (Middle/High School)

Carvell, M. (2002). *Who Will Tell My Brother?* New York: Hyperion.
A high school student—part Mohawk, part White—takes on his school's Indian mascot and endures racist taunts and cruel attacks from his peers as well as the callous indifference and condescension of adult leaders in his upstate New York community. (Middle/High School)

Cuthand, B. (2003). *The Little Duck/Sikihpsis*. Illustrated by Mary Longman. Bilingual (English-Cree) ed. Translated by Stan Cuthand. Vancouver, BC: Theytus; distributed by Orca Books.
A bilingual title for young children, this simple but deep story depicts a little duck that wants to be part of the Cree and attend the big dance. When he cannot understand the languages of the humans at the dance, he realizes he's better off with his own species. (Primary)

Dennis, Y. W., & Hirschfelder, A. (2003). *Children of Native America Today*. Foreword by Buffy Sainte-Marie. Watertown, MA: Charlesbridge.

Engaging photographs grace this sixty-four-page overview highlighting the diversity of American Indian life. Twenty-two nations, three confederacies, and urban Indians are covered. In addition to the usual "fast facts," the authors provide maps, information on arts and culture, brief biographies of notable members of each nation, and a list of organizations. (Intermediate)

Erdrich, L. (2005). *The Game of Silence*. New York: HarperCollins.

In this sequel to *The Birchbark House* (Hyperion, 1989), Omakayas is nine years old and taking on the responsibilities of an adult as she and the rest of her village must flee their island in what is now Lake Superior to escape the violence and diseases brought by White settlers. (Intermediate/Middle School)

Erdrich, L. (2002). *The Range Eternal*. Illustrated by Steve Johnson and Lou Fancher. New York: Hyperion.

In this poetic picture book, the acclaimed Ojibwe writer remembers the "range" in all its meanings at her grandparents' house on the Turtle Mountain Reservation in North Dakota. (Primary/Intermediate)

Grace, C. O., & Bruchac, M. M. (2001). *1621: A New Look at Thanksgiving*. Washington, DC: National Geographic Society.

The story of Thanksgiving is told from a Wampanoag perspective, with Wampanoag traditions and English colonial records used to challenge today's stereotypes and oversimplifications. (All ages)

Highway, T. (2001). *Caribou Song/atíhko níkamon*.

——. (2002). *Dragonfly Kites/pímíhákanísa*.

——. (2003) *Fox on the Ice/mahkesís mískwamíhk e-cípatapít*.

Illustrated by Brian Deines. Bilingual (English-Cree) ed. New York: HarperCollins.

The acclaimed Cree playwright Thomson Highway offers a trilogy of original bilingual stories collected as "Songs of the North Wind." They feature the adventures of two Cree brothers, their parents, their huskies, and their black dog living in the far north of Manitoba. The stories take place in different seasons—*Caribou Song* in spring, *Dragonfly Kites* in summer, and *Fox on the Ice* in winter. (Primary)

Lacapa, K., & Lacapa, M. (2001). *Less Than Half, More Than Whole*. Illustrated by Michael Lacapa. Chapel Hill, NC: Storytellers Publishing.

This is an excellent book that can be used to explain racial identity to children. Tony realizes that he is neither a White like his friend Scott, nor 100% Indian like Will. Tony's realization that he is more than whole is comforting to children who have ever felt "different." Storytellers Publishing has returned to print this classic, which first appeared in 1994. (Primary)

Lacapa, M. (2003). *Antelope Woman*. Illustrated by the author. Chapel Hill, NC: Storytellers Publishing.

Originally published in 1993, this is a poetic and visually stunning Apache folktale about a woman who falls in love with a strange man—in fact, an antelope in disguise. When her family rejects her choice, she goes to live with him and the rest of the antelopes. This is why the Apache refrain from hunting the antelope. (Primary)

Marshall, J., III. (2005). *How Not to Catch Fish and Other Stories of Iktomi*. Illustrated by Joseph Chamberlain. Eureka Springs, AR: Circle Studios.

Humor and wisdom characterize these seven traditional stories about the notorious trickster of Lakota legend. (Intermediate)

Medicine Crow, J., with H. J. Viola. (2006). *Counting Coup: Becoming a Crow Chief on the Reservation and Beyond*. Washington, DC: National Geographic.

The tribal historian of the Crow Nation offers vignettes of his childhood along with the rites of passage he experienced on his way to adulthood. (Intermediate/Middle School)

Messinger, C., with S. Katz. (2007). *When the Shadbush Blooms*. Illustrated by D. K. Fadden. Berkeley, CA: Tricycle Press.

A Lenni Lenape Indian family from long ago and one from today experience the cycle of the seasons through the twelve moons of the year. Accompanying the poetic text and exquisite illustrations are three pages of explanatory material. (Primary)

Moore, M. (2001). *Red Woman with Backward Eyes and Other Stories*. Candler, NC: Renegade Planets.

Ten short stories explore contemporary American Indian life and the experiences of women and girls from a Cherokee perspective. (High School)

Ochoa, A. P., Franco, B., & Gourdine, T. L. (Eds.). (2003). *Night Is Gone, Day Is Still Coming: Stories and Poems by American Indian Teens and Young Adults*. Cambridge, MA: Candlewick.

Indian teens and young adults describe their lives and dreams in poems, essays, and short stories. (High School)

Patent, D. H. (2006). *The Buffalo and the Indians: A Shared Destiny*. New York: Clarion.

The author explores the complex relationship between the Plains Indians and the buffalo, the impact of the animal's historic slaughter by White settlers, and efforts to restore buffalo herds today. (Intermediate/Middle School)

Sockabasin, A. (2006). *Thanks to the Animals*. Illustrated by Rebekah Raye. Gardiner, ME: Tilbury House.

A Passamoquoddy storyteller offers a warm tale about a boy who tumbles from his family's sled in the middle of winter but is saved by the animals. (Primary)

Rappaport, D. (2002). *We Are the Many: A Picture Book of American Indians*. Illustrated by Cornelius Van Wright and Ying-Hwa Hu. New York: HarperCollins.

Lively biographies accompanied by double-page full-color illustrations introduce sixteen American Indian people whose lives had an impact on American history, from the Tisquantum (Squanto) to Wilma Mankiller. (Primary/Intermediate)

Red Shirt, D. (2002). *Turtle Lung Woman's Granddaughter*. Lincoln: University of Nebraska Press.

The author, a Lakota poet, recounts her grandmother's stories, interspersed with her own poetry and stories from her mother's life. This intergenerational memoir chronicles changes in a landscape and a way of life from the mid-nineteenth century to the present. (High School)

Rivera, R. (2007). *Arctic Adventures: Tales from the Lives of Inuit Artists*. Illustrated by Jirina Marton. Toronto: Groundwood.

The four tales in this collection are based on traditional stories told and painted or sculpted by four Inuit artists. The author and illustrator place the Inuit artists' work in the context of their communities and include photos of the artists and their works. (Intermediate)

Rumford, J. (2004). *Sequoyah: The Cherokee Man Who Gave His People Writing*. Illustrated by the author. Bilingual (English-Cherokee) ed. Cherokee translation by Anna Sixkiller Huckaby. Boston: Houghton Mifflin.

On a road trip with his family, a Cherokee father tells the story of the Cherokee alphabet and the life of Sequoyah, its creator. (Primary/Intermediate)

Runningwolf, M., & Clark, P. C. (2003). *On the Trail of Elder Brother: Glous'gap Stories of the Micmac Nation*. Illustrated by Michael Runningwolf. New York: Persea.

This collection of sixteen creation stories comes from the five nations of the Wabanaki Confederation, not only the Mi'kmaq. Gluskabi, the Elder Brother and the embodiment of the Great Spirit's power, sets an example of both good and bad behavior for the humans to follow. (Intermediate/Middle School)

Savageau, C. (2006). *Muskrat Will Be Swimming*. Illustrated by Robert Hynes. Gardiner, ME: Tilbury House.

This 1996 classic, back in print, depicts an Abenaki girl who comes to live with her grandfather by a lake in Maine and endures the taunts of her wealthier White schoolmates who call her "Lake Rat." Her grandfather tells her the story of Muskrat and shows her the richness below the lake's surface. (Primary/Intermediate)

Slipperjack, R. (2002). *Little Voice*. Regina, Saskachewan: Coteau Books.
After her father dies and her family slides into poverty, ten-year-old Ray finds solace, community, and a source of strength in the summers she spends with her grandmother, an Ojibwa elder and healer. (Intermediate/Middle School)

Smith, C. L. (2002). *Indian Shoes*. Illustrated by Jim Madsen. New York: HarperCollins.
Six stories portray a Cherokee-Seminole boy and his relationship with his paternal grandfather. Set in Chicago and rural Oklahoma, the stories convey the traditions, humor, and warmth of a close extended family. (Intermediate)

Smith, C. L. (2001). *Rain Is Not My Indian Name*. New York: HarperCollins.
In this heartfelt novel by a young Muscogee author, a fourteen-year-old girl struggles with her grief over the sudden deaths of her mother and her best friend and with the expectations others have of her because she is Indian. (Middle School)

Sneve, V. D. H. (2003). *Enduring Wisdom: Sayings from Native Americans*. Illustrated by Synthia Saint James. New York: Holiday House.
The author collects traditional and contemporary American Indian quotations (and a few of her own) in the categories of "Mother Earth," "The People," "War and Peace," "Spirit Life," and "Enduring Wisdom." (All ages)

Sneve, V. D. H. (2000). *Grandpa Was a Cowboy and an Indian and Other Stories*. Lincoln: University of Nebraska Press.
This collection of brief stories retells traditional legends and myths, depicts moments in the history of the Plains Indians, and portrays the intergenerational bonds that serve as a model and support structure for Indian youth. (High School)

Sommerdorf, N. (2006). *Red River Girl*. New York: Holiday House.
A Métis girl must take charge of her younger siblings on a fur-trading expedition from present-day Quebec to St. Paul, Minnesota, after the death of her Ojibwa mother. Her desire to become a teacher clashes with her French Canadian father's expectations for her in this novel set in the mid-1800s. (Intermediate/Middle School)

Spalding, A. (2002). *Solomon's Tree*. Illustrated by Janet Wilson. Vancouver, BC: Orca Books.
A Tsimshian boy is devastated when his favorite tree is uprooted during a storm—until his uncle transforms the tree into a mask. Tsimshian maskmaker Victor Reece collaborated with the author and illustrator, and there is a photograph of the mask on which the story is based. (Primary)

Tingle, T. (2006). *Crossing Bok Chitto: A Choctaw Tale of Friendship and Freedom*. Illustrated by Jean Rorex Bridges. El Paso, TX: Cinco Puntos Press.
One of the stories included in *Walking the Choctaw Road* (Cinco Puntos Press, 2003), this original tale portrays a young Choctaw girl in the mid-nineteenth century who, defying her village's rules, crosses the Bok Chitto to the plantation on the other side. There, she befriends an enslaved boy and his family and ultimately helps them cross to the Indian side of the river to freedom. (Primary/Intermediate)

Tingle, T. (2006). *Spirits Dark and Light: Supernatural Tales from the Five Civilized Tribes*. Little Rock, AR: August House.
A master storyteller weaves traditional elements from Choctaw, Cherokee, Chickasaw, Creek, and Seminole folklore into a collection of entertaining original tales. (Middle/High School)

Tingle, T. (2003). *Walking the Choctaw Road: Stories from Red People Memory*. El Paso, TX: Cinco Puntos Press.

Twelve original stories, arranged chronologically from the early nineteenth century to the present, depict acts of great heroism, magic that can overcome insurmountable odds, and friendships that emerge from the most trying of circumstances. (Middle/High School)

Whitethorne, B. (2004). *Sunpainters: Eclipse of the Navajo Sun*. Illustrated by the author. Flagstaff, AZ: Salina Bookshelf.
A well-known Diné artist recounts through poetic text and striking color illustrations a solar eclipse he experienced while living on the Diné reservation as a young child. Interwoven with the child's account of the eclipse is the grandfather's story of the Little People who repaint the sun when it dies. (Intermediate)

Yamane, L. (1998). *The Snake That Lived in the Santa Cruz Mountains and Other Ohlone Stories*. Berkeley, CA: Oyate.
Seven traditional stories will delight readers of all ages. Yamane's earlier volume of traditional Ohlone pourquoi tales is entitled *When the World Ended, How Hummingbird Got Fire, How People Were Made: Rumsien Ohlone Stories* (Oyate, 1995). (All ages)

Yazzie, S. G. (2006). *Dibé Yázhi Táa'go Baa Hane'/The Three Little Sheep*. Illustrated by Ryan Huna Smith. Bilingual (Navajo-English) ed. Navajo translation by Peter A. Thomas. Flagstaff, AZ: Salina Bookshelf.
This retelling is a Navajo version of "The Three Little Pigs" in which a mother sends her little sheep out to become self-sufficient. One builds a grass hut, one builds a tepee, and one builds a hogan. With much humor, the author reflects on the construction and uses of these structures just before Coyote comes to test their durability. (Primary)

Zitkala-Sa/Bonin, G. (2003). *American Indian Stories*. Introduction by Susan Rose Dominguez. Lincoln: University of Nebraska Press.
Originally published in 1921, this is one of the first books entirely written by an American Indian woman without the intervention of a translator or editor. The Yankton Sioux author offers a collage of traditional stories, childhood memories, and essays. (High School)

CHAPTER SIX

NATIVE HAWAI'IANS
Concepts, Strategies, and Materials

You must not think that this is anything like olden times, that you are the only chiefs and can leave things as they are. Smart people have arrived from the great countries that you have never seen. They know our people are few in number and living in a small country; they will eat us up.

—David Malo, 1837

The experiences of Native Hawai'ians parallel those of other indigenous peoples whose cultures and traditional lifestyles were drastically altered by European contact. Like the American Indians, the numbers of Native Hawai'ians were sharply reduced in the past two centuries. Their culture was initially modified and finally overwhelmed by European and American settlers.

Native Hawai'ians often found it difficult to assume a viable role in a society in which Western practices were foreign to them. Values that for centuries had been hallmarks of Native Hawai'ian culture were often counterproductive in a Hawai'ian society run by foreigners. This conflict inevitably led to helplessness and despair for some of Hawai'i's original inhabitants.

Yet, the culture of Hawai'i has shown remarkable resiliency, despite the great odds against its survival. The Hawai'ian renaissance of the 1970s indicated that a revitalized consciousness of what it means to be Hawai'ian had developed. The Hawai'ian sovereignty movement in the late twentieth and early twenty-first centuries has shown that at least for some Hawai'ians, there is great dissatisfaction with the political status quo and their role in it. For some Native Hawai'ians, the

This chapter was contributed by **Carlos F. Diaz,** professor of education, Florida Atlantic University, Boca Raton, Florida. Professor Diaz is coauthor of *Touch the Future . . . Teach* (Allyn and Bacon, 2006). The bibliographies at the end of the chapter were written by **Jeffrey A. S. Moniz,** assistant professor of education, University of Hawai'i, Manoa.

American dream has borne fruit. For most, it has been largely deferred, and they remain the most economically disadvantaged group in Hawai'i. Students should be aware that although small in number, Native Hawai'ians have made unique and lasting contributions to the American saga.

In 1778, Captain James Cook's expedition landed on the islands that he named the Sandwich Islands, now called the state of Hawai'i. There, Cook found as many as 800,000 people living in relative isolation (Stannard, 1989). Since that time, Hawai'ian history has been fraught with the paternalism of Europeans and Americans, often to the detriment of Native Hawai'ians. This story is one of broken promises and the exploitation of Native Hawai'ians by foreigners that in some ways is similar to the plight of Native Americans.

Until foreigners started coming to Hawai'i, Native Hawai'ians did not have a word for *race*. There were two groups, Hawai'ians and strangers. They called themselves *kanakas* and referred to strangers as *haoles*. This total unimportance of race was to change with the coming of Europeans. The word *haole* came to mean "White" instead of "stranger" as Whites became more prevalent on the islands. The Hawai'ian people were forced to deal with an alien White economic, social, and legal system whose values often conflicted with their own.

NATIVE HAWAI'IANS: BEFORE EUROPEAN CONTACT

In the early subsistence economy of Hawai'i, the survival of Hawai'ians depended on a communal effort to reap the maximum benefits from the islands' scarce resources. The Hawai'ians were an agricultural and fishing people with a complex socioreligious structure. The islands were governed by the *ali'i,* who were powerful chiefs. The power of these chiefs was legitimized by the priests, or *kahuna,* who interpreted the religious doctrine set forth in the *kapu.* The common people, or *maka'ainana,* were extremely devoted to their chiefs. The high chief, or *ali'inui,* was the supreme ruler over his territory and was expected to provide protection for his people. People had the freedom to move to the district of another chief but rarely did so. Although sharing was a predominant practice, there was a considerable difference between the lifestyles of the chiefs and the common people.

There were two Hawai'ian customs that would lead to inevitable conflict with *haoles.* One was a system of sharing and bartering, in which products were exchanged from one island to another. The Hawai'ians did not use currency, so the accumulation of wealth in a market economy as we know it was unknown. The other custom was the notion that the land belonged to the gods, and therefore belonged to everyone, and could not be owned. The earliest visitors to the islands found the natives willing to share whatever they had. After all, that was the Hawai'ian way.

NATIVE HAWAI'IANS: HISTORICAL PERSPECTIVE

Important Dates	Events
1778	The beginning of European contact. Captain James Cook's expedition landed on the Hawai'ian Islands.
1795	The rise to power of King Kamehameha I, who united the Hawai'ian people under one ruler. This marked the beginning of the Kamehameha dynasty.
1820	The breaking of taboo against eating *kapu* by King Kamehameha II, which signaled the end of the ancient Hawai'ian religion as a state religion. The first missionaries arrived in Hawai'i from New England.
1835	King Kamehameha III granted an American firm the first long-term lease for a sugar plantation.
1845	The Great Mahele: all the land on the islands was divided between the king and 245 chiefs.
1893	Queen Liliuokalani was overthrown in a bloodless revolution led by American planters. The Republic of Hawai'i was established, with Sanford B. Dole as president. This government lasted until annexation by the United States.
1920	The Hawai'ian Homes Commission was started to benefit the Native Hawai'ians. Very little of this land was used for its stated purpose. By the 1930s, the commission was leasing half of its land to corporations or to non-Hawai'ians.
1954	For the first time since Hawai'i became a territory, the Democratic Party captured a majority in both houses of the legislature.
1959	Hawai'i became the fiftieth state of the United States.
1974	George Ariyoshi was the first non-*haole* elected governor of Hawai'i.
1975	The U.S. Congress passed a law recognizing Native Hawai'ians as a Native American group.
1976	The voyage of the Hawai'ian canoe Hokule'a from Hawai'i to Tahiti reinforced pride in the Polynesian roots of Hawai'ian culture.
	Daniel Akaka became the first Native Hawai'ian member of the U.S. House of Representatives.
1977	The first edition of the newsletter *Native Hawai'ian* was published, marking a growing Hawai'ian consciousness movement.
1978	The state government established the Office of Hawai'ian Affairs to help Native Hawai'ians secure their rights. Hawai'ian studies were mandated in the state's schools by a state constitutional amendment.
1980	The Hawai'ian tourist industry suffered its first decline since 1949. This fueled debate about diversification of the Hawai'ian economy.

Important Dates	Events
1986	John D. Waihee, the first governor of Hawai'ian ancestry, took office.
1993	President Clinton signs PL 103-150 into law, officially apologizing to the Hawai'ian people for the overthrow of the Hawai'ian monarchy.
1995	Seven hundred people demonstrate at the state capitol to pass a 600-million-dollar settlement to allow faster development of Hawai'ian homelands.
2000	The U.S. Supreme Court rules in *Rice* v. *Cayetano* that eligible voters in elections for Office of Hawai'ian Affairs trustees could not be limited to Native Hawai'ians.
2002	Linda Lingle becomes the first female governor of Hawai'i.
2006	The Akaka Bill, establishing a Native Hawai'ian "governing entity" to negotiate with the state and national governments, fails to pass the U.S. Senate. Governor Lingle is reelected.
2007	The Ninth U.S. Circuit Court of Appeals upheld the Hawai'ians-only admission policy of the Kamehameha Schools.

EUROPEAN CONTACT

The propensity of Hawai'ians to share eventually helped to seal their demise. Besides providing provisions for ships, Hawai'ians were quite willing to share their women, and Whites were eager to become intimate with them. These casual contacts over a long period of time had a decimating effect on the islands' population. The venereal diseases introduced by European and American sailors found little natural resistance among the Hawai'ians and, along with measles, cholera, and alcoholism, took a deadly toll.

An estimated 300,000 people inhabited the Hawai'ian islands at the time of European contact. By 1840, only about 100,000 Hawai'ians remained. Many Native Hawai'ians were naturally alarmed at what was taking place due to contact with the *haoles*. According to David Malo (cited in Jacobs & Landau, 1971), a Native Hawai'ian writer espoused this viewpoint: "The ships of the White man have come and smart men have arrived from the great countries. They know our people are few in number and living in a small country; they will eat us up" (p. 22). His prophecy came true eventually, but at that time it fell on deaf ears. When David Malo died, he was buried at his request in Lahaina, next to a school where he had received his education from missionaries.

The paternalism of *haoles* began with sea captains, who needed the islands as a place to replenish supplies and repair their ships. Often, chiefs were given a few metal items in return for supplies. As commercialism grew and the chiefs saw more European goods, there began to be a desire for these items. Sandalwood, which was plentiful on the islands, was in great demand for carving as well as for its aromatic qualities. It could be bought in Hawai'i for one cent per pound and sold lucratively in Canton, China, for 34 cents per pound (Kent, 1983, p. 18). As the Yankee traders increased their demands for sandalwood, many chiefs forced their subjects to cut more of the mountain trees and haul the lumber down steep slopes. Some chiefs also became fervent consumers of Western goods and kept their subjects away from their own food-producing activities in order to satisfy the sandalwood trade and their own avarice. This continued until the slopes of Hawai'i were nearly denuded of sandalwood trees. Today, they are scarce on the islands.

The ascension to power of King Kamehameha I marked the rise of the Kamehameha dynasty. According to Day (1968), "One of Kamehameha's greatest qualities was his ability to attract many White men to his service and retain their loyalty for years or even a lifetime" (p. 44). Even though Kamehameha was skillful in retaining power, this practice proved disastrous in the long run for his heirs, because often the *haole* advisers put their own interests ahead of the Hawai'ian people they were supposed to help.

Kamehameha I is often regarded as one of the greatest Hawai'ian monarchs because he conquered populations in other islands and unified the entire island chain under one rule. The weapons and technology he had obtained through contact with Westerners were of great assistance in this campaign.

After the death of Kamehameha I in 1819, his son, Liholiho, succeeded him. During the reign of Liholiho (Kamehameha II), he was pressured into abolishing the *kapu* system of taboos. This had far-reaching effects on Hawai'ian society. Although the *kapu* system was often oppressive and sometimes abused, its elimination began an erosion of Native Hawai'ian culture because there were no satisfactory substitutes provided.

Besides the traders and advisers of the chiefs, another group entered the Hawai'ian scene to lend its paternalistic hand. In 1820, the first groups of missionaries arrived in the islands from New England. Their goal was to Christianize the natives, but in most cases, their influence far surpassed the religious realm. According to Jacobs and Landau (1971), "Under increased influence of the missionaries on the king, more *haoles* were given the right to lease land for commercial enterprises. But these men did not want merely to lease the land, they wanted to own it outright so they could sell or lease it to others" (p. 26).

A further blow to the survival of Hawai'ian culture was dealt in 1848, when King Kamehameha III took the suggestions of his foreign advisers and decided to redistribute land in the Hawai'ian islands. This act by the king was known as the *Great Mahele*. Kent (1983) notes that, under its provisions, "60% of the land was allocated to the crown and government, 29% to the 208 chiefs, and less than 1% to 11,000 commoners" (p. 31).

After the Great Mahele, there was a steady decline in subsistence farming among the Native Hawai'ians. Alien concepts such as land deeds and property taxes clashed with the traditional Hawai'ian view that land was for the use and enjoyment of all the people. Slowly, even small plots of land owned by Native Hawai'ians passed into the hands of the *haoles*. This loss of control over their land by Native Hawai'ians somewhat parallels the saga of Native Americans.

As the sandalwood trade faded, the Hawai'ian economy began to rely more on supplying whaling ships with meat, vegetables, and water. Hawai'i also became a convenient location to make any repairs needed by whaling vessels on their long voyages. With the income earned from these activities, Hawai'i imported manufactured goods, mainly from the United States. When whaling in the Pacific began to decline, the Hawai'ian economy shifted to plantation agriculture.

During each of these phases, forces thousands of miles away from the islands always controlled the Hawai'ian economy. The interests and needs of the Native Hawai'ian population were inconsequential when compared to the potential for large profits.

The plantation system began to flourish in the latter part of the nineteenth century. Native Hawai'ians worked in the cane fields as laborers but were not as productive as plantation owners had expected. The dawn-to-dusk labor in the cane fields and rigid production quotas were difficult adjustments for Native Hawai'ians. Lacking a significant economic niche in their own islands, and slowly losing political control, the Native Hawai'ian population continued to decline.

From a population of 71,019 in 1853, the Native Hawai'ian population, including those of mixed ancestry, had dropped to 39,504 by 1896 (Lind, 1980). During this period, planters were importing field labor to the Hawai'ian islands from nearly the entire world. The first major group was the Chinese, soon followed by the Japanese, Filipinos, Portuguese, Koreans, Puerto Ricans, and immigrants from other nations.

The planters' strategy was to keep any one nationality of laborers from becoming too numerous and thus to thwart any type of labor organization. George H. Fairfield (cited in Takaki, 1983), manager of the Makee Sugar Company, stated the planters' strategy as follows: "Keep a variety of laborers, that is of different nationalities, and thus prevent any concerted action in case of strikes, for there are few, if any, cases of Japanese, Chinese, and Portuguese entering into a strike as a unit" (p. 24). Largely as a result of methods to keep laborers from uniting, Hawai'i's population was transformed into a multicultural one.

As the plantation economy matured, the "Big Five" emerged among planters that would eventually dominate the Hawai'ian economy for decades: Hackfield and Company (AMFAC), C. Brewer and Company, Theo Davis Company, Castle and Cooke, and Alexander and Baldwin. The nature of the sugar and pineapple plantations of the nineteenth and early twentieth centuries required a large concentration of land and capital as well as a disciplined workforce. Such large-scale operations also required that the political climate of Hawai'i be conducive to the interests of planters.

By the latter part of the nineteenth century, the practice of surrounding the Hawai'ian monarch with *haole* advisors made a mockery of political sovereignty. In 1873, the Hawai'ian throne was denied to Queen Emma by a group of planters who bribed, cajoled, and threatened electors into giving the crown to David Kalakaua. Pro-Emma supporters stormed the courthouse to register their outrage. This group was dispersed by U.S. Marines and British sailors whose assistance was requested by planter Charles Bishop to "quell the riotous mob" (Kent, 1983, p. 45).

In 1877, the planter oligarchy rewrote the Hawai'ian constitution and presented it to King Kalakaua for his signature under a state of armed siege. The constitution the king signed became known as the "bayonet constitution" to Hawai'ians. It made the king a ceremonial monarch, disenfranchised most Native Hawai'ians through strict property requirements, excluded all Asians from voting by declaring them aliens, and gave the vote only to U.S. citizens. After this action, the remaining days of even a ceremonial Hawai'ian monarchy were numbered.

Annexation

To paint a picture of something other than imperialistic motives by the United States in annexing Hawai'i would be doing a severe injustice to the facts. American military leaders saw Hawai'i as a coaling station for the Pacific fleet. Jacobs and Landau (1971) note, "The strength and influence of the pro-annexation Americans grew in Hawai'i and on the mainland, where the concepts of expansion and 'manifest destiny' were attracting a growing number of adherents" (p. 29). Manifest destiny, having reached the Pacific shore, seemed to set its sights on Hawai'i. The American planter oligarchy viewed annexation as an opportunity to guarantee, in perpetuity, the largest market in the world for Hawai'ian agricultural products. Expansionist, military, and economic motives worked collectively to end the last vestiges of Hawai'ian autonomy.

The first attempt at the deposition of the monarchy came on January 17, 1893. This coup was unofficially supported by U.S. troops and was led by Lorrin P. Thurston, a Honolulu publisher. U.S. minister John L. Stevens gave an order to disembark 162 troops from a U.S. Navy ship in Honolulu harbor ostensibly to protect American life and property. The troops had the coercive effect of forcing the queen's resignation. Controversy has always surrounded the issue of whether Minister Stevens acted on his own, or on direction from the U.S. government. Imperatore (1992) writes, "A review of Stevens' correspondence with the U.S. Secretary of State implies premeditation with the action simply awaiting opportunity" (p. 263).

Queen Liliuokalani ruled Hawai'i from 1891 to 1893. Her overthrow was an event from which Native Hawai'ians never recovered. The queen did not order her troops to battle the insurgents because the odds were overwhelmingly against her and she trusted the fairness of the United States. After losing her throne, the queen wrote a desperate plea to President Grover Cleveland to have it restored. President Cleveland sent an emissary, James Blount, to investigate the overthrow of the queen.

After receiving a report critical of the coup leaders, President Cleveland urged Sanford B. Dole and the conspirators to return the queen to her throne. Dole responded to Cleveland by telling him not to interfere in Hawai'ian affairs (Imperatore, 1992). This is ironic, since U.S. interference was largely responsible for the end of the monarchy.

The Republic of Hawai'i was established with Sanford B. Dole as its first and only president. Annexation by the United States was imminent. In 1898, under President William McKinley, the islands became part of the territorial possessions of the United States. Manifest destiny had triumphed again. The *haoles* who had once come as guests had managed to usurp the entire kingdom. Richard Olney (cited in Wright, 1972), the secretary of state under President McKinley, summarized the situation this way: "Hawai'i is ours," he said, "but as I look back upon the first steps in this miserable business and as I contemplate the means used to complete the outrage, I am ashamed of the whole affair" (p. 21).

From Territory to State

Once Hawai'i became a territory of the United States, its political and economic affairs were managed by forces on the mainland or by island elites responding to powerful people on the mainland. The territorial governorship of Hawai'i was a powerful position. The governor was appointed by the president of the United States. This appointment was heavily influenced by the recommendation of the U.S. Hawai'ian elite. The economy of the territory depended on favorable legislation from the U.S. Congress to subsidize Hawai'ian sugar and other agricultural products. The opening of the Panama Canal made it much easier for Hawai'ian products to reach markets on the East Coast of the United States. Favorable subsidies and market shares from the U.S. Congress made the Hawai'ian economy nearly totally reliant on sugar.

The Big Five corporations ran the economy of the islands through a variety of interlocking directorates and the vertical integration of businesses. To the average Native Hawai'ian, this world of Merchant Street in Honolulu was alien and remote. The original inhabitants of Hawai'i found themselves on the bottom rung of a plantation society, with little hope of improving their situation.

Prince Jonah Kuhio Kalanianaole became the territorial delegate to Congress by serving the interests of plantation owners. However, his frustrations would sometimes emerge, as they did in 1912, when he told a Hawai'ian audience (cited in Kent, 1983), "Under the political conditions in the territory, a man doesn't own his soul" (p. 45).

Native Hawai'ians' need for land was supposed to be reconciled in 1921 with the passage of the Hawai'ian Rehabilitation Act. Under the auspices of the Hawai'ian Homes Commission, 200,000 acres of land were to be distributed to landless Hawai'ians for small-scale farming. Most of the land actually distributed was not suitable for farming. Eventually, it passed into the hands of large plantation interests (Parker, 1989). The large amount of acreage devoted to export crops like sugar and pineapples meant that the traditional small-scale farming of the Native Hawai'ian was almost a relic from the past. Hawai'i had become a major importer of food from the mainland, even though historically it had been self-sufficient in food. Once again, actions purported to improve living conditions for Native Hawai'ians, like land distribution, resulted in benefits for other groups.

The plantation economy continued earning large profits with the support of the Republican Party, which had dominated island politics for the first fifty years of the twentieth century. On some plantations, managers monitored the actions of their workers by hanging pencils by strings from the ceilings of the voting booths. By noting in which direction the string moved, party preference could be determined. Anyone voting for a Democrat would be fired (Shaplen, 1982).

After World War II, political leaders in Hawai'i seriously began to discuss seeking statehood from the U.S. Congress. It was argued that becoming a state would guarantee the large U.S. market for Hawai'ian products. Hawai'ian leaders also believed that statehood would significantly increase the tourist industry and that many new construction and service jobs would be created.

While economic predictions turned out to be, in general, correct, Native Hawai'ians did not share proportionately in the new prosperity. As Joseph Keoloha, chairman of the State Office of Hawai'ian Affairs, observed, "Statehood was the final act following the confiscation of our land and the overthrow of our Queen, and Native Hawai'ians have mixed feelings about it" (Chrysler, 1984, p. 40).

NATIVE HAWAI'IANS TODAY

Social Class and Politics

Present-day Hawai'i is a polyglot of peoples with varied backgrounds. There are sizable communities of Japanese and Filipino Americans. There are smaller communities of Portuguese, Chinese, Korean, and Puerto Rican Americans, many of whom originally came to work in Hawai'ian agriculture. There are also a few thousand African Americans in Hawai'i, as well as the still powerful *haoles*. Americans of Japanese ancestry have been especially successful in the political arena. Chinese Americans have become business leaders in many areas. Asian Americans make up a majority of Hawai'i's population; it is the only U.S. state with this characteristic.

Upward mobility by Asian Americans in Hawai'i contrasts sharply with their primary status as agricultural workers a couple of generations ago. This change in status has caused some interethnic discord and ill feelings. Many Native Hawai'ians, who perceived the *haoles* as the holders of all-powerful positions, often see Japanese Americans in their place. Other groups besides Native Hawai'ians, who find themselves disproportionately represented in the lower economic classes, complain of difficulties in obtaining top jobs.

Dissatisfaction bred by the legacy of a caste system caused a major political movement. Organizers tried to convince workers that their future would best be served by identifying politically with their working-class brethren regardless of their ethnic origin. This movement achieved its first major success in 1954, when the Democratic Party broke the traditional Republican control in both houses of the territorial legislature. The man given a major share of the credit for this triumph was John A. Burns, who came to play an important role in Hawai'i's political future by lobbying vigorously for statehood and later becoming governor.

The 1954 victory was generally viewed as the beginning of a progressive movement in island politics. By 1970, the Democrats were the solidly entrenched party, and John Burns was a candidate for a third term as governor. The main opposition within the Democratic Party came from Tom Gill, who had been lieutenant governor under Burns. Gill charged that what may have started out as progressive political forces in 1954 had now become a power structure that was working together with the business and economic interests they originally opposed. The Gill campaign had a strong issue orientation, capitalizing on respect for Hawai'i's fragile environment. Governor Burns, with a network of loyal supporters on several islands, relied primarily on a media campaign and was successful in winning a third term.

In 1974, George Ariyoshi became the first non-*haole* governor of Hawai'i. He was also the first U.S. governor of Japanese or Asian ancestry. Ariyoshi was later reelected to second and third terms of office. Governor Ariyoshi was followed by John D. Waihee in 1986. Governor Waihee became the first person of Hawai'ian ancestry to hold this office and was reelected in 1990. Ben Cayetano was elected governor in 1994 and reelected in 1998. Cayetano was the first U.S. governor of Filipino ancestry. Linda Lingle, a *haole* Republican, became the first female governor of Hawai'i in 2003. Neither major political party in Hawai'i has a homogeneous political base. To make a viable appeal to a diverse society, each party has had leaders who represent most of Hawai'i's major ethnic groups.

The issues that are likely to dominate Hawai'ian politics in the foreseeable future are land use, tourism, economic diversification, Native Hawai'ian self-determination, and the preservation of Hawai'i's fragile natural environment. In 1996, 55% of all land in Hawai'i was privately owned (Hawai'i State, 1996), and 95% of that land was held by seventy-odd corporations or individuals (Bank of Hawai'i Reports, 1999, 2001; Shaplen, 1982). The zoning and distribution of land are likely to evoke strong feelings among many Hawai'ians. Tourism is clearly Hawai'i's largest source of income. In 1959, Hawai'i had only about 243,000 visitors each year. By 2005, the total number of annual visitors to Hawai'i was nearly 12 million, and their economic impact on the islands was almost 13.5 billion dollars (*State of Hawai'i Fact Book*, 2005).

Some critics of the tourist-dependent economy note that visitors cannot be relied on as a stable source of income. Hawai'i's tourist revenues were very adversely affected following the attacks on the World Trade Center and the Pentagon on September 11, 2001, as the overall air travel volume declined globally. Tourism has returned to normal levels since 2001, but Hawai'ians were reminded of the reliance of their economy on a single source.

There are many viewpoints, but no clear consensus on exactly how to diversify Hawai'i's economy. Agricultural land is too expensive for farming to ever regain its former prominence. Transportation and labor costs work against Hawai'i becoming a major manufacturing center. Meanwhile, tourism remains the mainstay of the economy but it is coupled with extensive real estate development. The numbers of timeshares and luxury real estate properties are rapidly increasing on the islands. When tourists come to Hawai'i, many of them are lured into presentations for purchasing timeshares. Affluent Americans from the mainland purchase pieces of Hawai'i because it is still an exotic enough locale that is not far out of the comfort zone of their hometowns and cities. The growth in development on the islands continues to place major strains on Native Hawai'ians.

Adapting Native Hawai'ian Values

The Hawai'ian spirit of *aloha aina* (love for the land) had a resurgence in response to growing developments through language revitalization, land restoration, and independence movements in the 1970s (Castanha, 1996; Kamana & Wilson, 1996; Tabrah, 1980). These activist movements led to the creation of the Office of Hawai'ian Affairs in 1978 by an amendment to the state constitution (Castanha, 1996).

The traditional value of *ohana* is a cooperative system of social relationships found within an extended family. This value of *ohana* is sometimes counterproductive to Hawai'ian children attending school, where cooperation on academic work may be perceived as "cheating." Also, Hawai'ian youngsters do not particularly relish the peer competition engendered in many school situations, and consequently they often do not respond well to competitive tasks.

The Hawai'ian value of *kokua* supports a traditional economic system based on cooperation, with some element of competition. Under this system, one expression of *kokua* (cooperation) should be repaid with another expression of *kokua*. In this manner, the status of the individual is enhanced (Ogawa, 1978). As the trend toward development continues in a state with limited natural resources, the spirit of *kokua* may point the way toward an accommodation among competing groups.

Another Hawai'ian value that could prove helpful in a multiethnic and growing society is *ho'oponopono*. Literally, this means "setting to right of wrongs" (Ogawa, 1978, p. 579). In early Hawai'i, *ho'oponopono* meant that all people had an opportunity to speak out on a problem until a solution was reached that would be binding on all parties. In Hawai'i today, *ho'oponopono* is frequently used—and some would argue misused—in institutions such as courts (Merry, 2001).

Native Hawai'ians: Population, Economic Standing, and Education

The classification of Native Hawai'ians is difficult because the overwhelming majority of them are part Hawai'ian. Estimates vary as to the number of part Hawai'ians. According to the 2000 census, 282,667 people identified themselves as at least part Native Hawai'ian or Pacific Islander, an increase of 74.2% from 1990. But 113,539 described themselves solely as a member of that group, a decrease of 30% (Dingeman & Bricking, 2001). These figures contrast sharply with the estimated 800,000 Native Hawai'ians on the islands when Captain Cook first visited in 1778.

Under current law, only people with 50% or more Hawai'ian blood are entitled to land and to medical and legal benefits. In 2007, it was estimated that only 50,000 to 60,000 people had this Native Hawai'ian blood quantum. A significant issue in Hawai'i is whether to lower the 50% requirement in order to allow more people to qualify for any program designated for Native Hawai'ians. Even if the current policy is followed, the matter of establishing Hawai'ian lineage to meet the 50% requirement often leaves the Office of Hawai'ian Affairs in a quandary.

U.S. Census Bureau data from 2005 show that Native Hawai'ians have a median family income of $49,453. This places them ahead of the median family income for all Pacific Islanders of $42,915 but slightly behind the median income for all U.S. families of $50,046 (Harris & Jones, 2005).

Native Hawai'ians have generally not adapted to the competitive nature of the dominant Western society. Rather, they are oriented toward affiliation, not competition. Friendship and family harmony, especially sibling relationships, are important social aspects for Native Hawai'ians. Research indicates that Hawai'ian schoolchildren achieve better when they are evaluated collectively rather than individually (McIntyre, 1996; Tharp & Yamauchi, 1994; Yamauchi, Ceppi, & Lau-Smith, 2000). Kathryn Au (1981) and Roland G. Tharp (1982), working in the Kamehameha Early Education Program (KEEP), found that both student participation and standardized achievement test scores increased when classroom teachers used strategies consistent with the cultures of Native Hawai'ian students and used the children's experiences in reading instruction.

The research described above has influenced the creation of schools whose curricula are based on Hawai'ian values. First among such schools was the Kamehameha School, a K–12 private school for children of Hawai'ian ancestry founded in 1887 (Clarke et al., 1996; Tharp & Yamauchi, 1994; Yamauchi, Ceppi, & Lau-Smith, 2000). The more recent charter school movement has further made it possible to offer publicly funded school programs based on bilingual and bicultural curricula. This offers the possibility for Native Hawai'ian students to acquire a strong background in Hawai'ian language and culture while at the same time developing traditional mainstream academic skills such as individual and field independent learning styles.

There are some scholars who have concerns about the implementation of the Native Hawai'ian studies program in the state's public schools. Kaomea (2005) is concerned that most teachers in the state are not Native Hawai'ian and have not had appropriate training to teach Native Hawai'ian studies. She believes that many teachers will focus on the exotic elements of ancient Hawai'ian culture and thus give students a skewed perspective of the topic. While Kaomea believes that you don't have to be a Native Hawai'ian to understand and teach Native Hawai'ian history, language, and culture, she is concerned about the lessons and images being presented by minimally trained teachers who may be teaching content about Native Hawai'ians merely to fulfill a mandate but don't believe in its legitimacy.

The Hawai'ian Sovereignty Movement

The Black civil rights movement, the anti-Vietnam protests, and the other movements for civil rights during the 1960s and 1970s stimulated the rise of the Hawai'ian sovereignty movement that has political as well as cultural aims (Castanha, 1996). Beginning in the 1970s, a militant grassroots movement for Native Hawai'ian rights began. A primary goal of these nationalist groups is to return lost economic and political power to people of Hawai'ian ancestry. Castanha (1996) gives an overview of the Hawai'ian sovereignty movement:

> In the 1980s and 1990s, major sovereignty organizations . . . formed to demand the return of lands, self-governance and independence based on the international rights of self-determination. In 1985, the Institute for the Advancement of Hawai'ian Affairs was created. In 1991, Hui Na 'auao, a coalition of 47 Hawai'ian groups focusing on sovereignty education, was organized. In 1992, the Ohana Council of Hawai'ian Kingdom . . . commenced. Also in 1992, the restored Kingdom of Hawai'i began. (p. 8)

Along with the Hawai'ian sovereignty movement, there has been a revision in Hawai'ian history that does not consider the whole era of Hawai'ian monarchy to be a glorious age of benevolent rule. Among some of these Hawai'ian nationalists, Kamehameha III is viewed as a ruler who broke up the traditional system of land ownership and started the islands on their steady slide toward *haole* control. Queen Liliuokalani is viewed as a great monarch who tried to retain power in the hands of Hawai'ians while facing insurmountable odds.

Militancy is reflected in the formation of such groups as the *Kokua* and the Hawai'ians. Membership in the *Kokua* is limited to non-*haoles*. This group espouses a transformative view of Hawai'ian society. The Hawai'ians limit their membership to people with at least some Hawai'ian blood. Their ideology is more moderate than the *Kokua*. The existence of these two groups has had little influence on the economic status of most Native Hawai'ians.

Another manifestation of sovereignty was the Free Kahoolawe movement in the mid 1970s. Kahoolawe, a small island owned by the military six miles off the coast of Maui, had been used for bombing practice since World War II. The movement began with an occupation of the island by a group of Native Hawai'ians who were joined by people from nearly all segments of Hawai'i's population. The goal of the Free Kahoolawe movement was the return of the island to state government jurisdiction and public access (Tabrah, 1980). In 1994, the Free Kahoolawe movement succeeded, and the U.S. Navy returned Kahoolawe to the state of Hawai'i. The Hawai'ian legislature designated Kahoolawe as a cultural and educational preserve. The Free Kahoolawe movement paralleled the conflict between the residents of Vieques Island (in Puerto Rico) and the U.S. Navy over the use of that island for maneuvers and as a bombing range. This conflict eventually ended similarly, with the U.S. Navy stopping its use of Vieques.

There can be little doubt that a true Hawai'ian renaissance occurred in the 1970s. This trend represented a sharp contrast to predictions that the Hawai'ian culture was slowly being extinguished. The renaissance went beyond a renewal of interest in cultural activities. It resulted in a new economic and political conscious-ness, an increasing involvement with other Pacific Island peoples (Kanahele, 1982), as well as an effort to revitalize the Hawai'ian language. Resulting from the latter were Hawai'ian immersion K–12 school programs and the development of new undergraduate and graduate programs in Hawai'ian studies and Hawai'ian lan-guage (Warschauer & Donaghy, 1997). Overall, it can be said that the Hawai'ian renaissance arrived at a propitious time, when Native Hawai'ian culture was being practiced less and less.

The issue of sovereignty for Native Hawai'ians has received added attention in recent years. Dudley and Agard (1990) chronicle the history of the Hawai'ian sov-ereignty movement and discuss various forms of possible Native Hawai'ian sover-eignty. Among the variations are (1) the American Indian model, (2) a broader model of "nation within a nation" that American Indians enjoy, or (3) restoration of the Hawai'ian nation.

There are strong differences of opinion on Hawai'ian sovereignty among Hawai'i's people, even among Native Hawai'ians. Those who favor it generally see the movement as a way to right historical wrongs. Those who oppose it often say that it will polarize Native Hawai'ians and non-Hawai'ians or are concerned that the outcome may be unfair to non-Hawai'ians.

The Hawai'ian Sovereignty Elections Council had planned to conduct an election in 1996, with the electorate being limited to persons of Hawai'ian ancestry over the age of 18. This election was successfully challenged by a rancher from Hawai'i Island, Fred Rice, in the case of *Rice* v. *Cayetano*. The Supreme Court ruled that the electorate for Office of Hawai'ian Affairs (OHA) trustees could not be limited to persons of Hawai'ian ancestry. Subsequently, an election was held with the full electorate eligible, and most of the trustees elected were individuals of Hawai'ian ancestry.

In 2001, Senator Daniel Akaka and Representative Neil Abercrombie spon-sored a bill that would establish a "governmental entity" to negotiate with the state government of Hawai'i and the U.S. government over resources for Native Hawai'ians. Supporters of the bill pointed to the example of Native Americans who are accorded similar rights of local self-government. Opponents said that this bill would set up a government based on racial classifications and would polarize Hawai'ian society. In 2006, the Akaka bill failed to get approval in the U.S. Senate. Some Native Hawai'ians opposed the Akaka bill because it didn't go far enough in granting sovereignty, while other opponents charged it went too far. Time will tell if the Akaka bill, or some modification of it, is revived in Congress.

Environmental Issues

Native Hawai'ians are vitally concerned with the future of their islands' natural envi-ronment. High real estate prices in Hawai'i promote vertical expansion of new dwellings, but the environment of the islands is particularly fragile. Foreign investment is playing an ever-increasing role in Hawai'i's economy. An important issue is whether absentee landlords will be appropriately concerned with the environmental impact of development, particularly if such measures reduce profit margins. These quality-of-life issues are important to all Hawai'ians but are particularly salient to Native Hawai'ians, whose culture is inextricably tied to the land.

In an environment where land is scarce and most of it is environmentally fragile, conflicts inevitably arise over appropriate uses for land. Compared to other states, much Hawai'ian land is leased as opposed to being owned. Development has to consider the ecological impact, but it must also ensure that land to be developed contains no ancient Native Hawai'ian burial sites. Development projects have been halted for the latter reason. Many Native Hawai'ians become quite concerned when development intrudes on final resting places. The indigenous perspective will continue to conflict with development in Hawai'i. As in many other locations, the economic imperative frequently trumps the cultural one.

Future Challenges and Native Resiliency

The story of Native Hawai'ians is a complex one. In spite of facing numerous obstacles since European contact, it can be argued that a key Native Hawai'ian characteristic is resiliency. They are confronted with daily paradoxes. They are employed in an economy heavily dependent on tourism (and thus on more development) while *aloha aina* (love for the land) suggests keeping land pristine. They participate in a modern and highly competitive society, yet many cling to the value of *ohana,* which favors group cooperation over competition. Like many other indigenous groups who were forced to cope with Western culture, Native Hawai'ians realize that many of their traditional values conflict with the norms of a society ruled by market forces.

TEACHING STRATEGIES

The concept of expansion can be illustrated in many ways. The Native Hawai'ians provide a classic case of the displacement of a native population because they were an obstacle to the expanding forces. Their story can be related to other native inhabitants who suffered a similar fate.

Concept

Expansion

Generalization: As a nation expands to obtain territory, often the rights of the native population are not protected.

1. After giving the students sufficient background information about the Native Hawai'ians, ask them to make a list of factors that apply both to the Native

Hawai'ians and the American Indians. These factors can include both past and present situations. Afterward, these points can be grouped, classified, and discussed.

2. Organize your students into small groups and present them with this hypothetical situation: One person in the group would be chosen to supervise and control the financial affairs of all the members. What problems might develop with such an arrangement? A tape could be made of their reactions. Later, this tape could be replayed and compared to what occurred between American advisers and Hawai'ian rulers.

3. Role-play the following situation, which occurred in Hawai'i in 1845. The *haole* adviser to the king is trying to persuade him to grant some land to Mr. Farmer, a prospective planter. Kaeo, a Native Hawai'ian, opposes the entire proposition. After the role-play situation, ask the students the questions that follow. The role descriptions are as follows:

> **King Kamehameha III:** He is indecisive over what to say to the planter, yet he greatly respects the advice of his *haole* counsel, Mr. George Bennett.
>
> **George Bennett:** Adviser to the king and a good friend of Mr. Farmer, whose interests he protects. He has been a missionary for nearly twenty years.
>
> **Floyd S. Farmer:** Planter and business tycoon. He intends to start sugar plantations in Hawai'i because of the predictably warm weather.
>
> **Kaeo:** A Native Hawai'ian and a member of the king's court. He vehemently opposes the granting of any more land to *haoles*.

Questions

1. Did George Bennett succeed in persuading the king to grant the land to Mr. Farmer? If so, why? If not, why?
2. Was Kaeo successful in his opposition to the land deal? Why or why not?
3. Did Mr. Farmer tell the king his plans for using native labor? Why or why not?
4. Did the king decide to grant the land lease to Mr. Farmer? If he did, what were his reasons? If he did not, why not?
5. Did Mr. Bennett use his position as a missionary to help his argument? Why or why not?

Concept

Adaptation

Generalization: When a native culture finds itself surrounded by a dominant culture, it becomes increasingly difficult to maintain the native culture.

Read the following story to the class and ask the questions that follow.

A HAWAI'IAN DILEMMA

The old ramshackle house had stood relatively unchanged since the family had obtained it more than forty years ago from the Hawai'ian Homes Commission. Around it were the two acres of vegetables that had provided subsistence for the Panui family during that time. Mary Panui lived on the property along with her sons, George and Eddie. Mr. Panui had died five years before and, since that time, things had not been the same. One afternoon George was weeding one of the vegetable patches when Eddie returned from a day in town. Feeling that he deserved some help, George asked his brother, "Hey, aren't you going to help out around here?"

Eddie answered, "No, I have gotten a job in town with the tourist agency. I will drive the mainland *haoles* around during the day, and in the evenings I will dance at the luaus."

George couldn't believe his ears. After all of those years that their father had taught them to respect their Hawai'ian heritage, his brother was suddenly changing. "Eddie, how can you do a thing like this?" George wondered. "It would have broken Dad's heart, and anyway, what will Mother say?"

Eddie looked at his brother casually and said, "I have been weeding taro root all of my life and I'm tired of it. I know Dad would probably say that I'm putting our culture up for sale but it's the only way to get ahead!"

The two brothers entered the home where Mary Panui was cooking dinner and told her of their conversation. The old woman with the creased brow was also unhappy with what Eddie was considering. However, she could not deny that the vegetable gardens would never provide more than a subsistence living.

Seeing his mother caught up in the dilemma, George tried one last time. "Eddie, can you imagine yourself in one of those flowered shirts selling shell necklaces to the tourists? Where is your pride?"

Eddie thought for a moment and answered smugly, "Pride doesn't fill your wallet; when will you realize that?"

With that, George started out of the door but stopped short and told his brother, "I may never have much money to my name, but I'll never be a practicing Hawai'ian!"

Questions

1. What would you have done if you had been Eddie Panui?
2. Do you think Eddie's brother is justified in calling him a practicing (commercialized) Hawai'ian?
3. Can you think of other ethnic groups in other settings that have had their culture commercialized? If so, how much was this trend sanctioned or resisted by the group?

REFERENCES

Au, K. (1980). Participation Structures in a Reading Lesson with Hawai'ian Children. *Anthropology and Education Quarterly, 11* (2), 91–115.

Castanha, A. (1996). The Hawai'ian Sovereignty Movement: Roles and Impacts on Non-Hawai'ians. Master's thesis, University of Hawai'i. Available online at http://www.hookele.com/non-hawai'ians/abstract.html.

Chrysler, K. M. (1984, August 27). Hawai'i: Youngest State Finds Its Place in the Sun. *U.S. News and World Report*, p. 40.

Clarke, M. A., Davis, A., Rhodes, L. K., & DeLott Baker, E. (1996). Conceptual Framework and Literature Review: Minority Status and School Success. In *Creating Coherence: High-Achieving Classrooms for Minority Students (HACMS)*. University of Colorado at Denver, Research Report, Chapter VI. Available online at http://carbon.cudenver.edu/~wdavis/chapt6_min.html.

Day, A. G. (1968). *Hawai'i and Its People*. New York: Meredith Press.

Dingeman, R., & Bricking, T. (2001, March 20). Census Lists More Native Hawai'ians Than Ever. *Honolulu Advertiser.*

Dudley, M. K., & Agard, K. K. (1990). *A Call for Hawai'ian Sovereignty*. Honolulu: Na Kane O Ka Malo Press.

Egan, T. (1990, January 20). Blood and Benefits: Hawai'i to Vote on Ancestral Rights. *Miami Herald,* p. 29A.

Harris, P. M., & Jones, N. A. (2005). *We the People: Pacific Islanders in the United States*. Washington, DC: U.S. Census Bureau.

Hawai'i Grappling with Sovereignty Movement. (1994, June 3). *Miami Herald,* p. 7A.

Hawai'i State, Department of Business, Economic Development and Tourism. (1998). *The State of Hawai'i Data Book: A Statistical Abstract, 1996*. In *Native Hawai'ian Data Book, 1998*, table 3.1. Available online at http://oha.org/databook/tab3-01.98.html.

Hawai'i State, Department of Health. (1996). *Vital Statistics Supplement, 1996*. In *Native Hawai'ian Data Book, 1998*, table 1.32. Available online at http://oha.org/databook/tab1-32.98.html.

Howard, A. (1974). *Ain't No Big Thing: Coping Strategies in a Hawai'ian American Community*. Honolulu: University Press of Hawai'i.

Imperatore, W. (1992, November/December). The Deposing of the Hawai'ian Monarch: The Changing Narrative in Textbooks. *The Social Studies, 83,* 261–266.

Jacobs, P., & Landau, S., with Pell, E. (1971). *To Serve the Devil: Colonials and Sojourners* (vol. 2). New York: Vintage.

Kamana, K., & Wilson, W. H. (1996). Hawai'ian Language Programs. In G. Cantoni (Ed.), *Stabilizing Indigenous Languages*. Flagstaff: Center for Excellence in Education, Northern Arizona University. Available online at http://www.ncbe.gwu.edu/miscpubs/stabilize/additional/Hawai'ian.htm.

Kanahele, G. (1982). *Hawai'ian Renaissance*. Honolulu: Project Waiaha.

Kaomea, J. (2005). Indigenous Studies in the Elementary Curriculum: A Cautionary Hawai'ian Example. *Anthropology and Education Quarterly, 36,* 24–42.

Kent, N. J. (1983). *Hawai'i: Islands under the Influence*. New York: Monthly Review Press.

Lind, A. (1980). *Hawai'i's People*. Honolulu: University Press of Hawai'i.

McIntyre, T. (1996). Does the Way We Teach Create Behavior Disorders in Culturally Different Students? *Education and Treatment of Children, 19* (3), 354–370.

Merry, S. E. (2001). Rights, Religion, and Community: Approaches to Violence against Women in the Context of Globalization. *Law and Society Review, 25,* 39–88.

Ogawa, D. (1978). *Kodomo No Tame Ni*. Honolulu: University Press of Hawai'i.

Parker, L. S. (1989). *Native American Estate: The Struggle over Indian and Hawai'ian Lands*. Honolulu: University Press of Hawai'i.

Population Reference Bureau. (2000). *United States Population Data Sheet of the Population Reference Bureau*. Washington, DC: Author.

Shaplen, R. (1982, September 6). A Reporter at Large: Islands of Disenchantment. *New Yorker,* p. 85.

Stannard, D. E. (1989). *Before the Horror: The Population of Hawai'i on the Eve of Western Contact*. Honolulu: Social Science Research Institute, University of Hawai'i.

State of Hawai'i Fact Book. (2005). Retrieved at www.hawaii.gov/debt.

Tabrah, R. (1980). *Hawai'i: A Bicentennial History*. New York: Norton.

Takaki, R. (1983). *Pau Hana: Plantation Life and Labor in Hawai'i*. Honolulu: University Press of Hawai'i.

Tharp, R. G. (1982). The Effective Instruction of Comprehension: Results and Description of the Kamehameha Early Childhood Education Program. *Reading Research Quarterly, 17* (4), 503–527.

Tharp, R. G., & Yamauchi, L. A. (1994). Effective Instructional Conversation in Native American Classrooms. *Educational Practice Report, 10.* Available online at http://www.ncbe.gwu.edu/miscpubs/ncrcdsll/epr10.htm.

Trask, H. K. (1992). Racism against Native Hawai'ians at the University of Hawai'i. *Amerasian Journal, 18* (3), 33–50.

U.S. Census Bureau. (2000a). Redistricting Data (P.L. 94-171). Summary File compiled by the Hawai'i State Department of Business, Economic Development and Tourism, Hawai'i State Data Center. Available online at http://www.Hawai'i.gov/dbedt/census2k/pltable3.html.

U.S. Census Bureau. (2000b). Summary File 1. Proximity Census 2000 School District General Demographic Characteristics Profile Geographic Area: State of Hawai'i. Available online at http://proximityone.com.

Warschauer, M., & Donaghy, K. (1997). Leokï: A Powerful Voice of Hawai'ian Language Revitalization. *Computer Assisted Language Learning, 10* (4), 349–362. Available online at http://www.gse.uci.edu/markw/leoki.html.

Woerner, B. (2000, August). Big Island's Charter Schools. *Waimea Gazette.* Available online at http://www.k12.hi.us/~bwoerner/ipcs/bigislandcharters.html.

Wright, T. (1972). *The Disenchanted Isles.* New York: Dial Press.

Yamauchi, L. A., Ceppi, A. K., & Lau-Smith, J.-A. (2000). Teaching in a Hawai'ian Context: Educator Perspectives on the Hawai'ian Language Immersion Program. *Bilingual Research Journal, 24*(4). Available online at http://brj.asu.edu/v244/articles/art5.html#theory.

ANNOTATED BIBLIOGRAPHY

Books for Teachers

Especially Recommended

Chun, M. C. (2006). *Ka Wana Series* [set]. Honolulu: Curriculum Research and Development Group, University of Hawai'i.
Eleven concise, yet rich, volumes on several Hawai'ian cultural traditions and practices that cover a range of subjects, including ethics and philosophy, leadership, education, health, management, protocol, and religious beliefs. The author, a cultural specialist, researcher, and scholar, uses traditional and historical examples to show behavior, thoughts, and values and then analyzes events in both traditional and contemporary contexts.

Hartwell, J. (1996). *Na Mamo: Hawai'ian People Today.* Honolulu: 'Ai Pohaku Press.
A collection of ten life histories of contemporary Hawai'ians, the author provides readers with an understanding of how native culture is being perpetuated by profiling Hawai'ians of various walks who are maintaining their heritage in today's society.

Kamakau, S. M. (1992). *Ka Po'e Kahiko: The People of Old.* Honolulu: Bishop Museum Press.
A translation of Samuel Kamakau's weekly newspaper articles from 1866 to 1871 that primarily focuses on ancient Hawai'ian customs and beliefs. Kamakau's work is considered one of three classics, along with both Davida Malo and John Papa Ii's works, which provide a composite picture of ancient times in transition.

Kame'eleihiwa, L. (1992). *Native Land and Foreign Desires: Pehea La E Pono Ai?* Honolulu: Bishop Museum Press.
A recounting of history, from a Hawai'ian perspective, that centers on the 1848 Great Mahele, the pivotal event that officially transformed the Hawai'ian system of land tenure from communal use to private ownership. Kame'eleihiwa's work is especially significant due to her focus on a native viewpoint and for her analysis of Hawai'ian metaphors and metaphoric shifts regarding land, politics, and religion.

Kanahele, G. H. S. (1986). *Ku Kanaka, Stand Tall: A Search for Hawai'ian Values.* Honolulu: University of Hawai'i Press.

A monumental work that gets to the heart of pressing issues; sample topics include Hawai'ian identity, feelings of inferiority, and pride. Kanahele concentrated on Hawai'ian achievements, basic beliefs, and values—especially *aloha*—as sources of identity and self-esteem for Hawai'ians.

King, S. P., & Roth, R. W. (2006). *Broken Trust: Greed, Mismanagement and Political Manipulation at America's Largest Charitable Trust*. Honolulu: University of Hawai'i Press.
This source examines how the board of trustees responsible for the multibillion-dollar trust for the Kamehameha Schools shirked its responsibilities.

McGregor, D. P. (2007). *Na Kua'aina: Living Hawai'ian Culture*. Honolulu: University of Hawai'i Press.
A history, drawn from oral history interviews, that describes a worldview and lifestyle found among the *kua'aina*, Native Hawai'ians who remain in rural communities, living apart from mainstream society in Hawai'i. McGregor describes these rural communities and emphasizes their importance as places where traditional Native Hawai'ian culture endures.

Osorio, J. K. K. (2002). *Dismembering Lahui: A History of the Hawai'ian Nation to 1887*. Honolulu: University of Hawai'i Press.
A political history that focuses on the effect Western law had on the national identity of Native Hawai'ians. Osorio provides a detailed account, from a Native Hawai'ian perspective, about the slow, insinuating, colonial invasion of people, ideas, and institutions. He also details the courageous and complex Native Hawai'ian response to the invasion.

Silva, N. K. (2004). *Aloha Betrayed: Native Hawai'ian Resistance to American Colonialism*. Durham, NC: Duke University Press.
Silva's book strongly refutes the myth that Native Hawai'ians passively accepted the loss of their nation and the erosion of their culture. She does this by using a wealth of material written in Hawai'ian as the basis to document the many forms of Native Hawai'ian resistance.

Trask, H. K. (1999). *From a Native Daughter: Colonialism and Sovereignty in Hawai'i*. Honolulu: University of Hawai'i Press.
Trask argues for Hawai'ian sovereignty and against institutional racism perpetrated against Native Hawai'ians. This collection of powerful pieces clearly presents these issues and provides an unmistakable and coherent vision for implementing Native Hawai'ian self-determination.

Young, K. G. T. (1998). *Rethinking the Native Hawai'ian Past*. New York: Garland.
An account that focuses on the changing roles of lower-ranked chiefs over time. The significance of this work is Young's use of a time-honored Hawai'ian method of composition as a method to interpret the past.

Other Books

Aoude, I. G. (Ed.). (1999). *The Ethnic Studies Story: Politics and Social Movements in Hawai'i—Essays in Honor of Marion Kelly*. Honolulu: University of Hawai'i Press.
A collection of interdisciplinary essays that address contemporary social, cultural, and political movements in Hawai'i.

Barrère, D. B., Pukui, M. K., & Kelly, M. (1980). *Hula: Historical Perspectives*. Honolulu: Bishop Museum Press.
A historical study of the hula, a vital expression of Hawai'ian culture through dance, chant, and instrumentation. It focuses on the role of the hula by describing the legends, myths, ceremonies, and performances associated with this cultural form.

Becket, J., & Singer, J. (1999). *Pana Oahu: Sacred Stones, Sacred Land*. Honolulu: University of Hawai'i Press.

A collection of photographs and descriptions of specific endangered ancient cultural sites on the island of O'ahu, Hawai'i.

Beckwith, M. W. (1972). *The Kumulipo: A Hawai'ian Creation Chant.* Honolulu: University of Hawai'i Press.
A translation of the sacred Hawai'ian creation chant with commentary.

Beckwith, M. W. (1970). *Hawai'ian Mythology.* Honolulu: University of Hawai'i Press.
A highly regarded scholarly work that is considered to be a valuable guide to Native Hawai'ian mythology.

Benham, M. K. P., & Heck, R. H. (1998). *Culture and Educational Policy in Hawai'i: The Silencing of Native Voices.* Mahwah, NJ: Erlbaum.
A history of public schools in Hawai'i that focuses on how educational policy and politics have marginalized Native Hawai'ians.

Budnick, R. (1992). *Stolen Kingdom: An American Conspiracy.* Honolulu: Aloha Press.
Budnick drew from official reports, correspondence, congressional testimony, and memoirs to recount the overthrow of the Hawai'ian kingdom by American businessmen.

Budnick, R. (2005). *Hawai'i's Forgotten History, 1900–1999: The Good . . . The Bad . . . The Embarrassing.* Honolulu: Aloha Press.
A chronology of 2001 important and little-known events researched from 300 books and 8,000 newspapers. Covering a variety of topics, this work is most significant for its reporting of interesting events in Hawai'i's ethnic and educational histories.

Coffman, T. (1998). *Nation Within: The Story of America's Annexation of the Nation of Hawai'i.* Kaneohe, HI: Epicenter.
This book by an independent writer and documentary filmmaker recounts the events around the U.S. annexation of Hawai'i by reexamining America's history in the Pacific.

Coffman, T. (2003). *The Island Edge of America: A Political History of Hawai'i.* Honolulu: University of Hawai'i Press.
A remarkably detailed history of politics in Hawai'i since the U.S. annexation.

Daws, G. (1976). *Shoal of Time: A History of the Hawai'ian Islands.* Honolulu: University of Hawai'i Press.
An interpretive history of Hawai'i from European contact to statehood. This often-referenced history of Hawai'i is popular for its readability and for the fact that it covers events from 1778 to 1959 in a single volume.

Day, A. G. (1984). *History Makers of Hawai'i: A Biographical Dictionary.* Honolulu: Mutual Publishing of Honolulu.
A reference volume containing the brief biographies of five hundred notable figures in Hawai'i history.

Dudley, M. K. (1990). *A Hawai'ian Nation I: Man, Gods, and Nature.* Honolulu: Na Kane O Ka Malo Press.
A concise description of Native Hawai'ian worship beliefs and practices drawn from Dudley's examination of published sources. The book provides an explanation of an ancient Hawai'ian worldview and is a prelude to its accompanying volume, *A Call for Hawai'ian Sovereignty.*

Dudley, M. K., & Agard, K. K. (1990). *A Hawai'ian Nation II: A Call for Hawai'ian Sovereignty.* Honolulu: Na Kane O Ka Malo Press.
This volume traces the history of injustices committed against Native Hawai'ians. It also presents the history of the sovereignty movement and an account of the movement at the time of its writing in the late 1980s.

Elbert, S. H. (Ed.). (1959). *Selections from Fornander's Hawai'ian Antiquities and Folk-Lore.* Honolulu: University of Hawai'i Press.

A collection of stories recorded in written Hawai'ian by Abraham Fornander in the 1860s and 1870s, including their subsequent English translations by Martha Beckwith.

Frazier, F. N. (2001). *The True Story of Kaluaikoolau: As Told by His Wife, Piilani*. Honolulu: University of Hawai'i Press.
An English translation by Frances Frazier of the story of Koolau. After contracting Hansen's disease, formerly known as leprosy, in 1892, Koolau fled to a remote valley and killed three authorities to avoid the forced separation that was the public health policy at the time. His story became a powerful symbol of resistance.

Fuchs, L. H. (1961). *Hawai'i Pono*. New York: Harcourt, Brace and World.
Perhaps the most highly regarded book on the social history of Hawai'i. It covers the period from annexation through statehood.

Furrer, R. P. (Ed.). (1993). *He Alo A He Alo (Face to Face): Hawai'ian Voices on Sovereignty*. Honolulu: American Friends Service Committee, Hawai'i Area Office.
A record of art, song, prose, and poetry of what Hawai'ian sovereignty means to a broad cross-section of Native Hawai'ians who submitted their thoughts, feelings, and impressions of the movement.

Grant, G. (1996). *Obake Files: Ghostly Encounters in Supernatural Hawai'i*. Honolulu: Mutual Publishing.
A compilation of supernatural stories collected by the author, who was a noted collector of ghost stories in Hawai'i. The tales, many of which involve Native Hawai'ian beliefs, provide a window through which one can glean interesting aspects of Hawai'ian culture.

Grant, G., & Hymer, B. (2000). *Hawai'i Looking Back: An Illustrated History of the Islands*. Honolulu: Mutual Publishing.
A large coffee table book of spectacular photos and artwork depicting aspects of life in Hawai'i. The illustrations are accompanied by captions and texts describing various events in Hawai'i and their historical contexts.

Halualani, R. T. (2002). *In the Name of Hawai'ians: Native Identities and Cultural Politics*. Minneapolis: University of Minnesota Press.
Halualani, a Native Hawai'ian born and raised in California, offers a perspective informed by critical, cultural, and postcolonial studies in this work that focuses on Native Hawai'ian identity, social agency, and power.

Handy, E. S. C., & Handy, E. G. (1991). *Native Planters in Old Hawai'i: Their Life, Lore, and Environment*. Honolulu: Bishop Museum Press.
An ethnographic study of traditional Native Hawai'ian culture that focuses on cultivation practices, beliefs, and rituals.

Handy, E. S. C., & Pukui, M. K. (1998). *The Polynesian Family System in Ka'u Hawai'i*. Honolulu: Mutual Publishing.
Considered the seminal study on Native Hawai'ian family values and relations, this work reflects the collaboration of anthropologist Handy with the Native Hawai'ian cultural specialist Pukui, the noted scholar who was also from the area studied.

Harden, M. J. (1999). *Voices of Wisdom: Hawai'ian Elders Speak*. Kula, HI: Aka Press.
A collection of the thoughts of leaders of the Hawai'ian renaissance. Twenty-two Hawai'ian elders and two on the cusp of becoming elders share life experiences in their own words. Photographs of the featured Native Hawai'ian leaders are included with the text.

Ii, J. P. (1959). *Fragments of Hawai'ian History*. Honolulu: Bishop Museum Press.
A compilation of writings by Ii, a leading citizen of the Hawai'ian Kingdom in the nineteenth century. This highly regarded collection covers a broad range, including history, customs, and events of his day.

Juvik, S. P., Juvik, J. O., & Paradise, T. R. (1998). *Atlas of Hawai'i, Deluxe Edition* (3rd ed.). Honolulu: University of Hawai'i Press.
This atlas contains an abundance of maps, graphs, photos, illustrations, and information about geographical, physical, biological, cultural, and social aspects of Hawai'i.

Kalakaua, D. (1990). *The Legends and Myths of Hawai'i: The Fables and Folk-Lore of a Strange People*. Honolulu: Mutual Publishing.
A compilation of mythology rich in historical narrative written by King David Kalakaua. Kalakaua led a cultural revival during his reign, and his book was an important contribution aimed at preserving Native Hawai'ian culture.

Kamakau, S. M. (1992). *The Works of the People of Old: Na Hana a ka Po'e Kahiko*. Honolulu: Bishop Museum Press.
This is the sequel to *Ka Po'e Kahiko: The People of Old*, which is mentioned in the Especially Recommended section. The collection is a translation of Kamakau's weekly newspaper articles from 1869 to 1870, which primarily focuses on accounts of the material culture of ancient Native Hawai'ians.

Kane, H. K. (1997). *Ancient Hawai'i*. Captain Cook, HI: Kawainui Press.
An excellent introduction to ancient Native Hawai'ian culture that is richly illustrated with full-color paintings. Kane, the author and illustrator, is a renowned artist who has contributed much to the recent Hawai'ian renaissance.

Kepelino. (1971). *Kepelino's Traditions of Hawai'i*. Honolulu: Bishop Museum Press.
The Hawai'ian and English texts of this treasured work are presented side-by-side. Kepelino, who was born in the mid-nineteenth century, described a version of the Hawai'ian creation story, stories about stars and dreams, and descriptions of Hawai'ian social roles and occupations.

Kinzer, S. (2006). *Overthrow: America's Century of Regime Change from Hawai'i to Iraq*. New York: Times Books, Henry Holt.
A narrative history that details the stories of how the United States has toppled fourteen governments around the world in order to advance its own political and economic goals. He recounts this pattern, which continues to today, starting with the overthrow of the Hawai'ian monarchy in 1893.

Kirch, P. V. (1985). *Feathered Gods and Fishhooks: An Introduction to Hawai'ian Archaeology and Prehistory*. Honolulu: University of Hawai'i Press.
The first major archaeological treatment of ancient Native Hawai'ian civilization by the foremost authority in Hawai'ian archaeology.

Kuykendall, R. S. (1947, 1966, 1967). *The Hawai'ian Kingdom* (vols. 1–3). Honolulu: University of Hawai'i Press.
A comprehensive history covering the time period from 1778 to 1893. Taking over forty years to complete, it is considered to be the most ambitious and definitive history of Hawai'i.

Leong, R. C. (Ed.). (2000). *Whose Vision: Asian Settler Colonialism in Hawai'i* [a special issue of] *Amerasia Journal, 26* (2).
A landmark issue of *Amerasia Journal* (Candace Fujikane and Jonathan Y. Okamura, guest editors) centers on the related matters of Hawai'ian sovereignty and Asian settler colonialism. The thesis is put forth that Hawai'i is made up of two kinds of people—settlers and those who are indigenous. Settlers of Asian descent are seen as unjustly benefiting from the domination of Native Hawai'ians.

Liliuokalani. (2004). *Hawai'i Story*. Honolulu: Mutual Publishing.
Considered a monumental contribution to Hawai'i literature by Hawai'i's last reigning monarch, Queen Liliuokalani. Originally published in 1898, she wrote the work as a plea for justice, providing details of her life and the final days of her kingdom.

Liliuokalani. (1997). *The Kumulipo: An Hawai'ian Creation Myth*. Kentfield, CA: Pueo Press.
   Queen Liliuokalani's English translation of the Hawai'ian creation chant, which was first
   published by her brother, King Kalakaua, in Hawai'ian. Translated in the time between her
   overthrow and U.S. annexation, the work served to refute the claim that Hawai'ians were
   ignorant savages who had no culture prior to the arrival of Europeans.

Malo, D. (1996). *Ka Mo'olelo Hawai'i: Hawai'ian Traditions*. Translated by M. N. Chun.
   Honolulu: First People's Productions.
   First translated in 1898, this book is a new translation of the classic work of Davida Malo,
   born in 1795. Davida Malo is considered to be among the three most significant authors of
   Native Hawai'ian history (with Ii and Kamakau).

Mast, R. H., & Mast, A. B. (1997). *Autobiography of Protest in Hawai'i*. Honolulu: University of
   Hawai'i Press.
   A collection of thirty-five oral histories of political activists in Hawai'i. While the collection also
   includes the oral histories of non-Native Hawai'ians, Native Hawai'ians are well represented.

Merry, S. E. (2000). *Colonizing Hawai'i: The Cultural Power of Law*. Princeton, NJ: Princeton
   University Press.
   A work that traces how the implementation of Western rule of law made striking changes in
   the everyday lives of nineteenth-century Native Hawai'ians.

Osborne, T. J. (1998). *Annexation, Hawai'i: Fighting American Imperialism*. Waimanalo, HI:
   Island Style Press.
   A study of the annexation of Hawai'i by the United States that focuses on opposition from
   those on the U.S. continent, not on resistance in Hawai'i or elsewhere, during the years after
   the overthrow and before eventual annexation (1893–1898).

Puku'i, M. K. (1983). *'Olelo No'eau: Hawai'ian Proverbs and Poetical Sayings*. Honolulu: Bishop
   Museum Press.
   A treasury of Native Hawai'ian sayings, expressed in Hawai'ian and English, that conveys
   wisdom and an essence of traditional Native Hawai'ian values.

Puku'i, M. K., & Curtis, C. (1996). *Hawai'i Island Legends: Pikoi, Pele, and Others*. Honolulu:
   Kamehameha Schools Press.
   A collection of legends and folktales associated with the Hawai'ian islands.

Puku'i, M. K., Elbert, & S. H., Mookini (1974). *Place Names of Hawai'i*. Honolulu: University of
   Hawai'i Press.
   A valuable reference for providing the meanings, in English, of important place-names,
   which are in Hawai'ian.

Puku'i, M. K., & Green, L. C. S. (1995). *Folktales of Hawai'i: He Mau Ka'ao Hawai'i*. Honolulu:
   Bishop Museum Press.
   A collection of Native Hawai'ian stories told by Mary Kawena Puku'i, arguably Hawai'i's
   foremost storyteller and Native Hawai'ian cultural expert.

Reeve, R. (1995). *Kaho'olawe: Na Leo o Kanaloa*. Honolulu: Ai Pohaku Press.
   This large coffee table book, dedicated to the island of Kaho'olawe, which had been used by
   the U.S. Navy for target practice, includes beautiful photographs depicting its rebirth. The
   book also includes stories about the island, a historical chronology, an excellent map, and an
   inspiring introduction by Emmett Aluli, one of the activists who played an instrumental role
   in returning the island to Native Hawai'ians.

Schutz, A. J. (1995). *The Voices of Eden: A History of Hawai'ian Language Studies*. Honolulu:
   University of Hawai'i Press.
   An account of Hawai'ian history from a language-centered point of view. The book also
   includes an exhaustive critique and analysis of nearly every work ever written about the
   Hawai'ian language.

Stannard, D. E. (1989). *Before the Horror: The Population of Hawai'i on the Eve of Western Contact*. Honolulu: University of Hawai'i Press.
> A very interesting work that employs an interdisciplinary approach to explore new data, refuting conventional estimates of Hawai'i's population when the first White men arrived in 1778. While the conventional estimate is about 300,000, Stannard contends that it was upward of 800,000.

Stannard, D. E. (2005). *Honor Killing: Race, Rape, and Clarence Darrow's Spectacular Last Case*. London: Penguin Books.
> A scholarly work that reads like a thriller about the alleged rape of a White naval officer's wife by Native Hawai'ians and other non-White men, and the subsequent string of controversial events, including the murder of one of the Hawai'ian men. Stannard's attention to matters of social class and race in Hawai'i is especially noteworthy.

Stillman, A. K. (1998). *Sacred Hula: The Historical Hula Ala'apapa*. Honolulu: Bishop Museum Press.
> A historical study focused on a particular genre of the ancient hula. It is significant in how Stillman distinguishes this distinctive form, moving from the use of the contemporary dichotomy of ancient or modern.

Trask, H.-K. (1999). *Light in the Crevice Never Seen* (2nd ed.). Corvallis, OR: Calyx Books.
> The powerful and moving poetry of an indigenous Hawai'ian leader and scholar reflects the social realities that affect indigenous Hawai'ians today.

Wei, D., & Kamel, R. (1997). *Resistance in Paradise: Rethinking 100 Years of U.S. Involvement in the Caribbean and the Pacific*. Philadelphia: American Friends Service Committee and Office of Curriculum Support, School District of Philadelphia.
> An outstanding curriculum guide that presents alternative voices in U.S. history. The guide focuses on reframing the Spanish-American War by examining the legacy of U.S. expansion. The perspectives of those who were colonized are given voice. The overview and the section on Hawai'i are of particular interest.

Books for Students

Armitage, K. A. (2001). *Na 'Olelo No'eau No Na Keiki: Words of Wisdom for Children*. Waipahu, HI: Island Heritage Publishing.
> A book of wise sayings in Hawai'ian and English, accompanied by beautiful, full-page color illustrations by Solomon Enos. (Primary)

Armitage, K. A. (2006). *Akua Hawai'i: Hawai'ian Gods and Their Stories*. Honolulu: Kamahoi Press.
> A book lavishly illustrated by Solomon Enos that provides an introduction to over thirty Hawai'ian gods. While it is a book for young readers, adults will also enjoy it. (Ages 9 and up/Intermediate)

Crowe, E. (2003). *Kamehameha: The Boy Who Became a Warrior King*. Waipahu, HI: Island Heritage Publishing.
> A tale about young Kamehameha rich with brilliant illustrations by Don Robinson. (Ages 9 and up/Intermediate)

Eyre, D. K. (2007). *White Rainbow, Black Curse*. Honolulu: Kamehameha Publishing.
> The first book in a twelve-part historical fiction series about the life of King Kamehameha I. (Young reader/Intermediate)

Goldsberry, U. (2004). *The Shark Man of Hana: O Ke Kane Mano O Hana*. Ewa Beach, HI: Beachhouse Publishing, LLC.
> A retelling of a classic Native Hawai'ian story, in both Hawai'ian and English. The tale is brought to life by Roy Chang's watercolor illustrations. (Ages 9 and up)

Kaopuiki, S. (1991). *The Secret of the Hawai'ian Rainbow: A Hawai'ian Story about Colors*. Wailuku, HI: Hawai'ian Island Concepts.

A fantastic tale about colors, involving *menehune,* which are Hawai'ian little people. Over the course of the story, colors are introduced in English, Hawai'ian, Japanese, and sign language. (Primary)

Kawai'ae'a, K. C. (1995). *Ke Nui A'e Au*. Hilo, HI: 'Aha Punana Leo.

A book written in Hawai'ian that shows some of the possible occupations that a child might choose growing up in Hawai'i. An English translation of the entire Hawai'ian text is included at the end of the book. (Primary)

Loebel-Fried, C. (2002). *Hawai'ian Legends of the Guardian Spirits*. Honolulu: University of Hawai'i Press.

Legends about family guardian spirits, which could take the form of animals or plants, are retold and illustrated with striking block prints. (Ages 9 and up/Intermediate)

Loebel-Fried, C. (2005). *Hawai'ian Legends of Dreams*. Honolulu: University of Hawai'i Press.

The companion volume to *Hawai'ian Legends of the Guardian Spirits,* this book retells legends about dreaming, which Native Hawai'ians believed was how they communicated with their family guardian spirits. (Ages 9 and up/Intermediate)

Loebel-Fried, C. (2006). *Lono and the Magic Land Beneath the Sea*. Honolulu: Bishop Museum Press.

The story of a Lono, a fisherman who dives beneath the sea to search for his missing fishhooks. The story is retold from an old Hawai'ian tale held in the Bishop Museum archives. (Ages 9 and up/Intermediate)

Menton, L., & Tamura, E. (Eds.). (1989). *A History of Hawai'i*. Honolulu: University of Hawai'i Press.

A textbook of Hawai'ian history from precolonial Hawai'i to the present. The emphasis placed on highlighting issues of concern to the state and its people makes this a better than average traditional text for high school students. (High School)

Morrison, S. (2003). *Kamehameha: The Warrior King of Hawai'i*. Honolulu: University of Hawai'i Press.

The story of King Kamehameha I is retold in this biography written for the middle grades. (Ages 9 and up/Intermediate)

Rayson, A., & Bauer, H. (1997). *Hawai'i: The Pacific State* (4th ed.). Honolulu: Bess Press.

This book provides a general and fairly current history of Hawai'i from the formation of the islands, the arrival of the first Hawai'ians, the European arrival in Hawai'i, the shift from monarchy to territory, and the political evolution through both world wars to the current sovereignty movement. A chapter lists and briefly explains island holidays and festivals. (Middle/Secondary)

Stone, S. C. (2003). *Yesterday in Hawai'i: A Voyage Through Time*. Waipahu, HI: Island Heritage.

This is a very readable and well-illustrated book that chronicles the history of Hawai'i from the days of European contact until shortly after statehood was achieved. (Middle/Secondary)

Thompson, V. L. (1971). *Hawai'ian Tales of Heroes and Champions*. Honolulu: University of Hawai'i Press.

A collection of "tall tales" about heroes and champions of the people of old Hawai'i. Noted Native Hawai'ian artist Herb Kane provided illustrations for the tales. (Ages 9 and up/Intermediate)

Thompson, V. L. (1990). *Hawai'ian Legends of Tricksters and Riddlers*. Honolulu: University of Hawai'i Press.

Twelve Native Hawai'ian trickster and riddler tales are recounted in this collection. (Ages 9 and up/Intermediate)

Tune, S. C. (1991). *Maui and the Secret of Fire*. Honolulu: University of Hawai'i Press.
    A retelling, illustrated by Robin Yoko Burningham, based on the Hawai'ian legend of Maui.
    (Ages 4–8/Primary)

Wight, K. (1998). *Illustrated Hawai'ian Dictionary*. Honolulu: Bess Press.
    A valuable reference for learning Hawai'ian that includes the words and definitions most
    commonly used by beginning students of the language. (Ages 9 and up/beginning Hawai'ian
    language learners)

Williams, J. S. (1991). *Maui Goes Fishing*. Honolulu: University of Hawai'i Press.
    A retelling of part of the legend of Maui that tells how he pulled up the Hawai'ian islands
    while using a magic fishhook. (Ages 4–8/Primary)

Williams, J. S. (1997). *From the Mountains to the Sea: Early Hawai'ian Life*. Honolulu: Kame-
    hameha Schools Press.
    This book describes the life and activities of people on the Hawai'ian Islands before Western
    contact. The text is accompanied by illustrations. (Ages 9 and up/Intermediate)

CHAPTER SEVEN

AFRICAN AMERICANS
Concepts, Strategies, and Materials

It is a peculiar sensation, this double-consciousness, this sense of always looking at one's self through the eyes of others. One feels his twoness— an American, a Negro; two souls, two unreconciled strivings; two warring ideals in one dark body, whose dogged strength alone keeps it from being torn asunder.

—William E. B. Du Bois (1903/1973)

Africans have had a unique experience in the Americas. They came with the earliest European explorers and settlers and were gradually enslaved in the North American colonies in the 1600s. When the eighteenth century began, slavery was flourishing in North America. The African experience in the United States has strikingly revealed the gross discrepancies between American ideals and reality. Throughout their history, African Americans have called on America to make its dream a reality. Their cries have usually fallen on deaf ears. African American history and culture must be studied to enable students to understand and appreciate fully the great conflicts and dilemmas in American society and to develop a commitment to help make America's ideals a reality.

AFRICAN EXPLORERS IN AMERICA

Africans have been in America for many centuries. Inconclusive evidence suggests that they established a colony in Mexico long before Columbus's voyage in 1492. Africans were with the first Europeans who explored America. Africans had been living in Europe for many years when European explorations of America began. The Moors, a North African people, invaded Europe in 711. They eventually conquered and ruled Spain. Other Africans were brought to Europe as slaves beginning in the 1400s. These Africans worked in private homes as servants, in banks and shipyards, and in mercantile establishments.

Diego el Negro was with Columbus on his last voyage to America in 1502. When Balboa arrived at the Pacific Ocean in 1513, his crew included a Black man, Nuflo de Olano. Africans explored present-day Kansas in 1541 with Coronado. Africans were also with many of the other early Spanish expeditions to the Americas. Estevanico, a Moor, is one of the most famous early Black explorers. Arriving in America in 1529, he explored present-day New Mexico and Arizona and paved the way for later Spanish explorations of the Southwest.

In addition to exploring America, Africans were among its first non-Indian settlers. Some of the settlers of the ill-fated South Carolina colony in 1526, San Miguel de Guadalupe, were African. Africans helped to establish St. Augustine, Florida, in 1565, the oldest non-Indian settlement in the United States. A number of colonies were established by Africans and the French. These groups settled in the Mississippi Valley in the seventeenth century.

AFRICAN AMERICANS: HISTORICAL PERSPECTIVE

Important Dates	Events
1565	Africans helped to establish a colony in St. Augustine, Florida.
1619	The first Africans arrived in the English North American colonies.
1808	The slave trade was legally ended, but illegal slave trading began.
1829	David Walker published his *Appeal,* in which he harshly denounced slavery and urged slaves to take up arms and rebel.
1831	Nat Turner led a slave revolt in which nearly sixty Whites were killed.
1850	The Fugitive Slave Act, which authorized the federal government to help capture runaway slaves, was enacted. It helped pave the way to the Civil War.
1857	The Supreme Court ruled in the *Dred Scott Decision* that slaves did not become free when they moved to free territory. It also held that African Americans were not and could not be citizens.
1861–1862	Congress enacted several Confiscation Acts designed to prevent the Confederacy from using slaves in its war efforts.
1863	Many African Americans in New York City were attacked and killed by largely Irish mobs that were protesting the draft laws and expressing anti-Black feelings.
	On January 1, 1863, President Abraham Lincoln issued the Emancipation Proclamation, which freed slaves in those states fighting the Union.
1865	Slavery was legally abolished throughout the United States by the enactment of the Thirteenth Amendment to the Constitution.
1866	The Fourteenth Amendment, which made African Americans United States citizens, was enacted. The Civil Rights Act of 1866 was enacted. It extended the African American's civil liberties in several areas.

Important Dates	Events
1870	The Fifteenth Amendment was enacted. It enabled many African Americans to vote.
1876	In the disputed Hayes-Tilden election, Hayes's supporters promised that he would remove the remaining federal troops from the South. This bargain symbolized the extent to which northern Whites had abandoned the southern African Americans.
1896	In a historic decision, *Plessy* v. *Ferguson,* the Supreme Court ruled that "separate but equal" facilities were constitutional.
1905	W. E. B. Du Bois and a group of African American intellectuals organized the Niagara Movement to promote civil rights for African Americans.
1910	The National Association for the Advancement of Colored People (NAACP) was organized. It successfully fought for African American legal rights.
1911	The National Urban League was founded to help the Black urban migrant adjust to city life and find jobs.
1914	Marcus Garvey organized the Universal Negro Improvement Association. Garvey urged African Americans to return to Africa.
1917	One of the worst riots in U.S. history occurred in East St. Louis, Illinois. Thirty-nine African Americans were killed.
1919	A series of riots occurred in a number of cities during the "Red Summer" of 1919. One of the most serious occurred in Chicago, in which thirty-eight people lost their lives.
1943	White violence directed at African Americans led to a serious riot in Detroit in which thirty-four people were killed.
1954	In a landmark decision, *Brown* v. *Board of Education,* the Supreme Court ruled that school segregation was inherently unequal.
1955	African Americans in Montgomery, Alabama, began a boycott of the city's buses that ended bus segregation there in 1956.
1957	Martin Luther King, Jr., and a group of Baptist ministers organized the Southern Christian Leadership Conference (SCLC).
	National Guardsmen were required to help integrate Central High School in Little Rock, Arkansas.
1960	On February 1, 1960, the sit-in movement, which desegregated public accommodation facilities throughout the South, began in Greensboro, North Carolina.
1961	The Congress of Racial Equality (CORE) led Freedom Rides throughout the South to desegregate interstate transportation.

Important Dates	Events
1963	More than 200,000 people participated in a "March on Washington for Freedom and Jobs."
	In a Birmingham demonstration led by Martin Luther King, Jr., civil rights demonstrators were violently attacked by the police.
1992	Carol Mosely Braun (Democrat, Ill.) became the first African American woman elected to the U.S. Senate.
1993	Toni Morrison was the first African American woman and the eighth woman to receive the Nobel Prize for literature.
2001	President George W. Bush appointed Condoleezza Rice national security adviser, Roderick Paige secretary of education, and Colin L. Powell secretary of state. These were the highest positions that African Americans held in any president's administration.
2007	Senator Barack Obama, Democrat from Illinois, was a serious candidate for president of the United States.
	The U.S. Supreme Court ruled that the desegregation plans implemented in Seattle (Wash.) and Louisville (Ky.) were unconstitutional.

THE SLAVE TRADE

The Arabs invaded Africa and enslaved Africans long before Europeans arrived on the continent. The European nations became involved in the African slave trade when they started trading with Africa in the 1400s. In the mid-fifteenth century, European monarchs sent explorers to Africa to obtain such goods as skins and oils. Many of these explorers brought back these wares as well as African slaves and gold as gifts for their rulers. These gifts greatly pleased the European monarchs. As more and more Europeans explored Africa and brought Africans back to Europe, the slave trade gradually gained momentum. Black slavery never became widespread in Europe, but it grew by leaps and bounds when Europeans started settling in America in the 1600s. Europeans developed large plantations in the West Indies that grew crops such as sugar, indigo, cotton, and tobacco. Sugar production reigned supreme over all other crops. To produce increasing amounts of sugar, the Europeans brought thousands of Africans to the West Indies.

The slave trade became highly lucrative. European nations competed aggressively to monopolize it. At first, the Portuguese dominated the slave trade. Portugal was eventually challenged by the Dutch. Gradually, more and more nations gained a toehold in Africa. However, England was dominating the slave trade when it peaked in 1700. The European nations greatly benefited from the slave trade. They obtained many raw materials from Africa that helped them to attain high levels of industrial growth. The ships that left Europe carried small items to use for exchange with the Africans. While in

Africa, the ships picked up wares such as gold, ivory, and dyewood as well as captives. The ships usually traveled from Africa to the West Indies, where the captives were sold and exchanged goods acquired. The goods were taken back to Europe. The journey from the West Coast of Africa to the West Indies was known as the "middle passage" because it was only part of a route that eventually led back to Europe.

When the slave trade in the West Indies began, European nations granted monopolies to a few favorite companies, such as the Dutch West India Company and the Royal African Company of England. Later, when these nations realized that they could make more money by allowing companies to compete, the monopoly system was abandoned. Before the monopolies ended in the late 1600s, the European colonists in North America were not able to obtain nearly as many Africans as they wanted. The major companies sold most of their Africans on the more profitable markets of the West Indian sugar plantations. However, the North American colonists were able to buy as many Africans as they wished when monopolies ended. The smaller companies were eager to trade with them.

Whereas the slave trade was profitable for European nations and contributed to their industrial growth and development, it was disastrous for the West African nations. When the trade first began, African rulers sold captives and criminals. Most of the captives had been taken from other tribes during warfare. There was no concept of "Africans" among the diverse groups that lived in Africa in the seventeenth century. The peoples of Africa identified with their clans or tribal groups, not with the continent (Ladson-Billings, 1994). As the Europeans sought more and more Africans, these sources became inadequate. The African rulers were so fascinated with the trinkets, rum, firearms, and other items they received in exchange for captives that they started warring to obtain captives, using the firearms they received from Europeans. Warring became increasingly frequent and destructive as the Europeans' desire for captives soared. As warring increased, some groups had to sell captives to acquire the firearms they needed to protect themselves. These wars adversely affected African political stability. The slave trade also drained off many of Africa's strongest and most productive young men and women. The slave traders wanted only healthy captives who could survive the horrible middle passage and the back-breaking work on the plantations in America.

The Beginning of Bondage

The captive's life was terrifying, brutal, and shocking. Slave catchers, who were usually Africans, raided the interior of the West African coast, looking for captives from other tribal groups. When Africans were caught, they were chained together and marched long distances, often hundreds of miles, to the European forts near the coast. Here they waited, sometimes for months, before being forced onto ships headed for America. The captives adamantly resisted bondage. Some of them escaped on the long march to the forts. Others jumped overboard once the ships were at sea. Mutinies occurred, both on the African shore and in midocean. In 1753 a group of captives seized a ship bound for America, killed the White crew, and forced the ship back to Africa. In 1839, the *Amistad*, a slave ship, was brought into New London, Connecticut, by a group of Africans who had revolted against their captors. Cinque, the young African leader, and his followers were granted their freedom by the U.S. Supreme Court (Ladson-Billings, 1994).

Conditions on the slave ships were degrading and dehumanizing. The captured Africans were packed into the ships like sardines. They were chained together with iron ankle fetters. The space for each slave was so small that they were forced to lie down in the ship. Because of the crowded and filthy conditions on the ships, diseases were rampant and took many lives. Many Africans died from scurvy, dysentery, and smallpox. Sometimes everyone on a ship was blinded by ophthalmia. Africans who became very sick were dumped into the ocean because sick Africans were worthless on the American slave market. Often more than half of the Africans died during the journey. Some historians estimate that one out of every eight captives died in the middle passage and never reached the Americas. This painful trip usually took from forty to sixty days.

Slavery in North America

The first Africans to arrive in the English North American colonies came in 1619 on a Dutch ship. These twenty Africans were not slaves but, like most of the Whites who came to the colonies during this period, were indentured servants. To pay for their passage to America, indentured servants agreed to work for their sponsors for a specified period of time. When they had completed their period of service, they became free. At first, the English colonists met their labor needs with indentured servants. Increasingly, the colonists began to feel that they were not obtaining enough workers with this system and that slavery had many more advantages. For one thing, indentured servitude was more expensive than slavery. The servants had to be provided certain goods and services, and eventually they became free. With slavery, the worker received few benefits and remained a servant for life. Also, the slaves' children would also be slaves. Clearly, slavery was a more profitable system than indentured servitude. The colonists deliberately decided to replace indentured servitude with African slavery for economic reasons.

Slavery existed in practice in most of the colonies long before it acquired legal status. The legal institutionalization of slavery was a gradual process. By 1630 in Virginia, laws and legal cases were beginning to evolve that would culminate in the legalization of slavery. In that year, a court sentenced a White man to a whipping for having sex with an African woman. The Virginia House of Burgesses passed a law in 1643 limiting the years for White indentured servants but not for African servants. The House enacted a law in 1662 that declared that children would inherit their mother's status. This law reversed English common law, which held that children inherited their father's status. A 1667 law enacted by the House enabled Christians to be slaves. A law passed in Maryland in 1664 openly declared that Blacks and their children would be slaves in that colony. By the end of the seventeenth century, slavery existed in fact as well as in law in colonial America.

American slavery was a unique institution in human history. It was designed to dehumanize Africans and to convince them that they were inferior and deserved the treatment they received. It was also designed to enable Whites to make maximum profits from African labor and to reinforce White supremacy. All of the laws, customs, and norms that developed around slavery reflected and reinforced its major goals. Slaves were regarded as property and were required to cater to the whims and wishes of their masters. A number of arguments and traditions emerged to justify slavery and to ensure its continuation. Because of their treatment of Blacks, and because of constant attempts by the captives to resist bondage, Whites developed a chronic fear of slave rebellions and retaliation. Sometimes, especially after a slave rebellion or when one was rumored, White fears of slave insurrections and uprisings became chronic, paranoid, and widespread. Consequently, the slave codes were made more severe, and the institutions and norms supporting bondage were revitalized.

Attempts by Whites to deny the African captives' humanity and to oppress them are reflected in the numerous slave codes enacted in colonies from New York to Georgia. These codes varied from colony to colony but tended to be most severe in the southern colonies. However, all of them were degrading and designed to reinforce bondage. In some colonies, slaves could not form groups without the presence of a White; they could not carry or own firearms, testify in court against a White person, or be taught to read or write. Some colonies prevented them from owning property or drinking liquor and did not recognize their marriages as legal. They were forbidden from leaving the plantation unless they had a special pass. Punishment for crimes was severe, although some planters did not welcome the death penalty because it deprived them of profitable workers. Slaves were subject to the death penalty for such crimes as rape, arson, and robbery.

Slaves worked in a wide variety of occupations, especially in the northern colonies. They worked as laborers and house servants in New England and also as skilled artisans. Many skilled slaves in the North hired themselves out and saved enough money to buy their freedom. Few skilled slaves in the South were allowed to keep the money they earned hiring themselves out. Although slaves in the South worked in many different jobs, especially in the cities, where many were skilled artisans, most worked on the large plantations owned by a few rich members of the southern aristocracy. Life on these large plantations, which specialized in such crops as tobacco and cotton, was hard and painful. Often driven by a merciless overseer and a driver, the slaves worked from sunup to sundown. They usually lived on the plantation in mud-floor shacks that were cold in the winter and hot in the summer. Their food consisted mostly of hominy and fatback. Their clothing was limited; men usually had little more than two shirts and two pairs of trousers.

Even though Whites tried to deny the slaves a human existence, Africans succeeded in developing a sense of community and a social life apart from the world of Whites. Slaves had stable marriages, even though they were not legally recognized by White society. These marriages usually occurred after long courtships. The family was important to slaves. Family members taught their children how to survive the harsh White environment as well as how not to submit totally to the whims of the master. Although Black fathers openly disapproved of the ways the Whites treated their families, they usually obeyed the master in order to avoid severe punishment or death. Many slave families that had developed strong bonds of love and kinship were broken up when the master sold family members to different buyers or sold only some members of the family. Some slaves escaped to search for members of their families when they were sold.

Most African captives never totally submitted to slavery or accepted it. They resisted it in both covert and blatant ways. To avoid work, slaves would sometimes feign illness. They sometimes destroyed farm equipment deliberately or cut up the plants when they were hoeing crops. A few slaves maimed themselves to avoid work. Some domestic slaves put poison in their masters' foods and killed them. Other slaves escaped. The number of runaways increased greatly when the Civil War began and when the Emancipation Proclamation was issued in 1863. Many slaves were helped to the North and Canada by a loosely organized system known as the Underground Railroad. Free Blacks, many of whom were escaped slaves, made numerous trips to the South to help Blacks escape. Africans such as Harriet Tubman and Josiah Henson helped hundreds of slaves follow the North Star to freedom. Many slaves traveled by night and were helped by "conductors" of the Underground Railroad. Other slaves escaped alone. These lone and brave captives were determined to escape bondage at any cost.

African captives also resisted slavery by rebellion (Genovese, 1979). Even though most slave uprisings were unsuccessful, partly because of slave informers, historical records indicate that at least 250 occurred (Aptheker, 1987). One of the most ambitious slave uprisings was planned by Gabriel Prosser in 1800. Prosser and a group of about 1,000 slaves armed themselves and headed for Richmond, Virginia. A heavy rainstorm stopped the rebels, and the authorities in Richmond, who had been alerted, were armed and waiting for them. Gabriel Prosser and thirty of the other captives died at the end of a rope.

Denmark Vesey, a free Black in Charleston, South Carolina, planned an insurrection in 1822. The group he led armed themselves and were prepared to take Charleston's two arsenals. The revolt was crushed before it got started, and the participants were hanged. The most successful slave revolt of the antebellum period was led by Nat Turner in 1831. Turner was a highly imaginative African American preacher who felt that he was destined by God to free his people from bondage. Turner organized and armed a crew that killed about sixty Whites, including his master and family. The Turner rebels caught their victims by surprise. Whites crushed the rebellion after it had raged for forty-eight hours. When they were seized, Turner and nineteen other rebels were hanged.

The Abolitionists

The first societies organized to agitate for the abolition of slavery were formed during and after the American Revolution. The earliest was founded in Philadelphia in

1775. The Quakers were the leading figures in this society. However, slavery was hotly debated among the Quakers. There were also Quakers in the South who owned slaves (Ladson-Billings, 1994). Other abolitionary societies were formed during this period. Most of the members of these early societies were propertied men who were sympathetic to the South. They spoke kindly of the South, were soft-spoken, and felt that slave owners who freed their slaves should be compensated. They advocated a gradual abolition of slavery. Because of the tactics they used, many Southerners supported these societies. These abolitionists did not believe in or practice social equality. Women and African Americans were excluded from their organizations.

The abolitionary societies organized in the 1800s were much more militant and aggressive than the earlier ones. They harshly denounced slavery and slave owners and demanded an immediate end to slavery. These groups were unpopular in both the North and the South. They became known as militants and extremists. Both Whites and Blacks participated in these societies, although the Whites, who did not believe in racial equality, tried to keep the African Americans in the background. Frederick Douglass, Robert Purvis, and Sojourner Truth were some of the leading African American abolitionists (Quarles, 1969; Yee, 1992).

One of the most militant societies was the American Anti-Slavery Society, organized in 1833. Although this society vigorously denounced slavery, it kept Blacks in the background. In its early years, it had no African American lecturers. Most of the policy was made by Whites. Members of the society discouraged African Americans when they started editing their own newspapers and lecturing. They wanted only a few Blacks to be visible in the organization for symbolic purposes. The African American abolitionists harshly condemned the White abolitionists, accusing them of discriminating against Blacks in their businesses and their daily lives.

The African American abolitionists often went their separate ways (Quarles, 1969). They edited newspapers and gave moving speeches giving Black views of abolition. Despite objections from White abolitionists such as William Lloyd Garrison, Frederick Douglass edited and published a paper, the *North Star*. Black abolitionists also expressed their views in the series of conventions they held in the antebellum period. At the National Negro Convention in 1843, Henry Highland Garnet gave a controversial speech in which he urged slaves to rise up and fight for their freedom. He later worked with William G. Allen to edit a newspaper, *The National Watchman*. Sojourner Truth and Harriet Tubman were also important African American abolitionists. Truth worked with other abolitionists, such as William Lloyd Garrison and Frederick Douglass. She also became active in the women's rights movement. Harriet Tubman was one of the most successful "conductors" on the Underground Railroad. She helped more than 300 captives escape to freedom.

As was to be the case in later years, African American and White participants in Black liberation movements in the 1800s often had different goals and aims, and they used different approaches. These divergent goals and methods inevitably led to conflict and hostility between these groups.

THE COLONIZATION MOVEMENT

In the early nineteenth century, a movement developed among Whites to deport African Americans to another country. The motives of the advocates of colonization varied. Some saw themselves as humanitarians and felt that because of White racism, African Americans would never be able to achieve equality in the United States. They believed that Blacks would have a much better chance in another nation. Other advocates of colonization were supporters of slavery and wanted to deport free Blacks because they felt that nonslave Blacks were a threat to slavery. Many southern Whites eagerly supported the American Colonization Society, organized in 1816 by a group of eminent White Americans.

Many influential Whites, such as Francis Scott Key and Henry Clay, supported colonization. A region in West Africa, named Liberia, was acquired by American colonizationists in 1822. Despite the enthusiastic support for the movement, it did not succeed. Fewer than 8,000 African Americans had immigrated to Liberia by 1852. Many of these were captives who had been granted their freedom on the condition that they immigrate to Africa. The colonization movement failed primarily because most African Americans were strongly against it. The American Colonization Society made its plans and solicited support from eminent White Americans but ignored the feelings of African Americans. African American leaders denounced the society, which often condoned racist practices. They argued that they would not leave the United States because their ancestors had helped to build the nation and they consequently had a right to live in the United States by birthright. The free African Americans who strongly opposed colonization saw it as an attempt by slave owners to get rid of them and thus make slavery more safe and secure. These leaders argued that their fate rested with the fate of their enchained brothers and sisters.

A few African Americans who became disillusioned with the United States began to advocate colonization. However, some of the leaders, such as Martin Delany, strongly criticized the American Colonization Society. Delany felt that the society's members were "arrogant hypocrites." He correctly perceived the White colonizationists' motives as being quite different from those of African American colonizationists, who wanted to leave the United States because they had become disillusioned and frustrated. Most White colonizationists hoped to deport African Americans so that they could get rid of a racial group they did not want in the United States.

From time to time, small groups of despairing African Americans thought seriously about colonization and sometimes took concrete actions to realize their aspirations. Paul Cuffe took thirty-eight Blacks to Sierra Leone in 1815. In 1859, Martin D. Delany obtained a piece of land in Africa for an African American settlement. A Black colonization group, the African Civilization Society, was organized by a group of eminent African Americans in 1858. Despite these attempts, African American colonizationists had no more success than White colonizationists, because most African Americans were determined to remain in the United States. Back-to-Africa advocates emerged later in the nineteenth and twentieth centuries. Marcus Garvey was a strong advocate of African colonization in the 1930s. However, these movements and advocates never gained widespread support.

Nonslave African Americans

Not all African Americans were slaves, either in the North or South, during the antebellum period. Many African Americans in the North hired themselves out and earned their freedom. Some in New England sued for their freedom in courts and won it. Some bondsmen were awarded their freedom after service in the Revolutionary War. A few African Americans were descendants of Black indentured servants and were never slaves. In the South, some slave masters left wills freeing their slaves on their deaths. Often these slaves were their children or other blood relatives as a result of forced sex with Black women captives. Some southern slaves were given their freedom after meritorious service to their communities. Others obtained their freedom by escaping. In both the North and the South, nonslave Blacks were harassed and demeaned and were often treated as if they were slaves. When Whites saw African Americans, they assumed that they were slaves. Nonslave Blacks had to prove that they were free. Free Blacks had to carry papers, which they usually had to purchase, that certified their freedom. However, they were often captured and enslaved whether they carried "free" papers or not.

Many of the legal limitations imposed on slaves also governed the nonslave African Americans. In many parts of the South, nonslave Blacks were forbidden to form groups without the presence of a White, were prohibited from testifying against a White, and were not allowed to own a gun or a dog. In the North, they were denied the franchise and prohibited by law from migrating to such states as Illinois, Indiana, and Oregon. The free African American could settle in other old Northwest states, such as Michigan and Ohio, only after paying bonds of up to a thousand dollars. Southerners regarded free African Americans as a nuisance and a threat to slavery. They blamed them for most of the slave rebellions and for encouraging slaves to escape. For these reasons, many southern Whites eagerly supported the movement to deport free Blacks to Africa.

Nonslave northern Blacks played an extremely important role in African American life. They strongly protested the racism and discrimination Blacks experienced. The Negro Convention Movement served as an important protest forum. Black conventions were held from 1830 up to the beginning of the twentieth century. At most of them, the delegates issued cogent statements demanding an end to racism in various areas of American life. The colonization movement, discrimination in northern schools, and segregation in the church were targets of Black protest.

Free African Americans also organized significant institutions, including the numerous self-help and mutual aid societies from which most of today's Black insurance companies grew. One of the earliest mutual benefit societies, the African Union Society, was organized in Newport, Rhode Island, in 1780. Like many similar societies organized later, it helped its members when they were out of work, gave them decent burials, and set up an apprentice program that trained young Blacks to be skilled artisans. Other mutual aid societies included the Masonic Order organized by Prince Hall in 1787 and the Grand United Order of Odd Fellows, established in 1843. These organizations were extremely important within the Black community.

African Americans also organized their own churches. They were forced to sit in separate pews in White churches and were sometimes interrupted in the middle of prayers if they were seated in the "wrong" sections. These kinds of indignities led Blacks such as Richard Allen and Absalom Jones to organize independent Black churches. In 1794, two Black Methodist churches were founded in Philadelphia, St. Thomas Protestant Episcopal Church and the Bethel African Methodist Episcopal Church. African American Methodist churches soon spread to many other cities. African American Baptists also established independent churches. The Black church became an extremely important institution in African American life. It trained most Black protest leaders, opened schools for Black children, gave Blacks practice in self-governance, and increased their self-respect. The church and the fraternal orders, which were affiliated with the church, were the key institutions within Black America. Today, the African American church still performs many of its historic functions and remains an important institution.

THE CIVIL WAR AND RECONSTRUCTION

African Americans viewed the Civil War as the God-sent conflict that would emancipate them from bondage. However, they were virtually alone in this view. Most White Americans, including President Lincoln and the U.S. Congress, viewed the war as a conflict to preserve the Union. When news of the war spread, northern Blacks rushed to recruiting stations and tried to enlist in the armed forces. Their services were rejected. Leaders thought that the war would last only ninety days. The war dragged on for four long years. When it became evident that the war would last much longer than was originally thought, the Union, and later the Confederacy, reluctantly allowed African Americans to take up arms.

Congress and President Lincoln took a number of steps to weaken the Confederacy. They realized that the slaves were being used to help the Confederate forces to maintain their strength. Consequently, Congress enacted a number of laws that undermined the Confederacy. In 1861, Congress enacted legislation enabling it to free slaves who were used to help the Confederate forces. In the summer of 1862, Congress passed a bill that freed slaves who had escaped and authorized the president to use Black troops. Captives had been escaping in large numbers ever since northern soldiers started coming to the South. President Lincoln also used his authority to weaken the Confederacy. On September 22, 1862, he announced that slaves in rebel states would be freed on January 1, 1863. Lincoln kept his promise and issued the Emancipation Proclamation, freeing those slaves in rebel states on January 1, 1863. Although African Americans and abolitionists rejoiced when the Emancipation Proclamation was issued, legally it did no more than the act that was passed by Congress in 1862. The thousands of slaves in states not fighting the Union were not freed, but the proclamation did give African Americans a moral uplift and motivated more captives to escape.

After four bitter years and the bloodiest war in U.S. history up to that time, General Lee surrendered at Appomattox on April 9, 1865, and the Civil War ended. On April 14, 1865, Lincoln was assassinated by John Wilkes Booth, and Andrew Johnson became president. President Johnson, like Lincoln, favored a lenient plan for readmitting the southern states back into the Union. However, the Republican Congress wanted to gain a toehold in the South so that the Republican Party could win future presidential elections. To obtain their objective, they franchised the newly freed African Americans so that they would develop an allegiance to the Republican Party. In a series of acts, Congress gave Black men the right to vote and extended their civil rights, thereby endearing the Republicans to them. In 1865, Congress enacted the Thirteenth Amendment, which abolished slavery throughout the United States, and passed a Civil Rights Act in 1866 that made African Americans citizens and granted them certain legal rights. The Fourteenth Amendment, enacted in 1866, also recognized Blacks as citizens.

The Reconstruction Act of 1867 divided the South into five military districts and required the Confederate states to enact constitutions that would be approved by Congress and to ratify the Fourteenth Amendment before they could be redacted into the Union. The South considered the Reconstruction Act especially galling.

Because they could now vote and run for public office, a number of African Americans held elected offices for brief periods during Reconstruction. Most of them held minor local offices. However, twenty-two served in the U.S. Congress, two as U.S. senators. Black elected officials were too few in number and their tenure too brief for them to play a leading role in shaping policy. However, the South established its most enlightened state constitutions during Reconstruction and enacted some of its most humane social legislation. For years after Reconstruction, southern apologists justified southern violence by arguing that the South was reacting to the former Black control of the southern states. However, African Americans never controlled any of the states' legal bodies and none were elected governors.

THE RISE OF WHITE SUPREMACY

The Republicans' plan to grab the Black man's vote was successful. Blacks in large numbers voted for the Republican presidential candidate in the election of 1868. However, by 1876 the Republicans, who were dominated by northern industrial interests, had new interests and no longer needed Blacks to attain them. In fact, African Americans stood in their way. Northern industrialists were now interested in extending their trade in the South and consequently wanted to court the southern Whites. To appease southern Whites, northern Whites decided to leave the fate of Blacks up to the South. The handling of the Hayes-Tilden election in 1876 indicated the extent to which northern Whites had abandoned African Americans. In that disputed election, an electoral commission named the Republican candidate, Hayes, president. To placate the South, Hayes's supporters promised White southerners that when he became president, Hayes would remove all of the remaining federal troops from the South.

Hayes kept this promise when he became president. By the time that the last federal troops were removed from the South, southern Whites were reestablishing their control of state governments throughout the South and had aggressively begun their campaigns to make African Americans chattel even though slavery had been legally abolished. One of the first acts of the state legislatures was to disenfranchise African Americans. A motley collection of ingenious methods was used to keep Blacks from voting. The Democratic primary election, the grandfather clause, literacy tests, and the poll tax were among the many ways in which African Americans, and, inadvertently, some poor Whites, were prevented from voting.

Determined to "put Blacks in their place," violence against African Americans became rampant. The goals of this violence were to intimidate African Americans to keep them from voting and to reestablish the caste system that had existed before the Civil War. African Americans became victims of a rash of riots that swept through the South between 1866 and 1898. When African Americans tried to obtain the right to vote in New Orleans in 1866, a riot erupted in which forty-eight Blacks were killed. A riot broke out in Savannah, Georgia, in 1872 when Blacks tried to end segregation on the city's streetcars. Thirty African Americans were killed in a riot that erupted in Meridian, Mississippi, in 1871. Forty-six died in a Memphis riot in 1866. Even though Blacks were usually innocent victims in these riots, they struck back at Whites in the Charleston Riot of 1876.

The Ku Klux Klan was reorganized in 1915 and became a prime leader of anti-Black violence. The lynching of African Americans also became widespread. About 100 Blacks met their death each year at the end of a rope during these difficult years.

Southern state legislatures also enacted most of their Jim Crow laws during this period. Laws were passed requiring segregation in schools, parks, restaurants, theaters, and almost all other public accommodation facilities. Tennessee passed a Jim Crow railroad car act in 1881. Most of the other southern and border states soon followed Tennessee's lead. In a series of cases, the Supreme Court upheld and legitimized the South's Jim Crow laws. In 1883 it ruled that the Civil Rights Act of 1875 was unconstitutional. In the *Plessy* v. *Ferguson* case of 1896, it upheld a Louisiana law that required segregation in railroad cars. The Court ruled that literacy tests and poll taxes required for voting were constitutional. It stripped the Fourteenth and Fifteenth Amendments of all their meaning as far as African Americans were concerned and encouraged White southerners to enact more racist laws.

Many African Americans expected to receive forty acres and a mule after the Civil War. However, most of the land confiscated from southern plantation owners was either given back to them or to other members of the southern aristocracy. Few African Americans were able to obtain land. Most of them became bound to the land and to White landowners in the sharecropping system. The sharecropper's life was little better than that of a slave's, and in some ways, worse. In theory, a sharecropper received a share of the crop. However, Black sharecroppers, who had to buy their merchandise from their boss's store, were severely cheated. Each year, when the crops were harvested, they found themselves further and further in debt and required to stay on the land until they paid their bill.

To make the system even more like slavery, southern state legislatures enacted a series of laws between 1865 and 1866 that became known as the Black Codes. These laws were similar to the old slave codes. In some states, Blacks could not testify in court against Whites, carry guns, or buy some types of property. African Americans who were unemployed could be arrested. Those who were unable to pay their fines were hired out. In some places, Black workers could not leave the farm without permission. By the beginning of the twentieth century, White Southerners had totally succeeded in reestablishing White supremacy, reducing African Americans to the status of peons. Black hopes born during the Civil War had been almost completely shattered. When the twentieth century opened, African Americans were deeply disillusioned and saw little hope for the future. They attempted to solve their problems by migrating north, still in search of the American dream.

MIGRATION AND CITY LIFE

After the Civil War, large numbers of African Americans began to migrate to urban areas in the South and to settle in the Southwest (Lemann, 1991). Because of the widespread discrimination they faced in the United States, some African Americans established all-Black towns. Nearly thirty such towns were established near the turn of the century, including Mound Bayou, Mississippi, in 1887 and Langston, Oklahoma, in 1891. Many African Americans also wanted to make Oklahoma an all-Black state, but this idea never materialized.

Although many African Americans settled in the South and Southwest, most who migrated near the turn of the century settled in large cities in the Midwest and East (Adero, 1993). New York City's Black population doubled between 1900 and 1910. During the same period, Chicago's increased by more than 30%. African Americans migrated to northern cities in large numbers in the early 1900s because of the severe economic, political, and social conditions in the South. Southern states had stripped African Americans of most of their legal rights. Disastrous floods, the boll weevil, and the sharecropping system combined to make life on the southern plantations nearly intolerable. The beginning of World War I had nearly stopped immigration from southern and eastern Europe. Consequently, northern manufacturers badly needed laborers. Some of them sent agents to the South to lure Blacks to the North. Black newspapers, such as the *Chicago Defender,* described the North as a land of milk and honey and urged African Americans to leave the South. These forces led nearly one-half million southern Blacks to head for the North during and immediately after World War I. This mass migration to the North greatly disturbed southern Whites because it deprived them of a cheap source of labor. They tried to stop Blacks from going North, but their efforts were futile.

When the African Americans arrived in midwestern and eastern cities, they had a rude awakening. Life in these cities was extremely difficult. African Americans were the victims of White violence and experienced gross discrimination in housing and employment. Many Blacks who moved into White communities were beaten and their homes were bombed. Because of a variety of techniques used by real estate agents, Blacks were excluded from many neighborhoods. Consequently, the Black urban community grew by leaps and bounds because African Americans were forced to live in areas that were predominantly Black. Also, many Blacks preferred to live in communities that had established Black churches, clubs, and fraternal orders.

As African Americans competed with Whites for housing and jobs, conflict and tension developed between them. Whites were determined to keep Blacks from their jobs and out of their communities. White aggression and violence in the early 1900s led to some of the bloodiest riots that the United States had experienced. One of the worst riots occurred in East St. Louis in 1917. The riot was started when a group of Whites fired into a Black neighborhood and Blacks retaliated. Thirty-nine African Americans and nine Whites were killed. During the same year, riots also occurred in Philadelphia and Chester, Pennsylvania. More than twenty riots occurred in cities throughout the United States in 1919. The gifted writer James Weldon Johnson called that summer the "Red Summer" because of the blood that ran in city streets. The most tragic riot that summer occurred in Chicago. The riot started when a Black youth was drowned after being chased by a group of Whites at a segregated beach on Lake Michigan. The riot lasted for almost two weeks. When it ended, thirty-eight people had been killed, twenty-three of them Black. More than 1,000 homes were destroyed, and 537 people were injured. In 1919, riots also occurred in such cities as Washington, D.C., and Longview, Texas.

WORLD WAR I

As they had with other wars, African Americans enthusiastically supported World War I and were impressed with President Woodrow Wilson's high-sounding rhetoric about fighting the war to "make the world safe for democracy." African Americans took Wilson seriously and joined the armed forces in massive numbers. However, it was not long before they realized that White Americans intended African Americans to be second-class citizens in the military. The discrimination that Black soldiers experienced during the war was blatant. When the United States first entered the war, no training camps were established for African American soldiers. Many Black professionals, like doctors, were made privates in the army. Most Black soldiers were given noncombatant assignments, although some fought on the battlefield. A tragic incident that occurred in Houston, Texas, in 1917, symbolized to African Americans more than anything else the status of the Black soldier. When a group of Black soldiers tried to board a segregated streetcar, a fight occurred in which twelve civilians died. Thirteen of the soldiers were sentenced to die, and fourteen were sent to prison for life. The fate of these soldiers shocked and dismayed the African American community.

ORGANIZATIONS

During these trying times a number of African American institutions and organizations emerged to help African Americans adjust to city life and to fight racism and discrimination in the courts. W. E. B. Du Bois, a militant spokesman for Black rights, and a group of Black intellectuals founded the Niagara Movement in 1905. The men in this movement issued a strong statement denouncing American racism. The Niagara Movement was short-lived. However, the National Association for the Advancement of Colored People (NAACP), organized in 1910, was an outgrowth of it. Although most of the officers of the NAACP were White, Black people strongly supported it. The NAACP concentrated on improving the African American's legal status. Under its leadership, the legal status of Blacks greatly improved. A group of social workers founded the National Urban League in 1911 to help Black migrants adjust to city life and to find employment. The Urban League worked against enormous odds because of job discrimination. However, it experienced some gains.

Whereas the NAACP and the National Urban League appealed greatly to middle-class and upwardly mobile African Americans, Marcus Garvey's Universal Negro Improvement Association (UNIA), organized in 1914, was a movement that strongly attracted the Black poor. Garvey preached Black pride and urged African Americans to return to Africa because they would never have equality in the United States. He also urged Blacks to establish businesses and to improve their own communities. The UNIA operated a number of businesses, including restaurants, grocery stores, and a hotel. Garvey was contemptuous of light-skinned and middle-class African Americans because he felt that they wanted to associate with Whites instead of other Blacks. The leading Black spokesmen and organizations were threatened by Garvey. Partly as a result of their efforts, he was jailed for irregularities in the handling of his Black Star Line. More than any other leader during this period, Garvey helped the lower-class African American to feel proud of being Black.

THE HARLEM RENAISSANCE

During the 1920s and 1930s, African American artists, writers, and musicians produced some of their best work. Like their counterparts in the 1960s, they deliberately tried to reflect the African American cultural heritage in their works. They emphasized Black pride and strongly protested racism and discrimination. Gifted poets, such as Claude McKay and Countee Cullen, penned angry poems that reflected Black aspirations and frustrations. Other African American writers during this period, such as Langston Hughes, Jean Toomer, and Zora Neale Hurston, wrote outstanding novels. African American musicians further developed blues and jazz. These two types of music became recognized throughout the world.

WORLD WAR II AND THE YEARS AFTER

African Americans did not expect World War II to bring them any great gains. Their memories of World War I were still too vivid and poignant. However, the war created additional jobs in the large cities, and masses of southern Blacks migrated during and after the war years. Many Blacks migrated to the West Coast as well as to the North. More than 150,000 African Americans left the South each year between 1940 and 1950. Black city migrants encountered problems similar to those experienced by African Americans who had migrated in earlier decades. Segregation in housing was still increasing. Many manufacturers with government contracts to make war-related materials refused to hire Blacks or hired them only for the lowest-paying jobs. President Franklin Roosevelt refused to take action to stop job discrimination until A. Philip Randolph threatened to march on Washington with 100,000 African Americans. To prevent the march, Roosevelt issued an executive order that outlawed discrimination in defense-related jobs and set up a federal committee on fair employment.

Violence and riots also erupted in the cities. The most serious riot during this period occurred in Detroit in the summer of 1943. It lasted for more than thirty hours. When the riot was over, thirty-four people were dead, twenty-five of them Black. During the same summer, riots also occurred in Los Angeles and in the Harlem district of New York City. These riots, especially the one in Detroit, greatly alarmed U.S. politicians. Mayors in many cities formulated commissions to study the causes of the racial outbreaks and to recommend ways to eliminate their causes.

President Truman

President Harry S. Truman, who won the presidential election in 1948 with heavy Black support, took a number of steps to improve race relations and helped to pave the way for the civil rights movement that reached its height in the 1960s. With the use of executive orders, he desegregated the armed forces and created a Committee on Civil Rights that investigated the condition of African Americans. The committee's publication, *To Secure These Rights*, recommended total integration in U.S. society. Truman also ordered industries doing business with the federal government to end discrimination. These measures were mainly symbolic and did not seriously affect the African American's status in the United States. However, they contributed significantly to setting an atmosphere of racial tolerance and the rising expectations of African Americans.

The Supreme Court

More important than Truman's action in improving race relations during the 1940s and 1950s were the actions of the U.S. Supreme Court. During the decades after the Civil War, the Supreme Court had consistently made decisions that denied African Americans civil liberties and legitimized and legalized racist practices. It now began to rule in favor of civil rights. In a series of cases, most of which were led or supported by the NAACP, the Court ruled for greater civil liberties for African Americans, thus reversing its racist tradition. In 1946, the Court ruled against segregation in interstate commerce and made a negative ruling regarding the restrictive covenants in 1948. In a number of cases related to African Americans attending segregated White universities in the southern and border states, it consistently ruled that Black Americans should be provided a higher education equal to that of Whites in their home states. These rulings forced many states to integrate their state universities. However, many of them created "instant" professional schools for African Americans. The landmark decision of this period was the *Brown* v. *Board of Education of Topeka* decision of 1954, which ruled that school segregation is inherently unequal. Perhaps more than any other single event, this decision by the high court helped pave the way for the civil rights movement of the 1960s and 1970s.

THE CIVIL RIGHTS MOVEMENT
OF THE 1960s AND 1970s

In the 1960s, African Americans began a fight for their rights that was unprecedented in the nation's history. However, the civil rights movement of the 1960s was closely related to the heritage of Black protest in America evident in slave rebellions and uprisings. Black Americans have always protested in ways consistent with the times in which they lived. David Walker, W. E. B. Du Bois, Ida B. Wells, and Ella Baker are a few of the many eminent African Americans who strongly protested against American racism through the years. In the 1960s, Martin Luther King, Jr., Malcolm X, and Fannie Lou Hamer joined this tradition of protest. The Black protest in the 1960s was unique in our history because the times were different. Black protest tends to reflect the times in which it occurs.

During the late 1940s and 1950s, events that occurred to elevate Black people's hopes for a better life in the United States included the actions of President Truman, the *Brown* decision of 1954, and the Civil Rights Act of 1957. As African Americans saw more and more signs indicating that social, economic, and political conditions were improving, they became increasingly impatient with their caste status. Signs of the African American's second-class status were rampant throughout the South when the Montgomery bus boycott began in 1955. The boycott was conceptualized and planned by Jo Ann Gibson Robinson and the Women's Political Council, a group of civic-minded African American women in Montgomery. Robinson gives her accounts of these events in her memoir (Garrow, 1987).

The boycott started when Rosa Parks, a Black seamstress, was jailed for refusing to move to the back of a city bus. Montgomery Blacks decided that they had taken enough and that they would fight the city's bus company until it eliminated segregation. They began a boycott of the bus line that did not end until a federal court outlawed racial segregation on Montgomery buses a year later. Martin Luther King, Jr., the young preacher who led the boycott, became the country's most influential civil rights leader and remained so until he was assassinated in 1968. Under his leadership and influence, the civil rights movement used direct action and nonviolent tactics to protest racism and discrimination in all areas of American life, including housing, education, and politics.

The civil rights movement actually began when four African American students—who sat down at a segregated lunch counter at a Woolworth's store in Greensboro, North Carolina, on February 1, 1960—refused to leave when they were not served. They had launched the sit-in movement. Within a short time, the sit-in movement had spread throughout the South, and African American college students were desegregating lunch counters and other public accommodation facilities in many cities below the Mason-Dixon line. African American student activists formed the Student Nonviolent Coordinating Committee (SNCC) in 1960 to coordinate their protest activities.

The student protests stimulated other civil rights groups to become more active. The Congress of Racial Equality (CORE), which had been organized since 1942, sponsored a number of freedom rides to Alabama and Mississippi in 1961 to test interstate transportation laws. The CORE riders were the victims of much hostility and violence. Many of them were beaten and jailed, and some of the buses in which they rode were burned. In 1957, King and a group of Black ministers organized the Southern Christian Leadership Conference (SCLC). SCLC trained its volunteers to use civil disobedience tactics and led numerous mass demonstrations. In 1963, King led a demonstration in Birmingham to protest racism and discrimination. The demonstrators were the victims of blatant police violence that was viewed throughout the United States and the rest of the world on television. Mass demonstrations culminated in the summer of 1963, when more than 200,000 people participated in the March on Washington for Freedom and Jobs.

These demonstrations resulted in some small but significant legal gains for African Americans. The historic March on Washington helped to rally public opinion for support of the Civil Rights Act, which finally passed in 1964 after much filibustering in Congress. A voting rights act was enacted in 1965 after King led demonstrations in Selma, Alabama. As a result of this act, which authorized federal workers to oversee elections in the South, the number of African American voters increased sharply in some southern states and counties. However, the mass of African Americans remained poor and without political power. By 1965, many young African American leaders, such as Stokely Carmichael and H. Rap Brown, who had been staunch supporters of nonviolent resistance, began to raise serious questions about this approach and to urge more militant action and different goals.

During a civil rights demonstration in 1966, Carmichael issued a call for "Black Power," and both the phrase and the ideas it signified spread throughout Black America like wildfire. Carmichael had coined a term that described a mood already pervasive within Black America. The concept of Black Power emerged during a time when the civil rights movement was losing momentum and when African Americans were becoming increasingly frustrated with the slow pace of the gains they had acquired using civil disobedience tactics. Black Power had different meanings for most Whites than for most African Americans. To most African Americans, it meant political power, pride in Blackness, Black control of schools and communities, and Black self-help organizations. To most Whites, the concept meant retaliatory violence and "Black racism." Malcolm X candidly articulated the concept to the Black masses. Black organizations such as the Black Panther Party, which was organized in Oakland, California, in 1966, tried to implement the concept. The Panthers attempted to protect the Black community and organized free lunch programs for African American children. The Nation of Islam (Black Muslims) also reflected the concept in its businesses, farms, schools, and weekly newspaper.

Black frustrations, which reached new highs in the mid and late 1960s, were manifested in a series of tragic race riots in U.S. cities. Unlike the earlier riots in which Whites attacked Blacks, these riots were different because they involved little contact between Whites and Blacks. Rather, urban Blacks directed their attacks toward the symbols of White society within their communities. They burned buildings owned by absentee landlords and looted stores run by merchants who they believed cheated them. The prestigious Kerner Commission, which was appointed by President Lyndon B. Johnson, concluded in 1968 that the riots were caused by the White racism that was rooted deeply in American life. Riots occurred in cities from New York to Los Angeles. Two of the most serious occurred during the summer of 1967 in Newark and Detroit. Twenty-three people lost their lives in the Newark riot; forty-three died in the Detroit outbreak. As in all of the riots during the 1960s, most of the victims were African Americans killed by White law officials. The Kerner Commission concluded in its massive report on the rebellions, "Our nation is moving toward two societies, one White, one Black—separate and unequal" (*Report of the National Advisory Commission on Civil Disorders*, 1968, p. 1).

Women in the Civil Rights Movement

With a history of activism and opposition to oppression trailing them, Black women embraced their legacy of active resistance and worked toward ending racial oppression during the civil rights movement. Despite sexism throughout U.S. society and within the civil rights movement itself, many Black women participated in organizational segments of the movement. Others provided direct and indirect leadership in civil rights organizations.

Black women formed the foundation of the organizational segment of the civil rights movement (Payne, 1993). In many civil rights organizations, they coordinated activities and also mobilized groups. These groups were often composed of large numbers of Black women who participated in voter registration, boycotts, and demonstrations. These grassroots activities, which took place throughout the South, enabled large numbers of African Americans to participate in and gain empowerment from the civil rights movement.

Although the civil rights movement worked against discrimination and exclusion, sexism existed within most of its organizations (Standley, 1993). Despite the small representation of women's leadership in some civil rights groups, a few women secured visible posts and others led groups indirectly. For example, Ella Baker helped to form and served as the chief adviser of the Student Nonviolent Coordinating Committee from 1960 to 1964. Fannie Lou Hamer was a cofounder of the Mississippi Democratic Freedom Party and ran as a candidate for Congress under the party's name. Septima Clark greatly influenced the civil rights movement through her role as the director of education and teaching for the Southern Christian Leadership Conference. She traveled throughout the South to educate African Americans in literacy and helped in voter registration.

Other women played significant roles in the civil rights movement through leadership in lesser-known organizations. Jo Ann Gibson Robinson and the other members of the Women's Political Council provided the organizational support for the Montgomery bus boycott (Garrow, 1987). Before the boycott they exposed the abuses against Blacks that occurred when they rode the city buses. In rural communities, women formed business cooperatives such as the Madison County Sewing Firm and the Hopedale Sewing Project. These small corporations provided jobs for women who had been fired for participating in civil rights activities (Crawford, 1993).

Black women's participation in civil rights activities placed in jeopardy not only their lives but also the livelihood of their families. They could lose their jobs and homes and become victims of terrorist activities. Black women who participated in the civil rights movement faced serious personal, social, and political challenges, which they were willing to take.

AFRICAN AMERICANS TODAY: PROGRESS AND PROBLEMS

Several major trends can be identified in the social, economic, and political condition of African Americans since the civil rights movement of the 1960s. African Americans experienced significant economic gains relative to Whites during the 1960s. During the 1970s the economic condition of African Americans relative to Whites stagnated. During the last two decades, African Americans have experienced both gains and setbacks (Clayton, 1996; Stoll, 2004).

Data released by the U.S. Census Bureau (2005) indicate that African Americans made educational, economic, and political progress between 1990 and 2005. However, these data also indicate that the Black community still faces important challenges in income, housing, and social mobility. The African American community is divided significantly along social class lines. While an important part of the Black community is middle and upper class, a large segment remains in inner-city, low-income communities with high rates of unemployment and female-headed households (Wilson, 1996). Many middle- and upper-status Blacks live in suburban communities.

In the last decade, African Americans made significant progress in educational attainment. In 2005, Blacks were close to parity with Whites in high school graduation rates, but the gap between college graduation rates was wide. In 2005, 80% of African Americans age 25 and over had completed high school, compared to 89% of non-Hispanic Whites (U.S. Census Bureau, 2005). In 1990, the rates for these population groups were 66% and 79%, respectively (U.S. Census Bureau, 1990). In 2005, the proportion of non-Hispanic Whites with at least a bachelor's degree (30%) was almost twice that of African Americans (17.5%). Among young adults with at least a bachelor's degree (25 to 29 years), the percentage of non-Hispanic Whites (34%) is twice that of their African American counterparts (17%) (U.S. Census Bureau, 2005).

In 2005, 31% of African American women and 21% of African American men worked in managerial and professional occupations, compared to 40% and 35% of their non-Hispanic White counterparts (U.S. Census Bureau, 2005). The 2005 median household income for African Americans was $31,041—in real terms—the highest ever recorded, yet still the lowest median income of any racial group (compared to $50,519 for non-Hispanic Whites) (U.S. Census Bureau, 2005). As of 2004, 54% of African American married-couple families had incomes of $50,000 or more, compared with 60% for their White, non-Hispanic counterparts (U.S. Census Bureau, 2005). Nearly 46% of African Americans were homeowners (U.S. Census Bureau, 2005).

Even though African Americans continue to make progress in many areas of American life, they still face serious challenges. In 2005, the average per capita income for Blacks was $16,326, compared to $28,760 for non-Hispanic Whites and $25,035 for the overall population (U.S. Census Bureau, 2005). Only 36% of all Black families—compared to 62% of all non-Hispanic White families—had incomes of $50,000 or more in 2005 (U.S. Census Bureau, 2006). Estimates by the U.S. Census in 2004 indicated that less than one-half (47%) of all African American families were married-couple families. Forty-five percent were maintained by women with no spouse present, while nearly 9% were maintained by men without a spouse (U.S. Census Bureau, 2004). The comparable figures for non-Hispanic White families are: 82% married-couple families, 13% maintained by women with no spouse present, and 5% maintained by men with no wife present.

A large proportion of African American families and children continue to be victims of poverty. In 2005, an average of 36.6 million Americans were living in poverty; 8.9 million were African Americans, and 16.3 million were non-Hispanic Whites. The poverty rate was 12.6% for the total population, 24.7% for African Americans, and 8.4% for non-Hispanic Whites (Denavas-Walt, Proctor, & Lee, 2006). In 2005, 34.5% of African American children under the age of 18 lived in poverty, compared to nearly 18% for all children and 10% for non-Hispanic White children. More than three times more African American children lived in poverty than non-Hispanic White children (Denavas-Walt, Proctor, & Lee, 2006).

A number of factors contribute to the large percentage of African American families and children that still live in poverty. One important factor is the substantial changes in the economy. Most low-skilled workers were able to obtain well-paying jobs a generation ago. However, as the U.S. economy has been transformed, fewer low-skilled jobs are available. Increasingly, available jobs require technical skills and knowledge. Black workers are disproportionately concentrated among low-skilled workers. The movement of many jobs out of the central cities and into the suburbs, as well as racial discrimination, are additional factors that have slowed the economic progress of African Americans.

African Americans in the Political System

African Americans have made substantial gains in politics since the voting rights legislation that resulted from the civil rights movement of the 1960s and 1970s. Their progress in politics is a direct result of African Americans being able to vote and run freely for office. Elected African American officials increased from a few dozen in 1940 to more than 6,800 in 1988 (Jaynes & Williams, 1989). In 1990 there were 300 African American mayors, 10% of whom were mayors of cities with at least 400,000 people (Shearer, 1990).

African Americans experienced both gains and losses in politics between 1990 and 2000. In 1998, Carol Mosley-Braun (Dem. Ill.)—who was the only African American U.S. senator—lost her reelection campaign and consequently her seat in the Senate. However, in January 1999, there were thirty-nine African Americans in the House of Representatives. At the state level, there were one governor, 156 state senators, and 427 representatives. Two African Americans were county executives; 794 were members of county governing boards. There were also 450 Black mayors and 3,498 members of city governing bodies in 1999 (Joint Center for Political and Economic Studies, 1999). In January 2005, Barack Obama, Democrat from Illinois, became the fifth African American Senator in U.S. history. He also became a very serious candidate for president of the United States in 2007. By July 2007, he had raised more money for his campaign than all other candidates in both parties, including his most important rival, Senator Hillary Rodham Clinton from New York.

Blacks Lose Ground with the Supreme Court

Although African Americans experienced significant political gains in the legislative branch of government during the 1990s and 2000s, they experienced serious setbacks in the judicial branch at the federal level. During his presidency George W. Bush stacked the Supreme Court with conservative judges, including Chief Justice John G. Roberts, Jr., and Associate Justice Samuel Alito. With the addition of two more conservatives to the Court and the resignation of Justice Sandra Day O'Connor in 2006—who was a Reagan appointee but a moderate conservative— the ardent conservatives gained control of the Court in 2006. The Court made many decisions in its 2007 term that favored the rich over the poor and that posed threats to civil liberties and civil rights. Its most important decision that challenged civil rights was its decision—in a five-to-four vote—that declared unconstitutional plans to racially desegregate schools in Seattle, Washington, and Louisville, Kentucky. Many Americans felt that the decision was regressive and threatened to turn back the gains that had been achieved as a result of the *Brown* v. *Board of Education of*

Topeka decision in 1954, the Court's historic case that declared school racial segregation unconstitutional.

Diversity in the African American Community

Immigration from Africa and the Caribbean since 1990 has significantly increased the diversity within the African American community. Blacks immigrating from sub-Saharan Africa to the United States more than doubled in the 1990s. Immigration from the Caribbean to the United States increased over 60 percent (Logan & Deane, 2003). Twenty-five percent of the growth in the African American population between 1990 and 2000 resulted from Black immigrant populations. Many of the immigrants from the Caribbean came from Jamaica, Haiti, and Guyana. Significant numbers of African immigrants came from Ghana, Nigeria, Ethiopia, and Somalia. Most Afro-Caribbean communities are found on the East Coast in the New York, Miami, and Fort Lauderdale metropolitan areas. The African communities are not as geographically concentrated as the Afro-Caribbean communities, although there are large communities in Washington, D.C., and New York. However, some African communities are in the West. For example, there is a significant number of Ethiopians in Seattle. The social and economic status of Afro-Caribbeans and Africans exceed that of African Americans by important margins. Their social and economic status is also above that of Hispanics (Logan & Deane, 2003). Table 7.1 shows immigrants to the United States from selected nations in the Caribbean and Africa between 1991 and 2005.

TABLE 7.1   African and Caribbean Immigrants to the United States from Selected Nations, 1991 to 2005 (in thousands; 104.9 represents 104,900)

AFRICA	
Nigeria	146.7
Ethiopia	114.7
Egypt	104.9
Ghana	75.0
South Africa	56.3
Somalia	39.8
CARIBBEAN	
Dominican Republic	720.5
Jamaica	463.4
Haiti	410.1
Trinidad and Tobago	131.2
Panama	60.9

Source: U.S. Census Bureau (2006), *Statistical Abstract of the United States, 2006* (125th ed.). Washington, DC: U.S. Government Printing Office, p. 11.

Social Class within the African American Community

A substantial number of African Americans have been able to enter the middle class as a result of opportunities and possibilities that resulted from the civil rights movement of the 1960s and 1970s (Cose, 1993). One of the most important developments in the social and economic situation of Blacks since the 1960s has been the development of substantial social class differences within the African American community and the increase of class differentiation (Wilson, 1996). Significant social class variation has existed within the African American community for many decades.

However, class variation within the African American community has never been as steep, nor have African Americans ever been as separated as much, in terms of neighborhoods and communities, on a social class basis. New careers, opportunities, and possibilities opened up for African Americans as a result of the civil rights movement and the affirmative action policies that followed it. Many of the African Americans who had the education and other skills to take advantage of these opportunities are now functioning in mainstream institutions as physicians, college professors and administrators, businesspeople, and corporation heads. Many of these individuals, like their White peers, have joined the exodus to the suburbs and are sending their children to predominantly White suburban public schools or to elite private schools. However, despite their social class mobility and high levels of acculturation, the Black middle class still experiences racism and discrimination (Feagin & Sikes, 1994).

African Americans from all cultures, social classes, and walks of life experience institutional racism and discrimination. The shared experiences of African Americans reinforce their sense of identity and peoplehood. Also, most middle- and upper-class African Americans want their children to know and to feel comfortable with other Blacks and with Black culture. Consequently, a number of middle- and upper-class African Americans encourage their children to attend historically Black colleges such as Fisk, Spelman, Morehouse, Howard, and Hampton.

Few careful studies have been done on social class variation within the African American community. Most articles and research on African Americans focus on the significant percentage of them who are low income. The wide social class variation within the African American community must be described in order to present an accurate description of Blacks in contemporary American life.

The New Century

When the twenty-first century began, African Americans were hopeful about their progress but deeply concerned about the large number of Black children living in poverty and about the conservative political forces in American society that were achieving significant political victories at all levels of government. However, a consensus has been developing within the African American community that it must and can take the leadership for its own improvement and that it has the resources to do so.

These resources have to be mobilized. African Americans have a significant middle class that functions in many of the nation's leading institutions. They have Black colleges with a distinguished record of academic excellence, and they have a strong tradition of self-help that has built impressive institutions and businesses. African Americans are working to help themselves and are thinking deeply about their future—and their children's future—in America.

TEACHING STRATEGIES

To illustrate how content related to African Americans can be used to integrate the curriculum, exemplary strategies are identified for teaching the following concepts at the grade levels indicated: *tradition* (primary grades), *Black protest* (intermediate and upper grades), and *separatism* (high school grades).

Primary Grades

Concept

Tradition

Generalization: African American songs and music are an important part of their cultural tradition and are passed down from generation to generation.

1. Ask the students, "What special days do you celebrate in your family?" List their responses on the board or butcher paper. Answers might include birthdays, Kwanza, Chinese New Year, Chanukah, the Fourth of July, and Thanksgiving.
2. Select several of their responses, such as birthdays, the Fourth of July, and Thanksgiving. Ask the children to give their ideas about why these special days are celebrated in their families. Ask them, "Which of the special days celebrated in your family are also celebrated (a) in other families, (b) in school, (c) throughout the nation?" Ask, "Why are these special days also celebrated by these other groups?"
3. Help the students to develop and state the idea that we celebrate these special days because they help us to remember and to honor important events in our personal histories (birthdays), the histories of our families (family reunions), or in the history of our nation (Thanksgiving and the Fourth of July).
4. Explain that the celebration of these special days helps us to remember and to honor our heritages and traditions. Explain that traditions are important ideas, events, and memories that are handed down from one generation to the next. Say, "Not only do families and nations have traditions, but so do groups of Americans such as African Americans, Mexican Americans, Japanese Americans, and Jewish Americans."
5. Tell the students that an important part of the heritage and traditions of African Americans is the song "Lift Ev'ry Voice and Sing," written by James Weldon Johnson and set to music by his brother, J. Rosamond Johnson. Tell the class that the song is often referred to by African Americans as the "Black National Anthem." Remind them that our national anthem is "The Star-Spangled Banner" by Francis Scott Key. Ask the students, "Why do you think that 'Lift Ev'ry Voice and Sing' is sometimes referred to as the 'Black National Anthem'?"

6. Working with the music teacher in your school, introduce your students to "Lift Ev'ry Voice and Sing." A beautifully illustrated version of the song makes up the book *Lift Ev'ry Voice and Sing* by James Weldon Johnson (1995), with moving illustrations by Jan Spivey Gilchrist.
7. Before teaching the students to sing the song, teach the words to them as a poem. Discuss the meaning of each stanza in the song. After the students have discussed each stanza in the song, summarize the lesson by explaining that the song describes the history and struggle of African Americans in the United States and that it is an important part of their traditions. Conclude the unit by teaching the students to sing "Lift Ev'ry Voice and Sing."

Intermediate and Upper Grades

Concept

Black protest

Generalization: African Americans have protested racism and discrimination throughout their history in America. The forms of protest reflected the times in which they occurred.

1. Begin this unit by showing and discussing with the students Part I of the videotape series *Eyes on the Prize* (or a similar one). In the discussion, focus on the reasons Black protest emerged and the forms that it took during the years covered in this videotape, 1954 to 1956.
2. Tell the students the story of the slave mutinies that occurred both on the West African coast and in midocean. Herbert Aptheker (1987), *American Negro Slave Revolts,* and Eugene D. Genovese (1979), *From Rebellion to Revolution: Afro-American Slave Revolts in the Making of the Modern World,* are well-researched and highly regarded sources of information on slave rebellions. Ask the students to act out, in role-play situations, the stories they have heard. After the role-play situations, ask them to hypothesize by responding to the following questions. Write their responses on the board.
   a. Why do you think the slaves were captured?
   b. Why do you think they started mutinies?
   c. Why didn't the mutinies end the slave trade?
   d. Do you think it was right for slaves to be captured? Why or why not?
   e. Do you think it was right for slaves to rebel? Why or why not?
      After the students have responded to these questions, read to them, or ask them to read, selections on the slave trade so that they can test their hypotheses.
3. Ask three different groups of students to research the following three topics:
   a. The Gabriel Prosser revolt of 1800
   b. The Denmark Vesey revolt of 1822
   c. The Nat Turner revolt of 1831
      To help them guide their research, ask the groups to focus on the following questions:
   a. Where did the revolt occur?
   b. Why did the revolt occur?
   c. Who led the revolt?
   d. Was the revolt successful? Why or why not?
   e. How were the rebels punished? Why were they punished?

Discuss the questions above with the entire class when the groups have presented their research. List the students' responses on the board. Through questioning, help the students see how the slave insurrections were both alike and different and why, of the three rebellions, only the Turner revolt was successful. After the class discussion, ask each group to plan and present to the class a dramatization showing the sequence of events in the rebellion they studied.

4. African Americans were active in the abolitionist movement and in the Underground Railroad, a loosely organized system that helped many slaves escape to the northern states and to Canada. Ask individual students to research the lives of and to "become," in a dramatization, one of the following people.

David Walker	James Forten
Henry Highland Garnet	Frederick Douglass
Robert Purvis	Harriet Tubman
Sojourner Truth	

When the dramatizations are presented, discuss the following questions with the class:

a. Why did African American abolitionists oppose slavery? How did their views differ from those of White abolitionists? Why did White abolitionists discriminate against Black abolitionists? Excellent sources on the Black abolitionists are Shirley J. Yee's (1992) *Black Women Abolitionists* and Benjamin Quarles's (1969) *Black Abolitionists*.

b. What was the Underground Railroad? How did it help slaves escape? Who were some of the outstanding "conductors" on the railroad? What risks did captives take when they escaped? Why did they take them? If you had been a slave, would you have tried to escape? Why or why not?

5. Ask individual students or groups of students to research the following organizations and movements and to describe ways in which they protested racism and discrimination.

a. The Negro Convention Movement (1800s)
b. The Niagara Movement (1905)
c. The National Association for the Advancement of Colored People (1910)
d. The National Urban League (1911)
e. The Universal Negro Improvement Association (1914)
f. The Black church in the 1800s

When their research is complete, the students should share it with the class. The class should discuss how these organizations and movements expressed discontent with the plight of African Americans, the actions they took to improve it, and the successes and failures they experienced and why.

6. Have the class role-play a civil rights conference in 1966 in which leaders of the organizations listed below debate the future directions of the movement. Each organizational representative should be thoroughly familiar with his or her organization's philosophical position in 1966. By that year, the civil rights movement was becoming increasingly radicalized, and deep factions had developed within the various organizations.

Southern Christian Leadership Conference (SCLC)
National Association for the Advancement of Colored People (NAACP)
National Urban League
Congress of Racial Equality (CORE)

Student Nonviolent Coordinating Committee (SNCC)
Black Panther Party
Revolutionary Action Movement (RAM)

7. Have the students role-play a meeting of the following people after a serious racial rebellion in a major city in 1967. These people have met to decide what can be done to eliminate the causes of city riots. Ask individual students to play specific roles. To structure this activity more tightly, write a role description for each character on a three-by-five-inch index card and give the cards to the student role-players.

Roles are as follows:
Mayor of the city
SCLC spokesperson
NAACP spokesperson
National Urban League spokesperson
CORE spokesperson
SNCC spokesperson
Black Panther Party spokesperson
RAM spokesperson
Young person who has participated in a riot

8. To enable the students to summarize this unit and to derive the key generalizations stated above, have them complete the data retrieval chart in Table 7.2.

TABLE 7.2   Black Protest: Data Retrieval Chart

FORM OF PROTEST, ORGANIZATION, OR MOVEMENT	GOAL OF PROTESTS	WAYS OF PROTEST	RESULTS OF PROTESTS
Slave mutinies			
Slave rebellions (in USA)			
Black abolitionary movement			
Underground Railroad			
Niagara Movement			
NAACP			
National Urban League			
SCLC			
CORE			
SNCC			
Black Panther Party			
RAM			

Valuing Activity

Read the following story to the class and ask the questions that follow.

Trying to Buy a Home in Lakewood Island

About a year ago, Joan and Henry Green, a young African American couple, moved from the West Coast to a large city in the Midwest. They moved because Henry finished his Ph.D. in chemistry and took a job at a big university in Midwestern City. Since they have been in Midwestern City, the Greens have rented an apartment in the central area of the city. However, they have decided that they want to buy a house. Their apartment has become too small for the many books and other things they have accumulated during the year. In addition to wanting more space, they want a house so that they can receive breaks on their income tax, which they do not receive living in an apartment. The Greens also think that a house will be a good financial investment.

The Greens have decided to move into a suburban community. They want a new house, and most of the houses within the city limits are rather old. They also feel that they can obtain a larger house for their money in the suburbs than in the city. They have looked at several suburban communities and have decided that they like Lakewood Island better than any of the others. Lakewood Island is a predominantly White community composed primarily of lower-middle-class and middle-class residents. There are a few wealthy families in Lakewood Island, but they are the exceptions rather than the rule.

Joan and Henry Green have become frustrated because of the problems they have experienced trying to buy a home in Lakewood Island. Before they go out to look at a house, they carefully study the newspaper ads. When they arrived at the first house in which they were interested, the owner told them that his house had just been sold. A week later they decided to work with a realtor. When they tried to close the deal on the next house they wanted, the realtor told them that the owner had raised the price $50,000 because he had had the house appraised since he had put it on the market and had discovered that his selling price was much too low. When the Greens tried to buy a third house in Lakewood Island, the owner told them that he had decided not to sell because he had not received the job in another city that he was almost sure that he would receive when he had put his house up for sale. He explained that the realtor had not removed the ad about his house from the newspaper even though he had told him that he had decided not to sell a week earlier. The realtor the owner had been working with had left the real estate company a few days ago. Henry is bitter and feels that he and his wife are victims of racism and discrimination. Joan believes that Henry is too sensitive and that they have been the victims of a series of events that could have happened to anyone, regardless of their race.

Questions

1. Do you think that the Greens were discriminated against in Lakewood Island? Why or why not?
2. What should the Greens do? Why?
3. If you were the Greens, what would you do? Why?
4. What can the Greens do to determine if they are victims of discrimination?

High School Grades

Concept

Separatism

Generalization: Black separatist movements emerge when African Americans experience acute discrimination and a heightened sense of racial pride.

1. Either through choice or force, Black separatism has always existed in America. Most of the social life of the slaves was confined to their communities. One of the earliest manifestations of Black separatism was the colonization movement led by African Americans. To begin this unit, ask several students to prepare and present research reports on the following topics:
   a. Martin R. Delany
   b. Paul Cuffe
   c. The African Colonization Society
      When the reports are presented to the class, the following questions should be discussed:
   a. Why did colonization movements emerge among African Americans?
   b. Were these movements popular and successful? Why or why not?
   c. Why did back-to-Africa movements fail to appeal to most African Americans?
   d. If early Black-led colonization attempts had succeeded, how do you think the subsequent history of African Americans would have been different?

2. Because of discrimination and the need for group solidarity, a number of African American organizations emerged in the 1800s. Ask a group of students to prepare short papers on the following topics and present them to the class in a panel discussion on separate Black institutions in the 1800s.

   The Black church
   Black fraternal and self-help organizations
   Black businesses
   Black schools and colleges
   The Negro Convention Movement

   Role-play a Negro Convention in the 1800s in which the participants draft a position statement detailing their major grievances about the plight of African Americans and a plan of action for social change. All of the delegates to the simulated convention must reach agreement on the position statement they prepare. The student role-players will need to be thoroughly familiar with the Negro Convention Movement and the various points of view that were presented in the series of Negro Conventions held in the 1800s.

3. The Niagara Movement was a Black protest organization organized in 1905 by W. E. B. Du Bois and a group of Black intellectuals. Ask a group of students to prepare a research report on this movement and present it to the class.

4. Most of the national civil rights organizations in the early 1900s were interracial. Ask the students to do required readings on the history and development of the NAACP and the National Urban League. When they have completed the readings, they should compare and contrast these two organizations with the Niagara Movement and earlier Black protest movements and organizations such as the Negro Convention Movement. Particular attention should be paid to (a) reasons the organizations emerged, (b) people who made major policy decisions and held key positions within

them, (c) types of problems that arose within the organizations, (d) the major goals of the organizations, and (e) ways in which the organizations succeeded or failed and why. While studying these organizations, the students should compare and contrast the ideas and actions of Booker T. Washington and W. E. B. Du Bois. To conclude this activity, ask two students to role-play a debate between Washington and Du Bois on the kind of education needed by African Americans. Two excellent references for this last exercise are *Up from Slavery* by Booker T. Washington and *The Souls of Black Folk* by W. E. B. Du Bois.

5. Ask a group of students to prepare a panel discussion on the ideas and actions of Marcus Garvey and the Universal Negro Improvement Association. Ask them to focus on the following questions:
   a. What social, economic, and political conditions made Garvey's movement particularly appealing to low-income African Americans?
   b. How did Garvey's ideas help to improve low-income Blacks' feelings about themselves?
   c. Why was Garvey's back-to-Africa movement unsuccessful?
   d. Why did conflict develop between Garvey and other Black leaders?
   e. Why was Garvey ultimately crushed as a leader?
   f. What was the main significance of Garvey's movement? The classic biography of Garvey is *Black Moses* by E. D. Cronon. Another excellent book for this activity is *Marcus Garvey and the Vision of Africa* edited by John Henrik Clarke.

6. When the Black revolt emerged in 1960, its major goal was to desegregate public accommodation facilities and other institutions. Action tactics and court battles achieved much desegregation. However, by 1965, many African Americans, especially young Black activists, were disillusioned with the attainments of the movement and realized that integration alone would not eliminate the African American's major social, economic, and political problems. These young activists felt that both the goals and tactics of the movement should be changed. They issued a call for Black Power.

   Ask the entire class to read excerpts from *Black Power: The Politics of Liberation in America* by Stokely Carmichael and Charles V. Hamilton. Discuss each excerpt with the class. The following questions and exercises can help guide class discussion and student research. An excellent reference for this activity is Joseph (2006), *Waiting 'til the Midnight Hour: A Narrative History of Black Power in America.*
   a. What did the concept "Black Power" mean? Did it mean the same things to African Americans and White Americans?
   b. Compare and contrast the goals of the Black Power movement and the goals of civil rights organizations like SCLC and the NAACP in the early 1960s.
   c. What kinds of economic, political, and social institutions were implied by the concept of Black Power?
   d. Compare and contrast the views of the following people:

David Walker	W. E. B. Du Bois
Martin R. Delany	Stokely Carmichael
Richard Allen	Malcolm X
Prentice Hall	Angela Y. Davis
Paul Cuffe	Jesse Jackson
Marcus Garvey	Fannie Lou Hamer
Al Sharpton	

7. Ask the students to research the Afrocentric movement in the 1990s and to state how it is similar to and different from early Black separatist movements. The ideas and work of Molefi K. Asante (1988) should be examined.
8. Conclude the unit by asking the students to present a dramatization that shows how Black separatism has developed and changed from the 1700s to the 2000s.

REFERENCES

Adero, M. (Ed.). (1993). *Up South: Stories, Studies, and Letters of This Century's African-American Migrations.* New York: New Press.

Aptheker, H. (1987). *American Negro Slave Revolts* (40th anniv. ed.). New York: International Publishers.

Asante, M. K. (1988). *Afrocentricity.* Trenton, NJ: Africa World Press.

Clayton, O. (Ed.). (1996). *An American Dilemma Revisited: Race Relations in a Changing World.* New York: Russell Sage Foundation.

Cose, E. (1993). *The Rage of a Privileged Class.* New York: HarperCollins.

Crawford, V. (1993). Beyond the Human Self: Grassroots Activists in the Mississippi Civil Rights Movement. In V. Crawford, J. A. Rouse, & B. Woods (Eds.), *Women in the Civil Rights Movement: Trailblazers and Torchbearers 1941–1965* (pp. 13–26). Bloomington: Indiana University Press.

Denavas-Walt, C., Proctor, B. D., & Lee, C. H. (2006). *Income, Poverty, and Health Insurance Coverage in the United States: 2005.* U.S. Census Bureau, Current Population Reports, P60–231. Washington, DC: U.S. Government Printing Office.

Du Bois, W. E. B. (1903/1973). *The Souls of Black Folk.* Millwood, NY: Kraus-Thomas.

Feagin, J. R., & Sikes, M. P. (1994). *Living with Racism: The Black Middle-Class Experience.* Boston: Beacon Press.

Garrow, D. (Ed.). (1987). *The Montgomery Bus Boycott and the Women Who Started It: The Memoir of Jo Ann Gibson Robinson.* Knoxville: University of Tennessee Press.

Genovese, E. D. (1979). *From Rebellion to Revolution: Afro-American Slave Revolts in the Making of the Modern World.* Baton Rouge: Louisiana State University Press.

Jaynes, G. D., & Williams, R. M., Jr. (1989). *A Common Destiny: Blacks and American Society.* Washington, DC: National Academy Press.

Johnson, J. W. (1995). *Lift Ev'ry Voice and Sing.* Illustrated by J. S. Gilchrist. New York: Scholastic.

Joint Center for Political and Economic Studies. (1999, January). Number of Black Elected Officials in the United States, by State and Office. Available online at http://jointcenter.org.

Joseph, P. E. (2006). *Waiting 'til the Midnight Hour: A Narrative History of Black Power in America.* New York: Holt.

Ladson-Billings, G. (1994). Review of *Teaching Strategies for Ethnic Studies* (5th ed.). Madison: University of Wisconsin, unpublished (prepared for 6th ed. rev.).

Lemann, N. (1991). *The Promised Land: The Great Black Migration and How It Changed America.* New York: Knopf.

Logan, J. R., & Deane, G. (2003, August 15). *Black Diversity in Metropolitan America.* Retrieved July 23, 2007, from http://mumford.albany.edu/census/BlackWhite/BlackDiversityReport/black-diversity01.htm.

McKinnon, J., & Humes, K. (2000, March). The Black Population in the United States: Population Characteristics. Washington, DC: U.S. Census Bureau. Available online at http:/ www.census.gov.

McKinnon, J. (2003, April). The Black Population in the United States: March 2002. In *Population Characteristics. Current Population Reports.* Washington, DC: U.S. Department of Commerce, Economics and Statistics Administration, U.S. Census Bureau.

Payne, C. (1993). Men Led, but Women Organized: Movement Participation of Women in the Mississippi Delta. In V. Crawford, J. A. Rouse, & B. Woods (Eds.), *Women in the Civil Rights Movement: Trailblazers and Torchbearers 1941–1965* (pp. 1–11). Bloomington: Indiana University Press.

Quarles, B. (1969). *Black Abolitionists*. New York: Oxford University Press.

Report of the National Advisory Commission on Civil Disorders. (1968). New York: Bantam Books.

Shearer, L. (1990, January 7). The Rise of Black Mayors. *Parade,* p. 14.

Standley, A. (1993). The Role of Black Women in the Civil Rights Movement. In V. Crawford, J. A. Rouse, & B. Woods (Eds.), *Women in the Civil Rights Movement: Trailblazers and Torchbearers, 1941–1965* (pp. 183–202). Bloomington: Indiana University Press.

Stoll, M. A. (2004). *African Americans and the Color Line*. New York: Russell Sage Foundation.

Stoops, N. (2004). *Educational Attainment in the United States, 2003. Current Population Reports*. Washington, DC: U.S. Department of Commerce, Economics and Statistics Administration, U.S. Census Bureau.

U.S. Census Bureau (1990). Census 1990. http://www.census.gov/main/www/cen1990.html.

U.S. Census Bureau. (2001, February 22). *Census Bureau Releases Update on Country's African American Population*. Available online at http://www.census.gov/Press-Release/www/2001/cb01–34.html.

U.S. Census Bureau. (2003). *Current Population Survey: Annual Social and Economic Supplement*. Washington, DC: Author, Population Division.

U.S. Census Bureau. (2004). *Current Population Survey: Annual Social and Economic Supplement*. Washington, DC: Author, Racial Statistics Branch, Population Division.

U.S. Census Bureau. (2005a). *Current Population Survey: Annual Social and Economic Supplement*. Retrieved February 12, 2007, from http://www.bls.census.gov/cps/asec/adsmain.htm.

U.S. Census Bureau (2005b). *American Community Survey, 2005: Select Population Groups*. Retrieved online July 7, 2007, from http://factfinder.census.gov/servlet/IPGeoSearchBy List-Servlet?ds_name=ACS_2005_EST_G00_&_lang=en&_ts=202048729223.

U.S. Census Bureau. (2006). *Current Population Survey: Annual Social and Economic Supplement*. Washington, DC: Author, Population Division.

U.S. Commission on Civil Rights. (2001, June 8). Voting Irregularities in Florida during the 2000 Presidential Election (draft report). Available online at http://www.usccr.gov.

Washington, B. T. (1956/1901). *Up from Slavery*. New York: Bantam. (Original work published 1901.)

Wilson, W. J. (1996). *When Work Disappears: The World of the New Urban Poor*. New York: Knopf.

Yee, S. J. (1992). *Black Women Abolitionists: A Study in Activism, 1828–1960*. Knoxville: University of Tennessee Press.

ANNOTATED BIBLIOGRAPHY

Books for Teachers

Especially Recommended

Appiah, K. A., & Gates, H. L., Jr. (Eds.). (2005). *Africana: The Encyclopedia of the African and African American Experience* (2nd ed.). New York: Oxford University Press.
This ambitious reference work, which has been expanded from one to five volumes in this second edition, was years in the making. It includes information and articles about Africans throughout the world. It contains a gold mine of information that is visually appealing and engaging because it is illustrated with photographs, some of which are in color.

Asante, M. K., & Mazama, A. (Eds). (2005). *Encyclopedia of Black Studies*. Thousand Oaks, CA: Sage.
This informative reference book is a rich source on myriad aspects of Black studies, the Black experience, and the connections of Black studies to Africa.

Bennett, L. (2007*). Before the Mayflower: A History of Black America* (New millennium ed.). Chicago: Johnson.
This classic and highly readable popular history of Blacks in the United States by the senior editor emeritus of *Ebony* magazine has been revised and updated.

Bobo, J., Hudley, C., & Michel, C. (Eds). (2004). *The Black Studies Reader*. New York: Routledge.
The essays in this scholarly collection of articles cover myriad aspects of Black studies and the Black experience, including Theorizing Black Studies, Black Feminism: Acts of Resistance, and Religion in Black Life.

Branch, T. (2006). *At Canaan's Edge: America in the King Years, 1965–1968*. New York: Simon & Schuster.
This is the third and final book in Taylor Branch's definitive history of Martin Luther King, Jr., and the civil rights movement. The first book in the trilogy, *Parting the Waters,* was a recipient of both the Pulitzer Prize and the National Book Critics Circle Award.

Claude, E. S., Jr. (2007). *In a Shade of Blue: Pragmatism and the Politics of Black America*. Chicago: University of Chicago Press.
The author, a scholar from the new generation of African American scholars, urges African Americans to address their social problems within the context of their experience and with a vision of the future.

Davis, B. D. (2006). *Inhuman Bondage: The Rise and Fall of Slavery in the New World*. New York: Oxford University Press.
This is a monumental and seminal book on slavery in the Americas by a highly respected author who has received the Pulitzer Prize and the National Book Award.

Franklin, J. H. (2005). *Mirror to America: The Autobiography of John Hope Franklin*. New York: Farrar, Straus, and Giroux.
A moving, insightful, and informative biography by one of America's most distinguished historians. It is a powerful testimony about the depth and power of institutionalized racism in the United States.

Franklin, J. H., & Moss, A. A., Jr. (2000). *From Slavery to Freedom: A History of Black Americans* (8th ed.). New York: McGraw-Hill.
This comprehensive history of African Americans is still one of the best. The senior author is one of the most highly regarded American historians in the United States.

Gates, H. L., Jr., & Higginbotham, E. B. (Eds.). (2004). *African American Lives*. New York: Oxford University Press.
This indispensable and comprehensive reference book includes hundreds of biographies of noted African Americans in both the past and present. Highly recommended for home, school, college, and university libraries.

Hine, D. C., Brown, E. B., & Terborg-Penn, R. (2005). *Black Women in America: An Historical Encyclopedia* (3 vols.). New York: Oxford University Press.
The definitive work on the experiences of African American women in the United States. An essential reference for school, college, and university libraries.

Hine, D. C., Hine, W. C., & Harrold, S. (2006). *The African American Odyssey* (3rd ed., combined vol.). Upper Saddle River, NJ: Prentice-Hall.
This engaging, well-researched, and beautifully illustrated college textbook is a good introduction to the history of African Americans in the United States.

Hine, D. C., & Thompson, K. (1998). *A Shining Thread of Hope: The History of Black Women in America*. New York: Broadway Books.

A highly readable historical overview of the sojourn of Black women in America. The first author is the best-known expert on the history of African American women in the United States.

Painter, N. I. (2006). *Creating Black Americans: African-American History and Its Meanings, 1619 to the Present*. New York: Oxford University Press.
In this innovative and well-crafted history of African Americans, art reproduced in full color is used to enrich the interesting text.

Other Books

Birnbaum, J., & Taylor, C. (Eds.). (2000). *Civil Rights since 1787: A Reader on the Black Struggle*. New York: New York University Press.
This comprehensive collection includes 188 selections in 935 pages. These documents can be used as resources for both teachers and students.

Carson, C. (Ed.). (2005). *The Papers of Martin Luther King, Jr.,* Vol. 5: *Threshold of a New Decade*. Berkeley: University of California Press.
The fifth volume of this ambitious publishing project includes the papers of Martin Luther King, Jr., from January 1959 to December 1960. The volumes are ably edited by Professor Clayborne Carson, the Stanford University historian, and his colleagues. Each of the volumes is an excellent teaching resource for high school, college, and university students.

De Graaf, L. B., Mulroy, K., & Taylor, Q. (Eds.). (2001). *African Americans in California*. Seattle: University of Washington Press.
The book consists of a collection of well-crafted and informative essays on African Americans in the most populous state in the United States.

Ellis, C., & Smith, S. D. (Eds.). (2005). *Say It Plain: A Century of Great African American Speeches*. New York: New Press.
This book contains a rich collection of speeches by eminent African Americans, such as Booker T. Washington, Marcus Garvey, Mary McLeod Bethune, and Lani Guinier. It includes two CDs with live recordings.

Fine, R., et al. (2003). *The Art of Romare Bearden*. Washington, DC: National Gallery of Art, in association with Harry N. Abrams.
This is a beautifully illustrated book (much of which is in four colors) about the work of an eminent American artist.

Forbes, J. D. (1993). *Africans and Native Americans: The Language of Race and the Evolution of Red-Black Peoples* (2nd ed.). Urbana: University of Illinois Press.
This seminal book by an eminent scholar describes intersections of the histories of Native Americans and African Americans throughout the Americas.

Gates, H. L., Jr. (2007). *Finding Oprah's Roots: Finding Your Own*. New York: Crown.
An interesting book for teachers and students interested in tracing their family histories. The author describes how genetic testing resources can help individuals trace their ancestors.

Guy-Sheftall, B. (Ed.). (1995). *Words of Fire: An Anthology of African-American Feminist Thought*. New York: New Press.
This richly textured and comprehensive anthology documents the experiences of African American women from 1831 to the present. Edited by a leading authority in Black women's studies, it also is appropriate for high school students.

Honey, M. K. (2007). *Going Down Jericho Road: The Memphis Strike, Martin Luther King's Last Campaign*. New York: Norton.
A well-researched and compassionate historical study of Black sanitation workers in Memphis, their strike, and King's trip to Memphis to support their struggle for human rights. This is an incisive and poignant account of King's last campaign.

Joseph, P. E. (2006). *Waiting 'til the Midnight Hour: A Narrative History of Black Power in America.* New York: Henry Holt.
> This well-researched and insightful history of Black power in the United States is an essential reference.

The Library of America. (2003). *Reporting Civil Rights* (vols. 1 and 2). New York: Author.
> These two valuable books contain original newspaper and magazine articles that cover civil rights issues and events. Volume 1 is titled *American Journalism 1941–1963*; volume 2, *American Journalism 1963–1973*.

McAdoo, H. P. (2002). *Black Families* (4th ed.). Thousand Oaks, CA: Sage.
> An informative and well-researched book by a noted sociologist.

Marable, M. (2006). *Living Black History: How Reimaging the African-American Past Can Remake America's Racial Future.* New York: Basic Books.
> This collection of essays by a highly respected social scientist and public intellectual is engaging and revealing.

Marable, M., Mullings, L., & Spencer-Wood, S. (2002). *Freedom: A Photographic History of the African American Experience.* New York: Phaidon Press.
> The powerful, engaging, and emotive photographs that make up this book are excellent tools for teaching and learning.

National Urban League. (Ed.). (2007). *The State of Black America: Portrait of the Black Male.* New York: Author.
> This informative and sobering report focuses on the poignant status of African American males in America and what needs to be done to improve their educational, economic, and social status in the United States.

Ransby, B. (2003). *Ella Baker and the Black Freedom Movement: A Radical Democratic Vision.* Chapel Hill: University of North Carolina Press.
> This is a major biography of one of the most influential women in the civil rights movement. Baker was a key figure in Martin Luther King, Jr.'s, Southern Christian Leadership Conference (SCLC).

Singh, N. P. (2004). *Black Is a Country: Race and the Unfinished Struggle for Democracy.* Cambridge, MA: Harvard University Press.
> In this important book on civil rights in the twentieth century, the author describes how radical thoughts and global dreams have been central to the history of Black struggle in the United States.

Books for Students

Adler, D. (2006). *Satchel Paige: Don't Look Back.* New York: Hyperion/Jump at the Sun.
> This well-written historical biography covers the life of a baseball player whose career spanned the Jim Crow era, the Negro Leagues, the integration of baseball, and the years of the civil rights movement. (Primary/Intermediate)

Adoff, J. (2005). *Jimi & Me.* New York: Hyperion/Jump at the Sun.
> A teenage boy whose record-producer father has recently been murdered and whose mother has moved him from Brooklyn to a small town in Ohio finds solace through the music of legendary African American rock guitarist Jimi Hendrix in this debut novel in verse. (Middle/High School)

Bolden, T. (2005). *Maritcha: A Nineteenth-Century American Girl.* New York: Abrams.
> Maritcha Lyons, who has a one-page memoir excerpt in Bolden's collection of oral histories for young readers, *Tell All the Children Our Story* (Abrams, 2002), is the subject of a full-length illustrated biography with extensive primary sources. Born a free Black in 1848, Maritcha

witnessed the 1863 Draft Riot in New York City that killed many of the city's African American residents and drove her and her family from the city. The next year, she lobbied the Rhode Island legislature for the right to attend an all-White public school. (Intermediate/Middle School)

Bolden, T. (2003). *Portraits of African-American Heroes*. Illustrated by A. Pitcairn. New York: Dutton. Unusual, highly detailed sepia-toned portraits accompany one-page biographies of eight women and twelve men who had an impact on their chosen fields and on African American history as a whole. (Intermediate/Middle School)

Bolden, T. (2003). *Wake Up Our Souls: A Celebration of Black American Artists*. New York: Abrams.
This is a well-researched, gracefully written, and handsomely produced introduction to the work of thirty-two African American artists, along with information about the economic and social conditions of the times in which they lived. (Middle/High School)

Bryan, A. (2003). *Beautiful Blackbird*. Illustrated by the author. New York: Atheneum.
The acclaimed artist and author adapts a Zambian folktale. His striking woodcuts that grace this work won the 2004 Coretta Scott King Award for Illustration. (All ages)

Cox. J. (2003). *My Family Plays Music*. Illustrated by E. Brown. New York: Holiday House.
Through lively illustrations, this book explores ten different genres of music, from classical to country, gospel to rock 'n' roll. Each member of the girl's African American family plays a different instrument, including the baby, who bangs on pots and pans. (Primary)

Davidson, D. (2005). *Played*. New York: Hyperion/Jump at the Sun.
This realistic novel depicts social and sexual pressures and the struggle to find true love among middle-class African American teens in a suburban high school. Davidson's earlier novel, *Jason & Kyra* (2004), portrays upper-middle-class African American teens dealing with the ups and downs of boy-girl relationships. (Middle/High School)

Draper, S. M. (2003). *The Battle of Jericho*. New York: Atheneum.
In an Ohio high school, a middle-class teenager must decide whether to join an elite secret society even though it means giving up a music competition for the initiation. A darker side of his choice emerges when he witnesses sexual harassment and bullying that becomes increasingly violent. (High School)

Draper, S. M. (2006). *Copper Sun*. New York: Simon & Schuster.
Set in colonial America, this novel portrays a fifteen-year-old Ashanti girl, Amari, who is captured into slavery, endures the Middle Passage, and is sold to a brutal plantation owner in the Carolinas who intends to use the girl for his son's sexual enjoyment. When the plantation owner's wife gives birth to a Black baby, Amari's friendship with a White indentured servant allows her to escape the owner's retaliation. Winner of the 2007 Coretta Scott King Award for Writing. (High School)

Dillon, L., & Dillon, D. (2002). *Rap a Tap Tap: Here's Bojangles—Think of That*. Illustrated by the authors. New York: Scholastic.
Using vivid gouache paintings in a style reminiscent of Harlem Renaissance artist Aaron Douglas, the author/illustrators pay tribute to the legendary African American tap dancer Bill "Bojangles" Robinson, who died in 1949 at the age of 70. (Primary)

Flake, S. G. (2004). *Who Am I Without Him? Short Stories About Girls and the Boys in Their Lives*. New York: Hyperion/Jump at the Sun.
Ten short stories tell what it is like to grow up Black and female in the United States today. Without preaching, Flake portrays the choices, good and bad, that girls make and how their romantic relationships often parallel those of their parents. (Middle/High School)

Freedman, R. (2006). *Freedom Walkers: The Story of the Montgomery Bus Boycott*. New York: Holiday House.

The author chronicles the origins, course, and key players of the year-long boycott that played a pivotal role in the early civil rights movement. (Middle/High School)

Freedman, R. (2004). *The Voice That Challenged a Nation: Marian Anderson and the Struggle of Equal Rights*. New York: Clarion.
Family pictures and other photos illustrate this inspirational biography of the talented singer who confronted racism and forged a friendship with Eleanor Roosevelt. (Intermediate/ Middle School)

Giovanni, N. (2005). *Rosa*. Illustrated by B. Collier. New York: Holt.
Poet/playwright Nikki Giovanni offers a lyrical tribute to the late civil rights leader whose 1955 act of resistance to segregation of public transportation sparked the Montgomery bus boycott. Bryan Collier won the 2006 Coretta Scott King Award for illustration as well as a Caldecott Honor. (Primary/Intermediate)

Govenar, A., & Miller, N. (2006). *Stompin' at the Savoy: The Story of Norma Miller*. Illustrated by M. French. Cambridge, MA: Candlewick.
Oral historian Govenar teams up with veteran dancer Miller to provide a personal story and a history of African American dance from the 1930s to the present revival of "swing." (Intermediate and up)

Grimes, N. (2002). *Bronx Masquerade*. New York: Dial.
An open-mike poetry activity in a high school classroom allows eighteen youngsters the opportunity to tell their life stories and express their dreams for the future. This novel-in-verse won the 2003 Coretta Scott King Award for writing. (Middle/High School)

Grimes, N. (2002). *Talkin' About Bessie: The Story of Aviator Elizabeth Coleman*. Illustrated by E. B. Lewis. New York: Scholastic/Orchard.
Winner of the 2003 Coretta Scott King Award for Illustration, this biography depicts the life of the early twentieth-century aviator through age twenty-one with fictionalized "eulogies" from the people who influenced Coleman's life (such as her father) and from those whose lives she touched. (Intermediate/Middle School)

Gunning, M. (2004). *A Shelter in Our Car*. Illustrated by E. Pedlar. San Francisco: Children's Book Press.
A girl and her mother, immigrants from Jamaica, end up homeless after the death of the girl's father. The author portrays with compassion the child's grief and homesickness as well as the close mother-daughter bond that is a source of strength in hard times. (Primary/Intermediate)

Hamilton, V. (2004). *The People Could Fly*. Illustrated by L. and D. Dillon. New York: Knopf.
This picture-book adaptation of Hamilton's classic folktale collection (1985) features pictures by award-winning illustrators Leo Dillon and Diane Dillon. The original collection is available in a handsome reissued edition published by Knopf (2000). (All ages)

Hathaway, B. (2004). *Missy Violet and Me*. Boston: Houghton Mifflin.
An eleven-year-old girl works with the local midwife in her small southern town in the 1930s and learns of life under slavery and emancipation, the use of healing herbs, caring for babies, and responding to crisis. The story is based on the life of the author's grandmother, who was a rural midwife in the South. (Intermediate)

Hoffman, M. (2003). *The Color of Home*. Illustrated by K. Littlewood. New York: Dial.
A refugee boy from Somalia finds an outlet for his loneliness and sadness in art class, where he paints his memories of his war-torn country and the life he and his family encounter in the United States. Caring teachers and friendly classmates ease his adjustment to his new land. (Intermediate)

Hubbard, C. (2005). *Catching the Moon*. Illustrated by R. DuBurke. New York: Lee and Low.
An African American girl, Marcenia Lyle, wants to become a professional baseball player and pursues her dream despite poverty and sexism; under the name Toni Stone, she became the first female member of an all-male pro team. (Primary/Intermediate)

Hudson, W. (2004). *Powerful Words: More Than 200 Years of Extraordinary Writing by African Americans*. Illustrated by S. Qualls. Foreword by M. W. Edelman. New York: Scholastic.
More than thirty African American writers, from Frederick Douglass and W. E. B. Du Bois to Toni Morrison and Lauryn Hill, are featured in this well-balanced anthology with attractive paintings and useful biographical and historical information. (Intermediate/Middle School)

Hurston, Z. N. (2006). *The Six Fools*. Illustrated by A. Tanksley. Adapted by J. C. Thomas. New York: HarperCollins/Amistad.
A man disgusted by his future in-laws' foolishness refuses to marry their daughter unless he can find three bigger fools. This folktale, gathered by Zora Neale Hurston in the 1920s, has been adapted in her folksy style for younger readers, accompanied by vibrant illustrations. (All ages)

Johnson, A. (2003). *The First Part Last*. New York: Simon & Schuster.
A prequel to her 1998 novel *Heaven*, which won the 1999 Coretta Scott King Award, *The First Part Last* tells the moving story of a teenage father charged with the responsibility of raising his daughter after her mother's death shortly after the child's birth. This novel won both the 2004 Coretta Scott King Award and the 2004 Michael L. Printz Award for outstanding young adult literature. (Middle/High School)

Johnson, A. (2005). *A Sweet Smell of Roses*. Illustrated by E. Velásquez. New York: Simon & Schuster.
In a story of children effecting social change, two girls join the 1963 March on Washington and are inspired by Dr. King's famous speech. (Primary)

Jones, T. L. (2006). *Standing Against the Wind*. New York: Farrar, Straus & Giroux.
In this gritty first novel, a studious eighth-grader moves from her grandmother's home in rural Georgia to her aunt's apartment in a Chicago public housing project, where she must deal with bullies, gangs, and other forces threatening to pull her down. (Middle School)

Lester, J. (2005). *Day of Tears: A Novel in Dialogue*. New York: Hyperion/Jump at the Sun.
The acclaimed author tells the story of the largest auction of enslaved people in U.S. history, which took place in Georgia in 1859, through the voices of those who witnessed that infamous event. (Middle/High School)

Marsalis, W. (2005). *Jazz A-B-Z: An A to Z Collection of Jazz Portraits*. Illustrated by P. Rogers. Cambridge, MA: Candlewick.
The notable jazz musician offers brief portraits of jazz greats and introductions to the different periods and styles of jazz, accompanied by realistic, posterlike illustrations. (All ages)

McDonald, J. (2004). *Brother Hood*. New York: Farrar, Straus & Giroux.
A sixteen-year-old boy is torn between his life as a scholarship student at a prestigious boarding school and loyalty to his brother and friends back in Harlem, who are courting danger in the drug trade. (Middle/High School)

McDonald J. (2006). *Harlem Hustle*. New York: Farrar, Straus & Giroux.
A budding hip-hop artist drops out of school and finds that, even with a well-to-do and connected girlfriend, making it in the real world is harder than he thought. (High School)

McKissack, P., & McKissack, F. (2003). *Days of Jubilee: The End of Slavery in the United States*. New York: Scholastic.
The authors use firsthand narratives of enslaved persons to describe the events of the Civil War and the end of slavery in various locales across the South. Also covered, more briefly, are revolts and escapes, the rise of the Ku Klux Klan, and the imposition of Jim Crow. (Intermediate/Middle School)

Morrison, T. (2004). *Remember: The Journey for School Integration*. Boston: Houghton Mifflin.
The Nobel laureate's first historical work for young people uses text and archival photos to tell the stories of the courageous children and adults who made integration happen. (Intermediate and up)

Moses, S. P. (2004). *The Legend of Buddy Bush*. New York: Simon & Schuster.
Through the eyes of a twelve-year-old girl, Moses offers a fictionalized account of a true incident from 1947. The girl's uncle Buddy, who lives in Harlem but is visiting his Southern relations, is falsely accused of raping a White woman. Buddy is tried, escapes from jail, and flees back North; his ordeal highlights the differences between African American life in the urban North and in the rural, Jim Crow–dominated South. (Middle School)

Mosley, W. (2005). *47*. New York: Little, Brown.
The acclaimed mystery writer makes a foray into young adult literature with the story of a young man born into slavery who meets the mythical High John the Conqueror and gains the strength to lead his people to freedom. (Middle/High School)

Muse, D. (Ed.). (2005). *The Entrance Place of Wonders: Poems of the Harlem Renaissance*. Illustrated by C. Riley-Webb. New York: Abrams.
A vividly illustrated introduction to the Harlem Renaissance, this collection features twenty poems by groundbreaking poets including Countee Cullen, Langston Hughes, Claude McKay, and James Weldon Johnson. (Primary/Intermediate)

Myers, W. D. (2004). *Here in Harlem*. New York: Holiday House.
The acclaimed author turns to poetry to portray the many voices he heard while growing up in Harlem in the 1950s. The fifty-four poems include well-known people such as Langston Hughes and the teachers, classmates, and neighbors who helped to shape Myers's character and dreams. (Intermediate/Middle School)

Myers, W. D. (2006). *Jazz*. Illustrated by C. Myers. New York: Holiday House.
Walter Dean Myers's poetry and son Christopher's surrealistic acrylic-and-ink illustrations offer homage to the greats of jazz and the places from which they came, from the early twentieth century to the present. (All ages)

Nelson, M. (2004). *Fortune's Bones: A Manumission Requiem*. Asheville, NC: Front Street Books.
Renowned poet Marilyn Nelson recounts in six poems the life of an enslaved man who died in Connecticut in 1798. His bones had been preserved by a local doctor, then lost, rediscovered, and displayed in a museum until 1970. Nelson gives her voice to Fortune, honoring his life, detailing (through the shape of his bones) his servitude, and conferring on him the dignity that those who enslaved him attempted to deny. (Middle School and up)

Nelson, M. (2005). *A Wreath for Emmett Till*. Illustrated by P. Lardy. Asheville, NC: Front Street Books.
Nelson honors Till's life through a heroic crown of sonnets—fifteen sonnets in which the last line of one forms the first line of the next, and each of those last/first lines comprises the final sonnet. The poems portray the promise of the young man's life, mourn his death by lynching in Mississippi in 1955, and place his death in the context of a human history of injustice and the struggle against it. (High School and up)

Nelson, V. M. (2003). *Almost to Freedom*. Illustrated by C. Bootman. Minneapolis: Lerner.
Dark, evocative illustrations complement this story of slavery and a family's night flight to freedom through the eyes of a young girl's doll, which gets separated from her child but eventually finds its way home as well. (Primary)

Nolen, J. (2003). *Thunder Rose*. Illustrated by K. Nelson. San Diego: Harcourt.
In this tall tale set in the Old West, a girl born during a violent thunderstorm and named, appropriately, Thunder Rose, develops supernatural powers and a fearless attitude that makes her the hero of her community and an inspiration to young readers. (Primary)

Perdomo, W. (2002). *Visiting Langston*. Illustrated by B. Collier. New York: Henry Holt.
In this historical picture book story set in Harlem in the mid-twentieth century, an African American girl anticipates her visit to the brownstone of acclaimed author Langston Hughes. Her poetic story reflects her admiration for Hughes and the way he has influenced her ambitions and her writing. (Primary)

Rappaport, D. (2006). *Nobody Gonna Turn Me 'Round: Stories and Songs of the Civil Rights Movement*. Illustrated by S. W. Evans. Cambridge, MA: Candlewick.
> True stories of heroes of the civil rights movement, interspersed with poetry, song excerpts, and powerful, expressive paintings, make up the final volume in a trilogy that includes *No More! Stories and Songs of Slave Resistance* (2001) and *Free at Last! Stories and Songs of Emancipation* (2003). (Intermediate/Middle School)

Richards, B. E. (2005). *Keep Climbing, Girls*. Illustrated by R. G. Christie. New York: Simon & Schuster.
> The author urges young African American girls to pursue their dreams through a poem about a girl who climbs a tree in defiance of elders who demand that she act like a lady. (Primary)

Roberts, B. C. (2004). *Jazzy Miz Mozetta*. Illustrated by F. Morrison. New York: Farrar, Straus & Giroux.
> Exuberant illustrations distinguish this story, set in an urban neighborhood in the mid-twentieth century and featuring an older neighbor who still has the energy to dance the jitterbug with her young friends. (Primary)

Roessell, D., & Rampersad, A. (Eds.). (2006). *Poetry for Young People: Langston Hughes*. Illustrated by B. Andrews. Series: Poetry for Young People. New York: Sterling.
> This series title combines twenty-six of Hughes's best-known and most accessible poems with colorful, stylized illustrations combining folk art and African motifs. The editors' introductions, notes from Hughes on the works, and biographical and historical information enhance the text. (Intermediate and up)

Shange, N. (2004). *Ellington Was Not a Street*. Illustrated by K. Nelson. New York: Simon & Schuster.
> The acclaimed poet and playwright offers a tribute to jazz great Duke Ellington and other legendary African American men whose work changed the culture of the United States in the twentieth century. Kadir Nelson won the 2004 Coretta Scott King Award for his illustrations. (All ages)

Stroud, B. (2005). *The Patchwork Path: A Quilt Map to Freedom*. Illustrated by E. S. Bennett. Cambridge, MA: Candlewick.
> The role of quilts in guiding enslaved people to freedom is the subject of this historical story about a 10-year-old girl who escapes with her father to Canada after her mother dies and her sister is sold. (Primary)

Taylor, G. (2006). *George Crum and the Saratoga Chip*. Illustrated by F. Morrison. New York: Lee and Low.
> Based on the life of the inventor of the potato chip, this story set in upstate New York in the 1830s chronicles the enterprise of an African American chef and restauranteur. (Primary/Intermediate)

Taylor, M. D. (2001). *The Land*. New York: Penguin Putnam.
> This prequel to Taylor's classic *Roll of Thunder, Hear My Cry* (1976) describes Paul Edward's life as a mixed-race slave on his father's plantation, his efforts to purchase his own farm in Reconstruction-era Mississippi, and his struggle to establish his identity as a person of biracial heritage. Winner of the 2002 Coretta Scott King Award for Writing. (Middle School/High School)

Thomas, J. C. (2004). *The Gospel Cinderella*. Illustrated by D. Diaz. New York: HarperCollins/Amistad.
> The author gives the familiar Cinderella story an African American flavor with a singing Cinderella, a Great Gospel Convention, and a Crooked Foster Mother who fails to silence the child's lovely voice. (All ages)

Vernick, A. G., & Gidaro, E. G. (2003). *Bark & Tim: A True Story of Friendship Based on the Paintings of Tim Brown*. Illustrated by T. Brown. Johnson City, TN: Overmountain Press.

A warm text about a boy's friendship with his dog highlights the work of Brown, a self-taught artist whose bright colors and simple shapes will appeal to young children and fans of "outsider" art. (All ages)

Weatherford, C. B. (2006). *Moses: Then Harriet Tubman Led Her People to Freedom.* Illustrated by K. Nelson. New York: Hyperion/Jump at the Sun.
Kadir Nelson's stunning illustrations, which won the 2007 Coretta Scott King Award for Illustration and a Caldecott honor, convey Tubman's perilous work as the most successful conductor on the Underground Railroad. (All ages)

Weatherford, C. B. (2005). *A Negro League Scrapbook.* Illustrated with photos. Foreword by Buck O'Neil. Honesdale, PA: Boyds Mills.
Archival photos, anecdotes, poetry, and team memorabilia grace this history of the Negro Leagues. (All ages)

Williams, M. (2005). *Brothers in Hope: The Story of the Lost Boys of Sudan.* Illustrated by R. G. Christie. New York: Lee and Low.
Since 2000, some 4,000 orphans of Sudan's civil wars have found asylum in the United States. Williams tells their story through a fictional eight-year-old who walked nearly a thousand miles to a refugee camp in Ethiopia, to another in Kenya when fighting broke out in Ethiopia, and waited more than a decade to enter the United States. (Intermediate)

Woods, B. (2002). *The Red Rose Box.* New York: Putnam.
A preteenage girl living in Louisiana in the mid 1950s sees a rift mended between her mother and her aunt, visits her wealthy aunt and uncle in Los Angeles, where she finds less prejudice than in the segregated South, and learns that there are more important things in life than comfort and material goods when her parents perish in a hurricane while she and her sister are traveling with the aunt. (Intermediate/Middle School)

Woodson, J. (2003). *Locomotion.* New York: Putnam.
A ten-year-old whose parents died in a house fire four years earlier uses different forms of poetry to express his sadness, reach out to others, and begin to heal. (Intermediate/Middle School)

·····

EUROPEAN AMERICANS

Concepts and Strategies

Part III consists of content, concepts, teaching strategies, and materials for teaching about European Americans. Most Americans are of European origin and descent. In 2005, the White non-Hispanic population of the United States numbered about 192.6 million people and comprised about 66.8% of the nation's population. However, the percentage of the nation's population of European ancestry had declined significantly since 1900, when it comprised 87.7% of the population. Demographers predict that the percentage of White non-Hispanic Americans in the U.S. population will continue to decline in future years. It is predicted that they will make up about 62% of the nation's population in 2025 and 53% in 2050 (Martin & Midgley, 1999).

White Americans of European descent are increasing at a slower rate than are other ancestry groups. The total population of the United States increased 15.9% between 1990 and 2005, while the White non-Hispanic population increased only 2.4%. This difference resulted primarily because a disproportionate number of Whites are middle class (and therefore have fewer children) and because Europeans comprised only 14.5% of the immigrants to the United States between 1990 and 2005 (U.S. Department of Homeland Security, 2006). Even though they are becoming a smaller percentage of the nation's population, Americans of European origin and descent still comprise the overwhelming majority of the nation's population and have the most influence on its culture, values, and ethos. A study of the sojourn of European immigrants across the Atlantic and of their journey in America is essential to a sound multicultural curriculum.

REFERENCES

Martin, P., & Midgley, E. (2006). Immigration: Shaping and Reshaping America (rev. 2nd ed.). *Population Bulletin, 61*(4). Washington, DC: Population Reference Bureau.

U.S. Department of Homeland Security. (2006). *Yearbook of Immigration Statistics: 2005.* Washington, DC: Author.

EUROPEAN ETHNIC GROUPS

Concepts, Strategies, and Materials

The poorest, the most miserable came here because they had no future over there. To them, the streets of America were paved in gold. They had what the Finns called kuum, *the American fever.*

—Andy Johnson, an immigrant

From Studs Terkel, *American Dreams: Lost and Found*

Between 1820 and 2006, 72,253,191 legal immigrants entered the United States. Most of them (38,546,705, or about 53%) were Europeans who belonged to many different religious, political, and cultural groups (U.S. Department of Homeland Security, 2006, 2007). The making of one society from so many different ethnic and nationality groups is one of the most amazing chapters in human history. Yet, social scientists, and therefore classroom teachers, have largely ignored the role of ethnicity in U.S. history and modern society. U.S. social scientists have been preoccupied with theories of assimilation and the melting pot concept. Nevertheless, scholars in the United States have given more attention to ethnicity as a variable in American life since the ethnic protest movements in the 1960s. However, a significant gap exists between scholarship and the school curriculum. The European ethnic experience is infrequently taught in the schools.

European ethnic groups should be included in a sound multicultural curriculum because the processes of acculturation and assimilation, which they have experienced and which many European ethnic groups are still experiencing, must be considered when students formulate concepts and generalizations about ethnicity and race in U.S. society. European Americans, like other Americans, often experienced ethnic rage, changed their names, and denied their ethnic heritages to gain social and economic mobility and to realize the American dream.

It is also important for students to study European ethnic groups because individuals of European origin comprise the bulk of the nation's population—67% in 2005 (Martin & Midgley, 2006). Additionally, Europeans continue to make up a significant proportion of the immigrants to the United States. Between 1997 and 2006,

TABLE 8.1 European Immigrants to the United States from Selected Nations, 1991 to 2005 (in thousands)

COUNTRY OF BIRTH	NUMBER	PERCENTAGE OF TOTAL IMMIGRATION	PERCENTAGE OF EUROPEAN IMMIGRATION
Poland	234.3	1.7	11.3
Ukraine	231.7	1.6	11.2
Russia	218.3	1.5	10.5
United Kingdom	214.4	1.5	10.3
Bosnia/Herzegovina	118.5	0.8	5.7
Soviet Union[a]	113.8	0.8	5.5
Germany	107.7	0.7	5.2
Romania	84.3	0.6	4.0
Ireland	66.4	0.5	3.2
Serbia/Montenegro	53.9	0.4	2.6
Albania	47.4	0.3	2.3
France	46.1	0.3	2.2
Armenia	45.9	0.3	2.2
Bulgaria	44.8	0.3	2.1
Italy	35.3	0.2	1.7
Portugal	28.6	0.2	1.3

[a]Prior to 1992, data include independent republics; beginning in 1992, data are for unknown republics only.

Source: U.S. Census Bureau (2007), *Statistical Abstract of the United States, 2007* (126th ed.). Retrieved July 12, 2007, from http://www.census.gov/prod/2006pubs/07statab/pop.pdf.

9,105,162 immigrants entered the United States (U.S. Department of Homeland Security, 2007). Of these, nearly 15% were Europeans. Even though 15% is a significant drop in the percentage of European immigrants that settled in the United States in prior decades, the number of European immigrants settling in the United States is still sizable.

The European immigrants who have entered the United States since 1997 are diverse in national origins and cultures. Table 8.1 shows the number of European immigrants who entered the United States between 1991 and 2005 from selected nations. As Table 8.1 indicates, a large number of immigrants came from Poland, Ukraine, Russia, and the United Kingdom. The challenge to communism that Poland experienced in the late 1980s and in 1990 and the collapse of the Soviet Union in 1991—in which the old political order crumbled—may have been factors that pushed immigrants from Poland and the various nations within the former Soviet Union, such as Ukraine (Bateman & Egan, 1993). Significant numbers of immigrants also came from Germany and Bosnia/Herzegovina between 1991 and 2005. Canada was also a major source of White immigrants; 154,660 Canadians immigrated to the United States between 1997 and 2006.

SPANIARDS IN THE AMERICAS

Spain was the first European nation to establish permanent settlements in the Americas. Spanish ships arrived in the Americas in 1492 under the leadership of Christopher Columbus. In 1496, Columbus and his brother Bartholomew founded the city of Santo Domingo on the island of Hispaniola. Santo Domingo was the first permanent continuing European settlement in the Americas. A number of Spanish explorers, including Coronado, Cortez, Cabeza de Vaca, and Ponce de Leon, followed Columbus. These and other Spaniards explored and settled in the Americas. In 1526, San Miguel de Gualdape, a Spanish colony in South Carolina, was established by Lucas Vasquez de Ayllon. Another Spaniard, named Pedro Menéndez de Avilés, founded the oldest permanent city in the United States, St. Augustine, Florida, in 1565. These early Spaniards influenced the language, religion, and other cultural aspects of the Americas.

Even though their influence in the Americas was great, few Spaniards came to the Americas. It has been estimated that no more than 300,000 Spaniards came to the Americas during the entire three colonial centuries, and many of these people stayed only a short time. Many of the Spaniards who remained in America fathered children with Indian women. These unions produced a new ethnic group in the Americas, the *mestizos* (see Chapter 10 on Mexican Americans). Today, the number of Spanish-born Americans is still small. Between 1989 and 2004, only 22,488 people immigrated to the United States from Spain (U.S. Department of Homeland Security, 2005).

EUROPEAN ETHNIC GROUPS: HISTORICAL PERSPECTIVE

Important Dates	Events
1565	Pedro Menéndez Avilés founded St. Augustine, Florida, on the site of an Indian village.
1607	English immigrants established their first permanent American colony at Jamestown, Virginia.
1620	The Pilgrims came to America from England on the *Mayflower* and established a settlement at Plymouth, Massachusetts.
1623	The Dutch West India Company settled New Netherland as a trading post.
1683	The first German immigrants to North America settled in Pennsylvania.
1718	The Scots-Irish began immigrating to the American colonies in large numbers.
1729	The Pennsylvania Colony increased the head taxes charged to entering immigrants to discourage further foreign settlement.

Important Dates	Events
1798	A Federalist-dominated Congress enacted the Alien and Sedition Acts to crush the Republican Party and harass aliens.
1803	The British Passenger Act was enacted to discourage immigration.
1825	Great Britain repealed laws that prohibited emigration. The first group of Norwegian immigrants arrived in the United States.
1845–1849	A series of potato blights in Ireland caused thousands of its citizens to immigrate to the United States.
1855	The antiforeign Know-Nothing movement reached its zenith and had a number of political successes in the 1855 elections. The movement rapidly declined after 1855.
	Castle Garden immigrant depot opened in New York.
1863	The Irish working classes expressed discontent with the Civil War and hostility toward urban Blacks in the New York Draft Riots, which lasted for four days.
1882	A congressional immigration act established a head tax of 50¢ and excluded lunatics, convicts, idiots, and people likely to become public charges.
1883–1885	An economic depression escalated nativistic feelings in the United States.
1885	The Foran Act outlawed the immigration of contract laborers.
1886	The Haymarket Affair in Chicago significantly increased fear of foreign "radicals" and stimulated the growth of nativistic sentiments in the United States.
	The Statue of Liberty was dedicated as nativism soared in the United States.
1891	Eleven Italian Americans were lynched in New Orleans during the height of American nativism after being accused of murdering a police superintendent.
1892	Ellis Island opened and replaced Castle Garden as the main port of entry for European immigrants.
1894	The Immigration Restriction League was organized in Boston by intellectuals to promote the passage of a bill that would require entering immigrants to pass a literacy test. The passage of the bill was urged to restrict immigration from southern and eastern Europe.
1899	William Z. Ripley's *The Races of Europe* was published. Ripley divided European people into three major racial groups, thus giving the nativists intellectual justifications for their movement.
1901–1910	Almost 9 million immigrants entered the United States, most of whom came from southern and eastern Europe. This mass immigration intensified significantly the activities of nativistic groups.
1907	A congressional act extended the classes of immigrants excluded from the United States. Victims of tuberculosis and individuals who had committed certain kinds of crimes were added to the list.

Important Dates	Events
1911	The Dillingham Commission, formed in 1907, issued its forty-one volume report in which it strongly recommended a literacy test for entering immigrants and made a marked distinction between the "old" and "new" immigrants.
1916	Madison Grant, a well-known naturalist, published *The Passing of the Great Race in America.* This popular book gave the nativists more ammunition.
1916–1919	The movement to Americanize aliens was widespread and intense.
1917	A comprehensive immigration bill was enacted that established the literacy test for entering immigrants, added to the classes of those excluded, and increased the head tax from $4 to $8. This act was a major victory for the nativists.
1919–1920	During the height of antiradical attitudes in America, hundreds of immigrant radicals were captured and deported in a movement led by A. Mitchell Palmer.
1921	The Johnson Act signaled a turning point in American history. It set up a nationality quota system and imposed the first numerical limits on European immigration to the United States.
1924	The Johnson-Reed Act established extreme quotas on immigration and blatantly discriminated against southern and eastern European and non-White nations.
1927	Two Italian radicals, Nicola Sacco and Bartolomeo Vanzetti, were executed during a period of extreme antiradical sentiment in America. Their execution set off a wave of reactions throughout the Western world.
1952	The McCarran-Walter Act, which allegedly removed racial barriers to immigration, essentially continued the policy established in 1924 and was in some ways more restrictive.
1954	The closing of Ellis Island marked the end of mass European immigration to the United States.
1965	A new immigration act, which became effective in 1968, abolished the national origins quota system and liberalized significantly U.S. immigration policy.
1984	Presidential and vice-presidential candidates of both major political parties appeared at the National Italian American Foundation dinner, indicating the continued importance of ethnicity to U.S. politicians.
1986	The centennial of the Statue of Liberty was commemorated.
1990	The Immigration Act of 1990 made some significant changes in immigration law. It set immigration at 675,000 annually (beginning in 1995) to consist of these categories: 480,000 family sponsored; 140,000 employment based; and 55,000 "diversity immigrants."
	Ellis Island National Immigration Museum opened to honor the nation's immigrants.

Important Dates	Events
1991	After disorder and fighting, the communist USSR fell, leaving its former republics to create democracy in the chaotic aftermath.
1991–1998	A significant number (386,327) of immigrants from nations in the former Soviet Union settled in the United States.
2006	Immigrants from Europe made up about 15% of the 9,105,162 documented immigrants that settled in the United States between 1997 and 2006.

MORE EUROPEANS COME TO AMERICA

Europeans began settling in America in significant numbers in the 1600s. The economic, social, and political conditions existing in Europe caused many of its inhabitants to cross the Atlantic searching for a new home. The main causes of the waves of immigrations were the drastic economic and social changes occurring in Europe. Serfdom had been the basis of European society for centuries. Most people were peasants who earned their living by farming. Throughout Europe, the old relationships between peasants and the land were changed, and the peasants suffered severely. The land owned by the village was divided into individual plots. With each succeeding generation, the land was further divided. Eventually, the plots of land became so small that younger sons were unable to make a living. Some peasants suffered when land holdings were consolidated by the landlords.

The peasants became landless or feared the loss of land and their place in the social order because they were attached to the land. Without it, they were unable to make a living or maintain a sense of well-being. The tremendous population growth Europe experienced in the seventeenth and eighteenth centuries increased the peasants' problems. Famine and crop failures also caused many people to immigrate.

The early settlers were a diverse group, although most of them were peasants. Many were unable to pay for their passage and became indentured servants in order to make the journey. However, merchants, artisans, professionals, and laborers comprised a small, but significant, part of the immigrants during the entire colonial period. Vagrants and convicts, who were unwanted by European nations, were also among the first settlers.

Although the bulk of the first European immigrants came to North America primarily for economic reasons, some came for religious and political reasons. Most European nations had established churches associated with the state. Religious dissenters who wanted to practice other religions sometimes immigrated to America. The Separatists who arrived in the colonies in 1620 on the *Mayflower* were seeking a place where they could freely practice their religion. The Jewish immigrants who settled in North America during the colonial period also were seeking religious and political freedom.

Once the European immigrations were under way, the movement itself produced forces that stimulated it. The letters settlers sent back to friends and relatives in Europe extolling the opportunities in America were a cogent factor that pulled more Europeans to America (Kamphoefner, Helbich, & Sommer, 1991). Guidebooks about wages and living conditions in America were distributed in Europe by travel and shipping agents and helped to motivate thousands of Europeans to immigrate.

The rise of the industrial revolution and scientific farming in the nineteenth century also stimulated European immigration to America. The development of industry put many artisans out of work. Modern farming methods displaced many farmers. These displaced workers tried to solve their problems by immigrating to America. Ship companies eager to get passengers, and U.S. states and railroad companies that wanted to settle sparsely populated areas in the nation, recruited European immigrants. European governments either discouraged or legally prohibited emigration in the 1600s and 1700s. However, these obstacles to immigration were largely removed in the nineteenth century. This, too, encouraged Europeans to immigrate. The development of more efficient and inexpensive ocean transportation also stimulated European immigration in the nineteenth century.

Although all of these factors contributed to European immigration to America, it was the search for a chance to earn a better living that caused most European immigrants to come to the United States. The tide of immigration rose and fell with economic conditions in the United States. When times were good, the immigrants came in great numbers. When depression set in, immigration dropped significantly. During some brief periods, the number of immigrants returning to Europe actually exceeded the number that arrived. Historians estimate that about one-third of the immigrants returned to Europe (Vecoli & Sinke, 1991). The key role that economic factors played in the European immigrations to North America make them similar to other mass movements to the United States from such nations as Canada, Mexico, the Philippines, China, and Japan.

Although some religious and political dissenters came to America so that they could freely practice their beliefs, this aspect of European immigration has been greatly exaggerated and oversimplified in textbooks and in the popular mind. Most came mainly for economic reasons. Most who were religious and political dissenters also hoped to improve their economic lot. The widespread belief that most of the first European settlers in America loved freedom and liberty has also been grossly exaggerated. The Puritans and other religious dissenters who settled in North America were not liberty-loving people but were doctrinaire groups who believed that their religions were the only true and valid ones. They were as intolerant of religious differences as those who protected the official churches in Europe (Jones, 1992). Their aim was to find a place where they could practice *their* religions freely and not to build a nation in which all religions would be tolerated.

Religious freedom and toleration developed in North America not because of the goals and wishes of the early colonists, but because the motley collection of religious groups that came to America competed for and won the right to practice their beliefs. The same is true about American democracy and the colonists. The colonists were Europeans in mind and spirit. They tried hard to establish European institutions and beliefs on American soil. They were not liberty-loving citizens who had a deep belief in democracy. Quite the contrary was true. They were the products of a hierarchical and class-structured society and had internalized these beliefs (Jones, 1992). That they failed to establish a highly stratified society in America was not because they did not try. Rather, a form of democracy emerged in the United States in part because the social and economic conditions that developed in North America made it impossible to establish a new Europe and fostered the development of a more open society. The ideas of the Enlightenment—which found a fertile ground in the British colonies—combined with the unique social, economic, and political conditions in the United States to produce American democracy.

The Passage to America

Especially in the seventeenth century, the journey from the peasants' European homes to the American port cities was hard and hazardous (Handlin, 1951). The peasants made the decision to come to America only after much thought. Often, only the threat of starvation or the loss of status compelled them to attempt the difficult journey. The trip was also expensive, especially during the first immigrations. Thus, even after they made the decision to come to America, they often had to save money for a long time before they could begin the trip.

The immigrants' first step in the journey to America was taking a long trip, usually by foot, to a European city that had a seaport from which ships sailed to America. Not everyone who started out was able to complete this stage of the journey. Many of those who made it to the European port cities were tired and battered. Once they arrived in the port city, the immigrants had to wait for weeks, and sometimes months, before the ship departed for America. The ship captains waited until the ships were full of goods and human cargo before they sailed for North America because the fuller ship was more profitable. During the long wait, the immigrants became restless and tired. Some were not able to board the ship when it was finally ready to depart. As each day went by during the long wait for the American departure, the food the immigrants had stored for the journey steadily dwindled. Renting a room at the European port city also took a large part of the meager funds they had saved for the trip.

Finally, the day came when the ship headed for America. The immigrants' joy at the departure was to be short-lived. The conditions on the ships were depressing and harsh. To maximize his profits, the ship captain packed the people in like sardines. Each family was assigned an extremely small space on the ship. The family spent most of its time in these dark, crowded compartments. Diseases were rampant on the vessels and took many lives. Dysentery, cholera, yellow fever, and smallpox were some of the more common ship diseases. The journey was long, often taking more than a month. Many families barely had enough food to last throughout the journey. Eventually, European nations passed laws requiring ship owners to provide a certain amount of food for the trip. However, ship captains who wanted to profit thought of many ingenious ways to evade these weakly enforced laws.

The Atlantic journey, especially before the time of the steamship, was a tremendous shock to the European immigrants. The family disruption that continued when they reached America began on the ship. Almost wholly dependent on the ship's crew, the father was unable to exercise his traditional role as leader and master of the family. The mother could not function in her traditional role either. When food was getting scarce, she had to try to keep the family fed. These transatlantic conditions severely strained family relationships.

The immigrants who survived the journey eventually landed at an American port city. The landing was eagerly awaited and celebrated. However, the immigrants still had some hurdles to overcome. They had to be checked and questioned by American immigration officials before they could travel freely in America. Wrong answers to questions or poor health could mean further questioning by officials and boards, a stay in a hospital, or even a trip back to Europe. In the earliest years, the inspection focused on physical health and ability to work. Gradually, questions related to the immigrant's morals and political beliefs were added. In 1917, Congress enacted a law requiring immigrants to demonstrate literacy in some language before they could enter the United States.

Many of the immigrants were broken, both financially and physically, when they arrived at American seaport cities. Some were the sole survivors in their families. Broken and lonely, some found asylum in poorhouses. Many immigrants who had planned to settle elsewhere never left the port cities in which their vessels landed. Thousands who had planned to settle elsewhere stayed in cities like Milwaukee, Chicago, and St. Louis. Some of the first settlers found work on construction projects in cities. Later, railroad construction provided work for immigrants. When the industrial revolution began, factory work became available. In all these lines of work, the immigrants were paid low wages and were exploited by their employers. Many of the immigrants settled in urban areas. However, a large percentage of the nineteenth-century immigrants settled on farms and became successful farmers. Many Germans, Scandinavians, Dutch, and Belgians settled in farm areas in the Midwest and successfully farmed (Vecoli, 1994).

The Urban Ghetto

Most European immigrants settled in cities, like most migrants from rural areas today. They had neither the means nor the desire to settle in rural areas. Like their modern counterparts, the new immigrants settled in blighted and dilapidated areas that became ethnic ghettos. Irishtowns, Germantowns, and Little Italys developed in most of the cities in the Northeast and Midwest. Ethnic organizations, like schools, newspapers, and churches, emerged within these communities. The immigrants, especially the more recent arrivals, usually lived in rundown housing near the business and manufacturing districts that had been vacated by suburban-bound, upwardly mobile residents when the manufacturing district sprawled outward into their communities.

When the upwardly mobile left the inner city, their old mansions were converted into multiple-family dwellings for the immigrants. The multiple-dwelling units became a source of quick profit for the owners. Little was done to make these dwellings comfortable. Profit, not comfort, was what the slum landlord sought. When these neighborhoods were deserted by the old residents, they were also forsaken by the street cleaners and sanitation crews. The smells from the garbage were pungent. The immigrants' habits of throwing garbage out of the window and keeping animals in their backyards made these communities even more unpleasant. High-rise apartments went up in some of the ethnic communities. Most of these buildings were crowded and uncomfortable. Many did not have interior plumbing or central heating. Some of the earliest ones had no toilets. There were only two toilets on each floor in some later apartment buildings. To help pay the rent, some families took in lodgers.

The immigrants looked forward to the day when their income would permit them to leave the ghetto and join the exodus to the suburbs. For most ethnic groups, this day eventually came. However, as one ethnic group vacated the ghetto, another group replaced it. In New York City, Italians took over old Irish neighborhoods. Jews from Russia and Poland occupied districts where the Germans had lived. After World War II, many of the urban areas that had been occupied by European ethnic groups received a large number of African Americans from the South, Mexican Americans from the Southwest, and migrants from Puerto Rico.

Immigrant Political Action

The participation of the immigrants in the urban political machines, though significant, was not the total of their importance in the U.S. political process. Early in U.S. political history, when the number of immigrants in U.S. cities became substantial and their votes had the power to sway or determine election outcomes, politicians became increasingly sensitive to the concerns and wishes of immigrant groups. Even politicians like Theodore Roosevelt and Woodrow Wilson, who felt rather negatively about the "new" immigrants, were forced on occasion to say positive things about them publicly. However, it was difficult for President Wilson to convince the southern and eastern European immigrants that he had had a change of heart.

Nevertheless, the major political parties began to vie aggressively for immigrant support and to include references to immigrants in their political platforms that reflected the specialized concerns of ethnic groups in the United States. These groups had many special concerns and aspirations, usually related to U.S. foreign policy and the ways in which the United States was treating their mother countries. Although many European immigrants did not have much of a sense of nationality when they arrived in the United States, intense nationalist movements developed among them.

According to Jones (1960), "There was a tendency among Irish political refugees as well as German Forty-eighters to look upon themselves as exiles and to use the United States simply as a base for promoting European causes. [These movements] afforded a means of group identification and self-assertion" (pp. 141–142).

Although the actions of these political refugees were probably extreme, most European immigrant groups did continue to see themselves as Europeans. The immigrants formed many groups to campaign aggressively for European causes and to sway U.S. foreign policy. In World War I, German Americans criticized Wilson's actions toward Germany and the Irish Americans became bitter because of Wilson's pro-British actions. The Irish voted strongly against Wilson in the subsequent election. The militant actions by some European American groups, especially German Americans, caused many Americans to question seriously their loyalties to the United States. However, even though some of these movements were radical and aggressively nationalistic, the most radical ones were unable to attract mass support because of the deep conservatism of most immigrants.

ANGLO-SAXON CULTURAL DOMINANCE

The early European settlements were highly ethnically mixed. English, Scots-Irish, Germans, French Huguenots, Africans, and Jews were among the earlier colonists. Writes Bailey (1961):

> The population of the thirteen colonies, though basically Anglo-Saxon, was perhaps the most mixed that could be found anywhere in the world. Counting [Africans], nearly 40% was of non-English origin, although New England boasted more native born and persons of English blood than the other sections. Of the 56 signers of the Declaration of Independence in 1776, 18 were non-English, and 8 of these had been born outside the colonies. (p. 67)

Ethnic conflict also developed early in the colonies. The English were dominant during the first years of colonial settlement. Consequently, they shaped the basic social and political institutions of colonial America. The English cultural dominance of the colonies was challenged by subsequent groups, but it remained the dominant social and political force in American life. Because of English political and cultural dominance, Anglo-Saxon culture became the ideal by which all subsequent ethnic groups were judged and by which levels of assimilation and acculturation were judged. To become *acculturated* became synonymous with acquiring Anglo-Saxon Protestant lifestyles, values, and language. The English language was dominant in almost every American colony by 1775.

Early in American colonial life, non-English groups began to be evaluated negatively. The New England colonies, which were predominantly English, took steps to bar the settlements of Roman Catholics. The French Huguenots became the focal point of English hostility. Later, the Scots-Irish and the German immigrants were the victims of English antagonism. An English mob prevented a group of Irish immigrants from landing in Boston in 1729. Several years later, another mob destroyed a new Scots-Irish Presbyterian church in Worcester, Massachusetts. The attitude that English culture and institutions were superior to all others profoundly shaped American life and was extremely significant in the nativistic movements that emerged after the Civil War. However, when the southern and eastern European immigrants began their mass exodus to the United States in the late 1800s, public opinion leaders extended the supposedly superior traits of the English to all northern and western European "races." In the nineteenth century, Europeans were considered to belong to several races, such as the Teutonic, the Alpine, and the Mediterranean (Jacobson, 1998). The races of northern and western Europe were considered superior to the races in southern, central, and eastern Europe. This extension was necessary to enable the old immigrants to band together to condemn the new immigrants. However, race assumed a new meaning when the southern and eastern European groups attained acceptable levels of assimilation in the twentieth century. All White races became one (Brodkin, 1998). Racial hostilities could now focus on non-White ethnic groups, such as African Americans, Asian Americans, Mexican Americans, and American Indians. Whites of southern and eastern European descent joined former adverse White ethnic groups to exclude people of color from full participation in U.S. life.

THE SOUTHERN AND EASTERN EUROPEAN IMMIGRANTS

Before 1892, most European immigrants who came to America were from northern and western European nations, such as England, Germany, France, and Sweden. Northern and western Europeans exceeded the number of immigrants from other parts of Europe up to the last decades of the nineteenth century. However, by 1896, a major change had taken place in the source of European immigrants to the United States. Most European immigrants to America now came from southern, eastern, and central Europe. Austria-Hungary, Italy, and Russia sent the largest number of new immigrants. Substantial numbers also came from such countries as Greece, Romania, Bulgaria, and Finland. Fifteen million European immigrants arrived in the United States between 1890 and 1914, most of them from southern and eastern Europe.

When immigrants from southern and eastern Europe began coming to the United States in significant numbers, a number of arguments evolved that were designed to distinguish them from immigrants who had come earlier from the northern and western parts of Europe. The southern and eastern immigrants became known as the "new" immigrants; the earlier immigrants were referred to as the "old" immigrants. The mass media, intellectuals, and politicians perpetuated the myth that the new immigrants were inferior to the older ones, that they caused major problems in the cities, and that steamship companies and U.S. industries eager for unskilled labor were the main causes of the new traffic. The Dillingham Commission, formed to investigate immigration in 1907, concluded that there was a fundamental difference in both the character and the causes of the new and old immigrations.

Repetition of this myth became evidence of its validity. It was eagerly embraced by writers, historians, and policymakers and significantly influenced the racist immigration legislation enacted in the 1920s. The nativistic movements reached their zenith in the 1920s and chose the southern and eastern European immigrants as their chief targets. Only the Asian immigrants in California were more harshly criticized. The distinctions made between the old and the new immigrants were artificial and based on inaccurate information and false assumptions. The southern and eastern European immigrants came to the United States for the same reasons that the earlier immigrants had come: to improve their economic conditions and to seek religious and political freedom. Steamship lines and U.S. industries played no greater role in stimulating immigration from southern and eastern Europe than they had in stimulating immigration from other parts of Europe. In both cases, their influence was rather meager and has been grossly exaggerated.

The types of new immigrants who came from southern and eastern Europe, like the older immigrants, were highly diverse. Some southern and eastern Europeans came to the United States for temporary work, not because of something unique about them but because the new steamship lines had so greatly reduced the length of the Atlantic trip that it was practical and possible to come to the United States for seasonal work.

Southern and eastern European immigrants were judged as being innately inferior to older Americans, partly because they started coming to the United States when the notion that the United States should be an asylum for the oppressed peoples of Europe was beginning to wane. When the Statue of Liberty was dedicated in New York City in 1886, many Americans had lost faith in the poetic words penned by Emma Lazarus about Europe's "huddled masses." They had also begun to question the melting pot theory and to raise serious questions about whether Europeans could be as readily assimilated as they had originally believed. The doubts about the new immigrants were not caused by their inability to be assimilated, but by the conditions and conceptions of foreigners emerging within American life. Thus, the rush of southern and eastern European immigrants to the United States was poorly timed. The internal conditions in the United States were giving birth to distinctly antiforeign attitudes. A scapegoat was needed to blame for urban blight, political corruption in the cities, and economic recession. The new immigrants were vulnerable and convenient targets. Consequently, they were judged intellectually and culturally inferior to the old immigrants and declared unassimilable. That they were an inferior "race" became widely accepted both in the intellectual community and in the popular mind.

NATIVISTIC MOVEMENTS

As early as 1727, nativistic feelings toward the Germans in Pennsylvania ran high. *Nativism* was a movement designed to restrict immigration to the United States and to protect the interests of the native-born. It was an extreme form of nationalism and ethnocentrism. To discourage further foreign settlement in the colony, Pennsylvania passed a statute in 1729 increasing the head tax on foreigners, allegedly to prevent persons likely to become public charges from entering the colony. Other antiforeign legislation emerged in the eighteenth century. In 1798, Congress, dominated by the Federalists, passed the Alien and Sedition Acts to crush the Republican Party by destroying its large base of immigrant support. These acts were also designed to silence criticism of the Federalists and to harass European immigrants. The Alien and Sedition Acts lengthened the time required to become a U.S. citizen from five to fourteen years and gave the president almost unlimited control over the behavior of immigrants, virtually nullifying the freedoms of speech and the press.

Nativistic sentiments continued to ebb and flow during the eighteenth and nineteenth centuries, although their most violent expressions did not arise until the late nineteenth and early twentieth centuries (Bennett, 1988). Nativism reached its zenith in the 1920s, culminating with the passage of the Johnson-Reed Act in 1924. The Know-Nothing movement, which emerged in the 1840s and reached its climax in 1855, was one of the most successful nativistic movements in the nineteenth century. The various secret organizations constituting this movement, such as the Order of United Americans and the Order of the Star-Spangled Banner, were strongly anti-Catholic and agitated for an extension of the period required for an immigrant to become a U.S. citizen and for the election of only "Americans" to political office. The movement, which became less secretive in 1855 and openly called itself the American Party, enjoyed tremendous political successes in a number of states in the 1855 elections. However, the Know-Nothing movement died as quickly as it had emerged. Conflict over slavery within the American Party severely strained and weakened it. Nativistic sentiments in the United States in the 1850s were not strong enough to sustain the Know-Nothing movement.

By the late 1800s, anti-Chinese agitation on the West Coast was virulent, and racist ideologies emerged to justify it (Takaki, 1993). The concept of the inferiority and superiority of various races became rampant in the West. In 1882, Congress passed the Chinese Exclusion Act, the first immigration bill specifically designed to exclude a particular race. Although many Americans viewed the case of the Chinese as separate from European immigration, the anti-Chinese act gave impetus to antiforeign attitudes throughout U.S. society. Three months after the anti-Chinese bill was passed, Congress enacted a bill further restricting the classes of Europeans who could enter the United States. Convicts, idiots, and lunatics, as well as those who might become public charges, were excluded.

Nativism grew more and more intense as the fear soared of a Catholic takeover of the federal government and of foreign radicals. The big jump in the number of southern and eastern European immigrants entering the United States in the 1900s added fuel to the fire. Cries of "100% Americanism" and "America for Americans" became widespread. Agitations for antiforeign legislation became intense, especially legislation that would exclude foreign "radicals" and require immigrants to pass a literacy test.

Congress, responding to pressure in 1885, passed the Foran Act, which prohibited the importation of contract labor from Europe. Violence also erupted during these turbulent times. Italians and Jews were frequently the victims of violent and outrageous acts. Eleven Italians were murdered in a mass lynching in New Orleans in 1891, when they were accused of killing a police superintendent. Riots directed at Jews in Chicago increased public paranoia about foreign "radicals." Congress further extended the classes of immigrants excluded from the United States in 1907. Imbeciles and victims of tuberculosis were now added to the list.

Nativistic movements, which were directed against most Irish Catholics and German radicals in the 1850s, began to focus increasingly on southern and eastern European immigrants as masses of them arrived in U.S. cities. The intellectual community legitimized the racist myths about the innate inferiority of southern and eastern Europeans (Tucker, 1994). William Z. Ripley was one of the leading intellectual nativists. His book, *The Races of Europe,* published in 1899, divided Whites into three major races: the Teutonic, the Northern blondes; the Alpine, the central race of stocky roundheads; and the Mediterranean, dark and slender longheads (Higham, 1972). The Teutonic was the superior race. Ripley warned against a racial mixture that would pollute the superior race with southern and eastern European racial groups.

Madison Grant (1916), a well-known naturalist, also argued for racial purity in his popular book, *The Passing of the Great Race in America,* published in 1916. Ripley and Grant, as well as other intellectuals and writers in the early twentieth century, provided the nativists with the scientific and intellectual justifications for their movements and issued a ringing plea for restrictive legislation (Higham, 1972; Smedley, 1993). As in other periods of mass hysteria in America, social and physical scientists justified and legitimized prevailing social attitudes and myths (Tucker, 1994).

When the twentieth century opened, nativist sentiments and attitudes had gained tremendous momentum in U.S. life. They did not subside until they culminated in the extreme restrictive legislation enacted in the 1920s. The Dillingham Commission, which issued its report in 1911, noted that the new European immigrants were essentially different from the old and strongly recommended the passage of a bill that would require immigrants to pass a literacy test. Agitation for a literacy test bill became intense, but the advocates of the bill faced repeated opposition in Congress and from President Wilson. As the United States prepared to enter World War I, nativism—directed especially at German Americans—became intense. Patriotic groups demanded that all aspects of German culture, including music and the names of streets and schools, be eradicated in the United States. Although most German Americans were loyal citizens during this period, they were often the victims of harassment. However, the abuses they endured were less severe than those suffered by Japanese Americans during World War II (see Chapter 13).

Just before the United States entered World War I, the literacy bill advocates finally mustered enough congressional votes to override a second Wilson veto, and the literacy bill was passed on February 5, 1917. Adult immigrants now had to be able to read a passage in some language before they could enter the United States. The bill was comprehensive. It codified existing legislation and added vagrants, chronic alcoholics, and psychopaths to the list of excluded aliens. The head tax was increased from $4 to $8 (Higham, 1972). Although nativists celebrated their victory, they began immediately to plan strategies to restrict further immigration to the United States.

Campaigns to "Americanize" aliens already in the United States became a national passion during World War I. When the war ended, Congress was pressured again to enact restrictive legislation. The law requiring immigrants to pass a literacy test did not halt immigration as much as the nativists had hoped for and expected. In fact, it reduced it very little. Consequently, nativists pushed for a quota system to restrict immigration. Antiforeign groups and organizations experienced tremendous growth in memberships. The Ku Klux Klan grew greatly in the South and Midwest. It had more than 2.5 million members by 1923. The phenomenal growth of the Klan was symptomatic of pervasive antiforeign attitudes in U.S. life.

Eventually, the nativistic forces gained congressional victories. The Johnson Act, enacted in 1921, marked a turning point in the history of American immigration. The Johnson Act established a nationality quota system and imposed the first numerical limits on immigration from European nations. The quota system was based on the various nationality groups in the United States. The most important immigration bill of this period was enacted in 1924, the Johnson-Reed Act. The quotas this act set were severe and blatantly discriminated against southern and eastern European and non-White nations. It stopped Asian immigration completely. After 1927, the act allowed only 150,000 Europeans to enter the United States each year, and they were "parceled out in ratio to the distribution of national origins in the White population of the United States in 1920." Because Europeans from the North and West represented the largest percentages of Whites in the United States in 1920, the authors of the Johnson-Reed Act had thought of an ingenious way to limit severely the number of immigrants from southern and eastern Europe, while ensuring that a significant number were allowed to enter from the North and West. Nativism had triumphed, and an important chapter in U.S. history had been closed.

SUBSEQUENT IMMIGRATION ACTS

There was little change in U.S. immigration policy from 1924 until the outbreak of World War II. A number of Europeans were displaced by the events of World War II and sought asylum as refugees in the United States. After much debate, a Displaced Persons Act was passed in 1948, which permitted about 400,000 refugees to enter the United States during a four-year period. The McCarran-Walter Act, passed in 1952, allegedly to remove racial barriers to immigration, essentially continued the policy established in 1924 and was, in some ways, more restrictive. In 1953, Congress passed a temporary measure, the Refugee Relief Act, to enable refugees from communist nations to settle in the United States. However, major reform in U.S. immigration policy was not made until 1965. President John F. Kennedy had strongly urged Congress to pass a progressive immigration act. After much discussion and vigorous debate, the bill finally became a reality during the Johnson administration, on July 1, 1968. This act abolished the national origins quota system and allowed 170,000 persons to enter the United States each year from the Eastern Hemisphere and 120,000 from the Western Hemisphere. Technical skill and family ties, rather than country of origin, became the major criteria for admitting immigrants to the United States. This bill was a major victory for progressive Americans and is a tribute to American democratic ideals. The Immigration Act of 1965 was one of the important consequences of the Black civil rights movement that emerged in the South in the 1950s and 1960s.

Congress enacted a comprehensive immigration bill, the Immigration Reform and Control Act, on November 6, 1986 (U.S. Immigration and Naturalization Service, 1998). This act allowed aliens who had been in the United States illegally since January 1, 1982, to attain temporary and then permanent resident status. It also established sanctions for employers who knowingly hired illegal aliens. The Immigration Act of 1990 initiated a major overhaul of immigration law. It increased immigration to a flexible limit of 675,000 annually, beginning in 1995. The 675,000 level was to consist of 480,000 family-sponsored immigrants, 140,000 employment-based immigrants, and 55,000 "diversity immigrants" (U.S. Immigration and Naturalization Service, 1998).

The U.S.A. Patriot Act—which was enacted by Congress forty-five days after the bombing of the World Trade Center in New York City and the Pentagon in Washington, D.C., on September 11, 2001—gives U.S. law enforcement officials broad authority to search the personal records of individuals, which weakens civil liberties. The act is part of what President George W. Bush called the "war on terrorism." The Patriot Act makes it much easier for U.S. authorities to regulate the financial transitions of immigrants and to deport immigrants suspected of terrorism.

EUROPEAN ETHNIC GROUPS IN U.S. SOCIETY

The mass settlement of Europeans in North America was a unique phenomenon in human history. Over 72 million legal immigrants (72,253,191) entered the United States between 1820 and 2006 (U.S. Department of Homeland Security, 2006, 2007). Most came from Europe and represented many religious, political, and cultural groups. Yet the United States, by forcing the immigrants to acquire the culture of the dominant society, was able to prevent the Balkanization of America and to establish a unified society. The immigrants paid a heavy price for cultural assimilation and acculturation. Nevertheless, a rather culturally homogeneous society emerged, although ethnicity is still a viable but complex force in U.S. life.

When European immigrants arrived on America's shores, their thoughts, feelings, aspirations, and attitudes were decidedly European. Many immigrants aggressively tried to build European institutions in the United States. They tried to maintain their religious life by building churches similar to those in Europe. They established parochial schools, ethnic newspapers, ethnic theaters, and self-help organizations in their attempts to hold on to the old order. Some groups, such as the German Americans, created ethnic colonies where their European cultures and ethnic kinships could flourish. Despite the concerted efforts by the immigrants to establish European institutions in the United States, these attempts were, by and large, destined to fail. Forces within American life worked against them and eventually eroded or greatly modified most European cultures in the United States.

The public schools, the U.S. press, and U.S. political institutions played key roles in mitigating the attempts to establish and maintain European institutions on U.S. soil. By the beginning of the nineteenth century, the English dominated most U.S. institutions, such as the schools, the courts, and the popular press. The immigrants and their children often found it necessary to acquire Anglo-Saxon cultural characteristics before they were allowed to participate fully in U.S. society. Schoolteachers demeaned foreign languages; employers often preferred to hire assimilated immigrants. European Americans, especially the second generation, often responded to these cogent forces by becoming ashamed of their ethnic cultures, deliberately denying them, such as by Anglicizing or changing their surnames, and actively seeking to assimilate. Many second- and third-generation immigrants became—in mores, values, and outlook—similar to Anglo-Saxon Protestants. These immigrants paid a tremendous psychological price for denying their cultures, languages, and identities. However, as Greenbaum (1974) has perceptively written, the larger society shamed the immigrants into abandoning their ethnic cultures but held out to them the hope of economic and structural inclusion into the mainstream society. White ethnic groups, unlike people of color, were able to attain full inclusion into the mainstream society and to experience social class mobility once they were culturally identical to Anglo-Saxon Protestants.

THE NEW ETHNICITY

During the 1950s, social scientists expected most ethnic characteristics eventually to disappear in the United States and a modernized, shared culture to evolve. In this common national culture, social class would persist but factors such as race and ethnicity would be largely unimportant.

Glazer and Moynihan, in their 1963 pathbreaking book *Beyond the Melting Pot* (1970), presented one of the first theoretical arguments that the melting pot conception of the United States was inaccurate and incomplete. They argued that ethnicity in New York was important and that it would continue to be important for both politics and culture. Significantly, they included case studies of the persistence of ethnicity among three White ethnic groups: the Jews, Italians, and Irish of New York City. They described how ethnicity persisted among these groups in politics and family structure.

During the 1960s, the civil rights movement emerged. This movement made ethnicity more legitimate. African Americans made claims on the federal government and other institutions because of the historic discrimination they have experienced in the United States. The Black civil rights movement stimulated ethnic revitalization movements among other ethnic groups, such as American Indians and Mexican Americans, and among White ethnic groups, such as Jews, Poles, Italians, and Greeks. Southern, eastern, and central European ethnic groups were the most active participants in the White ethnic revitalization movements that emerged in the early 1970s.

These ethnic groups, through leaders and organizations, began to articulate ways in which they had been victims of ethnic stereotypes and discrimination and how their histories and cultures had been omitted from history books and the school curriculum. They argued that, like Blacks, Indians, and Mexican Americans, they needed public policies that would enable them to acquire more equity and cultural democracy. Michael Novak, an articulate theologian and humanist, became the most prolific speaker and writer for what he called the "unmeltable ethnics." His book *The Rise of the Unmeltable Ethnics,* published in 1971, signaled the birth of the "new pluralism" among White ethnic groups.

In this widely reviewed and quoted book, Novak (1971) identified the "unmeltable ethnics" (Poles, Italians, Greeks, and Slavs), tried to explain how they were both different from and culturally alienated from Anglo-Saxon Protestants, and described how they were victims of discrimination, cultural arrogance, and the intellectual community. In moving prose, Novak also described how he and other Slavs were forced to deny their cultural identities. He wrote: "The estrangement I have come to feel derives not only from a lack of family history. Early in life, I was made to feel a slight uneasiness when I said my name. Liberal education tends to separate children from parents, from their roots, from their history, in the cause of a universal and superior religion" (pp. 64, 69).

Novak (1971) urged opinion leaders and politicians to recognize and respect the cultures of the White ethnics and predicted that they would be a powerful political force during the 1970s. He called the 1970s "the decade of the White ethnics." While Novak was arguing for the civil rights of White ethnics and attempting to mobilize them politically, researchers such as Andrew M. Greeley and William C. McCready (1974) were studying the extent to which ethnicity had survived among White ethnic groups, including the Irish Americans. In their 1974 article, they described significant differences among the Anglo-Saxons, the Irish, and the Italians on personality variables, political participation, and attitudes toward sexuality and drinking. Publications that focused on the new ethnicity of White ethnic groups also emerged. *Ethnicity,* a journal published between 1974 and 1982, included a number of articles describing the cultural differences among White ethnic groups.

The ethnic revitalization movements among White ethnic groups during the 1970s evoked considerable controversy. Some scholars argued that the White ethnic movement was not genuine but was a racist political movement designed to divert attention from the legitimate needs of ethnic groups of color, such as African Americans and Mexican Americans. Other critics argued that the movement was a "me-too," contrived movement. Critics of the new ethnic movements included scholars such as Orlando Patterson (1977), a Harvard sociologist, and distinguished historian Arthur Mann. Wrote Mann (1979): "The White ethnic revival was the product of a seriously divisive movement in history. Like previous revivals in America and elsewhere, secular as well as religious, the 1960s–1970s movement rested on the belief that the only way out for a troubled people lay in the return to a previous but languishing heritage" (pp. 41–42). Two anthropologists, Stein and Hill (1977), published a book-length work on the White ethnic movement in which they harshly criticized it. They wrote: "The New Ethnicity, then, is both a symptomatic expression of a disintegrated life and an attempt to cope with this sense of personal disintegration through regression to an earlier stage in individual development" (p. 9).

Scholars and civil rights leaders who defended the White ethnic movement argued that it was a genuine movement that had emerged in response to cultural assaults, discrimination, and epithets used to describe White ethnics by the liberal press. White ethnic leaders argued that those who dismissed the new pluralism as a "racist movement" had completely misunderstood its nature and complexity and were using a code word to dismiss it summarily.

WHITE ETHNIC GROUPS TODAY: INTO THE TWILIGHT OF ETHNICITY?

Most of the fervor of the ethnic revival movement of the 1970s has disappeared. Most European Americans, as they were in the 1970s, are continuing down the road toward assimilation into the mainstream society. The ethnic movement among White ethnic groups during the 1970s involved primarily ethnic leaders and intellectuals and not common men and women. As Alba (1985) indicates, the fact that ethnic leaders and intellectuals were able to articulate their rage and concerns in the mainstream media and intellectual community indicated that White ethnic groups had attained a significant level of structural inclusion into the mainstream society.

A lasting legacy of the White ethnic movement, and of the ethnic movements in the 1970s, is that ethnicity is more legitimate in the United States today than it was before the 1970s. Many Poles, Italians, and Yugoslavs no longer feel that they need to change their names or to become completely alienated from their ethnic culture in order to realize the American dream and attain economic and social mobility. While many members of White ethnic groups are becoming more assimilated into the mainstream society, continuing immigration from Europe infuses some European ethnic groups, such as Poles and Italians, with heavy doses of ethnic culture each year. Even though groups like the Poles and Italians may have entered the twilight of ethnicity, as Alba (1985) claims, new infusions of immigrants and various political and social events continue to renew ethnicity in the United States. The large number of immigrants that arrived in the United States from the nations of the former Soviet Union are the most recent examples of how White ethnic groups and cultures are continually becoming parts of the United States.

TEACHING STRATEGIES

To illustrate how content related to European Americans can be used to integrate the curriculum, exemplary strategies are identified for teaching these concepts at the grade levels indicated: *cultural contributions* (primary grades), *immigration* (intermediate and upper grades), and *nativism* (high school grades).

Primary Grades

Concept

Cultural contributions

Generalization: Our ancestors came from many different nations and belonged to many ethnic groups. All of these groups made outstanding contributions to American life.

1. To collect the information needed for this unit, duplicate the following letter and give each child one to take home. Tell the pupils to ask their parents to complete the form and return it to you the next day.

   Name of Child _____

   Ethnic Groups

English	Jewish (specify nation)
Scottish	African American
Welsh	American Indian
German	Mexican American
Irish	Asian American (specify nation)
Italian	Puerto Rican
Polish	Other(s) (please specify)
Russian	

   Dear Parents:

   To help our students understand and appreciate the contributions all ethnic groups have made to American life, we are studying about ethnic groups and their role in America. I want to make sure that we study the ethnic heritages of all of my students. To do this, I need your help. Would you please study the list above and place an "X" by the group indicating your child's ethnic heritage. If your child has a mixed heritage, such as "English" and "Russian," please check both of these. However, please try to limit your checks to three by checking only the main strains in your child's ethnic heritage. The list above is based on the categories used by the U.S. Bureau of the Census (2007). They represent the largest ethnic groups in the United States. However, many American ethnic groups are not included. If your child's ethnic heritage is not listed, please check "Other" and fill in the name(s) of your child's ethnic group(s), such as "Spanish" or "French."

   Please send this form back to me tomorrow morning. Thank you very much for your cooperation. I am sure that your response will help us to have a much better unit.

   Sincerely,
   Ms. Rosa Rivera
   Third Grade Teacher

2. When you have received the forms from the parents, make a table showing the ethnic groups represented in your class. Put the table on butcher paper or in a PowerPoint presentation and list the children's names under the appropriate ethnic categories. Your table might look like Table 8.2.

TABLE 8.2   Our Ethnic Heritages

ENGLISH	IRISH	ITALIAN	GERMAN	AFRICAN AMERICAN	POLISH
Susie	Cathy	Roy	*Pete	Jack	Linda
John	*Pete	Pat	Ray	Sam	Terry

*Pete has both Irish and German ancestors. Some of the children might be listed under several categories.

3. Discuss the table with the students, noting that our ancestors came from many different nations. Using a primary globe, locate and write the names of some of the nations and continents from which the children's ancestors came, such as Great Britain, Africa, Mexico, China, and Germany. Discuss these nations and continents with the students.

4. Using the photographs in a book such as *Ellis Island: An Illustrated History of the Immigrant Experience* by Ivan Chermayeff, Fred Wasserman, and Mary J. Shapiro (1991), tell the students the story of the great immigrations from Europe. Point out some of the reasons the immigrants came, how they came, and how they settled in the United States. The special case of the African Americans, as well as immigrants from other nations of color, should also be discussed.

5. Make another table on butcher paper or on a PowerPoint slide listing the major ethnic groups represented in your class and other major U.S. ethnic groups. Under each major group, list some famous Americans and the fields in which they have made outstanding contributions to American life. Your table might look like Table 8.3. Many books contain information about the ethnic backgrounds of famous Americans (see the annotated bibliographies in this chapter and in other chapters in Parts III through V of this book).

6. After you have completed the Famous Ethnic Americans table, making sure that all the children's ethnic heritages are represented, discuss the table with the students, and help them to formulate, in their own words, the following generalization: *Our ancestors came from many different lands and groups, and all these groups made many outstanding contributions to American life.*

TABLE 8.3   Famous Ethnic Americans

ENGLISH	ITALIAN	AFRICAN AMERICAN	POLISH
George Washington, *President*	Joe DiMaggio, *Baseball player*	Benjamin Banneker, *Scientist*	Helena Modjeska, *Actress*
Benjamin Franklin, *Scientist*	Frank Sinatra, *Singer*	Martin L. King, Jr., *Civil rights leader*	Edmund S. Muskie, *U.S. senator*

Make sure that each child knows at least one famous person who belongs to his or her ethnic group. This exercise must be modified in classrooms in which there is only one ethnic group. Use some famous Americans from the students' own ethnic groups, but also select heroes and heroines from at least five or six other ethnic groups not represented in your classroom.

Intermediate and Upper Grades

Concept

Immigration

Generalization: Europeans immigrated to the United States for various economic, political, and social reasons. Their experiences in the United States were both similar and different.

1. To help the students gain the needed content background to study American immigration, assign appropriate readings that will enable them to answer the following questions about the first or old immigrants to America:
   a. What European nations did the first immigrants to America come from during the colonial period?
   b. Why did they come?
   c. Was America like they expected? If so, in what ways? If not, why not? Explain.

2. After the students have completed their reading assignments, discuss the three questions above with the class. During the discussion, list on the board the reasons that various groups immigrated to the United States. When the reasons have been listed, group them, with the class, into three or four categories, such as "economic," "political," and "social" reasons.

3. Ask the students to read about the new immigrants who came to the United States from Europe in the late 1800s and early 1900s. These immigrants came primarily from southern and eastern Europe and included Ukrainians, Russian Jews, Poles, Italians, Greeks, and many other groups. The students should discuss the same three questions about these immigrants that they had discussed after reading about the old immigrants.

4. After the students have read and discussed the old and new immigrants, they should compare and contrast these groups. The following questions can be used to guide discussion:
   a. Did the old and new immigrants come to the United States for similar or different reasons? Explain.
   b. How did the new immigrants differ from the old? Why?
   c. How did American life differ at the times when the old and new immigrants came to America? How did this difference affect the adjustment of the newly arrived immigrants?
   d. Both the old and the new immigrants experienced problems on the trip across the Atlantic. How were these problems similar and different?
   e. How were the problems of settlement and finding jobs in America similar and different for the two groups of immigrants?
   f. Ethnic conflict developed early during the settlement of European nationality groups in America. What problems of prejudice and discrimination were experienced by the various groups? Which groups of immigrants were discriminated against the most? The least? Why?

TABLE 8.4　Generalizing about the Old and New European Immigrants

	OLD IMMIGRANTS			NEW IMMIGRANTS		
	English	Irish	Germans	Italians	Jews	Poles
Reasons for immigrating						
Kinds of people in group						
Problems on Atlantic journey						
Problems of settlement						
Prejudice and discrimination experienced						
Immigration laws in European country of origin						
Relationships *within* the nationality group						

　　The students can summarize this phase of the unit by making a data retrieval chart to summarize and compare information about major ethnic groups representing old and new immigrants, similar to Table 8.4.

5. To help the students gain a feeling for the harshness of the journey across the Atlantic that the immigrants experienced, read aloud to them Chapter 2, "The Crossing," in Oscar Handlin's (1951) classic book, *The Uprooted*. The class can develop a dramatization of the passage as described in Handlin and present it in a school assembly. The entire class should be involved in writing and presenting the dramatization.

6. European immigrants in the United States often wrote to their friends and relatives in Europe describing the wonders of America and, occasionally, their problems. These two books contain letters that German and Norwegian immigrants wrote home: Walter D. Kamphoefner, Wolfgang Helbich, and Ulrike Sommer (1991), *News from the Land of Freedom: Immigrants Write Home;* Solveig Zempel (1990), *In Their Own Words: Letters from Norwegian Immigrants.*

　　Read and discuss selected letters from these two books (or similar ones) with the class. Ask the students to pretend that they are new European immigrants in the United States in the 1800s. They should write to a friend or relative in Europe telling about their experiences. This activity can be correlated with the language arts.

7. Have the students role-play the situation below, which involves a poor Italian farmer and an agent of a steamship company who tries to persuade the farmer to immigrate to the United States. After the role-playing situation, ask the students the questions that follow.

Mr. Pareto, a poor Italian farmer in southern Italy in the 1800s

Mr. Pareto is in his thirties. He is a hard worker and is close to his family, which includes his wife, eight children, and both of his parents. For the past three years, Mr. Pareto has been unable to feed and clothe his family well because of severe crop failures. He has heard about the greatness of America and has often thought about going there. However, he knows that his father feels he should stay in Italy so that he can depend on him in his old age. He also realizes that, if he goes to America, he will have to leave his wife and children in Italy.

Mr. Rossi, an agent for a steamship company that makes trips to America

Mr. Rossi tries to persuade Italian men to immigrate to America. The more men that he can persuade to go to America on his company's steamship line, the more money he makes. He goes up to Mr. Pareto at the village market and tells him about the wonders of America and why he should go there. He tells him that he can obtain a job quickly in America and become a wealthy man. He knows that if Mr. Pareto goes to America he will not be able to take his family. However, Mr. Rossi tells Mr. Pareto that he will be able to send for his family within two or three months after he arrives in America.

Questions

1. Did Mr. Rossi persuade Mr. Pareto to go to America? Why or why not?
2. If Mr. Pareto goes to America, what do you think will happen to his family?
3. If Mr. Pareto stays in Italy, how do you think he will take care of his family?
4. How do you think his wife, parents, and children will react if Mr. Pareto goes to America? Why?
5. What else can Mr. Pareto do besides stay in his Italian village or immigrate to America?
6. If you were Mr. Pareto, would you immigrate to America? Why or why not? Explain.
7. Conclude this unit by viewing and discussing a DVD about European immigration.

Valuing Activity

Many European immigrants, especially those from southern and eastern Europe, changed their names and adopted Anglo-American cultural characteristics so that they could assimilate more quickly into the dominant society and experience rapid social, economic, and political mobility. Other immigrants, however, even though they were the victims of affronts by the larger society, tried to hold onto their names and ethnic cultural characteristics in America. In the following selection, written in 1939, a Polish American tells why he did not want to change his name. Read the selection to your students and ask them the questions that follow the selection.

I WAS ASHAMED OF MY NAME

Twenty-odd years ago I was ashamed of my Polish name and heritage. To the boys in the neighborhood I was the lone "dirty Polack." This rankled, burned, and developed in me a bitter sense of inferiority. There was no Poland . . . I was no Polack! I was American! I didn't want to be a Polack! I would not go to a Polish school! If my parents spoke to me in Polish, I would answer in English. I dreamed of going West, changing my name to Edward R. Edwards, and being American. The end of the war and the Versailles Treaty brought some consolation. Now there was a Poland! True, we didn't hear much about it, but we knew it was there. We had found peace.

In high school, a teacher who had trouble with my name started calling me Scott. Others followed suit. I tried to convince people my name wasn't Scott but Kostyra. Some refused to accept the more difficult name. Mail came to my home for me addressed to Scott. My parents soundly berated me because they considered the pseudonym an insult to them. I was in a quandary (*Polish American Review,* 1939).

Questions

1. What problems did Kostyra face?
2. Why do you think it was difficult for his family to accept a new name for him?
3. Why was Kostyra ashamed of his Polish name?
4. Why do you think some Americans refused to call Kostyra by his Polish name?
5. Do you feel that an individual should change his or her name under any circumstances? Why or why not? If so, under what circumstances?
6. What are some things that Kostyra could have done to solve his problems? What were probable consequences of each course of action?
7. What do you think Kostyra should have done? Why?
8. If you had been Kostyra, what would you have done? Why?
9. Have you ever been in a situation similar to the one that Kostyra was in? If so, what did you do? Why?

High School Grades

Concept

Nativism

Generalization: Negative feelings toward immigrant groups emerged early in colonial America. However, American nativism did not become widespread until the late nineteenth and early twentieth centuries. It eventually led to a virtual halt in European immigration.

1. Ask the students to read Chapter 2, "Ethnic Discord and the Growth of American Nationality," in Maldwyn Allen Jones (1992), *American Immigration,* and Chapter 1, "A Colonial Heritage," in David H. Bennett (1988), *The Party of Fear: From Nativist Movements to the New Right in American History,* and be able to discuss the following questions when they have finished the reading.
   a. Antiforeign attitudes were present in the early American colonies. What groups were the main victims of these negative feelings?

   b. What forms did nativism take in colonial America? What acts and laws were passed in colonial America that reflected antiforeign attitudes?

     When the students have completed these readings, discuss the above questions with the class. They will discover that the Irish, French, Huguenots, Catholics, and Germans were the main targets of early antiforeign attitudes in America. Record their responses to the questions above, in summary form, on the board.

2. Ask individual students or groups of students to prepare reports on the following topics and present them to the class.

- Know-Nothing movement in the 1850s
- Chinese Exclusion Act of 1882
- Immigration Act of 1882, which excluded certain classes of European immigrants
- Immigration Restriction League, formed in 1894
- Foran Act of 1885
- Haymarket Affair, 1886
- Lynching of eleven Italians in New Orleans, 1891
- William Z. Ripley's *The Races of Europe,* published in 1899
- Dillingham Commission, which issued its report in 1911
- Immigration Act of 1917
- Madison Grant, *The Passing of the Great Race in America,* published in 1916
- Johnson Act of 1921
- Johnson-Reed Act of 1924
- McCarran-Walter Act of 1952
- Immigration Act of 1965
- Immigration Reform and Control Act of 1986
- Immigration Act of 1990

    The books by Jones (1992) and Bennett (1988), cited above, are two excellent sources for information about the above topics. When the students are sharing their reports, help them identify some causes of nativistic movements. These causes should be noted on the board and in the students' notebooks. They include anti-Catholic attitudes, fear of foreign "radicals," economic recession and depression, the mass of new immigrants that arrived in the United States in the late 1800s and early 1900s, the belief that aliens were taking jobs away from American citizens, and the popularity of beliefs about the innate inferiority of southern and eastern European immigrants perpetuated by such writers as William Z. Ripley and the well-known naturalist Madison Grant.

3. Heated debates took place in Congress, as well as in other public forums, about the passage of a bill that would require immigrants to pass a reading test before they could enter the United States. Two opposing views of the literacy test are found in Chapter 8 of Oscar Handlin (1959), *Immigration as a Factor in American History.* Samuel Gompers defends the test and President Woodrow Wilson opposes it. Read these two accounts to the class. Ask the students to role-play a session of Congress in 1917 in which the bill is discussed. Different students should argue for and against the bill. After the speeches on the floor, the students should vote for or against the bill. After the voting, they should discuss why their final vote was similar to or different from the congressional vote in 1917.

4. Anthropologists and physical scientists divided Whites into various races in the 1800s (Tucker, 1994). William Z. Ripley (1899) and Madison Grant (1916) popularized

these views and argued that southern and eastern European immigrants were innately inferior to immigrants from the northern and western parts of Europe. Ask the class to compare the views of these writers with the racial views of contemporary scientists such as Richard J. Herrnstein and Charles Murray (1994). Excellent critiques of the views of Herrnstein and Murray are found in *The Bell Curve Debate: History, Documents, Opinions,* edited by Russell Jacoby and Naomi Glauberman (1995).

5. Social and physical scientists blamed the new immigrants for political corruption, urban blight, crime, and large welfare rolls. Ask the students to study writings about the immigrants during the 1800s and to compare these writings with writings today about new immigrants from nations such as Mexico and Haiti. The class can discuss the ways in which the old and new criticisms are alike and different and why they are alike and different. Oscar Handlin (1951), *The Uprooted,* Maldwyn A. Jones (1992), *American Immigration,* and David H. Bennett (1988), *The Party of Fear: From Nativist Movements to the New Right* contain information and references that will help students to carry out this activity.

6. The Johnson-Reed Act of 1924 marked the end of an era in the history of American immigration because it put a virtual end to immigration and discriminated blatantly against southern and eastern European immigrants and non-White nations. Duplicate a copy of this act for the class and ask them to discuss its legal, moral, and political implications. The students can then compare the Johnson-Reed Act with these acts: the McCarran-Walter Act of 1952, the Immigration Act of 1965, the Immigration Reform and Control Act of 1986, the Immigration Act of 1990, the USA Patriot Act of 2001.

Students can also compare nativism near the turn of the century directed against southern, central, and eastern European immigrants with the nativism that is directed against Asians and Hispanics today. For example, a number of states with large Hispanic populations have passed referenda that make English the official state language. In 1994, California voters passed Proposition 187, an initiative that denies undocumented workers and their children schooling and nonemergency medical care. You can conclude this unit by asking the students to write a five- to ten-page paper on "Nativism as a Factor in American Society: Today and Yesterday." This activity can be correlated with English or the language arts.

REFERENCES

Alba, R. D. (1985). *Italian Americans: Into the Twilight of Ethnicity.* Englewood Cliffs, NJ: Prentice-Hall.

Bailey, T. A. (1961). *The American Pageant: A History of the Republic* (2nd ed.). Boston: Heath.

Bateman, G., & Egan, V. (1993). *Encyclopedia of World Geography.* New York: Barnes & Noble.

Bennett, D. H. (1988). *The Party of Fear: From Nativist Movements to the New Right in American History.* Chapel Hill: University of North Carolina Press.

Brodkin, K. (1998). *How the Jews Became White Folks and What That Says about Race in America.* New Brunswick: Rutgers University Press.

Chermayeff, I., Wasserman, F., & Shapiro, M. J. (1991). *Ellis Island: An Illustrated History of the Immigrant Experience.* New York: Macmillan.

Glazer, N., & Moynihan, D. P. (1970). *Beyond the Melting Pot: The Negroes, Puerto Ricans, Jews, Italians, and Irish of New York City* (2nd ed.). Cambridge: M.I.T. Press.

Grant, M. (1916). *The Passing of the Great Race.* New York: Scribner's.

Greeley, A. M., & McCready, W. C. (1974, April). Does Ethnicity Matter? *Ethnicity, 1,* 91–108.

Greenbaum, W. (1974, August). America in Search of a New Ideal: An Essay on the Rise of Pluralism. *Harvard Educational Review, 44,* 411–440.

Handlin, O. (Ed.). (1951). *The Uprooted: The Epic Story of the Great Migrations That Made the American People.* New York: Grosset and Dunlap.

Handlin, O. (Ed.). (1959). *Immigration as a Factor in American History.* Englewood Cliffs, NJ: Prentice-Hall.

Herrnstein, R. J., & Murray, C. (1994). *The Bell Curve Debate: Intelligence and Class Structure in American Life.* New York: Free Press.

Higham, J. (1972). *Strangers in the Land: Patterns of American Nativism 1860–1925.* New York: Atheneum.

Jacobson, M. F. (1998). *Whiteness of a Different Color: European Immigrants and the Alchemy of Race.* Cambridge, MA: Harvard University Press.

Jacoby, R., & Glauberman, N. (Eds.). (1995). *The Bell Curve: History, Documents, Opinions.* New York: Times Books/Random House.

Jones, M. A. (1960). *American Immigration.* Chicago: University of Chicago Press.

Jones, M. A. (1992). *American Immigration* (2nd ed.). Chicago: University of Chicago Press.

Kamphoefner, W. D., Helbich, W., & Sommer, U. (Eds.). (1991). *News from the Land of Freedom: Immigrants Write Home.* Ithaca, NY: Cornell University Press.

Mann, A. (1979). *The One and the Many: Reflections on the American Identity.* Chicago: University of Chicago Press.

Martin, P., & Midgley, E. (2006). Immigration: Shaping and Reshaping America (rev. 2nd ed.). *Population Bulletin, 61*(4). Washington, DC: Population Reference Bureau.

Novak, M. (1971). *The Rise of the Unmeltable Ethnics: Politics and Culture in the Seventies.* New York: Macmillan.

Patterson, O. (1977). *Ethnic Chauvinism: The Reactionary Impulse.* New York: Stein and Day.

Polish American Review. (1939, July).

Ripley, W. Z. (1899). *The Races of Europe: A Sociological Study.* New York: Appleton.

Smedley, A. (1993). *Race in North America: Origin and Evolution of a Worldview.* Boulder, CO: Westview Press.

Stein, H. F., & Hill, R. F. (1977). *The Ethnic Imperative: Examining the New White Ethnic Movement.* University Park: Pennsylvania State University Press.

Takaki, R. (1993). *A Different Mirror: A History of Multicultural America.* New York: Little, Brown.

Terkel, S. (1980). *American Dreams: Lost and Found.* New York: Pantheon.

Tucker, W. H. (1994). *The Science and Politics of Racial Research.* Urbana: University of Illinois Press.

U.S. Census Bureau. (2007). *Statistical Abstract of the United States* (126th ed.). Available online at http://www.census.gov/statab/www/. Washington, DC: U.S. Government Printing Office.

U.S. Department of Homeland Security. (2005). *Yearbook of Immigration Statistics, 2004.* Washington, DC: Author.

U.S. Department of Homeland Security. (2006). *Yearbook of Immigration Statistics, 2005.* Washington, DC: Author.

U.S. Department of Homeland Security. (2007). *Yearbook of Immigration Statistics, 2006.* Washington, DC: Author.

U.S. Immigration and Naturalization Service. (1998). *Statistical Yearbook of the Immigration and Naturalization Service, 1998.* Washington, DC: U.S. Government Printing Office.

U.S. Immigration and Naturalization Service. (2000). *1998 Statistical Yearbook of the Immigration and Naturalization Service.* Washington, DC: U.S. Government Printing Office.

Vecoli, R. J. (1994). *Review of Teaching Strategies for Ethnic Studies* (5th ed.). (Comments prepared for author's revision of text for this 6th edition.)

Vecoli, R. J., & Sinke, S. (Eds.). (1991). *A Century of European Migrations, 1830–1930.* Urbana: University of Illinois Press.

Zempel, S. (Ed.). (1990). *In Their Own Words: Letters from Norwegian Immigrants.* Minneapolis: University of Minnesota Press.

ANNOTATED BIBLIOGRAPHY

Books for Teachers

Especially Recommended

Alba, R. (1990). *Ethnic Identity: The Transformation of White America.* New Haven, CT: Yale University Press.
In this informative and provocative book, Alba uses data from in-depth interviews with more than 500 people to examine the impact of ethnicity on the lives of White ethnics. He argues that ethnic-specific characteristics, such as those of Polish American and Italian American origin, are increasingly less important. However, a new collective White ethnic identity and group has emerged, which he calls "European Americans."

Daniels, R. (2002). *Coming to America: A History of Immigration and Ethnicity in American Life* (2nd ed.). New York: HarperCollins.
This excellent teacher resource is a complete study of immigration to the United States.

Fuchs, L. H. (1990). *The American Kaleidoscope: Race, Ethnicity, and the Civic Culture.* Hanover, NH: University Press of New England.
A rich, descriptive, and comprehensive treatment of the ethnic diversity that constitutes culture in the United States.

Howard, G. R. (2006). *We Can't Teach What We Don't Know: White Teachers, Multiracial Schools* (2nd ed.). New York: Teachers College Press.
Howard's book engages the reader on a journey of personal and professional transformation.

Jacobson, M. F. (1999). *Whiteness of a Different Color: European Immigrants and the Alchemy of Race.* Cambridge, MA: Harvard University Press.
The author engages in a historical analysis by investigating the past to create a narrative that explains "what," "why," and "how" the social constructions of race have changed over time and shaped government policies and individual/collective identity in the United States.

McKinney, K. (2005). *Being White: Stories of Race and Racism.* New York: Routledge.
A must read for teachers who are working to understand the thoughts and attitudes Whites have about racial identity. The book is a helpful tool for those interested in encouraging White students to recognize privilege and institutionalized racism in U.S. society.

Other Books

Alexander, J. G. (2004). *Ethnic Pride, American Patriotism: Slovaks and Other New Immigrants in the Interwar Era.* Philadelphia: Temple University Press.
New immigrants flocked to the United States in large numbers beginning around 1880. This book focuses on later eastern European immigration that occurred between World War I and World War II. The author emphasizes the sociohistorical context that existed as these new immigrants created community, negotiated unfamiliar linguistic barriers, and struggled to preserve ethnic pride and identity in future generations.

Amore, B. (2006). *An Italian American Odyssey: Lifeline-Filo della Vita: Through Ellis Island and Beyond.* Translated by F. Bagnolini. New York: Center for Migration Studies.
The author brings to life an epic story of the journey to the United States across seven generations of an Italian American family. Using a wide-ranging collection of family materials, such as letters, diaries, and historic photographs, Amore rewrites U.S. history from a new perspective.

Barton, H. A. (2007). *The Old Country and the New: Essays on Swedes in America.* Carbondale: Southern Illinois University Press.

The Old Country and the New offers a unique look at Swedish Americans. With chapters on the history of Scandinavians in North America, the testimony of immigrant letters, and the struggle for ethnic maintenance, this book describes the Swedish American experience.

Bukowczyk, J. J. (2006). *Polish Americans and Their History: Community, Culture, and Politics.* Pittsburgh: University of Pittsburgh Press.

This book describes the process by which the Polish changed, and were changed by, life in the United States. Bukowczyk uses the themes of community, culture, and politics to examine Polish American history.

Charitis, C. V. (2005). *Staten Island's Greek Community, New York.* Charleston, SC: Arcadia.

Staten Island received an influx of Greek immigrants during the early part of the twentieth century. This book illustrates the traditional aspects of Greek culture and highlights the many contributions of this group to the local community.

Cisek, J. (2006). *Polish Refugees and the Polish American Immigration and Relief Committee.* Translated by A. S. Juszczak. Jefferson, NC: McFarland.

The author describes the efforts of the Polish American Immigration and Relief Committee (PAIRC) during the post–World War II era. Founded in 1947, the group helped refugees fleeing Poland and the ensuing communist regime. Cisek's study includes both a detailed history and stories of individuals who reveal the struggles faced by this immigrant group.

Ebest, R. (2005). *Private Histories: The Writing of Irish Americans, 1900–1935.* Notre Dame, IN: University of Notre Dame Press.

This engaging book consists of personal narratives by Irish Americans. The stories push readers to reexamine Irish American life in the early 1900s.

Fine, M., Weis, L., Powell, L. C., & Wong, L. M. (Eds.). (1997). *Off White: Readings on Race, Power, and Society.* New York: Routledge.

This book places Whiteness at the center of analysis: Whiteness as race, as privilege, and as social construction. The contributors from fields of education and psychology unravel the racial hierarchies that shape our society by challenging the White norm that pervades our schools, communities, social research, and political movements.

Gardaphe, F. L. (Ed.). (2004). *Leaving Little Italy: Essaying Italian American Culture.* Albany: State University of New York Press.

This book examines Italian-American culture from early immigration to the present day.

Gutkind, L., & Herman, J. C. (Eds.). (2006). *Our Roots Are Deep with Passion: Creative Non-fiction Collects New Essays by Italian-American Writers.* New York: Other Press.

Weaving together stories of family, Catholicism, immigration, and language, this collection of essays speaks to life as an Italian American. Perhaps the book's best feature is that it challenges traditional stereotypes about Italian Americans.

Helbich, W. J., & Kamphoefner, W. D. (Eds.). (2004). *German American Immigration and Ethnicity in Comparative Perspective.* Madison: Max Kade Institute for German-American Studies, University of Wisconsin.

Using a comparative approach to study immigration and ethnicity, the authors test traditional stereotypes about various immigrant populations. This book examines the cultural patterns among German Catholics and other Catholic groups, the political activities of German and Irish immigrants during the nineteenth century, and the German American responses to the policies of Nazi Germany.

Houghton, G. (2004). *Ellis Island: A Primary Source History of an Immigrant's Arrival in America.* New York: Rosen.

An excellent classroom resource, *Ellis Island* provides primary documents concerning the more than 12 million immigrants from Europe, Southwest Asia, and Russia. This book is perfect for both students and teacher who desire firsthand accounts of those who, through this famous gateway, entered the United States for the first time.

Jaroszynska-Kirchmann, A. D. (2004). *The Exile Mission: The Polish Political Diaspora and Polish Americans, 1939–1956*. Athens: Ohio University Press.

This book uncovers the similarities and differences between two distinct Polish immigrant groups: those Polish Americans who were descendents of economic immigrants from the late 1800s and early 1900s, and Polish political refugees forced out after World War II and the communist takeover in Poland. The author attempts to understand the tensions between the two groups concerning nation and identity.

Kelly, M. C. (2005). *The Shamrock and the Lily: The New York Irish and the Creation of a Transatlantic Identity, 1845–1921*. New York: Lang.

Kelly's study is a significant contribution to the study of the Irish American experience in the postfamine decades.

Laliotou, I. (2004). *Transatlantic Subjects: Acts of Migration and Culture of Transnationalism between Greece and America*. Chicago: University of Chicago Press.

Laliotou reconstructs the history of Greek immigration to the United States.

Lee, J., & Casey, M. R. (2006). *Making the Irish American: History and Heritage of the Irish in the United States*. New York: New York University Press.

This engaging collection of essays documents the stories of Irish Americans and their contributions to U.S. culture. Besides an extensive look at Irish identities and expressions in music, sports, and literature, the book includes comments on the future of Irish Americans.

Moreno, B. (2004). *Encyclopedia of Ellis Island*. Westport, CT: Greenwood Press.

A great classroom resource, this is the first encyclopedia dedicated solely to Ellis Island. With more than 430 entries, this encyclopedia includes primary documents and personnel reports that record Ellis Island operations, building use, immigration laws, and organizations associated with immigration history.

Ray, C. (2001). *Highland Heritage: Scottish Americans in the American South*. Chapel Hill: University of North Carolina Press.

The author examines how and why we use memories of our ancestral pasts to provide a sense of identity and community in the present. This book is an original and insightful examination of what it means to be Scottish in the American South.

Sherman, A. F., & Mesenholler, P. (2005). *Augustus F. Sherman: Ellis Island Portraits: 1905–1920*. New York: Aperture.

This book compiles over one hundred portraits taken by Augustus F. Sherman, a registry clerk with the Immigration Division of Ellis Island.

Vecchio, D. C. (2006). *Merchants, Midwives, and Laboring Women: Italian Migrants in Urban America*. Urbana: University of Illinois Press.

Vecchio shares the compelling and notable histories of Italian American women in U.S. cities serving as midwives, laborers, and businesswomen. The author sets the stage through an exploration of women's working lives in Italy and contrasts those experiences with the women's new lives in the United States.

Books for Students

Bogomolny, A. (Ed.). (2006). *New to North America: Writing by U.S. Immigrants, Their Children and Grandchildren*. (2nd ed.). Santa Cruz, CA: Burning Bush.

This general anthology, with new works in its second edition, collects three generations of immigrant experiences from a variety of cultures. Poems, stories, and essays portray immigrants' and descendants' lives from 1840 to the present. (High School)

Clinton, C. (2005). *Simeon's Fire*. Cambridge, MA: Candlewick Press.

A boy is caught in the middle of a clash of cultures between the isolated, often misunderstood Amish community and the surrounding majority culture when a series of fires destroy the barns of Amish farmers. (Intermediate/Middle School)

Durbin, W. (2004). *The Darkest Evening.* New York: Orchard.
  Jake, a Finnish American boy living in Minnesota in the 1930s, resettles with his family in northern Russia when his father, a communist, answers Joseph Stalin's call to help establish an "independent" Finnish communist state. When the atrocities of Stalin's regime become apparent, it is too late for Jake and his family to leave. (Middle/High School)

Giff, P. R. (2003). *Maggie's Door.* New York: Random House.
  A sequel to *Nory Ryan's Song* (2000), this novel follows two boys who make a perilous journey from Ireland to the United States at the time of the potato famine. (Intermediate/Middle School)

Gundisch, K. (2001). *How I Became an American.* Chicago: Cricket Books.
  The immigration of a family from Austria-Hungary to the United States in the late nineteenth century is told from the perspective of a ten-year-old boy. Translated from German, this book won the 2002 Mildred L. Batchelder Award. (Intermediate)

Gutkind, L., & Herman, J. C. (Eds.). (2006). *Our Roots Are Deep with Passion: Creative Nonfiction Collects New Essays by Italian American Writers.* New York: Other Press.
  In a collection of 21 nonfiction narratives, writers reflect on their Italian-American heritage and tell stories that touch on family, food, music, folklore, values, and faith. (High School)

Hill, K. (2005). *Dancing at the Odinochka.* New York: Simon & Schuster.
  A Russian girl living in Russian America, now Alaska, in the middle of the nineteenth century observes the changes, as Native Americans, traders, and eventually American settlers come to this harsh land. (Middle School)

Hoobler, D., & Hoobler, T. (2003). *We Are Americans: Voices of the Immigrant Experience.* New York: Scholastic.
  This single-volume overview of the history of immigration to the United States from colonial times to the present offers testimony of immigrants along with a lively narrative. The book serves as a companion to the Hoobler's excellent Family Album Series (Oxford University Press, 1994–1997). (Intermediate and up)

Hopkinson, D. (2003). *Shutting Out the Sky: Life in the Tenements of New York, 1880–1924.* Illustrated with photos. New York: Orchard.
  The author describes the tenements and the families who lived in them, immigrants from Italy and Eastern Europe. She focuses on teenagers and their responses to the pressures and privations of tenement life. (Intermediate and up)

Huggins, P. (2006). *Trosclair and the Alligator.* Long Island City, NY: Star Bright Books.
  In this humorous Cajun trickster tale, a young boy defies his father and rows his pirogue into a dangerous swamp in pursuit of a hungry alligator known to eat pets. (Primary)

Hughes, P. (2004). *The Breaker Boys.* New York: Farrar, Straus & Giroux.
  The misfit son of a wealthy mine owner in Pennsylvania at the turn of the twentieth century finds friendship with the immigrant miners—until a bloody strike tests their bonds. (Middle School/High School)

Kirkpatrick, K. (2004). *Escape Across the Wide Sea.* New York: Holiday House.
  A French Hugenot family in the eighteenth century escapes religious persecution by taking a slave ship to America. (Intermediate/Middle School)

Lombard, J. (2006). *Drita, My Homegirl.* New York: Putnam.
  A refugee girl from Kosovo whose mother is mentally ill finds friendship and a common bond with an African American classmate whose mother has died and whose father has found a new girlfriend. (Intermediate/Middle School)

Martino, C. A. (2005). *Rosa, Sola.* Cambridge, MA: Candlewick.
  A ten-year-old Italian American girl living in Chicago in the 1960s prays for a baby brother or sister, but her prayers are answered with tragedy. Rosa endures the grief and anger of family members and questions her Catholic faith. (Intermediate)

Mead. A. (2005). *Swimming to America*. New York: Farrar, Straus & Giroux.
> A thirteen-year-old girl discovers that her Albanian immigrant family is in the United States illegally. (Middle School)

Paterson, K. (2006). *Bread and Roses, Too*. New York: Clarion.
> An Italian American immigrant girl is caught up in the 1912 strike in Lawrence, Massachusetts. (Middle School)

Russell, B. T. (2006). *Maggie's Amerikay*. Illustrated by J. Burke. New York: Farrar, Straus & Giroux.
> An Irish girl and her family move to New Orleans in 1898. When her sister contracts yellow fever, Maggie and an African American boy she has befriended try to raise money to help her immigrant family. (Primary)

Sandler, M. W. (2004). *Island of Hope: The Story of Ellis Island and the Journey to America*. New York: Scholastic.
> This engagingly written and comprehensive book offers an overview of the immigrant experience at the beginning of the twentieth century. The author describes conditions in the countries of origin, the various procedures at Ellis Island, and the world the immigrants encountered when they left Ellis Island to start their new lives. (Intermediate and up)

Testa, M. (2005). *Something About America*. Cambridge, MA: Candlewick.
> The author uses free verse to tell the story of a thirteen-year-old girl from Kosovo who adjusts to her new life in Maine as she heals from being burned in the war in her former country. (Middle School)

Thesman, J. (2003). *Rising Tide*. New York: Viking.
> In a sequel to *A Sea So Far* (2001), a seventeen-year-old Irish girl journeys to San Francisco to open a shop with her best friend, and the two girls encounter a mysterious diary, first love, and the aftermath of the 1906 earthquake. (Middle/High School)

CHAPTER NINE

JEWISH AMERICANS
Concepts, Strategies, and Materials

The journey of the Jews to success in America is part of American history; the survival of their Jewishness, and what definition of it they fashion or invent, is the stuff of Jewish history.

—Arthur Hertzberg

In 2006, about 6 million Jewish Americans lived in the United States, making up about 2% of the U.S. population of near 300 million (Sheskin & Dashefsky, 2006). They constitute a religious, cultural, and ethnic minority group that originated in the land that is today Israel. They are a diverse group, living in each of the fifty states, with about 55% in the Northeast and Midwest and 46% in the South and West. The population movement has continually been from the Northeast and Midwest to the South and West (Singer & Grossman, 2006).

Jewish Americans have been an integral part of American history since the days of Columbus, and they have contributed significantly in the arts and sciences, medicine, education, law, and other fields. American culture has been enriched by the works of Jewish novelists, playwrights, and critics who write from a Jewish perspective and on Jewish themes. Yet, the role of Jews in American history clearly transcends a mere listing of their contributions. Their presence is intimately intertwined with many fundamental themes and concepts that have characterized American history, such as religious freedom, the achievement of civic equality, and the struggle of a group to maintain its ethnic identity while assimilating into the U.S. mainstream.

This chapter was originally written by **Jerome L. Ruderman**, a former teacher and department head at Frankford High School in Philadelphia. It was revised by **Hallie Esbin Rosen**, director of visitor services at the Illinois Holocaust Museum and Education Center in Skokie, Ill.

HISTORICAL ROOTS

Jewish history, from Biblical times to the settlement of the first Jews in America, is a vast, complicated story woven into nearly 4,000 years of Western civilization. In the year A.D. 70, conquering Romans crushed the Jewish state in Palestine, driving most, but not all, of its inhabitants into exile. Many fled to Babylonia, where they established a community that soon outshone Palestine as a center of Jewish life. By the ninth century, the hub of the Jewish world had shifted to Spain, where the cooperative attitudes of the Moors encouraged a golden age of Jewish scholarship, literature, and science. This lasted until the thirteenth century, when Christian brutality against Jews replaced the tolerant Moorish rule. Entire Jewish communities were decimated, and countless numbers of Jews were forced or frightened into the Catholic church. Many professed Christianity but secretly adhered to Judaism. They were derisively referred to by the Spanish as *Marranos* (pigs). In 1492, the Spanish monarchs expelled the entire Jewish community, and nearly 150,000 Jews left Spain. A few made their way to America, where they laid the foundations of the Jewish community in America, which in time was to become the largest Jewish population in the world. Today approximately 40% of the world's 13 million Jews live in the United States, compared with 34% in Israel (Singer & Grossman, 2006).

The earliest Jews to reach America arrived with Christopher Columbus in 1492. By the sixteenth century, Jews were prominent in Portuguese Brazil, particularly in the city of Recife. In 1630, that city fell to the liberal Dutch, and the Jews joyfully abandoned the mask of Christianity. In 1654, when the Portuguese reconquered the city, they gave the Jews the choice of baptism or exile. Most chose exile. Twenty-three of them found their way to the Dutch colony of New Amsterdam. Since then, Jewish immigration to the United States has been nearly continuous.

The Colonies

In New Amsterdam, Governor Peter Stuyvesant wished to expel the Jews, but the Dutch West India Company disagreed. He was ordered to permit them to remain as long as they did not become a burden on the colony. However, Stuyvesant confined them to homes in a narrow street that came to be known as "Jews' Alley." He denied them equality with other people in New Amsterdam, even refusing them permission to build a synagogue. The Jews nonetheless formed a congregation (1656) and worshiped in private homes. With the transfer of power to the British in 1664, their status gradually improved. A synagogue was permitted and was completed in 1730. Ten years later, Parliament exempted Jews from saying the words "upon the true faith of a Christian" in the oath required for naturalization in the English colonies.

Jews were welcomed in other colonies such as Rhode Island, Pennsylvania, Georgia, and South Carolina. There, under the enlightened leadership of men like Roger Williams, William Penn, James Oglethorpe, and John Locke, Jewish communities were established. But, even in these colonies, Jewish participation in civic life was limited. Throughout the entire colonial period only one Jew, Francis Salvador of South Carolina, was elected (1774) to a representative congress or assembly. Nonetheless, Jews slowly gained the rights of domicile, trade, and religious organization. Where restrictions against them existed, they were usually ignored.

In some colonies, however, Jews were barred altogether. No Jewish community developed in Massachusetts, for example, until after the American Revolution. Virginia and Maryland, too, were unfriendly to Jews. Maryland was actually one of the last states to lift restrictions against Jews, in 1826.

JEWISH AMERICANS: HISTORICAL PERSPECTIVE

Important Dates	Events
1492	The Jews were expelled from Spain. Jews accompanied Columbus on his first voyage to America.
1654	Twenty-three Jewish immigrants from Brazil arrived in New Amsterdam. They established the first Jewish settlement in North America.
1730	New York Jews build the first synagogue, Shearith Israel, in North America.
1740	An act of Parliament exempted Jews from saying the words "on the true faith of a Christian" in the naturalization oath, enabling them to become citizens in English colonies.
1774	Francis Salvador was elected to the South Carolina Provincial Congress. He was the only Jewish delegate to any representative assembly in colonial times.
1786	The Virginia Statute of Religious Freedom was passed. It guaranteed religious equality to Jews in Virginia and became a model for other colonies.
1787	The Constitution of the United States barred religious tests for federal office.
1791	The First Amendment of the Bill of Rights prohibited congressional establishment of religion in the United States.
1809	Jacob Henry, a Jew, was allowed to retain his seat in the North Carolina House of Commons despite a state law limiting office holding to Protestants.
1815	The Congress of Vienna nullified the rights of German Jews, causing thousands to immigrate to the United States.
1826	The Maryland "Jew Bill" was passed. It ended religious tests against Jews in Maryland.
1848	The Revolution of 1848 in Europe caused many German Jews to come to America as political refugees.

Important Dates	Events
1862	Rabbis were permitted to serve as U.S. military chaplains. General Ulysses S. Grant issued General Order No. 11, which expelled Jews as a class from the Department of the Tennessee.
1868	The Fourteenth Amendment was adopted. Subsequent court decisions broadened it to guarantee religious equality in the states.
1877	Joseph Seligman, a Jewish manufacturer, and his family were excluded from a resort hotel, foreshadowing the pattern anti-Semitism was to take in the United States.
1881–1882	Discriminatory legislation and *pogroms* (government-sponsored attacks) against Russia's Jews spurred wholesale immigration to America.
1885	The Pittsburgh Platform was enunciated by Reform Jews. It stated their principles and beliefs.
1886	The Jewish Theological Seminary was founded by leaders of Conservative Judaism.
1915	Leo Frank, a Jew, was lynched in Georgia, a result of anti-Semitic hatred.
1916	Louis D. Brandeis was appointed to the U.S. Supreme Court
1921–1924	The Immigrant Acts of 1921 and 1924 drastically curtailed Jewish immigration to the United States.
1930–1940	Anti-Semitism, stimulated by Nazi propaganda, reached alarming levels in the United States.
1939–1946	Six million Jews were killed by the Nazis during World War II.
1948	President Harry S. Truman recognized the state of Israel immediately after its establishment.
1967	Jewish Americans strongly supported Israel during the Six-Day War.
1968	The Reconstructionist Rabbinical College is established.
1973	Jewish Americans contributed huge sums of money to Israel when the Yom Kippur War broke out.
1976	Jews throughout the world took pride in the heroic Israeli commando raid on Entebbe airfield in Uganda. This action freed hostages held by Palestinian terrorists.
1978	First woman rabbi was ordained.
1979	Egypt's President Anwar el-Sadat and Israel's Premier Menachim Begin signed a peace treaty, together with President Jimmy Carter, in a White House ceremony a few months after a thirteen-day conference at Camp David.
1981	Pressure generated by the New Right and Christian Right troubled many Jewish Americans as the "moral majority" and similar groups challenged the concept of separation of church and state.

Important Dates	Events
1982	Many Jewish Americans were privately critical of Israel's military thrust into Lebanon to end Palestine Liberation Organization terrorism, which thus reflected a shift from unquestioned support to criticism of the Begin government.
1985	American Jews were shocked by President Ronald Reagan's visit to a military cemetery in Bitburg, Germany, which contains the graves of forty-seven members of the Waffen SS (Hitler's elite armed guard).
1986	Elie Wiesel was awarded the Nobel Peace Prize.
1993	Israel signed a peace agreement with the PLO. The United States Holocaust museum was opened in Washington, D.C. Ruth Bader Ginsberg was appointed to the United States Supreme Court.
1994	Israel and Jordan signed a peace agreement. Steven Breyer was appointed to the United States Supreme Court.
1995	Israeli Prime Minister Yitzhak Rabin was assassinated at a Tel Aviv peace rally.
1997	Secretary of State Madeline Albright learned that at least three of her grandparents were Jewish and that they had perished in the Holocaust.
2000	Senator Joseph Lieberman ran and lost as the first Jewish American nominated as the Democratic vice presidential candidate.
2004	American Jews celebrate 350 years of American Jewish History.

Biblical Influence

Ironically, though few Jews lived in New England, Jewish influence there was pervasive and penetrating. The Puritan theocracy was modeled after that of ancient Israel, its early legal codes were patterned after the Law of Moses, and daily life and religious practices were influenced by the Hebrew Bible and the Judaic tradition. In New England, as was true throughout the colonies, there was considerable interest in the Hebrew language. Intelligent laymen studied it and frequently assembled collections of Hebraica. At Harvard and Yale, proficiency in Hebrew was required for graduation. In the eighteenth century, the New England clergy, often in the forefront of the drive for independence, frequently referred to the democratic principles in the Hebrew Bible, as did political pamphleteers like Thomas Paine. In their hands it became a political, as well as a religious, text.

THE AMERICAN REVOLUTION

At the outbreak of the Revolution, Jewish Americans numbered about 2,000 of a total population of two million. Many were merchants and traders. Others were doctors, manual laborers, candlemakers, watchmakers, shoemakers, silversmiths, wigmakers, bakers, or butchers. Like other colonists, Jews participated in a wide range of professions and occupations. The notion of Jews as a homogeneous population was as erroneous then as it is today.

When fighting broke out, most Jews participated in the struggle for independence, even those of the merchant-ship-owner class, whose commercial interests were in England. A few Jews were loyalists, but the majority participated as enlisted men and officers in the American army. Bernard Gratz of Philadelphia and other Jewish merchants signed nonimportation agreements. Aaron Lopez of Newport donated much of his personal fortune to the Continental cause. He and other ship owners outfitted their vessels with cannons and dispatched them against British ships. In Philadelphia, Haym Salomon was undoubtedly the most competent bill broker in America. As broker to the Office of Finance, he sold bills of exchange and government notes for the highest possible prices and the lowest commissions. His son and the sons and grandsons of numerous Jews of the Revolutionary period served in the War of 1812.

Uriah Phillips Levy is perhaps the best known of these men. He ultimately reached the rank of commodore in the U.S. Navy, despite a lifetime struggle to overcome anti-Semitism. Levy is best remembered for his crusade to end corporal punishment in the navy and for preserving Thomas Jefferson's home, Monticello, as a national shrine.

A result of the Revolution was that the colonists were no longer subjects of a king but enfranchised citizens of their own country. Important as that was for the colonists in general, it was even more important for the Jews because it legitimized the rights and privileges they had won. It was the first time in the history of Western civilization that they had been a legitimate part of the body politic, no longer excluded from the civic life of the community because of their religion. This transformation was eloquently expressed in 1790 by George Washington in a letter to the Jews of Newport, Rhode Island, in which he wrote, "Happily the government of the United States, which gives to bigotry no sanction, to persecution no assistance, requires only that they who live under its protection should demean themselves as good citizens."

Equality in the States

Constitutional guarantees of freedom of religion implicit in the Revolution were not automatically or universally guaranteed by the federal Constitution. Its protections were limited to suffrage and office holding at the federal level. The states were as free as ever to impose religious tests that, in some cases, remained on the statute books long after the adoption of the Constitution. In Pennsylvania, state office holding was limited to Christians; in New Jersey and North Carolina, it was restricted to Protestants. Not until the adoption of the Fourteenth Amendment in 1868 was a significant attempt made to limit the power of the states in this regard. Even then, it was many years before the Supreme Court wrote interpretations of the Fourteenth Amendment supporting the rights of religious minorities in the states. Thus, the struggle for full equality was thrown back to the states. In Virginia, Jefferson and Madison led the way with the Virginia Statute of Religious Freedom in 1786. By 1790, New York, Georgia, Pennsylvania, and South Carolina, states with established Jewish communities, had passed similar laws. Others tarried well into the nineteenth century.

In North Carolina, in 1809, Jacob Henry, a Jew, was reelected to the state House of Commons. He was challenged on the grounds that his election violated a state requirement that all public officials be Protestant and accept the divine authority of the Christian Bible. After a spirited defense, he was permitted to retain his seat, but only by a legal subterfuge. The law itself was not changed regarding Jewish Americans until 1868, when the North Carolina state constitution, which also enfranchised African Americans, was adopted by a Reconstruction government.

Similarly, the Maryland Constitution of 1776 required "a declaration of belief in the Christian religion" in order to hold state office. A protracted struggle by Maryland Jews, with the aid of a gentile, Thomas Kennedy, who was a member of the state legislature, resulted in the Maryland "Jew Bill" in 1826. It provided that any citizen could qualify for any public office by declaring "his belief in a future state of rewards and punishments." Though still a religious test of sorts, it was not specifically aimed at Jews. By the end of the Jacksonian period, the few religious disabilities that remained were largely unenforced and a friendly attitude toward Jewish Americans prevailed.

GERMAN-JEWISH IMMIGRATION

Though German Jews had predominated in the colonies since 1728, the years from 1820 to 1880 are considered the period of German-Jewish immigration. During those sixty years, about 200,000 Jews came to the United States from Germany and neighboring countries, where for centuries Jews had been vulnerable to recurring outbursts of mass hysteria and violence by the surrounding Christian population. Often confined to ghettos and forbidden to enter many skilled trades and farming, Jews had developed a close-knit society that emphasized study of the Bible and frequently turned to trade and commerce. In the eighteenth century, the Enlightenment and the reforms of Napoleon battered down their civic disabilities, and the Jews entered the secular worlds of France and Germany. However, their emancipation was short lived. In 1815, the Congress of Vienna sought to nullify their newly won rights, causing thousands to depart for America. They were actually part of an exodus of about 5 million Germans who sought political freedom and economic opportunity in the United States. After the Revolution of 1848, the number who came as political refugees increased.

The German immigrants spread out across the country, though most settled in the Ohio and Mississippi River Valleys. Many of them, Christians as well as Jews, turned to peddling, an occupation that required no training and little capital and that served the needs of rural and frontier America. From these humble beginnings, some peddlers managed to accumulate enough capital to acquire a cart, then a horse and wagon, and finally a small store, which in some cases evolved into modern department stores. Some stores founded by Jewish peddlers are Bamberger's, Bloomingdale's, Filene's, Magnin's, Gimbel's, and Macy's (a dry-goods business that Isidor and Nathan Straus turned into a giant department store). Other Jewish immigrants remained in the growing cities of the East and were frequently engaged in tailoring or shoemaking or dealt in secondhand clothing or dry goods.

A small number of Jews went West and became part of the saga of the frontier as buffalo hunters, ranchers, newspapermen, mayors (Galveston, Texas, had a Jewish mayor in 1850), miners, explorers, traders, artists, and photographers. Solomon Nunes Carvalho was a prominent Jewish artist and photographer who traveled with John Charles Fremont. Levi Strauss manufactured strong, copper-riveted denim trousers (Levi's) for the gold miners in California. By the mid 1850s, San Francisco had about 4,000 Jews.

The German-Jewish community in the nineteenth century was characterized by the multitude and variety of voluntary, self-help organizations that it established to meet a variety of social and political needs. A "Hebrew Benevolent Society" usually served many purposes in small communities. In larger cities, specific societies met unique needs, such as care of orphans or the poor. Five Jewish fraternal orders were born. The best known was B'nai B'rith, established in 1843. The Young Men's Hebrew Association (YMHA) was established at this time, as were a number of Jewish hospitals that provided kosher food to Jewish patients and training for Jewish medical students. During the Civil War, they admitted so many non-Jewish casualties that they became nonsectarian and have remained so to the present day.

Early attempts at Jewish schools met with little success. As public schools became popular, Jewish students attended them during the day and Jewish religious schools in the late afternoon or on Saturday or Sunday morning. This is still the most common form of Jewish education in the United States.

In 1843, the Reverend Isaac Leeser of Philadelphia founded a monthly publication, *The Occident.* Other Jewish periodicals appeared; the most important was *The Israelite,* published by Rabbi Isaac Mayer Wise, an outstanding Jewish leader and the father of Reform Judaism in America.

Reform Judaism

Most German Jews established their own congregations rather than join the existing Spanish congregations, whose ritual and liturgy differed somewhat from their own. Consequently, between 1850 and 1870 the number of congregations in the United States rose from 37 to 189.

Among the new congregations, demands were soon heard for shorter religious services, elimination of Sabbath observance, the use of English rather than Hebrew for prayer, modified dietary laws, and elimination of many traditional restrictions that had been part of Jewish tradition for centuries. Their demands were answered by the Reform movement, which, having begun in Germany, found fertile ground in America. Its leader, Rabbi Isaac Mayer Wise, preached that Judaism must adapt to the American environment or it would die. Notwithstanding the bitter opposition of traditionalists, who felt it wrong to tamper with sacred law and tradition, the new movement had become so much a part of Jewish life in America by 1885 that a panel of Reform rabbis met in Pittsburgh to codify their principles and beliefs. While adhering to the moral teachings of Judaism, the "Pittsburgh Platform" rejected traditional practices "not adapted to the views and habits of modern civilization."

THE CIVIL WAR

Before and during the Civil War, Judaism took no common position on the question of slavery. Then, as now, individual Jews and congregations were entirely free of hierarchical control. Pronouncements by individuals, even rabbis, represented no more than their personal opinions, which varied from those of fanatical abolitionists like Michael Heilprin of Philadelphia to champions of slavery like Judah P. Benjamin, secretary of state in the Confederate government and an intimate and influential adviser of Jefferson Davis.

Jewish merchants, whatever their inclination, played only a minimal role in the Atlantic slave trade. In the seventeenth century they were excluded from the Spanish and Portuguese colonies and banned from the French West Indies, areas of major slave trade activity. In the next century, when the slave trade was dominated by England, France, and Holland, Jewish names are virtually absent from the records. In general, geography determined the allegiance of American Jews, whose attitudes toward slavery reflected the culture in which they lived. Many Southern Jews, sensitive to proslavery pressures and concerned about anti-Semitism, prudently accepted the status quo. Others, steeped in the traditions of the South, embraced the Confederate cause promptly and enthusiastically. But Jews were not major slaveholders. Over 90% of the American slave population was concentrated in plantation districts, where Jews were a rarity. Those who did hold slaves generally lived in cities and owned small numbers of domestic servants. In the North, many Jews were recent immigrants from Germany, whose experience with persecution usually pitted them against slavery. When the fighting broke out, Jews in the North and South flocked to their respective colors. More than 6,000 Jewish soldiers and officers served in the Union forces, and several thousand Jews fought for the Confederacy, including twenty-four known staff officers.

Of greater significance than the number of Jewish participants in the war was the growth of anti-Semitism during this period. Though anti-Semitism had been present in American society since 1654, when the first Jews arrived in New Amsterdam, it was not until the Civil War that it became a national issue. The first incident occurred early in the war as Jewish soldiers in the Union army sought to have rabbis ordained as military chaplains. A furor of protest ensued as certain Protestant groups objected. In December 1861, the Reverend Arnold Fischel visited President Lincoln, who rectified the injustice.

But anti-Semitism would not be stilled. In December 1862, Ulysses S. Grant issued General Order No. 11. It expelled "the Jews, as a class" from the Department of the Tennessee without trial or hearing (the Department of the Tennessee was the district controlled by Grant's armies). Violators would be jailed until they could be deported as prisoners. Jews sent letters and telegrams to Jewish leaders all over the country. Cesar Kaskel, one of those deported, visited President Lincoln in Washington to protest. Lincoln was sympathetic. He directed Grant to cancel the infamous order.

The press of the country was divided. Newspapers supporting the administration generally defended Grant. Some printed anti-Jewish invective previously unheard in America. The *New York Times* condemned the order as "one of the deepest sensations of the war." Jewish Americans were stunned when the Senate and House of Representatives failed to pass resolutions castigating Grant's action. Partisan arguments in both houses obscured the moral and legal aspects of the matter. Grant never apologized for the order, but as president he displayed no antagonism toward Jewish Americans. Rather, he supported Jewish causes on a number of occasions and appointed Jews to public office.

In the Confederacy, verbal attacks against Jews were widespread. Jews were frequently accused of speculating in all manner of merchandise and thereby of causing the horrendous wartime inflation that paralyzed the South. A Jewish stereotype became the Confederacy's scapegoat, whereas the real causes of inflation—insufficient industrial base, heavy wartime demands on industry, and a successful Union blockade—were ignored.

POSTWAR ANTI-SEMITISM

The years following the Civil War witnessed the emergence of the chief forms of anti-Semitism that Jewish Americans have had to contend with: discrimination in certain professions and occupations and exclusion from certain residential areas, social clubs, fashionable resorts, private schools, and universities, particularly medical schools. Such anti-Semitic discrimination became more striking in the 1920s, 1930s, and 1940s.

As early as 1867, attempts by a number of insurance companies to deny Jews fire insurance became a public issue. Ten years later, Joseph Seligman, an eminent Jewish clothing manufacturer, and his family were excluded from a fashionable hotel in Saratoga, New York. At about the same time, the president of the Long Island Railroad declared, "We do not like Jews as a class." These incidents and the pattern of discrimination they foreshadowed must be viewed against a background of the improved social and economic status of Jews in America. By 1877, most Jews had left the ranks of the working class. But their rapid rise from humble origins made them abhorrent to high society. Moreover, thousands of eastern European Jews began immigrating to the United States after 1880. Their foreignness undoubtedly stimulated nativist tendencies and added to the determination of the White Anglo-Saxon Protestants in the country to exclude all Jews from their ranks.

Although anti-Semitism has never been an instrument of governmental policy in the United States, as has been the case in Europe, and though violence has never been a serious problem for Jewish Americans—even Grant's order produced no physical violence against them—the pattern of bigotry and hatred that characterized the post–Civil War years did lead to the Georgia lynching in 1915 of a Jew named Leo Frank.

CONSERVATIVE, RECONSTRUCTIONIST, AND ORTHODOX JUDAISM

By 1885, Reform Judaism had deviated drastically from received Jewish tradition. Even before that year, traditionalists, alarmed at its growing strength, had organized a countermovement that became known as Conservative Judaism. By 1886, it was strong enough to found the Jewish Theological Seminary in New York City. Though it made some concessions to the modern world, Conservative Judaism remained faithful to the core of Jewish law and ancestral traditions.

The early organizational efforts of Conservative Judaism were unimpressive, but with the arrival of one-half million Orthodox eastern European Jews by the end of the century, its prospects improved greatly. To many of the American-born children of the Orthodox, the Conservative movement offered an attractive compromise between their middle-class desire for social integration and their attachment to traditional Jewish culture. In 1901, Jewish philanthropists financed the reorganization of the Jewish Theological Seminary, which soon began graduating American-trained rabbis to satisfy the flourishing Conservative movement.

Shortly after this time, the smallest branch of American Judaism began. Reconstructionism, which began in the philosophy of Mordechai Kaplan, a graduate of the Jewish Theological Seminary, saw Judaism as a "religious civilization" emerging from the history and culture of the Jewish people. It is like Reform Judaism in its emphasis on reexamination of religious beliefs and similar to Orthodox Judaism in its commitment to preserve forms and symbols of religious practice.

But it was Orthodox Judaism that benefited most from the immigration of eastern European Jews. By 1900, most of the 850 congregations in the United States were Orthodox. Two years later, the Union of Orthodox Rabbis was organized to "place Orthodox Judaism in America on a firm basis." One of the educational institutions it supported became the nucleus of Yeshiva University.

Despite the growth of both the Reform and Conservative movements, Orthodox Judaism has maintained a significant place in the American Jewish community. Its numbers were augmented after World War I with the influx of thousands of Orthodox Jews from eastern Europe, many of whom settled in New York City.

THE NEW IMMIGRATION

Between 1881 and 1924, more than 2 million Jews left eastern Europe because of anti-Jewish legislation and *pogroms* (government-sponsored attacks) against them. In some years, they came to the United States at the rate of more than 100,000 per year. The vast majority, as was true of other immigrant groups, settled in the northeastern states, particularly in the port cities of New York, Boston, Philadelphia, and Baltimore. Others crowded into the great cities of the Midwest. The Jews moved into densely populated ethnic neighborhoods such as New York's Lower East Side, South Philadelphia, or Chicago's West Side. Data from 1908 to 1924 indicate that only 5% of Jews arriving in the United States returned to Europe, compared to 33% of the general immigration (Thernstrom, Orlov, & Handlin, 1980). Many found work in the new ready-to-wear clothing industry. They were attracted to it, not because of an inherent proclivity for tailoring, but because of the constant demand for cheap labor and the fact that many had had garment experience in Europe. Working conditions were deplorable. The highly competitive contract system and the sweatshops it generated regularly exploited the workers. The sweatshops were dark, airless, unsanitary firetraps in which whole families often worked to meet production quotas. Tuberculosis and other diseases were rampant. Laborers worked from 4:00 A.M. to 10:00 P.M. Men earned $6 to $10 a week; women and children much less.

Such conditions led to the formation in 1888 of the United Hebrew Trades in New York. It was the first organization to introduce Jewish immigrants to the trade union movement. After the turn of the century, Jewish clothing workers organized the powerful International Ladies' Garment Workers Union and the Amalgamated Clothing Workers of America. In 1911, a tragic fire at the Triangle Shirtwaist Factory in New York City underscored the need for better working conditions in the industry. Over the years, the International and the Amalgamated improved conditions and benefits and broke new ground in employer-employee relations. Since the end of World War I there has been a steady exodus of Jewish workers from the garment industry, but the legacy of the once largely Jewish unions remains an important chapter in the history of the American labor movement.

YIDDISH

Yiddish was the daily language of most of the eastern European Jews. Hebrew, the holy tongue, was reserved for prayer and study of the Bible. Though both use the Hebrew alphabet and are written from right to left, they are not the same. Yiddish is similar to German; Hebrew is a Semitic language.

Daily newspapers in Yiddish appeared in several U.S. cities, most notably the *Jewish Daily Forward* in New York. They taught the immigrants American history and civics in the language they understood best. Many read Yiddish fiction in America. The stories of Sholom Aleichem, one of the better-known Yiddish writers, inspired the hit Broadway musical *Fiddler on the Roof*. Yiddish theater, too, flourished and attained a high literary and dramatic level, producing a host of Yiddish dramatists. But the flowering of Yiddish was a phenomenon of the immigrant generation. By mid-twentieth century, it had fallen into disuse. Gifted writers like Waldo Frank, Ben Hecht, Ludwig Lewisohn, Michael Gold, and Abraham Cahan wrote about the Yiddish experience in English. The stories of the Yiddish writer Isaac Bashevis Singer are enjoyed in their English translations. Singer was awarded the Nobel Prize for literature in 1978.

Courses in Yiddish are offered in universities and adult education programs today in an attempt to preserve and revitalize Yiddish culture. The National Yiddish Book Center, founded in 1980, oversees the recovery, collection, and cataloging of Yiddish books from around the world that would otherwise be thrown away. By 2007, the center had collected 1.5 million books, instituted a Yiddish library development program, Yiddish musical and educational projects, and a series of public radio broadcasts of Yiddish stories in English translation (National Yiddish Book Center, 2007).

THE INTERWAR PERIOD

Following World War I, America's traditional hospitality toward immigrants suddenly changed. Undoubtedly, anti-Semitic factors account in part for the series of restrictive immigration laws that, by 1924, virtually stopped Jewish immigration. In that year, the Johnson-Reed National Origins Quota Act blatantly curtailed immigration from eastern Europe, where most Jews lived, from southern Europe, and from non-White countries. Its system of national quotas remained in effect until 1965.

The prosperity of the war years enabled many Jewish Americans to move to newer, middle-class neighborhoods, foreshadowing a later exodus to the suburbs. The less affluent, often more religious Jews tended to remain in older neighborhoods, where eastern European orthodoxy survived in its purest forms. Kosher restaurants flourished; late-afternoon Jewish schools, Yiddish publications, and Orthodox synagogues were abundant. In the newer neighborhoods, indifference, even skepticism, toward Jewish ritual was a common attitude. It seemed to foreshadow the demise of Judaism in America; yet that is not what happened. Instead, most Jewish Americans felt an overriding desire to preserve their Jewish cultural identity and pass it on to their children. This can be seen in their high rate of endogamous marriage and in the growth of congregations and Jewish schools in the newer Jewish neighborhoods during these years.

By 1940, Jewish Americans had transformed themselves from a working-class to a middle-class community of commercial, white-collar, and professional people who established an excellent record of achievement in the sciences, medicine, and other fields of endeavor.

For many Jews, education was a calculated means of social and economic improvement. But a more likely explanation of their drive for education is to be found in Jewish culture itself, which places a high priority on knowledge and learning for its own sake. Education was part of the value system that the Jewish immigrants brought with them, as well as part of the value system that sustained generations of pious Jews in their perpetual study of the Bible.

During these years, anti-Semitism assumed an ominous hue. The Ku Klux Klan reappeared. It burned fiery crosses in front of synagogues and smashed store windows of Jewish merchants. By 1925, it had more than four million members. In 1920, Henry Ford reprinted *The Protocols of the Elders of Zion* in his weekly newspaper, *The Dearborn Independent*. It was a clumsy fabrication, originally published in 1904 in Russia, purporting to be the minutes of a secret meeting of Jewish leaders in Prague, in the last years of the nineteenth century, who plotted the overthrow of the world. Many Americans were prepared to believe it. During the Great Depression, Jewish bankers were accused of controlling world finance. A *Fortune Magazine* survey in 1936 proved conclusively that Jews played, at best, a minimal role in national and international banking, yet the myth persisted. Later, in the 1930s, as the influence of Nazism was increasingly felt in the United States, and attempts to prove that Jews were biologically inferior were imported, anti-Jewish propaganda intensified. Hatemongers like Father Charles E. Coughlin, the Detroit "radio priest," revived the myth of a Jewish takeover of the world. But they made little headway in the United States, and with the end of World War II—when the full dimensions of the Nazi Holocaust were revealed—anti-Semitism ebbed to its lowest level in years.

Despite periodic ups and downs in reported anti-Semitic incidents due to, for instance, the situation in the Middle East, anti-Semitism in the United States continues at low levels. According to the Anti-Defamation League (2006), which has conducted an Audit of Anti-Semitic Incidents since 1979, through education and the diligent work of law enforcement, anti-Semitic incidents continue to decrease.

ZIONISM

The two most important events in the history of the Jewish people since their dispersion 2,000 years ago have been the Nazi Holocaust and the creation of the state of Israel in 1948. Modern political Zionism, as the proposal for the return of the Jewish people to Zion (Palestine) is known, is considered to have begun in 1897, when Theodore Herzl convened the first Zionist Congress in Basel, Switzerland. The Zionist movement in the United States drew its greatest support from the eastern European Jewish immigrants. A major factor in its growth was the emergence of Louis D. Brandeis as its leader, a role he held at the time of his appointment as associate justice of the U.S. Supreme Court in 1916. Yet, it was the Nazi Holocaust that brought the Zionist goal to fruition (Linenthal, 1995).

Six million of Europe's Jews and 5 million other people were killed by the Nazis in World War II (Berenbaum, 1993). The majority were systematically murdered in specially built death camps. The commander of Auschwitz estimated that 2.5 million victims were executed at that camp alone, and another 0.5 million died there of starvation and disease. Had it not been for America's restrictive immigration laws during these years, many lives could have been saved. Only a pitifully small number of Jewish refugees reached the United States in the 1930s. The best known was Albert Einstein. Ships carrying refugees from Germany were actually turned away from U.S. shores and sent back to the Nazi crematoria. The consistent refusal of the United States and other Western nations to accept Jewish refugees led to the near fanatical determination of Zionists the world over to reestablish a homeland in Palestine as a haven for persecuted Jews from any land. It also accounts for the passionate support of contemporary Jews for Israel. After the war, when the culpability of the Western nations in not accepting more refugees became evident, the general public endorsed the Zionist program.

When the state of Israel was proclaimed, President Harry S. Truman recognized the new nation immediately. Despite their emotional attachment to Israel, few Jewish Americans have moved to Israel, but Israel has long been a focal point of unity for the American Jewish community, particularly during the Six Day War in 1967 and the Yom Kippur War in 1973. In recent years, however, Israel has become a divisive communal issue. Policies toward the Palestinians, the peace process, and Israel's religious life all continue to be increasingly controversial, causing mixed feelings for some American Jews (Singer & Grossman, 2000). Despite the growing complexity of this relationship, one-third of Jewish Americans have visited Israel and 57% of Jewish Americans still believe that caring about Israel is a very important part of their Jewish identity (Second Thoughts. . . , 2007)

JEWISH AMERICANS TODAY

Today, Jewish Americans are enjoying another golden age. At the beginning of the twenty-first century, Jewish Americans have been accepted and have thrived in contemporary American society as never before.

Postwar prosperity and the end of educational quotas and social barriers after World War II opened up opportunities for Jews, who entered the academic world in disproportionate numbers. Jews currently make up 5% of all college students and 10% of college faculties—a figure that rises to at least 20% for the elite universities (Chanes, 2004). The same institutions that once discriminated against Jews, such as Harvard, Columbia, and Princeton, have all hired Jewish presidents in recent years.

In 2004, the average income of American Jews with children at home approached $80,000 a year (Chanes, 2004), which was well above the average national median household income of $46,000 (DeNaves-Walt et al., 2006).

Another symbol of Jewish success is the role of Jews in the upper echelons of government. For the first time in American history, the fact that someone was Jewish became irrelevant when being appointed to a high government position. Both Presidents George H.W. Bush and Bill Clinton appointed several Jewish cabinet members and ambassadors, and there are currently two Jewish Supreme Court justices, Ruth Bader Ginsburg and Stephen Breyer.

Being Jewish has also not kept Jews from seeking and securing various elective offices. In 2007 there were eleven Jewish senators and twenty-six Jewish members of Congress. While in the past Jewish politicians tended to represent the largely Jewish districts such as New York, this is no longer the case. For instance, Hawaii recently elected a Jewish governor, Linda Lingle, and the Jewish population in that state is just .5%. Although his Jewishness was significant, it did not keep Senator Joseph Lieberman from running as the Democratic candidate for vice president in the 2000 presidential election.

American Jews tend to be more liberal than the general population. Despite the shift in the early 1970s, when the U.S. political center moved to the right, carrying many Jews with it, the center of the Jewish political spectrum remained left of the national center. Today, American Jews are more likely (26% to 12%) to describe themselves as liberal than conservative, and 32% describe themselves as moderate. In 2005, 54% of American Jews affiliated with the Democratic Party and 29% with the Independents, as compared with 15% who registered as Republican (American Jewish Committee, 2006).

Although reasons for their liberal views are unclear, the commitment of Jews to reformist tradition no doubt has deep roots in their religious, economic, and political history and is related to their own struggle for equality and security from persecution. The generation of Jews that came after World War II was in the forefront of the civil rights movement and was active in liberal politics. Students, professors, and rabbis were especially prominent in the demonstrations, marches, sit-ins, and voter registration campaigns of the 1960s.

Jews continue to support liberal causes with an emphasis on civil rights and human rights. Much has been written about Black-Jewish relations, because the interests of these two communities were aligned on important civil rights issues during the 1950s and 1960s. However, several incidents that occurred during the late 1980s and through the 1990s—including Jesse Jackson's "Hymietown" remark, riots in Crown Heights, New York, and Louis Farrakhan's anti-Semitism—all seemed to drive these communities apart.

Fortunately, recent years have not been as contentious. High-profile Black anti-Semitism has almost disappeared. The Nation of Islam and Louis Farrakhan, who were so prominent in the 1990s, are no longer a Jewish communal concern. There are also long-lasting examples of common causes among Blacks and Jews. The two communities continue to represent the base of the Democratic Party. Together African Americans and Jews have mobilized support for a higher minimum wage and Medicaid expansion. While divisions still exist, the relationship between Blacks and Jews seems more realistic than ever before.

Since 2004, the American Jewish World Service (AJWS) has been in the forefront providing humanitarian aid, education, and advocacy on alerting the world and world leaders about the genocide taking place in Darfur. In 2006, AJWS and the U.S. Holocaust Memorial Museum organized a collaboration of faith-based and humanitarian organizations that drew 75,000 people to a Save Darfur rally in Washington, D.C., in April. Some 25,000 of those in attendance were Jews. The Jewish community's historical experience during the Holocaust as victims of genocide motivates them to empathize with current victims of ethnic cleansing and government-sponsored violence. Jewish groups throughout the United States, and particularly on college campuses, have been actively working on behalf of the beleaguered people of Darfur.

Jewish Americans are unquestionably more secure in U.S. society and more willing to demonstrate, protest, and lobby in their own self-interest as never before. Despite this security, eight out of ten American Jews believe that anti-Semitism is a problem in the United States (American Jewish Committee, 2006). Certainly groups such as the Ku Klux Klan, the American Nazi Party, and the neo-Nazis are a cause for concern, as is the growing number of websites devoted to White supremacy and hate groups that are found on the Internet. While anti-Semitism still exists, people and groups who hate Jews today are largely marginalized and powerless, leaving the daily impact on the lives of American Jews greatly lessened.

Many contend that a major threat to American Jewish life comes not from those who hate the Jews but from a culture that is so accepting it has eroded Jewish distinctiveness. Low birthrates, assimilation, and high intermarriage (or "out-marriage," the marriage of Jews to non-Jews) are all major concerns of the Jewish community in the twenty-first century. In 1990, the Council of Jewish Federations released their National Jewish Population Study (NJPS). Among its many findings, the most astonishing was that the rate of intermarriage in 1990 was 52%, up from 31% in 1974 (Kosmin et al., 1991). When the 2000 NJPS was released, it reported that the rate of intermarriage, while still increasing, had slowed down to 47% (Kotler-Berkowitz et al., 2004). Delayed marriage because of a desire to attain a higher education and establish a career has also contributed to low American Jewish fertility rates (fewer than two children per Jewish family). This lack of growth is startling when compared with population trends of the United States as a whole. In 1950 the American Jewish population was estimated at 3% of the total U.S. population. The number of Jews has barely increased over the last five decades, while the American population has soared.

Not surprisingly, a notable amount of concerned debate and discussion continues within the Jewish community about Jewish survival and continuity (Dershowitz, 1997). There have been two main responses to the Jewish continuity debate. The first is that communal resources should be used to encourage outreach to intermarried and unaffiliated Jews. Others believe that resources should be used to reach within the community to those who are already somewhat Jewishly connected. The hope is that by accentuating the positive, the current trend of unbridled assimilation can be reversed.

Despite these concerns, the American Jewish community remains an important ethnic and religious group in U.S. society, reflecting a wide diversity of social class, religious commitment, political outlook, and economic status.

TEACHING STRATEGIES

To illustrate how content related to Jewish Americans can be used to integrate the curriculum, exemplary strategies are identified for teaching these concepts at the grade levels indicated: *values* (primary and middle and upper grades), *immigration* (middle and upper grades), *ethnic organizations and institutions* and *ethnic identity* (high school grades).

Primary Grades

Concept

Values

Generalization: The values of Jewish Americans are reflected in their sacred writings and literature.

1. Distribute the following list of Jewish values to each student. Divide the students into small groups of four or five.
2. In their small groups, have the students discuss each value. For each value, the students should answer the following questions:
   a. What do you think that the value means?
   b. How does it relate to your own life?
   c. Have you ever learned a lesson similar to this value from your family, friends, or religion?
   d. Discuss an example of something you can do in your everyday life that would describe each value.
      After these activities, discuss the questions that follow the list of Jewish values with the whole class.

List of Jewish Values

1. Repairing or perfecting the world. (Aleynu prayer, Prayer Book)
2. You are not required to complete the task, nor are you free to desist from it entirely. (Pirkey Avot, *Ethics of the Fathers,* Chapter 2, Mishnah 21)
3. Humanity is created "in God's image." (Genesis, Chapter 1, Verse 27)
4. Guard your tongue from speaking evil. (Psalms, Chapter 34, Verse 14)
5. Do not look at the vessel, but rather at what it contains. (Pirkey Avot, *Ethics of the Fathers,* Chapter 4, Mishnah 27)
6. Love your neighbor as yourself. (Leviticus, Chapter 19, Verse 18)
7. What is hateful to you, do not do to your neighbor. (Tractate Shabbat, Talmud 31 A)
8. If I am not for myself, who will be for me? (Pirkey Avot, *Ethics of the Fathers,* Chapter 1, Mishnah 14)

Discussion Questions

1. What surprised you about these particular Jewish values? Do you think that these values apply only to American Jews? Explain. What are some of the lessons that these values teach?
2. Have the class prepare a list of things that they can do at their school or at home that would exemplify these values.

Second Strategy

1. Read the following books to the class:
   a. *The Treasure* by Uri Shulevitz (1986): This Caldecott Honor Book tells the story of an elderly man who travels a great distance to find a treasure that is already at his home.
   b. *Keeping Quilt* by Patricia Polaaco (2001): This autobiography tells the story of one family's keepsake that is passed from generation to generation. It shares family and religious traditions and shows how people can assimilate into a new country while maintaining rituals from their homeland.
2. Ask students to share family traditions and rituals with the class. Have students interview family members to learn the most important values from their own tradition that can be shared with the class.

Intermediate and Upper Grades

Concept

Values

Generalization: The values of Jewish Americans are reflected in their philosophy and literature.

1. Distribute the handout of Maimonides's Eight Steps of Giving Charity in a scrambled order to each student. Maimonides was a Jewish philosopher.
2. Ask the class to arrange the eight steps in the proper order, from the least to the most virtuous.
3. In small groups have the students explain the order of their lists.
4. In a large group, show the class the eight steps according to Maimonides. Conclude the discussion with the questions that follow the Eight Steps.

Maimonides's Eight Steps of Giving Charity

1. Give, but grudgingly.
2. Give less than is fitting, but willingly.
3. Give only after being asked to.
4. Give before being asked to.
5. Give in such a way that the giver does not know to whom he or she is giving.
6. Give in such a way that the one who receives does not know who has given to him or her.
7. Give in such a way that neither the giver nor the one who receives knows the identity of the other.
8. The highest form of charity is to help the poor become self-supporting by lending them money, taking them into partnership, or giving them work. In this way there is no loss of self-respect.

Questions and Activities

1. What surprised you about Maimonides's list? How did it compare to your own?
2. Do you agree that the highest form of charity is to help the poor become self-supporting? Why? How does this compare to welfare reform in our society?
3. Ask the students for examples of charity at each level.
4. Have students survey family and friends about the role of giving charity in their lives. Have the students compare the results with Maimonides's Eight Steps of Giving Charity.

5. Have students decide for themselves which of Maimonides's Eight Steps of Giving Charity is the highest. Have students organize a social action project at their school that exemplifies that particular step of giving (i.e., collecting food for a soup kitchen—the receiver would not know the giver).

Intermediate and Upper Grades

Concept

Immigration

Generalization: The Jews who immigrated to the United States a century ago are both alike and different from those who are settling in the United States today.

1. Distribute a copy of the last stanza of Emma Lazarus's poem "The New Colossus" to the class.
2. Explain that it was written in 1903 by Emma Lazarus, a young Sephardic Jew.
3. After the students have read the poem, ask the questions below.
4. Ask the students to write down their first thoughts about this poem.
5. Ask the students look up the underlined words in the dictionary so they fully understand the meaning of the poem.
6. Discuss the poem. Ask the students these questions: Who do you think is narrating the poem? Who is the narrator talking to? What is the "golden door?" Why is that image used?
7. Discuss how immigrants come to the United States today. List several of the reasons that they want to come to the United States.
8. Ask the students to rewrite the poem to reflect the immigrant experience today. Ask them: Who is narrating their poems and to whom are their poems speaking?

> *Give me your tired, your poor,*
> *Your <u>huddled</u> <u>masses</u> yearning to breathe free,*
> *The <u>wretched</u> <u>refuse</u> of your teeming shore.*
> *Send these, the homeless, tempest-tossed to me,*
> *I lift my lamp beside the golden door!*

High School Grades

Concept

Ethnic organizations and institutions

Generalization: Jewish Americans, like other U.S. ethnic groups, have created organizations to help them to maintain a sense of community and to fight discrimination.

1. Distribute the handout in Table 9.1 to each student.
2. Have the students complete the chart in Table 9.1 by listing parallel institutions of other ethnic or religious groups in column 2 and similarities and differences in columns 3 and 4.
3. After the students have completed the chart, discuss the following questions.

TABLE 9.1   Similarities and Differences in Jewish and Non-Jewish Organizations

JEWISH INSTITUTIONS/ ORGANIZATIONS	NON-JEWISH INSTITUTIONS/ ORGANIZATIONS	SIMILARITIES	DIFFERENCES
YMHA			
Jewish community centers			
Jewish day schools			
Synagogues			
Jewish hospitals			
Yiddish press			
Civil rights organizations			
Fraternal organizations			
Jewish publication society			
Service clubs			
Fundraising organizations			
Organizations for college students			

Discussion Questions
1. What surprised you about the information you found?
2. How are the various organizations funded (grants, private funds, etc.)?
3. Share some of the similarities you found among the various organizations.
4. Why do various ethnic and religious groups feel that it is necessary to maintain these organizations? Do you think they are necessary? Explain.
5. In some cases there may be overlap in the kinds of services these organizations provide. Should they merge? Why? Why not?

Concept

Ethnic identity

Generalization: Jewish identity within the United States is threatened by an increasing rate of out-marriage (which increased from 31% in 1974 to 52% in 2004), a low birthrate, and widespread assimilation among Jewish Americans.

1. Ask the students: Are Jews a nation, an ethnic group, a religious minority, a people, a race, all of these, some of these, or none of these? (The answer is "some of these." Jews are not a race.) The government of Israel in 1958 established a special committee to provide an answer to the perplexing question: "Who is a Jew?" The results were inconclusive. Have students conduct a survey or do a research paper to see if they can provide an answer. Students should include information about other ethnic groups so that they can conclude whether these groups have difficulty defining themselves.

2. Have students read and report on a book about Jews by a Jewish American author. Reports should tell how individuals or families they read about reconcile their desire to become Americanized with the desire to preserve their Jewish heritage. (These are among the authors the students can choose: Sholom Aleichem, Mary Antin, Pearl Abraham, Saul Bellow, Edna Ferber, Bernard Malamud, Tova Mirvis, Chaim Potok, Irwin Shaw, Leon Uris, Elie Wiesel, and Herman Wouk.)

3. Since 1948, Jewish Americans have become passionate supporters of Israel, despite the fact that few of them or their immediate ancestors were born there or plan to live there. Ask students to write essays that compare Jewish attitudes toward Israel with those of other ethnic minority groups to their country of origin. What similarities or differences exist? How do students account for them?

4. The rate of intermarriage for Jewish Americans has increased dramatically in recent years. Ask students to conduct an informal survey among their friends and families to determine if this is true of other ethnic and religious groups. Discuss and debate the pros and cons of intermarriage.

Valuing Activity

Read the following case studies to the class and ask the questions that follow.

BEING JEWISH IN SCHOOL

CASE STUDY 1—December Dilemma

Michelle is a ninth-grader who loves to sing. She is one of a growing number of Jewish students in a community that is very traditional in its celebration of Christmas. The school has recently included Chanukah songs in its repertoire for the Christmas concert. However, this year the school has an enthusiastic music teacher who is trying something different, more like a seasonal opera. The stars of the concert will have to dress as biblical characters. Michelle has been offered the best part as Mary. When she tells her parents, they insist that she cannot take the part, and they are not sure if this kind of concert is legal. Michelle wants to sing and does not understand her parents' reaction.

(Reprinted with permission from *Confronting Anti-Semitism, Trainer's Manual.* Copyright 2001, Anti-Defamation League of B'nai B'rith, New York. p. 89. www.adl.org.)

Questions

1. Have you ever experienced a similar situation? What happened? How did you feel?
2. Do you feel it is appropriate for a public school to sponsor a Christmas concert?

3. Prior to the concert, what can families and/or community members do to voice their concerns?
4. Is it better to participate in the program, even if it offends you, in order to avoid problems?
5. Are there outside organizations that Michelle can contact for assistance?

CASE STUDY 2—School Spirit
Scott, who is Jewish, plays soccer for the school team. The high school is getting ready for the soccer playoffs with a local school that has a large number of Jewish players. Scott's school is trying to create a high level of competitive school spirit for the upcoming pep rally, when Scott and his friend Justin notice a poster taped up in the hallway depicting the Jewish players of the opposing team as Holocaust victims in a train going to Auschwitz. The poster disgusts Scott, but Justin laughs and says Scott is being too serious. Justin says it is only a joke meant to illustrate that their school will "really kill those Jew bastards on the field." Scott is very angry about the poster and Justin's comments, but remains silent. As Justin walks away, Scott tears away the poster and throws it in the trash.

(Reprinted with permission from *Confronting Anti-Semitism, Trainer's Manual*. Copyright 2001, Anti-Defamation League of B'nai B'rith (New York), p. 104. Available online at www.adl.org.)

Questions
1. If this happened in your school, whom would you tell: the principal, a coach, and/or friends? What would you expect them to do?
2. Should Scott have taken down the offensive poster? Why or why not?
3. How might have Scott responded to Justin's comments?
4. Do you think that Justin's comments were anti-Semitic?

REFERENCES

American Jewish Committee. (2006). *Annual Survey of Jewish Opinion*. New York: American Jewish Committee.

Anti-Defamation League. (2006). *Annual Audit of Anti-Semitic Incidents*. New York: Anti-Defamation League.

Berenbaum, M. (1993). *The World Must Know: The History of the Holocaust as Told in the United States Holocaust Memorial Museum*. Boston: Little, Brown.

Chanes, J. (2004). *A Primer on the American Jewish Community*. New York: American Jewish Committee.

DeNaves-Walt, C., Proctor, B., & Lee, C. (2006). *Income, Poverty and Health Insurance Coverage in the United States, 2005*. U.S. Census Bureau *Current Population Reports*. Washington, DC: U.S. Government Printing Office.

Dershowitz, A. M. (1997). *The Vanishing American Jew: In Search of Jewish Identity for the Next Century*. New York: Little, Brown.

Hertzberg, A. (1998). *The Jews in America: Four Centuries of an Uneasy Encounter: A History.* New York: Columbia University Press.

Kosmin, B., Goldstein, S., Waksberg, J., Lerer, N., Keysar, A., & Scheckner, J. (1991). *Highlights of the CJF 1990 National Jewish Population Survey.* New York: Council of Jewish Federations.

Kotler-Berkowitz, L., Cohen, S., Ament, J., Klaff, V., Mott, F., & Peckerman-Neuman, D. (2004). *National Jewish Population Survey, 2000–01: Strength, Challenge, and Diversity in the American Jewish Population.* New York: Council of Jewish Federations.

Lazarus, E. (1889). *Poems* (vol. 2).

Linenthal, E. T. (1995). *Preserving Memory: The Struggle to Create America's Holocaust Museum.* New York: Viking.

National Yiddish Book Center. Retrieved July 23, 2007, from http://www.yiddishbookcenter.org.

Polaaco, P. (2001). *Keeping Quilt.* New York: Simon and Schuster.

Second Thoughts about the Promised Land. (2007, January 13). *Economist, 382* (8511), 53–56.

Shulevitz, U. (1986). *The Treasure.* Elgin, IL: Sunburst.

Sheskin, I. M., & Dashefsky, A. (2006). Jewish Population in the United States, 2006. In D. Singer & L. Grossman (Eds.), *American Jewish Year Book 2006* (vol. 106). New York: American Jewish Committee. Retrieved August 11, 2007, from http://www.jewishvirtuallibrary.org/jsource/US-Israel/usjewpop.html.

Singer, D., & Grossman,L. (Eds.). (2000). *American Jewish Yearbook* (vol. 100). New York: American Jewish Committee.

Singer, D., & Grossman,L. (Eds.). (2006). *American Jewish Yearbook* (vol. 106). New York: American Jewish Committee.

Thernstrom, S., Orlov, A., & Handlin, O. (Eds.). (1980). *Harvard Encyclopedia of American Ethnic Groups.* Cambridge, MA: Harvard University Press.

ANNOTATED BIBLIOGRAPHY

Books for Teachers

Especially Recommended

Carlson, R. (Ed.). (1999). *American Jewish Desk Reference.* Stevie Jewish Historical Society. New York: Random House.
This all-encompassing reference to Jewish life in the United States, from 1654 to the present, contains nearly 900 entries on all aspects of Jewish culture and brings together the events, personalities, themes, and issues of contemporary Jewish life in the United States.

Cohen, S., & Eisen, A. (2000). *The Jew Within: Self, Family, and Community in America.* Bloomington: Indiana University Press.
In response to current trends of out-marriage and assimilation in the Jewish community, the authors probe beneath the surface to explore the foundations of belief and behavior among moderately affiliated American Jews.

Goldstein, E. (2006). *The Price of Whiteness: Jews, Race, and American Identity.* Princeton: Princeton University Press.
A historical review of the uneasy place Jews have held in America's racial culture since the late nineteenth century. The book traces Jews' tumultuous encounter with race from the 1870s through World War II, when they became vested as part of America's White mainstream and abandoned the practice of describing themselves in racial terms.

Greenberg, C. L. (2006). *Troubling the Waters: Black-Jewish Relations in the American Century.* Princeton: Princeton University Press.

Tracing the growth, peak, and deterioration of Black-Jewish engagement over the course of the twentieth century, Greenberg shows that the history of this relationship is very much the history of American liberalism—neither as golden in its best years nor as absolute in its collapse as commonly thought.

Hertzberg, A. (1998). *Jews in America: Four Centuries of an Uneasy Encounter: A History.* New York: Columbia University Press.
A controversial examination of the Jewish "success story" in America that questions notions of identity, assimilation, and ethnicity.

Howe, I. (2005). *World of Our Fathers: The Journey of the East European Jews to America and the Life They Found and Made.* New York: New York University Press.
This story of more than 2 million Jewish immigrants in America in four decades begins with the 1880s. It also provides a detailed look at everything from Yiddish theater to the Jewish labor movement.

Pearl, J., & Pearl, R. (Eds). (2005). *I Am Jewish: Personal Reflections Inspired by the Last Words of Daniel Pearl.* Woodstock, VT: Jewish Lights Publishing.
When *Wall Street Journal* reporter Daniel Pearl was brutally murdered in Pakistan, many Jews were particularly touched by his last words affirming his Jewish identity. This compilation captures the richness of interpretation and inspires Jewish people of all backgrounds to reflect upon and take pride in their identity.

Sarna, J. (2005). *American Judaism.* New Haven: Yale University Press.
This authoritative work traces American Judaism from its origins in the colonial era through the present day, exploring how Judaism adapted, how American culture affected Jewish religion and culture, and how American Jews shaped their own communities and faith in the United States.

Telushkin, J. (1991). *Jewish Literacy.* New York: HarperCollins.
In 346 short entries, Rabbi Telushkin tells the most important things to know about the Jewish religion, essential trends, concepts, personalities, and culture.

Other Books

DeLange, N. (1997). *The Illustrated History of the Jewish People.* San Diego: Harcourt Brace.
The story of Judaism from its earliest beginnings to the present, as narrated by eight Jewish historians.

Dubner, S. (1999). *Turbulent Souls: A Catholic Son's Return to His Jewish Family.* New York: HarperCollins.
Dubner's parents were Jewish, but they both converted to Catholicism before they met. The devout Catholics raised their eight children in their new faith. Dubner eventually uncovered his parents' secret and set out in search of his spiritual and ethnic roots.

Feinstein, E. (Ed.). (2007). *Jews and Judaism in the 21st Century: Human Responsibility, the Presence of God, and the Future of the Covenant.* Woodstock, VT: Jewish Lights.
In this thought-provoking book, five celebrated leaders in Judaism, representing a broad spectrum of contemporary Jewish experience, reinterpret Jewish life, reenvision its institutions, and reimagine its future in the shadow of the events of the twentieth century.

Fishman, S. B. (2002). *Double or Nothing: Jewish Families and Mixed Marriages.* Waltham, MA: Brandeis University Press.
Recent population surveys have fixed the rate of mixed marriages in the Jewish community at about 50 percent, but they rarely prod the surface of that statistic. Fishman, however, employs a social scientist's eye to explore family dynamics in order to illuminate the larger social and psychological dimensions of mixed marriages.

Goldberg, J. J. (2005). *Jewish Power: Inside the American Jewish Establishment*. New York: Basic Books.
This is a study of Jewish organizations, money, and political power in the United States. Goldberg includes such topics as liberalism and American Jews; Jews and the cold war; and how Jews vote.

Kertzer, M. N. (Rev. by L. A. Hoffman). (1997). *What Is a Jew?* New York: Simon and Schuster.
Completely revised and reorganized, this guide to the traditions, beliefs, and practices of Judaism, written to inform both Jew and non-Jew, tackles a wide range of subjects in a question-and-answer format.

Kolatch, A. (2003). *Jewish Book of Why*. New York: Penguin.
In this complete, concise, fascinating, and thoroughly informative guide to Jewish life and tradition, Rabbi Alfred J. Kolatch clearly explains both the significance and the origin of nearly every symbol, custom, and practice known to Jewish culture, from Afikomon to Yarmulkes and from Passover to Purim.

Nathan, J. (2004). *Joan Nathan's Jewish Holiday Cookbook*. New York: Schocken.
Explaining their origins and the holidays that have shaped them, Nathan, an award-winning food writer, peppers these delicious recipes with delightful stories about the people who make them today. A classic Jewish cookbook.

Schwartz, S. (2006). *Judaism and Justice: The Jewish Passion to Repair the World*. Woodstock, VT: Jewish Light.
In this provocative exploration, the author sheds light on the relationship among Judaism, social justice, and the Jewish identity of American Jews.

Susser, B., and Liebman, C. S. (1999). *Choosing Survival: Strategies for a Jewish Future*. New York: Oxford University Press.
The authors examine what happens to Jews and Jewish identity when persecution, anti-Semitism, and gentile hostility no longer endanger them.

Wyman, D. (2007). *The Abandonment of the Jews: America and the Holocaust, 1941–1945*. New York: New Press.
A definitive account of American apathy regarding the Jewish plight during the Holocaust.

Books for Students

Adler, D. (1996). *The Kid's Catalog of Jewish Holidays*. Philadelphia: Jewish Publication Society.
Introduces the history and traditions of major Jewish holidays, including games, songs, crafts, stories, poems, riddles, jokes, and a wide variety of recipes, representing foods of several nations. It's well illustrated with sketches, cartoons, and photographs. (Primary/Intermediate)

Bierman, C. (2005). *Journey to Ellis Island: How My Father Came to America*. Illustrated by L. McGaw. New York: Hyperion.
The dramatic true story of a young Russian Jewish boy's journey with his mother and sister to America. Illustrated beautifully with evocative paintings and family photographs as well as period art and photos. (Intermediate)

Carmi, D., & Lotan, Y. (2002). *Samir and Yonaton*. New York: Scholastic.
Samir, a Palestinian boy is sent for surgery to an Israeli hospital where he has two other worldly experiences—making friends with an Israeli boy, Yonaton, and traveling with him to Mars, where he finds peace about this brother's death in the war. (Middle School)

Chametzky, J., Felstiner, J., Flazbaum, H., & Hellerstein, K. (Eds.). (2000). *Jewish American Literature: A Norton Anthology*. New York: Norton.
This rich anthology reconsiders Jewish American literature from its seventeenth-century origins to its flourishing present. It gathers the work of 145 writers in all genres—fiction, poetry, drama essays, journals, autobiography, song lyrics, and cartoons. (High School)

Charing, D. (2003). *Judaism.* (Eye Witness Books series).London: DK Publishing.
> Discover the history, faith, and culture that have shaped the modern Jewish world. With more than 50 million copies sold in eighty-eight countries and in thirty-six languages, Eye Witness Books are truly the ultimate visual information encyclopedias for the twenty-first century. (Primary/ Intermediate)

Chotjewitz, D. (2004). *Daniel Half Human and the Good Nazi.* New York: Simon and Schuster.
> In 1933, best friends Daniel and Armin admire Hitler, but as anti-Semitism buoys Hitler to power, Daniel learns he is half Jewish, threatening the friendship even as life in their beloved Hamburg, Germany, is becoming nightmarish. Also details Daniel and Armin's reunion in 1945 in interspersed chapters. (High School)

Cohen, J. (2000). *The Christmas Menorahs: How a Town Fought Hate.* Illustrated by B. Farnsworth. Morton Grove, IL: Albert Whitman.
> Describes how people in Billings, Montana, joined together to fight a series of hate crimes against a Jewish family. (Intermediate)

Finklestein, N. (2001). *The Other 1492: Jewish Settlement in the New World.* Lincoln, NE: iUniverse.
> Describes the causes, events, and aftermath of the expulsion of the Jews from Spain in 1492. (Middle School)

Frank, A. (1997). *The Diary of a Young Girl: The Definitive Edition.* Edited by O. H. Frank and M. Pressler. Translated by S. Massoty. New York: Bantam Books.
> This new edition of the *Diary of Anne Frank* restores passages that previously had been deleted. The new translation is far superior to earlier versions. (Middle School/High School)

Greene, B. (2006). *Summer of My German Soldier.* New York: Penguin Putnam.
> A twelve-year-old Jewish girl living in a backward Arkansas town forms a destructive friendship with a young German prisoner of war. When rebellious Patty hides the enemy-turned-friend, the town's communal wrath is swift and sure. (Middle School)

Hest, A. (2003). *When Jessie Came across the Sea.* Illustrated by P. J. Lynch. Cambridge, MA: Candlewick Press.
> Thirteen-year-old Jessie is given a one-way ticket from her eastern European shtetl to America. She overcomes the emotion of leaving her grandmother. In America she becomes a dressmaker and, in three years, saves enough money for a ticket for her grandmother. The emotions of separation, hope, and love will appeal to children. Strikingly illustrated. (Primary)

Jafee, N. (2000). *Tales for the Seventh Day: A Collection of Sabbath Stories.* Illustrated by K. Sutherland. New York: Scholastic.
> Includes seven tales tied to the Jewish Sabbath but reflective of different cultures and times and of different moods. Jaffee includes a careful introduction outlining the concepts of the Jewish Sabbath as well as an extensive bibliography. (Intermediate)

Kimmelman, L. (2000). *Dance, Sing, Remember: A Celebration of Jewish Holidays.* Illustrated by O. Eitan. New York: HarperCollins.
> Explains eleven major Jewish holidays and how they are celebrated. (Primary)

Kluger, S. (1998). *The Last Days of Summer.* New York: HarperCollins.
> The poignant story of Joey Margolis, the only Jewish kid in the building. Though regularly beaten up, he lives a charmed life and establishes a relationship with his hero, Charlie Banks, rookie third baseman for the Giants. The two have amazing adventures together. (High School)

Koss, A. G. (1998*). How I Saved Hanukkah.* Illustrated by D. deGroat. Minneapolis: Sagebrush Education Resources.
> Fourth-grader Marla Feinstein wants to know what Chanukah is all about. Her curiosity gets her mother into the spirit of the holiday, which leads to a big Chanukah party for all her friends, Jewish and non-Jewish alike. (Intermediate)

Lasky, K. (1997). *Marven of the Great North Woods*. Illustrated by K. Hawkes. Orlando, FL: Harcourt.
When his Jewish parents send him to a Minnesota logging camp to escape the influenza epidemic of 1918, ten-year-old Marven finds a special friend. (Primary/Intermediate)

Lasky, K. (1998). *Dreams in the Golden Country: The Diary of Zipporah Feldman, a Jewish Immigrant Girl*. New York: Scholastic.
Part of the Dear America series, this story of a Russian immigrant family in New York City in 1903 is told by twelve-year-old Zippy, who records events in her diary. This book deals with the Ellis Island experience as well as sweatshops, unionism, women's suffrage, and religious differences. (Intermediate)

Levine, K. (2003). *Hana's Suitcase*. Chicago: Whitman.
A biography of a Czech girl who died in the Holocaust is told in alternating chapters with an account of how the curator of a Japanese Holocaust Center learned about her life after Hana's suitcase was sent to her. (Middle School)

Naliboff, J. (2004). *The Only One Club*. Chicago: Flashlight Press
This heartwarming story explores the many ways in which children feel unique and special. (Primary)

Nye, N. (1999). *Habibi*. New York: Simon and Schuster.
When fourteen-year-old Liyanne Abboud, her younger brother, and her parents move from St. Louis to a new home between Jerusalem and the Palestinian village where her father was born, they face many tensions between Jews and Palestinians. (Middle School)

Polacco, P. (2000). *The Butterfly*. New York: Penguin.
During the Nazi occupation of France, Monique's mother hides a Jewish family in her basement and tries to help them escape to freedom. (Intermediate)

Polacco, P. (2002). *Christmas Tapestry*. New York: Penguin.
A tapestry that is being used to cover a hole in a church wall at Christmas brings together an elderly couple who were separated during World War II. (Primary)

Potok, C. (1996). *The Chosen*. New York: Random House.
This book chronicles the friendship between Danny Saunders, a boy from a Hasidic family, and the more assimilated Rueven Malter, as they come of age in Williamsburg, Brooklyn. (High School)

Rosen, S. (2001). *Speed of Light*. New York: Aladdin.
An eleven-year-old Jewish girl living in the South during the 1950s struggles with anti-Semitism and racism, which pervade her small community. (Middle School)

Schreiber, M., Schiff, A. I., & Klenicki, L. (Eds.). (2007). *The Shengold Jewish Encyclopedia*. Rockville, MD: Schreiber.
A revised and updated 50th edition of the *Junior Jewish Encyclopedia*. Covers American Jewish life, the contemporary Jewish world, and Jewish culture and history. Supported by an interactive website, with monthly updates. (Middle School/High School)

Schwartz, H. (2003). *The Day the Rabbi Disappeared: Jewish Holiday Tales of Magic*. Illustrated by M. Passicott. Philadelphia: Jewish Publication Society.
This retelling of twelve traditional tales from Jewish folklore features elements of magic and relates to holidays, including Rosh Hodesh, Sukkot, Tu b'shvat, and Shabbat. (Intermediate)

Sender, R. (2000). *To Life*. Illustrated by J. Coon. New York: Simon and Schuster.
A Holocaust survivor recounts her liberation from a Nazi concentration camp, her search for surviving family members, and a long and difficult ordeal of trying to immigrate with her husband and two children to America. (Middle School)

Sloan, S. R. (1998). *An Isolated Incident*. New York: Warner.

Set on fictional Seward Island in Puget Sound, this murder mystery deals with bigotry and prejudice as the evidence seems to point to Jerry Frankel, a newcomer to the island and one of a group of Jews protesting the high school's Christmas pageant festivities. (High School)

Spinelli, J., (2005) *Milkweed*. New York: Random House.
A tale of heartbreak, hope, and survival told through the bright eyes of a young orphan in Nazi-occupied Warsaw, Poland. (Middle School)

Stavens, I. (Ed.). (1998). *The Oxford Book of Jewish Stories*. New York: Oxford University Press.
A collection of stories by fifty-two Jewish writers from around the world. Themes include anti-Semitism, the Holocaust, domestic affairs, biblical subjects, inter-religious accounts, and ethnic relations. (High School)

Stein, T. (2005). *Light Years*. New York: Random House.
Caught between two vastly different worlds, Maya seeks balance between her tragic past in Israel and her present in Virginia as an astronomy student. Before leaving Israel to study abroad, Maya learns that a suicide bomber attacked the cafe where her boyfriend, Dov, was waiting for her. The story, however, reaches real depth when Maya reminisces about Israel as well as the everyday fears of people living there. (High School)

Wiesel, E. (2006). *Night*. New York: Hill and Wang.
An autobiographical narrative in which the author describes his experiences in Nazi concentration camps, watching family and friends die, and how they led him to believe that God is dead. (High School)

Woodruff, E. (1999). *The Memory Coat*. Illustrated by M. Dooling. New York: Scholastic.
In the early 1900s, two cousins leave their Russian *shtetl* with the rest of their family to come to America, hopeful that they will all pass the dreaded inspection at Ellis Island. (Intermediate)

Yolen, J. (2005). *Devil's Arithmetic*. New York: Penguin.
Hannah resents the traditions of her Jewish heritage until time travel places her in the middle of a small Jewish village in Nazi-occupied Poland. (Intermediate)

Zemach, M. (1990). *It Could Always Be Worse*. New York: Farrar, Straus, and Giroux.
Unable to stand his overcrowded and noisy home any longer, a poor man goes to the rabbi for advice. (Primary)

HISPANIC AMERICANS

Concepts and Strategies

Part IV consists of content, concepts, teaching strategies, and materials for teaching about three major Hispanic groups in the United States: Mexican Americans, Puerto Ricans, and Cuban Americans. Hispanics are one of the nation's fastest-growing ethnic groups. The number of Hispanics in the United States grew from 22.4 million in 1990 to 41.9 million in 2005, an 87% increase. Mexican Americans are the largest Hispanic group in the United States, and this group is growing faster than are Cubans or Puerto Ricans. Between 1990 and 2005, Mexican Americans increased 98.4%, compared to a 38.6% increase of Puerto Ricans and a 40% increase of Cuban Americans. The Hispanic population is growing more than five times faster than the rest of the U.S. population; the Hispanic population increased 87% between 1990 and 2005, compared to 15.9%, for the total U.S. population (U.S. Census Bureau, 2007). The rapid growth of Hispanics is due primarily to massive immigration and to a high birthrate.

CENTRAL AND SOUTH AMERICANS

A substantial number of immigrants from Central and South America entered the United States between 1990 and 2005. A significant number of these immigrants came from El Salvador, Guatemala, Colombia, Guyana, and Ecuador. Central and South Americans made up 12.7% of the Hispanic population of the United States in 2005 (U.S. Census Bureau, 2007). Figure A shows the percentage distribution of Hispanics in the United States in 2005. Table A shows the population and percentage for each group. It is misleading, however, to conceptualize these diverse groups of immigrants as one people, because they have significant cultural, racial, and ethnic differences.

297

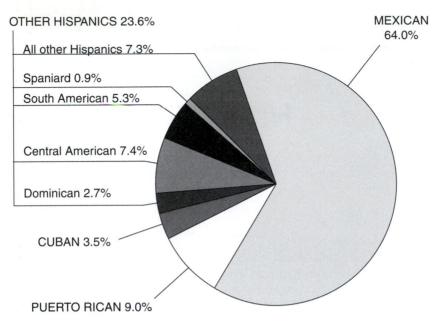

OTHER HISPANICS 23.6%

All other Hispanics 7.3%

Spaniard 0.9%

South American 5.3%

Central American 7.4%

Dominican 2.7%

CUBAN 3.5%

PUERTO RICAN 9.0%

MEXICAN
64.0%

FIGURE A   Percentage Distribution of the Hispanic Population by Type, 2005

Source: U.S. Census Bureau (2007), *American Community Survey, 2005: Selected Population Profile.* [Data file]. Available online from http://factfinder.census.gov/sevlet/IPCharIterationServlet?_ts=202649767048.

DEMOGRAPHIC CHARACTERISTICS OF HISPANICS

The Hispanic population, compared to the rest of the U.S. population, is young. The median age of Hispanics in 2005 was 27.2, compared to 38.4 for the non-Hispanic population (U.S. Census Bureau, 2007). The Hispanic population is also highly concentrated in the western and southern United States. In 2005, 42.9% of Hispanics lived in the West; 34.2%, in the South; 13.9%, in the Northeast; and 8.9%, in the Midwest (U.S. Census Bureau, 2007). Table B shows the Hispanic population for selected states in 2005 and the percentage of Hispanics in these states.

DIVERSITY AMONG HISPANICS

It is misleading to consider Hispanics as one ethnic group. Even though the various Hispanic groups share a past influenced significantly by Spain and the Spanish language, there are tremendous historical, racial, and cultural differences among and within them. Most Mexican Americans are *mestizos,* whereas some Cubans and Puerto Ricans are Black. Some Mexican Americans are native to the United States;

TABLE A   Hispanic Population by Type, 2005

SUBJECT	NUMBER	PERCENT
Hispanic or Latino Origin		
Total Population of United States	288,378,137	100.0
Hispanic or Latino (of any race)	41,870,703	14.5
Not Hispanic or Latino	246,507,434	85.5
Hispanic or Latino by Type		
Hispanic or Latino (of any race)	41,870,703	100.0
Mexican	26,781,547	64.0
Puerto Rican	3,781,317	9.0
Cuban	1,461,574	3.5
Other Hispanic or Latino	9,846,265	23.6
Dominican (Dominican Republic)	1,118,265	2.7
Central American (excludes Mexican)	3,084,580	7.4
Costa Rican	108,164	0.3
Guatemalan	758,898	1.8
Honduran	459,653	1.1
Nicaraguan	281,167	0.7
Panamanian	136,375	0.3
Salvadorian	1,239,640	3.0
Other Central American	100,683	0.2
South American	2,238,836	5.3
Argentinean	185,678	0.4
Bolivian	65,582	0.2
Chilean	102,911	0.2
Colombian	730,510	1.7
Ecuadorian	436,409	1.0
Peruvian	412,349	1.0
Venezuelan	164,903	0.4
Other South American	140,494	0.3
Spaniard	360,450	0.9
All other Hispanic or Latino	3,044,134	7.3

Source: U.S. Census Bureau (2007), *American Community Survey, 2005: Selected Population Profile.* [Data file]. Available online at http://factfinder.census.gov/servlet/IPCharIterationServlet?_ts=202649767048.

others, as well as some other Hispanics, arrived in the United States quite recently. Language is probably the most important factor that connects the various Hispanic groups. In 2005, 78.2% of Hispanics spoke a language other than English at home, predominantly Spanish for non-English speakers. The multicultural curriculum should help students understand the ways in which the various Hispanic groups are both alike and different.

TABLE B   Hispanic Population in Selected States, 2005

STATE	TOTAL POPULATION	HISPANIC AMERICAN POPULATION	PERCENTAGE OF TOTAL STATE POPULATION
California	35,340,566	12,534,628	35.5
Texas	22,250,152	7,882,254	35.4
Florida	17,363,653	3,433,355	19.8
New York	18,679,211	3,026,286	16.2
Illinois	12,441,864	1,807,908	14.5
Arizona	5,806,266	1,679,116	28.9
New Jersey	8,524,868	1,312,326	15.4
Colorado	4,540,639	895,176	19.7
New Mexico	1,886,789	827,940	43.9
Georgia	8,811,648	625,382	7.1
Nevada	2,376,017	557,370	23.5
Washington	6,157,786	546,209	8.9
North Carolina	8,397,785	544,470	6.5
Massachusetts	6,200,944	489,662	7.9
Pennsylvania	11,948,862	488,144	4.1
Virginia	7,320,848	440,988	6.0
Michigan	9,857,477	378,232	3.8
Connecticut	3,365,768	372,718	11.1
Oregon	3,560,922	360,000	10.1
Maryland	5,453,441	311,191	5.7
Indiana	6,081,212	273,004	4.5
Utah	2,452,149	264,010	10.8
Wisconsin	5,401,740	230,715	4.3
Ohio	11,146,050	253,014	2.3
Oklahoma	3,429,974	218,987	6.4

Source: U.S. Census Bureau (2007), *American Community Survey, 2005: Selected Population Profile.* [Data file]. Available online at http://factfinder.census.gov/servlet/IPCharIterationServlet?_ts=202649767048.

REFERENCE

U.S. Census Bureau. (2007). *American Community Survey, 2005: Selected Population Profile.* [Data file]. Available online from http://factfinder.census.gov/servlet/IPCharIterationServlet?_ts= 202649767048.

ANNOTATED BIBLIOGRAPHY

Arreola, D. (Ed.). (2004). *Hispanic Spaces, Latino Places: Community and Cultural Diversity in Contemporary America.* Austin: University of Texas Press.
This collection of scholarly articles shows how Latinos of varied nationalities live, work, and relate to their built and natural environment and how their environment affects them.

Browdy de Hernández, J. (Ed.). (2004). *Women Writing Resistance: Essays on Latin America and the Caribbean.* Cambridge, MA: South End Press.

Eighteen feminist writers explore and record the oppression experienced by women in Latin America and the Caribbean, including patriarchy, racism, poverty, and political repression. Among the pieces included are interviews, poems, letters, and diaries.

Candelaria, C. C., Aldama, A. J., Garcia, P. J., & Alvarez-Smith, A. (Eds.). (2004). *Encyclopedia of Latino Popular Culture.* Westport, CT: Greenwood.
In two volumes, this source covers Latino films, literature, music, and art; Latinos in sports, entertainment, and politics; and the topics Latinos of various backgrounds discuss as part of everyday life.

Cortés, E., & Barrea-Marlys, M. (Eds.). (2003). *Encyclopedia of Latin American Theater.* Westport, CT: Greenwood.
Filling a void, this reference title explores drama productivity throughout Latin America and the Caribbean, with a special focus on Puerto Rico, Mexico, and Cuba and on playwrights and other artists famous in their own countries but not in the United States.

Dávila, A. (2001). *Latinos Inc.: The Marketing and Making of a People.* Berkeley: University of California Press.
A critical exploration of how Latino artifacts, such as salsa dancing or food items, are taken up by corporate marketing as well as mainstream entertainment industries, while at the same time, economic parity and political enfranchisement of Latinos in the United States are lagging behind.

Díaz Soto, L. (Ed.). (2006). *The Praeger Handbook of Latino Education in the U.S.* Westport, CT: Praeger.
This two-volume set provides historical, demographic, pedagogical, political, social, and cultural information as well as references and statistics of use to all professionals who serve Latino/a youth and their families.

Dick, B. A. (2003). *A Poet's Truth: Conversations with Latino/Latina Poets.* Tucson: University of Arizona Press.
Sixteen poets are featured in this revealing set of interviews. Among the subjects addressed are the founding of the Nuyorican Poets Café, the life of the Latina/o poet in academia, and personal and intellectual journeys. Interviewed are, among others, Miguel Alargín, Martín Espada, Judith Ortiz Cofer, Carolina Hospital, Virgil Suárez, Gustavo Pérez-Firmat, and Pat Mora.

Garcia, E. E. (2005). *Teaching and Learning in Two Languages: Bilingualism and Schooling in the United States.* New York: Teachers College Press.
This text focuses on culturally responsive teaching for Spanish-speaking immigrant students. The history of bilingual education and current approaches are also covered.

Geron, K. (2005). *Latino Political Power.* Boulder, CO: Lynne Rienner.
This scholarly study examines the political involvement of various Latino groups and how they have shaped the political landscape of the United States, particularly in the debate over immigration.

Grandin, G. (2006). *Empire's Workshop: Latin America, the United States, and the Rise of the New Imperialism.* New York: Holt.
The author recounts the history of U.S. military interventions in Cuba, Venezuela, Brazil, Argentina, Chile, El Salvador, Nicaragua, and elsewhere, as well as the promotion of free market economies and free trade policies. The resulting impoverishment and repression have contributed greatly to Latin American migration to the United States.

Gutiérrrez, D. G. (Ed.). (2004). *The Columbia History of Latinos in the United States Since 1960.* New York: Columbia University Press.
This informative and well-researched book has chapters on various Latino groups as well as on topics that cut across the various groups, such as gender, religion, and citizenship. This is an excellent reference book.

Heide, R. (Ed.). (2003). *Under the Fifth Sun: Latino Literature from California.* Berkeley, CA: Heyday Books.
More than fifty authors living in California are featured in this anthology that includes poetry, short stories, essays, song lyrics, and more.

Kanellos, N. (2003). *Hispanic Literature of the United States*. Westport, Conn.: Greenwood.
Breadth of coverage is the strength of this reference source, which features short entries on a myriad of writers of Latin American and Latino heritage from the sixteenth century to the present. Included are essays on children's literature, publishing trends, and genres.

Montilla, R. E., & Medina, F. (2006). *Pastoral Care and Counseling with Latinos/as*. Minneapolis: Fortress Press.
Though geared to professional pastoral counselors, this guide has insights for all who work with Latino families. Topics covered include religious beliefs, special challenges facing recent immigrants and political refugees, race, and the diversity of Latinos' backgrounds and experiences.

Nevear, L. E. V. (2003). *The Rise of the Hispanic Market in the United States: Challenges, Dilemmas, and Opportunities for Corporate Management*. Armonk, NY: M. E. Sharpe.
Nevear provides insight into the diverse Latino/Hispanic market and strategies for appealing to consumers both in the United States and throughout Latin America.

Novas, H. (2007). *Everything You Need to Know about Latino History* (rev. ed.). New York: Plume.
The author offers an overview of Latino history and how Latino culture—both literary and popular—has influenced the United States. Lively writing and a question-and-answer format make this an accessible introduction for middle school and up.

Ochoa, E. C., & Ochoa, G. L. (2006). *Latino Los Angeles: Transformations, Communities, and Activism*. Tucson: University of Arizona Press.
Statistical, historical, and ethnographic perspectives highlight the successive migrations of Latinos to Los Angeles and how the immigrants have transformed the city's political culture.

Portales, R., & Portales, M. (2005). *Quality Education for Latinos and Latinas: Print and Oral Skills for All Students, K–College*. Austin: University of Texas Press.
Using compelling and powerful case studies to illustrate their arguments, the authors show how economic and language disparities can be overcome through good teaching.

Randle, J. W. (2003). *Issues in the Spanish-Speaking World*. Westport, CT: Greenwood.
Current controversies in the United States, Latin America, and Spain—for example, Columbus's exploration of the Americas, immigration, the drug trade, machismo, and environmental issues—receive thorough and nuanced coverage in this collection of articles.

Schon, I. (2003). *The Best of Latino Heritage: A Guide to the Best Juvenile Books about Latino People and Cultures, 1996–2002*. Lanham, MD: Scarecrow Press.
The director of the internationally respected Barahona Center for the Study of Books in Spanish for Children and Adolescents at California State University, San Marcos, has compiled an extensive annotated bibliography of books in English for those who work with young people at the K–12 level. The bibliography includes books about Latino children of various nationalities, arranged country-by-country, along with annotations that highlight important themes and subjects.

Suárez-Orozco, M. M., & Paez, M. (Eds.). (2002). *Latinos: Remaking America*. Berkeley: University of California Press.
This outstanding essay collection assesses the impact of migration from Latin America since 1960 on U.S. history, economy, politics, education, culture, and society.

West. L. A. (2004). *Color: Latino Voices in the Pacific Northwest*. Pullman: Washington State University Press.
The author explores the rich diversity of Latino heritages in one region of the United States.

York, S. (2002). *Children's and Young Adult Literature by Latino Writers: A Guide for Librarians, Teachers, Parents, and Students*. Worthington, OH: Linworth.
Using the same format as her *Picture Books by Latino Writers* (2002), the author covers chapter books, young adult novels, folklore and short story collections, drama, poetry, and nonfiction.

CHAPTER TEN

MEXICAN AMERICANS
Concepts, Strategies, and Materials

It would be a disservice to portray the future in idealistic terms. Hope is important, but the falsification of reality can immobilize a community.
—Rodolfo F. Acuña

Mexican Americans are the second largest ethnic group of color in the United States. They are also the largest Hispanic group. Mexican Americans comprised 64% of Hispanics in the United States in 2005 (U.S. Census Bureau, 2007). They are increasing at a much faster rate than are the other two major Hispanic groups, Puerto Ricans and Cubans. There were about 25,894,763 Mexican Americans living in the United States in 2004 (U.S. Census Bureau, 2007), up from about 13.5 million in 1990. The Mexican American population increased about 91% during that fourteen-year period.

The rapid growth in the Mexican American population results primarily from a higher birthrate, compared to other ethnic and racial groups, and significant and continuing immigration from Mexico. Between 1996 and 2005, 1,639,460 legal immigrants arrived in the United States from Mexico (U.S. Department of Homeland Security, 2006). In 2005, almost 11 million, or 31%, of the foreign-born residents in the United States were born in Mexico (U.S. Census Bureau, 2006). A large, but unknown, number of undocumented Mexican aliens in the United States are not reflected in these figures. In 2007, the *New York Times* estimated that there were 12 million illegal or undocumented immigrants living in the United States (Immigration Sabotage, 2007).

The Immigration Reform and Control Act of 1986 was designed to reduce the number of undocumented immigrants who enter the United States each year. The act imposes severe penalties on employers who knowingly hire illegal aliens. Under the conditions of this act, employers are required to ask job applicants for proof of citizenship. It was evident by 2007 that this act has not been successful in curbing the number of undocumented immigrants who enter the United States from Mexico or in prohibiting employers from hiring them. Illegal immigration was a hotly debated and divisive issue both among the general public and in Congress in 2007. Congress defeated a proposed immigration bill that would have allowed many undocumented immigrants to become citizens and authorized the extension of a fence between Mexico and the United States that would allegedly make it more difficult for immigrants to enter the United States.

The Mexican American population is highly concentrated in the West and Southwest, particularly in California and Texas. In 2005, 64% of all Mexican Americans in the United States lived in California and Texas; 39% lived in California, and 25% lived in Texas. Arizona and Illinois had the next largest concentrations of Mexican Americans, each having about 5%. The population and percentage of Mexican Americans in selected states are shown in Table 10.1. Even though Mexican Americans are highly concentrated in the states mentioned, pockets of them are found throughout the United States, including the South and the Northwest. In 2005, more than 652,387 lived in Colorado; 531,902, in Florida. Washington state, in the Northwest, had (in 2005) the eighth-largest population of Mexican Americans, 444,174. Mexican Americans are also becoming increasingly urbanized. Significant numbers are concentrated in large cities such as Los Angeles, Chicago, Milwaukee, and Detroit.

Mexican Americans were in the land that is now the United States before all other American groups, except the American Indians, Aleuts, Eskimos, and Native Hawai'ians. Their ancestors had settled in the region that is now the southwestern United States before Jamestown was settled by the English colonists in 1607. They became an ethnic minority when Texas was annexed by the United States in 1845. More of their territory was conquered by the United States during the Mexican American War, which lasted from 1846 to 1848. Their property, civic, and cultural rights were guaranteed by the Treaty of Guadalupe Hidalgo, the treaty that ended the war in 1848. In the decades after 1848, the treaty was blatantly disregarded, and Mexican Americans were made second-class citizens by Anglo-Americans who migrated and settled in the Southwest. There were about 80,000 Mexicans living in the territory Mexico ceded to the United States in 1848. Most modern Mexican American communities were formed by Mexican immigrants who came to the United States after 1910. The study of the conquest and subjugation of Mexican Americans and their resistance, which greatly intensified in the 1960s, is necessary to understand the nature of U.S. society and the genesis of the ethnic conflict and tensions in American life.

THE SPANISH CONQUEST

More than 25 million Indians were living in the Western Hemisphere when the Spanish conquistadores arrived in 1517. There were a wide variety of Indian cultures and groups in the region that is now Mexico. The Mayas and the Aztecs developed some of the most complex societies in the region. Mayan domestication and cultivation of corn significantly influenced agriculture in the Americas. A powerful military state and the most impressive contemporary cities were built by the Aztecs. Tenochtitlan, their capital city, has been called the most modern city in the world at the time of the Spanish conquest.

TABLE 10.1   Mexican American Population in Selected States, 2005

STATE	MEXICAN AMERICAN POPULATION	PERCENTAGE OF TOTAL STATE POPULATION
California	10,352,618	29.3
Texas	6,583,095	29.6
Arizona	1,481,707	25.4
Illinois	1,418,049	11.4
Colorado	652,387	14.3
Florida	531,902	3.1
Nevada	449,767	18.9
Washington	444,174	7.2
New Mexico	442,799	23.5
Georgia	417,452	4.7
New York	346,783	1.9
North Carolina	355,279	4.2
Oregon	302,852	8.5
Michigan	279,211	2.8
Indiana	215,217	3.5
Utah	192,270	7.9
Kansas	191,318	7.2
Oklahoma	185,966	5.4
Wisconsin	176,081	3.3
New Jersey	163,665	1.9
Minnesota	129,301	2.6
Ohio	124,721	1.1
Tennessee	113,787	2.0
Idaho	110,934	7.9
Virginia	109,073	1.5
Missouri	108,312	1.9
Nebraska	98,849	5.8
Arkansas	93,073	3.4
Pennsylvania	86,440	0.7
Iowa	85,142	3.0
South Carolina	84,059	2.0

Source: U.S. Census Bureau (2007), *American Community Survey, 2005: Selected Population Profile.* [Data file]. Available online at http://factfinder.census.gov/servlet/IPCharIterationServlet?_ts=202649767048.

Hernán Cortés, a Spanish explorer, led an expedition into Mexico in 1519. Before he reached the Aztec capital, he gained military help from other Indian civilizations by negotiation and conquest. After a two-year intermittent struggle with the Aztecs, Cortés finally seized Tenochtitlán on August 13, 1521, and the Aztec empire fell. Despite the Aztecs' military strength, the Spaniards were able to defeat them because they were helped by other Indian nations and had horses and superior firearms. Although the Spaniards were eventually successful in their conquest of much of the land stretching from southern South America to most of what is today the southwestern United States, this task was not easily accomplished. The Indians living in these areas fought hard to maintain their power and rebelled many times after the Spanish conquest. The Spaniards defeated most Indian groups only gradually and with the loss of many of their men.

MEXICAN AMERICANS: HISTORICAL PERSPECTIVE

Important Dates	Events
1519	Hernán Cortés, the Spanish conquistador, and a group of Spaniards arrived in the region that is now Mexico.
1521	Cortés, with the support of thousands of Indian allies, seized the Aztec capital city, Tenochtitlán, and the empire fell.
1598	Juan de Oñate established the first Spanish settlement in what is today New Mexico. The Spanish colonial period began.
1718	New Spain founded the mission and presidio of San Antonio.
1769	José Junípero Serra and Gaspar de Portolá established the mission and presidio of San Diego, the first in upper California.
1810	On September 16, 1810, Father Miguel Hidalgo sounded a battle cry known as the *El Grito de Dolores,* which signaled the beginning of the Mexican revolutionary era that eventually resulted in Mexican independence from Spain in 1821.
1836	Mexico's President Santa Anna and his troops defeated the rebelling Texans at the Alamo. Six weeks later, Santa Anna was defeated by Sam Houston and his Texan troops at San Jacinto. Texas declared itself independent and formed the Lone Star Republic.
1845	The United States annexed Texas, which had declared itself independent from Mexico in 1836. This was one key event leading to the Mexican-American War.
1846	On May 13, 1846, the United States declared war on Mexico, and the Mexican-American War began.
1848	The United States and Mexico signed the Treaty of Guadalupe Hidalgo, which ended the Mexican-American War. Mexico lost nearly one-third of its territory, and the United States acquired most of the territory that comprises the southwestern states.
1853	James Gadsden, representing the United States, purchased from Mexico 45,532 square miles of additional land, which was rich in copper, and opened a railroad route.
1859	Juan N. Cortina, who became a U.S. citizen under the provisions of the Treaty of Guadalupe Hidalgo, led a series of rebellions against Anglo-Americans in the Lower Rio Grande Valley of South Texas.

Important Dates	Events
1862	On May 5, 1862, French forces that had invaded Mexico were defeated at Puebla by Mexican forces led by Ignacio Zaragosa, a Texas Mexican. May 5 *(Cinco de Mayo)* is an important holiday observed by Mexican Americans.
1877	The El Paso Salt War occurred when Mexicans organized and rebelled against Anglos because of a dispute over rights to salt beds.
1910	A revolution starting in Mexico caused thousands of Mexicans to immigrate to the United States, looking for jobs and to escape political turmoil and persecution.
1924	Congress established the Border Patrol to monitor traffic across the Mexican-U.S. border. This border had previously been primarily open.
1929	The League of United Latin American Citizens was formed in Harlingen, Texas. Like other earlier Mexican-American civil rights organizations, the league stressed U.S. citizenship and assimilation.
1929–1935	Thousands of Mexican immigrants and their families were repatriated to Mexico, most without legal proceedings.
1942	The United States and Mexico made an agreement that authorized Mexicans to work temporarily in the United States. This project is known as the *bracero* program.
1943	The anti-Mexican "zoot-suit" riots occurred in Los Angeles during the summer.
1954	The U.S. Immigration and Naturalization Service began "Operation Wetback," a massive program to deport illegal Mexican immigrants to Mexico.
1965	A grape strike led by César Chávez and the United Farm Workers Association began in Delano, California, a town in the San Joaquin Valley.
	Rodolfo "Corky" Gonzales formed the Crusades for Justice in Denver. This important civil rights organization epitomized the Chicano movement that emerged in the 1960s.
	The U.S. Congress passed an immigration act limiting the number of Mexican immigrants to the United States to 20,000 annually.
1970	La Raza Unida Party was organized by José Angel Gutiérrez in Crystal City, Texas.
1976	Jerry Apodaca and Raul Castro were elected governors of New Mexico and Arizona, respectively.
1979	Luis Valdez's play *Zoot Suit* was the first Mexican American play produced on Broadway.
1982	Toney Anaya was elected governor of New Mexico.
1986	The Immigration Reform and Control Act of 1986 was passed. Designed to control the entry of undocumented (illegal) immigrants to the United States, it imposed severe penalties on employers who knowingly hired illegal immigrants.

Important Dates	Events
1992	President Bill Clinton named Henry G. Cisneros secretary of the Department of Housing and Urban Development.
	President Clinton named Federico Peña secretary of transportation.
2000	The 2000 census indicated that Mexican Americans were the largest (20,640,711) and fastest-growing Hispanic group. Their numbers increased 57.9% between 1990 and 2000.
2007	William Blaine "Bill" Richardson III was elected the thirtieth governor of New Mexico in 2002 and assumed office January 1, 2003. He was a candidate for president of the United States in 2007.

The Spanish Settlements

The Spanish settlements in Mexico and what is today the southwestern United States differed in several significant ways from the English colonies in the eastern parts of North America. For a number of complex reasons, more settlers from England than from Spain immigrated to the Americas. This was in part because, at the time of the conquest, Spain had a small population compared to other nations in Europe (Jiménez, 1994). It had, for example, about half the population of France. It is estimated that only about 300,000 Spaniards came to the Americas during three centuries of settlement (McWilliams, 1968). More English than Spanish colonists brought their wives, although a severe shortage of women was also a problem in the original English colonies. In 1619 the London Company sent 100 women who were willing to marry colonists to Virginia. Each man who married one of these women had to pay 54 kilograms (120 pounds) of the best tobacco. The serious shortage of women in the Spanish colonies was not dealt with as successfully as in Virginia. Writes Jiménez (1994):

> It is apparent that between 1493 and 1519 women represented less than 6 percent of all emigrants [to New Spain]. In the next twenty years they hardly surpassed this percentage. More favorable conditions in the colonies and the pressure exercised by the laws to encourage the emigration of women and the marriage of the conquistadors and settlers increased these ratios in the following years. (p. 79)

The unique characteristics of the Spanish settlers significantly influenced the physical and cultural development of the new "race" that was formed in the Americas. Because few women came to the colonies from Spain, most of the Spanish men had Indian concubines or wives. The offspring of these ethnically mixed unions were known as *mestizos*. The biological and cultural heritage of the Mexican American includes African strains although it is primarily Spanish-Indian. When they came to the Americas, the Spaniards had had long contact with a group of Africans called Moors. Moors came with the conquistadores to the Americas. Estevanico is perhaps the most famous. Nearly 200,000 African slaves were also brought to Mexico. They were so thoroughly mixed with the Spaniards and Indians by 1900 that they were no longer distinguishable as a separate racial group (Franklin & Moss, 2000). The Mexicans' biological heritage is more Indian than Spanish. Although the Spaniards imposed their culture and religion on the Indian nations, many Indian cultural elements survived and greatly influenced the development of Mexican culture. Thus, both the physical traits and culture of the Mexicans are primarily blends of Spanish and Indian influences. Writes McWilliams (1968): "To attempt to unravel any single strand from this pattern and label it 'Spanish' is to do a serious injustice to the Mexican and Indians . . . through whom . . . Spanish cultural influences survived" (p. 34).

The Texas Revolt

At the beginning of the nineteenth century, Mexico was in a perpetual state of political turmoil. Greatly concerned about the declining population in Texas, the Spanish, and later the Mexican government, encouraged Anglo Americans to settle there by making empresario land grants. The Spanish government gave an empresario grant to Moses Austin in 1821. His son Stephen received a reconfirmation of the original grant from the Mexican government in 1823. Because Texas was geographically close to the United States, it attracted a large number of Anglo immigrants who were interested in Texas's rich resources and open territory. Most Anglo settlers in Texas failed to keep the terms of their land-grant agreements with the Mexican government, such as becoming loyal citizens and Catholics, learning Spanish, and giving up their slaves. They were not interested in Mexican culture but wanted to establish Anglo institutions in the Mexican province and to control it.

Texas Mexicans were angry about President Santa Anna's attempts to centralize his power over the northern Mexican territories. The Anglo immigrants in Texas added fuel to the fire because of their disdain for the Mexican government. By permitting and encouraging U.S. citizens to settle in sparsely inhabited Texas, Mexico had inadvertently set the stage for revolt in the province and its eventual loss to the United States.

By the time Mexico realized that Anglo Mexicans were gaining control in Texas and took steps to undermine their power, antigovernment forces in Texas had already been firmly established. The Mexican government attempted to undermine Anglo power in Texas by abolishing slavery in 1829, by restricting Anglo immigration into Texas, and by enforcing customs regulations at the Texas-U.S. border. These actions greatly angered the Texas Anglo Mexicans and provoked attacks against the central government. Mexican federal troops arrived in Texas in 1835 after Texas proclaimed itself "conditionally independent." These troops were badly defeated. In 1836, President Santa Anna led several thousand Mexican troops into Texas. His army killed 187 Texans at a Franciscan mission in San Antonio called the

Alamo. The Mexican army had another victory at Goliad, but they were crushed at San Jacinto on April 21 by Sam Houston and his Texas troops, who shouted "Remember the Alamo!" After this victory, Texas sought world recognition of its independence and started the chain of events that eventually led to its annexation by the United States in 1845.

THE MEXICAN-AMERICAN WAR

When the Mexican government took serious steps to halt Anglo immigration to the Southwest, the United States had begun, in the name of Manifest Destiny, an aggressive campaign to annex all of Mexico's northern territories. The United States began a military conquest when negotiations failed and then angered Mexico by annexing Texas in 1845. The United States declared war on Mexico in 1846 when a boundary dispute developed between the two nations. The United States had defeated Mexico within two years and occupied California and New Mexico by the end of 1846. Mexico's northern provinces had little allegiance to the nation's capital. Anglo settlers who had a strong toehold in Mexican provinces such as California and New Mexico actively sought Mexico's defeat. Mexico was also greatly weakened by internal strife and its inability to rally internal support for the war.

The Treaty of Guadalupe Hidalgo

After Mexico was defeated by the United States, representatives of the two nations signed a treaty on February 2, 1848, in the Mexican village of Guadalupe Hidalgo. The United States forced Mexico to surrender its claim to Texas, which the United States had annexed in 1845, and to cede about one-third of its territory to the United States. This chunk of land included most of the territory now comprising the states of the U.S. Southwest, including Arizona, California, New Mexico, Utah, Nevada, and a section of Colorado. The United States paid Mexico $15 million for this large piece of land.

All Mexicans who remained in this newly acquired territory received the right to become U.S. citizens. Only about 3,000 of the nearly 80,000 people living in the area chose to leave their homes and move to the Mexican side of the border. The treaty guaranteed Mexican Americans "all the rights of citizens of the United States . . . [and] the free enjoyment of . . . liberty and property" (Treaty of Guadalupe Hidalgo, 1971). Write Meier and Rivera (1972):

> By this treaty the United States gained not only an immense new territory but also a large group of new citizens. Although they were left in their same geographic and cultural setting, these new citizens were now exposed to unfamiliar legal, political, and social institutions. Guaranteed full protection of property rights, they soon became enmeshed in a web of confusing Anglo laws which required proof of ownership unfamiliar to them. (p. 71)

After the Conquest: Oppression and Conflict

After 1848, forces were set in motion that were destined to make the Mexicans in the United States a conquered, powerless, and alienated ethnic minority. Although they were guaranteed property and citizenship rights by the Treaty of Guadalupe Hidalgo, it was only a matter of time before Anglo Americans, through a series of legal and financial maneuvers, had obtained control in all of the southwestern territories, and successfully reduced the native Mexicans to the status of second-class citizens.

The pattern of conquest differed somewhat in the various southwestern territories. Before the Anglos came to New Mexico, a rigid class structure existed that sharply divided the rich and the poor. The Anglos in New Mexico pitted the rich against the poor in order to gain control of the territory. Anglo dominance emerged more gradually in New Mexico than in California and Texas. A mass of Anglos immigrated to California during the gold rush of 1849 and in subsequent years. Mexicans were completely outnumbered. Anglos thoroughly dominated northern California by 1851, but domination of southern California was somewhat delayed, because most Anglo immigrants first settled in the northern part of the territory. However, Anglos eventually settled in the south and within a few years expanded their dominance over the entire state. There were more than 30,000 Anglos and only 5,000 native Mexicans in Texas as early as 1834. Anglos had controlled Texas since it became independent as the Lone Star Republic in 1836. This dominance continued after U.S. annexation in 1845.

The Anglo Americans were able to obtain most of the land owned by the Mexicans by imposing a series of legal and financial restraints. Land boundaries in Mexico had been rather loosely and casually defined. Many Mexicans had to appear in Anglo courts to defend their rights to the land they owned. Often they did not have the legal papers proving ownership of their land, and Mexican legal papers did not conform to superimposed U.S. law. In many cases they had to sell their land to pay taxes imposed by the new government or exorbitant fees to Anglo lawyers to argue their cases in court. Legal battles over land titles often dragged out in the courts for years and became expensive. Tactics such as these and the Congressional Land Act of 1851, which required U.S.-recognized proof of land ownership, had the ultimate effect of making the Mexicans largely landless and poverty-stricken.

Rioting, lynchings, burnings, vigilante action, and other forms of violence were directed at the country's "newest aliens" during this period of turmoil and Hispanic defeat in the Southwest. Moore (with Pachon, 1976) contends that "no other part of the United States saw such prolonged intergroup violence as did the Border States from 1848 to 1925" (p. 36). Many Anglo outlaws and social misfits settled in the Southwest during this period. They declared open season on Mexicans and often attacked them just for fun. There was little or no law enforcement in many parts of the Southwest during this period. In 1850, California passed a Foreign Miner's Tax that was designed to drive Mexicans out of the mines.

The Mexican Revolution of 1910 contributed to this atmosphere of hostility and violence. Banditry and filibustering (filibustering is pursuing military activity in a foreign nation for adventure) occurred on both sides of the border. Mexican-Anglo hostility reached new highs. Mexicans considered Anglo Americans "gringos," and Anglos called Mexicans "greasers." By the turn of the century, the Mexicans had been conquered and made foreigners within their homeland. Culturally, politically, and economically they were second-class citizens. Mexican Americans faced the beginning of the twentieth century suffering from a crushing second defeat in the Southwest.

NORTH FROM MEXICO

Early Immigrants

During the early development of agriculture in the Southwest, agribusinessmen depended on a large and cheap labor supply. This labor need was met in the late 1800s by the Chinese immigrants and later by immigrants from Japan and the Philippines (see Chapter 13). The expansion of irrigated farming in the Southwest at the turn of the century coincided with the Mexican Revolution of 1910. Many Mexicans were displaced by the revolution. They came north to the U.S. Southwest seeking job opportunities. They found jobs in truck farming, in cotton and sugar beet fields, in mines, in industry, and on the railroads. Hundreds of Mexican immigrants worked on the construction of railroad lines that crossed the West. Many Mexican American communities in the Southwest grew up around railroad campsites.

There was no legal agreement between Mexico and the United States that protected the rights of these immigrants. Consequently, they were often blatantly exploited by their employers. They were paid the lowest wages, given the worst jobs, and forced to live in the crudest shacks. Many became migrant workers who followed the crops. The mass of Mexican immigrants to the Southwest depressed wages so drastically that many native Mexican Americans migrated to midwestern cities, such as Detroit, Gary, and Chicago to obtain higher wages. The large number of Mexican immigrants who came to the Southwest between 1910 and 1930 laid the foundations for most modern Mexican American communities.

Many Anglo groups in the Southwest became alarmed by the large numbers of Mexicans who were entering the United States in the 1920s. Between 1920 and 1929, 498,900 Mexican immigrants entered the United States. Vigorous efforts were made to halt their immigration. Although the legal attempts to stop their immigration failed because of the powerful opposition from agribusinessmen who wanted them for cheap labor, other efforts were successful. The U.S.-Mexican border had historically been an open border, with Mexicans and U.S. citizens crossing it at will. The Border Patrol was established in 1924 by Congress to control traffic across the border.

When the Great Depression hit in 1929, and many Mexicans, like other Americans, lost their jobs and found it necessary to obtain welfare to survive, loud cries were heard against the Mexicans. Mexicans were regarded as "foreigners" who did not deserve welfare benefits. As with other immigrants of color who came before them, attempts were made to deport the Mexicans when their labor was no longer needed. Jobs became increasingly scarce as the dust bowl White immigrants fled to the Southwest to compete for the few available jobs. The U.S. Immigration Service, as well as state, county, and local governments, began an aggressive drive to repatriate immigrants.

In the eagerness to rid the United States of Mexicans in order to cut back on welfare rolls, many Mexican American citizens were "encouraged" or forced to go to Mexico. The civil rights of U.S. citizens of Mexican descent were violated seriously in this unfortunate repatriation movement. More than 64,000 Mexican aliens were returned to Mexico between 1930 and 1934 without legal proceedings. The Mexican population in the United States declined from 639,000 to 377,000 between 1930 and 1940 (Moore, with Pachon, 1976, p. 42).

The Bracero Program

When World War II began, a new demand for unskilled labor developed in the United States. Agribusiness leaders spoke vigorously about their desperate need for Mexican labor. Partly as a gesture to help with the war effort, Mexico agreed to a seasonal work program with the United States. The two nations signed an agreement in July 1942 that enabled Mexican citizens to work in the United States during work seasons. They were to return to Mexico when the work season ended. Unlike the earlier Mexican immigrants, these workers came under an agreement that guaranteed them specific conditions relating to such problems as wages, working conditions, transportation, and worker rights.

Although these contract stipulations helped reduce some of the extreme conditions experienced by earlier Mexican immigrants, their wages and living conditions were often depressing. The bracero program formally ended in December 1947. When it terminated, the number of undocumented immigrants crossing the U.S.-Mexican border soared. Smuggling undocumented immigrants across the border became a highly profitable business in which many "men snatchers" engaged and profited (McWilliams, 1968, pp. 178–179).

In 1954, the U.S. Immigration and Naturalization Service began a massive drive known as Operation Wetback to deport undocumented immigrants to Mexico. Operation Wetback grossly violated the civil rights of many Mexicans, as had the repatriation project in the 1930s. Hundreds of Mexican American citizens were arrested and harassed. They were threatened and forced to produce proof of their citizenship. Only a few of the thousands of Mexicans deported had formal hearings. Operation Wetback successfully attained its goal but alienated and outraged many Mexican American citizens. When the project ended, more than a million people had been deported to Mexico.

In 1951, the United States and Mexico jointly accepted a Migratory Labor Agreement known as Public Law 78. This agreement set forth conditions for a new bracero program. It contained conditions similar to the earlier bracero agreement. Public Law 78 was extended for various periods until it ended in December 1964. In

1965, the United States Congress passed a new immigration act, which became effective in 1968, that limited the annual immigration from Western Hemisphere nations to 120,000. Each nation, including Mexico, was given an annual quota of 20,000. This new act solved, at least for a time, problems concerning the number of Mexican nationals that could legally enter the United States.

Because of the chronic economic and population problems in Mexico, large numbers of undocumented Mexican immigrants enter the United States each year. The American Community Survey indicated that 40,459,196 Hispanics—14.2% of the U.S. household population—lived in the United States in 2004 (U.S. Census Bureau, 2007). However, the actual number of Hispanics who lived in the United States in 2004 was much higher than this figure because of the large numbers of undocumented immigrants who enter the United States from Mexico each year. The largest foreign-born group in the United States is Mexican Americans. Fifty-eight percent of all foreign-born Mexicans entered the United States since 1990 (U.S. Census Bureau, 2007).

Violence and Race Riots

In the 1940s, anti-Mexican feelings and stereotypes were rampant in the Southwest. The stereotypes, which depicted the Mexican American as criminal and violent, were perpetuated by the established Anglo press, especially the newspapers. The anti-Mexican press propaganda inflamed racial feelings and antagonisms toward the Mexican Americans. Anti-Mexican racism was the basic cause of the case of the Sleepy Lagoon and the zoot-suit riots that occurred in Los Angeles in the summer of 1943.

The Sleepy Lagoon Case

A young Mexican American, José Diaz, died mysteriously on August 2, 1942, apparently from a fractured skull. Without seriously seeking the facts of the case, the Los Angeles police immediately arrested twenty-four young men who were thought to be members of a Mexican gang accused of killing Diaz. All of them were charged with murder. A gravel pit, which became a central focus in the case, was dubbed "The Sleepy Lagoon" by a Los Angeles reporter. When seventeen of the twenty-four youths were convicted, the Sleepy Lagoon Defense Committee was organized. The committee, headed by journalist Carey McWilliams, successfully appealed the case. The case was dismissed because of insufficient evidence when the district court of appeals reversed the convictions on October 4, 1944.

The Zoot-Suit Riots

On June 3, 1943, eleven sailors were allegedly attacked by a group of boys in a predominantly Mexican neighborhood in Los Angeles. After this incident, the Los Angeles police conducted a raid that inflamed the community but failed to find the attackers. This incident kicked off a chain reaction resulting in one of the most serious series of race riots that has occurred in the United States. Encouraged by the actions of the police and the pervasive anti-Mexican attitudes in Los Angeles, about 200 sailors began to violently attack Mexican American youths on the night of June 4.

The police responded by arresting the victims of the attacks and keeping their hands off the sailors. The Los Angeles press warned that the dangerous zoot-suiters would retaliate the next night. Some Mexican American youths were referred to as "zoot-suiters" because of their style of dress during the 1940s. The press succeeded in alarming the public and in stirring up anti-Mexican feelings. On the night of June 7, hundreds of Anglos went into the streets and began a massive attack on Mexican American youths. Many zoot-suiters were beaten and stripped naked in the streets. The riot continued until military authorities intervened late on the night of June 7. Other riots occurred in cities as far away as Philadelphia, Chicago, and Detroit in the summer of 1943.

THE CHICANO MOVEMENT

Prior to the civil rights movement of the 1960s, *Chicano* was a term used to refer to lower-class Mexican immigrants from rural areas and small towns. The term was viewed negatively by the middle-class and elite Mexican Americans but not by the lower-class people who used it. During the 1960s, leaders of the Mexican American protest and civil rights movement used the term in a positive way to describe their new quest for political, social, economic, cultural, and educational equality. The term *Chicano* was also used to link Mexican American political activists and intellectuals to their Mexican Indian heritage. In the past, their Spanish heritage was usually emphasized. The Chicano movement was broad in scope: it had economic, educational, religious, and cultural goals. The push for bilingual education in the schools was one of its major goals. Including more Mexican American priests and other church officials in the Catholic church hierarchy was another.

The Chicano movement was also political. Its leaders saw political clout as one of the best ways to attain the other goals of the movement. Its leaders, who often differed on tactics, had a variety of goals. Many believed that Chicanos would be able to overcome oppression in the United States only when they had political power and control over the institutions, such as schools and courts, that influenced their lives and destinies.

It is inaccurate to interpret the Chicano movement as a protest force that suddenly arose in the 1960s or to refer to Chicanos as the "awakening minority"; neither can it be viewed in isolation. Often this was done in the 1960s. To understand the Chicano movement fully, we must view it as an important link in the long chain of resistance activities in which Chicanos have been involved since 1848. As historian Rodolfo Acuña (1972) pointed out in the 1970s, "Men like Juan Patron and J. J. Herrerra were the precursors of today's breed of rebels or insurrectionists. In understanding them . . . and others of their kind, we shall better understand the present, and the words of Reis Lopez Tijerina will take on more significant meaning" (p. 77).

Early Resistance to Anglo Dominance

Mexican Americans have resisted Anglo oppression and colonization since Anglo Americans conquered and occupied the Southwest. Chicanos such as Juan N. Cortina, Juan Jose Herrerra, and Juan Patron led organized resistance efforts in the 1800s. Cortina issued a "declaration of grievances" and urged Mexican Americans to "exterminate" their oppressors. Many Mexicans responded to the revolutionary calls issued by Cortina, Herrerra, and Patron (Acuña, 2007). Mexican American organizations, such as Las Gorras Blancas, fought Anglo leaders who were illegally taking land owned by Mexican Americans in New Mexico.

Unions and Strikes

In the first decades of the twentieth century, most Mexican Americans worked in agriculture, although many worked in mines, industry, and on the railroads. Farm workers were highly exploited by rich and powerful agribusinessmen. Mexican American workers aggressively opposed their conditions and organized unions and strikes, thus shattering the myth that they were docile workers. The period from 1900 to 1940 was characterized by active Mexican involvement in strikes and union organization. In 1927 the Confederacion de Uniones Obreras Mexicanas was organized in California. This union organized a strike in 1928 in the Imperial Valley. Farm owners and law officials, who formed coalitions, responded violently to the strike. They broke it up by deporting some strikers to Mexico and assaulting and intimidating others.

This pattern was used extensively by farm owners to crush strikes by Mexican Americans. However, strikes and union activities continued in the midst of these oppressive tactics. Meier and Rivera (1972) summarize this period: "Although Mexican Americans gained much labor union experience from 1900 to 1940, their organizations achieved only limited success. Some gains were made in wages and working conditions; however, the hopes and aspirations of Mexican-American workers continued to be frustrated by repression and discrimination" (p. 184).

Civil Rights Organizations

A number of civic, service, and political organizations have been organized since the late nineteenth century to promote the civil rights and interests of Mexican Americans. One of the first was a mutual-aid organization formed in Arizona in 1894, the Alianza Hispano-Americana. These early societies restricted membership to individuals of Mexican descent who were citizens of the United States. They were made up primarily of the middle and upper classes and promoted assimilation by urging their members to become loyal U.S. citizens. Cuellar (Moore, with Cuellar, 1970) argues that these organizations pursued a "politics of adaptation" rather than aggressively pushing for their political rights. They included the Order of the Sons of America, organized in San Antonio in 1921, and the League of United Latin-American Citizens, formed in Corpus Christi, Texas, in 1929.

Mexican Americans became more politicized in the post–World War II period. The organizations emerging during these years reflected acute political awareness and skill. The Community Service Organization, formed in Los Angeles in 1947, stressed political involvement and broad political participation. It organized a number of successful voter registration drives. The American G.I. Forum, founded in 1948, the Mexican American Political Association, organized in 1959, and the Political Association of Spanish-Speaking Organizations, formed in 1960, stressed political involvement. These organizations were direct predecessors of the Chicano movement that emerged in the 1960s.

The Militant Chicano Movement

Mexican Americans' protest activities, which had been going on historically, were intensified in the 1960s and 1970s and became collectively known as the "Chicano movement" (Meier & Ribera, 1993). In addition to being more intense than earlier Mexican American movements, the Chicano movement had other unique characteristics. It was more militant, often using forms of direct confrontation, and included a wide range of individuals among its ranks such as intellectuals, students, and community activists. Its goals were also more ambitious than the goals of traditional Mexican American civil rights groups. It sometimes demanded Chicano control of institutions within the Mexican American community. Some of its leaders argued that Chicanos in the United States were a colonized people who had been culturally and politically oppressed. They demanded redress of these grievances.

Chicano leaders also gave more attention to their mixed Mexican heritage than did earlier leaders. Their unique heritage, they argued, was to be celebrated and not denied, as was often done in the past by Mexican Americans who insisted on being viewed as "Spanish" instead of "Mexican." Much emphasis was placed on Mexican culture, values, foods, and especially on the speaking of Spanish. They demanded the right to speak Spanish in all U.S. institutions such as the school and church. Some Chicano leaders argued that "revolution" was necessary to liberate them.

Of the many local Chicano civil rights leaders, four young men epitomized the movement in the public view of the United States: Cesar Chávez, Reies Lopez Tijerina, Rodolfo "Corky" Gonzales, and José Angel Gutierrez. Chávez headed the United Farm Workers Organizing Committee, unionized farm workers, and successfully led the famous Delano grape strike in 1965, as well as many subsequent farm strikes. Tijerina demanded that Anglos in New Mexico return the lands they had taken from Mexican Americans in the 1800s. He formed the Federal Alliance of Free Cities in 1963 to push for the return of New Mexico lands to Chicanos or compensation to Chicanos for the loss of these lands. An important and militant civil rights group, the Crusade for Justice, was organized in Denver in 1965 by Gonzales. The crusade initiated successful projects related to improved education, better housing, and the elimination of police brutality in the Mexican American community. As a result of the activities of the political party La Raza Unida, organized in 1970 by Gutierrez, Mexican Americans exercised unprecedented political power in Crystal City, Texas, in the 1970s, which spread throughout the Lower Rio Grande Valley. These four charismatic leaders embodied the hopes and aspirations of millions of Mexican Americans.

MEXICAN AMERICANS TODAY

Mexican Americans, like African Americans and other people of color, made important educational and economic gains during the 1960s. However, many of these gains faded during the 1970s and 1980s. This loss during the 1970s and 1980s was caused by a number of factors, including the conservative national policies during the Reagan years and important changes in the U.S. economy. In previous decades, when industrial manufacturing was an important part of the U.S. economy, groups with few skills that were highly concentrated in the lower and working classes, such as Mexican Americans and African Americans, could move to large cities and obtain manufacturing jobs that paid well. There has been a substantial decrease in such jobs in the United States during the last forty years as the United States and other major Western nations have increasingly become societies characterized by high-technology and service occupations. These developments in the economy have had a disproportionately negative influence on job availability for groups heavily concentrated in the lower rungs of the economic and educational ladder, such as Mexican Americans, Puerto Ricans in the United States, and African Americans (Gregory & Sanjek, 1994; Wilson, 1996).

By the late 1980s, the militant Chicano movement of the 1960s had been transformed into more pragmatic forms of political organization. The various Hispanic groups, such as Mexican Americans, Puerto Ricans, and Cubans, worked cooperatively to form political, cultural, and business organizations to push for their collective rights and to improve the economic and educational status of U.S. Hispanics. These organizations included the National Association of Latino Elected and Appointed Officials, the Congressional Hispanic Caucus (composed of Hispanics in the U.S. Congress), the National Hispanic Chamber of Commerce, the League of United Latin American Citizens, and the Hispanic Policy Development Project, an organization that gathers data and analyzes public policy related to U.S. Hispanic groups. Many Mexican American organizations also remained viable, such as the Mexican-American Legal Defense and Education Fund. This organization made tremendous strides in size, scope, and influence.

Mexican Americans also reaped benefits in local and state elections and became more conscious of their potential political clout. In 1984, Eligio de la Garza (Texas), Manual Lujan, Jr. (New Mexico), and Matthew G. Martinez (California) were among the eleven Hispanics in the U.S. House of Representatives. Mexican American mayors of large cities included Henry G. Cisneros in San Antonio and Federico Pena in Denver. Toney Anaya was governor of New Mexico. Mexican Americans continued to make visible political gains during the Clinton administration in the 1990s, epitomized by Clinton's appointment of Henry G. Cisneros as secretary of housing and urban development in his administration.

In 2004, there were 5,205 Hispanic elected officials in the United States, including 234 state legislators and 27 in the U.S. House of Representatives (Latino Coalition, 2007). Three Hispanics served in the U.S. Senate, representing Colorado, Florida, and New Jersey. All were members of the Congressional Hispanic Caucus, formed in 1976. This is a bipartisan group that works to improve conditions for all Hispanics. Bill Richardson of New Mexico, who was the only Hispanic governor in the United States, was a candidate for the U.S. presidency in 2007. Five Hispanics have served as governors in three states. On May 17, 2005, Antonio R. Villaraigosa became the first Latino mayor of Los Angeles since Cristobal Aguilar in 1872.

Despite the political gains they had made from the 1980s to the 2000s, Mexican American leaders realized that their ethnic group had more potential political power than it was realizing. The nine states in which Hispanics are concentrated (California, Texas, New York, Florida, Illinois, New Jersey, New Mexico, Arizona, and Colorado) have 207 electoral votes, which is 76% of the 270 needed to put a presidential candidate in the White House. Yet, several factors worked against Mexican Americans realizing their potential political strength, including the low voter turnout rate among Mexican Americans and the fact that a significant percentage of Mexican Americans are not U.S. citizens.

The Mexican American population is becoming increasingly urbanized, although it is less urban than other Hispanic groups. More than 75% of Mexican Americans lived in metropolitan areas in 1960. By 1980, that number had increased about 10%, and about four of every five Mexican Americans lived in metropolitan areas (Bean & Tienda, 1987). By 2003 more than 90 percent of Mexican Americans lived in metropolitan areas (U.S. Census Bureau, 2004).

Large populations of Mexican Americans are concentrated in such cities as Los Angeles, Houston, Dallas, Denver, and Chicago. The Mexican American population, like the African American population, has also become more economically stratified since the 1970s. There has always been a middle class of Mexican Americans. However, a new group of middle-class Hispanics developed as a result of the economic and educational opportunities they gained during the civil rights movement of the 1960s and 1970s (Acuña, 2007).

This new middle-class group of Mexican Americans is composed of professionals and businesspeople. They frequently work in mainstream White institutions and live in predominantly White middle-class communities; consequently, they have little contact with the Hispanic barrio or with lower- and working-class Mexican American communities. The children of this new middle class often have little knowledge of the traditional Mexican American culture in the United States. Acuña (2007) has pointed out that these new middle-class professionals and businesspeople often have an identity with and use the term *Hispanic* to refer to themselves. These new middle-class Hispanics, according to Acuña (2007), are often more interested in business development than social action and see business leaders, rather than social activists, as the important movers and shakers in the Mexican American community.

During the 1980s, which some media writers called the "Decade of the Hispanic," the emphasis in the Mexican American community was often on educational and economic development rather than on the kind of strident social action that characterized the civil rights movement of the 1960s and 1970s. Presidents Ronald Reagan and George H.W. Bush appointed successful and visible Mexican Americans to important federal positions. President Reagan appointed a university president, Dr. Lauro F. Cavazos, to be secretary of the Department of Education. Cavazos was the first Hispanic appointed to a Cabinet post. Bush kept him in that position when he took office in 1989. In 1983, Reagan made history again when he appointed Linda Chavez to the U.S. Commission on Civil Rights. Both Bush and Jimmy Carter also appointed a number of Hispanics to important positions in their administrations. President Clinton appointed Henry Cisneros, the former mayor of San Antonio, secretary of housing and urban development. President George W. Bush appointed Alberto Gonzales U.S. attorney general in 2005.

Nativism in the 1990s: New Xenophobia

The so-called Decade of the Hispanics was not without its stresses and strains, emergent xenophobia (fear of foreigners), and subtle and sometimes blatant racism. The new xenophobia, nativism, and sometimes racism were triggered by several factors. Among them were the large influx of legal Asian and Latin American immigrants to the United States, the nation's inability to control the large but undetermined number of undocumented or illegal immigrants (some estimates put the figure at 200,000 annually), the radical changes in the U.S. economy discussed previously, and the escalating class schism in U.S. society.

Nativistic sentiments and proposals surfaced during the years of heated discussion that finally resulted in the passage of the Immigration Reform and Control Act of 1986, designed to curb the rapid flow of undocumented (illegal) immigrants who enter the United States each year by severely penalizing employers who knowingly hire undocumented workers. The enacted bill was a difficult compromise. Some of the voices heard during the strident debates over the proposed bill were decidedly anti-Hispanic. The English-Only movement, which came to the forefront during the 1980s, sometimes uses chilling language reminiscent of the nativistic movements at the turn of the last century. A major goal of this movement is to get enacted in as many states as possible referenda that make English the "official language." What these referenda exactly mean in a legal sense is ambiguous. However, important goals are to halt the growth of bilingual education programs and to send the message to native speakers of languages other than English, such as Spanish, that the only language accepted in the United States is English.

The English-Only movement is fostered by U.S. English, a political action group that has deep pockets and the endorsement of some influential Americans. The English-Only movement initially targeted states with large Hispanic populations for the passage of English-Only referenda. One of its major successes was the November 1986 passage of Proposition 63 in California, which made English the official language of the state. U.S. English knew that the stakes were high in California and spent more than $700,000 to get Proposition 63 passed there (Crawford, 1989). By the end of 2006, English had become the official language in twenty-eight states, including Colorado, Florida, and Arizona. In Arizona, the law was overturned in 1998 but was reinstated by voters in 2006.

California continued to be an influential center of nativistic activities and movements throughout the 1990s, perhaps because of its high concentration of Spanish-speaking and other immigrants. In 2005, over one-quarter of U.S. immigrants lived in California. About half of the foreign-born population lived in three states, California, New York, and Texas (U.S. Census Bureau, 2007). In 1994, feelings against immigrants surfaced and were sometimes encouraged by politicians. One outcome was the passage of Proposition 187 in California, dubbed by its supporters the "Save Our Children" proposition. This initiative denies undocumented workers and their children schooling and nonemergency medical care (*Encyclopaedia Britannica*, 1995). California governor Pete Wilson endorsed Proposition 187 and made it a key issue in his reelection campaign, but the proposition faced a legal challenge immediately after its passage. In 1998, California voters approved Proposition 227, called "English for the Children," or the Unz Amendment after its main sponsor, Ron K. Unz, a former businessman and political activist. The law requires all public school instruction to be in English and bans bilingual education.

Mexican Americans face several important challenges in the years ahead, including the need to increase the educational status of their youth, to close the income gap between Mexican Americans and the total U.S. population, and to work with other Hispanic groups to influence political elections and national policy. There are encouraging signs that the Mexican American community will face these challenges creatively.

TEACHING STRATEGIES

To illustrate how content about Mexican Americans can be used to integrate the curriculum, three key concepts have been identified and exemplary strategies are given for teaching them. Strategies are presented for teaching *stereotypes*, *immigration*, and *social protest* for the primary, intermediate and upper, and high school grades, respectively.

Primary Grades

Concept

Stereotypes

Generalization: People have many stereotypes about what makes a person an American. These stereotypes often cause hurt and harm.

1. Read the following story to the class and ask the questions that follow.

CHILD FROM ANOTHER LAND

Manuel and Maria Gonzales are descendants of Indian, Mexican, and Spanish people who have lived in the state of New Mexico for at least a century. The Gonzaleses are proud to be Americans but are just as proud of their Mexican American heritage. In their upper-middle-class community in the Southwest, their eight-year-old son, Ramon, went to a public elementary school that had a 20% Mexican American population. Ramon felt at home at the school and was sorry when he learned that his father, an engineer, was moving to the Midwest to accept an important job at a well-known computer company. Mrs. Gonzales, a high school English teacher, was also able to get a job in the midwestern city to which the family was moving.

Manuel and Maria were excited about the move to the Midwest because of the opportunity it offered Manuel. Ramon was very sorry to leave his friends and the only home and community he had ever known. He had decided, however, that he would try to make the best of the move. Ramon was the only Mexican American child in the third grade in his new school. There were only five Mexican American children in the entire school. During the first several days in his new school, Ramon fared okay but felt awkward when the teacher had trouble pronouncing his name and several children asked him, "What country are you from?"

Questions
1. How do you think Ramon felt about leaving his friends?
2. How do you think he felt in his new school? Why did he feel that way? Have you ever felt that way?
3. How do you think Ramon felt when the teacher had trouble pronouncing his name?
4. Why did the children ask Ramon, "What country are you from?"
5. Why do you think the children thought Ramon was from another country?

2. Introduce the concept *stereotype* to the students. Tell the students that a stereotype is a rigid and simplified way of thinking about a group of people and that it often causes harm to individuals and groups. Explain to the students how stereotypes lead to prejudice and discrimination. Ask them to list some of the stereotypes of different groups they may have, such as stereotypes about boys, girls, rich people, poor people, and fat people.
3. Explain to the students that the children thought Ramon was from a different country because he was a person of color who had a Spanish name. Explain that the children had a stereotypic notion of what an American is. Tell the students that Americans are of all racial, ethnic, and cultural origins and provide several examples. Also, show them pictures of African Americans, Mexican Americans, and Asian Americans. Summarize the lesson by asking the children to list the hurt and harm that stereotypes cause.

Intermediate and Upper Grades

Concept

Immigration

Generalization: Social, economic, and political conditions have influenced Mexican immigration to the United States. Mexican immigrants in the United States have been the victims of racism, deportation, and labor exploitation.

1. Tell the students that about one million Mexican immigrants came to the United States between 1910 and 1930. Ask them to state hypotheses to explain why so many Mexicans immigrated to the United States during this period. List their responses on the board. When the students have finished stating their hypotheses, ask them to group their hypotheses into several categories, using symbols such as "−" and "+" to indicate statements that should be grouped together. When the statements have been grouped, ask the students to label the groups. The hypotheses might be grouped into such broad categories as "social reasons," "political reasons," and "economic reasons." These categories need not be mutually exclusive. In this initial exercise, you will be teaching your students how to hypothesize and conceptualize, which involves three major steps: listing, grouping, and labeling.

2. When the first exercise is completed, the students should record their hypotheses and categories in their notebooks. They will need to refer to them later in this exercise, when the hypotheses are tested. The students should now collect and study data to test their hypotheses. Their readings should include information on the Mexican Revolution of 1910 and the tremendous need for agricultural labor that had developed in the Southwest by the turn of the century. The Mexican Revolution caused many displaced Mexican peasants to come to the United States looking for jobs after 1910. The wealthy farmers in the Southwest wanted a large and cheap labor supply.

3. Students should investigate the conditions of the early Mexican immigrants to the United States. Most became migrant workers who followed the seasonal crops. Many of their dreams were shattered in the United States. Their problems are vividly and poignantly revealed in Manuel Gamio (1971), *The Life Story of the Mexican Immigrant*. Ask four students to read and dramatize for the class the accounts by these migratory laborers: Gumersindo Valdez, Juan Berzunzolo, Elias Garza, and Nivardo del Rio. Accounts by these writers are found on pages 141–159 of the Gamio book.

4. When the Great Depression struck in 1929, a movement began to deport Mexican immigrants to Mexico. Ask one student to prepare a class presentation giving the views of the U.S. Immigration Service and another to prepare a report revealing how different segments of the Mexican American community felt about this massive repatriation movement. The class should discuss the problem after these two presentations have been given.

5. Beginning in 1942, Mexican immigrants entered the United States under the terms of an agreement between the United States and Mexico. Ask the students to pretend that it is January 1942 and that the bracero bill is being debated in the U.S. Congress. Ask different members of the class to play the roles of various kinds of people in the Mexican American community (old settlers, new immigrants, etc.), southwestern agribusinessmen, and representatives of major unions in the United States. Ask the students playing the assigned roles to argue for or against the bill before the simulated

Congress. The class should vote to decide the fate of the bracero bill of 1942 after they have heard the arguments. The class should then compare the results of their vote with the bill passed by Congress in 1942.

6. Ask several students in the class to make reports on Public Law 78, the Migratory Labor Agreement, and Operation Wetback, which began in 1954. Conduct a class discussion on the legal, social, and moral implications of these two activities that were implemented by the U.S. government. Particular attention should be given to how they affected U.S. citizens of Mexican descent.

7. During the debates and discussion on the passage of the Immigration Reform and Control Act of 1986, many problems of undocumented immigrants to the United States were revealed. Ask the students to research the debates that took place when the proposed act was being discussed, to describe the main goals of the act, and to determine the extent to which the act has been successful.

8. Because of the economic problems in Mexico today, a large number of people (both documented and undocumented) are entering the United States from Mexico. In 2005, 161,445 legal Mexican immigrants entered the United States. A large but unknown number of undocumented immigrants also enter the United States each year.

   Ask the students to investigate the economic conditions in Mexico today that cause large numbers of Mexicans to leave their nation and head for the United States. Unlike the past, most of these immigrants settle in large U.S. cities such as Los Angeles, Dallas, and Houston. Ask the students to find out what kinds of jobs these immigrants obtain in U.S. cities, the problems they encounter, and their general status in U.S. society.

9. Summarize the unit by asking the students to take out the hypotheses they formulated at the beginning of this unit and evaluate them, using the information they have collected and discussed. They should determine which hypotheses can remain as they were originally stated, which ones must be modified, and which ones must be totally rejected on the basis of the evidence collected.

10. Culminate the unit by showing and discussing a videotape or DVD on the experiences of Mexican Americans. See Appendix C for the descriptions and annotations of available videotapes and films. In the discussion, focus on social, economic, and political conditions that have influenced Mexican immigration to the United States.

Valuing Activity

Read the following story to the class and ask the questions that follow.

THE SANCHEZ FAMILY AND THE GRAPE STRIKE

Mr. and Mrs. Sanchez and their seven children came from Mexico to live in California four years ago. Mr. Sanchez had been told by relatives who had been to the United States that he could make money very quickly if he came to California. When Mr. Sanchez arrived in California, he found that it was hard to make a living working in the fields. Since the Sanchez family has been living in California, the family has had to move many times in order to follow the crops and find work. The family has traveled as far as Texas and Michigan to work in the fields.

The work in the fields is very hard. Everyone in the family, except little Carlos, works in the fields so that the family can make enough money. Even Mrs. Sanchez, who used to stay at home and take care of the home when they lived in Mexico, now must work in the fields. The pay for the work is low. Mr. and Mrs. Sanchez find that they become further and further in debt each year.

The Sanchez family is now living in the San Joaquin Valley in California. The family went to live there to work in the grape fields. For a while everything there was okay. Recently, a lot of things have been happening in the valley that Mr. and Mrs. Sanchez do not fully understand. Most of the field workers have said that they will not go to work next week because the Mexican American Union, led by Juan Gonzalez, who is popular with the workers, has called a strike. The union is demanding that the owners of the grape fields pay the workers more money and give them better worker benefits. The workers who belong to the union are threatening to attack any worker who tries to go to work while the strike is on.

Mr. Sanchez is not a member of the union. He wants very much to go to work next week. He has many bills to pay and needs money for food and clothing. The family simply cannot get by with the small amount of money that the union has promised to give Mr. Sanchez if he joins it and refuses to work next week. Mr. Sanchez also realizes that, if the grapes are not picked within the next two weeks, they will rot. He has heard that these strikes sometimes last for months. His boss told him that if he wants to go to work next Monday morning—the day the strike is to begin—he will protect him from the unionized workers. Mrs. Sanchez thinks that Mr. Sanchez should support the strike so that he can make higher wages in the future.

Questions

1. Do you think that Mr. Sanchez and his family will go to work in the fields next Monday? Why or why not?
2. If Mr. Sanchez does go to work, what do you think will happen to him and his family?
3. If Mr. Sanchez does not go to work in the grape fields next Monday, what do you think he might do to earn money?
4. What do you think Mr. Sanchez should do? Why?
5. What would you do if you were (a) Mr. Sanchez, (b) Mrs. Sanchez, (c) the children? Why?
6. Tell whether you agree or disagree with this statement and why: "The head of a family should never let his or her spouse and children do without the food and clothing they need."

High School Grades

Concept

Social protest

Generalization: Since the Anglo-American conquest of the Southwest, Mexican Americans have used a variety of means to resist oppression and discrimination. This resistance intensified and assumed new characteristics in the 1960s and 1970s.

1. The teacher can begin this unit by having the students read and dramatize the epic poem of the Chicano movement, *I Am Joaquin/Yo Soy Joaquin,* by Rodolfo Gonzales (1972). This poem is a powerful statement of the history and culture of Chicanos, with emphasis on their oppression and struggle for freedom. Among the many references made in the poem related to social protest are Father Miguel Hidalgo and *El Grito de Dolores* of 1810, Cinco de Mayo, the Treaty of Guadalupe Hidalgo, and the Anglo conquest of the Southwest in the 1800s. This poem will stimulate many questions students can pursue while studying Chicano resistance to oppression. The teacher may also want to show the film based on the poem *I Am Joaquin.*

2. References are frequently made to the Treaty of Guadalupe Hidalgo by Chicano leaders. After students have studied the events that led to the treaty, have them examine the treaty in detail and give their interpretations of it. They should compare their interpretations of the treaty with interpretations given by contemporary Chicano leaders. The complete text of the treaty is found in *A Documentary History of Mexican Americans* (Moquin, with Van Doren, 1972).

3. Ask a group of students to prepare and present to the class a dramatization portraying the positions and statements of early Mexican American militant leaders, such as Juan Patron, J. J. Herrerra, and Juan N. Cortina.

4. Some of the earliest Chicano resistance activities were unionization and strikes. Ask a group of students to prepare short reports on the various strikes and union activities during the period from 1900 to 1940. The strike in the California Imperial Valley in 1928 should be highlighted.

5. The earliest Mexican American civil rights organizations pursued what Cuellar (Moore, with Cuellar, 1970) has called a "politics of adaptation." Mexican American civil rights organizations became more politicized in the post–World War II period. Militant Chicano organizations emerged in the 1960s. Ask the students to research the goals, tactics, and strategies used by the following Mexican American civil rights groups. They will discover the trends described above.
   a. Order of the Sons of America (formed in 1921)
   b. League of United Latin-American Citizens (1929)
   c. Community Service Organization (1947)
   d. American G.I. Forum (1948)
   e. Federal Alliance of Free Cities (1963)
   f. Crusade for Justice (1965)

6. Ask the class to research the following questions: How was the Chicano movement similar to other Mexican American protest movements? How were its goals and strategies different? When did the movement emerge? What problems did it help to solve? What had happened to the movement by the late 1980s? Why? In what ways was the Chicano movement similar to, and different from, civil rights movements that emerged within other ethnic minority communities in the 1960s? What long-term effects do you think the Chicano movement has had and is having on U.S. society?

7. The union activity led by César Chávez during the 1960s and 1970s was an integral part of the Chicano movement. You may begin a study of these events by reading to the class the brilliant and poignant letter that Chávez wrote to E. L. Barr, Jr., president of the California Grape and Tree Fruit League, reprinted in Fusco and Horwitz (1970), *La Causa: The California Grape Strike.* The moving photographs in this book will evoke many questions and comments about the strike. The students can also read the excellently written book on the strike by John Gregory Dunne (1967), *Delano: The Story of the California Grape Strike.*

8. After the students have read and discussed accounts and interpretations of Mexican American resistance and the Chicano movement, ask them to write and present a dramatization on "Mexican American Resistance to Oppression in the United States, 1848 to the Present."

REFERENCES

Acuña, R. (1972). *Occupied America: The Chicano's Struggle toward Liberation.* San Francisco: Canfield Press.

Acuña, R. (2007). *Occupied America: A History of Chicanos* (6th ed.). New York: Harper and Row.

Banks, J. A., with Clegg, A. A., Jr. (1990). *Teaching Strategies for the Social Studies: Inquiry, Valuing, and Decision-Making* (4th ed.). White Plains, NY: Longman.

Bean, F. D., & Tienda, M. (1987). *The Hispanic Population of the United States.* New York: Russell Sage.

Crawford, J. (1989). *Bilingual Education: History, Politics, Theory, and Practice.* Trenton, NJ: Crane.

Dunne, J. G. (1967). *Delano: The Story of the California Grape Strike.* New York: Farrar, Straus & Giroux.

Encyclopaedia Britannica. (1995). *1995 Book of the Year.* Chicago: Author.

Franklin, J. H., & Moss, A. A., Jr. (2000). *From Slavery to Freedom: A History of Negro Americans* (8th ed.). New York: McGraw-Hill.

Fusco, P., & Horwitz, G. D. (1970). *La Causa: The California Grape Strike.* New York: Collier.

Gamio, M. (1971). *The Life Story of the Mexican Immigrant.* New York: Dover.

Gonzales, R. (1972). *I Am Joaquin/Yo Soy Joaquin.* New York: Bantam.

Gregory, S., & Sanjek, R. (Eds.). (1994). *Race.* New Brunswick, NJ: Rutgers University Press.

Immigration Sabotage (editorial). (2007, June 4). *New York Times,* p. A22.

Jiménez, A. (1994). The Spanish Colonial Model. In A. Jiménez (Ed.), *Handbook of Hispanic Cultures in the United States: History* (pp. 66–95). Houston: Arte Público/University of Houston.

Kanellos, N. (1994). *The Hispanic Almanac: From Columbus to Corporate America.* Detroit: Gale Research.

Latino Coalition. Facts about the Latino Community. Retrieved April 16, 2007, from http://www.thelatinocoalition.com/misc/Facts_About_The_Latino_Community.pdf.

McWilliams, C. (1968). *North from Mexico: The Spanish-Speaking People of the United States.* New York: Greenwood Press.

Meier, M. S., & Rivera, F. (1993). *Mexican Americans/American Mexicans: From Conquistadors to Chicanos.* New York: Hill & Wang.

Meier, M. S., & Rivera, F. (1972). *The Chicanos: A History of Mexican Americans.* New York: Hill and Wang.

Moore, J. W., with Cuellar, A. (1970). *Mexican Americans.* Englewood Cliffs, NJ: Prentice-Hall.

Moore, J. W., with Pachon, H. (1976). *Mexican-Americans* (2nd ed.). Englewood Cliffs, NJ: Prentice-Hall.

Moquin, W., & Van Doren, C. (Eds.). (1972). *A Documentary History of the Mexican Americans.* New York: Bantam.

Treaty of Guadalupe Hidalgo. In W. Moquin, with C. Van Doren (Eds.) (1971), *A Documentary History of Mexican Americans* (pp. 241–249). New York: Bantam.

U.S. Census Bureau. (1993). *We, the Foreign Born.* Washington, DC: U.S. Government Printing Office.

U.S. Census Bureau. (1994). *Statistical Abstract of the United States: 1994* (114th ed.). Washington, DC: U.S. Government Printing Office.

U.S. Census Bureau. (2000). *Statistical Abstract of the United States: 2000* (120th ed.). Washington, DC: U.S. Government Printing Office.

U.S. Census Bureau. (2001). Available online at http://www.census.gov.

U.S. Census Bureau. (2004). *Current Population Survey: Annual Social and Economic Supplement, 2003*, table 4.15: Foreign-Born Population from Latin America by Metropolitan-Nonmetropolitan Residence, Sex, and Sub-region of Birth, 2003. Washington, DC: Immigration Statistics Staff, Population Division.

U.S. Census Bureau. (2006). *Statistical Abstract of the United States, 2006*. Washington, DC: U.S. Government Printing Office.

U.S. Census Bureau. (2007). *The American Community—Hispanics, 2004: American Community Survey Reports*. Washington, DC: U.S. Department of Commerce, Economics and Statistics Administration.

U.S. Department of Homeland Security. (2006). *Yearbook of Immigration Statistics, 2005*. Washington, DC: Author, Office of Immigration Statistics.

Wilson, W. J. (1996). *When Work Disappears: The World of the New Urban Poor*. New York: Knopf.

ANNOTATED BIBLIOGRAPHY

Books for Teachers

Especially Recommended

Acuña, R. (2007). *Occupied America: A History of Chicanos* (6th ed.). Boston: Addison-Wesley Longman.
  The author presents the complex history of Mexican Americans from a variety of sources. The cultural, economic, and political strategies that Chicanos/as used to resist colonization are described by the author.

Alarcón, A. (2004). *The Border Patrol Ate My Dust*. Houston, TX: Arte Público Press.
  The author, a Los Angeles–based journalist, compiles testimonies of thirty undocumented immigrants from Mexico and Central America, giving silenced people a voice and revealing the courage and sacrifice of those who come to the United States for a better life.

Anzaldúa, G. (1999). *Borderlands/La Frontera: The New Mestiza* (2nd ed.). San Francisco: Aunt Lute Books.
  This classic title explores the cultural, psychological, sexual, and spiritual borderlands within the self using the U.S. Southwest–Mexican border as a starting point. Written from a Chicana feminist perspective, it has an introduction by scholar Sonia Saldívar-Hull and an interview with the late Gloria Anzaldúa.

Cisneros, S. (2002). *Caramelo*. New York: Knopf.
  The acclaimed author of *The House on Mango Street* (1984) returns with a kaleidoscopic novel that depicts a Mexican American family as its members travel from Mexico to various destinations in the United States. The teller of the story is Lala, the perceptive youngest child of seven, whose engaging voice invites the reader into the life of her family.

Coerver, D. M., Pasztor, S. B., & Buffington, R. M. (2004). *Mexico: An Encyclopedia of Contemporary Culture and History*. Santa Barbara, CA: ABC-CLIO.
  In a single volume, this valuable reference work offers an overview of Mexican history; articles on individuals, recent events, literature, art, music, religion, culture, politics, economics, and more; and separate entries for each of Mexico's states.

Cull, N. J., & Carrasco, D. (Eds.). (2004). *Alambrista and the U.S.-Mexico Border: Film, Music, and Stories of Undocumented Immigrants* (rev. ed.). Albuquerque: University of New Mexico Press.
  This book and DVD package explore the lives of undocumented migrant workers from Mexico, from the 1970s to the present.

Gonzales, M. G., & Gonzales, C. M. (Eds.). (2000). *En Aquel Entonces: Readings in Mexican-American History.* Bloomington: Indiana University Press.

This book offers an interdisciplinary overview of various aspects of Mexican American life experiences and is, at the same time, an introduction to Chicana/o historiography. An anthology of thirty-one journal articles, it represents the important works in Mexican American history from the 1960s to 2000.

Macias, T. (2006). *Mestizo in America: Generations of Mexican Identity in the Suburban Southwest.* Tucson: University of Arizona Press.

Data and discussion explore third- and fourth-generation Mexican Americans who have joined the middle class but experience cultural conflicts with White colleagues and struggle to pass on their culture to their children.

Meier, M., & Gutierrez, M. (2003). *The Mexican American Experience: An Encyclopedia.* Westport, CT: Greenwood.

This important single-volume encyclopedia gives readers an overview of Mexican and Mexican American history and information about significant individuals and aspects of culture. A brief guide to Mexican American slang is another useful feature.

Ortega, C. (2006). *The Eyes of the Weaver/Los ojos del tejedor.* Illustrated with photos by P. E. García. Albuquerque: University of New Mexico Press.

Adults and children alike will delight in this description of a young New Mexico girl being introduced to the art of weaving by her grandfather, the acclaimed weaver Juan Melquiades Ortega. Spanish words, the grandfather's stories, and photos of daily life in this close extended family add to the enchantment of this book.

Taylor, J. I., & Taggart, J. M. (2003). *Alex and the Hobo: A Chicano Life and Story.* Austin: University of Texas Press.

A collaboration between a Chicano social activist and a history professor, this unusual book contains an autobiographical story about a boy and his family trying to maintain their culture within mainstream American society, along with a more scholarly analysis of Mexican American family, community, and social structures.

Villaseñor, V. (2004). *Burro Genius.* New York: HarperCollins.

The acclaimed author of books for children and adults narrates his story of growing up in the United States as a boy of Mexican heritage, touching on discrimination, stereotypes, learning disabilities, and finding the strength to overcome all obstacles.

Other Books

Alcaraz, L. (2004). *Migra Mouse: Political Cartoons on Immigration by Lalo Alcaraz.* New York: Akashic Books.

The syndicated cartoonist offers a Mexican American perspective on the immigration issue as well as a sardonic portrait of immigrant life, especially in California.

Anaya, R. (2004). *Serafina's Stories.* Houston, TX: Arte Público Press.

From a master storyteller comes a collection of *cuentos* (short stories) that explore the Hispanic and indigenous roots of New Mexico.

Carroll, P. J. (2003). *Felix Longoria's Wake: Bereavement, Racism, and the Rise of Mexican American Activism.* Austin: University of Texas Press.

The author explores the death of World War II soldier Felix Longoria, the refusal of the Anglo elite to hold a ceremony for him when his remains were returned to Texas in 1949, and the civil rights struggle to give this war hero a dignified burial. Through the intervention of Senator Lyndon B. Johnson, Longoria was eventually buried in Arlington National Cemetery.

Castillo, D. A., & Tabuenca Cordoba, M. S. (2003). *Border Women: Writing from La Frontera.* Minneapolis: University of Minnesota Press.

Critical essays examine the works of Mexican and Mexican American women who write about living on the border, including Alicia Gaspar de Alba, Helena María Viramontes, and Demetria Martínez.

Dalton, F. J. (2003). *The Moral Vision of César Chávez.* Maryknoll, NY: Orbis Books.
The spiritual foundation of Chávez's nonviolent activism is the subject of this biography.

Davis, M. (2001). *Magical Urbanism: Latinos Reinvent the U.S. City.* New York: Verso.
This book examines the Latinization of the United States as well as the militarization and violence at the border crossings.

Deverell, W. (2004). *Whitewashed Adobe: The Rise of Los Angeles and the Remaking of Its Mexican Past.* Berkeley: University of California Press.
This well-written study explores conflicts between Anglos and Mexicans and how, from the mid-nineteenth century onward, Anglo elites misused, misrepresented, and disempowered the Mexican Americans of the Los Angeles basin.

Dohan, D. (2003). *The Price of Poverty: Money, Work, and Culture in the Mexican American Barrio.* Berkeley: University of California Press.
The impact of poverty and the social institutions created by residents in Mexican immigrant communities of San Jose and East Los Angeles, California, are the subjects of this socio-logical study that also addresses reverse migration, the underground economy, and attitudes toward public assistance.

Durand, J., & Massey, D. S. (2004). *Crossing the Border: Research from the Mexican Migration Project.* New York: Russell Sage Foundation.
The authors offer valuable quantitative data on Mexican migration to the United States, past and present.

Espinoza, A. (2006). *Still Water Saints.* New York: Random House.
The lives of characters in a Mexican American community in Los Angeles revolve around a *botánica* and its charismatic 72-year-old owner, Perla Portillo, in this richly textured debut novel.

García, N. (2004). *¡Chistes! Hispanic Humor of Northern New Mexico and Southern Colorado.* Santa Fe: Museum of New Mexico Press.
A collection of stories, practical jokes, pranks, hyperbole, and double entendres reveals the Hispanic culture of this region.

González, A. (2002). *Mexican Americans and the U.S. Economy: Quest for Buenos Dias.* Tucson: University of Arizona Press.
Written in layman's prose, this book by an economist explores the labor situation in Mexico and for Mexican immigrants to the United States, as well as the upward mobility experienced by the children of immigrants. He concludes that economic opportunities are real and Mexican Americans have achieved considerable success with each generation.

González, R. (2006). *Butterfly Boy.* Madison: University of Wisconsin Press.
The poet and essayist offers a coming-of-age story that depicts extreme poverty, strong family ties, his beloved mother's death when he was twelve, and his growing awareness of his homosexuality in a culture that abuses and endangers those who do not conform to the macho image.

Guilbault, R. C. (2006). *Farmworker's Daughter.* Berkeley, CA: Heyday Books.
This wonderfully detailed memoir recounts the author's journey from a bordertown child-hood in Nogales, Mexico, to award-winning journalist. After escaping an abusive marriage, the author's mother moves to California with her only daughter and marries a laborer; the three work in fields and canneries to survive and to send Rose to college.

Haney-López, I. F. (2003). *Racism on Trial: The Chicano Fight for Justice.* Cambridge, MA: Harvard University Press.

The trial of thirteen community leaders and college students from East Los Angeles, stemming from a 1968 protest, was a watershed moment in the Chicano civil rights movement, as depicted in this fascinating historical narrative.

Lagasse, M. H. (2004). *The Fifth Sun.* Willimantic, CT: Curbstone Press.
The story of three generations of women begins in Mexico, continues in New Orleans, and crosses the border multiple times, capturing the nature of Mexican migration as well as the often conflicting struggles of women to gain independence, support their families, and nurture their children.

León, L. D. (2004). *La Llorona's Children: Religion, Life, and Death in the U.S.-Mexico Borderlands.* Berkeley: University of California Press.
Borderland religion, as symbolized by La Llorona, the Weeping Woman endlessly searching for the children she drowned, is the subject of this study that examines traditional and modern religious expression among various Mexican American groups.

Martín-Rodríguez, M. M. (2003). *Life in Search of Readers: Reading (in) Chicano/a Literature.* Albuquerque: University of New Mexico Press.
Taking as its premise the hypothesis that Chicano/a literature is defined as much by readers as by the text, this study examines the readership of classic works from colonial times to the present. Other topics discussed include literature by women and recovery efforts of the past two decades.

Medina, L. (2004). *Las Hermanas: Chicana/Latina Religious-Political Activism in the U.S. Catholic Church.* Philadelphia: Temple University Press.
The author examines the history of Mexican American women's participation and social activism in the U.S. Catholic church, beginning with the founding of the feminist organization Las Hermanas in 1971.

Oakland Museum of California. (2005). *El Corazón de la Muerte: Altars and Offerings for Days of the Dead.* Berkeley, CA: Heyday Books.
More than a hundred color photographs illustrate aspects of this important Mexican holiday, as practiced by people in Mexico and those of Mexican heritage in the United States.

Ochoa, G. L. (2004). *Becoming Neighbors in a Mexican American Community: Power, Conflict, and Solidarity.* Austin: University of Texas Press.
The author examines encounters, conflicts, and alliances between recent immigrants from Mexico and Mexican Americans who have lived in the United States for several generations.

Pérez-Torres, R. (2006). *Mestizaje: Critical Uses of Race in Chicano Culture.* Minneapolis: University of Minnesota Press.
The role of race and mixed-race identity in Chicano culture is the subject of this analysis of literature, music, art, and film.

Perlmann, J. (2006). *Italians Then, Mexicans Now: Immigrant Origins and Second-Generation Progress, 1890–2000.* New York: Russell Sage Foundation.
A comparative study highlights immigration expectations, assimilation, family structure, economic status, and educational attainment among two different immigrant groups during two separate periods of U.S. history.

Ponce, M. H. (2006). *Hoyt Street.* Albuquerque: University of New Mexico Press.
This memoir describes the home and neighborhood outside of Los Angeles where Ponce grew up, capturing the indoor and outdoor spaces, the people, the stories, and the blend of Spanish and English that contributed to her love of place, characters, and words.

Rivas-Rodríguez, M. (Ed.). (2005). *Mexican Americans and World War II.* Austin: University of Texas Press.
This anthology addresses various aspects of Mexican American participation in the Second World War, from workers in war industries to those who fought with courage on the front lines.

Romo, D. D. (2005). *Ringside Seat to a Revolution: An Underground Cultural History of El Paso and Juarez, 1893–1923*. El Paso, TX: Cinco Puntos Press.

> The author explores the history of the Mexican Revolution, its precursors, and its aftermath through the lives of residents of two cities on either side of the border. Engaging writing and period photographs bring the stories to life.

Smith, R. C. (2006). *Mexican New York: Transnational Lives of New Immigrants*. Berkeley: University of California Press.

> The workings and impact of serial migration from a village in Mexico to New York City from the last third of the twentieth century to the present are the subject of this accessible scholarly study.

Trevino, R. R. (2006). *The Church in the Barrio: Mexican American Ethno-Catholicism in Houston*. Chapel Hill: University of North Carolina Press.

> The author chronicles the way in which Houston's Mexican American Catholics struggled against and eventually transformed the city's predominantly Anglo church hierarchy and practices.

Books for Students

Abraham, S. G., & Abraham, D. G. (2004). *Cecilia's Year*. El Paso, TX: Cinco Puntos Press.

> Two sisters offer a semibiographical tale of their mother's childhood on a small farm in Derry, New Mexico, in the 1930s. In her fifteenth year, Cecilia resists pressures to quit school and become a farmer's wife; she dreams instead of attending high school and moving to El Paso. Cecilia Gonzales Abraham's story continues through her adolescence to adulthood in *Surprising Cecilia* (Cinco Puntos Press, 2005). (Middle School/High School)

Alarcón, F. X. (2005). *Poems to Dream Together/Poemas para soñar juntos*. Illustrated by P. Barragán. New York: Lee and Low.

> Vibrant illustrations and short, vivid poems on topics that range from family and community to ecology and world peace to heroes such as César Chávez make this bilingual collection an ideal introduction to poetry for the youngest readers. (Primary)

Alegría, M. (2006). *Estrella's Quinceañera*. New York: Simon and Schuster.

> Estrella's Quinceañera party creates a challenge for a scholarship student at a snooty Catholic school, who wants to be friends with the popular Anglo girls, chafes against the rules laid down by her conservative parents, and is attracted to a funny and handsome boy from her *barrio*. (Middle/High School)

Anaya, R. (2004). *The Santero's Miracle*. Illustrated by A. Córdova. Albuquerque: University of New Mexico Press.

> The noted writer and storyteller offers an endearing bilingual Christmas tale set in the Sangre de Cristo Mountains of New Mexico. A ten-year-old boy visiting his grandfather experiences a violent winter snowstorm, and a miracle is needed to save the life of his grandfather's neighbor. (Intermediate and up)

Andrews-Goebel, N. (2002). *The Pot That Juan Built*. Illustrated by D. Díaz. New York: Lee and Low.

> Fascinating photographs and bold, stylized illustrations by an award-winning artist accompany this cumulative pattern book that describes the work of Juan Quezada, a famous Mexican potter. (All ages)

Bernier-Grant, C. T. (2005). *César: ¡Si, se Puede! Yes, We Can!* Tarrytown, NY: Marshall Cavendish.

> In a series of lyrical and inspiring free-verse poems, this book narrates the life of the labor leader, touching on his public and private life, his influence on others, and his values. David Díaz's stylized folk-art-based illustrations add to the emotional power of this unusual biography. This book received Pura Belpré Honor Awards for both writing and illustration. (Intermediate)

Bertrand, D. G. (2005). *Upside Down and Backwards/De cabeza y al revés*. Illustrated by P. R. Howard. Houston, TX: Piñata Books.
Four short stories presented in English and Spanish celebrate young people's unique bonds with family, friends, teachers, and the community as a whole. (Middle School)

Canales, V. (2005). *The Tequila Worm*. New York: Random House.
A girl devoted to her family and community in South Texas receives a scholarship from an exclusive boarding school and has to convince herself and her family that leaving home is the best move for her future. This book won the 2006 Pura Belpré Award for Writing. (Middle School)

Cohn, D. (2002). *Si, Se Puede! Janitor Strike in L.A.* Illustrated by F. Delgado. El Paso, TX: Cinco Puntos Press.
The 2000 janitors strike in Los Angeles is told in fiction, through the eyes of a boy whose mother joins the strike and becomes a leader. The book includes an informative classroom poster and is an excellent introduction to political activism and why people become involved. (Primary/Intermediate)

Cumpiano, I. (2005). *Quinito's Neighborhood/El vecindario de Quinito*. Illustrated by J. Ramirez. San Francisco: Children's Book Press.
A Mexican American boy guides young readers to his multiethnic neighborhood and the people who make it an exciting and comfortable place to live. (Primary)

de Anda, D. (2004). *Kikiriki/Quiquiriqui*. Illustrated by D. Lechón. Houston, TX: Piñata Books.
Sisters conspire to save a rooster that their grandfather has brought home for dinner in this humorous family tale in English and Spanish. (Primary)

Garza, X. (2005). *Lucha Libre: The Man in the Silver Mask*. Illustrated by the author. El Paso, TX: Cinco Puntos Press.
A Mexican American boy travels with his father to Mexico City to see *lucha libre* (a style of professional wrestling popular in Mexico); they are supposed to see the boy's uncle, who does not appear until after the end of the match, and for a very good reason. This bilingual story showcases the *lucha libre* illustrations of San Antonio–based artist Xavier Garza. (Intermediate)

Grande, R. (2006). *Across a Hundred Mountains*. New York: Atria Books.
A Mexican girl makes a harrowing journey into the United States in search of her father, who crossed the border years earlier and hasn't been heard from since. (High School)

Hayes, J. (2004). *Ghost Fever/Mal de fantasma*. El Paso, TX: Cinco Puntos Press.
The veteran storyteller, best known for his rendition of *La Llorona/The Weeping Woman* (Cinco Puntos Press, reprint edition, 2006), returns with a bilingual ghost novel set in Arizona in the 1950s. After her father loses his job and her mother abandons the family, ten-year-old Elena moves to a haunted house. There, she is tormented by a vision of a dead girl her age, and she turns to her beloved grandmother for help. (Intermediate)

Krull, K. (2003). *Harvesting Hope: The Story of César Chávez*. Illustrated by Y. Morales. San Diego: Harcourt.
This inspiring biography, a Pura Belpré Honor Title for Illustration, focuses on two periods of Chávez's life—his youth as a migrant worker and his first major victory as a labor organizer, the 300-mile walk from Delano, California, to Sacramento. (All ages)

López, L. (2006). *Call Me Henri*. Willimantic, CT: Curbstone Press.
A recent immigrant from Mexico living in a tough southern California neighborhood dreams of learning French rather than English, at the same time as he tries to hold his troubled family together and avoid the gangs that target him after he witnesses a drive-by shooting. (Middle School)

Marsden, C. (2003). *Mama Had to Work on Christmas*. Illustrated by R. Casilla. New York: Viking.

A nine-year-old girl is disappointed that her father, a migrant worker, and her mother, a hotel housekeeper, have to work on Christmas Day; on top of that, she experiences the disdain of a wealthy girl in the hotel restaurant. A trip to her grandmother's house in Mexico after work that evening helps the girl to see that a close family is more important than money. (Intermediate)

Medina, J. (2004). *The Dream on Blanca's Wall/El sueño pegado en la pared de Blanca*. Illustrated by R. Casilla. Honesdale, PA: Boyds Mills Press.
The author captures the immigration experience in a series of moving poems, accompanied by subtle charcoal drawings. (Intermediate)

Mora, P. (2005). *Doña Flor: A Tall Tale About a Giant Woman with a Great Big Heart*. Illustrated by R. Colón. New York: Knopf.
This tale set in the southwestern United States portrays a generous giant woman who protects the people of her village but is almost bested by a small puma. Raúl Colón's illustrations for this delightful folk story won the 2006 Pura Belpré Award for Illustration. (Primary)

Morales, Y. (2003). *Just a Minute: A Trickster Tale and Counting Book*. Illustrated by the author. San Francisco: Chronicle Books.
Winner of the 2004 Pura Belpré Award for Illustration, this original tale about a grandmother who delays a skeleton asking her to "come along" draws from traditional Mexican folkloric elements related to the Day of the Dead. (Primary)

Pérez, A. I. (2002). *My Diary from Here to There/Mi diario de aquí hasta allá*. Illustrated by M. C. González. San Francisco: Children's Book Press.
In poetic language in English and Spanish, a young girl describes her sadness on leaving her Mexican village, her journey across the border, and her impressions of life in the United States, where she has come to be reunited with her father. (Primary/Intermediate)

Pérez, A. I. (2007). *Nana's Big Surprise/Nana ¡Qué Sorpresa!* Illustrated by M. C. González. San Francisco: Children's Book Press.
After Tata (grandfather) dies, Nana comes from Mexico to stay with a young boy's family. The boy's father builds a chicken coop, and in raising chickens with her grandchildren, Nana works through her grief and teaches the children about their culture. (Primary)

Pérez, L. K. (2002). *First Day in Grapes*. Illustrated by R. Casilla. New York: Lee and Low.
Despite some plot elements that do not ring true, this beautifully illustrated picture book depicts the disruption and uncertainty of migrant children who have to start over at a new school each time their parents relocate to harvest a new crop. (Primary)

Reich, S. (2005). *José! Born to Dance: The Story of José Limón*. Illustrated by R. Colon. New York: Simon and Schuster.
Reich focuses on the childhood of the Mexican-born choreographer, who struggled to learn English and find friends in his new land, helped to support his family when his mother died, and discovered his life's passion as a young adult. (Primary/Intermediate)

Rodríguez, A. (2006). *The King of Things/El rey de las cosas*. Illustrated by the author. El Paso, TX: Cinco Puntos Press.
The Mexican game of *lotería* is the subject of this engaging bilingual book created by a well-known woodcut artist based in Los Angeles. (Primary)

Ryan, P. M. (2004). *Becoming Naomi León*. New York: Scholastic.
The award-winning author of *Esperanza Rising* (Scholastic, 2000) returns with the story of a shy, unpopular preteen, the daughter of a Mexican father and an Anglo mother, whose journey with her younger brother to find their father in Mexico also helps her to discover who she is. (Intermediate/Middle School)

Saénz, B. A. (2004). *Sammy and Juliana in Hollywood*. El Paso, TX: Cinco Puntos Press.

This compelling coming-of-age story portrays a teenager in a poor *barrio* of Las Cruces, New Mexico, in the late 1960s, when he and his friends have to navigate family violence, prejudice at school, drugs, and the draft for the Vietnam War. (High School)

Serros, M. M. (2006). *Honey Blonde Chicas*. New York: Putnam.

An example of the popular "chick-lit" genre, but with Latina characters and frequent code-switching, this light-hearted novel presents fast-living upper-class California high school girls in a rivalry with more recent (upscale) arrivals from Mexico. (High School)

Soto, G. (2000). *Mercy on These Teenage Chimps*. San Diego: Harcourt.

The groundbreaking, award-winning author captures the insecurities and cataclysmic changes of early adolescence in this heartwarming story about friendship and first love among a group of suburban Mexican American teens. *Accidental Love* (Harcourt, 2006) explores similar themes, with more emphasis on romance. (Middle School/High School)

Stork, F. X. (2006). *Behind the Eyes*. New York: Dutton.

Sent to a juvenile detention center after trying to avenge his brother's killing, a teenager's toughness is tested and he learns to break the cycle of violence that has afflicted his family. (Middle School/High School)

Torres, E., & Sawyer, T. L. (Eds.) (2005). *Stories of Mexico's Independence Days and Other Bilingual Children's Fables*. Albuquerque: University of New Mexico Press.

Fables, presented in English and Spanish, embody values passed from Mexican grandparents and parents to their children. (Intermediate and up)

Villareal, R. (2006). *My Father, the Angel of Death*. Houston, TX: Piñata Books.

The teenage son of a famous Mexican American professional wrestler must deal with frequent moves, his father's hectic travel schedule, and classmates whose adulation of his father makes him wonder if he has any real friends. (Middle School)

CHAPTER ELEVEN

PUERTO RICANS IN THE UNITED STATES

Concepts, Strategies, and Materials

Colonialism has always played an important role in the Puerto Rican experience. Puerto Rico and the United States are connected through colonial ties, and this gives the [Puerto Rican] migration a unique character.

—Sonia Nieto

Puerto Ricans are the second largest Hispanic group in the United States. Their 2005 population (3,781,317) made up 9% of the total population of documented Hispanics living in the United States (U.S. Census Bureau, 2007a). The Puerto Rican population increased 40% between 1990 and 2005, from 2.7 million to nearly 3.8 million (U.S. Census Bureau, 2007a). This rate of growth was considerably greater than the rate of increase for the total U.S. population and for Whites but below the rate of growth for the total Hispanic population (87%). The 40% population increase experienced by Puerto Ricans between 1990 and 2005 was due primarily to a high birthrate rather than to migration. Puerto Rican migration to the United States peaked in 1953, with about 75,000 net arrivals. Since that time, net migration between Puerto Rico and the United States has ebbed and flowed with economic conditions in the two nations (Rodriguez, 1991; Van Middeldyk, 2006).

Santiago-Valles and Jiménez-Muñoz (2004) describe three components of migration between the United States and Puerto Rico. The first component, "the cyclical migration of semi- and lower-skilled labor from the island to the United States and back to the island again" (p. 120), makes up the bulk of migration between the island and the United States. The second component is highly skilled individuals, primarily Anglo-Americans and Cubans, who migrate from the United States and other parts of the world to Puerto Rico. The third component is highly skilled individuals who migrate from Puerto Rico to the United States, which creates a "brain drain" from the island. In 1983, 80% of the graduates of prestigious engineering schools migrated to the United States. Puerto Rican teachers and hospital workers were recruited by school districts and hospitals in significant numbers during the 1990s (Santiago-Valles & Jiménez-Muñoz, 2004).

The Puerto Rican population on the U.S. mainland is growing faster than the population in Puerto Rico. In 2005, Puerto Rico's population was nearly 3.9 million (Population Reference Bureau, 2007), compared to a U.S. Puerto Rican population of nearly 3.8 million. The island's population increased just over 11% between 1990 and 2005, whereas the U.S. Puerto Rican population increased about 40% (U.S. Census Bureau, 2007b). Not all of the people who lived on the island, however, were of Puerto Rican descent. Puerto Rico has a sizable immigrant population, including many Cubans. Some population experts predict that if the current disproportionate rate of population growth on the island and the mainland continues, the number of Puerto Ricans on the U.S. mainland will soon exceed the number on the island.

Content about Puerto Ricans should be included in the mainstream curriculum because they are an integral part of U.S. society. Knowledge of their experiences on the mainland can help students master important social science concepts, such as *migration, cultural diversity, racism,* and *colonialism.*

When studying about Puerto Ricans on the U.S. mainland, students can compare and contrast their experiences with those of other migrant and immigrant groups. In some ways, Puerto Rican migration is similar to the movement of other groups to the United States. Puerto Ricans are culturally uprooted, like European immigrants were when they migrated to the United States. However, their migration is also unique in U.S. history in several ways. When large numbers of Puerto Ricans began to migrate to the U.S. mainland, automation had greatly decreased the need for manual labor in the United States. Unlike other groups, Puerto Ricans are U.S. citizens when they set foot on U.S. soil. Their migration is the first "airborne migration" in U.S. history. Puerto Ricans bring racial attitudes to the United States that are considerably different from those they find here. The study of the complex nature of the Puerto Rican migration and experience on the U.S. mainland provides students with excellent opportunities to formulate generalizations that are essential components of a sound multicultural curriculum.

THE ISLAND BACKGROUND

Puerto Rico

Puerto Rico, called San Juan Baptista by Christopher Columbus, is a beautiful, small tropical island in the Caribbean Sea. The island, which sits on the top of a large underwater mountain, is smaller than the state of Connecticut. It is about 35 miles wide, 100 miles long, and its total area is slightly more than 3,400 square miles. Puerto Rico, which has become one of the favorite vacation places for U.S. tourists, has one of the highest population densities in the world, 1,137 persons per square mile in 2006. Almost four million (3.9 million) people lived on this attractive island in 2006 (Population Reference Bureau, 2007).

Puerto Rico's history is just as interesting as its terrain and demography. During the last four centuries, its fate has been determined by two faraway nations that ruled it the way absentee landlords govern a slum. Spain ruled the country from the sixteenth century up to the Spanish-American War in 1898, when the United States took control. It governed Puerto Rico awkwardly and ambiguously. Although the Commonwealth of Puerto Rico has existed since July 1952, Puerto Rico's relationship with the United States is still shaky and unclear (Trías Monge, 1997). Puerto Rico, which is neither a state nor an independent nation, continues to suffer from the burden of colonialism, and its ambiguous colonialist status is likely to continue for some years to come, especially as cries for independence keep emerging in Puerto Rico, even if they are voiced only by a determined, forceful few.

In a plebiscite—a vote by the electorate to make a decision on an important issue—held in 1993, Puerto Rico's current commonwealth status won by only a slim margin. In a plebiscite held on December 13, 1998, the citizens voted as follows on the five choices: (1) territorial commonwealth (0.1%), (2) free association (0.3%), (3) statehood (46.5%), (4) independence (2.5%), and (5) none of the above (50.3%). More voters chose none of the above than the other options, with statehood receiving the next largest percentage of votes (Elections in Puerto Rico, 2007).

Since 1917, Puerto Ricans have been U.S. citizens. In the period between the two world wars, they started migrating to the mainland in large numbers, mainly to New York City. In 1990, about 39% of all Puerto Ricans lived on the U.S. mainland. About half of the mainland Puerto Ricans were born in the United States. The number of Puerto Ricans on the U.S. mainland is significant and increases at every census count, growing from 900,000 in 1960 to 3.8 million in 2005.

PUERTO RICANS IN THE UNITED STATES: HISTORICAL PERSPECTIVE

Important Dates	Events
1493	Columbus landed on the island of Boriquén, November 19, 1493. Boriquén was the home of the Taíno (or Arawak) Indians, the native inhabitants of Puerto Rico.
1508	Juan Ponce de León became the governor of Puerto Rico.
1511	The Taíno Indians unsuccessfully rebelled against the Spanish system of forced labor.
1513	African slaves were introduced on Puerto Rican plantations.
1868	El Grito De Lares, a group of Puerto Rican revolutionaries, called for independence and planned an unsuccessful revolt.
1873	Slavery was abolished in Puerto Rico.

Important Dates	Events
1898	Spain ceded Puerto Rico to the United States under the terms of the Treaty of Paris, the treaty that formally ended the Spanish-American War.
1900	Under the terms of the Foraker Act, the United States established a government in Puerto Rico, to which the president of the United States appointed the governor and the Executive Council. The House of Delegates and the resident commissioner were to be elected by popular vote.
1910	The U.S. Census indicated that there were 1,513 native Puerto Ricans living in the United States.
1917	The Jones Act was passed by the U.S. Congress. It made Puerto Ricans U.S. citizens and subject to the U.S. draft. The act also provided for the popular election of both houses of the Puerto Rican legislature.
1920	11,811 persons born in Puerto Rico were living in the United States. That number increased to 58,200 in 1935.
1937	Twenty people were killed in a tragedy known as the "Ponce Massacre" on Palm Sunday.
1947	The U.S. Congress amended the Jones Act of 1917. Puerto Ricans were granted the right to elect their own governor. The governor was given the right to make most of the appointments for high public offices.
1948	Luis Muñoz Marin became the first elected governor of Puerto Rico. He was governor of Puerto Rico until 1964.
1952	On July 25, Governor Luis Muñoz Marin led the inaugural ceremonies establishing the Commonwealth of Puerto Rico, or the Associated Free State.
1961	ASPIRA of America (now the ASPIRA Association, Inc.) was founded.
1965	With the passage of the Civil Rights Act of 1965, Puerto Ricans in the United States were no longer required to pass an English literacy test to vote in the state of New York.
1967	In a plebiscite, Puerto Ricans voted to maintain the commonwealth status. Statehood and independence were the second and third choices, respectively.
1970	Herman Badillo was elected to the U.S. House of Representatives. He was the first mainland Puerto Rican elected to Congress.
1971	Cuban representatives to the United Nations proposed a resolution to have U.S. colonialism in Puerto Rico debated during a meeting of the United Nations Trusteeship Council.
1972	The United Nations Decolonization Committee declared that Puerto Rico is a colony of the United States.
1974	The legal case *ASPIRA of New York, Inc. et al.* v. *Board of Education of the City of New York, Inc. et al.* ended when the two parties reached an agreement, legally termed a "consent decree." The Board of Education agreed to provide bilingual instruction for Puerto Rican students.

Important Dates	Events
1992	The New Progressive Party, which supports statehood, won the governorship.
1998	In a plebiscite, more voters chose "none of the above" than the other options, with statehood receiving the next largest percentage of votes.
2003	Responding to the pressure from the people living on Vieques Island, the U.S. Navy left the island in May 2003, ending sixty years of using it to conduct tests.

The Taino Indians

Puerto Ricans have three major racial heritages—Indian, African, and Spanish. The island was inhabited by a group of Indians called the Tainos when the Spanish arrived in the fifteenth century. Because they left no written records, little is known about the Tainos except what archaeologists have been able to detect from potsherds and skulls (Rouse, 1992). Some social scientists believe that there were about 40,000 Tainos on the island when the Spanish arrived and that they had straight black hair and copper-colored skin (Babin, 1971). Their culture was based on farming, hunting, and raising animals. Religion was also an important part of the Taino culture. The Spaniards caught the Indians by surprise and totally without the kinds of weapons they needed to fight men who fought with swords (Wagenheim, 1975).

The Coming of the Spaniards

In search of a new route to India, Columbus arrived in the Americas in 1492. When he came back to the Americas in 1493, he landed on the island of Boriquen, home of the Taino Indians. Columbus's arrival on the island foreshadowed the Spanish takeover. When Juan Ponce de Leon was made governor of the island in 1508, the Spanish occupation of Puerto Rico was well under way. From the time of the arrival of the Spanish conquistadors, life for the native Indians became increasingly more difficult. Eventually, they were almost totally exterminated. The Spanish set up a kind of forced labor, known as the *encomienda* system. Under this system, each Spanish colonizer was given a group of Indians to work for him. The Spanish colonizer was supposed to "teach" the Indians Spanish "culture" in return for their work.

At first, the Indians did not fight back. They thought the Spaniards were immortal. Eventually, a group of Taino Indians decided to find out if the Spanish were actually immortal. They tried to drown a young Spaniard and succeeded. Once they discovered that the Spaniards died like other men, they started fighting back. A number of Indian rebellions occurred in various parts of the island and many

Spaniards were killed in these skirmishes. The Tainos also ran away from the Spanish settlements. The conquistadors searched for them, often with little success. So many Indians were killed by the Spaniards and their diseases, and so many escaped from the island, that by 1777 they had all but disappeared from Puerto Rico.

Spanish Rule

By the late nineteenth century, Puerto Rico was one of the most neglected colonies in the Western Hemisphere. For nearly 400 years, Spain had ruled the colony from across the Atlantic like an absentee landlord and had woefully neglected it. Puerto Rico's last series of Spanish governors were incompetent and autocratic. They ineptly governed the island with an oppressive, heavy hand. When Spain and the United States entered the Spanish-American War in 1898, Spain's 400-year neglect of her small Caribbean colony was painfully visible. The masses of the people were peons, and the country's wealth was concentrated in the hands of the small upper class. No middle class existed, most of the people were illiterate, and 92% of the children were not in school. Contagious diseases were widespread, and public health facilities were almost totally absent. Nearly 80% of the draftable Puerto Rican males failed the physical test given by the U.S. military during World War I.

Spain's neglect and mistreatment of Puerto Rico had led to an aggressive movement for home rule by the 1800s. In 1868, the famous Lares Revolt occurred. A group of independence advocates took the city of Lares and proclaimed it the "Republic of Puerto Rico." The revolt failed, but the agitation for home rule continued, even though it was often sporadic and poorly organized. Eventually, the movement bore fruit. On November 28, 1897, Puerto Rico was granted autonomy by Spain. This proved to be one of the shortest and most meaningless political changes in history. Barely before the new Puerto Rican government could begin to function, U.S. troops landed on the island.

The Spanish-American War

Spain declared war on the United States on April 24, 1898. A truce was signed on August 12 of that same year. Spain was a pushover for the United States. The two nations formally ended the war with the Treaty of Paris, signed on December 10, 1898. At the meeting, the United States reigned supreme. Spain ceded the Philippines and Puerto Rico to the United States and gave up rights to Cuba. The United States also acquired American Guam.

As had been the case for 400 years, nobody asked Puerto Rico about its political future. Its fate was determined by the United States and Spain. After the meeting, Puerto Rico lost the little autonomy that Spain had granted it in 1897 and became a United States possession. Puerto Rican independence leaders were shocked and dismayed. They had thought that their neighbor from the North had come to free them from colonialism. It was a rude awakening to discover that the United States, the "citadel of freedom and democracy," would also subjugate Puerto Rico just as Spain had done.

UNITED STATES RULE

When the U.S. government took control of Puerto Rico in 1898, it had little experience in governing colonies. In fact, "self-determination of nations" had been one of the main ideas voiced by the U.S. government. However, with the emergence of the doctrine of Manifest Destiny, the United States began to go after foreign lands rather aggressively. It acquired nearly one-third of Mexico's territory in 1848 and increasingly saw how important Caribbean possessions would be, both financially and militarily. When the United States entered the Spanish-American War, it hoped to acquire a toehold in the Caribbean Sea. By defeating Spain and gaining Puerto Rico, the U.S. government was better able to make claims to supremacy in the Western Hemisphere and show the world that it was a powerful military force.

The U.S. relationship with Puerto Rico was awkward and ambiguous during the first two years of U.S. rule. Military governors from the United States ran the island. This type of government did not prove satisfactory. Congress attempted to establish a more workable relationship with Puerto Rico in 1900. That year it passed the Foraker Act. Under the terms of this act, Puerto Rico became "the People of Puerto Rico." Puerto Ricans were not U.S. citizens nor was the nation independent. The governor and the Executive Council (the upper house) were to be appointed by the president of the United States. The House of Delegates (the lower house) and the resident commissioner were to be chosen by popular election. The resident commissioner's job was to present the island's views on issues in the U.S. House of Representatives, although he would be unable to vote. Any action taken by the elected House of Delegates could be vetoed by the U.S. Congress. The Circuit Court of Boston was named the high court for the island. Puerto Rican leaders were shocked by this arrangement, which they interpreted as a slap in the face. They had hoped that when the United States took over the island, its people would be able to decide their own political destiny with a plebiscite. The Foraker Act shattered their hopes.

The Struggle for Self-Governance

Cries for independence were heard throughout Puerto Rico during the sixteen years that the Foraker Act was in effect. Anti-U.S. feelings continued to grow and spread on the island. The island's factional parties shared the belief that Puerto Rico had been betrayed by the United States. As anti-American feelings escalated, the president and Congress decided that action had to be taken. The then-resident commissioner in Washington, Muñoz Rivera, wanted to poll Puerto Rico's citizens to determine what they felt should be the political status of the island, but Muñoz's arguments were ignored. Instead, Congress decided to deal with the problem by making Puerto Ricans U.S. citizens with the Jones Act in 1917. This act only further alienated the Puerto Ricans, who wanted self-governance on the island. The act not only "forced" citizenship on Puerto Ricans, but it also made them obligated to serve in the U.S. Armed Forces. Many Puerto Ricans resented the forced U.S. citizenship and the fact that they had no voice in the matter. They could resist U.S. citizenship, but resistance meant that they would lose many benefits and become aliens within their homeland. Because of the Jones Act, 140,000 Puerto Ricans fought in World War I.

The Nationalist Party

The Nationalist Party, the radical party that strongly advocated the independence of Puerto Rico, emerged out of the forces that opposed how the United States was handling Puerto Rico's affairs. The party leaders felt, with some justification, that the major Puerto Rican parties were too sympathetic to U.S. interests and that party members could not deal with the United States effectively by using traditional means such as the ballot and appealing to the U.S. conscience. Pedro Albizu Campos emerged as the militant leader of the party. A graduate of Harvard, Albizu knew U.S. politics well. The party became a target of the Puerto Rican and U.S. governments, who considered it extreme and dangerous.

At a parade sponsored by the Nationalist Party on Palm Sunday, March 21, 1937, a shot fired into a crowd resulted in a massacre in the streets of Ponce. When the Nationalists' initial request for a parade permit to march in San Juan was denied, they decided to move the parade to Ponce. The mayor of Ponce granted the parade request because the Nationalists agreed to keep the march peaceful. Despite a last-minute attempt by Governor Blanton Winship to prevent the parade, the Nationalists marched. The marchers did not carry arms, but the police were heavily armed. In the ruckus that occurred after the shot was fired, 20 people lost their lives and more than 100 were wounded. A inquiry by the Brookings Institution revealed that the police instigated the gunfire and were excessively brutal (Nieto, 1995). This infamous event in Puerto Rican history is known as the "Ponce Massacre." It symbolizes the independence struggle in Puerto Rico.

Luis Muñoz Marin: Governor of Puerto Rico, 1948–1964

Between 1900 and 1946, Puerto Rico was headed by a series of fifteen U.S. governors appointed by the president of the United States. With only a few exceptions, they were unimpressive men and differed little from the Spaniards who had ruled Puerto Rico prior to 1898. Medical, educational, and economic conditions on the island reflected poor leadership. By 1940, conditions in Puerto Rico were not substantially different from conditions in 1898. Persistent expressions of dissatisfaction with the governors by Puerto Rican leaders led the United States to grant Puerto Rico the opportunity to elect its own governor in 1947. In 1948, Luis Muñoz Marin was elected governor of Puerto Rico. He was the first elected governor in Puerto Rico's history.

THE COMMONWEALTH OF PUERTO RICO

Muñoz was destined to change decisively the course of Puerto Rican history. More changes occurred in Puerto Rico during his sixteen years as governor than had taken place during the previous four centuries of Spanish rule. Without question, Muñoz's influence on the island was unprecedented. Like any political leader who gets things done and shapes history, he was a charismatic and controversial figure.

Once in office, Muñoz took a position on the polemical status question. He favored what later became known as the Commonwealth, or the *Estado Libre Asociado* (Free Associated State). With this status, Puerto Rico would maintain a tie with the United States but would have a degree of governmental autonomy. Muñoz fought hard to make the Commonwealth a reality. The people approved it in a plebiscite on June 4, 1951. Muñoz led an inauguration ceremony for the Commonwealth of Puerto Rico on July 25, 1952.

The Commonwealth did not solve the status question, and the controversy continued. Both statehood and independence advocates opposed the new status. Many people refused to go to the polls, claiming that the plebiscite was a hoax because the voters were presented with only two choices. They had to vote either to maintain the status quo or to initiate the proposed Commonwealth. Thus, the meaning of the plebiscite was bitterly debated. To this day, the status question is still one of the hottest political issues on the island and tends to dominate and overshadow other issues (Trías Monge, 1997).

Urbanization and Operation Bootstrap

Muñoz also set Puerto Rico on a new economic course. He felt that income from the island's three main cash crops—sugar, tobacco, and coffee—was inadequate to support Puerto Rico. Muñoz wanted to industrialize the island by luring U.S. manufacturers to set up plants in Puerto Rico. He formed "Operation Bootstrap" to attract U.S. industry to Puerto Rico. He offered generous benefits, such as lower wages and tax exemptions for up to ten years. Many U.S. companies established plants in Puerto Rico under this program. Like most changes that Muñoz implemented, the program was both successful and controversial. The changes that Operation Bootstrap stimulated in Puerto Rico were truly amazing. By 1971, the program had recruited 2,000 plants and millions of dollars in investments. Income from manufacturing was more than three times that from agriculture, although agriculture was still important in the island's economy. The island's per capita income jumped from $188 a year in 1940 to $1,234 a year in 1969.

The Operation Bootstrap reforms and modernization of Puerto Rico that occurred during the 1940s, 1950s, and 1960s were mixed blessings. Urbanization brought the usual problems in housing and created a new poverty class—the urban poor. Although Operation Bootstrap was designed to help solve the problem of unemployment, it actually increased it. Industrialization displaced small farmers, who migrated to the cities and became unemployed. Many Puerto Ricans left the island and migrated to the U.S. mainland to look for work. Migration from the island to the United States peaked during the 1950s, a time when Operation Bootstrap was booming.

The Puerto Rican economy remains precarious. The island has a high level of unemployment. Even when Operation Bootstrap was booming, the large numbers of Puerto Ricans who migrated to the United States each year helped maintain a healthy economy on the island. Urbanization has pulled many families looking for work to the cities and has created city slums, housing congestion, and other problems associated with urban growth. The percentage of persons living below the poverty level in Puerto Rico is considerably above the percentage for Puerto Ricans on the U.S. mainland. In 2005, the U.S. Census Bureau estimated that 13.3% of all people on the U.S. mainland were living in poverty, compared to 44.9% of all people in the Commonwealth of Puerto Rico. On the U.S. mainland in 2005, the poverty rate for non-Hispanic Whites was 9.0%, 25.6% for African Americans, and 22.4% for Hispanics. The poverty rates for children are even more alarming. In 2005, 18.5% of children (under the age of 18) on the U.S. mainland were living in poverty, compared to 54.7% of children in the Commonwealth of Puerto Rico. On the U.S. mainland in 2005, the poverty rate for non-Hispanic White children was 10.8%, 36% for African American children, and 29.1% for Hispanic children (U.S. Census Bureau, 2007a,b).

Although urbanization created a middle class in Puerto Rico and bedroom suburban communities, Muñoz's critics correctly note that Operation Bootstrap brought the greatest benefits to the upper class and to U.S. industrialists. U.S. companies take the bulk of the money they earn on the island back to the United States. Many of them are now deserting Puerto Rico for nations in Asia where they can find cheaper labor. Urbanization in Puerto Rico, like so many other developments, has done little to change the living conditions of the poor, except perhaps to show them how to live in a poor urban rather than a poor rural style. Despite the mixed blessings of the Muñoz reforms, his sixteen-year reign made a tremendous difference in Puerto Rico's present and future.

Controversy on Vieques Island

The U.S. Navy conducted land, sea, and air exercises on Vieques Island in Puerto Rico in the late 1990s and in 2001. When a security guard was accidentally killed in one of the navy's exercises in 1999, many residents on the island became angry and were reminded of what they interpret as Puerto Rico's colonial relationship with the United States. In a local and non–legally binding referendum on the island on July 29, 2001, 68% of the residents of Vieques Island favored an immediate end to the exercises. Civil rights advocates on both the island and the mainland and many members of the Hispanic Congressional Caucus, as well as Governor Calderon of Puerto Rico, publicly opposed the exercises and said they should be ended.

Responding to the protests against the exercises and public pressure, President George W. Bush agreed to withdraw the navy from Vieques Island in May 2003. However, the September 11, 2001, tragedies that occurred at the World Trade Center in New York City and at the Pentagon in Washington, D.C., were used by some supporters of the exercises to bolster their argument. Grayson (2001) wrote on the editorial page of the *Wall Street Journal:* "With America at war, the future of Vieques must be considered. Congress should act immediately to spike the Nov. 6 referendum and quash plans to boot the Navy in 2003" (p. A15). The controversy on Vieques Island opened deep wounds about the status of Puerto Rico with the United States. Responding to the pressure from the people living on Vieques Island, the U.S. Navy left the island in May 2003, ending sixty years of using it to conduct tests (Vieques Island, 2007).

LIFE ON THE MAINLAND

The Migration

After the United States gained control of Puerto Rico, the stage was set for the mass movement of islanders to the U.S. mainland. A few Puerto Ricans, such as cigarmakers and merchant seamen, had settled in New York before the 1920s, but Puerto Ricans did not begin to migrate to the United States in significant numbers until the 1920s and 1930s. When Mills, Senior, and Goldsen (1967) published their pioneering study in 1950, most Puerto Ricans in New York City had come during the years between the two world wars. The number of Puerto Ricans migrating to the United States decreased considerably during World War II because of the closing of transportation routes between New York and Puerto Rico.

After the war, the number of Puerto Ricans migrating to the United States increased. In 1945, only 22,737 Puerto Ricans came to the United States, but that number increased to 101,115 in 1947. Puerto Rican migration to the United States has always reflected economic trends. A significant number of migrants usually return to the island when the mainland economy is depressed. During the Great Depression of the 1930s, the net migration back to the island reached 8,694 people in a four-year period (Mills, Senior, & Goldsen, 1967). *Net migration* is the difference between the number of Puerto Ricans who enter the United States and the number who leave within a specific time period. It can be a positive (+) or a negative (–) figure. When the U.S. economy is booming, Puerto Rican migration usually increases and return migration decreases considerably.

Rodriguez (1991) describes three major periods of Puerto Rican migration to and from the U.S. mainland. The first significant number of migrants arrived between 1900 and 1945. Most of these migrants settled in New York City. The second period of migration took place between 1946 and 1964. During this period, the largest number of migrants from Puerto Rico settled on the U.S. mainland. Rodriguez (1991) calls the third period of Puerto Rican migration, from 1965 to the present, "the revolving-door migration." During this period, migration to the mainland has varied with economic developments on the island and the mainland. Migrants have also dispersed to other regions in the United States, such as New Jersey, Illinois, and California.

The lack of legal barriers is a major factor in Puerto Rican migration to and from the U.S. mainland. The Jones Act of 1917 made Puerto Ricans U.S. citizens. As U.S. citizens, they can move freely from the island to the mainland and within various parts of the United States. Their migration to the United States is not limited by restrictive quotas, as is the case in Mexico and in the various Asian nations. Many Puerto Ricans take advantage of their freedom of movement to migrate to the United States. Although the movement of Puerto Ricans to the mainland has many of the sociological characteristics of an immigration, Puerto Ricans are technically migrants rather than immigrants because they are citizens of the United States.

Easy and inexpensive transportation to the mainland also facilitates Puerto Rican migration. In the 1930s, Puerto Ricans could make a boat trip from San Juan to New York City in the relatively short period of three and a half days and for as low as $40 (Chenault, 1938). After World War II, plane transportation from the island became more available and inexpensive. During this period, a migrant could fly from San Juan to New York City for as low as $35 (Mills, Senior, & Goldsen, 1967). Today, transportation from the island is more convenient and still inexpensive. Whereas the flight from San Juan to New York City took eight bumpy hours in the 1940s, the trip could be made as quickly as three hours and for as low as $140 in 2007. Convenient and inexpensive transportation has not only stimulated migration from the island to the mainland but has also helped make Puerto Ricans transients between the island and the United States. Many Puerto Ricans in New York return to the island to visit relatives, to vacation, or to take care of business for short periods.

The "Americanization" of Puerto Rico since 1898 and economic factors have played major roles in motivating Puerto Ricans to migrate to the United States. Since Puerto Rico became an American colony, U.S. culture and institutions have greatly influenced Puerto Rican culture and lifestyles. Americans forced the teaching of English in Puerto Rican schools for years and introduced textbooks that venerated George Washington and Abraham Lincoln rather than Puerto Rican leaders (Negron de Montilla, 1975). These books also described the United States as the neighbor in the North in which "democracy and freedom" flourished. American stores such as J. C. Penney and Sears dot the streets in San Juan as they do in Chicago.

During the period of high migration to the U.S. mainland in the 1950s, many Puerto Ricans who returned to the island told their relatives and friends about the "great" new life in New York City. The availability of jobs in New York City during periods of intensive migration and the higher pay Puerto Ricans could earn in New York, compared to San Juan, lured many Puerto Ricans from the island to the mainland.

Since the great period of migration to the U.S. mainland from Puerto Rico between 1946 and 1964, migration to and from the U.S. mainland has followed economic trends. When economic times are good on the mainland, the number of migrants from Puerto Rico increases. However, migrants tend to return to the island during economic hard times on the mainland. In 1953, migration from Puerto Rico to the mainland peaked at 74,000. Since the mid 1960s, migration from Puerto Rico to the mainland has been fluctuating. A deep drop occurred around 1976 when there was an economic downturn in the United States.

The population increase in the Puerto Rican mainland community today results primarily from new births rather than from migration, although migration still occurs. However, much of it consists of unemployed individuals who circulate from the island to the mainland and back again. These migrants often cannot find jobs on the island or the mainland.

Although the migration of Puerto Ricans from the island to the mainland is similar in many ways to other movements of peoples to the United States, it is unique in several ways. As Fitzpatrick notes, it was the first "airborne migration" in U.S. history (Fitzpatrick, 1987, p. 20). Puerto Ricans, unlike many of the earlier immigrants, are also U.S. citizens when they arrive in the United States. Puerto Ricans bring attitudes toward race that are different from and more complex than those in the United States. They also started migrating to the United States at a time when automation had eliminated most of the jobs requiring unskilled laborers. Most of these factors, along with the racism and discrimination they experience in the United States, have increased rather than mitigated their problems in the United States.

The Family

The family, which is important in traditional Puerto Rican culture, is experiencing tremendous changes on the island. Cultures are not static in modernized societies but are dynamic and changing. As Puerto Rico becomes increasingly urbanized, many of its traditional rural values—including those related to the family—are changing. While the Puerto Rican family and its values are changing on the island, the family faces even more conflicts and problems when it moves to the U.S. mainland. It becomes part of a U.S. mainstream culture that is often unaware of and unsympathetic to traditional Puerto Rican values related to family and community. The racism and discrimination that the Puerto Rican family experiences in the United States also create adjustment problems.

The serious economic problems that faced the Puerto Rican community by the mid 1990s affected the family. In 1993, about 32.5% of Puerto Rican families were living below the official government poverty level (U.S. Bureau of the Census, 1994). This percentage was greater than that of all other Hispanics and also greater than that of African Americans and Whites. By 2005, the poverty rate for Puerto Rican Americans dropped significantly, to 23.1% (U.S. Census Bureau, 2007a,b).

A deep sense of family remains within the Puerto Rican community despite the economic problems it faces. A number of values are still strongly held within Puerto Rican families, including respect for the elderly and for parents and extremely strong bonds within the family, particularly with the mother (Sanchez-Ayendez, 1988). The family, rather than the individual, tends to be the primary focus of identification. The extended family is important, and all family members tend to feel obligated to care for and be responsible for one another. The protection of children, especially girls, is very important to the family. This protection is often viewed as overprotection by people outside the culture. These traditional values of Puerto Rican families are being challenged by modernization, urbanization, and the levels of assimilation occurring among the current generation of Puerto Ricans in the United States. However, they still have a great deal of tenacity in the Puerto Rican community.

Despite the problems that they face there, many Puerto Rican migrants remain in the United States. A few return to the island for many different reasons, including the lack of a job, alienation, discrimination, and longing for their homeland, family, and friends. Most Puerto Ricans who remain in the United States retain important aspects of their culture but re-create and change their culture in ways that reflect their participation within U.S. society. How Puerto Ricans use language illustrates this process of cultural adaptation and change. While learning English, most Puerto Ricans also continue to speak Spanish. In 2004, 47.2% of Puerto Ricans were non-English speakers at home but spoke English very well; 22.0% were non-English speakers at home and did not speak English very well; 30.6% of Puerto Ricans reported speaking only English at home (U.S. Census Bureau, 2007c, p. 14).

The Issue of Race and Racism among Puerto Ricans

Although racism exists in both Puerto Rico and the U.S. mainland, race is highly complex in Puerto Rico, and *social race* has different meanings in the two cultures. Scholars such as Zenon Cruz (1975) and Betances (1972) believe that social scientists have exaggerated the differences between racism in the United States and in Puerto Rico. These two researchers believe that most social scientists have underestimated the extent to which Blacks are victimized by racism in Puerto Rico. They believe that racism is an important part of Puerto Rican society. Although Zenon Cruz and Betances provide a needed perspective on race relations in Puerto Rico, social class status in Puerto Rico interacts with race in complex ways. Upper-class Whites tend to exclude both poor Whites and poor Blacks from their social gatherings. However, poor Whites and poor Blacks tend to mix more freely in Puerto Rico than in the United States. Even though Whites tend to marry other Whites in Puerto Rico, racial intermarriage occurs more often in Puerto Rico than in the United States.

The primary identity for most Puerto Ricans is culture rather than race, whereas race has primacy in the United States. Most Puerto Ricans tend to think of themselves first as Puerto Rican and secondarily as members of a racial group. Writes Rodriguez (1991): "Perhaps the primary point of contrast was that, in Puerto Rico, racial identification was subordinate to cultural identification, while in the United States, racial identification, to a large extent, determined cultural identification" (p. 52).

Puerto Ricans on the U.S. mainland are forced to fit into one of two racial categories: Black or White, categories that are often less meaningful in the Puerto Rican community. Puerto Ricans, both on the island and on the mainland, recognize and use a number of different racial categories, such as *blanco* (Whites), *prieto* (dark-skinned), *negro* (Blacks), and *trigueño* (tan) (Wagenheim, 1975). Other words they use to make color distinctions among themselves are *indio, grifo,* and *de color* (Padilla, 1958). When determining an individual's color, Puerto Ricans consider hair color and texture as well as skin color. Also, color classification is determined primarily by physical traits rather than by the color of parents or relatives. Within one family there can be individuals who are considered *blanco, negro,* and *trigueño.* Also, social status can be an important factor in racial classification. In general, the higher the social status, the less likely the individual will be considered *negro.*

The different ways in which color is recognized and treated on the mainland cause problems for the Puerto Rican migrant, especially for those who are intermediate in skin color. In their community, they are neither Black nor White but are often considered Black by outsiders. This causes the intermediate individual to feel alienated from both the White and Black communities in the United States. A study by Mills, Senior, and Goldsen (1967) indicated that Puerto Rican migrants who were intermediate in color experienced more adjustment problems in the United States than did individuals who were clearly identified as either Black or White.

On the 2000 U.S. Census, Puerto Ricans were asked to indicate the racial category to which they belonged. Most people (95.8%) responded to the question, with 80% indicating they were White; 8%, Black; 12%, mulatto; and 0.4%, Indian or Alaska Native (Puerto Rico, 2007). The respondents may have been limited in their self-descriptions by the U.S. Census categories from which they had to select responses. Racial categories in Puerto Rico and on the U.S. mainland differ in significant ways.

The Puerto Rican Mainland Community

When they first started migrating to the United States, most Puerto Ricans settled in New York City. However, the percentage of Puerto Rican migrants settling in New York City has steadily decreased in recent decades, while the percentage settling in other mainland cities and states has increased. In 1940, 88% of the Puerto Rican population in the United States lived in New York City. By 1960, that number had declined to 69%. In 2005, 72% of Puerto Ricans lived outside New York state.

While more than half (56.3%) of Puerto Ricans in the United States lived in the states of New York, New Jersey, Pennsylvania, Massachusetts, and Connecticut in 2005, many lived in other parts of the nation. A considerable number of Puerto Ricans (29.9%) lived in Florida, Illinois, California, Texas, and Ohio. In 2005, most Puerto Ricans (86.2%) were concentrated in these ten states: New York, Florida, New Jersey, Pennsylvania, Massachusetts, Connecticut, Illinois, California, Texas, and Ohio (see Table 11.1).

Pockets of Puerto Ricans in U.S. cities constitute ethnic neighborhoods. The Puerto Rican community is usually a poor community, with the characteristics of people who are poor. In 2005, Puerto Ricans had the lowest median family income of the major Hispanic groups and the largest percentage of persons below the poverty level (U.S. Census Bureau, 2007a,b). The median family income was $34,116 for Puerto Ricans, compared to $35,464 for Mexicans and $38,395 for Cuban Americans. In 2005, about 25.3% of Puerto Ricans lived below the poverty level, compared to 22.0% of Mexican Americans, 15.8% of Cubans, 25.6% of African Americans, and 10.4% of Whites.

The sound of Spanish, *bodegas,* travel agencies, and Pentecostal storefront churches are familiar sounds and sights in most Puerto Rican mainland neighborhoods. Although Puerto Rican mainland culture is decidedly different from Puerto Rican island culture, certain parts of the old culture are retained on the mainland.

TABLE 11.1   Puerto Rican Population in Selected States, 2005

STATE	TOTAL POPULATION	PUERTO RICAN AMERICAN POPULATION	PERCENTAGE OF TOTAL STATE POPULATION
New York	18,655,275	1,057,423	5.7
Florida	17,382,511	645,240	3.7
New Jersey	8,521,427	388,283	4.6
Pennsylvania	11,979,147	260,580	2.2
Massachusetts	6,182,860	217,347	3.5
Connecticut	3,394,751	204,616	6.0
Illinois	12,440,351	174,770	1.4
California	35,278,768	147,076	0.4
Texas	22,270,165	87,534	0.4
Ohio	11,155,606	74,348	0.7

Source: U.S. Census Bureau (2007), *American Community Survey, 2005: Selected Population Profile.* [Data file]. Available online from http://factfinder.census.gov/servlet/IPCharIterationServlet?_ts= 202649767048.

Hispanos, as many Puerto Ricans call themselves, usually speak Spanish at home and English when talking with outsiders. To obtain the foods to prepare favorite ethnic dishes, such as rice and beans, fried plaintains, or dried codfish, the family may shop at the *bodega,* the little corner grocery store usually run by Puerto Ricans. Increasingly, however, supermarkets are carrying Puerto Rican foods and other goods. Herbs and plants needed to cure illnesses or to fight the "evil eye" can be bought at the *botanicas.* Tickets for an air trip back home can be bought at the local travel agency, perhaps on easy terms. The Pentecostal church, a fast-growing institution in the Puerto Rican mainland community, serves the spiritual needs of the migrants. The Puerto Rican community, with its *bodegas, botanicas,* and Pentecostal churches, helps to ease the culture shock for the migrants and helps them to develop roots in their new land.

THE FUTURE

On most major indices—such as occupational status, education, and income—Puerto Ricans fall far behind the general U.S. population and most other Hispanic groups. Yet, the future of the Puerto Rican community can be shaped by educational, political, and social action. Puerto Ricans in the United States are a young and growing population. In 2005 they had the second youngest median age, 29.2, of U.S. Hispanic groups (U.S. Census Bureau, 2007a,b). Mexican Americans were the youngest group, with a median age of 25.5. There are signs that the Puerto Rican community is becoming more politically and legally active than it has been in the past. The New York Puerto Rican community is playing an increasingly important role in local, state, and national elections.

A number of Puerto Rican educational and civic organizations are working to strengthen the Puerto Rican community. One of the most important is the ASPIRA Association, an organization founded in 1961 to promote educational achievement and leadership development among youths. Today, it is an important, active, and effective organization within the Puerto Rican community (ASPIRA Association, 2007). Other important Puerto Rican organizations include the National Puerto Rican Coalition (http://www.bateylink.org/about.htm), which coordinates a group of organizations and works to improve the social and economic conditions of Puerto Ricans in the United States, and the Puerto Rican Legal Defense and Educational Fund (http://www.prldef.org), which litigates for Hispanics who live in the Northeast. The National Congress for Puerto Rican Rights (http://www.columbia.edu/~rmg36/NCPRR.html) works to obtain "civil and human rights for Puerto Ricans."

The future of Puerto Ricans in the United States will be heavily influenced by political, economic, and social developments on the island. These two communities are integrally bound. Many Puerto Ricans view the existence of Puerto Ricans on the island and on the mainland as indicating a divided nation. Consequently, the status question that haunts the island cogently influences the ideologies, debates, and visions of mainland Puerto Ricans.

TEACHING STRATEGIES

Content related to the Puerto Rican experience can be incorporated into a conceptual curriculum. Three key concepts related to the Puerto Rican experience and sample strategies for teaching them are presented. Strategies are described for teaching *cultural conflict, racial categories,* and *colonialism* in the primary, intermediate and upper, and high school grades, respectively.

Primary Grades

Concept

Cultural conflict

Generalization: The Puerto Rican migrant family in the United States experiences many conflicts and problems because it encounters new norms, values, and roles on the mainland that conflict with those in Puerto Rico.

1. Read the following case study to the students and ask the questions that follow. During the discussion of the story, help the children to state the generalization in their own words.

THE RAMOS FAMILY

Mr. and Mrs. Ramos and their two children, Maria, age three, and Carlos, age seven, live in New York City in an area called El Barrio. The Ramos family moved to New York two years ago from San Juan, Puerto Rico. When the family lived in San Juan, Mr. Ramos worked in a factory. Mrs. Ramos stayed at home and took care of the children and house.

Both Mr. and Mrs. Ramos were happy living in San Juan until some of their relatives moved from San Juan to New York City. First, Mrs. Ramos's two sisters, whom she likes very much, moved to New York. Later, Mr. Ramos's brother moved to New York. Mr. and Mrs. Ramos missed their relatives very much. They wanted to be able to see them more often, so they decided to go to New York to pay their relatives a visit.

When Mr. and Mrs. Ramos arrived in New York to visit, their relatives were very glad to see them. Mrs. Ramos kissed her two sisters. She told them about all the news back home. Her sisters told her about New York City. They liked it very much. Mrs. Ramos became very excited about New York City as she listened to her sisters talk about it. Mr. Ramos and his brother were also glad to see each other. Mr. Ramos told his brother how the family was doing in San Juan. Mr. Ramos's brother told him about how good things were in New York. He told Mr. Ramos that he could make twice as much money in New York as he made in San Juan! Mr. and Mrs. Ramos enjoyed New York City for two weeks. When they left, they had decided that they would move to New York City as soon as they got back home.

When the Ramos family got to New York again, things were not as nice as they thought they would be. The family was not as happy as it had been in San Juan. They had to live with Mr. Ramos's brother for two months because they could not find a nice apartment right away. When they did find one, it cost much more than they had paid for rent in San Juan. Mr. Ramos looked a long time before he could find a job. To help the family pay its bills, Mrs. Ramos got a job in a garment factory. Mrs. Ramos was the only person in the family working. She began to make more and more decisions for everyone in the family.

Mr. Ramos spent most of each day looking for a job. He spoke good Spanish but many companies would not hire him because he spoke little English. Since Mrs. Ramos was working and Mr. Ramos was job hunting, Carlos and Maria had to spend a lot of time without either parent. Sometimes they would get into trouble with the neighborhood children.

Carlos became sad when he started to school. He was a top student in Puerto Rico. However, he did poorly in school in New York. He could not read English well. He fell further and further behind in school each week. The teacher called him "Charlie" instead of "Carlos." The children teased him because he spoke "funny." Carlos tried hard to speak English, even at home. His parents wanted him to speak Spanish at home so that they could understand him.

After looking for three months, Mr. Ramos found a job in a hotel. The family then moved into their own apartment. Things got better then. Mr. Ramos wanted Mrs. Ramos to quit her job and stay at home with the children. Mrs. Ramos wanted to keep working because she felt that it took more money to live in New York than in San Juan. Sometimes the family wished that they had stayed in San Juan.

The Ramos family has now been in New York City for two years. They are much happier now, but they still miss their friends and relatives in San Juan. Mr. Ramos understands why Mrs. Ramos wants to work. Carlos is speaking better English and getting better grades in school. The family is planning to visit Puerto Rico during the Christmas season. Carlos is counting the days until Christmas!

Questions
1. Why did the Ramos family move from San Juan to New York City?
2. Was New York City like the family expected it to be? Why or why not?
3. What problems did each of the family members have in New York City that he or she did not have in San Juan?

4. Which family member faced the greatest problems in New York? Why?
5. Which family member faced the fewest problems in New York? Why?
6. What problems do you think the family faced in New York City that are not brought out in the story? Why?
7. How do you think the family will feel about New York a year from now? Do you think that the family will move back to Puerto Rico? Why or why not?

Intermediate and Upper Grades

Concept

Racial categories

Generalization: Racial categories differ in Puerto Rico and on the U.S. mainland. These differing racial categories make the experience of Puerto Rican migrants to the mainland more difficult.

1. Find old copies of magazines such as *Ebony, Hispanic, Essence, Black Enterprise,* and *Life.* Locate pictures of people who look (a) obviously European American, (b) obviously African American, and (c) like fair-skinned African Americans. Mount these pictures on cardboard.
2. Show the students three of the pictures, one that will fit into each of the categories described above. Ask the students to name the "race" of the person in each picture. They will most likely say that one of the pictured persons is "White," and that the other two are "Black" or "African American." Ask: "Why do we use only two categories to classify the people in these pictures?" With the use of careful questions, explain that in the United States any person, regardless of physical appearance, is considered "Black" or "African American" if he or she has any *known* African ancestry.
3. Show the class mounted pictures of (a) a fair-skinned African American male adult, (b) a fair-skinned African American female adult, (c) a dark-skinned African American male child, and (d) a female child who looks Caucasian.
4. Ask the students to name the "race" of each of the pictured persons. After discussing their responses, tell the class that the pictures represent a Puerto Rican family that recently moved from San Juan to New York City. In the pictures are mom, dad, brother, and sister. Point out that, even though we may call the parents and the son "Black," Puerto Ricans have words to describe each color. Introduce these words. They would call the parents *trigueño,* the son *negro* or *de color,* and the daughter *blanca.* Tell the students that in Puerto Rico "color" has a special meaning that is different from its meaning in the United States. Ask the students what race the different family members would belong to in the United States and why. Through questioning, bring out that all of them would be considered "Black" or "African American" and why.
5. Ask: "Now that the family is in New York City, what kinds of racial problems might they encounter?" "Why?" Through questioning, reveal that mother and father will be considered "Black" on the mainland even though they were intermediates (*trigueños*) in Puerto Rico. Discuss with the class the kinds of identity and social problems that the couple will face on the mainland and how they might cope with them. Ask the class the following questions:
   a. How do you think the mother and father will feel when mainland Whites call them "Black" or "African American"?

    b. How do you think they will feel when African Americans call them "Black"? Do you think they will identify with the Black struggle for civil rights? Why or why not?

    c. Do you think they will want to be called "White" or "Black"? Why? What problems might they encounter when seeking to obtain their preferred racial identification? Why? How might they go about solving them?

6. With these and other questions, bring out the generalization that Puerto Rican migrants to the mainland who are intermediate in color have serious racial and adjustment problems because they are neither White nor Black in Puerto Rico but are forced to be "Black" on the mainland. Ask the class these valuing questions: Do you think that it is right to consider intermediates on the mainland "Blacks"? Why or why not? Do you think they should be considered "White"? Why or why not? If you were an intermediate Puerto Rican on the mainland, would you want to be considered "White" or "Black"? Why? When asking such valuing questions, accept all responses and maintain an open classroom atmosphere. Ask the class these questions:

    a. What special identity and racial problems might the son have in his family? In school? In the community? Why? How might he deal with them?

    b. What special racial and identity problems might the daughter have in the family? In school? In the community? Why? How might she deal with them?

Read the following case study to the class and ask the questions that follow.

MR. DIAZ AND MR. SEDA ON THE MAINLAND

Mr. Diaz looks Caucasian. In Puerto Rico, he and Mr. Seda, who is *de color*, were close friends. They both now live in New York City. When they first came to New York City, they would visit each other often, as they had done in Puerto Rico. Eventually Mr. Diaz started visiting Mr. Seda less and less and would often act unfriendly when Mr. Seda came to visit him, especially when his White friends were over. Mr. Diaz's White friends would always give Mr. Seda strange looks when he came over. Mr. Diaz began to understand that in New York City he was expected to mix socially with Whites only. Now, Mr. Diaz never visits Mr. Seda, and Mr. Seda goes to Mr. Diaz's house very seldom. When he does, he stays only a short time. The last time that Mr. Seda visited Mr. Diaz's home, Mr. Diaz left in the middle of the visit with a White American friend. He told Mr. Seda that he and his White American friend had to go out and take care of some important business.

Questions
1. What is the main problem in this case study?
2. What kind of relationship did Mr. Diaz and Mr. Seda have in Puerto Rico?
3. Why did their relationship change when they moved to the mainland?
4. If you were Mr. Diaz, would you act as he acted when he moved to the mainland? Why or why not?
5. If you were Mr. Seda, would you act as he acted when he moved to New York City? Why or why not?

Valuing Activity

Ask the students independently to complete these open-ended sentences. After they have completed them, discuss their responses and summarize the lesson by highlighting the generalization about the racial problems Puerto Rican migrants experience on the U.S. mainland.

1. Mr. Diaz should _____.
2. Mr. Seda should _____.
3. Mr. Diaz values _____ more than_____.
4. Mr. Seda values _____ more than _____.
5. If I were Mr. Diaz, I would _____.
6. If I were Mr. Seda, I would _____.

High School Grades

Concept

Colonialism

Generalizations: Since the late fifteenth century, Puerto Rico has been controlled by foreign powers. This has caused rebellions, political ambiguity, and instability on the island.

1. Give the students a copy of the questions below and ask them to read a selection about the Taino Indians prior to 1493. One source is Irving Rouse (1992), *The Tainos: Rise and Decline of the People Who Greeted Columbus.* Tell them to be able to respond to these questions when they have finished their reading. After the students have completed the reading assignment, discuss the questions.
   a. How did the Tainos obtain food?
   b. What kind of political system did they have?
   c. What kind of religion did they have?
   d. What was a typical day like for (1) a Taino adult female, (2) a Taino adult male, (3) Taino children?
   e. What kinds of relationships did the Tainos have with other American Indian groups?
   f. What kinds of weapons did the Tainos use when they were at war with other Indian tribes?
2. Divide the class into research groups and ask them to prepare and give short reports on each of the following topics. They should be encouraged to present their reports to the class in the form of debates, simulations, and role-play situations, using visual aids such as charts and graphs.
   a. Columbus's trip to North America and his relationship with the native populations
   b. The establishment of Spanish domination in Puerto Rico in the 1500s
   c. The *encomienda* system of forced labor that the Spanish established in Puerto Rico during the early years of domination
   d. Ways in which the Tainos resisted Spanish colonization by rebelling and running away
   e. Spanish domination in Puerto Rico in the 1600s, 1700s, and 1800s
   f. *Grito de Lares* of 1868
   g. The political, economic, and social status of Puerto Rico in 1898
   h. The Spanish-American War (causes and effects)

    i. The American takeover of Puerto Rico in 1898

    j. The Treaty of Paris, 1898

       After the students have a basic understanding of Puerto Rican history up to 1898, they can then become involved in activities like those below to gain a better understanding of the island's political and economic status today.

3. Ask the students to pretend that they are members of the U.S. Congress in 1898. Spain has just ceded Puerto Rico to the United States. Their job is to decide on specific political and economic policies for their new territory. They must develop a plan for governing the island and have it approved by majority vote. After this exercise is completed, ask the students to compare their plan with the plan the United States used to govern Puerto Rico during the first two years of U.S. rule and with the plan delineated in the Foraker Act of 1900. Ask the students to discuss the similarities and differences in the three plans and possible reasons for them.

4. Ask the students to research the positions advocated by the following political parties regarding the political status of Puerto Rico:

    a. The Independence Party (independence)

    b. The New Progressive Party (statehood)

    c. The Popular Party (Commonwealth)

       After this research, ask three students to role-play an advocate of each status position. The advocate of each position should argue his or her position in front of the class. The three speakers will debate the status question and answer questions posed by the class. After the debate and discussion, each class member will vote for one of the three following positions: (a) the Commonwealth, (b) statehood, or (c) independence. After the voting, conduct a class discussion in which the class will compare their choice with the choice made by the citizens of Puerto Rico in a plebiscite held in 1998. (See the chronology at the beginning of this chapter.) The students should discuss the reasons for the similarities and differences in their choice and the choice made by Puerto Rican citizens.

5. Ask a group of students to role-play a discussion between the individuals named below about what should be the future of Puerto Rico. Conduct a class discussion about the role-play situation when it ends.

    a. Pedro Albizu Campos

    b. Luis Muñoz Marin

    c. Luis A. Ferré

    d. Rafael Hernandez Colon

    e. A U.S. businessperson who is president of a company that owns several factories in Puerto Rico

    f. A southern U.S. senator

    g. A U.S. congressional representative from the Midwest

6. Since the Spanish colonized Puerto Rico in the sixteenth century, there have been uprisings and rebellions against oppression on the island. Ask the students to prepare a short research paper on forms of resistance to oppression in Puerto Rico since the sixteenth century. Make sure that they note resistance as exemplified by (a) the Taino Indians, (b) the Lares Rebellion of 1868, (c) the Nationalist Party, (d) the university student uprisings in Puerto Rico in the 1960s, (e) the protests over the navy exercises and the death of a security guard on Vieques Island in Puerto Rico that occurred in 1999 and continued into 2001.

7. After the students have completed and discussed their papers, ask them to write and present a dramatization about "The Struggle for Home Rule in Puerto Rico." They can invite another class or their parents and friends to attend the presentation.

REFERENCES

ASPIRA Association. Retrieved July 22, 2007, from http://en.wikipedia.org/wiki/Puerto_Rico.

Babin, M. T. (1971). *The Puerto Ricans' Spirit*. Translated by B. Luby. New York: Collier Books.

Betances, S. (1972, Winter; 1973, Spring). The Prejudice of Having No Prejudice in Puerto Rico. Part 1, *The Rican*, 41–52; Part II, *The Rican*, 22–37.

Chenault, L. R. (1938). *The Puerto Rican Migrant in New York City*. New York: Columbia University Press.

Elections in Puerto Rico: 1998 Status Plebiscite Vote Summary. Retrieved July 22, 2007, from http://electionspuertorico.org/1998/summary.html.

Fitzpatrick, J. P. (1987). *Puerto Rican Americans: The Meaning of Migration to the Mainland* (2nd ed.). Englewood Cliffs, NJ: Prentice-Hall.

Grayson, G. W. (2001, October 12). A Call to Patriotism: Keep Vieques Open. *Wall Street Journal*, p. A15.

Mills, C. W., Senior, C., & Goldsen, R. K. (1967). *The Puerto Rican Journey: New York's Newest Migrants*. New York: Russel and Russel.

Negron de Montilla, A. (1975). *Americanization in Puerto Rico and the Public School System 1901–1920*. Rio Piedras: University of Puerto Rico Press.

Nieto, S. (1995). Unpublished review of J. A. Banks, *Teaching Strategies for Ethnic Studies* (5th ed.). Boston: Allyn and Bacon, 1991.

Padilla, E. (1958). *Up from Puerto Rico*. New York: Columbia University Press.

Population Reference Bureau. (2007). *Puerto Rico: Statistics*. Retrieved June 27, 2007, from http://www.prb.org/Countries/PuertoRico.aspx.

Puerto Rico. Retrieved July 22, 2007, from http://en.wikipedia.org/wiki/Puerto_Rico.

Rodriguez, C. E. (1991). *Puerto Ricans Born in the U.S.A.* Boulder, CO: Westview.

Rouse, I. (1992). *The Tainos: Rise and Decline of the People Who Greeted Columbus*. New Haven, CT: Yale University Press.

Sanchez-Ayendez, M. (1988). The Puerto Rican American Family. In C. H. Mindel, R. W. Haberstein, & R. Wright, Jr. (Eds.), *Ethnic Families in America: Patterns and Variations* (3rd ed., pp.173–195). New York: Elsevier.

Santiago-Valles, K. A., & Jiménez-Muñoz, G. M. (2004). Social Polarization and Colonized Labor: Puerto Ricans in the United States, 1945–2000. In D. G. Gutiérrez (Ed.), *The Columbia History of Latinos in the United States Since 1960* (pp. 87–145). New York: Columbia University Press.

Trías Monge, J. (1997). *Puerto Rico: The Trials of the Oldest Colony in the World*. New Haven, CT: Yale University Press.

U.S. Census Bureau. (1990). *Current Population Reports, Population Characteristics, P23–183*. Washington, DC: U.S. Government Printing Office.

U.S. Census Bureau. (1993). *We, the American Hispanics*. Washington, DC: U.S. Government Printing Office.

U.S. Census Bureau. (1994). *Statistical Abstract of the United States: 1994* (114th ed.). Washington, DC: U.S. Government Printing Office.

U.S. Census Bureau. (2000). *Poverty Rate Lowest in 20 Years, Household Income at Record High, Census Bureau Report*. Available online at http://www.census.gov/Press-Release/www/2000/cb00–158.html.

U.S. Census Bureau. (2001). *The Hispanic Population: Census 2000 Brief.* Available online at http://www.census.gov.

U.S. Census Bureau. (2007a). *2005 American Community Survey: Select Population Profile in the United States.* Retrieved June 27, 2007, from http://factfinder.census.gov/servlet/IPCharIterationServlet?_ts=201015035938.

U.S. Census Bureau. (2007b). *2005 Puerto Rico Community Survey.* Retrieved June 27, 2007, from http://www.census.gov/acs/www/SBasics/FlyerPR.htm.

U.S. Census Bureau. (2007c). *The American Community—Hispanics, 2004. American Community Survey Reports,* no. 3. Washington, DC: U.S. Department of Commerce, Economics and Statistics Administration.

Van Middeldyk, R. A. (2006). *The History of Puerto Rico: From the Spanish Discovery to the American Occupation.* Charleston, SC: BiblioBazaar.

Vieques Island, Puerto Rico. Retrieved July 22, 2007, from http://topuertorico.org/city/vieques.shtml.

Wagenheim, K. (1975). *Puerto Rico: A Profile* (2nd ed.). New York: Praeger.

Zenon Cruz, I. (1975). *Narcisco Descubre Su Trasero.* Homacao, PR: Editorial Furidi.

ANNOTATED BIBLIOGRAPHY

Books for Teachers

Especially Recommended

Acosta-Belén, E., Cruz, J. E., Santiago, C. E., Rodriguez, C. E., Gonzalez-Rodriguez, Y., Benitez, M., Santiago-Rivera, A., & Sjostrom, B. R. (Eds.). (2000). *Adiós, Borinquen querida: The Puerto Rican Diaspora: Its History and Contributions.* Albany: University of Albany Press.
This book offers an overview of the historical, cultural, and political development of Puerto Rican immigrant communities within and outside of the United States (Cuba, the Dominican Republic, Mexico, and St. Croix). The contributors are distinguished scholars and writers in the field of Puerto Rican Studies.

Acosta-Belén, E., & Santiago, C. E. (2006). *Puerto Ricans in the United States: A Contemporary Portrait.* Boulder, CO: Lynne Rienner Publishers.
A follow-up to *Adiós, Borinquen querida,* this book focuses on Puerto Rican communities on the mainland—why the Puerto Ricans came, the lives they have made, and their efforts to preserve their culture across generations.

De Wagenheim, O. J., & Wagenheim, K. (2001). *The Puerto Ricans: A Documentary History* (rev. ed.). New York: Markus Wiener.
This book is a documentary and analysis of Puerto Rico's history from the beginning of the island's settlement by the Spanish to the mass migration to the United States after World War II.

Márquez, R. (Ed.). (2007). *Puerto Rican Poetry: An Anthology from Aboriginal to Contemporary Times.* Amherst: University of Massachusetts Press.
This wide-ranging and comprehensive collection includes the work of sixty-four poets from the fifteenth century to the present, including poets living in the mainland United States. Introductory essays for each era (1400–1820, 1821–1950s, 1950s-1970s, and 1970s to the present) and biographical sketches make this an important historical and critical work as well.

Nieto, S. (Ed.). (2000). *Puerto Rican Students in U.S. Schools.* Mahwah, NJ: Erlbaum.
This is a collection of reflective essays, research studies, and poems about the education and schooling of Puerto Rican students in the United States. The authors address issues of identity, culture, ethnicity, language, gender, social activism, community involvement, and policy implications.

Rivera, C. (2000). *Kissing the Mango Tree: Puerto Rican Women Rewriting American Literature.* Houston, TX: Arte Publico Press.

Accessible critical essays explore the works of mainland Puerto Rican women writers Esmeralda Santiago, Nicholasa Mohr, Rosario Morales, Aurora Levins, Sandra María Esteves, Luz María Umpierre-Herrera, and Judith Ortiz Cofer.

Sanchez-Korrol, V. (1999). *Teaching U.S. Puerto Rican History*. Washington, DC: American Historical Association.
This text offers a comprehensive historical overview of the Puerto Rican experience in the United States. Special attention is given to pedagogical strategies for teaching Puerto Rican American history.

Santiago-Valles, K. A., & Jiménez-Muñoz, G. M. (2004). Social Polarization and Colonized Labor: Puerto Ricans in the United States, 1945–2000. In D. G. Gutiérrez (Ed.), *The Columbia History of Latinos in the United States Since 1960* (pp. 87–145). New York: Columbia University Press.
An excellent overview of the history, demographic, economic, educational, and social status of Puerto Ricans in the United States between 1960 and the early 2000s. This chapter is carefully researched, informative, and highly readable.

Other Books

Barreto, A. A. (2001). *The Politics of Language in Puerto Rico*. Gainesville: University Press of Florida.
This book describes Puerto Rican language policies and examines the connections between language, cultural identity, and politics.

Dávila, A. (2004). *Barrio Dreams: Puerto Ricans, Latinos, and the Neoliberal City*. Berkeley: University of California Press.
The author examines the connections between cultural symbols, cultural politics, and conflicts over the gentrification of New York City's predominantly Puerto Rican Spanish Harlem neighborhood.

Figueredo, D. H. (Ed.). (2005). *Encyclopedia of Caribbean Literature*. Westport, CT: Greenwood.
Many Puerto Rican poets, novelists, essayists, playwrights, musicians, and children's authors are among the literary figures featured in this two-volume encyclopedia.

Flores, L. (2000). *From Bomba to Hip-Hop: Puerto Rican Culture and Latino Identity*. New York: Columbia University Press.
This book explores how Puerto Ricans in New York have created a unique identity for themselves. The author describes architecture, literary traditions, musical styles, and cultural movements and compares them to those of the city's other ethnic and racial minority groups.

Griffith, D., & Valdés Pizzini, M. (2002). *Fishers at Work, Workers at Sea: A Puerto Rican Journey Through Labor and Refuge*. Philadelphia: Temple University Press.
This ethnographic study utilizes over 100 life histories to analyze how fishing men and women in Puerto Rico balance their traditional life's work with the need to supplement their household income with wage labor.

Grosfoguel, R. (2003). *Colonial Subjects: Puerto Ricans in a Global Perspective*. Berkeley: University of California Press.
In this important contribution to migration studies, the author examines the political economy of the island, Puerto Rican communities in the United States, and migration patterns not only to the United States but to Europe as well.

Hernández, C. D. (1997). *Puerto Rican Voices in English*. New York: Praeger.
This book presents a collection of interviews with fourteen of the most prominent Puerto Rican writers living in the United States.

Kasinitz, P., Mollenkopf, J. H., & Waters, M. C. (Eds.). (2004). *Becoming New Yorkers: Ethnographies of the Second Generation*. New York: Russell Sage Foundation.

Puerto Ricans are among the groups featured in this collection of essays on second-generation assimilation and cultural practices in New York City. Topics include education, employment, community life, religion, family relationships, and language.

McCaffrey, K. T. (1999). *Military Power and Popular Protest: The U.S. Navy in Vieques, Puerto Rico*. Piscataway, NJ: Rutgers University Press.
The author offers an overview of the conflict over Vieques Island, where the United States for years conducted bombing trainings, depriving fishermen of their livelihood, and where, in 1999, a stray bomb killed a civilian base employee.

Méndez-Méndez, S., & Cueto, G. A. (2003). *Notable Caribbeans and Caribbean Americans: A Biographical Dictionary*. Westport, CT: Greenwood.
Important Puerto Ricans on the island and the mainland—political leaders, writers, entertainers, artists, sports figures, business leaders, scientists, journalists, and educators—are among the figures included in this reference source.

Montero, M. (2005). *Captain of the Sleepers*. New York: Farrar, Straus and Giroux.
A boy who witnesses his mother's affair with a ship's captain, which leads to her suicide, carries his desire for revenge through his life. Set in Puerto Rico, the novel spans a half century of the island's turbulent history.

Pérez y González, M. E. (2000). *Puerto Ricans in the United States*. Westport, CT: Greenwood.
This book examines the experiences of Puerto Rican immigrants in the United States and the development of Puerto Rican urban culture in America.

Rodríguez Julia, E. (2000). *Cortijo's Wake/El Entierro de Cortijo*. Durham, NC: Duke University Press.
A cycle of poems chronicles the wake and funeral of the Afro–Puerto Rican musician Rafael Cortijo (1928–1982), with commentary on human nature, politics, race, class, and the role of art in keeping one's spirit alive.

Sánchez-González, L. (2001). *Boricua Literature: A Literary History of the Puerto Rican Diaspora*. New York: New York University Press.
This book offers a historical analysis and overview of Puerto Rican or Boricua literature.

Thomas, P. (1997). *Down These Mean Streets*. New York: Vintage.
A classic memoir about growing up in Spanish Harlem as a dark-skinned Puerto Rican child in a family that refused to acknowledge its African heritage.

Trías Monge, J. (1997). *Puerto Rico: The Trials of the Oldest Colony in the World*. New Haven: Yale University Press.
An informative and readable history that argues that Puerto Rico is the oldest colony in the world.

Torres, A., Velazquez, J. E., & Pantojos-Garcia, E. (Eds.). (1998). *The Puerto Rican Movement: Voices from the Diaspora*. Philadelphia: Temple University Press.
This anthology discusses the history of organizations and social movements of the 1960s and 1970s that emerged to promote Puerto Rican independence from the United States.

Whalen, C. (2001). *From Puerto Rico to Philadelphia: Puerto Rican Workers and Postwar Economies*. Philadelphia: Temple University Press.
This book describes the experiences of Puerto Rican immigrants to Philadelphia and analyzes the contract labor programs, state policies, changes in regional and local economies, social networks, and individual decisions that structure the lives of the immigrants.

Books for Students

Acosta González, A. (2006). *Mayte and the Bogeyman/Mayte y el Cuco*. Illustrated by C. Rodríguez. Houston, TX: Piñata Books.
This tale in English and Spanish depicts a colorful assortment of street vendors, all of whom have a special relationship with Mayte, except a mysterious ice cream vendor that she believes is the bogeyman. Elements from Puerto Rican folklore enrich the adventure. (Primary)

Bernier-Grand, C. T. (1999). *In the Shade of the Níspero Tree*. New York: Orchard.
A Puerto Rican preteen learns unpleasant truths about race and class when her darker-skinned best friend and later she too are excluded from the island's elite social circles. (Middle School)

Bernier-Grand, C. T. (2002). *Shake It, Morena: And Other Folklore from Puerto Rico*. Illustrated by L. Delacre. Brookfield, CT: Millbrook.
This attractive book contains games, rhymes, songs, stories, riddles, and more that the author learned as a child growing up in Puerto Rico. Most of the items in this collection appear in both English and Spanish. (Intermediate)

Caraballo, S. (2002). *Estrellita se despide de su isla/Estrellita Says Good-bye to Her Island*. Illustrated by P. Torrecilla. Houston, TX: Piñata Books.
A girl leaving Puerto Rico for the mainland says good-bye to the things she loves—the beaches, the forests, the colorful roosters, and the coquí, a nearly transparent frog found only on the island. (Primary)

Caraballo, S. (2004). *Mis abuelos y yo/My Grandparents and I*. Illustrated by D. N. Cruz. Houston, TX: Piñata Books.
This simple and tender bilingual book portrays a young boy's day with his grandparents in Puerto Rico as they go to the beach, visit museums, cook a meal, and tend the garden. (Primary)

Carlson, L. M. (2002). *The Flamboyant*. New York: HarperCollins.
This historical novel tells the story of the island's first woman aviator, Laura Demarest, who moves with her father to Puerto Rico as a child after her mother's death in 1917. (High School)

Espada, M. (2003). *Alabanza: New and Selected Poems, 1982–2002*. New York: Norton.
The award-winning poet culls the best of a twenty-year career, including poems about his father, about Latino/Latina American struggles for justice, and, in the title poem, about the Puerto Rican and other immigrant restaurant workers who lost their lives at the Windows on the World restaurant atop the World Trade Center on September 11, 2001. (High School)

Hoyt-Goldsmith, D. (2004). *Three Kings Day: A Celebration at Christmastime*. Illustrated with photos by L. Migdale. New York: Holiday House.
A Puerto Rican family in Queens, New York, prepares for the Feast of the Three Kings, the January 6 festival that concludes the Christmas season, in this appealing photo-essay. Special foods, a parade reenacting the arrival of the Three Wise Men, and gifts are among the features of this traditional Puerto Rican holiday. (Primary/Intermediate)

Manzano, S. (2004). *No Dogs Allowed!* Illustrated by J. J. Muth. New York: Simon and Schuster.
This lighthearted picture book written by the *Sesame Street* actor depicts a close extended family that travels from their home in the Bronx to a state park where they are shocked to discover that the family dog is not allowed. Family members take turns dog-sitting in the parking lot. (Primary)

Martinez, A. (2004). *Poe Park*. New York: Holiday House.
An eleven-year-old boy living in the Bronx witnesses the shooting of his best friend and must choose between the local gang and his strict but supportive family. Arriving from Puerto Rico, his older half-brother is faced with the same choice. (Intermediate/Middle School)

Miller-Lachmann, L. (Ed.). (2003). *Once Upon a Cuento*. Willimantic, CN: Curbstone Press.
Notable Puerto Rican children's authors Carmen T. Bernier-Grand and Nicholasa Mohr are among the Latino authors featured in this collection of seventeen short stories about heritage, family, and friendship. (Intermediate/Middle School)

Mohr, N. (1986). *Going Home*. New York: Dial.
This sequel to *Felita* focuses on the dilemmas faced by a Nuyorican girl who returns to Puerto Rico. (Middle School). Other books by Nicholasa Mohr for this age group include *Nilda* (1973), *El Bronx Remembered* (1975), *Felita* (1979), and *In Nueva York* (1977).

Mohr, N., & Martorell, A. (1995). *The Song of el Coquí and Other Tales of Puerto Rico*. New York: Viking.
This collection of stories reveals the rich ancestral traditions of Puerto Rican culture. (All ages)

Ortíz Cofer, J. (2003). *The Meaning of Consuelo*. New York: Farrar, Straus & Giroux.
A teenager growing up on the island in the 1950s must take care of her mentally ill younger sister at the same time as she witnesses changes in the economy and culture of her area and in the expectations for women. Vivid, lyrical writing distinguishes this memorable coming-of-age novel. (Middle School/High School)

Ortíz Cofer, J. (1998). *The Year of Our Revolution*. Houston, TX: Arte Público.
Entertaining and revealing poems and short stories describe the author's experience of growing up in the Puerto Rican barrio of Paterson, New Jersey, in the turbulent 1960s. This book begins approximately where Ortíz Cofer's acclaimed memoir of her life on the island, *Silent Dancing: A Partial Remembrance of a Puerto Rican Childhood* (Arte Público, 1990), ends. (Middle School/High School)

Ortíz Cofer, J. (Ed.). (2004). *Riding Low on the Streets of Gold: Latino Literature for Young Adults*. Houston, TX: Piñata Books.
The award-winning Puerto Rican writer offers twenty-two poems and short stories by Latino authors from the past and present, providing readers with an overview of Puerto Rican, Mexican American, Cuban American, and other Latino literature and a celebration of bilingualism and biculturalism. (Middle School/High School)

Padilla, Z. (2004). *The Night We Almost Saw the Three Kings*. Illustrated by G. Ramirez. Long Beach, NY: Libros.
The night before Three Kings Day—January 6, when Puerto Rican children traditionally get their presents—two sisters decide to stay up all night hoping to catch the Three Kings delivering toys. (Primary)

Santiago, E. (2004). *The Turkish Lover*. Cambridge, MA: Da Capo Press.
The author of *When I Was Puerto Rican* (Perseus, 1993) and *Almost a Woman* (Perseus, 1998) continues her life story of achievement against all odds. The memoir begins in her early twenties, when she breaks off with an abusive older lover and wins a scholarship to attend Harvard University. It ends with her graduation from Harvard, when she makes a symbolic purchase of a fountain pen because no one from her family is there for the ceremony or to encourage her career. (High School)

Starr, M. (2002). *Alicia's Happy Day*. Illustrated by C. Van Wright and Y. Hu. New York: Star Bright Books.
It's a young girl's birthday, and as she walks through her Puerto Rican neighborhood collecting birthday greetings, she imagines dancing salsa, seeing flags fly in her honor, having taxis stop for her, and reading a "happy birthday" written in the sky. (Primary)

Vázquez, L. (2004). *Bestiary: Selected Poems, 1986–1997*. Tempe, AZ: Bilingual Review Press.
Arranged in chronological order, Vázquez's poems examine her roots in Santurce, Puerto Rico, and the experiences of women confronting repression, abandonment, and betrayal. This bilingual edition is well translated into English, with an introduction by Rose Alcalá. (High School)

Wallner, A. (2000). *Sergio and the Hurricane*. Illustrated by the author. New York: Holt.
In San Juan, Puerto Rico, Sergio is excited about a coming hurricane until he helps his family prepare and in this way learns about the destructive power of nature. (Primary)

Winter, J. (2004). *Roberto Clemente: Pride of the Pittsburgh Pirates*. Illustrated by the R. Colón. New York: Simon and Schuster.
Winter's inspiring biography of the baseball player covers his childhood, growing up in poverty on the island; his years with the Pirates, where he overcame prejudice to become the team's best all-round player; and his hero's death in a plane crash while delivering supplies to the victims of an earthquake in Nicaragua. (Primary)

CHAPTER TWELVE

CUBAN AMERICANS
Concepts, Strategies, and Materials

*If in things concerning my country I should be given a choice above all
others this would be the good I would choose: I should want the
cornerstone of our Republic to be the devotion of Cubans to
the dignity of humankind.*

—José Marti

This chapter discusses the background and experience of a small but significant group of Hispanics in the United States. Cubans have lived in small communities in New York, Tampa, and Key West, Florida, since the latter part of the nineteenth century. Large numbers did not immigrate to the United States until after Fidel Castro assumed power in the revolution that occurred in 1959.

To fully comprehend Cuban Americans in the United States today, one must understand the circumstances that led them to emigrate. While levels of intensity may differ, there is a near-universal dislike among Cuban Americans of the communist government of Cuba. However, as time passes and there are more Cuban Americans who are born in the United States, those with more moderate perspectives increase in number. This chapter illustrates how Cuban immigrants have sought the American dream while simultaneously maintaining a passion for their homeland.

CUBAN IMMIGRANTS TO THE UNITED STATES

Since the 1960s, Cubans have been one of the largest groups immigrating to the United States. Of the foreign nationals entering the United States from Spanish-speaking nations, they have been the second largest immigrant group, surpassed

This chapter was contributed by **Carlos F. Diaz,** professor of education, Florida Atlantic University, Boca Raton, Florida. Professor Diaz is coauthor of *Touch the Future . . . Teach* (Allyn and Bacon, 2005).

CUBAN AMERICANS: HISTORICAL PERSPECTIVE

Important Dates	Events
1959	Fidel Castro took over the reins of power in Cuba from the government of dictator Fulgencio Batista.
1961	Diplomatic relations between the United States and Cuba were severed. The Cuban exile brigade 2500 landed at the Bay of Pigs on the southern coast of Cuba in an ill-fated attempt to overthrow the Castro regime.
1962	Commercial air flights between the United States and Cuba were ended. Immigration to the United States became strictly clandestine. The Cuban missile crisis prompted President John F. Kennedy to blockade Cuba. The Soviet Union eventually withdrew the missiles from Cuban soil.
1965	Beginning of the Cuban Refugee Airlift program. The U.S. government sponsored flights from Cuba to Miami, Florida.
1973	Termination of the Cuban Refugee Airlift program. Immigration to the United States returned to a clandestine status or took place through a third country, such as Spain or Mexico.
1977	The United States established diplomatic interest sections as well as Cuban governments in the embassies of third countries. Cuba used the Czechoslovakian embassy in Washington, and the United States used the Swiss embassy in Havana. This move was strongly opposed by most Cuban Americans. Fidel Castro allowed U.S. citizens and their Cuban dependents living in Cuba who wished to leave to depart Cuba.
1980	125,000 Cubans arrived in the United States via a boatlift from Mariel. Reaction in the United States ranged from welcome to open hostility.
1984	The Immigration and Naturalization Service ruled that Cubans who entered the United States via Mariel with the classification of "entrant" would be permitted to apply for permanent resident status under the Cuban Refugee Readjustment Act of 1966.
1985	In response to Radio Martí broadcasts beamed at Cuba, Fidel Castro stopped familial visits of Cuban Americans and abrogated the agreement with the United States to repatriate Mariel Cubans who were being held in American jails. Xavier Suarez was elected mayor of Miami, Florida. He was the first Cuban American to be elected to that office.
1987	Mariel refugee inmates imprisoned in Atlanta, Georgia, and Oakdale, Louisiana, rioted and took hostages on learning they might be deported. Riots ended after the U.S. government set up a review process for anyone facing deportation.

Important Dates	Events
1989	Representative Ileana Ros-Lehtinen became the first Cuban-born member of the U.S. Congress in a special election to replace the late representative Claude Pepper. Florida followed the precedent set in California, Illinois, and other states and voted 84% to 16% to amend the state constitution declaring English the state's official language. Cuban Americans largely opposed this measure.
1994	Fidel Castro announced that he would not stop Cubans attempting to flee the island. A massive rafting exodus followed, with the U.S. Coast Guard interdicting Cubans and sending them to camps at the Guantanamo naval base.
1995	Cuba and the United States negotiated an agreement that would slowly bring refugees from Guantanamo and Panama to the United States. Future entry visas for Cubans were set at 20,000 per year.
2000	The case of Elian Gonzalez riveted national attention for several months. Ultimately, courts ruled that Elian be returned to his father to live in Cuba.
2006	Fidel Castro cedes the Cuban presidency to his brother Raul when he has to undergo abdominal surgery. Speculation abounds regarding policy changes by the new president and when/whether Fidel will return to the presidency.

only by Mexicans. The number of Cubans immigrating to the United States between 1971 and 1980 (276,800) was 28% larger than the number that settled in the United States between 1951 and 1960 (78,300) (U.S. Immigration and Naturalization Service, 2000). After the 125,000 entrants from the Mariel boatlift in 1980, Cuban immigration declined during the remainder of the decade. Immigration from Cuba has been a sporadic process since 1959. In 1994, the Cuban government temporarily suspended enforcement of Cuban law forbidding Cuban citizens from leaving national territory by "illegal means." This temporary window of opportunity resulted in tens of thousands of *balseros* (rafters) openly launching their rafts in an effort to reach Florida, or at least a U.S. Coast Guard cutter. This window was closed after negotiations between the Clinton administration and the Cuban government established that Cuba would again enforce its law forbidding illegal exit and the United States would fill all or most of its allotment of 20,000 visas for legal Cuban entrants.

Cuban Americans are a group with low visibility because their relocation has occurred almost exclusively in a few large urban areas. In 2007, they numbered around 1.3 million, or about 3.5% of the Hispanic population of the United States. The largest Cuban American community is in the greater Miami, Florida, area and includes more than 500,000 people. Other large concentrations are found in the New York City metropolitan area and in the greater Los Angeles area (see Table 12.1).

TABLE 12.1   Cuban American Population in
Selected States, 2005

STATE	POPULATION
United States	1,461,574
Florida	1,000,151
California	83,205
New Jersey	77,451
New York	66,687

Note: The population of Cuban Americans in other states
is fewer than 65,000.

Source: U.S Census Bureau (2007), *American Community
Survey, 2005: Selected Population Profile.* Available online
at http://www.factfinder.census.gov.

The Cubans' brief history on U.S. soil shares some common elements with older
and more established immigrant groups. Yet many unique differences distinguish
their exodus. Most Cubans have migrated to the United States since the Castro revolution of 1959. Those who came did so primarily because they felt threatened by the
political situation they experienced in Cuba. This contrasts with most other American
immigrants, who came to the United States searching mainly for economic improvement for themselves and their families.

Another characteristic of the Cuban influx is that those who left the island in
search of a political haven are not a representative sample of the Cuban population
at large. A demographic study by Fagen, Brody, and O'Leary (1968) indicated that
"a disproportionate number of refugees come from the middle and upper strata of
pre-revolutionary society" (p. 16). People in the lower socioeconomic strata who
opposed the revolution had fewer resources at their disposal to turn their dissatisfaction into some viable action.

The middle and upper strata of Cuban society were most heavily represented in
the first wave of immigration during the early 1960s. As time progressed, Cuban
immigrants became a more representative sample of the Cuban population. However, the total number of Cuban immigrants in the United States still contains a
higher proportion of business and professional people than are present in the Cuban
population.

This overrepresentation of the Cuban middle and upper classes among immigrants can be partly explained by the fact the people in these classes felt particularly
threatened by governmental changes that eroded their economic position. Most
Cuban Americans were never part of the elite in their homeland, so their departure
cannot be attributed to a loss of great wealth. They left their native land primarily
because of their genuine opposition to the political system and for reasons of family
reunification.

Another group that is overrepresented in the Cuban American population is older people. Barriers to their exit from the island were considerably fewer than those for younger Cubans. Another factor contributing to this demographic trend is that many Cuban families sent for their parents or grandparents after they gained an economic foothold in the United States.

The ethnic and racial composition of Cuban Americans is also disproportionate to the Cuban population. According to Pérez (1980), "Black Cubans were probably less likely to emigrate because of their perception that race relations in the United States are less satisfactory than they are in socialist Cuba" (p. 257). Even though Black Cubans are underrepresented among immigrants, their numbers increased significantly after the Mariel influx in 1980. Caucasian and Chinese Cubans are found in greater proportions among Cubans in the United States than in the Cuban population. In prerevolutionary Cuba, Caucasian and Chinese Cubans were more prevalent in the middle and upper economic strata of society. Conversely, Black Cubans were more likely to be present in the lower economic class. Most Cuban Americans, regardless of racial and ethnic background, share an opposition to the Castro regime in Cuba. Among those who immigrated as adults, it is difficult to describe the depth and emotional nature of their sentiments. The desire for political as well as economic stability has shaped the dreams of Cuban immigrants to the United States.

The Cuban immigrant has generally accepted and lived by the predominant American ethos that hard work will ultimately be rewarded. Considering the deprived economic conditions with which most started, the results have been notable. Their accomplishments have caused some observers to tout them as a "model minority," much like their Japanese American counterparts. Yet the success of Cubans should not be construed so as to obscure the general plight of Spanish-speaking Americans. For most, this success has not occurred without hardship. Their accomplishments do not mean that Cuban Americans do not have problems. Their median income still lags behind the national average although it is higher than that of most Hispanic groups. To attain their median income, a disproportionate number of working wives are found in Cuban American households. Also, the cohesive nature of the Cuban family has sometimes suffered because of economic pressures.

The assimilation of Cubans has occurred at different levels among people living in various locations in the United States. Like other immigrant groups, assimilation has been less for the older segment of the population and for Cubans living in cities with large Cuban communities. The continuum of assimilation ranges from the almost perfectly integrated to some who have failed to accept the permanence of their U.S. surroundings.

LIFE IN CUBA

On January 1, 1959, the city of Havana, Cuba, rocked with the effects of a drastic change. The regime of dictator Fulgencio Batista had been deposed by *la Revolucion,* led by a bearded young rebel named Fidel Castro. His triumphal entry into the capital city was seen by nearly everyone as the coming of a new messiah. His popularity was more than that of a political figure; he had all the markings of a charismatic leader.

Promises of economic prosperity and of uniting the Cuban people were among the many Fidel Castro made. The synthesis of the Cuban revolution took place in a slow, deliberate series of steps, to the delight of some and the disillusionment of others. The Agrarian Reform confiscated large holdings of land in private hands. This land became government property, and farmers became government employees.

As the course of the revolution drifted politically left, a marked polarization of Cuban society began to occur. A person either supported the revolution or was thought of as a *gusano* (worm), a parasite to progress without whom the revolution was better off. True to the Cuban sense of humor, the expression *abrir los ojos* (see the light) marked a person who took exception to revolutionary policies. These political divisions permeated the family unit and caused bitter disagreements among those relatives who advocated for the revolution and those who opposed it. Many of these rifts remain today. The Cuban revolution affected everyone, regardless of his or her place in society. Fundamental changes reached the economic, political, social, and religious sectors of Cuban life.

The educational system in Cuba was affected fundamentally by the revolution. The number of schools in rural areas was increased in a campaign to end *analfabetismo* (illiteracy), and new high schools were built primarily in rural areas. Some urban students had to board a school bus to a rural school in order to obtain a secondary education. In the public schools, instruction in the humanities and the natural and physical sciences was fraught with political socialization, which placed a premium on loyalty to the revolution. The Cuban educational system, despite limited financial resources, tends to produce high-quality graduates. A study analyzing Cuban education found that Cuban education is child-centered and allows for long-term relationships between students and teachers. The curriculum is conceptually oriented. Elementary school students in Cuba outperform their Latin American peers (Carnoy, 2007). Along with expanding education, the Cuban government has expanded access to health care well beyond what it was before 1959. Clinics are more readily available in cities and rural areas, and access to these facilities is free. There are occasional shortages of medicines, but in general, Cubans have access to better health care than other Latin American populations.

The Cuban economy today deemphasizes consumer goods in favor of products for export. As a result of this emphasis, as well as of production lags, rationing is fairly common. The following ration limits per person were obtained by interviewing a Cuban immigrant and were in effect in 2007 (author's interview with a person who visited Cuba in 2006):

rice	5 pounds per month
beans	6 ounces per month
coffee	1 ounce per week
meat	not available through the rationing process
eggs	5 per month

sugar	4 pounds per month
bread	$\frac{1}{4}$ pound per day
soap	$\frac{1}{2}$ bar every 3 to 4 months (if available)

FOR CHILDREN

| 0–7 years of age | 1 liter of milk per day (not available for those over 7) |

CLANDESTINE MARKET

1 pound of rice	5 pesos
1 pound of pork	26 pesos
1 liter of milk	3 pesos
1 liter of gasoline	25 pesos
1 egg	2 pesos

The official exchange rate in 2007 was 26 pesos to one dollar.

Since the collapse of the Soviet empire, most of the favorable trading or bartering agreements Cuba had with former communist nations have collapsed. New goods must be purchased with hard currency, which the Cuban peso is not. Daily life in Cuba, particularly the procurement of sufficient food, has become increasingly difficult when compared to food availability prior to 1992. Salaries in 2007 ranged from approximately 550 pesos ($22.00) per month for a physician to 180 pesos ($7.00) per month for an office worker. Pensioners typically receive around 100 pesos ($4.00) per month. The imbalance between legal wages and the prices of necessities has forced many Cubans to turn to the clandestine market or to barter.

Some fortunate individuals receive dollars or other foreign currencies from relatives abroad. These may be used in "dollar stores" where the Cuban peso is not accepted. In these stores, one can purchase soap, toiletries, and many other goods that are not available in the regular stores.

In addition to the rationing, Cubans must plan on spending a fair amount of time waiting to buy their food items. It is not uncommon for a shopper to spend two hours or more per day making food purchases. Whenever something extra can be obtained, people do so for friends or relatives. Any outing from the home is a potential shopping trip. Because the availability of products is often sporadic, the shopping bag (*jaba*) is a constant companion.

Socioeconomic mobility in Cuba is accomplished by a mixture of individual talent, effort, and loyalty. The last of these factors creates some wrenching psychological dilemmas for certain individuals. To hold most of the managerial and many professional positions, the person must be a card-carrying *militante* (militant). Some people hold this status out of conviction for communist or revolutionary beliefs and others because the card is convenient for upward mobility in society. These people must be particularly careful of their associations.

A constant dilemma for the "militants of convenience" is whether their activities or associations will help or hinder their image as militants. It is also assumed that people with militant status will be prepared to serve on any international mission to which they may be assigned. This is also true for people studying any of the professions, particularly those in the health fields. These missions may last two or three years, and some couples have been separated for that long.

Other adaptations to revolutionary society include having most salaries in the nation specified by the government. Purchasing food and major consumer goods requires a ration book or government coupon. Entrepreneurial activity (small factories, renting rooms, home restaurants) requires government permission.

Salary laws require workers to meet a production quota of either goods or services. If this quota is not reached, the worker's salary can be reduced by a proportional amount. In addition to a worker's obligatory job, there is volunteer labor available on Sundays or holidays. This volunteer work may consist of cleaning details, construction projects, or harvesting sugar cane, as well as many other tasks. Workers who want to purchase a major item, such as a refrigerator, often accumulate many hours of volunteer labor.

Leaving the country entails many sacrifices. Invariably, relatives are left behind. This point is particularly significant when one realizes the close-knit nature of the Cuban extended family, which makes it difficult for members to break from the family unit.

Forfeiture of all possessions is another factor to consider. Everything a person has worked for in a lifetime finds its way into government hands. Also, there is the prospect of starting over in a new nation. For most immigrants to the United States, this happens without command of the English language. Despite all these difficulties, however, more than a million Cubans have felt compelled to leave their homeland.

Opinions about the Castro regime vary within Cuba. Supporters point out that the Cuban government has vastly expanded health care and education (Carnoy, 2007). Cubans on the island who are strong supporters of the Castro government and its philosophy cite wide gaps in living standards between the elite and common people in other Latin American nations. These issues, however valid, are not very salient with the Cuban American population. For most of them, the ills perpetrated by the Castro government outweigh any of its positive measures (Sung-Chang & Grenier, 2004).

In the early 1960s, the United States accepted as a political refugee any Cuban who could reach its shores. In 1966, the Cuban Readjustment Act gave Cuban refugees the status of parolees and allowed a change to permanent resident status after two years with good behavior in the United States. This law also gave Cubans special immigration status so their number would not be limited or counted against the limits allowed for other nations in the Americas.

This remained U.S. policy until the Refugee Act of 1980 removed special immigration status from Cuban immigrants. In order to accommodate the influx of Cubans in 1980, President Carter created a special immigration category of "entrants." People who held this entrant status remained as temporary residents of the United States until late 1984, when the Immigration and Naturalization Service decided to allow them to apply for permanent residency status. Today, Cubans no longer hold officially favored immigration status.

DEPARTURE

Prohias and Casal (1973) have identified three stages in the migration of Cubans to the United States:

> They are as follows: A first stage, between January 1959 and October 1962, when commercial flights between Cuba and the United States were available; a second stage, between October 1962 and December 1965, with a corresponding slowdown of the migration rate as Cubans had to resort to unconventional means (small boats, rafts, etc.) or flights through third countries to come to the United States; a third stage, with daily air flights between Varadero and Miami throughout most of the period. (p. 257)

The third stage, known as the Cuban Refugee Airlift, was terminated in January 1973. From 1973 to 1980, Cubans reverted to the unconventional means of the second stage. In 1980, a temporary policy change by the Cuban government produced a fourth stage, resulting in a wave of 125,000 Cubans coming by sea from Mariel to Key West, Florida. At the conclusion of this boatlift in May 1980, Cubans reverted to second-stage methods.

In 1988, the Cuban American National Foundation received permission from the U.S. Immigration and Naturalization Service to sponsor Cubans living outside of Cuba. This effort was to reunite them with relatives living in the United States. The visas granted to these individuals stipulated that their relocation would occur at no cost to the national, state, or local government. Today, nearly all Cubans immigrating to the United States legally have won a lottery for a U.S. visa. The number of visas issued yearly cannot exceed 20,000, although fewer have been awarded in many years.

The trauma of leaving Cuba varies greatly with the particular experience. Leaving by commercial airline in 1960 was fairly conventional. However, escaping in a small boat meant jeopardizing one's life. Also, the date of departure determined how much difficulty an exile would encounter in leaving the island. In general, the longer a family waited before making the decision to leave, the more obstacles it would have to face before it could secure permission to exit. In the early 1960s, many families sent their children out of Cuba via Catholic or other religious relief agencies in the hope that the parents could follow later. This effort was called Operation Peter Pan. Most of these families were reunited; a few are still waiting.

Many Americans have heard of Cubans reaching U.S. shores in small boats or rafts, but little publicity is given to the fact that many never made it, having encountered a patrol boat or perished drifting away in the Gulf Stream current.

THE MARIEL IMMIGRANTS OF 1980

In April 1980, more than 10,000 Cubans sought political asylum in the Peruvian embassy in Havana. The Cuban government's initial response was to allow them permission to leave Cuba via Peru or other willing Latin American nations, such as Costa Rica. Within days, that policy was changed to allow the exit of those people, as well as others who had sought to immigrate, directly to the United States. The Cuban American community in the United States saw this temporary respite in Cuban immigration policy as an opportunity to reunite with relatives whom they had been trying to join for years.

A small port city on the northern coast of Cuba, Mariel, became the staging area for people waiting for transportation to the United States. On May 5, 1980, President Carter stated that the United States would receive the refugees "with an open heart and open arms." Nine days later, a presidential order forbade boats going to Cuba to pick up refugees. By then, hundreds of boats were on their way to Mariel or were there waiting. Many Cuban American families spent their savings or pooled their earnings to pay for passage on a boat for relatives in Cuba.

The hundreds of boats that had crossed the Straits of Florida found a chaotic situation at the port of Mariel. Most boats had to anchor and wait, sometimes for weeks, until the government indicated that a group of people was ready for loading. Boat captains brought lists of people they came to transport, but often the lists were ignored or only one or two people on the list would be permitted to leave.

Meanwhile, food and supplies began to run low on board these vessels. Provisions had to be purchased from the Cuban government at three to six times their price in the United States. As time passed, tempers began to flare in the Mariel harbor.

People who had declared a willingness to leave via Mariel were gathered from all parts of Cuba. In some instances, people departing were publicly humiliated by zealous supporters of the revolution. Some people who declared a desire to leave through Mariel were not able to do so for logistical or other reasons. Their declaration caused them to lose their jobs, and many could not find other jobs.

The return crossing of the Straits of Florida was often a perilous ordeal. As a rule, boats were loaded beyond their capacity. Some captains objected to this, as well as to carrying people for whom they had not come. When the Cuban authorities insisted on both points, boat captains faced the dilemma of violating these directives or violating U.S. directives to stop the boatlift when they returned to Florida. More than fifty people died during these crossings. Some drowned when boats capsized in heavy seas, and others succumbed to carbon monoxide fumes in the holds of overloaded vessels. A frequently repeated ritual consisted of Cuban refugees kissing the ground after arriving in Key West, Florida.

As the flood of refugees continued, they were housed in a variety of temporary holding centers, including the Orange Bowl in Miami, Florida. People with immediate relatives were the most likely to be released quickly. Others without relatives waited patiently for relocation in other parts of the United States. As the numbers of refugees increased, a backlash of public opinion began. A Gallup poll conducted nationally in late May 1980 found that 59% of respondents felt that Cuban emigration was bad for the United States (Alpen, 1980). In the Miami area, a similar survey conducted by the *Miami Herald* in May 1980 found that 68% of the non-Latino White population and 57% of the African American population surveyed felt that the new wave of Cuban refugees would have a negative influence on the local community (Morin, 1980, p. 1).

The Cuban community in Miami raised more than $2 million in cash and other assistance to help accommodate the new arrivals. Nevertheless, the size of the influx made it necessary to relocate many Cubans in holding centers outside southern Florida. As Cuban refugees were relocated on military bases in predominantly rural areas of Arkansas, Pennsylvania, Wisconsin, and Florida, residents of those areas vehemently protested the Cuban presence.

There was a higher proportion of Black Cubans, single males, and blue-collar workers among the Mariel boatlift immigrants than in previous groups of Cubans who settled in the United States. Much has been written about the undesirable or criminal element that came to the United States during the boatlift. The Cuban government seized the opportunity to rid itself of people who had committed serious crimes or suffered mental or physical problems, but people in these categories constituted fewer than 5% of the 125,000 entrants. Also, spending time in a Cuban jail could have been either for criminal or political activities. Consequently, not all criminals would have had that label if they had been living in the United States. Most of the Mariel Cubans originally detained were eventually released. In 2007, a few of these prisoners still remain at the Atlanta Federal Penitentiary.

Most Cubans who came via the 1980 boatlift were of humbler origins than their predecessors but were just as determined to improve themselves. A few gave the term *Marielito* a pejorative connotation. Unfortunately, that connotation has sometimes tainted the majority of Mariel Cubans who have worked hard and respected the law. Today, nearly three decades after their arrival, nearly all Mariel Cubans have adjusted well to U.S. society.

THE CUBAN RAFTERS OF 1994

While Cubans have been risking their lives trying to cross the Straits of Florida in makeshift rafts for decades, some unusual events occurred in the summer of 1994. The sequence began with a small Cuban vessel that was hijacked by a group of Cubans seeking to come to Florida. In the process, a Cuban military officer was killed. The vessel eventually made its way to Florida.

The Castro government protested that the United States was harboring hijackers and should return the group to Cuba. When the United States refused to do so, Fidel Castro retaliated by refusing to stop any Cubans who tried to leave the nation by sea. Tens of thousands of Cubans took to the ocean, mostly in makeshift rafts. The United States Coast Guard was rescuing thousands of Cubans each day at the peak of this exodus.

President Clinton issued a proclamation that Cubans leaving in rafts would no longer be granted entrant status to the United States. The last vestiges of the Cuban Refugee Readjustment Act of 1966 had been nullified. Cuban rafters were confined in a camp at the military base in Guantanamo, Cuba. Some Cubans were transferred to a camp in Panama.

After negotiations between Cuban and U.S. authorities in New York, the Cuban government agreed to enforce Cuban law prohibiting exit from the country without documentation. The United States agreed to give all or nearly all of the 28,000 yearly visas to Cubans promised under an earlier accord negotiated in 1984. An average of 2,000 to 3,000 visas per year were granted between 1984 to 1994. The fate of those Cubans detained in Guantanamo and Panama was resolved by an accord reached in 1995 between the United States and Cuba. Cubans in the Guantanamo and Panama camps would be slowly resettled in the United States, beginning with children and those who had close family relations in the United States. Cubans in Cuba were to apply for U.S. entry visas. The United States promised to issue at least 20,000 per year.

THE CASE OF ELIAN GONZALEZ

On Thanksgiving Day of 1999, two men fishing off the coast of Fort Lauderdale, Florida, found five-year-old Elian Gonzalez clinging to an inner tube. Two other adult survivors from the same boat that brought Elian were rescued off the coast of Miami. Elian's mother and nine other Cuban refugees perished in an effort to reach the shores of Florida. Thus began a protracted family and diplomatic struggle over the future of a five-year-old boy that was chronicled throughout the world.

Elian was turned over to his great-uncle, Lazaro Gonzalez, and his family, who resided in Miami. Shortly afterward, Elian's biological father, Juan Miguel Gonzalez, requested that Elian be returned to live with him in Cuba. The family of Lazaro Gonzalez refused the request, and an international custody battle ensued.

Many observers who heard about this case on the news found the controversy perplexing. After all, when viewed strictly as a child custody issue between a father and a great-uncle, wouldn't the law always support granting custody to the natural father, providing he is a fit parent?

If Juan Miguel Gonzalez had resided in the United States, there would have been no controversy. However, because he was a citizen of Cuba, it was understood by all parties that if his father was granted custody, Elian would definitely return to Cuba. Elian's return to Cuba was very problematic for many Cuban Americans who felt that if this occurred, Elian's mother would have died in vain and her desires would be ignored. They also felt that Elian's future would be far more promising if he was allowed to remain in the United States.

Ultimately, this issue was resolved in the courts. Over a period of months and through various hearings and appeals, the attorneys representing Juan Miguel Gonzalez were prevailing. Meanwhile, Lazaro Gonzalez and his family had received temporary custody of Elian from the Immigration and Naturalization Service (INS). The Justice Department plan was to have a voluntary transfer of Elian to INS custody and transport him to Washington, D.C., where he would reside with his father until a final determination was made by the courts.

While this scenario was playing out in the United States, many demonstrations were held in Cuba involving hundreds of thousands of Cubans demanding that the United States "free Elian" and "return Cuba's son." Elian was frequently featured in the Cuban media with commentary that his continued stay in the United States amounted to an "international kidnapping."

In March of 2000, U.S. district judge Michael Moore threw out a political asylum lawsuit that cleared the way for Elian Gonzalez to be returned to his father in Cuba. Elian's Miami family attorneys appealed Judge Moore's decision to the 11th U.S. Circuit Court of Appeals in Atlanta.

While all parties waited for this decision, the Immigration and Naturalization Service revoked Lazaro Gonzalez's custody of Elian, but Lazaro did not voluntarily turn Elian over to INS custody. After protracted discussions between the Miami family's lawyers and the Justice Department, Attorney General Janet Reno gave permission for Elian to be removed from Lazaro Gonzalez's home in the early morning of April 22, 2000. The dramatic raid caused consternation in many circles but particularly among Cuban Americans in Miami, some of whom demonstrated in the streets. Elian became a hero in Cuba and was befriended by Fidel Castro, the president of Cuba.

On June 1, 2000, a three-judge panel of the Circuit Court of Appeals upheld Judge Moore's original ruling, and the way was cleared for Juan Miguel Gonzalez to return to Cuba with Elian. He did so on June 28, 2000.

ADAPTATION TO LIFE IN THE UNITED STATES

Most immigrants to the United States have come with the unwavering conviction of making this country their permanent home. In contrast, many Cubans arrived in the United States hoping to return to their homeland as soon as the political climate changed. Although grateful to the United States for their asylum, their ultimate plans were not to remain in the United States. Thus, they did not feel the immediate need to assimilate into the mainstream culture. With the passing of time, only the most optimistic clung exclusively to this viewpoint. As the Castro regime has shown strong signs of longevity, exiles have tried to adapt to their new environment.

The adaptation of Cubans to American life has often been difficult. This process has been more extensive in areas where the Cuban population is small. In a city like Miami, with its large Cuban community, it is possible to live without crossing the boundaries of the ethnic neighborhood, and assimilation is not imperative. One major change has been to forsake the more leisurely mood of the Cuban lifestyle. According to a *New York Times* article (Morin, 1980), "Conversion to the pace of American life has threatened to disrupt the traditional Cuban way of life.

The initial cultural shock was compounded by the dizzying social changes under way in the United States that perplexed most Americans" (p. 1).

The high percentage of Cuban American working wives has had a significant social, as well as economic, impact on the Cuban community. Richmond (1980) found that "resources of the wife, particularly as they compared favorably to the resources possessed by her husband, were found to be an additional influence in the absorption of a more egalitarian ideology" (p. 115). The traditional dominant role of the husband in the Cuban household has undergone some modification, particularly in locations where families live in a largely non-Cuban community.

One problem encountered by Cuban parents was having their children adhere to Cuban values, norms, and customs. These permitted less freedom than their American peers enjoyed. This gap was felt more acutely by daughters in Cuban families than sons, because traditionally girls have been more closely supervised by parents.

Where Cubans resettled in large numbers, they were received in a variety of ways. A former Cuban lawyer related his impression in the following manner: "There are many people in Miami who still resent the Cubans settling here," he said, "but for the most part, since we have been the most successful immigrants in American history, Americans find it hard to look down their noses at us because we arrived here loaded with American characteristics. We are just too outgoing and enterprising and hard-working for them to stay mad at us" (Morin, 1980, p. 1).

The reactions experienced by Cuban immigrants depend on the time and location of their immigration. People who were relocated to cities and towns with small Hispanic populations experience little negative reaction. The influx of a few families is probably noticed little in most communities. Among Cubans who settled in areas like Miami, Florida, initial opposition to their arrival came from people in unskilled and blue-collar jobs. These new arrivals were perceived as an economic threat. People with higher socioeconomic positions were relatively unconcerned and often praised the hard-working émigrés who competed with others for low-wage jobs.

With time and increasing command of English, Cubans began to climb the socioeconomic ladder and to assert themselves economically and, to a lesser extent, politically. In 1969, Dade County (Miami) had 3,449 Hispanic businesses. By 1977, that figure had become 8,248, and in 1985 it had grown to 15,000. The Hispanic (mostly Cuban) population of Dade County had an annual income in 1985 of $6.7 billion (Oppenheimer, 1985). In 2007, the economic output of the Dade County Hispanic business community exceeded that of Hispanic businesses in Los Angeles, which has more than double the Hispanic population of Miami.

When Cubans started to become a potent economic force in Miami, and in other cities where their numbers were significant, they encountered difficulties from segments of the community that traditionally held most of the economic and political influence and wanted no change. Many of these people had been relatively unconcerned a decade or two before. More recently, they have realized that Cuban Americans are a viable economic entity and a competitive force. Competition is not always welcomed.

Like many immigrant groups, Cuban Americans have formed their own organizations to promote common interests. Groups such as the Latin American Chamber of Commerce were formed in Miami and claim the greatest membership among Cuban American businesspeople. While many members of this association may also join the Greater Miami Chamber of Commerce, the Latin Chamber is expected to continue in the foreseeable future.

In 2005, the median income of Cuban Americans ($38,395) was higher than the median for all Hispanics ($36,278) and below the median income ($46,242) for the entire nation (U.S. Census Bureau, 2005). When compared to other Hispanics, the higher Cuban median income was partly explained by an unusually high percentage of Cuban American women in the workforce and the higher average age of the Cuban American population.

In 1980, the entrance of thousands of Mariel Cubans into predominantly low-skill jobs temporarily decreased Cuban American median income. However, Cuban American economic status increased sharply within ten years. According to Olson and Olson (1995), Mariel Cubans "were proving to be as successful in learning English, finding jobs and building businesses as the earlier generation of Cuban immigrations after only 10 years in the United States" (p. 91).

When they tried to pursue their former occupations in the United States, many Cubans ran into difficulties. The main obstacle to white-collar employment was mastery of the English language, which most did not have. In the professional fields, degrees earned in Cuba were often not recognized, and individuals frequently returned to college if they wanted to obtain work related to their former professions. Even though many Cubans have regained their former occupational status, and some have even surpassed it, a slight loss of occupational status remains.

The typical newly arrived exile family in the 1960s received some assistance from the Cuban refugee program while it existed. Afterward, Cubans took whatever employment was immediately available, anticipating that their preferred work could be obtained later. When the concentration of Cubans in the Miami area became substantial, the government started a resettlement program. This program offered jobs and one month's free rent to immigrants who agreed to move outside Florida. In recent years, some Cubans who had been relocated trickled back into the south Florida area after they had achieved a financial foothold to make relocation in Miami possible.

Many Cubans arriving via the 1980 boatlift had a more difficult time, especially single males with no family in the United States. Many waited months behind camp fences, looking for an organization or person to sponsor their release. As time passed, frustration grew and even erupted into hostility at some camps. Even after being released in the care of a sponsor, some Mariel Cubans found it difficult to adjust to a competitive capitalist society with opportunities but few guarantees. After decades of working in a socialist economic system, some were unaccustomed to or unsure of work patterns and habits in the United States. Others adapted quickly and easily.

At times, a rift developed between the older, established Cuban immigrant and the Mariel émigré. The former sometimes felt that the latter were insufficiently driven to succeed or grateful for the assistance received. This situation is similar to the relationship that developed in the latter part of the nineteenth century between the established German American Jews and the new arrivals from eastern Europe.

Another analysis of this group reveals that non-White Mariel immigrants have had a more difficult time with socioeconomic adjustment, as evidenced by somewhat lower median incomes compared to White Mariel immigrants. Relatively few Mariel immigrants chose to resettle in the greater Miami area; they were much more likely to live in Cuban communities in other areas such as Tampa, Los Angeles, or New York (Skop, 2001).

The children who entered via Mariel also had to make major adjustments, as did the school systems in which they enrolled. Writes Silva (1985): "In absolute numbers, the Dade County Public Schools faced integrating a school population larger than 95% of the school districts in the United States" (p. 23). The Dade County schools enrolled more than 11,500 Cuban refugee children in the 1980–1981 school year. Students were divided between two entrant facilities established exclusively for Mariel students. The remaining students attended special programs in schools designated as entrant centers, as well as neighborhood schools.

Mariel Cubans often miss a sense of closeness and spirituality in life in the United States. Many centered their lives in Cuba on these qualities, which helped them endure hardships and privations. They see themselves as distinct from the older émigrés, some of whom they view as living in a "frozen Cuban culture." This frozen culture is based solely on Cuban values, beliefs, and attitudes; all aspects of contemporary life are compared to this Cuban cultural baseline. These people exist as a subculture within a subculture.

The process of assimilation has been most difficult for the elderly Cuban population. They represent an unusually high percentage of the Cuban immigrant population because older people could leave the island more readily. This elderly population faced the usual problems of the aged, compounded by an environment that many found perplexing. Those elderly whose families had strayed from traditional Cuban customs venerating the aged missed being the center of the family. Elderly persons living alone are found in larger-than-expected numbers in the Cuban American community. Many Cuban elderly who live in extended families provide the crucial day-care function that allows many Cuban women to join the labor force.

As might be expected, the Cuban American elderly are the least culturally assimilated segment of the Cuban community in the United States. Most speak minimal or no English and can only participate in limited aspects of American life. Their children and grandchildren are often their link to the non-Cuban community. Some, though not most, of the elderly belong to what has been described earlier as the "frozen culture."

News from relatives in Cuba keeps Cuban Americans of all ages aware of life in their former country. They feel deeply the difficulties and privations that loved ones may be experiencing, and they do whatever they can to help ameliorate the circumstances. In 1979, the Cuban government began to allow familial visits. Tens of thousands of Cubans in the United States returned to the island with suitcases bulging with clothes, food, and gifts for relatives. These visitors were described by the Cuban population as belonging to "the community." The stories of their lives in the United States were sometimes exaggerated, representing more affluence than truly existed, but these visits were crucial to many families because relatives brought badly needed items as gifts. These visits were curtailed to one every three years under the administration of President George W. Bush. This limitation created a rift in the Cuban American community between those who wanted a tighter embargo and those who felt maintaining family ties was more important.

Politically, Cuban Americans have been generally more conservative than most recently arrived immigrants. However, this conservatism should not be equated unequivocally with traditional American conservatism. Cuban Americans are conservative on foreign policy issues, especially if those issues concern Cuba or communism. They tend to be considerably more moderate on domestic social issues.

In the Miami metropolitan area, Cubans are becoming an increasing portion of the electorate through naturalization. In the fall of 1981, Raul Martinez was elected mayor of Hialeah, Florida, thus becoming the first Cuban American mayor of a large U.S. city. Until 1982, no Cuban American had been elected to the state legislature of Florida, even though Cuban Americans comprised approximately one-half of Miami's Dade County. In 1982, Florida changed from multimember to single-member legislative districts, and a number of Cuban Americans were elected to serve in the state house of representatives. The mid and late 1980s saw Xavier Suarez elected mayor of Miami, followed by Joe Corollo. In 2006, Marco Rubio, a Cuban American, was chosen speaker of the Florida House of Representatives.

At the national level, Ileana Ros-Lehtinen was elected to the U.S. House of Representatives in 1989, becoming the first Cuban American member of Congress. Two fellow Cuban Americans, Lincoln Diaz-Balart and Mario Diaz-Balart, both from Miami, later joined her. By 2007, there were two Cuban American U.S. senators: Robert Menendez of New Jersey and Mel Martinez of Florida. As more Cuban Americans become naturalized citizens and turn their attention to U.S. politics, their political participation and influence should grow proportionately.

THE SECOND GENERATION

The Cuban American community now has a significant population that immigrated to the United States when they were young children or were born in the United States. This second generation represents a unique group of English-dominant bilingual persons who function well in both the Cuban American community and within mainstream society. They range approximately from ages twenty to fifty and are found in nearly every walk of life.

They are sometimes referred to as YUCAs (young upwardly mobile Cuban Americans). The term has a double meaning, because the *yuca* is a starchy root that

Cubans frequently eat. The perspectives of this second generation are neither those of their parents nor those of their American peers. One American-born young woman in her early twenties commented, "The Cubans consider me an American, and the Americans consider me a Cuban." Another American-born young man observed, "I didn't realize how Cuban I was until I left South Florida for Boston to attend college." Many of these young people understand the anachronisms in Cuban American culture but are respectful of the persons who hold them.

Cuba is not a personal experience or memory for most of these individuals. They know of Cuba only from their parents' accounts, which typically grow fonder with each telling. It is thus understandable that most do not hold as strong an attachment as their parents for a place and a way of life that appears mythical.

Most of this second generation is fundamentally pragmatic. They are generally less politicized and conservative than their parents, but they still see themselves as culturally distinct (Sung-Chang & Grenier, 2004). Their identity as Cuban Americans often does not include thinking of themselves as minority group members. They sometimes are surprised when they interact with other young Hispanics who identify with minority group status.

As a rule, the YUCAs see the perpetuation of the Spanish language through their own children as a desirable goal, even if some of their own command of Spanish grammar is rudimentary. A study by Garcia and Diaz (1992) of language use among Hispanic (mostly Cuban American) high school seniors in Miami confirmed that most of the youth spoke English in formal and informal settings; Spanish predominated in familial settings. The one exception to this pattern was that English was used more than Spanish as the preferred language among siblings. The continued use of English among siblings suggests that the family setting is no longer the sole province of the Spanish language. Time will tell whether this generation of Cuban Americans will be able to pass on significant knowledge of Spanish to its children.

Politically, slightly more than half of U.S.-born Cuban Americans register as Democrats or Independents. They are more likely than their parents' generation to oppose the embargo on Cuba and have a more compromising attitude toward U.S.-Cuban relations. They are also less likely to consider a candidate's position on Cuba as an overriding consideration when voting. In short, U.S.-born Cubans, while influenced by their parents, are developing their own cultural and political profile (Sung-Chang & Grenier, 2004).

CUBAN AMERICANS: LOOKING AHEAD

After nearly five decades from the beginning of the first wave of Cuban immigration to the United States in 1959, Cuban Americans represent a community in transition. While still keenly interested in matters affecting Cuba, many more Cuban Americans than before are focused on domestic issues. The older immigrants who represent the core of the "exile community" are fewer in number. Cuban Americans who came to the United States as children are now among the leadership in various communities.

These immigrants, along with U.S.-born Cuban Americans, are generally well assimilated but face some dilemmas. The great majority of Cuban Americans view themselves as persons who can function equally well in American society as in Cuban or Hispanic circles. This requires a person who is generally bilingual, biliterate, and bicultural. They view English-Spanish biliteracy as a definite economic and educational asset for themselves and their children. "Cuban Americans see learning of the non-English language as one of the three most important things a child can learn in school" (Baratz-Snowden, Rock, Pollard, & Wilder, 1988, p. 47). While biliteracy is a difficult goal to master, Cuban Americans view it as desirable.

This conception of American nationality is somewhat at odds with the one that prevailed at the beginning of the twentieth century. Immigrants from this era were encouraged to lose their original language and culture and replace them with English and American culture. This historical notion of the immigrant is at odds with what most Cuban Americans view as practical. They generally favor assimilation, which is a process of "language and cultural addition," not "language and cultural replacement." While Cuban Americans are generally very law abiding, they also feel empathy for fellow immigrants who are trying to adapt to American society, a role they know only too well.

During the debate over immigration changes in 2007, Cuban American members of Congress generally supported changes in immigration law that would provide for better border control without being unduly punitive to those who were in the United States without proper documentation. Since the immigration bill failed in the U.S. Senate, Congress will have to revisit this issue in the future. Cuban Americans generally felt uncomfortable with nativist and xenophobic tendencies unleashed by this immigration debate. While most are fairly well assimilated, the immigrant experience still resonates, and Cuban Americans are leery of anti-immigrant rhetoric, especially when it crosses the line from illegal immigration to immigrants in general. Cuban Americans are keenly aware of efforts like antibilingual ordinances or English-only groups, which most view largely as thinly veiled efforts to limit Hispanics in the United States.

Another major issue in the future of the Cuban American community is what will happen in Cuba when Fidel Castro dies. He was so ill in 2006 that he ceded the presidency of Cuba to his brother Raul. There has been speculation among Cuban Americans that Raul could not make any significant changes in Cuba while Fidel remains alive. Another view is that Raul will not change anything when Fidel dies. The question of whether there will be any significant political change in Cuba after Fidel—and whether this change will be violent or peaceful—is a topic of much debate among Cuban Americans. Relatively few Cuban Americans would return to Cuba to live under a different system, but most of them are strongly interested in Cuba.

Cuban Americans, like many immigrants to the United States before them, continue to look for a balance between being productive citizens in the United States—a nation they revere—and keeping significant elements of the culture and language that make them unique.

TEACHING STRATEGIES

Concept

Immigration

Generalization: Many Cuban immigrants found themselves unable and/or unwilling to live with the Castro government and chose to leave their homeland instead.

1. Divide your class into small groups and instruct them as follows: Your family is forced to move to a country in which the language and customs are alien. Each of you is allowed to take only a small amount of clothes. All of your possessions are left behind and forfeited because you cannot return. Describe what your life might be like where you are going. What clothing would you take with you? Why? How well do you think your family would fare? What adjustments would all of you have to make? The students' reactions can be taped or written. The taping would provide more spontaneous responses. Afterwards, compare and discuss reactions among groups.

2. After sufficient background information is presented, ask each student to write an essay titled "If I Had Been a Cuban in 1959, What Would I Have Done?"

3. Organize a debate in which one side takes the position that deposing the Castro regime is feasible and the other feels it is impossible.

4. Read the following story to the class and ask the questions that follow.

THE PINA FAMILY

Ernesto Pina was a fisherman who lived in Cardenas, on the north coast of Cuba. He and his wife, Iliana, had never been wealthy, but fishing had always provided for the necessities of life. Ernesto always seemed to be able to return with fish of one type or another.

They had been happy to see the tyrant Batista deposed by the Castro revolution. Ernesto felt that Fidel Castro had the interests of the "little man" like himself at heart. One day when he returned to the fishery to sell his catch, Ernesto was informed that part of it would go to the government. Officials said that his fish would be exported and the goods received in return would help the revolution. Ernesto did not want to be considered greedy, but he needed his entire catch to support his family. At the risk of being caught, he would hide some fish and sell them privately to his friends.

The family's only son, Jose, was sixteen and had been forced to join the militia. Neither parent liked this, but it could not be helped.

One night Ernesto and Iliana were talking and she suggested going to the United States. Yet both knew that they could not depart legally, because Jose was of military age. Obviously, they could not leave their only son behind. So the three decided to try to escape in the fishing boat one night. They knew they would be shot in the water if discovered, but decided to take the risk anyway.

The eventful night came, and the Pina family slipped away from the harbor. Ernesto was sailing the craft because he did not want the noise of the engine to be heard. He had been quite careful to wait for the proper tide and a moonless night. After a short time, they heard an engine; the sound kept coming closer. It was the shore patrol! He lowered the sail quickly, and they hid in the bottom of the boat. The patrol boat passed within fifty yards but had not spotted them. They had been saved by the darkness!

When morning came, Ernesto started his small engine because the breeze had faded. He hoped for the best because he did not have much gasoline. After two days at sea he was beginning to worry. His family was sunburned, he was out of gasoline, and he had not yet spotted the Florida coast. Yet they kept their faith. They were lucky to be seen by a U.S. Coast Guard cutter, which towed them into port. As the three stepped off the boat onto American soil, they each said a prayer for having been so fortunate.

Questions
1. If you had been one of the Pina family and found yourself in their circumstances, would you have taken the risk they did? Why or why not?
2. What problems did Mr. Pina encounter that made him decide to leave Cuba?
3. Why didn't the Pina family attempt to leave Cuba by legal means?
4. What kind of future do you foresee for the Pina family in the United States?
5. Have students (either in writing or orally) describe the circumstances of a political situation in the United States that would cause them to escape to a foreign nation at a risk to their lives.

Concept

Intergenerational conflict

Generalization: The second generation of any immigrant group is going to absorb from the larger society values, beliefs, and priorities that are sometimes at odds with their parents' beliefs.

Read the following story to the class and ask the questions that follow.

THE RODRIGUEZ FAMILY

Carlos Rodriguez is a young, successful, professional person working in the Miami branch of a major American corporation. His wife, Maria, teaches in the public schools; their daughters, Gloria and Cecilia, are ages three and four.

Both Carlos's and Maria's parents live within a twenty-minute drive. Maria's parents provide the much-needed day care for their granddaughters, and Carlos's parents are happy to substitute if needed. Most other family members who left Cuba are also living in the greater Miami area; family gatherings are frequent and well attended.

One day Carlos tells his wife of a possible promotion, which would involve moving to Minneapolis. Carlos can choose to accept the promotion or can stay in his current job.

Carlos and Maria decide to inform their parents before deciding. As expected, both sets of parents are opposed to the family's moving. They point out that Carlos and Maria's combined income enables them to live comfortably and that in Minneapolis the girls would be cared for by strangers and their contact with their grandparents would be limited. Maria's father also remarks that some things are more important than higher positions and more money, such as family.

Questions
1. What is the value system that is prompting the objections from the Rodriguez grandparents?

2. How do the grandparents' values compare with the predominant values in U.S. society regarding advancement and mobility?
3. When you think of the term *family,* do you think of it as a nuclear or an extended family?
4. If you think Carlos and Maria should remain in Miami, give at least three reasons.
5. If you think the Rodriguez family should move to Minneapolis, give at least three reasons.

Concept

Nativism

Generalization: A new group of immigrants arriving in the United States is likely to encounter rejection from some segments of the population.

The following is an example of letters to the editor that appeared in South Florida newspapers in response to the 1994 influx of Cuban immigrants on rafts and small boats. Read the sample letter to the students and ask the questions that follow.

SOUTH FLORIDA SATURATED

As a citizen of South Florida for the past ten years, I strongly object to the masses of Cuban refugees being dumped on our shores. I am also distressed at the lack of response by national and state elected officials to stop this alien infusion.

We are having sluggish economic times, and adequate housing is scarce for American citizens. How can we continue to be "nice guys" and accept more Cubans and Haitians? We already have enough!

We, the tax-paying public of Florida, are being forced to subsidize these unwanted refugees that should either stay in their own country or go elsewhere. Included among these refugees are Castro's gifts of criminals, insane, and other undesirables.

I also understand that Cubans are training military groups on Florida soil. Why can't we prosecute these people? Meanwhile, many of our own Americans around the country need the assistance being given to these people we don't want.

Why can't we take care of our own first and forget about the headaches of other nations?

Name withheld by request

Questions
1. What facts does the letter's author use to substantiate his or her positions?
2. Compare the positions in the letter with the idea that the United States is the land of immigrants.
3. Do you agree or disagree with the author's positions? Which ones? Explain the reasons for your responses.
4. As a comparative exercise where library facilities permit, ask students to look for letters to the editor in major newspapers concerning immigration around 1910. Afterward, ask the students to compare reactions to immigration in 1910 to the letter above.

REFERENCES

Alpen, D. (1980, May 26). Carter and the Cuban Influx. *Newsweek,* p. 25.

Baratz-Snowden, J., Rock, D., Pollack, J., & Wilder, G. (1988). *Parent Preference Study.* Princeton, NJ: Educational Testing Service.

Barberis, M. (1982). Hispanic America. (Editorial Research Reports), *Congressional Quarterly.* Washington, DC: U.S. Government Printing Office.

Carnoy, M. (2007). *Cuba's Academic Advantage: Why Students in Cuba Do Better in School.* Stanford, CA: Stanford University Press.

Diaz, W. (1984). *Hispanics: Challenges and Opportunities.* New York: Ford Foundation.

Fagen, R. R., Brody, R. A., & O'Leary, T. J. (1968). *Cubans in Exile.* Stanford, CA.: Stanford University Press.

Garcia, R. L., & Diaz, C. F. (1992). The Status and Use of Spanish and English among Hispanic Youth in Dade County (Miami), Florida. *Language and Education,* 6(1), 13–22.

Kelly, J. (1981, May 18). Closing the Golden Door. *Time,* p. 27.

Morin, R. (1980, May 11). Dade Fears Refugee Wave, Poll Shows. *Miami Herald,* p. 1; originally printed in *New York Times,* April 16, 1971, p. 4.

Olson, J. S., & Olson, J. E. (1995). *Cuban Americans: From Trauma to Triumph.* New York: Twayne.

Oppenheimer, A. (1985, August 25). Dade's Latins Feel a Separate Economy. *Miami Herald,* p. 1.

Pérez, L. (1980). Cubans. In S. Thernstrom, A. Orlov, & O. Handlin (Eds.), *Harvard Encyclopedia of American Ethnic Groups* (pp. 256–261). Cambridge, MA: Harvard University Press.

Prohias, R. J., & Casal, L. (1973). *The Cuban Minority in the U.S. Cuban Minority Planning Study.* Boca Raton: Florida Atlantic University.

Richmond, M. L. (1980). *Immigrant Adaptation and Family Structure among Cubans in Miami, Florida.* New York: Arno Press.

Silva, H. (1985). *The Children of Mariel: Cuban Refugee Children in South Florida Schools.* Washington, DC: Cuban American National Foundation.

Skop, E. H. (2001, Summer). Race and Place in the Adaptation of Mariel Exiles. *International Migration Review,* 35(2), 449–471.

Sung-Chang, C., & Grenier, G. (2004, November). Anti-Castro Political Ideology Among Cuban Americans: Cohort and Generational Differences. *Latino Research N D 2* (1), 1–9.

U.S. Census Bureau. (2005). *American Community Survey, 2005.* Retrieved August 2, 2007, from http://www.census.gov/acs/www/index.html.

U.S. Department of Commerce. (1993). *We, the American Hispanics.* Washington, DC: U.S. Government Printing Office.

U.S. Immigration and Naturalization Service. (2000). *Statistical Yearbook of the Immigration and Naturalization Service, 1998.* Washington, DC: U.S. Government Printing Office.

ANNOTATED BIBLIOGRAPHY

Books for Teachers

Especially Recommended

Carnoy, M. (2007). *Cuba's Academic Advantage: Why Students in Cuba Do Better in School.* Stanford, CA: Stanford University Press.

This book describes the system of education in Cuba today. Despite limited resources, Cuban schools produce students who are highly competent. A small and personalized teaching approach is coupled with a conceptual imagination of the curriculum. This book is very useful for anyone who wishes to understand Cuban education and apply some of its approaches to other educational settings.

Chavez, L. (2005). *Capitalism, God, and a Good Cigar*. Durham, NC: Duke University Press.
This edited source analyzes currents and changes in Cuban life since the dissolution of the Soviet Union. It focuses on how changes have affected the lives of ordinary Cubans.

Eire, C. (2006). *Waiting for Snow in Havana: Confessions of a Cuban Boy*. New York: Simon and Schuster.
This novel chronicles the youth of a Cuban immigrant who left Cuba alone as a youth with Operation Peter Pan. Eire flashes back to his relatively idyllic life in Cuba as he faces adaptation in the U.S. without his family. This source can also serve senior high school students.

García, M. C. (1994). Cuban Women in the United States. In A. Jiménez (Ed.), *Handbook of Hispanic Cultures in the United States* (pp. 203–217). Houston, TX: Arte Público Press.
An informative and comprehensive overview of the experiences of Cuban American women.

Garcia, M. C. (1996). *Havana USA: Cuban Exiles and Cuban Americans in South Florida, 1959–1994*. Berkeley: University of California Press.
An excellent and well-documented source about the major trends in the Cuban American community of Miami, Florida.

Grenier, G. J., & Pérez, L. (2003). *The Legacy of Exile: Cubans in the United States*. Boston: Allyn and Bacon.
An informative historical overview of the Cuban American sojourn in the United States.

Olson, J. S., & Olson, J. E. (1995). *Cuban Americans: From Trauma to Triumph*. New York: Twayne.
This book provides a comprehensive discussion of Cuba and the migration and settlement of Cuban Americans in the United States. It includes chapters on the Mariel Cubans and on the status of Cuban Americans in 1995.

O'Reilly Herrera, A. (2001). *Remembering Cuba: Legacy of a Diaspora*. Austin: University of Texas Press.
This collection of short essays is organized around a series of themes such as "Crossing the Generational Divide" and "the Culture Wars." The authenticity of these essays provides an excellent snapshot of the Cuban immigrant experience.

Poyo, G. E., & Díaz-Miranda, M. (1994). Cubans in the United States. In A. Jiménez (Ed.), *Handbook of Hispanic Cultures in the United States* (pp. 301–320). Houston, TX: Arte Público Press.
Cuban immigration, Cuban communities in the United States, Cuban women, and Cubans of color are among the topics in this informative historical overview of the Cuban American saga. Includes a helpful bibliography.

Stepick, A., Grenier, G., Castro, M., & Dunn, M. (2003). *This Land Is Our Land: Immigration and Power in Miami*. Berkeley: University of California Press.
This book discusses the social, economic, and political conditions among Cuban Americans in Miami. It also delves into the causes of ethnic conflict.

Other Books

De La Torre, M. (2003). *La Lucha for Cuba*. Berkeley: University of California Press.
An excellent source for readers who wish to understand the "Cuban exile mentality" in Miami and elsewhere in the United States. The book ends with speculations on postexilic Cubans in the United States.

Font, M., & Quiroz, A. (2006). *The Cuban Republic and Jose Marti*. Lanham, MD: Rowman and Littlefield.
This edited source describes Marti's ideas in many areas such as race, gender, education, and human rights. The essays show how the left and right have used Marti's writings and political legacy.

Greenbaum, S. (2002). *More Than Black: Afro-Cubans in Tampa*. Gainesville: University Press of Florida.
This is one of the few available sources that focus on Afro-Cubans. It traces the Afro-Cuban presence in Tampa, Florida, from the beginning of the twentieth century to the start of the twenty-first century. The source analyzes the divided lives Afro-Cubans experienced interacting with the Cuban, African American, and White communities.

Grillo, E. (2000). *Black Cuban, Black American*. Houston, TX: Arte Público Press.
Grillo's memoir discusses his life in Ybor City (Tampa), Florida, in the 1920s, '30s, and '40s, and navigating the cultural norms of the Cuban, African American, and White communities.

Lopez, A. (2006). *Jose Marti and the Future of Cuban Nationalisms*. Gainesville: University Press of Florida.
A short analysis of the life and philosophy of Cuba's most famous intellectual: Jose Marti. The author delves into the role Marti's ideas have played in forming the Cuban consciousness in Cuba as well as outside Cuba.

Miller J. (2003, October 27). Trouble in Miami if Bush Doesn't Watch Out, He Could Lose the Cuban Americans. *National Review 55*, 1–3.
This article explores concerns of the Cuban American community with changes in Cuba policy made by the George W. Bush administration.

Ojito, M. (2005). *Finding Manana: A Memoir of a Cuban Exodus*. New York: Penguin Press. The author gives a personal account of the massive exodus of more than 125,000 people from Cuba's Mariel harbor to the United States in 1980.

Ortiz, R. (2007). *Cultural Erotics in Cuban America*. Minneapolis: University of Minnesota Press. The author examines the Cuban immigrant experience by focusing on communities in the United States outside of Miami, Florida. He analyzes the legacies of sexism and homophobia in Cuban culture as well as focusus on smaller Cuban communities in the United States, such as Los Angeles, Chicago, and New York.

Pérez Firmat, G. (1995). *Next Year in Cuba*. New York: Anchor Books/Doubleday.
This book was authored by someone who came to the United States as a child. He grew up in Little Havana and left South Florida to become an academic. This book chronicles that journey.

Books for Students

Ada, A. F. (1998). *Under the Royal Palms: A Childhood in Cuba*. New York: Atheneum.
The Cuban-born author describes her childhood in Cuba in the 1940s by means of the many colorful individuals who passed through her life. Winner of the 2000 Pura Belpré Award for Writing. (Intermediate/Middle School)

Boza, M. (1998). *Scattering the Ashes*. Tempe, AZ: Bilingual Review Press.
For mature readers, this memoir describes the isolation and homesickness that led Boza's father, an influential Cuban journalist before the revolution and a popular exile writer in Miami afterward, to take his own life in 1989. (High School)

Camarello, D. (2003). *Cuban Americans*. Chashassen, MN: Children's World.
A well-illustrated and concise source about Cuban adaptation to American life. (Middle School)

Caseley, J. (2000). *Praying to A. L.* New York: HarperCollins.
The culturally diverse relatives of a girl of mixed Cuban American and Jewish American background help her to cope with the long illness and death of her father. (Middle School)

Condé, Y. (1999). *Operation Pedro Pan: The Untold Exodus of 14,048 Cuban Children*. New York: Routledge.

A powerfully presented history of the evacuation of thousands of children to the United States after Castro's victory, written by one of those who experienced firsthand the separation from her parents and the dislocations of a new language and culture. (High School)

Engler, L. (2005). *Cubans in America*. Minneapolis, MN: Lerner Publishing Group.
This source examines the impact of Cuban immigration on the United States and describes historical events and famous Cuban Americans. It also contains useful websites. (Elementary)

Figueredo, D. H. (1999). *When This World Was New*. Illustrated by E. O. Sanchez. New York: Lee and Low.
A boy immigrates with his parents from his warm green island in the Caribbean to a wintry northern city where he sees snow for the first time. Based on the Cuban American author's own experiences as an immigrant in the 1960s. (Primary)

García, P. (1997). *From Amigos to Friends*. Houston, TX: Piñata Books.
Three friends from diverse class backgrounds in Cuba are separated by the revolution; two end up in Miami but follow separate paths. (Middle School/High School)

Hoobler, D., & Hoobler, T. (1995). *The Cuban American Family Album*. New York: Oxford University Press.
This informative, interesting, and well-illustrated book includes photographs and other primary resources. (Intermediate and up)

Kent, D. (2005). *Cuban Refugees: Cuban Roots, American Dreams*. Chashassen, MN: Children's World.
Part of the Hispanic Library series, this book examines the Elian Gonzales case and examines the adaptation of Cuban Americans in the United States. (Upper Elementary/Middle School)

Limon, J. (2005). *Cuban Americans: Exiles from an Island Home*. Broomall, PA: Mason Crest Publishers.
Part of the illustrated Hispanic American series, this book describes the passions of Cuban immigrants objectively. (Upper Elementary/Middle School)

Muñoz, E. M. (1998). *Brand New Memory*. Houston, TX: Arte Público.
An assimilated Cuban American teenager learns about family, heritage, love, and loss when her grandmother comes from Cuba for a visit. (High School)

Suárez, V. (1997). *Spared Angola: Memories from a Cuban-American Childhood*. Houston, TX: Arte Público.
The acclaimed novelist describes growing up in Cuba in a family opposed to the revolution, his years in exile in Spain, and his arrival in Los Angeles as a young teenager unable to speak English or to fit into the tough barrio culture. (High School)

ASIAN AMERICANS AND ARAB AMERICANS

Concepts and Strategies

This part consists of content, concepts, teaching strategies, and materials for teaching about Asian Americans and Arab Americans. Although different in many ways, these groups also share similarities. Each term—*Asian American* and *Arab American*—describes diverse groups that vary in significant ways. The Japanese are very different from the Hmong, just as the Iranians and the Lebanese differ in important ways. Edward Said (1978) describes how the Europeans constructed the idea of "Orientalism" to refer to peoples in Asia as well as in the Middle East. Writes Said:

> Taking the late eighteenth century as a very roughly defined starting point Orientalism can be discussed and analyzed as the corporate institution for dealing with the Orient—dealing with it by making statements about it, authorizing views of it, describing it, by teaching it, settling it, ruling over it: in short, Orientalism as a Western style for dominating, restructuring, and having authority over the Orient. (p. 3)

He continues: "In brief, because of Orientalism the Orient was not (and is not) a free subject of thought and action" (p. 3).

When teaching about Asian Americans and Arab Americans, teachers can use Said's concept of Orientalism to help students examine the ways in which this concept was used historically and is being used today to construct ideas of the Japanese, the Chinese, the Iranians, and the Lebanese as "different." By having students examine and deconstruct images of Asian Americans and Arab Americans that are widespread within the popular media and the wider society, teachers can help students understand the ways in which the concept of Orientalism still functions in Western societies and why its destructive power needs to be questioned and replaced with transformative, multicultural knowledge.

REFERENCE

Said, E. (1978). *Orientalism*. New York: Vintage Books.

PART V

ASIAN AMERICANS AND ARAB AMERICANS

Concepts and Strategies

CHAPTER THIRTEEN

ASIAN AMERICANS
Concepts, Strategies, and Materials

In America, Asian immigrants and their offspring have been actors in history. Their dreams and hopes unfurled here before the wind, all of them—from the first Chinese miners sailing through the Golden Gate to the last Vietnamese boat people flying into Los Angeles International Airport—have been making history in America.

—Ronald Takaki

This chapter consists of content, concepts, teaching strategies, and materials for teaching about three of the oldest Asian groups in the United States: the Chinese Americans, Japanese Americans, and Filipino Americans.

Asian Americans, one of the most diverse and interesting ethnic groups in the United States, are rarely studied in the elementary and high school grades. When discussed in textbooks and in the popular media, they are often used to illustrate how an ethnic group of color can succeed in the United States. Because of their tremendous educational, occupational, and economic success, Asian Americans are often called the "model minority" in the popular media. It is true that some Asian American groups are better educated, have a higher occupational status, and earn more money than other Americans, including White Americans. However, the model minority concept is problematic for several reasons.

PROBLEMS WITH THE MODEL MINORITY CONCEPT

A focus on the economic success of Asian Americans results in several problems. It obscures the tremendous economic diversity within Asian American communities and the problems Asians have. When we look at only the group characteristics of Chinese Americans, for example, the serious economic problems of the new immigrants are overlooked. In 2004, about 48% of Chinese Americans had menial service, low-skilled, and blue-collar jobs. About 52% had managerial, professional, and related jobs (U.S. Census Bureau, 2007a). Takaki (1998) has called the unskilled Chinese immigrant workers "a colonized labor force" (p. 425). Many Chinese immigrant women work as seamstresses in San Francisco and in New York for long hours at very low wages. The model minority concept also obscures the stories of successful members of other ethnic groups, such as upwardly mobile African Americans and Hispanics. Finally, when overly emphasized, the model minority argument can divert attention from the racism and poverty that Asian Americans and other people of color in the United States still experience (Takaki, 1998). The poverty rate for Asian Americans (12%) is higher than for non-Hispanic Whites (9%) (U.S. Census Bureau, 2007b). Daniels (1988) states that diverting attention from racism was one intent of William Petersen (1966), the writer who first used the concept of the model minority in a *New York Times Magazine* article.

RAPID INCREASES IN THE ASIAN AMERICAN POPULATION

The Asian American population doubled between 1990 and 2005, from 7.2 million to 14.4 million, compared to a 90.6% increase for Hispanics, 32.7% for African Americans, and 19.5% for the total U.S. population (U.S. Census Bureau, 2007b). The number of Asians immigrating to the United States has increased substantially since the Immigration Reform Act became effective in 1968. Five Asian nations—the Philippines, India, China, Vietnam, and Korea—were among the top twenty-five nations from which immigrants came to the United States in 2000 (Camarota, 2002). Table 13.1 shows the number of immigrants to the United States from 1990 to 2000 from selected Asian nations.

The United States now has a sizable population of Vietnamese Americans (1,418,334), which increased by 26.3% between 2000 and 2005. After U.S. participation in the Vietnam War ended (1973) and the communists took control of that nation (1975), thousands of Vietnamese refugees rushed to the United States. Only 226 Vietnamese immigrated to the United States in 1965, but more than 87,000 came to the United States in 1978. Between 1990 and 2000, the number of Vietnamese immigrants that settled in the United States increased by 82%, from 543,262 in 1990 to 988,174 in 2000 (U.S. Census Bureau, 2006).

The number of Chinese immigrants settling in the United States from China and Hong Kong has also increased substantially since 1965. In 1965, for example, 4,769 immigrants from China settled in the United States. Between 1990 and 2000, the number of immigrants that settled in the United States from China increased by 87%, from 529,837 in 1990 to 988,857 in 2000 (U.S. Census Bureau, 2006).

The Chinese—with a population of 2.8 million in 2005—remained the largest Asian American population (U.S. Census Bureau, 2007a). However, Asian Indians outgrew all of the other Asian populations; they increased 38% between 2000 and 2005, from 1,678,765 to 2,319,222 (U.S. Census Bureau, 2007a). The demand for

TABLE 13.1   Asian Immigrants to the United States from Selected Nations, 1990–2000

COUNTRY OF BIRTH	TOTAL	PERCENTAGE OF ASIAN IMMIGRATION
Philippines	1,369,070	16.6
India	1,022,552	12.4
China[a]	988,857	12.0
Vietnam	988,174	12.0
Korea	864,125	10.5
Japan	347,539	4.2
Taiwan	326,215	3.9
Iran	283,226	3.4
Pakistan	223,477	2.7
Laos	204,284	2.4
Hong Kong	203,580	2.4
Thailand	169,801	2.0
Cambodia	136,978	1.6

[a] Data for Hong Kong and Taiwan included with China for 2000.

Source: U.S Census Bureau (2006), *Historical Census Statistics on the Foreign-Born Population of the United States: 1850 to 2000.* Washington, DC: U.S. Government Printing Office.

highly skilled workers in the United States and the lack of high-tech jobs in India were major reasons for the rapid increase in the Asian Indian population.

KOREAN AMERICANS

The number of Korean and Asian Indian immigrants to the United States has also increased tremendously since the Immigration Act of 1965 became effective in 1968. The Korean American population increased from 10,000 in 1960 to more than 1.2 million in 2005 (U.S. Census Bureau, 2007b). The first Koreans who came to the United States arrived in 1885. Later, between 1890 and 1905, sixty-four Korean students came to study in the United States (Kim, 1980). A significant number of Koreans were recruited to work in the sugar plantations in Hawaii in the early 1900s. However, few Korean immigrants settled in the United States until the 1970s. Only 6,231 Koreans immigrated to the United States between 1951 and 1960, and 34,526 between 1961 and 1970 (U.S. Immigration and Naturalization Service, 1985). However, more than 864,125 immigrated to the United States between 1990 and 2000 (U.S. Census Bureau, 2006).

Koreans are one of the largest immigrant groups settling in the United States. Like the new immigrants from the Philippines, many of the new Korean immigrants are college-educated professionals. In 2005, immigrants from Korea had one of the highest percentages of a population holding a bachelor's degree or higher, 53.4%, compared to 53.6% for immigrants from the United Kingdom, 31.6% for immigrants from Germany, and 25.5% for immigrants from Vietnam (U.S. Census Bureau, 2007b).

ASIAN INDIAN AND PAKISTANI IMMIGRANTS

Only a small number of immigrants from India settled in the United States prior to 1965. A total of about 130,000 came during the period between 1820 and 1976 (Takaki, 1998). Most of the immigrants who came during the nineteenth century were professionals, adventurers, merchants, and monks (Jensen, 1980). A few thousand agricultural workers came to California between 1904 and 1923. Only 1,973 immigrants from India came to the United States between 1951 and 1960; 31,200 immigrated to the United States between 1961 and 1979 (U.S. Immigration and Naturalization Service, 1985).

Since 1971, immigrants from India have been entering the United States in substantial numbers. More than 1,022,552 Indian immigrants settled in the United States between 1990 and 2000 (U.S. Census Bureau, 2006). A significant number of immigrants from Pakistan have also entered the United States since 1960. About 223,477 Pakistani immigrants settled in the United States between 1990 and 2000 (U.S. Census Bureau, 2006).

The U.S. Census indicates that 2.3 million Asian Indians were living in the United States in 2005. In contrast to East Asian Americans, who tend to concentrate in areas near the Pacific Coast, like California, Asian Indians were evenly spread throughout the United States: for example, in 2005, 449,722 lived in California, 336,423 lived in New York, and 176,608 lived in Texas. Asian Indians are now the largest Asian American group in more than twenty U.S. states, including New Jersey (228,250) and Illinois (157,126) (U.S. Census Bureau, 2007a). Asian Indians are English speaking and are a highly educated group. Among the immigrants are a large number of engineers, scientists, physicians, dentists, and other professionals. Like the new Filipino immigrants, they are settling in the United States primarily because of the paucity of professional job opportunities in their native land and the need for highly skilled workers in the United States.

SOUTHEAST ASIAN AMERICANS

The Southeast Asians who have settled in the United States have come from three contiguous nations, Vietnam, Kampuchea (Cambodia), and Laos. The Europeans referred to this area as Indochina because it had been historically influenced by India and China. The Southeast Asian Americans consist of Vietnamese, Laotians,

Cambodians (Kampucheans), Hmong, and ethnic Chinese refugees who fled to the United States in the aftermath of the Vietnam War. In the decade before 1975, only about 20,000 Vietnamese immigrated to the United States (Wright, 1989). It is not known how many immigrants came from Laos and Kampuchea (Cambodia) during this period. The first refugees from Southeast Asia fled to the United States in 1975. Their journey to the United States was directly related to the ending of the Vietnam War and the resulting communist governments in Vietnam, Laos, and Kampuchea.

The Southeast Asians, like the Cuban refugees from 1959 to 1962, sought refuge in the United States when communist governments came to power in their homelands. A large number of Southeast Asian refugees were resettled in the United States between mid-May 1975 and December 31, 1978. This was one of the largest emergency resettlement programs in the nation's history.

The number of Vietnamese, Laotians, and Kampucheans in the United States grew significantly between 1990 and 2000. Vietnam was one of the ten nations that sent the most legal immigrants to the United States during this period. More than a million (1,192,458) immigrants from Vietnam and Laos settled in the United States between 1990 and 2000 (see Table 13.1). Most of these immigrants (82%) came from Vietnam. The Vietnamese population in the United States is one of the nation's fastest-growing populations. There were 1,122,528 Vietnamese living in the United States in 2000 and 1,418,334 in 2005, a 26.3% increase within this five-year period. A number of developments have contributed to the rapid growth in the Indochinese population in the United States. Indochinese refugees continued to come to the United States from refugee camps in Southeast Asia between 1981 and 1989. Many Vietnamese, including Amerasian children (children of American fathers and Vietnamese mothers) and their close relatives have been permitted to immigrate to the United States by federal policies designed to facilitate family reunification. About 10,000 Amerasian children were scheduled for resettlement in the United States in 1989.

The Southeast Asians came to the United States for many different reasons. Singular political, economic, or personal concerns motivated some of the refugees to leave their homeland. Others were motivated by many factors. Many of the Southeast Asian refugees had been directly touched by the trauma of the Vietnam War (1954–1975) or its aftermath. The Southeast Asians left their nations as refugees and are now in the process of becoming Americans.

ASIAN AMERICANS: A DIVERSE GROUP

Asian Americans are one of the most highly diversified ethnic groups in the United States. They vary greatly in both cultural and physical characteristics. The attitudes, values, and ethnic institutions often differ within Japanese American, Chinese American, Filipino American, and Asian Indian communities. However, the first waves of Chinese, Japanese, and Filipino immigrants had some parallel experiences in the United States. For example, their immigration began when there was a need for cheap labor, but they were harassed and demeaned, and eventually immigration laws were passed to exclude them. After the Chinese Exclusion Act was passed in 1882, there

TABLE 13.2   Resident Population of Asian Americans, 2005

COUNTRY OF BIRTH	POPULATION	PERCENTAGE OF ASIAN IMMIGRATION
Chinese	2,889,280	23.1
Asian Indian	2,319,222	18.6
Filipino	2,282,872	18.3
Vietnamese	1,418,334	11.3
Other Asian[a]	1,408,076	11.2
Korean	1,246,240	10.0
Japanese	833,761	6.7

[a] Asian in combination with one or more other races.

Source: U.S. Census Bureau (2007), *American Community Survey, 2005: Selected Population Profile.* [Data file]. Available online at http://factfinder.census.gov/servlet/IPCharIterationServlet?_ts=202658644174.

was still a desire for cheap laborers in Hawaii and California. Consequently, Japanese immigrants began arriving in California in significant numbers in the 1890s. When the Gentlemen's Agreement of 1908 and the Immigration Act of 1924 halted Japanese immigration, California farmers imported Filipinos from Hawaii and the Philippines to work in the fields. Anti-Filipino forces emerged on the West Coast and culminated in 1934, when Congress limited Filipino immigration to fifty people per year. This quota constituted, in effect, the virtual exclusion of Filipino immigrants.

Because of their tremendous diversity, similarities, and unique experiences in the United States, the study of Asian Americans can help students increase their ethnic literacy and develop a respect for cultural differences. Table 13.2 shows the percentage distribution of the Asian American population for selected groups in 2005.

THE CHINESE, JAPANESE, AND FILIPINO AMERICANS: OVERVIEW

This section of this chapter discusses content, concepts, strategies, and materials for teaching about the three Asian American groups that have lived in the United States the longest: the Chinese Americans, Japanese Americans, and Filipino Americans. These groups have important similarities as well as differences. Each group that came to the United States sought the American dream, satisfied important labor needs, and became victims of an anti-Asian movement designed to prevent their further immigration to the United States. Chinese Americans, Japanese Americans, and Filipino Americans have also experienced tremendous economic, educational, and social mobility and success in U.S. society.

The number of Chinese, Japanese, and Filipino immigrants that settled in the United States between 1951 and 1960 was small compared to the numbers from

Europe. However, the number of immigrants to the United States from China and the Philippines has increased enormously since the Immigration Reform Act of 1965 became effective in 1968. The number of Japanese immigrating to the United States since 1968 has remained moderate. Between 1951 and 1960, 19,300 immigrants from the Philippines and 25,200 from China and Hong Kong settled in the United States. Between 1990 and 2000 the numbers were 1,369,070 from the Philippines, 203,580 from Hong Kong, and 988,857 from China. (See Table 13.1.)

As a result of the increasing number of immigrants from China, Hong Kong, and the Philippines, as well as from other Asian nations, the Japanese are becoming an increasingly smaller percentage of the Asian American population. In 1970, Japanese Americans were the largest Asian American group, followed by the Chinese and the Filipinos. By 2005, however, the Japanese were one of the smallest Asian American groups, exceeded in size by the Chinese, Filipinos, Asian Indians, Vietnamese, and Koreans. The Japanese were the only one of these groups with a population of less than one million. (See Table 13.2.)

The story of the Chinese, Japanese, and Filipinos in the United States has been largely one of success, if we measure success by the educational, income, and occupational levels these groups have attained. They have achieved tremendous educational, income, and occupational success even though they have historically been the victims of racism and discrimination and are still often the victims of subtle discrimination. The stories of the Chinese, Japanese, and Filipinos in the United States can help students understand how the American dream can be pursued and attained. However, when these groups are studied, the problems that Asian Americans still face in U.S. society, such as cultural conflict, identity, and attaining a balance between their ethnic cultures and the mainstream culture, should not be glossed over. The poverty that exists in many Asian American communities, especially in urban ethnic communities, where newly arrived immigrants settle in large numbers, should also be studied.

When studying about Asians in the United States, students should examine and analyze the new wave of racism that has been directed against Asian Americans and Arab Americans. This new wave of racism, which emerged in the 1980s, has been expressed in a number of ways, including ugly racial incidents on college campuses. The rising number of Asian students at some of the nation's most prestigious colleges and universities has evoked comments that some Asians have interpreted as a call for restrictive quotas. In the 2006–2007 academic year, Asian Americans made up 24% of the total undergraduate student body at Stanford, 41% of the total undergraduate student body at the University of California at Berkeley, and 14% of the total undergraduate student body at Harvard (America's Best Colleges, 2007).

Many Americans, particularly unemployed auto workers, blame Japan for the stiff competition from Japanese car manufacturers. This hostility has sometimes been directed at Japanese Americans, because some Americans do not distinguish Japanese nationals and Japanese Americans. This hostility has taken diverse forms, including bumper stickers that read "Unemployment—Made in Japan" and statements such as "Auto unemployment is an economic Pearl Harbor" (Daniels, 1988, p. 342). An odious incident occurred on June 19, 1982: an unemployed auto worker,

Ronald Ebens, and his stepson beat Vincent Chin to death in a Detroit suburb. Ebens thought Chin was a Japanese American. Despite their success—and sometimes because of it—Asian Americans are still victims of racism and discrimination. Some Americans still consider Asian Americans "strangers from a different shore" (Takaki, 1998). In 2007, Toyota, the Japanese car manufacturer, exceeded the worldwide sales for General Motors for the first time in history.

CHINESE AMERICANS

Immigration

When the news reached the Guandong Province in southeast China that there was a "Golden Mountain" across the Pacific, a number of young men violated both Chinese law and tradition and headed for the promised land. The decision to leave China for a foreign land was a serious one, because it was illegal to immigrate and violators could be severely punished. Also, Confucian doctrine, an integral part of Chinese life during this period, taught that a young man should value his family above all else and thus should not leave it. However, both the promises of the land of the Mountain of Gold and the severe living conditions in the Toishan district in Guandong, from which most of the first Chinese immigrants hailed, helped push the young immigrants across the Pacific.

Political upheaval, famine, local warfare, excessive taxes, a severely depressed economy, and a rugged terrain in Toishan inimical to farming motivated young Chinese males to seek better opportunities in an unknown land where, according to a pervasive myth, one could easily strike gold and return to China a rich man. Most of the Chinese who headed for California were young married men. They were self-proclaimed "sojourners" who intended to earn their fortunes in the United States and return to their families in China. Because of tradition and the rough voyage across the Pacific, their families were left behind.

CHINESE AMERICANS: HISTORICAL PERSPECTIVE

Important Dates	Events
1850	The U.S. Census showed 450 Chinese immigrants in the United States. This number increased to 34,933 in 1860. The California legislature passed a discriminatory Foreign Miner's Tax, which forced Chinese immigrants to pay a highly disproportionate share of the state taxes.
1859	Authorities in the Guangdong Province legalized the recruitment of Chinese laborers.
1882	The Chinese Exclusion Act was enacted by Congress. It stopped the immigration of Chinese laborers for ten years.

Important Dates	Events
1974	The U.S. Supreme Court ruled in *Lau* v. *Nichols* that the San Francisco Unified School District was denying Chinese American students who did not speak English "a meaningful opportunity to participate in the public educational program." This ruling by the high court established a legal basis for bilingual educational programs. Such programs were later established in various parts of the nation.
1980	The U.S. Census indicated that the Chinese were one of the largest groups that immigrated to the United States between 1970 and 1980. The Chinese population in the United States increased 88% between 1970 and 1980, compared to 11% for the total population and 6% for Whites.
1982	Vincent Chin was beaten to death in a Detroit suburb by an unemployed auto worker and his stepson. Ronald Ebens, the unemployed auto worker, thought Chin was of Japanese descent.
1992	More than 49,000 immigrants from China and Hong Kong entered the United States, which made the Chinese the second largest Asian group immigrating to the United States. The Filipinos were the largest immigrating Asian group.
2005	The U.S. Census indicated that Chinese Americans were the largest group of Asian Americans. With a population of 2,797,966, they made up 23.1% of the Asian American population. The second largest group were Asian Indians, who made up 18.6% of Asian Americans.

The journey across the Pacific was rugged and hazardous. On their arrival in California, the Chinese immigrants experienced a rude awakening. Although White Americans expressed little overt hostility toward the Chinese when they first started immigrating to the West Coast in substantial numbers in the 1850s, they considered them exotic, strange people. Whites thought that the Chinese were strange because of their traditional Chinese clothing, language, queue hairstyle (which Whites called pigtails), and skin color. Almost from the beginning, the Chinese were the victims of curiosity and racism. Writes Melendy (1972): "From almost the first moment the Chinese landed in San Francisco in the 1850s, they were subjected to harsh treatment. The aim was to exclude them from the United States because of basically *racist* fears and beliefs" (p. 20, emphasis added).

Labor.   In addition to receiving a curious and strange welcome from Californians, the Chinese immigrants found that the mines in which they had to dig for gold had already been thoroughly gone over by White gold diggers. They had to dig for the scraps of gold left by Whites. However, some Chinese immigrants managed to secure respectable sums of money by remining White claims.

When Congress decided to build a railroad linking the Missouri River to the Pacific Coast in 1862, the Central Pacific issued a call for men to build the western portion of the railroad. Because of the backbreaking work involved in building a railroad over the rugged Western terrain, few Whites would take the work. But the Chinese took up the challenge and almost single-handedly built the Pacific portion of the transcontinental railroad. While the nation celebrated the completion of the railroad on May 10, 1869, 25,000 laborers, most of them Chinese, lost their jobs.

It was not easy for the Chinese immigrants to save money because of the large debts they had incurred when they arranged to come to California. Most of them came to the United States through a credit-ticket system, which was similar to the indenture system used to bring many European immigrants to North America. In this system, a moneyless Chinese man could borrow money from a relative or fellow villager to pay for his passage to California. Chinese organizations, such as the Hui Kuan or Landsmanner, collected the money from the immigrant and sent it to the individuals from whom it was borrowed.

The leaders of the Hui Kuan also provided the immigrants with a place to eat and sleep on their arrival in San Francisco and sent groups of them to work in the mines. Before the worker received his wages, the amount he owed for his passage was deducted. Because of the credit-ticket system, some immigrants ended up worse off financially than they had been before they came to California. Some found that their return to China was indefinitely delayed. What at first promised to be a nation of gold turned out, for many, to be a land of disillusionment and shattered dreams. Writes Melendy (1972): "The Chinese existed at a poverty level, receiving low wages for their work. Even so, they gained materially a bit more than they had in China. The dream of coming to the Golden Mountain to make a fortune and return home still seemed possible to most. For many, however, this was the impossible dream" (p. 20).

Despite the difficulties the Chinese immigrants experienced, many were able to find enough work in a wide range of occupations that most Whites found unpalatable—such as domestic work, work on railroads, and intensive farming—to save enough money to return to China to visit their families and to father children, hopefully sons. The immigrants who returned to China usually told about the promises of California but said little about its difficulties. Also, the home folks were impressed with what seemed like sizable sums of money the sojourners brought back to China. As the news about the Mountain of Gold spread, and immigrants returned home with money or sent money home to their families, the number of Chinese immigrating to California rose tremendously.

Anti-Chinese Agitation

According to the 1860 census, there were 34,933 Chinese in the United States. By 1880, that number had risen to 105,465. Although the increase was sizable, there were still few Chinese immigrating to the United States compared to the number of European immigrants. Between 1820 and 1930, 38 million immigrants entered the United States, mostly from Europe. However, many Whites became alarmed at the number of Chinese entering the United States, and a vicious movement developed to keep them out. Although leaders of the anti-Chinese movement claimed that the Chinese could not be assimilated and that they competed unfairly with Whites on the labor market, racism was one of the main forces behind the anti-Chinese movement. As Saxton (cited in Melendy, 1972) has pointed out, "The Chinese inherited the long-standing hostility of Whites against people of color, particularly Blacks. White Californians, conditioned to the notion that Blacks were inferior persons and servile workers, easily transferred these perceptions to the Chinese" (p. 18).

Led by Dennis Kearney and the California Workingmen's Party, "The Chinese Must Go" became the rallying cry of the anti-Chinese movement. Leaders of all types joined in the movement to push the Chinese out of the West. Labor leaders were among the most staunch anti-Chinese advocates. Politicians jumped on the bandwagon in order to gain votes. As the hostility against the Chinese mounted, they became increasingly defenseless. Unlike the Japanese, they did not have a strong nation that could threaten the balance of world power when its citizens in the United States were ill treated.

The anti-Chinese movement spread as the Chinese moved to such states as Washington, Oregon, Colorado, and Wyoming. Anti-Chinese activities took the form of racist newspaper stories; violent attacks against defenseless men, women, and children; and highly discriminatory laws aimed particularly at the Chinese, such as the Queues Ordinance, the Laundry Ordinance, and the 1876 Cubic Air Law. One of the most blatantly discriminatory laws was the Foreign Miner's Tax passed by the California legislature in 1850. Applied most effectively against the Chinese, it forced them to pay a highly disproportionate share of the taxes collected under the law. Taxes paid by the Chinese largely financed the California state and county governments during this period (Chun-Hoon, 1973). The movement to ban the immigration of Chinese culminated with the passage of the Immigration Act of 1882. This bill stopped the immigration of Chinese laborers for a period of ten years. A victory for the anti-Chinese leaders, it was followed by a series of similar bills that drastically reduced Chinese immigration for decades. The number of Chinese entering the United States dwindled from 39,579 in 1882 to 472 in 1893.

Violence and Riots.   Violence directed against the Chinese was widespread in the late 1880s. An anti-Chinese riot occurred in San Francisco as early as 1869. A White mob in Los Angeles attacked a Chinese community in 1871. When the conflict ended, nineteen Chinese Americans had been killed and their community was in shambles. Another anti-Chinese riot exploded in Denver, Colorado, in 1880. One Chinese was killed and most of the homes in the Chinese community were wrecked during the riot. A serious anti-Chinese riot occurred in Rock Springs, Wyoming, in 1885. Twenty-eight Chinese were killed, fifteen were wounded, and many were driven from their homes. The value of property destroyed was estimated at $150,000. Most of the White aggressors in these riots went unpunished, partly because testimony against a White person by a Chinese was inadmissible in the courts.

Chinatowns

The Chinese responded to this violence by moving farther eastward, to the Northeast (where they also became the victims of violence), and by retreating into ethnic communities in urban areas. Writes Lyman (1970): "By the end of the nineteenth century, the

California Chinese had, for the most part, died off, returned to China, moved eastward or settled into the ghettos of American cities referred to as 'Chinatowns'"(p. 14).

Despite its outer glitter, life in Chinatown was and is tough and depressing. Because most of the male immigrants did not bring their wives to California and were unable to marry Caucasians because of miscegenation laws, Chinatown was made up primarily of desperate and lonely men who sought their recreation in the form of prostitution, gambling, and opium smoking. Because of the high population of lonely and virile men, and the scarcity of females, prostitution loomed large in Chinatown in the 1800s. It was controlled by the Chinese secret societies that paid off police officials so that they could "safely" practice their business. Competition among the various Chinese societies for power, women, and money was keen, and violence among them often erupted. These conflicts were sensationalized by the White press and were popularized as "tong wars." Such stories made good copy and were eagerly sought by many journalists. These news stories played into the hands of the anti-Chinese racists and were fully exploited.

Prostitution, tong wars, gambling, and opium smoking are largely things of the past in Chinatown. However, powerful antiquated Chinese organizations that care little about the masses still exercise considerable power. Poverty, squalor, and disease are rampant in some Chinese urban communities. San Francisco's Chinatown has one of the highest population densities in the nation. Many women in San Francisco's Chinatown work in the garment industry for very low wages. Housing and education in San Francisco's Chinatown are among the worst in the nation. The power elite in Chinatown, which profits from the misery of the masses, has helped obscure its outrageous conditions and publicize its glitter. Chinatown has been described as a "gilded ghetto whose tinseled streets and brightly lit shops barely camouflage a pocket of poverty in the metropolis" (Lyman, 1970, p. 8).

Chinese Americans Today

Chinatown served as a port of entry for most of the earlier immigrants; it provided them with a sense of security, ties with the old world culture, and a partial escape from discrimination. Many Chinese Americans who are descendants of these earlier immigrants have experienced upward social and economic mobility and are leaving Chinatown. They have joined the exodus to the suburbs (Horton, 1995). However, the American Chinatowns are still viable and important communities. The newly upwardly mobile Chinese Americans who are moving to suburban communities are being replaced in Chinatown by new waves of immigrants from China and Hong Kong. In 2004, 40.5% of the Chinese Americans were foreign-born, compared to 11.4% of the Japanese (U.S. Census Bureau, 2007b). In his anthropological study of New York's Chinatown, Wong (1982) identifies four groups that live there: (1) old overseas Chinese, (2) American-born Chinese and naturalized Chinese Americans, (3) jump-ship sailors and refugees, and (4) disenchanted/disenfranchised youths. The refugees from Southeast Asia face tremendous economic hardships and work long hours each day, sometimes from eighteen to twenty hours.

The new immigrants who have entered the United States since the Immigration Reform Act of 1965 have been bipolar in their social class backgrounds. In 2004, about 48% of Chinese Americans were menial service, low-skilled, and blue-collar workers; 52% were managerial and professional workers (U.S. Census Bureau, 2007b). Even though the economic and educational levels of the total Chinese population are high, a large group of the new immigrants have low-paying jobs that are highly concentrated in restaurants and textile work. The bipolar nature of the Chinese community is also reflected in where they live. Many of the lower-level workers live in Chinatown, whereas many of the professional and upper-status workers live in suburban communities. Monterey Park, California, a suburban community of Los Angeles that had a population of 61,000 in 1988, had 50% Chinese residents. It had become "America's first suburban Chinatown" (Horton, 1995; Takaki, 1998, p. 425).

The social, educational, and economic characteristics of the total population of Chinese Americans in 2005 were impressive. Most Chinese Americans (about 82.7%) who were twenty-five years or older were high school graduates, compared to 86.6% for Whites, and 84.2% for all persons (U.S. Census Bureau, 2007b). The median family income of Chinese Americans in 2005 was $71,416, compared to $55,832 for all persons. Chinese Americans were also highly concentrated in managerial, professional, and technical jobs in 2005: 53.9% of them held managerial and professional specialty jobs, compared to 34.1% for all persons. In addition, 21.2% of them held sales and office occupations in 2005, compared to 25.9% for all persons. On most leading indicators of success in 2005, the Chinese in the United States exceeded the general population (U.S. Census Bureau, 2007b).

Because of the educational, occupational, and economic success of Chinese Americans, many of them have moved out of Chinatown to other areas within the city, but they are still primarily urban and metropolitan dwellers. In 2005, most lived in metropolitan areas such as Boston, New York, San Francisco, Los Angeles, Houston, Seattle, Chicago, Philadelphia, and Portland. Almost all poor Chinese, aged bachelors, and most recent immigrants live in Chinatown. Other groups, however, also live there. Although many Chinese Americans have joined the larger society, the Chinatowns of the nation are still viable communities that satisfy important human and cultural needs. Even the highly assimilated Chinese American occasionally returns to Chinatown on the weekend for a good ethnic meal or to buy certain Chinese products unavailable in predominantly White communities.

The Chinese community has experienced an influx of immigrants since the passage of the Immigration Act of 1965, which gave a liberal quota of 170,000 to people who lived in Eastern Hemisphere nations. A chain migration has developed. Once they are in the United States and have become citizens, many Chinese send for relatives under the provisions of the immigrant act that allow families to join other family members. The process multiplies. Between 1970 and 1980, the Chinese population in the United States increased 88%, while the White population increased 6%. In 1965, only 4,769 Chinese immigrants entered the United States, whereas 70,000 individuals born in China (mainland and Taiwan) and Hong Kong immigrated to the United States in 2005. The Chinese American population in 2005 was 2.9 million, which made them the largest Asian American group. They made up 23.1% of the Asian American population. (See Figure 13.1.)

Despite the tremendous increase in the Chinese American population since 1965, Asians comprised only a small percentage of the U.S. population in 2004. The 13.4 million Asians made up 4.7% of the U.S. population of 281 million in 2004. The Chinese population in the United States grew 15% between 2000 and 2005, compared to 18.6% for Hispanics and 15.9% for the total U.S. population. The rapid growth of the Chinese population in the United States is likely to have a number of important consequences. One possible consequence is that U.S. foreign policy will focus more on Asia. Although Asian Americans make up only a small percentage of the total U.S. population, they are highly concentrated in Hawai'i and the West Coast states. Figure 13.1 shows the percentage distribution of Asian American population for selected groups in 2005.

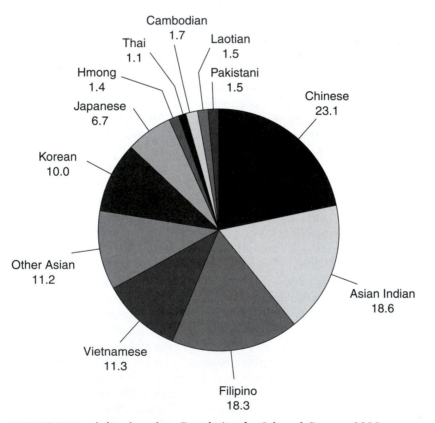

FIGURE 13.1   **Asian American Population for Selected Groups, 2005 (percentage distribution)**

Source: U.S. Census Bureau (2007), *American Community Survey, 2005: Selected Population Profile.* [Data file]. Available http://factfinder.census.gov/servlet/IPCharlterationServlet?_ts=202658644174.

JAPANESE AMERICANS

Immigration

Because of overpopulation, depressed farming conditions, and political turmoil in Japan in the late 1800s, its citizens began immigrating to Hawai'i and the U.S. mainland in search of better economic opportunities. The arrival of 148 Japanese contract laborers in Hawai'i in 1868 to work on the plantations violated Japanese law. Japanese immigrants did not arrive in the United States and Hawai'i in significant numbers until the Japanese government, because of internal problems, legalized immigration in 1886. There were 55 people of Japanese ancestry in the United States in 1870; 2,039 in 1890; and 111,010 in 1920 (Lyman, 1970). The largest number of Japanese immigrants arrived in the United States between 1891 and 1924; about 200,000 came during this period (Kitano, 1976).

JAPANESE AMERICANS: HISTORICAL PERSPECTIVE

Important Dates	Events
1868	Japanese contract laborers totaling 148 arrive in Hawai'i .
1869	The unsuccessful Wakamatsu Colony, made up of Japanese immigrants, was established in California.
1906	The San Francisco Board of Education ordered all Asian children to attend a segregated Oriental school.
1907–1908	The United States and Japan made the Gentlemen's Agreement, which was designed to reduce the number of Japanese immigrants entering the United States.
1913	The California legislature passed a land bill making it difficult for Japanese immigrants to lease land.
1924	An immigration bill was passed by Congress that stopped Asian immigration to the United States.
1930	The Japanese American Citizenship League was founded.
1941	Japan attacked Pearl Harbor on December 7.
1942	On February 19, President Franklin D. Roosevelt issued Executive Order 9066, which authorized the internment of Japanese Americans who lived on the West Coast.
1946	The last internment camp was closed.
1948	The Japanese American Evacuation Claims Act, signed by President Harry S. Truman, authorized some compensation for the financial losses incurred by Japanese Americans during the internment. The U.S. government eventually compensated the Japanese Americans for property loss at the rate of about 10¢ per dollar.

Important Dates	Events
1952	The McCarran-Walter Immigration Act was passed by Congress. It ended the total exclusion of Asian immigrants, which had begun with the passage of the Immigration Act of 1924. Asian Americans were granted naturalization rights.
1972	Statistics indicated that 47% of the Japanese Americans living in Los Angeles were married to non-Japanese spouses.
1986	A U.S. Court of Appeals reinstated the claim that the U.S. government illegally took property from a group of Japanese interned during World War II. This case made it possible for claims by survivors to be heard in court.
1988	The American Civil Liberties bill was passed by Congress and signed by President Ronald Reagan. It provided an apology for the internment of Japanese Americans during World War II and a $20,000 payment for each survivor of the internment.
2005	The U.S. Census indicated that the Japanese American population increased slightly between 2000 and 2005, from 796,700 to 833,761.

After the anti-Chinese forces had successfully stopped Chinese immigration with the Chinese Exclusion Act of 1882, there was still a need for seasonal farm laborers in the developing West. The Japanese immigrants filled the labor void in agriculture and in other areas that had been created by the cessation of Chinese immigration. Why Whites on the West Coast halted the immigration of one group of Asians and then encouraged the coming of another is a curious and complex historical event. However, it was only a matter of time before the anti-Asian forces, already mobilized, began to attack aggressively the Japanese Americans as they had earlier attacked the Chinese.

Most of the first Japanese immigrants were young men, some of whom were married. They hoped to earn a small fortune in the United States and return to Japan. Like the Chinese, however, most of them remained in North America. There were many similarities in the experiences of Japanese and Chinese immigrants to the United States. However, there were some significant differences that profoundly influenced the development of the Chinese American and Japanese American communities. Organizations emerged within the Little Tokyos of America, as in early Chinatowns, to help the new immigrants secure lodging, food, and jobs.

There were also few women among the first Japanese immigrants. Like the Chinese, the men had to share the women who were available. However, the man–woman ratio never became as imbalanced within the Japanese American community as it became in the Chinese community because the Japanese immigrants were able to marry Japanese women, despite the exclusion laws directed against

Japanese immigrants. Although the men were in the United States and the women in Japan, marriages were arranged with photographs. The wives would later join their husbands, whom they had never seen, in the United States. These women became known as "picture brides."

The picture-bride custom was similar in some ways to the "tobacco-bride" custom that was practiced in the Jamestown colony. The Virginia Company sent ninety European women to Virginia in the spring of 1620. Each man who married one of the women had to pay 120 pounds of the best tobacco to help pay for his bride's transportation costs from Europe. In later years, the company continued to send more "maids" to Virginia to marry the lonely male colonists.

Although the picture-bride marriage practice was opposed vigorously by anti-Japanese groups, it was consistent with Japanese custom and continued until outlawed in Japan in 1920. Many parents of second-generation Japanese Americans (*nisei*) were married in a "picture" ceremony. (Japanese Americans use specific terms to designate each generation: *issei, nisei, sansei,* and *yonsei* refer to the first, second, third, and fourth generations, respectively.) These marriages worked amazingly well, partly because traditionally romantic love had not been a major factor in Japanese marriages, which were more the joining of two families rather than two individuals. This Japanese proverb expresses cogently this attitude toward marriage: "Those who come together in passion stay together in tears."

Although most of the issei men were much older than their picture brides, the fact that they were able to marry helped the Japanese to establish strong families in the United States. Some writers consider the Japanese family the most significant factor in the social and economic mobility of Japanese Americans. Strong families developed early in the Japanese American community, partly because of the picture-bride custom, and a large and assertive second generation of Japanese Americans emerged. Such a generation did not develop among the Chinese for several decades because of their lack of family life. There were few Chinese women available, and Chinese men were unable to marry Whites. Because of exclusion laws that prohibited the immigration of Chinese females, family life in the Chinese American community developed slowly. As a result, the Chinese community was made up primarily of destitute, lonely, aging, and exploited men for several decades.

When they arrived on the West Coast, the Japanese immigrants worked in a variety of fields, including agriculture, the railroads, domestic work, gardening, small businesses, and industry. Because of job discrimination, they worked mainly in self-employment types of occupations. Consequently, they made their greatest impact in such fields as agriculture, gardening, and small business. Of all these areas, their accomplishments in agriculture, and especially truck farming, were the most impressive. Much of the land they were able to farm was considered unarable and largely useless by most White farmers. With a great deal of ingenuity and the use of intensive farming techniques, the Japanese began to dominate certain areas of California truck farming. They produced 90% of the state's peppers, strawberries, celery, and snap beans in 1941. In the same year, they raised a large percentage of California's cucumbers, tomatoes, cabbage, carrots, lettuce, and onions (Melendy, 1972).

The Japanese immigrants were often praised for their industry and eagerness when they first arrived in California. However, their tremendous success in agriculture eventually alarmed and frightened Anglo-American farmers, who no longer saw the Japanese merely as ambitious workers and servants but rather as tough competitors in the marketplace. To halt their success and to drive them out of California, White farmers and labor leaders inflamed anti-Asian feelings and warned of a new "Yellow Peril."

Some familiar faces and organizations, such as Dennis Kearney and the California newspapers, renewed their anti-Asian tactics. Anti-Japanese attitudes were pervasive on the West Coast, and almost every institution was affected. In 1906, the San Francisco Board of Education ordered all Asian American children, including the Japanese, to attend the segregated Oriental school. Japan was upset by this order and considered it a gross insult. Because of Japan's growing military strength, President Theodore Roosevelt thought the order might cause a serious conflict with Japan. Consequently, he intervened and persuaded the school board to rescind it.

To help mitigate the pervasive anti-Japanese feelings on the West Coast, the United States and Japan worked out an agreement designed to reduce drastically the immigration of Japanese laborers to the United States. This agreement, which became known as the Gentlemen's Agreement, was completed in 1908. Japan agreed to halt the immigration of laborers to the United States, and the United States agreed to end discrimination against the Japanese. After this agreement, the number of Japanese entering the United States was reduced drastically. However, the anti-Japanese movements continued unabated. The most extremist groups wanted nothing less than total exclusion of the Japanese.

"The Japs Must Go!" became the rallying cry of the anti-Japanese movements. Racist headlines in the press, attacks on Japanese businesses, and other forms of violence occurred. The anti-Japanese forces won a major victory when the California legislature passed the Alien Land Bill in 1913. Japanese immigrants were considered "aliens ineligible for citizenship." This bill, designed to drive the Japanese out of farming, prohibited the issei from leasing land for more than three years. Although the Japanese found this law devastating, they were able, to some extent, to circumvent it. Consequently, it did not have the impact its architects had hoped. Many issei used their children's names to secure land or obtained land with the help of White friends. In 1920, the California legislature passed a more severe law, which was destined to have the effects the legislators had hoped the 1913 law would have. This law prevented the issei from leasing land and prohibited them from using their children's names to lease land they could not legally lease themselves. This law served as the prototype for laws later passed in such states as Arizona, New Mexico, Oregon, Utah, and Wyoming.

Even though the Alien Land Law of 1920 successfully reduced the number of Japanese Americans in agriculture, the anti-Japanese movement continued in full force. The groups comprising this movement wanted a total victory, which they viewed as a complete halt of Japanese immigration to the United States and the removal of the Japanese from California. They claimed that despite the Gentlemen's

Agreement, the picture brides were swelling the Japanese population in the United States and that the Japanese were having an alarming number of children. The phobia of these groups was totally unfounded. The proportion of Japanese immigrants in the United States has always been small. From 1915 to 1924, when the movement to exclude Japanese immigrants was intense, 85,197 Japanese immigrants entered the United States, which comprised only 2.16% of all immigrants during this period (Petersen, 1971). A total of 45,533,116 immigrants came to the United States between 1820 and 1971, but only 370,033 of these were Japanese. In 1920, there were only 111,010 Japanese immigrants in the United States. Thus, the "problem" was clearly fiction. Politics, economic competition, and racism—not the number of Japanese immigrants—caused alarm about the "swelling" Japanese population in the United States.

The anti-Japanese forces experienced a long-awaited victory when the Immigration Act of 1924 was passed. This act fixed quotas for European countries on the basis of the percentages of their immigrants living in the United States and prohibited the immigration of aliens ineligible for citizenship. The act, in effect, stopped Asian immigration. Writes Kitano (1976): "The 1924 immigration act was a major victory for racists, nativists, and exclusionists, and there is little doubt that it was resented by an insulted and bewildered Japan, which having understood that she was to become an important member of the family of nations, did not now understand this slap in the face" (p. 28).

The Internment

On December 7, 1941, Japan attacked Pearl Harbor. Hysteria emerged on the West Coast as the anti-Japanese groups spread rumors about the so-called fifth column and espionage activities among the Japanese (Daniels, 1971). Some Whites argued that all Japanese Americans were still loyal to their mother country; others claimed that it was impossible to tell a "good Jap" from a "bad Jap." Rumors, which spread like wildfire, suggested that the United States was in danger of being attacked by a fleet of Japanese soldiers and that Japanese Americans were helping to plan the attack. A tremendous fear of what came to be known as the Yellow Peril haunted the Pacific Coast. Daniels notes that the fear of conquest by Japan was irrational and racist (Daniels, 1971, p. 29). The press reinforced and perpetuated the fear by printing highly fictionalized and sensationalized news stories about the Japanese "threat."

It is significant to note that White California farmers and politicians played key roles in creating and perpetuating myths about the Yellow Peril. The farmers had long wanted to drive the Japanese out of California; politicians used the issue to gain votes and to divert attention from real political and social issues. It is also worth noting that we know of no sabotage activities in which Japanese Americans were involved during the war. In his perceptive study of the internment, Daniels (1971) argues that the decision to remove the Japanese from the West Coast was a political rather than military decision. Military officials knew during the war that the Japanese on the West Coast were not a security risk. However, because anti-Japanese groups in California urged the removal of the Japanese, it was politically expedient to intern them.

The uproar on the West Coast and the fear that spread throughout other parts of the nation resulted in the issuance of Executive Order No. 9066 by President Franklin D. Roosevelt on February 19, 1942. This order authorized the secretary of war to declare military areas "from which any or all persons may be excluded, and with respect to which, the right of any person to enter, remain in, or leave shall be subject to whatever restrictions the Secretary of War . . . may impose in his discretion." Although mention of the Japanese Americans by name is notably absent from the document, the order was clearly aimed at them. It authorized the secretary of war to remove Japanese Americans from the West Coast (declared a "military area") and to set up federal concentration camps to which they would be forcibly removed.

The Japanese were first sent to assembly centers, which served as temporary living quarters. Later, a total of 110,000 Japanese Americans (two-thirds of whom were citizens of the United States) were located in these ten concentration camps: Tule Lake and Manzanar in interior California, Minidoka in Idaho, Topaz in Utah, Poston and Gila River in Arizona, Heart Mountain in Wyoming, Granada in Colorado, and Rohwer and Jerome in Arkansas. Most of the camps were located in desolate and barren areas that had hot weather in the summer and cold weather in the winter. They were fenced in with barbed wire and guarded by soldiers.

The internment had some adverse effects on the culture and life of the Japanese Americans. Because of the wide differences in the cultures of Japan and the United States, the issei and nisei had been less able to understand each other than most other immigrants and their children. The camp experience increased their alienation. The position of the issei was further undermined in the camps because often their children, who were U.S. citizens, were able to obtain responsible jobs for which the issei did not qualify. This was a severe blow to the self-image and confidence of the issei male, because for centuries the oldest Japanese male had been the undisputed head of the household.

Other events undermined the strength and cogency of the Japanese family, which traditionally had been the pivotal force within the Japanese community. The female often made as much money as the male, and the family had to eat in a communal dining room. The father was unable to exercise his usual authority because of such situations. Consequently, family solidarity was lessened in the camps.

Widespread conflict developed within the camps over the question of loyalty. The nisei often questioned the loyalty of the issei. Japanese nationals accused the leaders of the Japanese American Citizenship League, who cooperated with the War Relocation Authority, of participating in the oppression of the Japanese. In their eagerness to prove their loyalty to the U.S. government, some Japanese helped federal authorities to conduct witch hunts for "suspected" Japanese. The internment showed how a dehumanizing experience could demoralize a group that had traditionally had high group solidarity and trust and cause mistrust and suspicion within it.

Japanese Americans Today

The U.S. Japanese population has never been very large. Japanese immigration was halted by the Immigration Act of 1924 and did not resume until the ban on Asian immigration was lifted when the McCarran-Walter Act was passed in 1952. Although this act set a quota of only 185 Japanese immigrants per year, Asian immigrants were no longer totally excluded.

Compared to the other Asian immigrant groups, few Japanese have immigrated to the United States since the passage of the Immigration Reform Act of 1965. This is because of the highly developed nature of the economy of Japan and its ability to provide jobs for large numbers of technical and professional workers. Most of the immigrants who come to the United States from nations such as the Philippines, Korea, and India—and many of those from China and Hong Kong—are professional workers who are unable to find jobs consistent with their educations in their native lands. This is not the case in Japan. Between 1990 and 2000, 347,539 immigrants came to the United States from Japan, compared to 1,369,070 from the Philippines, 988,857 from China, and 1,022,552 from India. (See Table 13.1, p. 395.)

As a result of its small immigrating population and low birthrate, Japanese Americans are one of the smallest of the Asian American groups and have one of the smallest foreign-born populations. In 2004, most Japanese Americans (about 58.1%) were U.S.-born citizens (U.S. Census Bureau, 2007a).

The Japanese American population was 833,761 in 2005, a slight increase of 37,061 since 2000. Because they have a relatively low immigration rate, Japanese Americans had a lower level of foreign-born among their population than any other group of Asian Americans in 2005 (39.3%). Japanese Americans are highly culturally assimilated. This is indicated by their high rate of out-marriage with other groups (Kitano & Daniels, 1995). In 1989, the out-marriage rate for Japanese Americans living in Los Angeles County was 51.9%. It was 58.3% for women and 41.7% for men.

The Japanese Americans have been termed the so-called model American ethnic minority because of their success in education, social class mobility, and low levels of crime, mental illness, and other social deviances. In 2005, the Japanese median family income was $74,301 compared to $55,832 for all Americans (U.S. Census Bureau, 2007b). The Japanese also had high educational achievement in 2005; 93.2% of Japanese twenty-five years or older were high school graduates or higher, compared to 84.2% for all persons in the United States. The Japanese were also highly concentrated in managerial, professional, and related occupations in 2005 (employed persons age sixteen and older); 49.8% of the Japanese had managerial and professional specialty occupations, compared to 34.1% for all persons. In addition, 27.3% of the Japanese had sales and office occupations, compared to 25.9% for all persons (U.S. Census Bureau, 2007b).

Writes Petersen (1971): "By almost any criterion of good citizenship that we choose, not only are Japanese Americans better than any other segment of American society, including native Whites of native parents, but they have realized this remarkable progress by their own almost unaided effort. Every attempt to hamper the progress of Japanese Americans, in short, has resulted in enhancing their determination to succeed" (pp. 4–5).

Breaking Silence and the Future of the Japanese in U.S. Society

The silence that many Japanese Americans had kept about their internment during World War II was broken during the hearings before the Commission on Wartime Relocation and Internment of Civilians (CWRIC). Congress created the commission "to determine whether a wrong was committed against those American citizens and permanent residents relocated and/or interned as a result of Executive Order Numbered 9066 and other associated acts of the Federal Government, and to recommend appropriate remedies." The commission held twenty days of hearings and took testimony from more than 750 witnesses between July and December 1981. Many people who spoke before the commission were Japanese Americans who had been interned. They told about their experiences in poignant and moving language.

In December 1982 the commission issued its report, *Personal Justice Denied* (Report of the Commission on Wartime Relocation and Internment of Civilians, 1982). The report condemned the internment and in June 1983 recommended that Congress allow $1.5 billion to provide personal redress to the Japanese who were interned during the war years. The commission stated in its report:

> The promulgation of Executive Order 9066 was not justified by military necessity and the decisions which followed from it—detention, ending detention and ending exclusion—were not driven by analysis of military conditions. The broad historical causes which shaped these decisions were race prejudice, war hysteria and a failure of political leadership. Widespread ignorance of Japanese Americans contributed to a policy conceived in haste and executed in an atmosphere of fear and anger at Japan. A grave injustice was done to American citizens and resident aliens of Japanese ancestry who, without individual review or any probative evidence against them, were excluded, removed and detained by the United States during World War II. (p. 18)

It was a long road of debate and controversy, both within and outside of Congress, between the commission's recommendation of redress for internees in June 1983 and the enactment of the American Civil Liberties bill by Congress in August 1988. The bill offered the Japanese Americans an apology for their internment and provided a payment of $20,000 for each internee. The payments, which were scheduled to begin in 1990, were to be made over a ten-year period, were to go to older persons first, and could be made to survivors' descendants in the event of the survivor's death. Because the payments were to be made over a ten-year period, many internees would die before the total payment was made. President Ronald Reagan praised the Japanese who served in World War II when he signed the bill and said that the nation was gravely wrong when it interned the Japanese Americans.

The success of the Japanese in U.S. society is indisputable. However, the future of Japanese culture, values, and behaviors in the United States is uncertain. Their success is probably a result largely of traditional Japanese values, attitudes, and beliefs. With a high out-marriage rate and a relatively low rate of immigration, cultural and structural assimilation into the mainstream society may erode the most important values that have taken the Japanese down the road to success. However, a more hopeful possibility is that as they become structurally integrated into the mainstream society, they will enrich it with traditional Japanese values and will remain, to some extent, culturally Japanese as they become full participants in U.S. society.

FILIPINO AMERICANS

Early Filipino Settlement in the United States and Hawai'i

Filipinos came to Hawai'i and the United States in the first decades of the twentieth century seeking work and better opportunities. An early community of Filipinos in Louisiana has been documented by Espina (1988). Espina's research cites October 18, 1587, as the earliest known date when Filipino sailors aboard a Spanish galleon landed in what is known today as Morro Bay, San Luis Obispo County, California. Eventually, these sailors—"Manilamen"—jumped ship to escape Spanish domination and, around 1763, founded the first permanent Filipino settlement in the bayous of Louisiana. These men developed a dried shrimp industry in their Louisiana settlement.

FILIPINO AMERICANS: HISTORICAL PERSPECTIVE

Important Dates	Events
1587	Filipino sailors landed in Morro Bay, San Luis Obispo County, California. They were among the first Asians to cross the Pacific Ocean for the North American continent because of the Manila galleon trade between Mexico and the Philippines.
1763	The first permanent Asian settlements in the continental United States were Filipino villages in the bayous of Louisiana. Filipino sailors escaped from Spanish colonizers.
1898	Filipinos fought Spanish rule, established the Malolos Congress, and elected Emilio Aguinaldo as the first Philippine president.
	The United States refuted Philippine claims to independence and purchased the islands for $20 million under the terms of the Treaty of Paris, which ended the Spanish-American War.
1899–1901	Filipinos fought for independence from the United States in the Filipino-American War.

Important Dates	Events
1902	The Organic Act of July 1902 recognized the Philippines as an unincorporated territory of the United States.
1906	More than 200 Filipino contract laborers, *sakadas,* were brought to Hawai'i by the Hawaiian Sugar Planters Association.
1911	The Filipino Federation of Labor was founded in Hawaii.
1929	An anti-Filipino riot occurred in Exeter, California, in which more than 200 Filipinos were assaulted.
1930	Fermin Tobera, who later became a Filipino martyr, was killed in an anti-Filipino riot in Watsonville, California.
1934	Congress passed the Tydings-McDuffie Act. This act promised the Philippines independence in ten years and limited Filipino immigration to the United States to fifty per year.
1935	President Franklin D. Roosevelt signed the Repatriation Act on July 11. This act offered free transportation to Filipinos who would return to the Philippines. The 2,190 who took advantage were unable to return to the United States except under the quota system.
1940	Under the terms of the Nationality Act of 1940, Filipino immigrants to the United States could become citizens through naturalization. U.S. citizenship was extended to other categories of Filipino Americans on July 2, 1946.
1941	Japan attacked the Philippines.
1946	On July 4, 1946, the Philippines became independent.
1965	Larry Itliong organized Filipino farm laborers.
1965	The Immigration Reform Act of 1965 opened the door for an influx of Philippine professionals to the United States. More than 32,000 Filipinos immigrated to the United States in 1974.
1990	The Immigration Act of 1990, Section 405, gave Filipino servicemen who were trained in the Philippines and who fought for the United States during World War II between 1939 and 1946 the opportunity to apply for U.S. citizenship.
1992	More than 61,000 Filipino immigrants entered the United States, making them the second largest national group to enter the United States that year, after Mexicans.
2005	The U.S. Census indicated that Filipinos were the third largest Asian group in the United States and the largest Asian group immigrating to the United States between 1990 and 2000.
	The Asian Indian population was slightly larger than the Filipino American population.

Significant numbers of Filipinos did not settle in the United States and Hawai'i until the turn of the century. Most Filipino immigrants were categorized as *pensionados* or *sakadas,* although some were neither. *Pensionados* were government-sponsored students who returned to the Philippines to apply the knowledge they had acquired in the United States. *Sakadas* were contract laborers who were recruited to work in the sugar fields of Hawai'i for three years and either returned to the Philippines, remained in Hawai'i, or ventured to the mainland. *Sakadas* were cheap and exploited field hands lured by the promise of a better life in America.

The Philippine revolution against Spanish domination began in 1896. By 1898, Spain and the United States were fighting the Spanish-American War. With the bulk of Spain's military forces concentrated in the Caribbean, its weakened position in the Philippines led the United States to seek control of the Philippines. The refusal of the United States to accept the Filipinos' claim to independence in 1898 launched the Filipino-American War. In 1902, the United States assumed guardianship over the Philippines, thus establishing Filipinos as nationals.

Immigration

The magnet that pulled Filipinos to Hawai'i and the United States came primarily from without rather than from within. Immigration from the Philippines during the 333 years that the islands were ruled by Spain was virtually nil. However, when the United States acquired the Philippines after the Spanish-American War in 1898, it was only a matter of time before farmers in Hawai'i and the United States would successfully lure Filipinos away from the islands to work as cheap and exploited field hands. Recruiting and transportation agents lured Filipinos away from their homeland with high-pressure propaganda about the promises of Hawai'i and the United States. Because of chronic unemployment and widespread poverty in the islands, thousands of Filipinos left their native land in search of the dream.

Because Chinese immigration had come to an abrupt end in 1882, Japanese immigrants had been the main source of cheap labor for plantation owners in Hawai'i and big farmers on the U.S. West Coast. However, the Gentlemen's Agreement of 1907–1908 substantially reduced Japanese immigration, and the Immigration Act of 1924 virtually stopped it. When Japanese immigration ended, a new source of cheap labor was desired by farmers in Hawai'i and in the United States. The United States had recently annexed both Puerto Rico and the Philippines. Each nation was regarded as a promising source of cheap labor. However, the attempt to start large-scale immigration from Puerto Rico failed, and the farmers turned to the Philippines, where they had considerable success. The powerful Hawai'ian Sugar Planters Association became so alarmed when the Gentlemen's Agreement restricted Japanese immigration in 1907–1908 that it brought more than 200 Filipino workers to Hawai'i that year. The association wanted to make sure that, when Japanese immigration stopped, there would be a new source of labor just as abundant and cheap.

Filipino immigration to Hawai'i continued and escalated after 1907. However, until the 1920s, most of the Filipino immigrants remained in Hawai'i and did not come to the U.S. mainland. In 1920, there were only 5,603 Filipinos in the United States. However, from 1923, when Filipino immigration to the United States gained momentum, until it reached its peak in 1929, large-scale immigration to the mainland occurred. In 1929 alone 5,795 Filipinos entered California. Between 1907 and 1910, about 150,000 immigrants left the Philippines and headed for Hawai'i or the United States. Although the highly glorified and exaggerated tales spread by recruiting and transportation agents were the magnet that pulled hundreds of Filipinos from their homeland, the letters and money sent back home by immigrants, as well as the desire to get rich quickly, helped to motivate them to leave the poverty-stricken islands.

Filipino immigrants in the United States had some unique group characteristics that were destined to make their lives on the West Coast harsh. As the third wave of Asian immigrants, they were victims of the accumulated anti-Asian racism. They were also a young group. According to McWilliams (1943), they were the youngest group of immigrants in U.S. history. They ranged in age from about sixteen to thirty; most, 84.3%, were under thirty. Also, most of the immigrants were sojourners who hoped to return to the Philippines after attaining the riches of America. Like the other Asian sojourners, the longer they stayed in the United States, the more their hope waned that they would ever be able to return home.

The immigrants were predominantly male. The sex ratio was imbalanced, as it was in early Chinese American communities, because few Filipino women immigrated because female immigration violated tradition. In 1930, there was one woman for every 143 men. The Filipinos immigrated from a country that was a U.S. colony in which the American myth of "all men are created equal" was taught in the schools. Thus, unlike the other Asian groups, they came to the United States expecting to be treated like equals. Their acceptance of this myth made their adjustment in the United States more difficult.

Work.   Like other Asian immigrants, the Filipinos came to Hawai'i and the United States to do work the Whites disdained and refused to do. They were hired, usually under a contract system, to pick asparagus and lettuce and to do other kinds of "stoop" field work. In addition to farming, the Filipinos, especially after World War II, worked as domestics. They cooked, washed dishes, and worked as house servants. Some worked in the fishing industry and in canneries.

The Filipino Community.   Unlike the Japanese and Chinese, the Filipinos were unable to develop tightly knit ethnic communities. The Little Manila districts in cities such as Los Angeles and San Francisco were primarily entertainment centers and stopping places for the field hands between seasons. The Filipinos could not establish highly cohesive communities because their jobs kept them moving and because, like the Chinese immigrants, they were unable to have much of a family life because of the small number of Filipino females.

The types of entertainment and recreation that emerged within Filipino American communities reflected the sociological makeup of young, unmarried males searching for meaning in life in a hostile and racist atmosphere. Prostitution, cockfighting, and gambling were favorite pastimes for the lonely, alienated men. The Filipino-owned dance halls, in which White girls danced and sold or gave other favors to the immigrants, were popular and a source of widespread tension between Filipinos and White men. Whites passed laws prohibiting Filipinos from marrying White women. However, these laws had little effect on biological drives and mutual attraction between White women and Filipino men. Stockton, California, was dubbed the Manila of the United States because so many Filipinos settled there. It was the site of much conflict and tension between Filipinos and Whites. Although there were few tightly organized Filipino communities, a strong sense of group solidarity and sense of peoplehood emerged among Filipinos. Strong nationalism, as the gifted Filipino American writer Carlos Bulosan epitomized (San Juan, 1972), was widespread among Filipinos in the United States.

Anti-Filipino Agitation.   As the third wave of Asian immigrants to the West Coast, Filipinos inherited all of the anti-Asian prejudice and racism that had accumulated since the Chinese started immigrating to the United States in the 1850s. When Filipino immigration reached significant levels in the 1920s, familiar anti-Asian screams about the Yellow Peril were again heard. These anti-Asian movements were, again, led by organized labor and patriotic organizations such as the American Federation of Labor and the Native Sons of the Golden West. The arguments were identical to those that had been made against the Chinese and Japanese; the victims were different but the victimizers were the same. Labor groups claimed that Filipinos were "unfair competition"; patriotic groups argued that they were unassimilable and would pollute the "pure" White race. One exclusionist warned (cited in Divine, 1957, p. 70), "This mongrel stream is small, but when it is considered how rapidly it multiplies and grows it is clear that the tide must be stemmed before it gets beyond control."

Labor and nativistic groups had succeeded in halting Chinese and Japanese immigration by urging Congress to pass exclusion laws. However, the Filipinos presented a different problem. They could not be excluded as "aliens" under the provisions of the Immigration Act of 1924 because of their peculiar and ambiguous legal status. Because the United States had annexed the Philippines in 1898, its citizens were not aliens. However, unlike Puerto Ricans, they were not citizens of the United States either. Filipinos were "nationals" or "wards" of the United States. Consequently, they could not be excluded with the immigration laws that applied to foreign nations. Representative Richard Welch of California nevertheless fought hard to get an outright exclusion act through Congress in 1928. The attempt failed, but Welch succeeded in rallying widespread support for the anti-Filipino cause.

The failure of the Welch bill convinced the leaders of the exclusion movement that they had to try another strategy. The desire for independence within the Philippines had become intense by the late 1920s. The Philippines' independence movement gave the exclusionists new hope for a cause that had become an obsession: to exclude and deport Filipinos. They jumped on the independence bandwagon. If the Philippines became independent, they correctly reasoned, its citizens could be excluded under the provisions of existing immigration laws. The passage of the Tydings-McDuffie Act on March 24, 1934, was a significant victory for the exclusionists.

In addition to promising the Philippines independence, the Tydings-McDuffie Act limited Filipino immigration to the United States to fifty people per year. This act, as was the intention of its architects, virtually excluded Filipino immigration to the United States. Even this bill did not totally satisfy the exclusionists. They not only wanted Filipino immigration stopped, but they also wanted Filipinos deported. They pushed the so-called Repatriation Act through Congress. President Franklin D. Roosevelt signed the act on July 11, 1935. Under the terms of the act, any Filipino could obtain free transportation back to the Philippines. However, there was an insidious catch to this inducement. Once they returned, they could not reenter the United States. Few Filipinos were seduced by this act. Only about 2,000 returned to the Philippines under its provisions.

Riots and Anti-Filipino Violence.   Both before and after the Filipino exclusion and deportation acts, anti-Filipino Whites carried out a vicious and active campaign of violence against Filipinos in the western states. One of the first anti-Filipino riots broke out in Yakima, Washington, on September 19, 1928. Some of the most serious riots occurred in California, where most Filipino immigrants first settled. On October 24, 1929, Whites attacked and assaulted more than 200 Filipinos and did considerable property damage in Exeter, California. Fermin Tobera, a lettuce picker, was killed in a riot that occurred in Watsonville, California, in January 1930. Tobera's murder greatly disturbed people in his native homeland, and a National Humiliation Day was declared in Manila. Some Filipinos felt that Tobera had been ruthlessly slain by a "mob of blood-thirsty Americans" (Wallovits, 1966, p. 124). Three people were shot in a riot that occurred near Salinas, California, in August 1934. An anti-Filipino riot occurred as late as June 1939 in Lake County, California. Writes McWilliams (1943): "No reparations or indemnities were ever made for these repeated outrages; nor were the culprits ever punished" (p. 240).

Filipino Americans Today

Between 2001 and 2005, Filipinos were the fourth largest group immigrating to the United States, exceeded only by immigrants from Mexico, India, and China. The number of Filipinos entering the United States increased from 3,130 in 1965 to 60,748 in 2005 (U.S. Department of Homeland Security, 2006). The Filipino population in the United States increased 23.3% between 2000 and 2005, while the total U.S. population, in contrast, increased by 15.9% (U.S. Census Bureau, 2007b). In 2005, there were about 2,282,872 Filipinos living in the United States. Significant percentages lived in California and Hawai'i; most lived in urban areas.

Most Filipinos who came to the United States in the 1920s were unskilled laborers. The Immigration Act of 1965 not only significantly increased the number of Filipino immigrants to the United States but also changed the characteristics of the immigrants. The majority of the immigrants now entering the United States from the Philippines are professional, technical, and kindred workers. These immigrants come to the United States to seek jobs that are more consistent with their training than those they can obtain in the Philippines. A significant number of them are specialists in the health professions. Professional and technical workers from the Philippines have encountered some difficulties obtaining licenses to practice their crafts in the United States and have experienced language problems and discrimination. Sometimes doctors, dentists, and pharmacists must take lower-level jobs out of their fields until they can obtain the licenses needed to practice their professions in the United States. Many Filipinos who eventually practice their professions in the United States have obtained additional training in U.S. schools.

The significant number of professionally trained Filipinos who have immigrated to the United States since the Immigration Act of 1965 was enacted has changed substantially the social and demographic characteristics of the Filipino Americans. In 2005, 66.2% of Filipinos in the United States were foreign born. In terms of numbers, there were more foreign-born Americans of Filipino origin than of any other group other than Mexicans. There were 1,512,211 foreign-born Filipinos and 10,826766 Mexicans. However, the Filipinos did not have the highest percentage of foreign-born persons among the Asian Americans; 75.8% of Koreans were foreign born and 73.3% of Asian Indians were foreign born (U.S. Census Bureau, 2007b).

Before 1970, Filipinos were heavily concentrated in the lower strata of the population on most indices, such as education, income, and job status. However, data from the American Community Survey indicate that the group characteristics of Filipino Americans in 2005—based on several criteria related to education, income, and job status—do not differ significantly from the Japanese, Chinese, and other Asian groups in the United States. Like the Chinese and Japanese, Filipinos are ahead of the general population on most of these indices. In 2005, the median family income for Filipinos was $75,722, compared to $55,832 for all persons in the United States. The percentage of Filipino high school graduates, twenty-five years or older, was 90.9%, compared to 84.2% for all persons in the United States (U.S. Census Bureau, 2007b).

Kim's (1978) study of Filipinos in Chicago indicates why the median family income of Asian families might be higher than that of White families. In many Asian families, both parents are highly trained and have professional jobs. Kim describes the typical Filipino in her study as follows:

> In broad terms, the Chicago Pilipino [sic] respondent can be categorized as young, well-educated, and fairly well-off financially: he [or she] is in his early thirties, has finished college, and may have a graduate or professional degree. Unlike most of the other groups in the study, it does not matter in this area whether the Pilipino respondent is male or female. In either case, the educational level and job level—skilled, white-collar, or professional—will probably be about the same. The Pilipino female will also be just about as likely as her male counterpart to have a full-time job, or to hold more than one job. (p. 172)

A study of the Chinese, Japanese, and Filipinos in the United States will help students to understand how these groups resisted racism and discrimination and attained success in U.S. society. However, their success was attained and is maintained by hard work, tenacity, and the will to overcome. Despite their success in U.S. society, Asians are still the victims of racism and discrimination, both subtle and blatant. Violent incidents against Asian Americans received national attention in 1985. A *New York Times* article, for example, was entitled "Violent Incidents against Asian-Americans Seen as Part of Racist Pattern" (Butterfield, 1985). Part of the violence may have its roots in the U.S. response to competition from the Japanese; some Americans blur the distinction between Japanese Americans and foreign Japanese. The violence may be partly a response to the significant number of Asian immigrants now entering the United States. Regardless of the cause of this new wave of anti-Asian violence, it reminds us that racism is an integral part of U.S. society that can victimize any racial or ethnic group, no matter how successful. However, despite its problems, the success and mobility of Asian American groups in the United States indicate its promise and that it is still a land in which many dreams of immigrants are actualized.

TEACHING STRATEGIES

Concepts such as *immigration, discrimination,* and *cultural diversity* are highlighted in the historical overviews. This part of the chapter illustrates strategies for teaching three concepts, *similarities and differences, immigration,* and *discrimination.* An infinite variety of strategies can be used to teach each of these concepts. However, these activities are illustrative and can serve as a guide to teacher planning. Although each concept can and should be taught at all grade levels, these concepts are discussed for particular grade levels: *similarities and differences* in the primary grades, *immigration* in the intermediate and upper grades, and *discrimination* in the high school grades.

Primary Grades

Concept

Names (similarities and differences)

Generalization: We all have names. However, our different names often give other people clues about our different origins, cultures, and experiences.

Introduction

Similarities and *differences* are two concepts that can be effectively taught in the primary grades. These concepts can be understood by young children when they are taught with concrete examples. A unit on names can help primary-grade children learn that even though we all have names (a similarity), our names often give other people clues about our different origins, experiences, and cultural backgrounds. It is appropriate to help children better understand the nature and origins of names when they are studying Asian Americans because teachers and students often find some Asian names, such as Vietnamese names, difficult to pronounce and understand.

1. Begin this unit by telling the class that the people who live in our nation, the United States (point it out to the children on a primary globe), came from many different nations and lands. Ask the students: "Can you name some of the nations from which the people in the United States came?" Record accurate responses on the board or butcher paper.

   Using a primary globe, show the students some of the nations and continents from which immigrants to the United States came. Ask the students if any of them have ever traveled or lived in any of these nations and continents. If any of them have, ask them to tell briefly about their life in these countries or their trips to them.

   Say to the class: "The ancestors of American Indians came to what is now the United States thousands of years ago. The ancestors of many Jews and Italians came to the United States almost 100 years ago. Other Americans, such as many Cubans and Vietnamese, have lived in the United States for fewer than fifty years. People from different parts of the world have many different ways of living, often believe different things, eat different kinds of food, and have different religions. Often people from various nations keep some of their differences after they have lived in the United States for many years. People in various nations often have different kinds of names. Many Americans, whose ancestors came from many different nations or who came from different nations themselves, have names that sound and look different from the names of other groups. These different kinds of names give us clues about the homelands of their ancestors or about their homelands, and about their ways of life and beliefs."

   Write the following names on the board or butcher paper:

Susan Schmidt	Ito Matsuda
Juan Rivera Sanchez	Wing Chu
Jennifer Kim	Katherine Ann Shilenski
Patrick O'Shea	Hoang Hy Vinh

   Say to the class: "Here are the names of eight of the children in Mrs. Gonzales's third-grade class in a school in Los Angeles. Do their names give us any clues about where their ancestors came from, about what foods they might eat, and about which holidays they might celebrate?"

   After giving the students an opportunity to state their ideas about what the children's names reveal about them, tell them a little about each of the eight students in Mrs. Gonzales's class. A brief description of each student follows.

   Susan Schmidt. Susan's ancestors came to the United States from Germany in the 1820s. However, Susan says she is a *complete* American. She has no German characteristics that she knows about.

   Ask the class: "Why do you think Susan has an American, rather than a German, given name? Why does she consider herself completely American rather than part German? Do any of you have German names? If so, do you feel totally American or part German? Why?"

   Juan Rivera Sanchez. Juan was born in Mexico and moved to Los Angeles last year. Unlike Susan's name, Juan's name includes both his father's surname (Rivera), and his mother's maiden surname (Sanchez). This is a common practice in Spanish-speaking nations. In Mexico, it is correct to call Juan "Mr. Rivera."

Ask the class: "Why do you think that in Spanish-speaking nations children's names often include both their father's surname and their mother's surname before marriage? If your name included both of your parents' surnames (and not just your father's), how would your name be written? If you don't know your mother's surname before she married, ask a parent or another adult whom you live with tonight and be prepared to share your name written with your father's surname and your mother's surname before she married." (Note: Some of the children's mothers might use their maiden surnames, rather than the surnames of their spouses. Some of them may also be single parents who have never used any other surname.)

Jennifer Kim. Jennifer's grandparents came to the United States during the Korean War in 1952. Jennifer does not speak Korean but enjoys Korean foods. She also likes to visit her relatives who speak Korean and talk about what life was like in Korea.

Ask the class: "Why do you think Jennifer has an American, rather than a Korean, given name? Do you think Jennifer feels like a total American, or part Korean and part American? Why do you think she feels this way?"

Patrick O'Shea. Patrick's great-grandparents came to the United States from Ireland. He thinks of himself as both Irish and American—as an "Irish American."

Ask the class: "Why do you think Patrick feels more Irish than Susan feels German?"

Ito Matsuda. Ito was born in Japan and came to the United States when he was two years old. Ito speaks Japanese and English. He feels that he is both Japanese and American. At home, the Matsuda family usually eats Japanese, rather than American, food. Most of the time the Matsudas speak Japanese, rather than English, when talking to each other.

Ask the class: "Why do you think Ito is more Japanese than Jennifer is Korean?"

Wing Chu. Wing's family moved from China to the United States last year. Wing is still learning to speak English. Most of his family's friends are Chinese. He lives in a Chinese neighborhood.

Ask the class: "Do you think Wing feels Chinese and American, or Chinese? Why do you think he feels this way?"

Katherine Ann Shilenski. Katherine's grandparents came to the United States from Poland before her parents were born. Katherine does not speak Polish and knows only a little about the Polish culture. She has often heard her parents talk about the problems of the people in Poland. Katherine is interested in learning more about the culture and language of her ancestors. She hopes to visit Poland some day.

Ask the class: "Why do you think Katherine feels more Polish than Susan feels German?"

Hoang Hy Vinh. Vinh came to the United States with his parents from Vietnam three years ago. Vinh's name is different in one important way from the names of his classmates. His surname (Hoang) is written first, his middle name (Hy) next, and his first or given name last (Vinh). Because of respect for him and his ancestors, the people in Vietnam would not address Vinh by his surname (Binh, 1975). Rather, they would call him "Vinh" or "Mr. Vinh."

Point out to the class how Susan's, Jennifer's, Juan's, and Patrick's names, and most of their names, are written differently from Vinh's. Ask the students to write their names in the Vietnamese way and read them aloud.

Ask the class: "What problems do you think Vinh's teachers and classmates might have with his name? How do you think these problems make Vinh feel? If you moved to Vietnam and went to school, what do you think the teachers and students would call you? Why? How do you think this would make you feel?"

2. Tell the students to ask their parents to tell them the national origins of their surnames. End this unit by making a chart on butcher paper (or on the board) that shows each student's surname and the nation from which it came. Ask the children to tell as much as they can about the nations from which their surnames came, and whether their families eat foods, celebrate holidays, or have customs related to those nations. Second- and third-grade students can do research on these nations using a source such as the Internet.

Note: Some children in your class might not be able to find out the nations from which their surnames came. It is difficult, for example, for most African Americans to find out the national origins of their surnames. In these cases, label their names *American* on the class chart and ask these students to tell what *American* customs their families practice.

Intermediate and Upper Grades

Concept

Immigration

Generalization: The first groups of Asians to immigrate to the United States came to improve their economic conditions and to fulfill labor needs in Hawai'i and in the continental United States.

1. Read to the class accounts that describe the early immigrations of Chinese, Japanese, and Filipinos to the United States (see the bibliography at the end of this chapter for appropriate references).

Students should be able to answer the following questions when they have finished the readings:

a. What economic, social, and political problems did the Chinese, Japanese, and Filipinos have in China, Japan, and the Philippines?
b. What were the labor needs on the West Coast of the United States?
c. Why did the immigrants leave China, Japan, and the Philippines?
d. Was the United States what they expected? Why or why not?

2. Carefully study the historical summary on Filipino Americans in this chapter and read Chapter 9, "Dollar a Day, Dime a Dance: The Forgotten Filipinos," in Ronald Takaki (1998), *Strangers from a Different Shore: A History of Asian Americans.* Prepare a two-page summary of the economic, social, and political conditions of the early Filipino immigrants who went to Hawai'i and the United States. Assign this summary to the students as a third reading.

TABLE 13.3   Data Retrieval Chart on Asian American Immigrants

	CHINESE IMMIGRANTS	JAPANESE IMMIGRANTS	FILIPINO IMMIGRANTS
Economic situation in homeland when immigration began			
Political situation in homeland when immigration began			
Social conditions in homeland when immigration began			
Labor needs on U.S. mainland when immigration began			
Labor needs in Hawai'i when immigration began			

3. After the students have read and discussed each of the three readings, have them complete Table 13.3.

4. When the students have completed the chart, have them summarize and generalize about why many Chinese, Japanese, and Filipinos immigrated to Hawai'i and the United States, and about the labor needs they satisfied there.

5. Have the students role-play the situation below, which involves a representative of the Hawai'ian Farmers Association trying to persuade a Filipino worker to go to Hawai'i to work on a sugar plantation in 1910. After the role-play situation, ask the students the questions that follow. The role descriptions follow.

Mr. Howard Smith, the Hawai'ian Sugar Planters Association Representative

Mr. Smith has been hired to recruit workers for the association. He realizes that his job depends on his success in recruiting workers. He also realizes that if he truthfully explains the situation in Hawai'i, he will obtain few workers. He therefore decides to paint a rosy picture of the work on the sugar plantation in Hawai'i. He explains to Mr. Ilanos that the contract is for three years and that the association will pay his transportation from the Philippines to Hawai'i.

Mr. Jose Ilanos, a Filipino Who Lives in the Philippines

Mr. Ilanos is a young man with a wife and two children. He is a hard worker. However, in the last few years he has not been able to make enough money to support his family. He has heard about Mr. Smith and is interested in talking to him. However, his wife does not want him to leave the Philippines. Moreover, he has heard from friends that the work in Hawai'i is hard and that the pay is rather low.

Questions

1. Did Mr. Smith succeed in persuading Mr. Ilanos to go to Hawai'i to work? Why or why not?

2. If Mr. Ilanos decides to go to Hawai'i, do you think that Mrs. Ilanos would go with him? Why or why not?

3. If Mr. Ilanos decides to go to Hawai'i, what do you think will happen to him? Why? Do you think he might eventually immigrate to the United States? Why or why not?

4. If Mr. Ilanos decides to remain in the Philippines, what do you think will happen to him? Why?

5. Were there any other options open to Mr. Ilanos besides keeping his same job or going to Hawai'i to work on the sugar plantations? If there were, what were they? If there were not, why?

6. If you were Mr. Ilanos, would you have accepted a contract from Mr. Smith? Why or why not?

Valuing Activity

Read the following story to the class and ask the questions that follow.

FATHER AND SON

Mr. Robert Morimoto is a second-generation Japanese American who lives in an upper-middle-class, predominantly White suburban community near Los Angeles. He is a successful businessman. Mr. Morimoto is proud to be an American and believes that even though our country has problems, any person, regardless of his or her race, can make it in the United States if he or she really tries. Mr. Morimoto does not like to talk about the years that he spent in the Heart Mountain federal concentration camp in Wyoming during World War II. The internment, he feels, is a thing of the past. Japanese Americans should not dwell on it too much today. Mr. Morimoto is impatient with those sansei who talk about the internment all of the time. He feels that they have had it easy and do not have much right to criticize their country the way that they do.

Mr. Morimoto and his son have many fights because of their different beliefs. Henry is a student at a local university and is president of the Asian American Student Association on campus. Henry believes that the United States is a racist nation that oppresses all people of color, including the Japanese Americans. He often talks about the internment and harshly criticizes Japanese Americans like his father who try to "sweep it under the rug." Henry believes that all people of color should join together to fight oppression and racism in America. When they had their last verbal fight, Henry told his father that even though he was successful in business, he had no political power in America and was Yellow on the outside but was White on the inside. Mr. Morimoto became very upset with Henry. He told Henry that he would either have to start treating him with respect or move out of his house.

Questions

1. Why do you think Mr. Morimoto feels the way he does?
2. Why do you think Henry feels the way he does?
3. Do you think that Henry is treating Mr. Morimoto fairly?
4. Do you think that Mr. Morimoto is treating Henry fairly?
5. If you were Henry, what would you do? Why?
6. If you were Mr. Morimoto, what would you do? Why?

High School Grades

Concept

Discrimination

Generalization: Asian Americans have been the victims of widespread prejudice and highly discriminatory immigration and migration laws.

Initiate this unit by showing the students a videotape or DVD about the internment, such as *Rabbit in the Moon* (see Appendix C for details about this videotape). This powerful and informative videotape describes the powerful human effects that the internment had on Japanese American communities. After viewing the videotape, ask the students to write one-sentence reactions to it. Divide the class into groups of three to five to discuss their written reactions to the videotape. Each group should be asked to develop a written reaction to be shared later with the entire class.

1. Ask individual students or small groups of students to prepare short research reports on the following topics and present them to the class:
   a. the California Foreign Miner's Tax of 1850
   b. anti-Chinese riots that occurred in the 1800s
   c. the Chinese Exclusion Act of 1882
   d. anti-Asian groups that developed on the West Coast in the late 1800s and continued through the 1930s, such as the Native Sons of the Golden West
   e. the California Alien Land Laws that prohibited Japanese immigrants from owning or leasing land
   f. the internment of Japanese Americans
   g. the Immigration Act of 1924
   h. anti-Filipino riots that occurred in the 1920s and 1930s
   i. the Tydings-McDuffie Act of 1934
   j. the Repatriation Act of July 11, 1935
2. When students share their reports, have them list on a master chart (a) ways in which all of the laws and actions were similar, (b) ways in which they were different, and (c) ways in which they discriminated against Asian Americans. Through the use of higher-level questions, help the students derive the key generalization stated previously.
3. Have your students role-play a session of Congress in which the Chinese Exclusion Act of 1882 is debated. The entire class can participate. However, assign several specific students to lead the debates. For example, ask one student to play the role of a California senator who is anxious to be reelected, and thus is strongly in favor of the act. Ask another student to argue against the act. Before the role-playing begins, read and discuss the act with the class. It is reprinted in Alexander Yamato, Soo-Young Chin, Wendy L. Ng, and Joel Franks (Eds.), *Asian Americans in the United States* (vol. 1) (Dubuque, Iowa: Kendall/Hunt, 1993), pp. 235–240.

   When the main speakers start debating, the other class members can participate both by asking them questions and by arguing on the floor. When the discussion of the act is complete, the students should then vote on it. After the voting, the role-playing should be discussed, as well as the actual historical events. The students should discuss why their voting results were similar to or different from that of Congress in 1882 and why. In this activity, try to help the students recreate the political and social atmosphere of the late 1800s. One way this can be done is to ask each student to pretend that he or

TABLE 13.4   Asian Immigrants in the United States

PERIOD	NUMBER	PERCENTAGE OF ALL IMMIGRANTS
1861–1880		
1880–1900		
1900–1914		
1914–1925		
1925–1940		
1940–1960		
1960–1970		
1970–1980		
1980–1990		
1990–2000		

she is a senator from a specific state with a particular mandate from his or her constituency.

4. Ask a group of students to do research and complete Table 13.4. After the students have completed the table, ask them to (a) write a generalization about the percentage of Asian immigrants that came to the United States between 1861 and 1960 and the total number of immigrants that came to the United States during this period; and (b) discuss, using the completed chart, whether White Americans on the West Coast had valid reasons to fear what was called the Yellow Peril. Ask them to discuss their answers to this question: "If Whites on the West Coast had no valid reasons to fear a Yellow Peril, why do you think that Asian Americans were the victims of so much hostility and harassment?"

5. Ask the students to read a book on the internment. Some recommended books follow:
   - Gary Y. Okihiro (2006). *Whispered Silences: Japanese Americans and World War II*. Seattle: University of Washington Press (photographs and text).
   - Charles Kikuchi (1993). *The Kikuchi Diary: Chronicle from an American Concentration Camp*. Edited by John Modell. Urbana: University of Illinois Press.
   - Michi Nishiura Weglyn (1995). *Years of Infamy: The Untold Story of America's Concentration Camps* (updated ed.). Seattle: University of Washington Press.

6. After they have read a book on the subject, ask them to do the following:
   a. compare the interpretation of the internment in the book read with the interpretation in a high school American history textbook or some other source
   b. discuss why they think the internment occurred
   c. discuss the role of the Japanese American Citizenship League during the internment

     d. discuss the roles of the following men in the internment:
       (1) President Franklin D. Roosevelt
       (2) Secretary of War Henry L. Stimson
       (3) Lieutenant General John L. DeWitt
       (4) Assistant Secretary of War John J. McCloy
       (5) Colonel Karl R. Bendetsen
       (6) Major General Allen W. Gullion

7. Role-play a meeting of the men listed in 6.d. discussing whether the Japanese should be interned during World War II.

8. Discuss the moral implications of the internment, that is: Should the internment have occurred? Why or why not? Who was responsible for the internment? What does the internment teach us about our society? Do you believe that an ethnic minority group could be interned today? Why or why not? Why were the Japanese interned and not the Germans?

9. Ask the students to review the hearing and testimony made before the Commission on Wartime Relocation and Internment of Civilians and to identify the factors that resulted in the passage of the American Civil Liberties bill in 1988. The hearing and testimony are summarized in Report of the Commission on Wartime Relocation and Internment of Civilians (1982), *Personal Justice Denied*.

10. To summarize this activity, ask the students to write an essay on "The Meaning of the Internment—Then and Now."

11. Asian American authors, like other American writers, often express their reactions to and experiences with prejudice and discrimination in their writings. Literary works by Asian Americans can provide students with insights that cannot be gained from factual sources. To help your students understand better the reactions of Asian Americans to discrimination, have the class read and discuss selections from the following books:

    a. John Okada (1981), *No-No Boy*. A powerful and well-crafted novel about a Japanese American who refused to fight in World War II.

    b. Carlos Bulosan (1973), *America Is in the Heat*. A poignant, beautiful, and revealing book that can serve as an excellent springboard for a discussion about anti-Filipino discrimination in the United States.

    c. Frank Chin et al. (Eds.) (1974), *Aiiieeeee: An Anthology of Asian-American Writers*. Includes stories, poetry, and excerpts from novels.

    d. Asian Women of California (1997), *Making Waves: An Anthology of Writings by and about Asian Women*. (Part 6 of this excellent anthology is called "Thunderstorms: Injustice." The readings provide firsthand accounts of the injustice experienced by Asian American women.)

    e. Mine Okubo (1983), *Citizen 1366*. An individual who was interned describes her experiences.

REFERENCES

America's Best Colleges, 2007: College Search. *U.S News and World Report*. [Data file]. Retrieved August 12, 2007, from http://www.usnews.com/usnews/edu/college/tools/search.php.

Binh, D. T. (1975). *A Handbook for Teachers of Vietnamese Students: Hints for Dealing with Cultural Differences in Schools*. Arlington, VA: Center for Applied Linguistics.

Butterfield, F. (1985, August 31). Violent Incidents against Asian-Americans Seen as Part of Racist Pattern. *New York Times*, p. 8.

Camarota, S. A. (2002) *Immigrants in the United States, 2002: A Snapshot of America's Foreign-Born Population*. Washington, DC: Center for Immigration Studies.

Chun-Hoon, L. K. Y. (1973). Teaching the Asian American Experience. In J. A. Banks (Ed.), *Teaching Ethnic Studies: Concepts and Strategies* (pp. 119–147). Washington, DC: National Council for the Social Studies.

Daniels, R. (1971). *Concentration Camps USA: Japanese Americans and World War II*. New York: Holt.

Daniels, R. (1988). *Asian America: Chinese and Japanese in the United States since 1850*. Seattle: University of Washington Press.

Divine, R. A. (1957). *American Immigration Policy, 1924–1952*. New Haven, CT: Yale University Press.

Espina, E. (1988). *Filipinos in Louisiana*. New Orleans: Laborde.

Horton, J. (1995). *The Politics of Diversity: Immigration, Resistance, and Change in Monterey Park, California*. Philadelphia: Temple University Press.

Jensen, R. (1980). East Indians. In S. Thernstrom, A. Orlov, & O. Handlin (Eds.), *Harvard Encyclopedia of American Ethnic Groups* (pp. 296–301). Cambridge, MA: Harvard University Press.

Kim, B. C. (1978). *The Asian Americans: Changing Patterns, Changing Needs*. Montclair, NJ: Association of Korean Christian Scholars in North America.

Kim, H. (1980). Koreans. In S. Thernstrom, A. Orlov, & O. Handlin (Eds.), *Harvard Encyclopedia of American Ethnic Groups* (pp. 601–606). Cambridge, MA: Harvard University Press.

Kitano, H. H. L. (1976). *Japanese Americans: The Evolution of a Subculture* (2nd ed.). Englewood Cliffs, NJ: Prentice-Hall.

Kitano, H. H. L., & Daniels, R. (1995). *Asian Americans: Emerging Minorities* (2nd ed.). Englewood Cliffs, NJ: Prentice-Hall.

Lyman, S. M. (1970). *The Asian in the West*. Reno, NV: Desert Research Institute.

McWilliams, C. (1943). *Brothers under the Skin*. Boston: Little, Brown.

Melendy, H. B. (1972). *The Oriental Americans*. New York: Hippocrene Books.

Okada, J. (1981). *No-No Boy*. Seattle: University of Washington Press.

Petersen, W. (1966, January 6). Success Story, Japanese Style. *New York Times Magazine*, pp. 20ff.

Petersen, W. (1971). *Japanese Americans*. New York: Random House.

Report of the Commission on Wartime Relocation and Internment of Civilians. (1982, December). *Personal Justice Denied*. Washington, DC: U.S. Government Printing Office.

San Juan, E., Jr. (1972). *Carlos Bulosan and the Imagination of the Class Struggle*. Quezon City: Philippines Press.

Takaki, R. (1998). *Strangers from a Different Shore: A History of Asian Americans* (rev. ed.). Boston: Little, Brown.

U.S. Census Bureau (2006) *Historical Census Statistics on the Foreign-Born Population of the United States: 1850 to 2000*. Washington, DC: U.S. Government Printing Office.

U.S. Census Bureau (2007a). The American Community—Asians: 2004. *American Community Survey Reports*. Washington, DC: U.S. Department of Commerce, Economics and Statistics Administration.

U.S. Census Bureau (2007b). *American Community Survey, 2005: Selected Population Profile*. [Data file]. Retrieved August 12, 2007, from http://factfinder.census.gov/servlet/IPCharIterationServlet?_ts=202658644174.

U.S. Department of Homeland Security. (2006). *Yearbook of Immigration Statistics: 2005*. Washington, DC: Author.

U.S. Immigration and Naturalization Service. (1985). *Statistical Yearbook of the Immigration and Naturalization Service, 1984*. Washington, DC: U.S. Government Printing Office.

Wallovits, S. E. (1966). *The Filipinos in California*. Unpublished master's thesis, University of Southern California.

Wong, B. P. (1982). *Chinatown: Economic Adaptation and Ethnic Identity in Chinatown*. New York: Holt.

Wright, J. W. (Ed.). (1989). *The Universal Almanac, 1990*. Kansas City, MO: Andrews and McMeel.

ANNOTATED BIBLIOGRAPHY

Books for Teachers

Multiethnic

Amerasia Journal. Published by the Asian American Studies Center, 3230 Campbell Hall, University of California, Los Angeles, CA 90095-1546.

> *Amerasia* is a scholarly journal that publishes papers that deal with historical and contemporary Asian American experiences in the United States.

Ancheta, A. N. (2006). *Race, Rights, and the Asian American Experience.* New Brunswick, NJ: Rutgers University Press.

> Written from an intimate perspective, this thoughtful book contributes to the discussion on race relations in the United States with an emphasis on experiences of racial discrimination faced by Asian Americans.

Chang, V. (Ed.). (2004). *Asian American Poetry.* Urbana: University of Illinois Press.

> An appealing compilation of poetry by a new generation of young Asian American writers. These poets reflect diversity in voice and perspective, reminding the reader not to essentialize the experiences of Asian Americans.

Cohen, W. I. (2002). *Asian American Century.* Cambridge, MA: Harvard University Press.

> Cohen's book is essential reading for those who want to understand more about cultural exchange between the United States and East Asia. In just three chapters, the author presents a modern history of U.S.–East Asian relations with special attention paid to the countless Asian influences that have become staples in American life: Chinese restaurants, Buddhism, and spreading forms of art and architecture.

Danico, M. Y., & Ng, F. (2004). *Asian American Issues.* Westport, CT: Greenwood Press.

> Offering a comprehensive overview of the Asian American experience, the authors discuss the model minority myth, transnationalism, issues of panethnicity, and stereotyping.

Davé, S., Nishime, L., & Oren, T. G. (Eds.). (2005). *East Main Street: Asian American Popular Culture.* New York: New York University Press.

> Asian Americans are one of the country's most rapidly growing non-White populations, and their influences on popular culture should not be ignored. This book considers a range of these influences on food, music, film, dance, and video games.

Duncan, P. (2003). *Tell This Silence: Asian American Women Writers and the Politics of Speech.* Iowa City: University of Iowa Press.

> This book analyzes the complex relationships between race, gender, sexuality, and nation. The author argues for an inclusion of Asian American women into the mainstream feminist conversation in order to challenge traditional meanings of silence and speech.

Garrod, A., & Kilkenny, R. (Eds.). (2007). *Balancing Two Worlds: Asian American College Students Tell Their Life Stories.* Ithaca, NY: Cornell University Press.

> This book contains fourteen first-person narratives from Asian American college students. Their intriguing accounts detail experiences with educational stereotyping and personal struggles with the model minority myth.

Han, A., & Hsu, J. Y. (2004). *Asian American X: An Intersection of 21st Century Asian American Voices.* Ann Arbor: University of Michigan Press.

> An extensive collection of essays written and edited by young Asian Americans, this book is an important resource for teachers working with students. Many of these essays speak to the feeling of the individual being pulled in sometimes opposite directions—by the United States and Asian cultures.

Huang, G. (2006). *The Columbia Guide to Asian American Fiction*. New York: Columbia University Press.
A great classroom resource for language arts and literature teachers who want to introduce students to Asian American writing. This guide covers six genres—anthology, memoir, drama, fiction, poetry, and short fiction—explains key terms, and offers a list of major Asian American writers and their work.

Kurotsuchi, K., & Inkelas, K. (2006). *Racial Attitudes and Asian Pacific Americans: Demystifying the Model Minority*. New York: Routledge.
This study compiles research on racial attitudes and ethnic identity by exploring the views of Asian American college students on controversial issues: affirmative action, social inequities, and ethnic identification.

Lawrence, K., & Cheung, F. (Eds.). (2005). *Recovered Legacies: Authority and Identity in Early Asian American Literature*. Philadelphia: Temple University Press.
This book uses traditional and contemporary readings in a variety of forms—such as poetry, drama, and prose—to examine and appreciate Asian American writing from the late 1800s to the 1960s. This collection of literature exposes the diversity of literature and argues for the adoption of these works into the dominant literary canon.

Lee, J., & Zhou, M. (Eds.). (2004). *Asian American Youth: Culture, Identity, and Ethnicity*. London: Routledge.
An important book for those who work with young people that addresses a wide range of topics: immigration, cultural negotiations, the pressure to assimilate, intermarriage, and sexuality.

Lien, P., Conway, M., & Wong, J. (2004). *The Politics of Asian Americans: Diversity and Community*. New York: Routledge.
The authors carried out the nation's first multiethnic, multilingual, and multiregional political survey on Asian Americans. The results and analysis counter many prevailing stereotypes about Asian Americans and present a significant contribution to our understanding of race, ethnicity, politics, and Asian Americans.

Min, P. G., & Kim, J. H. (Eds.). (2001). *Religions in Asian America: Building Faith Communities*. Lanham, MD: Alta Mira Press.
This book provides a comprehensive overview of the religious practices of Asian Americans and how their religions differ from Western religions. It describes how religious communities deal with issues related to gender, race, transnationalism, economics, social services, and the passage of an ethnic identity to future generations.

Min, P. G. (Ed.). (2006). *Asian Americans: Contemporary Trends and Issues*. Thousand Oaks, CA: Pine Forge Press.
A complete collection of modern issues facing Asian Americans. Contributing scholars write about labor, economic status, educational achievements, settlement patterns, and intergroup relations. The photo essays included truly engage the reader.

Natividad, I., & Gall, S. B. (Eds.). (2003). *Asian American Almanac*. Farmington Hills, MI: Thomson Gale Publishing.
This book describes the cultures and histories of the diverse groups of people descending from Asian and Pacific Island nations. It is comprehensive in scope and detail. The editors include primary documents, compelling photographs, and high-quality maps.

Ono, K. A. (2005). *A Companion to Asian American Studies*. Malden, MA: Blackwell Publishing.
This book consists of twenty previously published essays that focus on myriad issues, including class, sexuality, and identity.

Park, C. C., & Chi, M. M. (Eds.). (1999). *Asian-American Education: Prospects and Challenges*. Westport, CT: Bergin and Garvey.
This book is an inclusive survey that describes the linguistic and sociocultural aspects of seven Asian American groups: Cambodian, Chinese, Filipino, Hmong, Japanese, Korean,

and Vietnamese. The contributors, who wrote intimately about their respective ethnic groups, share insights about needs, educational issues, and challenges faced by each group.

Park, C. C., Lee, S. J., & Goodwin, A. L. (Eds.). (2000). *Asian American Identities, Families, and Schooling*. Greenwich, CT: Information Age Publishing.
A vital resource for teachers who want to learn more about current research on Asian Americans. This anthology consists of twelve contributing scholars who explore issues of ethnic identity development, family relationships, and the educational experiences of Asian American children.

Park, C. C., Endo, R., & Goodwin, A. L. (Eds.). (2006). *Asian and Pacific American Education: Learning, Socialization, and Identity*. Greenwich, CT: Information Age Publishing.
This collection of research analyzes the experiences of Asian American students in schools, communities, and the society at large. Scholars come together to shed light on important Asian American issues. Teachers will find this research anthology especially valuable and informative.

Purkayastha, B. (2005). *Negotiating Ethnicity: Second-Generation South Asian Americans Traverse a Transitional World*. New Brunswick, NJ: Rutgers University Press.
This insightful sociological analysis of race and ethnicity focuses on second-generation young people of Indian, Pakistani, Bangladeshi, and Nepalese origin in the United States.

Robles, R. (2006). *Asian Americans and the Shifting Politics of Race*. London: Taylor and Francis.
A case study that explores the political and rhetorical struggles surrounding race-based admissions in an elite public high school in San Francisco. The author analyzes a lawsuit filed by a group of Chinese Americans against the San Francisco Unified School District and describes the impact of the case on the views about race, diversity, and affirmative action held by White, Chinese, Black, and Latino students.

Rondilla, J. L., Spickard, P. R., Agvateesiri, L., & Chum, M. (2007). *Is Lighter Better? Skin-Tone Discrimination among Asian Americans*. Lanham, MD: Rowman and Littlefield.
This book extends the traditional race relations framework of the Black-White model to include racial attitudes and discrimination within the Asian American community. The authors include personal narratives by Asian American women on the topic of colorism and a chapter dealing with the contemporary issue of cosmetic surgery.

Tong, B. (Ed.). (2004). *Asian American Children: A Historical Guide*. Westport, CT: Greenwood Press.
The presence of Asian immigrants in the United States and their subsequent enrollment in the nation's schools are increasing, requiring teachers to develop a knowledge and understanding of new student groups. This book provides important information on family structures, labor, refugees, and biculturalism.

Ty, E., & Goellnicht, D. C. (Eds.). (2004). *Asian North American Identities: Beyond the Hyphen*. Bloomington: Indiana University Press.
The author describes how Asian Americans have created new ways of seeing and thinking about themselves, avoiding imposed stereotypes. The book offers new views of race, identity, and nation.

Wen-Chen, E., & Omatsu, G. (2006). *Teaching about Asian Pacific Americans: Effective Activities, Strategies, and Assignments for Classrooms and Communities*. Lanham, MD: Rowman and Littlefield.
An accessible resource for classroom teachers, this book offers support for transforming standard curriculum and tools for instruction such as lesson plans and activities.

Zhou, M., & Gatewood, J. V. (Eds.). (2000). *Contemporary Asian America: A Multidisciplinary Reader*. New York: New York University Press.
A valuable resource, this broad collection of theoretically grounded accounts of Asian American experiences provides insights into contemporary issues of assimilation and transformation.

Chinese Americans

Cassel, S. L. (Ed.). (2002). *The Chinese in America: A History from Gold Mountain to the New Millennium*. Lanham, MD: Alta Mira Press.
Chinese Americans have been called "model workers" but have also been perceived as perpetual foreigners in the United States. Contributors to this book describe labor immigration history and policies that define the Chinese American experience.

Chan, S. (2006). *Chinese American Transnationalism: The Flow of People, Resources, and Ideas between China and America during the Exclusion Era*. Philadelphia: Temple University Press.
This book describes the many ways in which the Chinese living in the United States stayed connected to their homeland. The author takes a thoughtful look at the exchange of people, economic resources, and political and cultural ideas during this difficult era.

Chang, I. (2003). *The Chinese in America: A Narrative History*. New York: Viking Press.
Chang's epic story spans 150 years of Chinese American history concluding in the present day. A poignant narrative, *The Chinese in America* offers a unique look at the perseverance of an ethnic community in the United States while illustrating the many accomplishments, from building the transcontinental railroad to important scientific contributions.

Chen, S. (2002). *Being Chinese, Becoming Chinese American*. Urbana: University of Illinois Press.
An informative book with a specific emphasis on how Chinese immigrants searched for identity and created community between 1911 and 1927.

Jung, M. (2006). *Coolies and Cane: Race, Labor, and Sugar in the Age of Emancipation*. Baltimore: Johns Hopkins University Press.
The author analyzes the thousands of Chinese migrants who worked in the fields next to African Americans in Louisiana just after the Civil War. Jung considers the "coolies'" role in re-creating notions of race and nation in the United States.

Lai, H. M. (2004). *Becoming Chinese American: A History of Communities and Institution*. Walnut Creek, CA: Alta Mira Press.
This book is a well-written and comprehensive collection of essays concerning the social and historical development of Chinese American life in the United States. Lai is a renowned scholar of Chinese American history and a reliable resource for teachers.

Lau, E. T. (2006). *Paper Families: Identity, Immigration Administration, and Chinese Exclusion*. Durham, NC: Duke University Press.
Chinese Americans were the first immigrant group officially excluded from the United States with the passing of the Chinese Exclusion Act of 1882. This book uncovers how exclusion forced Chinese Americans to find loopholes in the system, leading to the complex "paper families" plan. Weaving together immigration case files, legislative policy, and transcripts, the author reveals how Chinese Americans circumvented racist immigration policies.

Louie, V. S. (2004). *Compelled to Excel: Immigration, Education, and Opportunity among Chinese Americans*. Stanford, CA: Stanford University Press.
This is an important book for teachers. The author challenges the "model minority" myth and argues that race and class matter for education and upward social mobility. Through extensive interviews with second-generation Chinese American students, Louie found that American students share stories of opportunity and challenge experienced by other immigrant students in the United States.

Mao, L. M. (2006). *Reading Chinese Fortune Cookie: The Making of Chinese American Rhetoric*. Logan: Utah State University Press.
This book examines how bilingual and multilingual speakers contribute to the transformation of the English language. Mao's work has implications for the teaching of writing in English and for understanding Chinese immigrant students who are learning to speak English.

Pan, L. (Ed.). (1999). *The Encyclopedia of Chinese Overseas*. Cambridge, MA: Harvard University Press.
   This encyclopedia is a historical description of the overseas Chinese. The chapter on the United States provides an historical overview of migration and heritage.

Pfaelzer, J. (2007). *The Forgotten War against Chinese Americans*. New York: Random House.
   Investigating a racist campaign in 1885 to expel Chinese immigrants in Northern California, this book evokes a great deal of emotion as the author exposes a little-documented episode of racial purging and the Chinese community's refusal to abandon their claims in the face of ensuing violence.

Praeger, E. (2001). *Wu Hu Diary: On Taking My Adopted Daughter to Her Hometown in China*. New York: Random House.
   The search for a Chinese child's identity creates a deeper emotional bond between a Caucasian mother and her adopted Chinese daughter.

Tong, B. (2003). *The Chinese Americans*. Boulder: University Press of Colorado.
   This book, often referred to as the definitive source on the Chinese American experience, describes the history of the largest Asian ethnic group in the United States. The text includes Chinese American contributions to art, literature, and film, as well as a helpful analysis of the negotiation of identity.

Welland, S. (2006). *A Thousand Miles of Dreams: The Journeys of Two Chinese Sisters*. Lanham, MD: Rowman and Littlefield.
   The author chronicles the stories of two Chinese sisters, Amy Ling Chen and Ling Shuhua, who took very different paths in life—one in the United States and the other in China. The narrative combines family sources, detailed research, and the critical reading of Shuhua's fiction to create an engaging story of culture and the struggle for identity.

Wong, W. H. (2006). *American Paper Son: A Chinese Immigrant in the Midwest*. Edited by B. Tong. Urbana: University of Illinois Press.
   Different from the traditional focus on the West Coast experience, Wong writes in a descriptive style about his family's experiences as Chinese Americans living in the Midwest.

Yung, J., Chang, G. H., & Lai, H. M. (Eds.). (2006). *Chinese American Voices: From the Gold Rush to the Present*. Berkeley: University of California Press.
   A powerful teacher resource that consists of an extensive list of primary documents and stories by Chinese Americans from the 1800s to the present day. The compilation includes accounts from railroad workers, stories of individuals detained during the immigration process, tales of life in Chinatown, and thoughts on becoming American.

Japanese Americans

Asada, S. (2007). *Culture Shock and Japanese American Relations: Historical Essays*. Columbia: University of Missouri Press.
   A noted Japanese historian analyzes U.S. and Japanese relations between 1890 and 2006. The author finds that cross-cultural communication between the two nations has been complex and provides an interesting look at both American and Japanese perceptions focusing on naval strategy, racism, and the atomic bomb controversy.

Asakawa, G. (2004). *Being Japanese American: A JA Sourcebook for Nikkei, Hapa . . . and Their Friends*. Berkeley, CA: Stone Bridge Press.
   This is an important book for teachers learning about Japanese Americans. Using facts, features, recipes, songs, and memories, Asakawa brings the Japanese American culture to life for readers. The book includes sections on Japantown communities, interviews with famous Japanese Americans, and advice for travel to Japan.

Creef, E. T. (2004). *Imaging Japanese America: The Visual Construction of Citizenship, Nation, and the Body.* New York: New York University Press.

The author, a women's studies professor at Wellesley College, examines the ways in which popular images of Japanese Americans have been formed. The book includes an in-depth analysis of internment camp photographs, an investigation of Hollywood's representation of Japanese Americans, and a case study contrasting the media portrayal of two public figures—a Japanese American woman and a Japanese woman.

Daniels, R. (2004). *Prisoners without Trial: Japanese Americans in World War II.* New York: Hill and Wang.

This book provides a detailed account of the decision to move the Japanese Americans from the West Coast into ten different concentration camps during World War II. The author explores this shameful chapter in the nation's history and responsibly questions the possibility of history repeating itself.

Ichioka, Y. (2006). *Before Internment: Essays in Prewar Japanese American History.* Edited by G. H. Chang & E. Azuma. Stanford, CA: Stanford University Press.

This is a final collection of essays from renowned historian Yuji Ichioka who recently passed away. The essays examine Japanese Americans prior to World War II and investigate controversial and important issues such as the meaning of "loyalty" in a racist society.

Inada, L. F. (Ed.). (2000). *Only What We Could Carry: The Japanese American Internment Experience.* Berkeley, CA: Heyday Books.

This book contains a collection of documents from writers who share their voices through diverse literary forms, including narratives, letters, stories, and graphic arts. The writers reveal the victims' powerful emotions and struggles during wartime hysteria.

King-O'Riain, R. C. (2006). *Pure Beauty: Judging Race in Japanese American Beauty Pageants.* Minneapolis: University of Minnesota Press.

This book examines the low rate of immigration and high rate of interracial marriage among Japanese Americans today. Within these ethnic communities, the question has surfaced: "Who is Japanese American?" The author offers new answers to the question of cultural authenticity through the use of ethnographic methods to study Japanese American beauty pageants held in Honolulu, Los Angeles, San Francisco, and Seattle.

Lange, D. (2006). *Impounded: Dorothea Lange and the Censored Images of Japanese American Internment.* Edited by L. Gordon & G. Y. Okihiro. New York: Norton.

This important book combines the work of historians Linda Gordon and Gary Okihiro and photographer Dorothea Lange, providing a vivid analysis of 119 images, originally censored by the U.S. Army, many of which have never before been published. The images uncover the harsh reality of life in the internment camps, while the historians tell the story of thousands of lives uprooted by the racial animosity during World War II.

Neiwert, D. (2005). *Strawberry Days: How Internment Destroyed a Japanese American Community.* New York: Palgrave Macmillan.

This powerful narrative combines documents, interviews, and storytelling to expose the destruction of a Japanese immigrant community just outside of Seattle, Washington. This book unpacks racist methods that prevented the Japanese from reclaiming land after the internment.

Niiya, B. (Ed.). (2001). *Encyclopedia of Japanese American History.* New York: Facts on File.

An A-to-Z reference from 1868 to the present. This is a rich and excellent resource for teachers, with an introductory essay by Gary Okihiro.

Simpson, C. C. (2001). *Absent Presence: Japanese Americans in Postwar America.* Durham, NC: Duke University Press.

In five essays, the author argues that the mass media's description of the Japanese American internment in the late 1940s and early 1950s ignored the larger issues of racial discrimination and displacement. The book shows how the internment experience tended to be an "absent presence" in the minds of White writers in the postwar era.

Filipino Americans

Bautista, V. (2002). *Filipino Americans (1763–Present): Their History, Culture and Traditions.* Naperville, IL: Bookhaus Publishers.
    This book provides a general and basic overview of Filipinos in the United States from 1763 to the present. A rich resource for teachers because it also includes a wealth of cultural information.

Bulosan, C. (1973). *America Is in the Heart.* Seattle: University of Washington Press.
    This classic book describes the inner thoughts and personal journey of a Filipino laborer's struggle to become an American. Bulosan, a Filipino American laborer who lived during the colonialization and postcolonialization era, was a self-taught and talented writer.

Espiritu, A. F. (2005). *Five Faces of Exile: The Nation and Filipino American Intellectuals.* Stanford, CA: Stanford University Press.
    This book examines U.S. colonialism of the Philippines from the perspectives and lived experiences of the colonized. Five distinct Filipinos who feel at home neither in the Philippines nor in the United States discuss issues of identity, ethnicity, and race.

Espiritu, Y. L. (2003). *Home Bound: Filipino American Lives across Culture, Communities, and Countries.* Berkeley: University of California Press.
    Despite being one of the largest Asian immigrant groups, Filipino Americans have been rarely studied. Espiritu interviews more than one hundred Filipinos in California to expose how these individuals are changed by migration and how they negotiate the new social context of life in the United States.

Filipinas Magazine. Published by Filipinas Publishing, Inc., 1580 Bryant St., Daly City, CA 94015.
    A current events magazine, *Filipinas* describes Filipino Americans' contemporary social, cultural, economic, and political issues.

Isaac, A. P. (2006). *American Tropics: Articulating Filipino America.* Minneapolis: University of Minnesota Press.
    In this book, race and identity are examined through the history of U.S. imperialism. Isaac investigates the ways in which popular images of Filipinos are created.

Jamero, P. M. (2006). *Growing Up Brown: Memoirs of a Filipino American.* Seattle: University of Washington Press.
    The author shares stories of his life "growing up Brown" in a White-dominated society. Jamero explores issues of ethnic identity development, negotiations of home and dominant culture, and social activism.

Lott, J. T. (2006). *Common Destiny: Filipino American Generations.* Lanham, MD: Rowman and Littlefield.
    This book compares and contrasts various generations of Filipino Americans. The author includes sections on the first Filipino immigrants to the United States, as well as an analysis of post-1965 Filipino immigrants.

Okamura, J. Y. (1998). *Imagining the Filipino American Diaspora: Transnational Relations, Identities, and Communities.* New York: Garland.
    After eighteen years of research on Filipino Americans, Okamura reconceptualizes the Filipino American population as a transnational diaspora rather than as an immigrant or ethnic minority. This book presents a refreshing perspective and analysis of Filipino Americans as a marginalized minority within a global diaspora.

Root, M. P. (Ed.). (1997). *Filipino Americans: Transformation and Identity.* Thousand Oaks, CA: Sage.
    Through a collection of essays and scholarly contributions, this book addresses the historical impact of colonialism on ethnic identity formation, race and human relations, and contemporary issues that affect the identity and definition of Filipino Americans.

Rosal, P. (2006). *My American Kundiman: Poems*. New York: Persea Books.
This collection of poems by gifted young Filipino poet Patrick Rosal is a rich resource for teachers who want a more personal look at the culture of Filipino Americans.

San Juan, E., Jr. (2000). *After Postcolonialism: Remapping Philippines–United States Confrontations*. Lanham, MD: Rowman and Littlefield.
An intellectual analysis of modern issues facing the Philippines—the continued and varied effects of diaspora, globalization, and U.S. racial formation.

Tiongson, A., Gutierrez, E. V., & Gutierrez, R. V. (Eds.). (2006). *Positively No Filipinos Allowed: Building Communities and Discourse*. Philadelphia: Temple University Press.
This powerful book challenges traditional narratives of Filipino American history. The authors explore the ways in which the colonialism of the Philippines influences Filipino American ways of life, both individually and communally.

Villanueva, M., & Cerenio, V. (Eds.). (2003). *Going Home to a Landscape: Writings by Filipinas*. Corvallis, OR: CALYX Books.
This is a collection of essays about struggle, acculturation, and survival. Fifty-two Filipinas share stories of their desire to maintain transnational identities and the power of culture despite thousands of miles and many generations of separation from the Philippine homeland.

Books for Students

Multiethnic

Chiu, C. (1996). *Lives of Notable Asian Americans: Literature and Education*. The Asian American Experience series. New York: Chelsea House.
This collection of brief biographies is illustrated with photographs of the subjects. (Intermediate and up)

Hong, M. (Ed.). (1993). *Growing Up Asian American*. New York: William Morrow.
Thirty-two classic stories by new and established writers. (High School)

Lee, J. F. J. (1991). *Asian Americans: Oral Histories of First- to Fourth-Generation Americans from China, the Philippines, Japan, India, the Pacific Islands, Vietnam, and Cambodia*. New York: New Press.
These oral histories are a rich and informative source. (High School)

Pak, S. (1991). *A Place to Grow*. Illustrated by M. Truong. New York: Scholastic.
A Korean American author and a Filipino American illustrator team up to create a picture book that captures both their and other Asian Americans' immigration experiences. (Primary)

Yamanaka, L.-A. (1999). *Name Me Nobody*. New York: Hyperion.
The gritty lives of Hawai'i's multiethnic teens are detailed in frank language and pidgin dialect in this and other novels by the acclaimed author, including *Heads by Harry* (Farrar, Straus, and Giroux, 1999) and *Blu's Hanging* (Farrar, Straus, and Giroux, 1997). (High School)

Chinese Americans

Cheng, A. (2004). *Honeysuckle House*. Asheville, NC: Front Street Books.
A recent immigrant from China reaches out to a Chinese American girl who doesn't speak Chinese, has never been to China, and wants to be part of the popular crowd. (Middle School)

Cheng, A. (2005). *Shanghai Messenger*. Illustrated by E. Young. New York: Lee and Low.
Half Chinese and half Caucasian, an eleven-year-old girl learns about her mother's side of the family when she visits relatives in Shanghai over the summer. (Primary)

Cummings, M. (2006). *Three Names of Me*. Illustrated by L. Wang. Morton Grove, IL: Whitman.
A girl adopted from China tells the story of her life through a scrapbook in this beautifully illustrated book that conveys the adoption experience through the adopted child's eyes. (Primary)

Hall, B. E. (2004). *Henry and the Kite Dragons*. Illustrated by W. Low. New York: Philomel.
 Set in the early twentieth century, this charming book portrays a conflict between two groups of recent immigrants—the Chinese youngsters who want to fly their elaborate kites in the park and the Italian boys whose homing pigeons are frightened by the kites. (Primary)

Lee, M. (2006). *Landed*. Illustrated by Y. Choi. New York: Farrar, Straus & Giroux.
 The author tells her father-in-law's immigration story, when at the age of twelve he came to America with his father and was unexpectedly detained, examined, and questioned at Angel Island. Another good Angel Island story for this age group is K. G. Currier's *Kai's Journey to Gold Mountain,* illustrated by G. Utomo (Tiburon, CA: Angel Island Association, 2005). (Primary/Intermediate)

Look, L. (2005). *Uncle Peter's Amazing Chinese Wedding*. Illustrated by Y. Heo. New York: Atheneum.
 A girl's favorite uncle is getting married in a traditional Chinese wedding in America, and she is jealous of his new wife. (Primary)

Marsden, C., & Loh, V. S. (2006). *The Jade Dragon*. Cambridge, MA: Candlewick.
 A second-grader in search of a friend who shares her Chinese heritage finds a kindred spirit in a Chinese-born classmate adopted by White parents, but a coveted jade dragon threatens to tear them apart. (Intermediate)

Mochzuki, K. (2006). *Be Water, My Friend: The Early Years of Bruce Lee*. Illustrated by D. Lee. New York: Lee and Low.
 Poetic text and detailed, compelling artwork distinguish this biography of the famous martial artist, which focuses primarily on his childhood in Hong Kong. (Primary/Intermediate)

Namioka, L. (2003). *Half and Half*. New York: Delacorte.
 A girl with a Scottish mother and a Chinese father has to balance two sets of cultural expectations when both sets of grandparents come to visit. (Intermediate)

Simonds, N., Swartz, L., & the Boston Children's Museum. (2002). *Moonbeams, Dumplings, and Dragon Boats: A Treasury of Chinese Holiday Tales, Activities, and Recipes*. San Diego, CA: Harcourt.
 The authors go beyond the Chinese New Year to offer a complete picture of a cultural tradition, with a wide range of activities for students to learn and celebrate. (All ages)

Yang, B. (2004). *Hannah Is My Name*. Illustrated by the author. Cambridge, MA: Candlewick Press.
 An immigrant girl from Taiwan senses her parents' anxiety as they wait for the green card that will allow them to live and work in the United States. (Primary)

Yang, G. L. (2006). *American-Born Chinese*. New York: Roaring Brook Press.
 In this graphic novel, winner of the 2007 Michael L. Printz Award, Yang interweaves three plot lines in the story of a Chinese American teenage boy to address questions of race, stereotyping, identity, and acceptance. (Primary)

Japanese Americans

Asakawa, G. (2004). *Being Japanese American: A JA Sourcebook for Hikkei, Hapa . . . and Their Families*. Berkeley, CA: Stone Bridge Press.
 Hip, impressionistic writing characterizes this guide for young adults seeking information about their Japanese roots. (High School)

Cooper, M. (2002). *Remembering Manzanar: Life in a Japanese Relocation Camp*. New York: Clarion.
 The author of *Fighting for Honor: Japanese Americans and World War II* (Clarion, 2000) returns with a readable and moving account of Japanese Americans' experiences of relocation, drawn from diaries, journals, and newspaper accounts. (Intermediate and up)

Kadohata, C. (2005). *Kira-Kira*. New York: Atheneum.
> Winner of the 2005 Newbery Award, this novel set in Georgia in the 1950s features two Japanese American sisters, one with a terminal illness and the other trying to keep up her spirit and do the right thing after her sister's death. (Middle School)

Kadohata, C. (2006). *Weedflower*. New York: Atheneum.
> A girl sent with her family to a relocation camp in the Arizona desert during the Second World War befriends a Mohave boy and learns that the internment camp is built on Mohave land. (Intermediate/Middle School)

Lee-Tai, A. (2006). *A Place Where the Sunflowers Grow*. Illustrated by F. Hoshino. San Francisco: Children's Book Press.
> Presented in English and Japanese, this moving book tells the story of a family deported to the Topaz Relocation Camp during World War II and a young girl's struggle to overcome the trauma of relocation and the harshness of her new home. (Primary/Intermediate)

Patneaude, D. (2004). *Thin Wood Walls*. Boston: Houghton Mifflin.
> Although he is a U.S. citizen, an eleven-year-old boy is interned with his mother at the Tule Lake camp during the Second World War while his father is transferred from camp to camp and his older brother enlists in the U.S. Army. (Intermediate)

Filipino Americans

Brainard, C. M. (Ed.). (2003). *Growing Up Filipino: Stories for Young Adults*. Santa Monica, CA: Philippine American Literary House.
> A wide range of experiences and insights about being young and Filipino American are included in this anthology of short stories and personal essays. Brainard also edited *Fiction by Filipinos in America* (New Day Publishers, 1993), a collection of stories by twenty-three Filipino American authors. (High School)

Espiritu, Y. L. (1995). *Filipino American Lives*. Philadelphia: Temple University Press.
> An informative collection of first-person narratives. Pre- and post-1965 immigrants share their sojourns in the United States. (High School)

Gilles, A. A. (2001). *Willie Wins*. Illustrated by C. Angel. New York: Lee and Low.
> Willie hears his father's stories of growing up in the Philippines and receives for a school contest an *alkansiya,* a bank made from a coconut shell. Other children make fun of Willie's bank, but the *alkansiya* contains a special treasure. (Primary)

Robles, A. (2006). *Lakas and the Makibaka Hotel/Si Lakas at ang Makibaka Hotel*. Illustrated by C. Angel. San Francisco: Children's Book Press.
> Presented in English and Tagalog, this colorfully illustrated book depicts a group of immigrant Filipinos who live in a hotel and the young boy whose cleverness allows them to stay when the landlord sells the hotel. (Primary)

Robles, A. (2006). *Lakas and the Manilatown Fish/Si Lakas at ang Isdang Manilatown*. Illustrated by C. Angel. San Francisco: Children's Book Press.
> This first-ever English and Tagalog picture book set in the United States is a lively and humorous fantasy about a boy who dreams of, then finds, a magical fish in a Filipino neighborhood's fish market. (Primary)

Korean Americans

Kent, R. (2007). *Kimchi and Calamari*. New York: HarperCollins.
> A Korean boy adopted by culturally conscious Italian American parents learns surprising things about his birth country and himself when assigned by his teacher to research his family tree. (Middle School)

Na, A. (2006). *Wait for Me*. New York: Putnam.
> Children of a Korean American family are pushed so hard to bring to fruition their parents' dreams that they turn to lying and cheating on exams, and one of them has to choose to tell the truth or to allow a Mexican American coworker to take the blame. This is the second young adult novel by An Na, whose *A Step from Heaven* (Front Street Books, 2001) won the 2002 Michael L. Printz Award for Outstanding Young Adult Literature.

Park, F., & Park, G. (2002). *Good-bye, 382 Shin Dang Dong*. Illustrated by Y. Choi. Washington, DC: National Geographic.
> Drawing on their older sister's immigration experience, the authors offer a nostalgic look at a girl leaving a much-loved way of life and trying to reproduce it in a new land. (Primary)

Park, F., & Park, G. (2005). *The Have a Good Day Cafe*. Illustrated by K. Potter. New York: Lee and Low.
> When Mike's grandmother comes from Korea to live with his family, she misses her foods from home. Mike's family operates a food stand selling favorite American foods, but Mike and his grandmother cook up Korean meals that become a big hit. (Primary)

Park, L. S. (2005). *Bee-bim Bop!* Illustrated by H. B. Lee. New York: Clarion.
> The award-winning author, also a food critic, describes a Korean American girl and her mother making bee-bim bop, a favorite Korean dish. (Primary)

Park, L. S. (2005). *Project Mulberry*. New York: Clarion.
> Working with a White classmate on a science project to raise silkworms, a Korean American girl meets an African American man who grows the mulberry trees that feed the worms. She worries about her mother's reaction to the Black man. Mock interviews between the girl and Park before each chapter are an interesting plot device in this novel that addresses identity and race. Park is the author of the historical novel set in Korea *A Single Shard* (Clarion, 2001), which won the 2002 Newbery Award. (Intermediate/Middle School)

Recorvits, H. (2003). *My Name Is Yoon*. Illustrated by G. Swiatkowska. New York: Farrar, Straus & Giroux.
> Recently arrived in the United States with her family, young Yoon resists learning English and adopting American ways. She thinks the Korean characters look better than Roman letters, but her teacher's encouragement of her art leads her to write in English. (Primary)

Yoo. P. (2005) *Sixteen Years in Sixteen Seconds: The Sammy Lee Story*. Illustrated by D. Lee. New York: Lee and Low.
> The author tells the true story of a son of Korean immigrants who pursues his dreams of becoming a medical doctor and competing as a diver for the United States in the Olympic Games. (All ages)

South Asian Americans

Banerjee, A. (2005). *Rani and the Fashion Divas*. Renton, WA: Mirrorstone.
> Rani, a brainy high school freshman, longs to fit in with the popular girls and gets her chance when she is selected to take part in the school fashion show. Peer and family pressures come into conflict as Rani learns to be true to herself. Banerjee's *Maya Running* (Random House, 2004) examines similar themes, portraying a Indian girl who has lived in Manitoba, Canada, since she was a small child but still finds herself still treated as an outsider because of her dark skin. (Intermediate/Middle School)

Budhos, M. (2006). *Ask Me No Questions*. New York: Atheneum.
> After September 11, 2001, a Bangladeshi Muslim girl living in New York City watches in horror as men in her community are rounded up, imprisoned, and/or deported. The family tries to flee to Canada, but her father is arrested, her mother stays in a shelter until his release, and she and her older sister must return to New York alone, where they are greeted with suspicion and hostility. (Middle/High School)

Fleming, C. (2005). *Lowji Discovers America*. New York: Atheneum.
> After immigrating to the United States, an Indian boy discovers that he cannot have a pet where he lives, and his happy dreams of his new home are shattered until he uses his ingenuity to change his landlady's mind. (Intermediate)

Heine, T. (2004). *Elephant Dance: Memories of India*. New York: Barefoot Books.
> Indian American children learn from their visiting grandfather about life in India. (Primary)

Hidier, T. D. (2003). *Born Confused*. New York: Scholastic.
> When her immigrant parents start to arrange meetings with "suitable" Indian boys, a seventeen-year-old Indian American girl resists until one of those "suitable" boys turns out to be rather "unsuitable." (Middle/High School)

Krishnaswami, U. (2006). *Bringing Asha Home*. Illustrated by J. Akib. New York: Lee and Low.
> A boy whose father was born in India describes how his American family has adopted an Indian girl at the same time as he celebrates Rakhi Day, an Indian holiday that celebrates the brother-sister bond. Krishnaswami is also the author of *The Closet Ghosts* (Children's Book Press, 2006), where a young girl looks to Hanuman, a character from Indian mythology, to help her cope with a new home and school. (Primary)

Krishnaswami, U. (2004). *Naming Maya*. New York: Farrar, Straus & Giroux.
> An Indian American girl and her mother travel to India to sell her late grandfather's estate. (Middle/High School)

Staples, S. F. (2005). *Under the Persimmon Tree*. New York: Farrar, Straus & Giroux.
> An Afghanistan-born doctor and his American wife, who has converted to Islam, travel to his native country to help people caught up in the 2001 war; among them is a preteenage girl who has lost her entire family. (Middle/High School)

Southeast Asian Americans

Ly, M. (2005). *Home East*. New York: Delacorte.
> A ten-year-old girl emigrates with her father from Cambodia to California after her mother abandons the family. Along with missing her mother, she copes with language and cultural misunderstandings at her new school. (Intermediate)

Marsden, C. (2006). *The Quail Club*. Cambridge, MA: Candlewick.
> A Thai American fifth-grader wants to perform a Thai dance for her school's talent show, but her best friend insists on performing a popular American dance. (Intermediate)

Warren, A. (2004). *Escape from Saigon: How a Vietnam War Orphan Became an American Boy*. New York: Farrar, Straus & Giroux.
> This is a moving and informative book about an orphaned eight-year-old Amerasian boy who was airlifted to the United States in 1975, grew up in New Jersey, and eventually became an ER doctor. (Middle School)

■■■■■

CHAPTER FOURTEEN

ARAB AMERICANS
Concepts, Strategies, and Materials

The more I answered to Arab, the more I puzzled over the discrepancy between what most people believed about Arabs and what I knew of Arab Americans. The stereotypes just didn't fit. Terrorist, oil sheik, master of the seraglio—it was impossible to connect these terms with my uncle who baked blueberry muffins for his wife's breakfast and washed out her [clothes] by hand, or with my other uncle who belonged to the Rotary Club, voted Republican, and was a deacon in the Baptist church.

—Evelyn Shakir (1997, p. 1)

Never deny it [that you are Arab American]. Maybe [after 9/11] Arab Americans are twice as sad as other people. But we are still proud of everything peaceful and beautiful that endures. Then speak beauty if we can—the beauty of culture, poetry, tradition, memory, family, daily life.

Because men with hard faces do violent things, because fanaticism seizes and shrinks minds, is no reason for the rest of us to abandon our songs. Maybe we need to sing louder.

—Naomi Shihab Nye (cited in Lee, 2002, p. 14)

Arabs have been becoming Americans for well over a century. Yet for much of that time, both in popular literature and in the national conversations on ethnicity, as well as in school curricula, they have been invisible to most Americans. Toward the end of the twentieth century, the invisibility gave way to negative stereotype, and they found that they—or at least people from their countries of origin—were portrayed largely as caricatures: the terrorist, the oil sheik, the belly dancer. Their contributions to American economic, social and public life, the development of their

This chapter was contributed by **Paula Hajar**, Ed.D., an educator and long time activist, researcher, and writer in the Arab American community. Professor Hajar received her undergraduate degree from Radcliffe College, and graduate degrees from Antioch University and Harvard Graduate School of Education. She is currently senior professional development specialist of New York City's Bronx Charter School for Better Learning, a school she helped to found in 2003.

institutional life, and their extraordinarily strong family values were, according to Helen Hatab Samhan, "the best kept ethnic secret in America" (Hatab, n.d.).

The achievements of Arab Americans, their reasons for coming to America, and their struggles are in many ways similar to those of other immigrant groups. In the wake of 9/11, their position has become both more precarious and at the same time more grounded. In the name of national security, laws have been enacted that, when executed, strip Arabs of their civil rights. Yet curiosity about Arabs has grown, and many civic and cultural institutions and discourses have begun to open up to them or seek them out. Arab Americans have spent the last 125 years striving first for inclusion and now for self-definition. This chapter is the story of that struggle.

WHO IS AN ARAB?

Language defines the Arab: an Arab is a person whose mother tongue is Arabic or who descends from such a person. Though spoken in local dialects in over twenty countries, the Arabic language is unified by a standard (classical) written form, which is also used orally in formal situations, including on television and radio. The countries where Arabic is the official language stretch from the Arabian Peninsula in southwest Asia across North Africa to the Atlantic. Figure 14.1 shows the nations that make up the Arab world.

The terms *Muslim* and *Arab* are not interchangeable. *Muslim* is a religious descriptor. Muslims are followers of Islam, the religion that claims that there is only one God and that Muhammad is his prophet. Of the total number of Muslims in the world (about 1.1 billion), Arabs account for no more than 20%. While the vast majority (95%) of Arabs are Muslim, there are also millions of Arab Christians and prominent communities of Arab Jews. Both of these groups have made important contributions to Arabic—and Muslim—culture and history.

When Arabs first began to immigrate to the United States, the overwhelming majority—over 90%—were Christians. In recent years, more Arab Muslims than Christians have immigrated to the United States, but Christians still comprise the majority of Arab Americans, about 75% (El-Badry, 1994).

There has always been a discrepancy between the number of people who report Arab ancestry on the U.S. Census and scholarly estimates of the size of the Arab community. While the official count was close to 1.5 million Arab Americans in the 2000 U.S. Census, Arab American researchers estimate the population at 3 to 4 million. In any case, the 2005 American Community Survey of the U.S. Census Bureau indicated that 33.1% had Lebanese ancestry, 12.8% were Egyptian, 11% were Syrian, and 4.7% were Palestinian. Another 18.9% claimed to be "Arab" or "Arabic," and 19.4% were "Other Arab," meaning from one of the other Arab counties, such as Kuwait, Algeria, Tunisia, and Libya (U.S. Census Bureau, 2007). Figure 14.2 shows the percent distribution of the Arab American population by

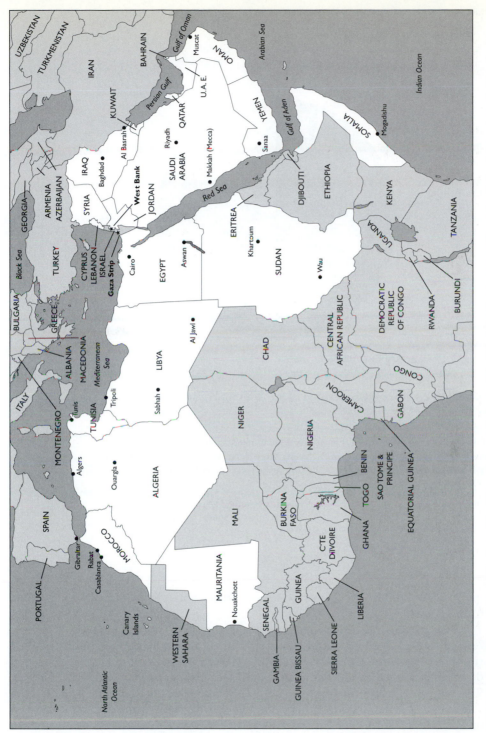

FIGURE 14.1 Map of Arab Nations The Gaza Strip and parts of the West Bank are currently under Palestinian control. The final status of the borders, the final status of Jerusalem, and the future of Palestinian refugees are still under Palestinian-Israeli negotiation.

Source: A. Ameri & D. Ramey (2000), *Arab American Encyclopedia*. Farmington Hills, MI: Gale Group. Reprinted with permission of the Gale Group.

447

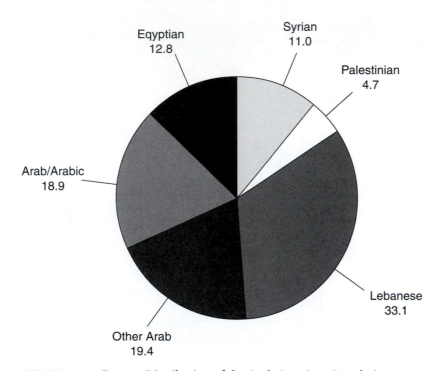

FIGURE 14.2   Percent Distribution of the Arab American Population by Type, 2005

Note: "Other Arab" includes Americans from Algeria, Bahrain, Comoros Islands, Djibouti, Iraq, Jordan, Kuwait, Libya, Morocco, Oman, Qatar, Saudi Arabia, Tunisia, the United Arab Emirates, and Yemen. Iraqis, Moroccans, and Jordanian Americans each accounted for approximately 3% of the Arab American population as of the 2000 census.

Source: U.S. Census Bureau (2007), *American Community Survey, 2005: Selected Population Profile.* [Data file]. Available online at http://factfinder.census.gov/servlet/IPCharIterationServlet?_ts=202649767048.

type in 2005. Table 14.1 shows the population with Arab ancestry by detailed group.

Western civilization has inherited a great deal from the Arabs. Much of Western science, medicine, architecture, music, and mathematics is built on what originated or was developed in the medieval Arab world during the 800 years (AD 700 to 1500) when Arabs dominated the Mediterranean (Hayes, 1983; Shabbas, 1998; Tschanz, 1997; Dalrymple, 2007). Learning about the achievements and contributions of Arabs and other Muslims during these centuries casts light on crucial parts of Westerners' own history, including such periods as the European Renaissance.

TABLE 14.1   Population with Arab Ancestry, by Detailed Group

DETAILED GROUP	ARAB ANCESTRY ALONE		ARAB ANCESTRY ALONE OR IN COMBINATION WITH ANOTHER ANCESTRY	
	NUMBER	PERCENTAGE OF U.S. POPULATION	NUMBER	PERCENTAGE OF U.S. POPULATION
Total	850,027[a]	0.30	1,189,731[b]	0.42
Lebanese	244,525	0.09	440,279	0.16
Egyptian	123,489	0.04	142,832	0.05
Syrian	75,517	0.03	142,897	0.05
Palestinian	61,691	0.02	72,112	0.03
Jordanian	36,104	0.01	39,734	0.01
Moroccan	30,352	0.01	38,923	0.01
Iraqi	29,429	0.01	37,714	0.01
"Arab" or "Arabic"	167,166	0.06	205,822	0.07
Other Arab	81,754[c]	0.03	82,337[d]	0.03

[a]Includes people who reported Arab ancestry only, regardless of whether they reported one or two Arab ancestries.

[b]Includes people who reported one or two Arab ancestries and people who reported both an Arab and non-Arab ancestry. The total is less than the sum of the rows because most people reporting two Arab ancestries are tabulated in two categories, but only once in the total. People who reported two Arab ancestries not listed above (e.g., Algerian and Tunisian) are tabulated once in the "Other Arab" category.

[c]Includes 68,614 people who reported one Arab ancestry not listed above and 13,140 people who reported two Arab ancestries, whether listed above or not.

[d]Represents the number of people who reported one or two Arab ancestries excluding the ancestries listed above. The total 82,337 includes 68,614 people who reported one Arab ancestry not listed above (e.g., Yemen), 1,862 people who reported two Arab ancestries not listed above (e.g., Algerian and Tunisian), and 11,861 people who reported an Arab ancestry not listed above and a non-Arab ancestry (e.g., Kuwaiti and German).

Note: Confidence intervals are not displayed because they round to the percentages shown in the table. Data based on sample. For information on confidentiality protection, sampling error, nonsampling error, and definitions, see www.census.gov/prod/cen2000/doc/sf4.pdf.

Source: A. Brittinghamm and G. P. de la Cruz (2005, March), *We the People of Arab Ancestry in the United States: Census 2000 Special Reports.* Washington, DC: U.S. Census Bureau. Retrieved July 20, 2007, from http://www.census.gov.

EARLY ARAB IMMIGRATION TO THE UNITED STATES

The first Arab presence in North America dates back to the sixteenth century, when the Moor Estivanico, a pathfinder, led caravans of 600 Spanish explorers overland from Florida to Mexico and northward (Younis, 1995). However, Arabs didn't begin immigrating to the United States in significant numbers until the late

1870s. In the first wave, which lasted until the early 1920s, 90 to 95% were Christians. They came from what was, until the end of World War I, the Ottoman province of Syria, an area that included what are now the countries of Syria, Lebanon, Jordan, and Palestine/Israel. With the demise of the Ottoman Empire in 1917, this area came under French and British League of Nations mandates. Lebanon and Syria achieved independence from France in 1943 and 1946, respectively; Jordan gained independence from Britain in 1961; and Palestine was subsumed under Jordanian and Israeli rule when Israel was established in 1948. Well into the 1950s, the immigrants from all these areas and their descendants referred to themselves as Syrian.

Immigration from Syria was spurred by a number of pull-and-push factors. One pull factor was the American missionary movement. Early in the nineteenth century, Christian missionaries had begun traveling to Lebanon, Syria, and Palestine to convert Muslims (as well as Eastern-rite Christians) to Protestantism. In addition to proselytizing, they established hospitals, clinics, and schools, including, in 1866, the Syrian Protestant College, later known as the American University of Beirut. The missionaries' accounts of U.S. democratic values and practices made Syrians eager to seek their fortunes in America.

Another pull factor was the Arabs' experience in three American world fairs: Philadelphia, in 1876; Chicago, in 1893; and St. Louis, in 1904. Arabs brought to these fairs elaborate re-creations of scenes from Arab life; they returned to their hometowns with tales of the economic opportunities that awaited the adventurous in America (Younis, 1995).

Among the push factors were the land squeeze that resulted from improved health conditions on Mount Lebanon; fear (after 1908) of Ottoman conscription; and the famine that devastated Lebanon during World War I. In a society in which so much emphasis was placed on family status, some scholars have concluded that the most compelling reason to emigrate was to be able to send money home to secure the economic well-being of the immigrant's family. According to Tannous (1943), "By 1925, practically every household in every village in the Lebanon Mountains had at least one of its members living as a permanent emigrant somewhere in the Americas" (p. 265). In 1907, the U.S. Immigration Committee reported to the Senate that Syrian immigrants were sending home more money per capita than the immigrants of any other nationality (Hitti, 1924). Though the earliest Syrian immigrants were primarily single men who came to the United States for a brief economic adventure, by the early 1900s whole families were coming to start new lives.

THE FIRST GENERATION

Many, if not most, of the earliest Syrian immigrants began work in America as peddlers, mostly of dry goods. Some eventually settled and opened small businesses. By 1908 the Syrian Businessman's Directory could list 3,000 Syrian-owned businesses scattered throughout every state (Mokarzel & Okash, 1908). The Syrian-Lebanese

ARAB AMERICANS: HISTORICAL PERSPECTIVE

Important Dates	Events
1876	The Centennial Exposition in Philadelphia was the first of three world fairs to bring to the United States merchants from the Arab world, many of whom stayed, becoming peddlers, importers, and, later, U.S. citizens.
1878	The first Arab American family, the Arbeelys, immigrated to the United States.
1886–1891	Immigration from Turkey began to increase, leaping in a single year from 15 (1886) to 208 (1887); by 1891, the year's total was 2,448.
1907	Universal military conscription was declared by the Ottoman Turkish government, ending Syrian Christians' exemption from conscription and further encouraging Syrian emigration.
1908	The Syrian Business Directory was published, listing Syrian-owned businesses in every state in the United States. It contained 3,000, demonstrating the entrepreneurial spirit of the Syrian immigrants.
1909	A case challenging Syrian immigrants' rights to American naturalization on racial grounds, because they were from Asia, was brought in a South Carolina court. It was not settled until 1915.
1914–1918	World War I left Lebanon devastated by famine, further encouraging emigration.
1920	France and England divided areas of the former Ottoman Empire after their victory in World War I, creating new semicolonies known as mandates: Syria, Lebanon, Transjordan, and Palestine.
1920	Ar-Rabitah Al-Qalamiyah (the Pen League) was formed in New York City by Kahlil Gibran. This émigré literary society had an unparalleled impact on the course of Arabic literature, especially poetry.
1924	The Johnson-Reed Act drastically curtailed immigration from outside northwestern Europe, including from the Arab world.
1947–1948	The British withdrew forces and government apparatus from Mandate Palestine without resolving territorial disputes between Palestinian Arabs and Zionist Jews. War broke out. The Jewish population seized Palestinian lands far in excess of those specified in the 1947 U.N. General Assembly partition solution. Hundreds of thousands of Palestinians became refugees. The state of Israel was declared. Some Palestinians emigrated to North America.
1960	St. Jude's Hospital was founded in Memphis, Tennessee, by Lebanese American entertainer Danny Thomas, with the help of the Syrian Lebanese and general Arab American community.
1967	War between Israel and the Arab states broke out in June. This event caused further Palestinian immigration to the United States.
1967	The Association of Arab-American University Graduates (AAUG) was established to enlarge the discourse with regard to the troubles in the Middle East.

Important Dates	Events
1972	"Operation Boulder" was instituted by the Nixon administration to combat "terrorism" in the United States. This operation resulted in the surveillance and harassment of many "ethnic Arabs."
1972	The National Association of Arab Americans (NAAA) was founded as a political lobby in Washington, D.C.
1973	As a result of the October Arab-Israeli war, the Organization of Petroleum Exporting Countries (OPEC) shut off oil from the American market. American oil companies sharply increased prices, creating a bogus oil shortage, and Arabs were blamed for the high prices. Stereotyping of Arabs intensified in the news and entertainment media.
1974	James Abourezk was elected the country's first Arab American senator.
1980	The American-Arab Anti-Discrimination Committee (ADC) was founded in Washington, D.C.
1983	In the U.S. presidential elections, Arabs participated significantly in the Rainbow Coalition, the first time they were a critical mass at a national political convention.
1984	The Arab American Institute (AAI) was formed in Washington, D.C., to encourage Arab Americans to participate in the electoral process and to promote access to the political parties.
1989	The Arab American contingent of the Jesse Jackson delegates to the Democratic National Convention put the Palestinian homeland issue on the agenda.
1990	On August 2, Iraq invaded Kuwait, the United States began a military buildup in the Persian Gulf, and public hostility against Arabs and Arab Americans rose.
1993	The World Trade Center in New York City was bombed; the perpetrators convicted in court were Arabs or non-Arab Muslims.
1995	On April 19, the bombing of the Alfred P. Murrah Federal Building in Oklahoma initially stirred up anger and violence directed at Arab and Muslim communities. Congress opened a discussion of a broad antiterrorism bill that would unconstitutionally restrict the civil liberties of some Arab Americans and Arabs residing in the United States.
1995	Congress passed the Antiterrorism and Effective Death Penalty Act.
	Congress passed an immigration bill that allowed for the use of secret evidence against immigrants and foreign visitors in order to deport them. Over a dozen Arabs were held on secret evidence for up to four years.
2000	The Second Intifada (uprising) by Palestinians under Israeli occupation and the Israeli response to it resulted in hundreds of Palestinian civilian deaths and generated anti-Arab reporting in the American media. It also mobilized new political activism among Arab Americans across the United States.

Important Dates	Events
2001	On September 11, the Twin Towers of the World Trade Center in New York, the Pentagon, and United Airlines Flight 93 were attacked in a coordinated terrorist operation that involved nineteen Arab men, resulting in the deaths of nearly 3,000 people. Hate crimes against Arab Americans and others rose precipitously and included physical attacks, arson, destruction of property, and murder.
2003	On the pretext of destroying weapons of mass destruction, toppling the regime of Saddam Hussein, and bringing democracy to the Middle East, the United States invaded Iraq. Arab Americans, some once hopeful of the goals of the war, now despaired of the U.S. role in the Middle East.
2005	In Dearborn, Michigan, home to the largest concentration of Arab Americans in the United States, the National Arab American Museum, the first of its kind, opened its doors.

penchant for business, particularly the family business, continued to characterize the group until the end of the twentieth century. Among the early Syrian American communities, New York was the first and, for sixty years, the largest and most influential. Boston was second in size and strength, and there were other enclaves in New England and upstate New York.

Religion was the nexus of early Syrian identity. As former Ottoman subjects who had been ruled according to their religious affiliation, the non-Muslim Syrian immigrants strongly identified with their Christian sects, and churches were among the first Syrian American institutions. Most of the early immigrants belonged to one of three Eastern Christian rites: Antiochian Orthodox, Melkite Catholic, and Maronite Catholic. The first two trace their roots to the earliest Christian traditions (and, in fact, until 1724 were one and the same); the Maronites became recognized as a separate rite in the eighth century. The liturgies of the Antiochian Orthodox and Melkite churches are in Arabic, and the Maronite liturgy is in Aramaic, the language spoken by Jesus.

The Arabic-language press also played a role in helping Syrians maintain their identification with their origins. The Golden Age of the Arabic-language press was from 1900 to 1930. Between 1890 and 1930, about seventy-five Arabic-language periodicals came and went out of existence in the United States (Hatab, 1974). Many were organs of the various religious sects, but most worked to keep the culture alive while helping the immigrant community assimilate. The community's leading intellectuals edited and wrote for these journals. In 1920 they organized themselves into the New York–based Ar-Rabitah al-Qalamiyya, or the Pen League. One of the leaders was Kahlil Gibran, best known for his book *The Prophet*, still widely read today. Though Gibran was closely identified with Boston, to which he had emigrated from

Lebanon with his family in 1895 at age twelve, from 1911 until his death in 1931 he lived and worked much of the year in New York City, mingling with the American art community there as well as with Arabic-speaking émigré writers.

Gibran and the other *mahjar* (émigré) poets were greatly influenced by the work of Walt Whitman. In their experimentation with free verse, the *mahjar* poets liberated Arabic poetry from its traditional constrictions of form. Their work revolutionized Arabic writing in the Arab world, and today the *mahjar* poets are studied in high schools and colleges throughout the Middle East. Ironically, with the obvious exception of Gibran, these poets are virtually unknown among U.S.-educated Arab Americans (Orfalea, 1984).

Some of the earliest Syrian organizations were based on village or town of origin—for example, Aleppian Clubs (Aleppo) and Homsian Clubs (Homs). Later Syrians added American models—a Syrian Girl Scout troop in Boston, a Syrian Junior League chapter in Brooklyn. Among the most enduring Syrian organizations were women's clubs (Shakir, 1987). Both New York and Boston had Syrian Ladies Aid Societies, established in 1907 and 1917, respectively. In the 1950s, the National Federation of Syrian Lebanese Clubs was formed. This was the Syrian community's earliest effort to organize on a national scale. The federation led the way in presenting to the public and elected officials the Arab community's concerns about conditions in the Middle East and the influence of United States policies there (Hagopian, 1969).

The relatively smooth assimilation of Syrians into U.S. society was marred by a series of court cases that began in 1909 and lasted until 1915. The cases challenged the right of Syrians to become U.S. citizens because they were Asians and therefore non-White. These cases were tried mainly in the circuit courts of southern states. The issue culminated in the *Dow* case (1915), in which it was reasoned that as Semites, Syrians were, like Jews, White and therefore eligible for naturalization (Naff, 1985; Younis, 1995). In the South, however, through the segregation era, racism against Syrians, as "colored," cropped up from time to time.

In 1924, the Johnson-Reed Act drastically curtailed the flow of immigrants from countries outside of northern and western Europe. This had the effect of cutting Syrians off from the constant cultural rejuvenation that aids in cultural maintenance and accelerated their assimilation. In fact, most of the early immigrants had been eager to assimilate. With the exception of the naturalization cases, there had been little systematic or overt discrimination against Arabs; yet, in a general climate of nativism, Syrians were encouraged in many ways to "Americanize," and they seem to have complied, at least outwardly (Hitti, 1924).

By the 1940s, the Arabic press had lost much of its readership. By the 1950s and 1960s, for newer generations of American-born Arabs, even the spoken Arabic language had become "the language of old people." In fact, its forms and expressions were the now fossilized ones that the immigrant generation had brought with them a half century before. Although the Arabic churches were streamlining their liturgies and replacing Arabic with English, many second-generation Syrians were finding Protestant and Roman Catholic churches more accessible. By the 1960s, out-marriage had become four times more common than marrying within the group (Kayal & Kayal, 1975). To be Syrian, at that point, meant little more than eating Syrian food and dancing the *debkeh* at Syrian weddings. Arabic identity in the United States was disappearing.

THE POST-1965 IMMIGRANTS

A confluence of factors saved the Arab American community from cultural extinction. First, there was the coming of age of the third generation of Arab Americans who—like a number of grandchildren of immigrants influenced by the civil rights and ethnic revitalization movements—were seeking a "return" to their roots. Second, and more important, there was the lifting of immigration restrictions in 1965, after which Arab immigration numbers began to climb. Third, crises in the Middle East, beginning with the Arab-Israeli War of 1967 and American public reaction to it, compelled many assimilated Arabs to reevaluate their ties to their origins and renew their sense of ethnicity.

Most of the new immigrants came to the United States searching for economic, professional, and educational opportunities. The outbreaks of wars between Israel and nations in the Arab world and the continuing civil strife between Israel and the Palestinians had increased the pressure to emigrate. By the beginning of the new century (2000), there were large communities of Palestinians, Lebanese, Syrians, Jordanians, Moroccans, Egyptians, and Iraqis throughout the United States, including San Francisco and Southern California, New York City and vicinity, northern New Jersey, Dearborn and Detroit, Chicago, Boston, Houston, Cleveland, Toledo, Columbus, Cincinnati, and Akron. When the new century began, the foreign born were about 54% of those identifying as Arab Americans (Brittingham & de la Cruz, 2005).

Arabs who settled in the United States after 1965—both Muslim and Christian—were, on the whole, much more educated than the pioneers who came in the early 1900s. They were also more cosmopolitan, politically astute, and critical of U.S. policies than many of the descendants of the early wave. Some were less willing than earlier immigrants to give up their Arab values and perspectives. In contrast to the third- and fourth-generation descendants of the earliest immigrants, who were now mostly middle class (Kayal & Kayal, 1975; Naff, 1985; Zogby, 1990, 1995; Brittingham & de la Cruz, 2005), there was more economic diversity among the new immigrants—that is, both more visible prosperity and more poverty.

Because the new immigrants were coming from sovereign Arab countries, they were more secure in their Arab identities than the earliest immigrants had been. Muslim and Christian in roughly equal numbers, they established mosques and increased the rolls of the Arabic churches, in many cases making Arabic once again the main language of their liturgies. In 2007, those claiming Lebanese origins still comprised a plurality of the Arab American community, but the numbers and influence of Arabs from other countries were growing. Palestinians in particular were becoming stronger in political and cultural influence and were particularly active within new Arab American organizations in bringing Arab issues to the attention of the general public.

THE GROWTH OF THE ARAB MUSLIM COMMUNITY IN AMERICA

Muslims did not participate in significant numbers in the earliest Arab immigration movement to the United States, largely because of the difficulties of practicing their faith in a secular society. They were concerned that the materialistic and individualistic American lifestyle contradicted the more spiritual and family-centered orientation of Islam. Praying (five times a day) and fasting (one full month each year during daylight hours) were often hard to maintain in a society for which these practices were not the norm. Muslim norms of modesty contrast with the freer dress and behavior of the secular American mainstream.

For a variety of reasons (among them perhaps a new spirit in the United States of multicultural tolerance), when immigration restrictions were lifted in 1965, Muslims overcame their hesitancy to immigrate to the West. By the end of the twentieth century, immigration of Arabs and other Muslims, as well as American conversions, had made Islam one of the fastest-growing religions in the United States (Eck, 2001). A study on mosques by the Council on American-Islamic Relations indicated that by 2001 there were 1,250 mosques in the United States, an increase of 50% over the previous seven years, with 75% of them experiencing an increase in the number of participants (Council on American-Islamic Relations, 2001).

During these years Muslim immigrants took the lead in reviving Arabic language in the United States. They established Islamic schools in which their children could learn Arabic, something only rarely done by first-wave Syrian Christians. By 2001, the number of U.S. chapters of the Muslim Student Association had almost doubled, from 240 to 473 (Council on American-Islamic Relations, 2001). By the beginning of the new millennium, Islamic educational advisory councils were more active than textbooks and the media in American cultural and political discourse.

A national survey released in the spring of 2007 by the Pew Research Center reported that two-thirds of U.S. Muslims surveyed (including the 24% that were Arabs) felt it was difficult to be a Muslim in America. A large percentage had been the victims of discriminatory behavior (such as airport profiling and being called names). Despite these and the more serious effects of "war on terror" policy initiatives—such as the increased surveillance of mosques, the detentions of Muslims and Arabs based on secret evidence, and the rejection of citizenship applications based on secret evidence, as well as abuses of the civil rights of Arabs—they reported that they were satisfied with their lives. They had adopted American attitudes and values (and felt anyone who lives in the United States should do so), felt their efforts were rewarded in the workplace, had income and educational attainments that were at least as high as those of Americans at large, and they liked the communities they were living in. Significantly, most felt there was no conflict between practicing their faith and living in American society.

ARAB AMERICAN CULTURAL VALUES

Muslim parents worry that their children will find American individualism appealing and will abandon their own traditions, but this has always been a concern of Arab Americans generally. There are many contrasts between Arab and mainstream American cultures. Like others in traditional cultures, Arabs tend to stress the needs of the family over the preferences of the individual. More social engineering by elders is tolerated—and even expected—than is the norm in mainstream American society. For example, some traditional Arab families still arrange marriages, particularly in places where there are high concentrations of Arabs, such as Dearborn, Michigan (Abraham & Shryock, 2000). Even among American-born Arabs, however, parental desires are rarely discounted, and marriage is still considered by many to be as much a union of two families as of two individuals.

There is a more pronounced differentiation of parental roles in most Arab American families than in American, at least as families interface with the public. The father is still seen as the family's principal breadwinner and its public representative. Although it is now common for Arab American women to work outside the home, they do so less than the population at large (Brittingham & de la Cruz, 2005).

The culture of the extended family, specifically, the expectation of supporting and being supported by relatives, survives among many Arab Americans. It is still not uncommon for Arab Americans to go to uncles and cousins and siblings for employment, for help with tuition expenses, for start-up financing for new businesses, and for support for the aged.

Hospitality is another bedrock Arab value, and is one way Arabs have traditionally demonstrated their sense of self-worth. Elaborate Arab hospitality is legendary; for some Arabs it is the essence of "being Arab." Hosting guests for unlimited stays, having weddings that last for several days, and taking time from work to escort visiting friends and relatives around town are common practices in Arab countries. However, they are usually out of the question in the competitive work- and self-oriented climate of the United States (Hajar, 1993).

Modesty is another value highly prized among Arabs, and "immodest" behavior by a woman in particular can seriously jeopardize not only her name but also her family's social status. Though more young Muslim Arab American women have elected to wear the *hijab* (the veil) than several decades ago, most do not. How modesty is defined differs from one family to another, but the "talk of people" is a serious social constraint in Arab society. An important source of tension for Arab Americans is the freedom Americans have versus the constraints in the Arab family culture.

It is important to point out here that, while most Americans see Arab women as oppressed, most women in Arab society are neither powerless nor retiring. Precisely because of the constraints under which they live, their social skills and intuitions are highly developed, and they are articulate, assertive, and resourceful in finding ways to shape their own fates and direct the fortunes of their families (Shakir, 1997). In addition, their highly valued and specified roles and responsibilities as mothers and wives and economic partners to their husbands relieve them of many confusions and discontents that mainstream U.S. women have experienced since the sexual revolution of the 1960s, though for many the proximity of such a different culture causes discontent (Hajar, 1993).

The challenges many post-1965 Arab immigrants have had to face as they adjust to American society have led to the establishment of Arab family centers in many cities, including Chicago, New York, Washington, D.C., Toledo, and San Francisco. The largest and most well known is the Arab Community Center for Economic and Social Services (ACCESS) in Dearborn, Michigan, a suburb of Detroit. Since 1971, ACCESS has been providing Arab families with emergency food programs; help with entitlements; job referrals and training; workshops on health, American culture, and assimilation; as well as tutoring, language classes, and counseling. In 2007 ACCESS opened the Hope House, a psychosocial rehabilitation center. This new institution reflects a rise in interest and competence in serving the particular mental health needs of the Arab community, especially as those needs are exacerbated by U.S. interventions in their countries of origin. In 2005, ACCESS opened the National Arab American Museum, the first of its kind in the United States. It houses 500 artifacts from Arab Americans and the Arab world, serves as a cultural and performing arts center, and is a resource for scholars on the Arab American experience. The goal of the museum is to educate the public on the contributions of Arab Americans and the roles they have played in building the United States.

ANTI-ARAB STEREOTYPING—WHY?

Negative stereotyping has been one of the most troubling problems for Arab Americans. Throughout history, and long before 9/11, Europeans have portrayed Arabs as "the other," a phenomenon Palestinian American scholar Edward Said called "Orientalism" (Said, 1978). During eight centuries of Arab cultural and economic domination of Spain and the Mediterranean region, Europeans had mixed views of the Arabs, eagerly borrowing from them culturally but also resenting them because of their economic power. During the Crusades (wars that were supposedly about religion but which, like most wars, had economic roots), Europeans portrayed Muslims as practitioners of a "false religion" and referred to Muhammad, its prophet, as the anti-Christ. Twentieth- and twenty-first-century tensions may have their roots in this medieval history.

Today, both foreign and domestic politics—some of which arise out of the complex relationship the United States has with Israel—as well as Hollywood entertainments, fuel anti-Arab attitudes among the public. One modern-day trigger for negative Arab stereotypes was the 1973 Arab-Israeli War and the ensuing oil embargo. Although at the time the United States was importing only 6% of its oil from Arab countries, oil companies used the opportunity to raise oil prices.

Through their advertising, they generated the idea that the Arabs were the cause of the long gas lines.

Since then negative stereotyping of Arabs has only increased. As it did during the Crusades, the image of "the Arab" now serves a multitude of cultural, political, and economic purposes. Like the Europeans before them, Americans have used the Arab as a way of defining who they (Americans) are not; they have created in the media (political cartoons, movies, fiction) a matrix of descriptors of Arabs (craven, backward, dirty, devious, sexually predatory) that are supposed to stand in opposition to the qualities (bravery, intelligence, cleanliness, principled discretion, and honesty) that White Americans use to define themselves.

In works of fiction, the movies, television, and advertising, Arabs are still invariably typed as the villain (Michalak, 1988; Sabbagh, 1990; Stockton, 1994; Shaheen, 1988, 1997, 2001). It is with this media bombardment as text and backdrop that anti-Arab attitudes are enacted in daily life (Shrag & Javidi, 1995). Stereotypes permeate the language and provide the context for anti-Arab hate crimes, cases of defamation, and incidents of job discrimination. Long before 9/11, Arab as terrorist had become standard fare in adult movies. By the 1980s, the Islamic militant was the stock character of many B-movies (*Delta Force, Wanted Dead or Alive, Iron Eagle*), and by the nineties it was high-profile blockbusters such as *True Lies, The Mummy, The Siege,* and *Rules of Engagement* that were perpetuating the anti-Arab messages.

The producers of children's programs have perpetuated some of the most damaging images of Arabs. Cartoons and cartoon movies, particularly those made by the Disney company, have been particularly offensive (Shaheen, 1980, 1988, 2001). Several Disney movies released in the 1990s included gratuitous "bad Arab" characters (for example, *The Father of the Bride II* and Disney's *Aladdin*). These films and others have been the focus of organized protest efforts by the community. The negative Arab stereotypes common in children's programming are particularly dangerous. Any story seen or heard in the early years of a child's life constitutes a "first story," a narrative structure against which all later narratives are judged. When individuals learn through these narratives that Arabs are evil, they internalize the evil images as norms and carry them their entire lives (Shrag & Javidi, 1995).

News reporting, by omission and/or selectivity or sticking to stock story frames, has been complicit in perpetuating stereotypes of Arabs. These images went unchallenged until a new generation of Arab American organizations set about to fight them.

Many teachers have worked to present accurate information on Arabs and the Arab world. However, most social studies and history texts used in the United States—either by omitting treatment of the Arab world altogether or by treating Arabs in a superficial or pejorative way—have actually contributed to the stereotyping and the misinformation. One common distortion found in textbooks is the emphasis on nomadic life. Though Bedouin nomads account for no more than 2% of Arab society today, the traditional Bedouin lifestyle is commonly treated as if it were representative of all Arabs (Shabbas, 1998). Another distortion is the omission of the Palestinian perspective in textbook treatments of the Arab-Israeli wars; usually the conflict is treated solely from the Israeli perspective. Another distortion in textbooks results from the failure to discuss the close links between Islam, Judaism, and Christianity, three faiths that share many beliefs and texts (Barlow, 1994).

ANTI-ARAB HATE CRIMES

Since 1979, when Americans were taken hostage by Iranian students (whom Americans mistakenly believed to be Arab), there has been a rise in violence against Middle Easterners in the United States. Since then, whenever there is an incident involving Americans and Middle Easterners anywhere in the world, there is often a domestic reaction against Arabs and Arab Americans in the United States. Across the United States, on radio talk shows and in political speeches, anti-Arab and anti-Muslim stereotypes and rhetoric surface, and various forms of hate crimes against Arabs increase. The violence against Arabs has included bombings, shootings, arson attacks, beatings, death threats, harassment, intimidation, and murder (Ekin & Gorchev, 1991; *ADC Special Report,* 1995; Ibish, 2003). The most significant example of this type occurred in the fall of 1985, when Alex Odeh (western regional director of the American-Arab Anti-Discrimination Committee in Santa Ana, California) was killed by a bomb trip-wired to his office door.

Even when Arabs have nothing to do with an incident, there is an anti-Arab reaction. In the immediate aftermath of the 1995 Oklahoma City bombing, which involved a White American, there was a dramatic increase in anti-Arab hate crimes (*ADC Special Report,* 1995).

Arab Americans were as stricken as all Americans by the 9/11 terrorist attacks. They were among the victims and among the first responders. Like Americans across the country, they mourned the losses and raised money for the victims; their leaders issued statements condemning the attacks. Arab Americans felt a double burden: like all Americans they were horrified; but they knew that they would be scrutinized and their loyalty doubted because of their ties to the Arab world. Though the attacks were "the work of a fringe group that emerged from one sectarian version of Islam, extremists who [did] not represent the Arab or Muslim mainstream and certainly [did] not represent Arab Americans or American Muslims" (Wingfield, 2006), nevertheless the entire ethnic group was branded, a clear by-product of American ignorance of Arabs and Arab Americans.

In the days following the September 11 attacks, despite firm statements to the nation by many elected and administration officials and the FBI warning the general population against backlash, there was a dramatic increase in hate crimes of all sorts against Arab Americans and Muslims and much hate speech on the radio and even in the halls of Congress. In the first nine weeks after 9/11, the American Arab Anti-Discrimination Committee reported 700 violent incidents and more than 800 incidents of employment discrimination. For a time, some Arab Americans were afraid to leave their homes (Ibish, 2003).

In response, many Americans reached out to Arab Americans to offer their support. In cities across the United States, individuals volunteered to serve as escorts to Arab children and their mothers as a form of protection. Some American women even donned the *hijab* (veil) to show solidarity with Muslim women, and organizations and individuals across the country raised money to help pay for the vandalism that was perpetrated on Arab American institutions, including mosques and churches, in the aftermath of the tragedy (Ibish, 2003).

EROSION OF CIVIL RIGHTS

The abridgment of Arab Americans' civil rights did not begin with 9/11 but had been going on for almost three decades. Since the 1970s, in times of crisis or tension, Arab Americans were subjected to FBI surveillance. This occurred during the Nixon years with Operation Boulder (Abraham, 1994) and during the Gulf War (*ADC Special Report*, 1995). In 1996, Congress passed the Antiterrorism and Effective Death Penalty Act, which gave the FBI expanded surveillance powers over the legal and peaceful activities of immigrant communities and organizations. That year Congress also passed an immigration bill that allowed for the deportation of noncitizens if they were suspected of links to organizations abroad that the U.S. government had designated as terrorist. The bill made it illegal to donate funds to humanitarian programs linked to the designated organizations, with ten-year prison sentences as punishment. Most alarming has been the use, beginning in 1996, of secret evidence to detain individuals considered by the government to be a threat to U.S. security. In the late 1990s, over twenty men, all Arabs and/or Muslims, were held without formal charges for up to four years. When the cases finally came to trial, the U.S. government failed to win a single one of them because the courts found secret evidence to be a violation of due process.

In the years since 9/11, the erosion of their civil rights has become of even greater concern to Arab Americans than hate crimes, as new laws, new executive orders, and new Justice Department initiatives have been enacted in the name of waging the war on terror. Among the new practices launched by the USA Patriot Act have been secret detentions (5,000 Arab and Muslim men were detained in the first two years after 9/11); hearings and deportations; alien registration of 80,000 men based on national origin and ethnicity; "voluntary interviews" of young Arab men; the monitoring of international students; discriminatory visa screening procedures for young Arab men; and the selective deportation of Middle Eastern "absconders."

Other threats to justice include indefinite detention of foreign nationals without process or appeal; new search and surveillance powers, with insufficient judicial review; measures providing for guilt by association; eavesdropping on attorney-client communication; military tribunals; suspension of constitutional rights of U.S. citizens without due process or appeal; domestic law enforcement spying on lawful political and religious activities; and seizure of assets without due process, especially from Muslim American charities. Other social justice threats include "Operation TIPS" (Terrorist Information and Prevention System) and other programs encouraging Americans to spy on each other; arbitrary and abusive stops and detentions by the police; abuse of detainees; and racial profiling and stereotyping by police and the FBI (Ibish, 2003).

According to law professor David Cole, "None of the 80,000 men called in for Special Registration or the more than 5,000 foreign nationals the administration admitted to detaining in the first two years after September 11 stands convicted of a terrorist crime today" (Cole, 2007). While Muslims, particularly those whose dress identifies them as such, have suffered the brunt of this backlash, these policies and practices can be applied to anyone and are most often applied to people of color. Arab Americans have joined with other ethnic groups and human rights organizations such as the American Civil Liberties Union and the Center for Constitutional Rights to protest the governmental overreach and hold the government accountable for its treatment of all citizens, residents, and immigrants.

NEW ARAB AMERICAN ACTIVISM: THE MATURING OF AN ETHNIC COMMUNITY

For decades, crises have been the organizing force among Arab Americans. Out of crises have come new incentives for education and coalition building. In the wake of the 1967 Arab-Israeli War, the Association of Arab-American University Graduates (AAUG) was formed to enlarge the discourse around the ongoing strife in the Middle East. Its highly educated membership, strengthened by new immigrants, held conferences and symposia and published books and monographs about the community and the issue of Palestine. Several of the earliest modern studies of the Arab community in the United States were sponsored by this organization.

In 1972, the National Association of Arab Americans, or "N-Triple A" (NAAA), was established to lobby the U.S. government on its Middle East policies. AAUG and NAAA were among the first to use the word *Arab* as a self-identifier by Arabic-speaking Americans, including people who had previously called themselves Syrian or Lebanese or Syrian-Lebanese. This name change reflected both the presence of many new Arab Americans who are not necessarily Syrian or Lebanese and the recognition that there is strength in identification with a larger group. In fact, identifying with this larger ethnicity is a way that new immigrants enter the American mainstream, for it is through ethnicity politics that they have been able to make their voices and concerns heard.

In 1980 James Abourezk, the first Arab American senator, formed the third national Arab American organization, the American-Arab Anti-Discrimination Committee (ADC). The need for an organization such as ADC had become clear by 1979, after the FBI initiated a sting operation called ABSCAM, in which FBI officials posing as rich Arab sheiks attempted to bribe American elected officials. Dismayed by the stereotypes implicit in such an operation, the outgoing Senator Abourezk created ADC to combat racism, discrimination, and the stereotyping of Arabs in government as well as in entertainment, the news media, and education. Reaction to ABSCAM, the continuing crises in the Middle East, the presence of a critical mass of new and educated Arab American activists, and the populism and pluralism spawned by the civil rights movement of the 1960s produced significant growth in the ADC. Within three years it had grown into the nation's largest Arab American organization. By 2007, it had chapters in forty states and members in all fifty states. Members learned to write letters to editors and political representatives, organize protests, and meet with politicians and the CEOs of companies with offensive ad campaigns. The organization has a research arm that provides information for educators as well as the general public.

For many years, Arab Americans were virtually excluded from the political process. Sometimes individual Arab Americans had their campaign contributions spurned because candidates "feared being associated with 'Arab interests'" (Abourezk, 1989). At other times candidates were criticized if they met with Arab groups, and "Arab money" was viewed as tainted (*ADC Special Report,* 1995). To remedy this political exclusion, and stimulated by the receptivity of Jesse Jackson's Rainbow Coalition to Arab American participation in 1984, a fourth national Arab American organization, the Arab American Institute (AAI), was established in 1985. Its goals were to organize Arab Americans to participate effectively in all aspects of the political process—namely, as issue advocates, as voters who rally for targeted candidates, and as political candidates themselves. AAI's successes are reflected in the fact that several dozen new Arab American political clubs across the United States have been able to send over fifty Arab American delegates to each national convention since 1988.

The 1988 presidential campaign was a watershed event in Arab Americans' struggle for full political participation and visibility. After several years of intensive organizing by AAI, Arab American Democrats won local races as Jackson delegates to the Democratic National Convention. The Jackson campaign's Arab American delegation was second in size only to that of the African American delegation. In the platform debate, the Arab American delegates helped to place on the agenda a discussion of the right to self-determination for Palestinians. The plank was not submitted to a vote, but the fifteen-minute debate was a political first, demonstrating the difficulties Arab Americans had faced around any discussion of U.S. policies in the Middle East (Samhan, 1989).

Since the 2000 elections, Arab Americans have been running for office in growing numbers—particularly in Michigan, Ohio, Illinois, and California—and a significant number of them have been foreign born. By 2007 there were over a hundred elected officials of Arab ancestry at all levels across the nation (state senators and representatives, judges, city council members, mayors, governors), as well as over 120 party leaders and activists.

One of the newest Arab American organizations is APAAM—Association of Patriotic Arab Americans in the Military. Started by Marine gunnery sergeant Jamal Baadani, its goal is to educate the American people about the continuous military service and sacrifices of Arab Americans in all ranks of the military. Arabs have served in the American military ever since the American Revolution, for which Syrian immigrant Private Nathan Badeen gave his life only six weeks before American independence was declared. In 2007, there were 3,500 Arab Americans in uniform. The most well-known was General John Abizaid, a Lebanese American who for four years directed American military operations in Iraq.

THE CONTRIBUTIONS OF ARAB AMERICANS TO AMERICAN LIFE

Philip Hitti, an eminent historian of the Middle East, called the early Syrian American immigrants "ready made Yankees" (1924). Largely middle class or aspiring to it, they were devoted to the work ethic. Though the majority operated businesses that started with peddling, others worked in factories such as the textile mills on the East Coast and the Detroit auto plants. Arabs helped build the U.S. labor movement. Perhaps their chief distinction was their deep devotion to family life; most were low-profile solid citizens of their communities.

When Arab Americans have been more high profile, they have often been pioneers and mavericks, and they have made contributions to every aspect of American life. Besides poet Kahlil Gibran, such pioneers include Ralph Nader, whose consumer advocacy accomplishments will probably be as great a legacy as that of any American in history; Senator James Abourezk, known during his term in the 1970s as the most radical senator in the Senate; Senate majority leader and peace negotiator George Mitchell; heart surgeon Dr. Michael DeBakey, who pioneered the heart bypass operation; Michael Shadid, founder of the first cooperative hospital; Candy Lightner, founder of Mothers Against Drunk Driving; and Christa McAuliffe, first teacher in space, who died on the ill-fated *Challenger*.

Other famous Arab Americans include Jacques Nasser, former CEO of Ford Motor Company; Paul Orfalea, founder of Kinko's; John Zogby, a nationally respected pollster; fashion designers Joseph Abboud and Norma Kamali; radio personality Casey Kasem; opera singer Rosalind Elias; pop singers Paul Anka, Gloria Estefan, and Paula Abdul; actors F. Murray Abraham, Kathy Najimi, and Tony Shalhoub; and poet Naomi Shihab Nye. Lebanese American entertainer Danny Thomas made a significant and lasting contribution when he founded St. Jude's Children's Research Hospital in Memphis, Tennessee, in 1962. The acronym of its fund-raising arm is ALSAC, which stands both for Aiding Leukemia Stricken American Children and for Association of Lebanese-Syrian American Charities. Perhaps the most important institution in the world in the battle against childhood leukemia, St. Jude's treats its young patients at no expense to their families. Schoolchildren may know about this hospital through the annual national St. Jude's Math-a-thon.

ARAB AMERICANS TODAY

For Arab Americans it is "the best of times and the worst of times." As a group, their prosperity continues to grow, at least by broad economic and educational averages. In 1999, the median household income of Arab Americans was $52,318, compared to $50,000 for the total U.S. population. Most are well educated: 41% are college graduates, compared to 24% of all Americans (Brittingham & de la Cruz, 2005).

Arab Americans are also making gains politically. Since the 1970s, there have been four U.S. senators and thirteen U.S. representatives who have claimed Arab heritage. Since the 1980s, four Arab Americans have held cabinet-level positions: Reagan's chief of staff John Sununu; Clinton's secretary of health and human services Donna Shalala; George W. Bush's secretary of management and budget Mitch Daniels, and Bush's secretary of energy, Spencer Abraham. As an ethnic group, Arab Americans were courted by serious candidates for public office and were represented on the national councils of both major political parties. Clearly, the days of political exclusion are over.

What has made it "the worst of times" has been the anti-Arab stereotyping and misinformation that is still deeply embedded in American popular culture and attitudes: the USA Patriot Act and the attendant anti-Arab and anti-Muslim policies and directives, which have weakened the civil rights of Arab Americans, particularly immigrants, and the problematic policies of the U.S. government in Iraq, Palestine, and Lebanon.

Regardless of whether their ties to their countries of origin are strong, many Arab Americans find themselves, like other Americans, questioning a continuing war effort that is costing the lives of tens of thousands of Iraqis and Americans. They deplore also the use of their tax dollars to purchase weapons and other material that are ultimately used against people in their families' countries of origin (e.g., Lebanon, Palestine). The problem is especially intensified for Palestinian Americans, as the long-standing commitment of the United States to Israel has provided financial and military support of what Palestinians consider to be an occupation of their land.

Because of the issues described above, in the last decades of the twentieth century more and more Arab Americans became involved in human rights and political action activities. Their goal was to bring an Arab American perspective on events in the Middle East to the attention of other Americans and elected officials. These activities included protest demonstrations, vigils, and teach-ins when Israel occupied Lebanon in 1982, during the first Gulf War in 1991, in 2000 when the second *intifada* began in Jerusalem, and again in the summer of 2006 when Israel invaded Lebanon.

Within the last ten years, education and the arts have become new politics. Arab Americans have taken their places in multicultural events and curriculum committees and have demanded to be depicted accurately in teaching materials. In the last few decades, Arab American parents, activists, and educators have presented their concerns to school boards and publishers. There are now teacher workshops that help teachers identify unwarranted assumptions and distorting language about Islam and the Arab world. Arab Americans have learned that the price of not doing this work is very great.

Arab Americans have also turned their energies toward creating and supporting all forms of Arabic culture, both the traditional and the new, for its own sake and as a way to work against ignorance, discrimination, and stereotyping. In the 1990s and into the new millennium, Arab festivals, lasting from one evening to one month, spread across the United States. These festivals have included traditional performance arts such as music and dance, storytelling and poetry reciting, and Arabic films. Museums and theaters are offering space to Arab cultural events and exhibits (for example, see Benson & Kayal, 2002, for the exhibit "A Community of Many

Worlds: Arab Americans in New York City," a six-month installation at the Museum of the City of New York in 2002). Arabic food, a cuisine that has been winning over the palates of non–Arab Americans for at least a generation, is usually a major attraction at these events. Arab music and instrumentation can be heard in new music performances in mainstream concert halls and radio stations.

There has also been, in the last two decades or less, an outpouring of new Arab American literature. There are now significant anthologies of stories and poetry, much of it by women, that tell of the Arab American experience with humor and insight. New plays are being written and performed around the nation and off Broadway (see, for example, *Roar,* by Betty Shamieh). Arab stand-up comedy has begun to flower as well, signaling a new confidence born of the difficulties of recent times. Perhaps more light will be shed on the Arab American experience through the short story, poem, and play than through a mass of academic studies and symposia.

After generations of keeping their ethnicity quiet and in spite of the trauma of 9/11—or perhaps because of it—more and more Arab Americans are publicly expressing pride in their heritage. In their literature, poetry, films, and plays, Arab Americans are sharing their lives and, in so doing, creating new and more nuanced images of themselves in the minds of other Americans. In the words of poet Naomi Shihab Nye, they are learning to "sing louder" (Nye, cited in Lee, 2002, p. 14).

TEACHING STRATEGIES

To illustrate how content related to Arab Americans can be used to integrate the curriculum, exemplary strategies are identified for teaching these concepts at the grade levels indicated: *adaptation and resourcefulness* (primary grades), *contributions* (intermediate and upper grades), and *stereotyping* (high school grades).

Primary Grades

Concept

Adaptation and resourcefulness

Generalization: Arabs who came to the United States were willing to overcome major obstacles to realize their American dreams.

Background: Early Arab immigrants arrived with a determination to achieve the American dream, despite the hard work involved. Finding factory work too confining, most started as peddlers. They developed regular routes and clientele and, despite their humble appearance, were soon earning more annually, on average, than the American farm, factory, or mine worker (Naff, 1985). Their success depended on their resourcefulness and quickwittedness, goodwill, cooperation with each other, and willingness to endure hardships and even danger.

1. Read to the students chapters from Naff's *The Arab Americans* (1988), which deals with the early immigrant peddlers. Students who have high reading skills should read "On the Road" (Chapter 5, pp. 161–200) in Naff's *Becoming American* (1985). You can summarize or retell the funniest anecdotes from this book to younger students.

2. As you share these readings, list with the class the kinds of difficulties the Syrian peddlers encountered on the road and the ways they dealt with them. Have the students
use notes from this list to write and act out various peddling scenarios, making props
and costumes and taking the roles of the peddlers and their American customers.
Make sure there are no good guys or bad guys, because the difficulties were usually
humorous and arose from language gaps on all sides.

3. Have a discussion about the period of adjustment migrants and immigrants experience when they first arrive in a new place. Talk about the jobs many immigrants or
people new to an area take when they first arrive and how they are often willing
to do almost any kind of work to get started. Have students go home and investigate what the immigrants or other ancestors in their families did to earn their first
dollar.

4. While it is common to picture the wife in a family as taking care of the house and the
children, the Syrian wife was usually behind the cash register taking care of the customers and the books. Discuss with the students family cooperation, including in
business ventures. Ask them to share examples of relatives who helped each other
build businesses or to overcome economic hard times. This will be a good opportunity for the students to interview family members and report their findings to the
class.

Intermediate and Upper Grades

Concept

Contributions

Generalization: Arab Americans have made many contributions to world civilization and
to American life.

1. Using Naff's *The Arab Americans* (1988) as the main text, have students choose a
topic and do individual or group research projects on various contributions of the
Arabs to world civilization. Topics could include Arab architecture, art, science, medicine, mathematics, and astronomy. The *Arab World Notebook* and AWAIR (Arab
World and Islamic Resources), its distributor, have many suggestions for materials for
this lesson.

2. Have students report to the class or build exhibits that present their findings. Have a
fair on "What the Western World Learned from the Arab East."

3. Have the students read "Meeting the Challenge" (the final chapter in Naff's *The Arab
Americans*), "Some Lebanese Americans of Note" (the chapter on Arab Americans in
the *Arab World Notebook*), or the September/October 1986 issue of *Aramco World
Magazine*. Ask each student to choose one individual to research. Encourage the students to be ingenious about sources (e.g., besides checking already-published materials, they might create a list of questions to put in a letter to send to the subject, if still
alive, or to his or her family or someone in the same field, if deceased). Possibilities:
heart surgeon Michael DeBakey; consumer advocate Ralph Nader; Top 40 disk
jockey Casey Kasem; Academy Award–winning actor F. Murray Abraham; Heisman
Trophy winner Doug Flutie; singers Paula Abdul, Tiffany, and Gloria Estefan; actors
Kathy Najimy and Tony Shalhoub; the biographers of Kahlil Gibran, Jean and Kahlil
Gibran; actress Marlo Thomas on her late father, the comedian and actor Danny
Thomas, founder of the St. Jude's Research Hospital.

Valuing Activity

Background for teachers: essay on Arab and Lebanese families by Abudabbeh and Simon in McGoldrick et al., *Ethnicity and Family Therapy* (2000), or sections on the Arab (or Syrian) family in Naff's *Becoming American* (1985). Arab family relations are extremely close. Interdependence, rather than independence, is promoted in many ways. Ask the students to research Arab family values by reading about Arab families in Naff's *The Arab Americans* (1988) or by watching *Tales from Arab Detroit,* a videotape produced by Joan Mandell. Ask the students to make a list of practices they have read about that seem unusual. Then divide the class into small groups. Ask each group to compare an Arab practice with an American behavior or custom, discuss it, and list the advantages and disadvantages of each. Ask the students to share their results in a whole-class discussion.

Possible Topics

the chaperoning of girls

arranged or approved marriages

living at home until marriage

living at home after marriage

helping relatives start businesses

taking responsibility for educating relatives' children

working in the family business rather than starting one's own career

putting relatives up who need a place to stay

parents supervising children's attire

parents supervising children's friendships

Using this material, ask the students to write a "Dear Amal" column (Amal instead of Ann, as in Ann Landers). Ask them to write letters from parents and children who are experiencing the cultural clash over various issues (most having to do with freedom and limits—freedom corresponding to individualism, limits corresponding to the constraints imposed by the interests of an extended family).

High School Grades

Concept

Stereotyping

Generalization: Many Americans view Arabs through the negative clichés and stereotypes that are institutionalized in the media.

1. Have students research and discuss in groups—comprised in a way appropriate and meaningful to them (racial, ethnic, or gender)—the stereotypes about them or their group. Discuss the ways that stereotypes oversimplify the complexity of groups and individuals. Ask the students to describe ways in which individuals within a group differ from the stereotypes about it. Ask the students to summarize their discussion.

2. Have students read at least one of Jack Shaheen's essays on the Arab's image in the media: *The TV Arab* (1984), *The Influence of the Arab Stereotype on American Children* (1980), a chapter in *Arab and Muslim Stereotyping in American Popular Culture* (1997), or the introduction to *Reel Bad Arabs: How Hollywood Vilifies a People* (2001).

3. Ask the students to look for images of Arabs in the following: political cartoons, political commentary, movies, television shows, textbooks, advertisements, news reports, and political discourse. (They can also look in the same venues for images or mention of Islam and Muslims.) Ask the students to keep a scrapbook of these images for a period of time (e.g., one month), noting positive, negative, and neutral language. Analyze and report to the class. You might also want to rent from a video store several of the movies mentioned by Shaheen or the American-Arab Anti-Discrimination Committee (ADC) and ask students to look for stereotypes in them.

4. Contact the American-Arab Anti-Discrimination Committee for news on their current antidefamation campaigns (1732 Wisconsin Avenue NW, Washington, D.C. 2008. Phone: 202-244-2990. Fax: 202-244-7968. E-mail: adc@adc.org. Website: http://www.adc.org). Ask the students to discuss the merits of the case and decide whether to take the action ADC recommends, such as writing a letter to the CEO of the offending companies. Track responses.

REFERENCES

Abourezk, J. (1989). *Advise and Dissent: Memoirs of South Dakota and the U.S. Senate*. Chicago: Lawrence Hill.

Abraham, N. (1994). Anti-Arab Racism and Violence in the United States. In E. McCarus (Ed.), *The Development of Arab American Identity* (pp. 155–214). Ann Arbor: University of Michigan Press.

Abraham, N., & Shryock, A. (Eds.). (2000). *Arab Detroit: From Margin to Mainstream*. Detroit: Wayne State University Press.

ADC Special Report: Anti-Arab Racism in the United States—1995. (1995). Washington, DC: American-Arab Anti-Discrimination Committee.

Barlow, B. (Ed.). (1994). *Evaluation of Secondary-Level Textbooks for Coverage of the Middle East and North Africa*. Ann Arbor, MI: Middle East Studies Association and the Middle East Outreach Council.

Benson, K., & Kayal, P. (Eds.). (2002). *A Community of Many Worlds: Arab Americans in New York City*. New York and Syracuse: Museum of the City of New York/Syracuse University Press.

Brittingham, A., & de la Cruz, P. (March, 2005). *We the People of Arab Ancestry in the United States*. Washington, DC: U.S. Department of Commerce.

Cole, D. (2007, July 19). The Grand Inquisitors. *New York Review of Books*, 54(12), 53–56.

Council on American-Islamic Relations. (2001). Available online at http://www.cair-net.org.

Dalrymple, W. (2007, July 19). The Venetian Treasure Hunt (on the Metropolitan Museum of Art, New York, exhibit, "Venice and the Islamic World, 828–1797). *New York Review of Books*, 54(12), 29–31.

Eck, D. (2001). *A New Religious America: How a "Christian Country" Has Become the World's Most Religiously Diverse Nation*. New York: HarperSanFrancisco.

Ekin, L., & Gorchev, L. (Eds.). (1991). *ADC Special Report: 1991 Report on Anti-Arab Hate Crimes: Political and Hate Violence against Arab Americans during the Gulf War*. Washington, DC: American-Arab Anti-Discrimination Committee Research Institute.

El-Badry, S. (1994, January). The Arab-American Market. *American Demographics*, pp. 22–30.

Gibran, G. K. (1923). *The Prophet*. New York: Knopf.

Hagopian, E. (1969). The Institutional Development of the Arab-American Community of Boston: A Sketch. In E. Hagopian & A. Paden (Eds.), *The Arab-Americans: Studies in Assimilation* (pp. 67–83). Wilmette, IL: Medina University Press International.

Hajar, P. (1993). Arab Immigrant Parents and American School People: An Ethnography of a Cross-Cultural Relationship. Cambridge, MA: Harvard Graduate School of Education. Unpublished doctoral dissertation.

Hatab, H. (n.d.). *Arabs in the U.S.: No Longer the Best Kept Secret in Ethnic America* (pamphlet). Washington, DC: American-Arab Anti-Discrimination Committee.

Hatab, H. (1974). Syrian-American Ethnicity: Structure and Ideology in Transition. Unpublished master's thesis. American University of Beirut, Beirut, Lebanon.

Hayes, J. R. (Ed.). (1983). *The Genius of Arab Civilization: Source of the Renaissance.* Cambridge: MIT Press.

Hitti, P. (1924). *The Syrians in America.* New York: Doran.

Ibish, H. (2003). *Report on Hate Crimes and Discrimination against Arab Americans: The Post September 11 Backlash, September 11, 2001–October 11, 2002.* Washington, DC: American-Arab Anti-Discrimination Committee.

Kayal, P., & Kayal, J. (1975). *The Syrian-Lebanese in America: A Study in Religion and Assimilation.* Boston: Twayne.

Lee, M. (2002*). Healing the Nation: The Arab American Experience after September 11.* Washington, DC: Arab American Institute.

McGoldrick, M., Giordano, J., & Garcia-Preto, N. (Eds.). (2005). *Ethnicity and Family Therapy.* New York: Columbia University Press.

Michalak, L. (1988). *Cruel and Unusual: Negative Images of Arabs in Popular Culture.* Occasional paper no. 15. Washington, DC: American-Arab Anti-Discrimination Committee.

Mokarzel, S., & Okash, H. F. (1908). *The Syrian Business Directory: 1908–1909.* New York: Al-Hoda.

Naff, A. (1985). *Becoming American: The Early Arab Immigrant Experience.* Carbondale: Southern Illinois University Press.

Naff, A. (1988). *The Arab Americans.* New York: Chelsea House.

Orfalea, G. (1984). *U.S.-Arab Relations: The Literary Dimension.* Occasional paper series no. 2. Washington, DC: National Council on U.S. Arab Relations and Arab American Cultural Foundation.

Pew Research Center. (2007). *Muslim Americans: Middle Class and Mostly Mainstream.* Retrieved August 5, 2007, from http://pewresearch.org/assets/pdf/muslim-americans.pdf.

Sabbagh, S. (1990). *Sex, Lies, and Stereotypes: The Image of Arabs in American Popular Fiction.* Issues paper no. 23. Washington, DC: American-Arab Anti-Discrimination Committee.

Said, E. (1978). *Orientalism.* New York: Random House.

Samhan, H. H. (1989). Arab Americans and the Elections of 1988: A Constituency Come of Age. In B. Abu-Laban & M. Suleiman (Eds.), Arab Americans: Continuity and Change, *Arab Studies Quarterly* (special issue). Belmont, MA: Association of Arab-American University Graduate and Institute of Arab Studies.

Shabbas, A. (Ed.). (1998). *Arab World Studies Notebook.* Berkeley, CA: AWAIR (Arab World and Islamic Resources and School Services); Washington, DC: Middle East Policy Council.

Shaheen, J. (1980). *The Influence of the Arab Stereotype on American Children.* Issue paper no. 2. Washington, DC: American-Arab Anti-Discrimination Committee.

Shaheen, J. (1984). *The TV Arab.* Bowling Green, OH: Bowling Green State University Popular Press.

Shaheen, J. (1988). *ABSCAM: Arabiaphobia in America.* Issue paper no. 1. Washington, DC: American-Arab Anti-Discrimination Committee.

Shaheen, J. (1997). *Arab and Muslim Stereotyping in American Popular Culture.* Washington, DC: Center for Muslim-Christian Understanding, History and International Affairs, Edmund A. Walsh School of Foreign Service, Georgetown University.

Shaheen, J. (2001). *Reel Bad Arabs: How Hollywood Vilifies a People.* New York: Olive Branch Press.

Shakir, E. (1987). Good Works, Good Times. In E. Hooglund (Ed.), *Crossing the Waters* (pp. 133–143). Washington, DC: Smithsonian Institution Press.

Shakir, E. (1997). *Bint Arab: Arab and Arab-American Women in the United States.* Westport, CT: Praeger.

Shrag, R. L., & Javidi, M. N. (1995). Through a Glass Darkly: American Media Images of Middle Eastern Cultures and Their Potential Impact on Young Children. In Y. R. Kamalipour (Ed.), *The U.S. Media and the Middle East: Image and Perception* (pp. 212–221). Westport, CT: Praeger.

Stockton, R. (1994). Ethnic Archetypes and the Arab Image. In E. McCarus (Ed.), *The Development of Arab-American Identity* (pp. 119–153). Ann Arbor: University of Michigan.

Tannous, A. (June, 1943). Acculturation of an Arab-Syrian Community in the Deep South. *American Sociological Review, 8*(3), 264–271.

Tschanz, D. (1997, May/June). The Arab Roots of European Medicine. *Aramco World Magazine,* 20–31.

U.S. Census Bureau. (2007). *American Community Survey, 2005: Selected Population Profile.* [Data file]. Available online from http://factfinder.census.gov/servlet/IPCharIterationServlet?_ts=202649767048.

Wingfield, M. (2006). Arab Americans: Into the Multicultural Mainstream. *Equity and Excellence in Education, 39*(3), 253–266.

Younis, A. (1995). *The Coming of the Arabic-Speaking Peoples to the United States.* New York: Center for Migration Studies.

Zogby, J. (1990). *Arab America Today.* Washington, DC: Arab American Institute.

Zogby, J. (1995). *Arab American Demographics.* Utica, NY: Zogby International.

ANNOTATED BIBLIOGRAPHY

Books for Teachers

Especially Recommended

Haddad, Y. Y. (2004). *Not Quite American? The Shaping of Arab and Muslim Identity in the United States.* Waco, TX: Baylor University Press.

Haddad is a leading authority on Islam and Muslims in the West. This short book includes an overview of their early history in the United States, as well as their assimilation, institution building, and their post-9/11 experiences.

Handal, N. (2001). *The Poetry of Arab Women: A Contemporary Anthology.* New York: Interlink Books.

This excellent compendium includes the poetry of twenty-one Arab American women, including Naomi Shihab Nye, Mohja Kahf, Lisa Suhair Majaj, Suheir Hammad, and D.H. Milhelm.

Hooglund, E. J. (Ed.). (1985). *Taking Root/Bearing Fruit* (vol. 2). Washington, DC: American-Arab Anti-Discrimination Committee.

The second of two volumes of community studies sponsored by ADC, this volume includes stories about Vicksburg, Mississippi; Shaw, Mississippi; New Castle, Pennsylvania; Providence, Rhode Island; and Ross, North Dakota (home of the first mosque built in North America). These are real stories, quirky and beautifully written.

Hooglund, E. J. (Ed.). (1987). *Crossing the Waters: Arabic-Speaking Immigrants to the United States before 1940.* Washington, DC: Smithsonian Institution Press.

Eleven original essays and case studies on Arab Americans in such diverse communities as El Paso, Boston, Waterville (Maine), and Birmingham (Alabama). Not the usual overviews, these delightful essays are about specific immigrants, or aspects of immigrant life, and are wonderfully written.

Ibish, H. (2003). *Report on Hate Crimes and Discrimination against Arab Americans: The Post–September 11 Backlash, September 11, 2001–October 11, 2002.* Washington, DC: American-Arab Anti-Discrimination Committee.

A compelling resource, as ADC and CAIR (Council on American Islamic Relations) were the organizations that logged most comprehensively the incidents in question.

Kaldas, P., & Mattawa, K. (Eds.). (2004). *Dinazard's Children: An Anthology of Contemporary Arab American Fiction.* Fayetteville: University of Arkansas Press.

An extraordinary collection of short stories by Arab Americans, mostly about the multifaceted experiences of being Arab American. Writers include Evelyn Shakir, Joseph Geha, Nabil Abraham, Diane Abu Jabar, and more than a dozen others.

Kamalipour, Y. R. (Ed.). (1995). *The U.S. Media and the Middle East: Image and Perception.* Westport, CT: Praeger.
This collection of essays and reports is one of the most creative in print on many aspects of this topic. It probes the sources of the negative images of Arabs in U.S. culture and offers fascinating history as well as theories about the reasons for these images.

Lee, M. (2002). *Healing the Nation: The Arab American Experience after September 11.* Washington, DC: Arab American Institute.
Includes sections on the Arab American response to the September 11 attacks, the subsequent backlash, the nation's response to it, and civil rights issues that followed.

McCarus, E. (Ed.). (1994). *The Development of Arab-American Identity.* Ann Arbor: University of Michigan Press.
The essays in this authoritative and up-to-date collection on Arab American life are comprensive, well researched, and well written. The book includes probing articles on the development of the Arab stereotype and the progression of anti-Arab violence, as well as essays on politics, art, religion, identity, and assimilation.

Naff, A. (1987). *Becoming American: The Early Arab Immigrant Experience.* Carbondale: Southern Illinois University Press.
This book is another classic. One of the few that is not an anthology, it focuses on Arabs who came to the United States in the pre-1950 period. Naff is an authority in this field; her account weaves in 125 interviews with the early immigrants.

Nydell, M. K. (2006). *Understanding Arabs: A Guide for Modern Times* (4th ed.). Boston: Intercultural Press.
This engaging and highly readable book describes the values and cultures of the Arab world. It includes an informative chapter on "Arabs and Muslims in the West." It is appropriate for adults as well as upper grade and high school students.

Shabbas, A. (Ed.). (1998). *Arab World Notebook.* Berkeley: Arab World and Islamic Resources (AWAIR); Washington, DC: Middle East Policy Council.
This is a wonderful collection of essays and teaching resources on the Arab world, past and present. It has many ideas for lesson plans and includes a section on Arab Americans. Shabbas gives workshops to teachers nationwide and can be reached through her website: www.awaironline.org. (AWAIR stands for Arab World and Islamic Resources and School Services.)

Shaheen, J. (1997). *Arab and Muslim Stereotyping in American Popular Culture.* Georgetown, VA: Center for Muslim-Christian Understanding, History, and International Affairs, Edmund A. Walsh School of Foreign Service, Georgetown University.
Shaheen is one of the noted experts in the field of the Arab image in the media. His works are quite readable and the substance is informative and illuminating.

Shaikh, M., & Mansuri, S. (Eds.). (1995). *Teaching about Islam and Muslims in the Public School Classroom.* Fountain Valley, CA: Council on Islamic Education.
This handbook is essential for anyone intending to teach about Islam or who has Muslim students. It has clear information as well as a useful glossary and an excellent and extensive list of resources for teachers as well as for students of all ages.

Shakir, E. (1997). *Bint Arab: Arab and Arab-American Women in the United States.* Westport, CT: Praeger.
This beautifully written book interweaves a memoir and portrait of the author's mother with a well-told general history of Arab America. The book contains interviews with about thirty Arab American women.

Wingfield, M. (2006). Arab Americans: Into the Multicultural Mainstream. *Equity and Excellence in Education, 39*(3), 253–266.
> This is a sophisticated overview of Arab American history and anti-Arab discrimination. It weaves an analysis according to the Banks model of multicultural education and contains specific advice to educators about systematically integrating Arab American materials into the curriculum.

Zogby, J. (Ed.). (1984). *Taking Root/Bearing Fruit: The Arab-American Experience* (vol. 1). Washington, DC: American-Arab Anti-Discrimination Committee.
> The first volume of essays on the community published by ADC, it reports on Allentown, Pennsylvania; Boston; Brooklyn; Detroit; Houston; Portland, Maine; San Francisco; Utica, New York; and Worcester, Massachusetts. It also provides regional surveys and includes a collection of famous essays (some of them from the early *mahjar* period) on or by members of the community.

Other Books

Abourezk, J. (1989). *Advise and Dissent: Memoirs of South Dakota and the U.S. Senate.* Chicago: Lawrence Hill.
> This autobiography of the first Arab American senator and founder of the American-Arab Anti-Discrimination Committee is both entertaining and informative. It gives insight into the political experiences that shaped a key perspective.

Abraham, N., & Shryock, A. (Eds.). (2000). *Arab Detroit: From Margin to Mainstream.* Detroit: Wayne State University Press.
> This superb anthology of essays creates a richly detailed portrait of Arab Americans in Detroit. Food, music, religion, and identity politics are among the topics; analysis, memory, poetry, and biography are among the approaches taken.

ADC Special Report: Anti-Arab Racism in the United States—1995. (1995). Washington, DC: American-Arab Anti-Discrimination Committee.
> This report chronicles and analyzes hate crimes against Arabs after the Oklahoma City bombing.

Antonius, G. (1965, 2001). *The Arab Awakening.* New York: Capricorn.
> This is the fascinating and brilliantly told story of the late-nineteenth-century Arab National Movement that eventually led to the first great immigration movement from Syria. It starts with the Turkish conquest and ends just after World War I. The detail is astonishing, and the book reads like a novel.

Gibran, J., & Gibran, K. (1974). *Kahlil Gibran: His Life and World.* Boston: New York Graphic Society.
> This is the definitive work by the subject's cousin and namesake and the cousin's wife. The authors' access to Gibran's extensive correspondence makes this an intimate portrait.

Haddad, Y. (1994). Maintaining the Faith of the Fathers: Dilemmas of Religious Identity in the Christian and Muslim Arab-American Communities. In E. McCarus (Ed.), *The Development of Arab-American Identity* (pp. 61–84). Ann Arbor: University of Michigan Press.
> This is an overview of the religions of Arab Americans.

Haiek, J. (Ed.). (2003). *Arab American Almanac.* Glendale, CA: News Circle.
> This excellent reference includes essays on the history of the Arab American community and has directories, by subject and state, of various types of Arab American institutions.

McGoldrick, M., Giordano, J., & Pearce, J. (Eds.). (1996). *Ethnicity and Family Therapy* (2nd ed.). New York: Guilford.
> This wonderful resource on the family dynamics of various ethnic groups contains a chapter on Arabs by N. Abudabbeh and a separate one on the Lebanese by J. Simon.

Orfalea, G. (Ed.). (1982). *Wrapping the Grapeleaves: A Sheaf of Contemporary Arab-American Poets.* Washington, DC: American-Arab Anti-Discrimination Committee.

This book contains eleven poems by Arab Americans—eight of them about family relationships. This is an excellent classroom resource.

Orfalea, G. (1988). *Before the Flames: A Quest for the History of Arab Americans.* Austin: University of Texas Press.

This personal account of the author's quest to find out what it means to be Arab American in these times blends historical background with family stories and quotes from the author's interviews with the famous and not-quite-famous, including actor F. Murray Abraham and the late entertainer Danny Thomas.

Orfalea, G., & Elmusa, S. (Eds.). (1999). *Grapeleaves: A Century of Arab American Poetry.* Northampton, MA: Interlink.

This poetry anthology introduces some of the major poets, living and dead, of Arab America. It contains biographical and autobiographical commentary. Poets who write from the Arab American experience include Naomi Shihab Nye, D. H. Milhem, Sam Hazo, and Lawrence Joseph. All of these poets have also published their own volumes.

Saudi Aramco World Magazine (formerly *Aramco World*). Address: Saudi Aramco World, Post Office Box 2106, Houston, TX 77252-2106.

Educators are encouraged to subscribe to this glossy bimonthly. It has wonderful photographs, and subscriptions are free. Articles are about aspects of the Arab world and occasionally cover Arab Americans and their accomplishments.

Shaheen, J. G. (2001). *Reel Bad Arabs: How Hollywood Vilifies a People.* New York and Northhampton: Olive Branch Press.

An engaging 500-page compendium of original reviews of over 900 films, showing how the vast majority of them dehumanize Arabs. It also includes best and worst lists, as well as a list of films Shaheen recommends.

Suleiman, M. (Ed.). (1999). *Arabs in America: Building a New Future.* Philadelphia: Temple University Press.

This book has sections on Arabs and the American legal system, Arab American youth and family, the Palestinian community in Chicago, the Arab Shiite community in the United States, Arab American health and welfare issues and political activism, and several pieces on Arab American identity.

Younis, Adele L. (1995). *The Coming of the Arabic-Speaking People to the United States.* New York: Center for Migration Studies.

Though not published until 1995, this book contains information that many researchers on the Arab American community relied on when it was still a dissertation. Younis did much of the original work on the early Arab American experience. This book also contains Philip Kayal's most up-to-date Arab American bibliography.

Books for Students

Ameri, A., & Ramey, D. (Eds.). (2000). *Arab American Encyclopedia.* Detroit: ACCESS/Gale Group.

Articles cover every aspect of Arab American life and include essays on history, immigration, language, religion, work, education, family, holidays, health, civil rights, organizations and political activism, music, literature, arts, media, and community portraits. (Primarily for Middle School, but could be used both for Upper Elementary and High School)

Ashabranner, B. K. (1991). *An Ancient Heritage: The Arab American Minority.* New York: Harper-Collins.

This book tells the story of the Arab Americans through their own words and the memories of the author growing up with them in Oklahoma. It also shows the connection they still have with their homelands. It contains many photographs. (Intermediate)

Geha, J. (1990). *Through and Through: Toledo Stories*. St. Paul, MN: Graywolf Press.
This amusing book contains eight short stories depicting life in the Syrian-Lebanese community in Toledo, Ohio, from the 1930s to the present, and themes ranging from the domestic to the criminal. (High School)

Menconi, E. (2002). (Consulting Ed.). *Arab Americans*. Peterborough, NH: Cobblestone.
This issue (May, vol. 23) of the Discovering American History series in this well-known children's magazine includes introductory articles about Arab American history, identity, religion, language, discrimination, and contributions. (Elementary)

Nader, R. (2007). *The Seventeen Traditions*. New York: HarperCollins.
A memoir in which the famous consumer-advocate reflects warmly on the roots of his passionate citizenship—his own upbringing by his Arab Lebanese parents and the culture of his New England hometown. (High School)

Naff, A. (1988). *The Arab Americans*. New York: Chelsea House.
Part of the Peoples of America series, this is an excellent, rich, and comprehensive overview of the Arab American story by one of the leading chroniclers of this ethnic group. It does not shy away from presenting or interpreting complicated issues. It is an excellent book for the teacher new to the topic. It also contains good pictures. (Middle School/High School)

Nye, N. S. (1994). *Sitti's Secrets*. New York: Four Winds Press.
This is a poetic story of a little girl who visits her grandmother in her village on the West Bank and blends in with the lives of her relatives there. The writing and the pictures are extraordinary. (Primary)

Nye, N. S. (1997). *Habibi*. New York: Simon & Schuster.
This is the semiautobiographical story of a young Arab American teenager who returns for a year with her American family to live in her father's hometown near Jerusalem. It shows her difficulties in adjusting to attitudes different from the ones she grew up with in America. It is a pleasure to read. (Intermediate/Middle School)

Peduzzi, K. (1990). *Ralph Nader: Crusader for Safe Consumer Products and Lawyer for the Public Interest*. Milwaukee, WI: Gareth Stephens Books.
One of the People Who Have Helped the World series, this book explores the ways that the Arab American consumer advocate Ralph Nader and those he has inspired take on the wealthiest and most powerful organizations in America to defend the safety, health, and consumer rights of all Americans. (Upper Elementary/Middle School)

Schur, J. B. (2004). *The Arab Americans*. Immigrants in America series. Detroit: Lucent Books, Gale Group.
This account covers early immigrants to recent refugees from political conflict and is a good overview of the contemporary Arab American community. (Middle School/High School).

ETHNIC GROUPS IN U.S. HISTORY
A Chronology of Key Events

*Indicates an important immigration act.

DATE	EVENT
1513	Juan Ponce de León landed on the Florida peninsula while en route from Puerto Rico. The relationship between Europeans and Indians north of Mexico began.
1519	Hernán Cortéz, the Spanish conquistador, and a group of Spaniards arrived in the region that is now Mexico.
1565	The Spaniards established the St. Augustine colony in Florida, the first settlement organized by Europeans in present-day United States.
1619	The first Africans arrived in the English North American colonies.
1620	The Pilgrims came to America from England on the *Mayflower* and established a settlement at Plymouth, Massachusetts.
1637	More than 500 American Indians were killed by the colonists in a massacre known as the Pequot War.
1654	The first Jewish immigrants to North America settled in New Amsterdam to escape persecution in Brazil.
1683	German immigrants settled in Pennsylvania.
1718	The Scots-Irish began immigrating to North America in large numbers.
1754–1763	The French and Indian War occurred.
1798	A Federalist-dominated Congress enacted the Alien and Sedition Acts to crush the Republican Party and to harass aliens.
1812	The War of 1812, a war between the United States and Britain, caused deep factions among the Indian tribes because of their different allegiances.

DATE	EVENT
1815	The first mass immigrations from Europe to North America began.
1830	Congress passed a Removal Act, which authorized the removal of Indians from east to west of the Mississippi.
1831	Nat Turner led a slave revolt in which nearly sixty Whites were killed.
1836	Mexico's President Santa Anna and his troops defeated the Texans at the Alamo. Six weeks later, Santa Anna was defeated by Sam Houston and his Texan troops at San Jacinto.
1845	The United States annexed Texas, which had declared itself independent from Mexico in 1836. This was one key event that led to the Mexican-American War.
1846–1848	A series of potato blights in Ireland caused thousands of its citizens to immigrate to the United States.
1846	On May 13, 1846, the United States declared war on Mexico and the Mexican-American War began.
1848	The United States and Mexico signed the Treaty of Guadalupe Hidalgo that ended the Mexican-American War. Mexico lost nearly one-third of its territory, and the United States acquired most of the territory that comprises its southwestern states.
1850	The California legislature passed a discriminatory Foreign Miner's Tax that forced Chinese immigrants to pay a highly disproportionate share of the state taxes.
1855	Castle Garden, an immigration station, opened in New York City. The antiforeign Know-Nothing Movement reached its zenith and had a number of political successes in the 1855 elections. The movement rapidly declined after 1855.
1859	Juan N. Cortina, who became a U.S. citizen under the provisions of the Treaty of Guadalupe Hidalgo, led a series of rebellions against Anglo-Americans in the Southwest.
1863	On January 1, 1863, President Abraham Lincoln issued the Emancipation Proclamation, which freed slaves in those states still fighting the Union.
1864	Nearly 300 Cheyennes were killed in a surprise attack at Sand Creek, Colorado. This event is known as the Sand Creek Massacre.
1869	The transcontinental railroad, linking the United States west to the east, was completed. Chinese laborers did most of the work on the Pacific portion of the railroad.
	The unsuccessful Wakamatsu Colony, made up of Japanese immigrants, was established in California.

DATE	EVENT
1871	A White mob in Los Angeles attacked a Chinese community. When the conflict ended, nineteen Chinese were dead and their community was in shambles.
1876	In the disputed Hayes-Tilden election, the Democrats and Republicans made a political bargain that symbolized the extent to which northern Whites had abandoned southern Blacks.
	Sioux tribes, under the leadership of Sitting Bull, wiped out Custer's Seventh Cavalry at Little Big Horn. This was one of the last victories for American Indian tribes.
*1882	The Chinese Exclusion Act was enacted by Congress.
	Another congressional immigration act established a head tax of fifty cents and excluded lunatics, convicts, idiots, and those likely to become public charges.
1885	A serious anti-Chinese riot occurred in Rock Springs, Wyoming. Twenty-eight Chinese were killed, and many others were wounded and driven from their homes.
1886	The Apache warrior Geronimo surrendered to U.S. forces in September 1886. His surrender marked the defeat of the Southwest tribes.
	The Haymarket Affair in Chicago increased the fear of foreign "radicals" and stimulated the growth of nativistic sentiments in the United States.
	The Statue of Liberty was dedicated as nativism soared in the United States.
1887	Congress passed the Dawes Severalty Act, which was designed to partially terminate the American Indians' special relationship with the U.S. government.
1888	The Scott Act prohibited the immigration of Chinese laborers and permitted only officials, teachers, students, merchants, and travelers from China to enter the United States.
1890	Three hundred Sioux were killed in a conflict at Wounded Knee Creek in South Dakota.
1891	Eleven Italian Americans were lynched in New Orleans during the height of American nativism, after being accused of murdering a police superintendent.
1892	Ellis Island opened and replaced Castle Garden as the main port of entry for European immigrants.
1893	Queen Liliuokalani of Hawai'i was overthrown in a bloodless revolution led by American planters.
	The Republic of Hawai'i was established, with Stanford B. Dole as president.

DATE	EVENT
1896	In a historic decision, *Plessy* v. *Ferguson,* the Supreme Court ruled that "separate but equal" facilities were constitutional.
1898	Hawai'i was annexed to the United States.
	Under the terms of the Treaty of Paris, the treaty that ended the Spanish-American War, the United States acquired Puerto Rico, Guam, and the Philippines. Cuba became independent of Spain but was placed under U.S. tutelage.
1900	With the Foraker Act, the United States established a government in Puerto Rico to which the president of the United States appointed the governor and the Executive Council.
1901–1910	Almost 9 million immigrants entered the United States, most of whom came from southern and eastern Europe.
1908	The United States and Japan made the Gentlemen's Agreement, which was designed to reduce the number of Japanese immigrants entering the United States.
1910	The National Association for the Advancement of Colored People (NAACP) was organized.
	A Mexican revolution caused many Mexican peasants to immigrate to the United States looking for jobs. Other immigrants came to escape political turmoil and persecution.
1913	The California legislature passed a land bill that made it difficult for Japanese immigrants to lease land.
1917	Thirty-nine African Americans were killed in a bloody riot in East St. Louis, Missouri.
	*A comprehensive immigration bill was enacted that established a literacy test for entering immigrants.
	The Jones Act was passed by the U.S. Congress, making Puerto Ricans U.S. citizens and subject to the draft.
1920	The Hawai'ian Homes Commission was started to benefit the native Hawai'ians, but little of the land involved was used for its stated purpose.
	The number of people born in Puerto Rico and living in the United States was 11,811. That number increased to 58,200 in the year 1935.
*1924	The Johnson-Reed Act established extreme quotas on immigration and blatantly discriminated against southern and eastern European and non-White nations.
1925	A large number of Filipinos began to immigrate to Hawai'i and the U.S. mainland to work as field laborers.

DATE	EVENT
1927	The Filipino Federation of Labor was organized in Los Angeles.
1928	The League of United Latin American Citizens was formed in Harlingen, Texas.
1929	An anti-Filipino riot occurred in Exeter, California, in which more than 200 Filipinos were assaulted.
1930	The Japanese American Citizenship League was organized.
*1934	Congress passed the Tydings-McDuffie Act, which promised the Philippines independence and limited Filipino immigration to the United States to fifty per year.
1935	President Franklin D. Roosevelt signed the Repatriation Act. The act offered free transportation to Filipinos who would return to the Philippines. Those who left were unable to return to the United States except under a severe quota system.
1942	On February 19, 1942, President Franklin D. Roosevelt issued Executive Order 9066, which authorized the internment of Japanese Americans who lived on the West Coast.
	The United States and Mexico made an agreement that authorized Mexican immigrants to work temporarily in the United States. This project is known as the *bracero* program.
1943	White violence directed at African Americans led to a serious riot in Detroit, in which thirty-four people were killed.
	The anti-Mexican "zoot-suit" riots occurred in Los Angeles during the summer.
1946	On July 4, 1946, the Philippines became independent.
*1952	The McCarran-Walter Immigration and Nationality Act was passed by Congress. It eliminated race as a factor in immigration. However, the national origins quota system remained but was liberalized.
1954	The Refugee Relief Act permitted 5,000 Hungarian refugees to enter the United States.
	In a landmark decision, *Brown* v. *Board of Education,* the Supreme Court ruled that school segregation was inherently unequal.
	The U.S. Immigration and Naturalization Service began Operation Wetback, a massive program to deport illegal Mexican immigrants.
1959	Fidel Castro took over the reins of power in Cuba from the government of Fulgencio Batista. After this revolution, many Cuban refugees entered the United States.
	Hawai'i became the fiftieth state of the United States.

DATE	EVENT
1960	On February 1, 1960, the sit-in movement, which desegregated public accommodation facilities throughout the South, began in Greensboro, North Carolina.
1961	The National Indian Youth Council was organized.
1962	Commercial air flights between the United States and Cuba ended. Immigration from Cuba to the United States became strictly clandestine.
1963	More than 200,000 people participated in a "March on Washington for Freedom and Jobs."
1964	The Civil Rights Act of 1964, the most comprehensive civil rights bill in American history, was enacted by Congress and signed by President Lyndon B. Johnson.
1965	With the passage of the Civil Rights Act of 1965, Puerto Ricans were no longer required to pass an English literacy test to vote in New York state.
	*The Immigration Reform Act of 1965 was passed by Congress. This act, which became effective in 1968, abolished the national origins quota system and liberalized American immigration policy. Immigration from Asia and Latin America increased after this act was passed.
	A grape strike led by César Chávez and the National Farm Workers Association began in Delano, California, a town in the San Joaquin Valley.
	Rodolfo "Corkey" Gonzales formed the Crusade for Justice in Denver. This important civil rights organization epitomized the Chicano movement that emerged in the 1960s.
	The Cuban Refugee Airlift program began. Flights from Cuba to Miami, Florida, were sponsored by the U.S. government. The program was terminated in 1973.
1965–1968	A series of riots occurred in U.S. cities in which African Americans expressed their frustrations and discontent.
1966	Stokely Carmichael issued a call for Black Power during a civil rights demonstration in Greenwood, Mississippi.
1970	Herman Badillo was elected to the U.S. House of Representatives, the first Puerto Rican elected to Congress.
1973	African Americans were elected mayors in Detroit, Atlanta, Los Angeles, and other cities.
1974	The U.S. Supreme Court ruled in the *Lau* v. *Nichols* case that schools should provide students with instruction in their native language. This ruling gave bilingual-bicultural education in the United States a tremendous boost.

DATE	EVENT
1975	U.S. participation in the Vietnam War had ended (1973), and communist governments took control of Vietnam and Cambodia (Kampuchea). Many Indochinese refugees settled in the United States. Between 1971 and 1978, 110,200 Vietnamese refugees immigrated to the United States.
1978	In the case of *Regents of the University of California* v. *Bakke*, the Supreme Court of the United States upheld the idea of affirmative action but ruled against strict racial quotas. The Court concluded that the affirmative action program at the medical school of the University of California at Davis was unconstitutional.
1980	The 1980 U.S. Census indicated that the population of some ethnic groups in the United States increased dramatically in the decade between 1970 and 1980. Mexicans, Koreans, and Chinese were among the groups whose population increased the most. While the White population increased only 6% between 1970 and 1980, the population of Asian and Pacific Islanders more than doubled (from 1.5 million to 3.5 million), and the Hispanic population increased more than 60%.
	The Refugee Relief Act of 1980 was enacted. It enabled more refugees to enter the United States.
*1986	The Immigration Reform and Control Act of 1986 was passed by Congress and became law. The act imposed severe penalties on employers who knowingly hired illegal immigrants, and it gave amnesty to many illegal immigrants who had been living in the United States since January 1, 1982.
1988	The Civil Liberties Act of 1988 was passed by Congress and signed by President Ronald Reagan. The act provided compensation for the Japanese Americans and the Aleuts of the Pribilof Islands and the Aleutian Islands for the losses they incurred for being forcibly relocated during World War II.
*1990	The Immigration Act of 1990 made some significant changes in immigration law. It set immigration at 675,000 annually (beginning in 1995), to consist of 480,000 family-sponsored, 140,000 employment-based, and 55,000 "diversity" immigrants. It revised political and ideological grounds for exclusion and deportation.
1994	Nativistic sentiments throughout the nation were epitomized by the passage of Proposition 197 in California. This proposition denied undocumented workers and their children schooling and nonemergency medical care.

DATE	EVENT
2001	After the September 11 tragedy in which almost 3,000 people were killed by terrorists belonging to an Islamic fringe group, a number of Arab Americans were victims of racist attacks in the United States. President George W. Bush spoke out against these attacks and appealed to Americans to treat fellow citizens fairly.
2006	The U.S. Census indicated that the population of ethnic minorities of color in the United States had reached 100 million, out of a national population of just over 300 million.
2007	In *Parents Involved in Community Schools* v. *Seattle District No. 1 et al.*, the Supreme Court ruled on June, 28, 2007, that the desegregation plans implemented in the Seattle (Wash.) and Louisville (Ky.) school districts were unconstitutional and that race could not be used as a factor when making student assignments to desegregate schools. The 5-to-4 decision was typical of many others made by this sharply ideologically divided court during the first full term of George W. Bush's two conservative appointees, Chief Justice John Roberts and Associate Justice Samuel Alito.

INTERNET RESOURCES FOR TEACHING ABOUT ETHNIC AND CULTURAL DIVERSITY

Notice: Between the time website information is gathered and then published, it is not unusual for some sites to have closed. Also the transcription of URLs can result in unintended typographical errors. The publisher would appreciate notification where these occur so that they may be corrected in subsequent printings and editions. Thank you.

GENERAL MULTICULTURAL

Applied Research Center

http://www.arc.org
ARC is a public policy, educational, and research center that focuses on issues of race and social change. ARC produces a magazine called *Colorlines,* available online along with numerous other articles and perspectives by staff members. Additionally, ARC has several projects designed to foster worldwide and national awareness and action.

Center for Multicultural Education, University of Washington, Seattle

http://depts.washington.edu/centerme/home.htm
Based at the University of Washington, the Center for Multicultural Education focuses on research projects related to equity issues, intergroup relations, and the achievement of all students. The center's site lists its publications, research projects, upcoming and past events, conferences, lectures, degree programs, courses, and faculty. The center's publications include the *Handbook of Research on Multicultural Education* (2nd ed.) (Jossey-Bass/Wiley, 2004) and *Democracy and Diversity: Principles and Concepts for Educating Citizens in a Global Age.* James A. Banks is the director of the center.

Digital History

http://www.digitalhistory.uh.edu
Based at the University of Houston, this comprehensive website includes over 600 documents, audio files, historic newspaper articles, and photographs spanning the history of the United States. An entire section, titled "Ethnic Voices," includes primary and secondary documents concerning the lives and contributions of Mexican Americans, American Indians, Asian Americans, and African Americans in the United States.

Ed Change

http://www.edchange.org
This program is coordinated by a team of enthusiastic and experienced educators who pursue social justice in schools through professional development, project sharing, and scholarship. The website is easily accessible and helpful for practicing teachers. The "Teacher's Corner" provides definitions of multicultural concepts and philosophies as well as an abundance of lesson plans and classroom activities.

Educational Justice

http://www.edjustice.org
This program's mission is to "promote access to quality education for students from all racial and cultural groups." Sharing resources is an important part in its goal. This page provides massive amounts of resources. Included are topic-specific resources as well as a curriculum page for all subjects and groups or cultures.

Facing History and Ourselves

http://www.facinghistory.org/campus/reslib.nsf
Facing History and Ourselves encourages teachers and students to examine history and legacies of prejudice and discrimination. This site contains a massive resource section, including study guides to go with films and lectures, books, and multimedia. There are also excellent resources on teaching about the Holocaust, which help teachers and students to understand the Holocaust in the context of prejudice and discrimination in U.S. society today. There is also a teacher in-service component.

Family Search

http://www.familysearch.org
This website, maintained by the Church of Jesus Christ of Latter-day Saints, is reported to be "the largest collection of free family history, family tree, and genealogy records." Easy and accessible, this site allows the viewer to enter information

concerning deceased relatives, create and share a family tree, and collaborate with other people interested in genealogy. A great classroom resource, Family Search includes the Personal Ancestral File (PAF), which is a free, downloadable program that allows one to collect and organize family history information.

Immigration History Research Center

http://www.ihrc.umn.edu
Based at the University of Minnesota, the Immigration History Research Center makes available to the public its archival and published materials related to immigration and ethnicity. This site is particularly useful for eastern, central, and southern European groups.

MAVIN Foundation—The Mixed-Race Experience

http://www.mavinfoundation.org
The MAVIN foundation advocates for mixed-race people in the United States. The website investigates the experiences of "mixed-heritage people, transracial adoptees, interracial relationships, and multiracial families." Speakers and consultants are available through the website, as is information about ongoing projects and events in communities nationwide.

The National Association for Multicultural Education (NAME)

http://www.nameorg.org
NAME is a national professional organization that provides resources and support that help educators implement "a philosophy of inclusion and promote cultural and ethnic diversity as a national strength." NAME organizes an annual conference that deals with issues of diversity and multicultural education. It also has a number of regional organizations that sponsor conferences.

National Clearinghouse for English Language Acquisition and Language Instruction Educational Programs

http://www.nclea.gwu.edu
The U.S. Department of Education's Office of Minority Language Affairs funds this organization. Its goal is to provide information related to "the effective education of linguistically and culturally diverse learners in the U.S." The site includes links such as the online library, database, language and educational links, and classroom materials.

National Women's History Project

http://www.nwhp.org

In an attempt to provide teachers with information and materials regarding women's perspectives and contributions to society, the National Women's History Project offers much more than an online catalog. It also offers a learning page where teachers can discover resources and teacher support, student-specific links, and current events such as National Women's History Month. A significant part of the project's materials deal with women of color.

The Population Reference Bureau

http://www.prb.org

The Population Reference Bureau provides basic population and demographic data for the United States and the world. Many of its reports focus on U.S. ethnic groups. Recent reports include *International Migration: Facing the Challenge; New Marriages, New Families: U.S. Racial and Hispanic Intermarriage;* and *Immigration: Shaping and Reshaping America*. The site also includes specialized lesson plans and educational articles on different topics.

REACH Center

http://www.reachctr.org

The REACH Center provides training and learning experiences in multicultural education and ethnic history for school districts, schools, and individuals. The cross-cultural training REACH offers helps participants gain knowledge and understanding of different racial and ethnic groups. The goal of REACH is to help all people function well in a diverse society. Gary Howard, the director of the REACH Center, is the author of *We Can't Teach What We Don't Know: White Teachers, Multiracial Schools* (2nd ed.) (Teachers College Press, 2006).

Rethinking Schools

http://www.rethinkingschools.org

Rethinking Schools is devoted to reforming urban schools and addressing issues involving race. Rethinking Schools is "committed to equity and to the vision that public education is central to the creation of a humane, caring, multiracial democracy." The site includes a searchable index of all articles that have appeared in its periodic publication, *Rethinking Schools*. Rethinking Schools was founded by and is run by classroom teachers.

Social Studies School Service

http://www.socialstudies.com

The Social Studies School Service is a distributor of social studies teaching materials. It publishes a multicultural catalog that covers immigration, ethnic studies, diversity, and human relations. The online catalog provides searches and links by region. Other topics include religions and specific American histories such as women's history and Native American history.

Teaching for Change

http://www.teachingforchange.org
Teaching for Change is part of the Network of Educators on the Americas. The site provides teachers with resources to help integrate diverse cultures and experiences into the curriculum and updated material and resources on specific topics and current events. The site contains an online catalog.

Teaching Tolerance

http://www.teachingtolerance.org
The goal of this site is to fight hate and promote tolerance. Specific pages for teachers, parents, and students provide materials and information to foster equity within schools and society. This site is excellent for providing relevant current events and plans of action to help foster classroom discussion and exploration.

United States Census Bureau: Minority Links

http://www.census.gov/pubinfo/www/hotlinks.html
Minority Links provides easily accessible data on minority populations in the United States. In addition to basic census data, the site includes social characteristics, economic characteristics, profiles, news releases, and other related topics.

AMERICAN INDIANS AND ALASKAN NATIVES

The Alaska Native Knowledge Network

http://www.ankn.uaf.edu
The Alaska Native Knowledge Network is designed to serve as a resource for collecting and sharing information related to Alaska Native knowledge systems and ways of understanding. It has been established to assist Native people, government agencies, educators, and the general public in learning about and understanding Alaska Native people.

The Cradleboard Teaching Project

http://www.cradleboard.org
This teaching project is based on linking Indian and non-Indian children through the learning process. The Cradleboard curriculum and lessons are designed to be interactive multimedia Native studies lessons in which partner classes are linked through technology and learn together. In addition, Cradleboard offers numerous links to

tribal Web pages, a question-and-answer forum, and five core curriculum samples from a Native American perspective from elementary to high school level.

Living Voices, Voces Vivas—Smithsonian National Museum of the American Indian

http://www.nmai.si.edu/livingvoices/voices.html
This website highlights over forty interviews with a variety of American Indian and Native Hawai'ian people from the United States, Canada, Mexico, and Panama. Each three- to five-minute interview is coupled with the original transcript for further analysis. The site is easy to navigate and is an important resource for both teachers and students who are learning about indigenous populations.

National Congress of American Indians

http://www.ncai.org
The National Congress of American Indians (NCAI) serves as a forum for policy development among its 250 tribal government members. NCAI informs the public and the federal government about tribal self-government, treaty rights, and a wide range of federal policy issues affecting tribal governments.

The National Museum of the American Indian, Smithsonian Institution National Museum

http://www.nmai.si.edu
The National Museum of the American Indian presents in-depth, activity-based educational programs. It has an online Resource Center that provides a bibliography of suggested books and links to other sites relating to Native Americans.

Native Village

http://www.nativevillage.org
Native Village was created as an educational and current events resource for Native youth, teens, families, educators, and friends. The writers of this site publish two weekly news editions: *Native Village Drum* and *Native Village Youth and Education News.* Each issue shares Indian news from all parts of the Americas.

Native Web

http://www.nativeweb.org
Native Web is an educational organization dedicated to using technology to disseminate information from and about indigenous cultures throughout the world. This site is complete with a comprehensive resource center, including Web links, books, music, a nation index, and a geographical region index.

Virtual Library on Native Americans

http://www.hanksville.org/NAresources/
This Virtual Library on Native Americans provides a comprehensive index of Native American teaching resources on the Internet. The links provided allow teachers and students to explore the multitude of resources available on the Web.

NATIVE HAWAI'IANS

Hawai'ian Independence

http://www.hawaii-nation.org/index.html
This site is dedicated to issues revolving around Hawai'i as an independent and a sovereign state. The historical and archived information is excellent, as is the list of links and cultural information.

Native Hawai'ians

http://www.nativehawaiians.com
This site answers the question "Who are native Hawai'ians?" and provides a historical time line, the latest news, articles, lesson plans, and a press kit. There are links to a few other sites, including the Office of Hawai'ian Affairs.

AFRICAN AMERICANS

BlackPast.org—Remembered & Reclaimed

http://www.blackpast.org
This site was developed and is maintained by Professor Quintard Taylor, who is on the faculty in the department of history at the University of Washington, Seattle. It provides reference materials on over 600 years of African American history. Also accessible is an online encyclopedia, important speeches, primary documents, and links to other scholarly websites pertaining to African Americans.

Born in Slavery: Slave Narratives from the Federal Writers' Project, 1936–1938

http://www.lcweb2.loc.gov/ammem/snhtml/snhome.html
This powerful and important Library of Congress website offers 2,300 firsthand accounts of slavery and over 500 photographs collected in the 1930s by the Works Project Administration during President Roosevelt's New Deal. With transcripts and detailed notes available for each interview and photograph, students and teachers will be taken back in time to a shameful part of United States history to grapple with the experiences and legacies of slavery.

Civil Rights in Mississippi Digital Archive

http://www.lib.usm.edu/~spcol/crda/oh
This resource provides over 150 oral history interviews with people on both sides of the civil rights movement. Document collections include pamphlets, journals, and arrest records. The website is continually updated and maintained by the University of Southern Mississippi. It also includes links to many other civil rights websites.

Images of African Americans from the Nineteenth Century

http://digital.nypl.org/schomburg/images_aa19
The Schomburg Center for Research in Black Culture makes over 500 good-quality images available to viewers. The images highlight the economic, political, and cultural world of African Americans during the nineteenth century. Personal collections and school photographs are many of the unique images that are on this website.

EUROPEAN AMERICAN ETHNIC

American Institute of Polish Culture

http://www.ampolinstitute.org.ic.pl/_engine/page_render.asp
The American Institute of Polish Culture maintains a good website of its own, but its list of links to other pages about Polish culture is an excellent resource for any subject.

Center for Migration Studies

http://www.cmsny.org
CMS is committed to studying all aspects of human migration including historical, economic, political, and sociodemographic. This site includes a documentation center with a comprehensive library as well as numerous links to related European websites and others in the Federation of Centers for Migration Studies.

Center for the Study of White American Culture

http://www.euroamerican.org
The Center for the Study of White American Culture is a multiracial organization that examines different racial and cultural groups of White Americans. The center promotes the idea that "Knowledge of one's own racial background and culture is essential when learning how to relate to people of other racial and cultural groups." This site has a great list of links, including one about European American heritage, where people can learn about ethnic heritages. Additionally, there is a White studies library that can be searched by subject.

One Stop Italian American Culture and Heritage

http://www.osia.org
This site offers a good variety of resources from literature to current events. There is even an Italian American magazine available to read.

Slovak-American International Culture Foundation

http://www.slovakculture.org/home.html
This foundation is designed to provide information about Slovak American and Slovak contributions to society. The site provides good cultural background information.

JEWISH AMERICANS

Jewish Americans: History and Bibliography for Children and Young Adults

http://falcon.jmu.edu/~ramseyil/muljew.htm
This is primarily a site with links to other sources for children's books, bibliographies, and publishers. Some of the specific categories listed are biographies, Jewish holidays, the Holocaust, professional resources, and history.

Jewish Women's Archive

http://www.jwa.org
Valuable when examining the experience of Jewish women in the United States, this website focuses on sixteen women and their contributions to society. Students and teachers can learn more about these Jewish women's struggles with gender identity, discrimination, and values as well as the activism and rewards that resulted from the challenges these women faced.

Multicultural Research: Jewish American/Judaic Research

http://www.union.edu/PUBLIC/LIBRARY/guide/mcjewish.html
This site has been put together by the Multicultural Resource Center of the Schaffer Library Union College for the purpose of providing sources and tools for academic research. It is primarily a site with numerous links to other sources for Jewish culture and history, such as private centers, societies and organizations, communication networks with worldwide news updates, and an online book catalog.

National Museum of American Jewish History

http://nmajh.org/exhibitions/
The National Museum of American Jewish History site offers virtual tours of online exhibitions.

MEXICAN AMERICANS

A History of the Mexican-American People

http://www.jsri.msu.edu/museum/pubs/MexAmHist/
An online version of a highly acclaimed textbook originally published in 1977. Commonly used in high school and university settings in both history and ethnic studies courses, *A History of the Mexican-American People* provides a wealth of information. The book examines Indian-Spanish heritage, the effects of foreign intrusion into Mexico, and Mexican heritage in the United States. The current edition continues to describe the pursuit of Mexican Americans for social justice.

Cultural Resources for Mexican American Education—ERIC Digest

http://www.ericdigests.org/2000–4/mexican.htm
A great place to begin initial research or curriculum development, this website is dedicated to supporting teachers. The goal of the digest is to help teachers integrate Mexican American culture and history into the traditional curriculum of schools. The site summarizes the content of a number of helpful resources and includes both academic and commercial websites.

Chicano Art Life

http://www.chicano-art-life.com/index2.html
This site presents the many voices of today's Chicanos through traditional art and multimedia exhibits. A teacher's guide to the exhibitions is easily accessible on the website, and students can examine some of the artwork online. The resource includes links to "The Chicano Facts Sheet" and background information on the Chicano movement.

Chicano.org

http://www.chicano.org/newsite
This online magazine covers current issues important to the Mexican American community. There is an online forum where one can respond to articles and engage in discussions with others.

UCLA Chicano Studies Research Center

http://www.chicano.ucla.edu
Founded in 1969, the UCLA Chicano Studies Research Center houses a library and special collections archive, establishes community-based partnerships, and conducts research projects. The website offers access to scholarly reports, journals, books, and visual media.

PUERTO RICANS IN THE UNITED STATES

Puerto Rico and the American Dream

http://www.prdream.com/index.html
Puerto Rico and the American Dream is an extremely thoughtful site on the history, culture, and politics of Puerto Rico. The site includes a film section, an online gallery, discussion boards, historical time lines, oral histories, and announcements and current event postings.

Selected Reference Sources on Puerto Rico and Puerto Ricans in the W. E. B. Du Bois Library

http://www.library.umass.edu/instruction/handouts/prbiblio.html
This site includes almanacs and bibliographies. Other resources provide information on topics such as culture, economics, education, health, and race relations.

Welcome to Puerto Rico

http://www.topuertorico.org
This site, created by Magaly Rivera, a Puerto Rican in the United States, is a good place for initial research and information about Puerto Rico. History, geography, people, culture, and government are just a sample of the topics under which the author provides a wealth of information, visual images, and links to additional sites.

Yale–New Haven Teachers Institute

http://www.yale.edu/ynhti/curriculum/units/1991/2/91.02.06.x.html
The content of this site is a curriculum called "The Heritage and Culture of Puerto Ricans" by the Yale–New Haven Teachers Institute. It was designed to supplement social studies in grades 3 and 4, but may be adapted for all levels.

CUBAN AMERICANS

Institute for Cuban and Cuban American Studies

http://www6.miami.edu/iccas/
This site is quite possibly the most comprehensive place to visit if you are looking for links relating to Cuban Americans. The Institute for Cuban and Cuban American Studies offers researchers an opportunity to examine the Cuban Family and History Genealogy Project and Cuba Online, among others. The Cuban Family and History Genealogy Project aims to preserve cultural links to and documentation about Cuba. Cuba Online is a comprehensive, full-text, online database containing information on Cuba.

Latin American and Caribbean Center

http://lacc.fiu.edu

The Latin American and Caribbean Center (LACC) is part of Florida International University. This site describes the center, public education and outreach efforts (including teacher training workshops, faculty development in foreign language education, and distance learning), publications and resources, grants and research, and news and events. The Cuban Research Institute is within the LACC and offers degree programs, symposiums, and information on current events.

Simon Fraser University Library

http://edocs.lib.sfu.ca/projects/Cuba/

This site provides an annotated bibliography of novels written in English about Cuba/Cubans/Cuban Americans from 1851 to 2000, compiled by the Simon Fraser University Library. It is a good resource for secondary teachers but does not include children's or young adult fiction.

ASIAN AMERICANS

The Asian American Curriculum Project (AACP)

http://www.AsianAmericanBooks.com

The mission of the AACP is to educate the public about the Asian American experience by offering materials for all age groups, all levels of education, and all Asian ethnic groups. The AACP publishes an excellent and comprehensive catalog of materials for teaching about Asian Americans. This is an excellent nonprofit organization that has been engaged in its important work since 1970. Florence M. Hongo is the general manager of AACP.

Asian American Studies Center, UCLA

http://www.sscnet.ucla.edu/aasc/

This center is on the UCLA campus and contains much more than just class listings. This excellent research center provides updates on important events and functions.

The Chinese in California, 1850–1925

http://lcweb2.loc.gov/ammem/award99/cubhtml/cichome.html

A powerful website illuminating the challenges and achievements of Chinese American settlement in California during the late nineteenth and early twentieth centuries. This source has a wealth of primary and secondary documents, including diaries, letters, legal documents, business records, music, and art making, and is a wonderful resource for student research.

East and Southeast Asia: An Annotated Directory of Internet Resources

http://newton.uor.edu/Departments&Programs/AsianStudiesDept/
This site includes links to a vast amount of information about many Asian groups. These links are divided into categories such as multiculturalism, general information, political and social issues, media, communities, culture and arts, immigrations, and academic resources.

Filipino American National Historical Society (FANHS)

http://www.fanhs-national.org
FANHS provides information about many aspects of Filipino issues today. Some of the beneficial information on this site includes ongoing research, public forums, exhibits, journals, film and book reviews, and bibliographies of resources.

Japanese Legacy Project

http://www.densho.org
The Japanese Legacy Project includes over 200 hours of video interviews encompassing the Japanese internment during World War II. With the goal of preserving the testimonies of Japanese Americans who were held in relocation camps solely because of their ancestry, this site encourages the use of the resources to increase awareness of Japanese history and help members of society to think critically about social justice and democratic principles. Topics addressed on the site include race and racism, community, resistance, and identity.

USC Archival Research Center

http://www.usc.edu/isd/archives/arc
Based at the University of Southern California, this website provides a detailed look at the history of Los Angeles. The documents include artifacts from early Chinese American settlement, photographs of Japanese American relocation during World War II, and audio files describing Korean American history in the United States.

Vietnamese American Council

http://www.viet-nam.org
The mission of this organization is to promote the advancement of Vietnamese Americans in American society while maintaining their Vietnamese cultural heritage. This site contains a valuable page of links, culture, history, and current events.

Wing Luke Asian Museum, Seattle, Washington

http://www.wingluke.org/index.htm
This Seattle museum home page has access to a research center that contains links to information in categories such as Asian Pacific American, Chinese American, Filipino American, and Japanese American.

ARAB AMERICANS

Arab American Institute

http://www.aaiusa.org
This site includes news and views and general information regarding Arab Americans. Additionally, the site includes a bibliography for further research.

Araboo—The Arab Guide

http://www.araboo.com
This site, heralded as the "premier Arab World directory," includes news and Web resources for Arab Americans. Students will find this to be an accessible website, with links to the arts, business, society and culture, recreation, travel, and tourism.

Book Links: The Arab World and Arab Americans

http://www.ala.org/booklinksbucket/arabworld.htm
Book Links is designed to connect the library to the classroom. This site offers a bibliography of books designed to help teachers learn about and teach Arab Americans.

National Council of Arab Americans

http://www.arab-american.net
The National Council of Arab Americans was established in 2003 to be a unifying vehicle for Arab Americans across gender, race, religion, national identity, and socioeconomic backgrounds. The website includes information on Arab American culture and history, political analysis on current events concerning Arab Americans, and community news and resources.

PUBLISHERS OF MULTICULTURAL BOOKS AND MATERIALS

Anti-Defamation League Resources

http://www.adl.org
The Anti-Defamation League offers a resource catalog of materials that help teachers and parents teach about communication and respect among diverse groups.

These resources are designed to confront prejudice, hatred, bigotry, and discrimination while teaching the value of diversity and tolerance.

Arte Público Press

http://www.arte.uh.edu
Arte Público specializes in publishing contemporary and recovered literature by Hispanic authors in the United States. It offers general catalogs as well as specific catalogs for such categories as women's/feminist titles, drama, poetry, reference, piñata books for children and young adults, and recovering the U.S. Hispanic literary heritage.

Children's Book Press

http://www.childrensbookpress.org
This is a nonprofit publisher that specializes in bilingual and multicultural literature, publishing stories that reflect "the traditions and cultures of the emerging majority in the U.S." Additionally, the teaching and learning page provides examples of workshops given by the authors and online resources created by teachers to accompany the books.

Intercultural Press

http://www.interculturalpress.com
The Intercultural Press provides books, simulations, videos, and training material about crossing cultures designed for a variety of audiences. The Education and Theory section is of particular interest.

Lee and Low Books

http://www.leeandlow.com
Lee and Low is an independent children's book publisher specializing in multicultural themes with which children of color, as well as all children, can identify. The search engine allows you to search by title, author, illustrator, or subject. There is also a teacher resource center and a book talk link.

The New Press

http://www.thenewpress.com
The New Press is a nonprofit company created as an alternative to large commercial publishers. It is committed to publishing works of educational, cultural, and community value. Its site includes a "tools for teachers" section complete with free teacher guides.

Northland Publishing

http://www.northlandbooks.com
Based in Arizona, Northland Publishing specializes in themes of the West and Native American material. There is a specific section for children's literature, which includes tools for teachers.

South End Press

http://www.southendpress.org
This nonprofit publisher works to provide material to readers who are interested in social change. The goal of South End Press is to print books that encourage critical thinking and constructive action. This site also provides links to magazines, radio shows, and organizations that share the goals of South End Press.

Temple University Press

http://www.temple.edu/tempress/
Temple University Press publishes books in the social sciences and humanities that address social justice issues and produces a specific catalog for ethnic studies. Its website provides links to award winners, best sellers, and series. Many of the books the press publishes are interdisciplinary and can fit into several categories.

VISUAL MEDIA ON RACE, U.S. ETHNIC GROUPS, AND MULTICULTURAL EDUCATION

FOR TEACHERS AND TEACHER EDUCATION

African American Lives. Producer/Distributor: PBS Video. Phone: 800-344-3337. Website: http:www.shopPBS.com/teachers.

Harvard professor Henry Louis Gates uses genealogical and DNA research to trace the racial backgrounds of eight famous African Americans in this DVD that is appropriate for both adult audiences and upper-grade and high school students. It is available in both DVD and VHS. However, because it consists of approximately four hours, teachers will have to use it selectively.

Culture, Difference, and Power (Multimedia CD-ROM for Windows and Macintosh). Author: Christine Sleeter. Publisher: Teachers College Press, NY. Website: www .teacherscollegepress.com.

This innovative and interactive electronic book, designed for future and practicing teachers, contains forty-five original readings by the author, an instructor's manual, and eighty videoclips that feature five classrooms, seven teachers, one school leadership team, five noted theorists, and two artists.

Good Morning Miss Toliver. Producer/Distributor: Foundation for Advancements in Science and Education (FASE), 4801 Wilshire Boulevard, Suite 215, Los Angeles, CA 90010. Website: www.fasenet.org.

In this half-hour videotape, viewers visit the classroom of Kay Toliver, a creative and perceptive teacher in New York City's East Harlem Tech/P.S.72. She teaches engaging math lessons by creating math problems that relate to the East Harlem community.

Mirrors of Privilege: Making Whiteness Visible. Distributor: Teaching for Change. Phone: 800-763-9131. Website: www.teachingforchange.org.

White activists describe stories of how they confronted their personal racism and experienced transformation in this fifty-minute DVD.

Off Track: Classroom Privilege for All. Authors: Michelle Fine, Bernadette Anand, Markie Hancock, Carlton Jordan, & Dana Sherman. Publisher: Teachers College Press, NY. Website: www.teacherscollegepress.com.

Viewers witness students learning in an untracked world literature course in which use of a critical pedagogy of groupwork, collaboration, and serious individualized attention creates an innovative classroom in which all students learn at high levels.

Overcoming Personal Racism: What Can I Do? Distributor: Insight Media, 2162 Broadway, New York, NY 10024. Website: http://www.insight-media.com/IMHome.htm.

The distinguished counselor and educator Derald Wing Sue describes ways in which people can recognize and take steps to overcome personal racism in this sixty-minute DVD.

Rabbit in the Moon: A Documentary Memoir. Producers: Emiko Omori and Chizuko Omori. Distributor: New Day Films, Honokus, NJ. Website: www.newday.com.

This is a powerful presentation of the internment of Japanese Americans that blends a rewriting of history with a description of the erosive effects of the internment on the Japanese American community. The legacy of these effects remains.

Race: The Power of an Illusion. (2003). Distributor: California Newsreel, San Francisco, CA. Website: www.newsreel.org.

A three-part series analyzing an often unasked but extremely important question: What is race? *Episode 1: The Difference Between Us* examines science and race, challenging the commonly held assumption that humans can be divided into groups based on genetics. *Episode 2: The Story We Tell* analyzes the changing meaning of race throughout U.S. history. *Episode 3: The House We Live In* uncovers the consequences of the social construction of race in politics, economics, and society. This series is essential, both for practicing teachers and students.

FOR STUDENTS

Act of War: The Overthrow of the Hawaiian Nation. Distributor: CrossCurrent Media, San Francisco. Website: www.naatanet.org.

The struggle of Native Hawaiians to reclaim their land and the historical events that led to their current situation are described in this one-hour program.

The American Story. Producer/Distributor: Anti-Defamation League, New York. Website: www.adl.org.

The lives of twelve families from different ethnic groups are profiled in this series. Titles in the series include families from these U.S. ethnic groups: Puerto Rican, Japanese, Polish, Mexican, Native American, Jewish, Greek, and Italian. This series is excellent for involving students in discussion. The range of ethnic groups covered in the series is another strong characteristic. Each video presentation is twenty-three minutes, which makes the set excellent for teaching purposes.

Arab Americans. Distributor: AWAIR (Arab World and Islamic Resources), P.O. Box 174, Abiquiu, NM 87510. Fax: 505-68504533. E-mail: awair@igc.org. Website: http://www .awaironline.org.

Based on the Chelsea House series "People of North America," this thirty-minute video, primarily geared to upper elementary and secondary school students, examines Arab American immigration against the larger backdrop of the entire American immigration story.

Becoming Americans. Producers: Ken and Ivory Waterworth Levine. Distributor: New Day Films, Honokus, NJ. Website: www.newday.com.

This documentary film focuses on the Hmong refugees from Laos. It is a powerful presentation that is excellent for stimulating discussion. Available in both thirty-minute and sixty-minute versions.

Before Columbus: Native Americans Tell Their Own Story. Producer/Distributor: Films for the Humanities and Sciences, Princeton, NJ. Website: www.films.com.

Each of the five parts of this program consists of twenty-eight minutes. Titles in the series are *Invasion; The Right to Their Own Land; Temples into Churches; Teaching Indians to Be White; Rebellion;* and *The Indian Experience in the 20th Century.*

Benaat Chicago (Daughters of Chicago): Growing Up Arab and Female in Chicago. (1996). Distributor: American Friends Service Committee, 637 S. Dearborn, Chicago, IL 60605. Phone: 312-427-2533. Fax: 312-427-4171. E-mail: jbing-canar@afsc.org. Website: www.afsc.org.

Produced by Jennifer Bing and Mary Zerkel of the Chicago Office of the American Friends Service Committee and the Arab-American Community Center of Chicago, this thirty-minute video documents the lives of Arab American teenagers growing up on Chicago's southwest side. It depicts the source of pride of Arab American young women and addresses issues of stereotypes and racism against Arabs.

Breaking the Silence: Asian American Students Speak Out. Distributor: Teaching for Change. Phone: 800-763-9131. Website: www.teachingforchange.org.

Cambodian and Tibetan heritage students speak about the educational challenges they experience in this forty-one-minute DVD.

Brothers and Others: The Impact of September 11 on Muslims, Arab, and South Asians. Producer: Baraka Productions, New York. Distributor: Arab Film Distributors, 4022 Stone Way North, Seattle, WA 98103. Phone: 206-547-4687. Fax: 206-547-6455. E-mail: info@arabfilm.com. Website: www.arabfilm.com.

Directed by Nicholas Rossier, this sixty-minute video presents a powerful documentary about the "hidden victims of 9/11—the thousands detained without trial." It follows several immigrant and American families struggling in a climate of suspicion and addresses the need to balance security with civil liberties and the rule of law.

Chicana. Distributor: Women Make Movies, New York. Website: www.wmm.com.

The important roles and contributions of Mexican American women are described in this twenty-three-minute videotape.

Collecting Stories from Exile: Chicago Palestinians Remember 1948. (1999). Distributor: American Friends Service Committee, 637 S. Dearborn, Chicago, IL 60605. Phone: 312-427-2533. Fax: 312-427-4171. E-mail: jbing-canar@afsc.org. Website: www.afsc.org.

Produced by the Chicago Office of the American Friends Service Committee and the Arab-American Action Network of Chicago, this twenty-eight-minute oral history project documents the lives of Chicago Palestinians who survived the 1948 Arab-Israeli War.

Different and the Same. Producer/Distributor: Family Communications, Pittsburgh, PA. Website: www.misterrogers.org.

This series of videotapes is designed to teach children in grades 1 through 3 about racial and ethnic differences and to develop respect for differences. The nine-program segments are contained within three videotapes. Puppets are central characters in these effective and useful videotapes for use with young children. Program segment titles include *Sticks and Stones, Proud to Be Me,* and *I Am American, Too.*

Dollar a Day, Ten Cents a Dance: A Historic Portrait of Filipino Farmworkers in America. Distributor: CrossCurrent Media, San Francisco. Website: www.naatanet.org.
This thirty-minute program describes the Filipino immigrants who settled in the United States in the 1920s and 1930s. Their community consisted primarily of men.

Eyes on the Prize: America's Civil Rights Years. Series I and II. Producer: PBS Video. Distributor: Social Studies School Service, Culver City, CA. Website: www.socialstudies.com.
This is an outstanding series of fifty-seven-minute color videotapes that cover the civil rights movement in depth from 1954 through the mid 1980s. Part I (six videotapes) covers the period from 1954 to 1965. Part II (eight videotapes) covers the period from 1965 through the mid 1980s. Every school system, as well as college and university media center, should purchase this outstanding series.

A History of Hispanic Achievement in America. Producer/Distributor: PBS Video. Phone: 800-344-3337. Website: http:www.shopPBS.com/teachers.
This four-hour DVD tells the story of the contributions that Hispanics have made to the development of the United States in various areas, including civil rights, politics, education, entertainment, and business.

In Black and White: Conversations with African American Writers. Producer: California Newsreel, San Francisco. Website: www.newsreel.org.
This set of six videotapes (151 minutes total) features six African American authors: Charles Johnson, Gloria Naylor, Toni Morrison, Alice Walker, August Wilson, and John Wideman.

In No One's Shadow: Filipinos in America. Distributor: CrossCurrent Media, San Francisco. Website: www.naatanet.org.
This twenty-eight-minute videotape describes the historical saga of Filipinos in the United States, with emphasis on the twentieth century.

In the White Man's Image. Distributor: PBS Video, Arlington, VA. Website: www.pbs.org.
The Carlisle School for Indian Students, founded in the early part of this century, is profiled in this fifty-eight-minute videotape.

Japanese American Women: A Sense of Place. Distributor: Women Make Movies, New York. Website: www.wmm.com.
In this twenty-seven-minute videotape, Japanese American women describe the conflict of cultures and identity they experience in America.

The Language of Life. Distributor: AWAIR (Arab World and Islamic Resources), P.O. Box 174, Abiquiu, NM 87510. Fax: 505-68504533. E-mail: awair@igc.org. Website: http://www .awaironline.org.
This fifty-minute videotape features Bill Moyers and Arab American poet Naomi Shihab Nye. She reads her poetry and discusses her family's Palestinian past and her work in the United States today. The African American poet Sekou Sundiata is also included in this video, which is appropriate for seventh grade to adult.

The Latino Family. Distributor: Films for the Humanities and Sciences, Princeton, NJ. Website: www.films.com.
Changes in the traditional Mexican American family are revealed by depicting three generations of one family.

Mighty Times: The Children's March. Producer/Distributor: Southern Poverty Law Center, 400 Washington Avenue, Montgomery, AL 36104. Website: http://www.tolerance.org/ index.jsp.
This DVD tells the story of a youth group in Birmingham, Alabama, who reignited the

civil rights movement in 1963 when they stood up against fire hoses and police dogs to protest segregation and other forms of discrimination. Their bravery moved the nation and played a role in the introduction and passage of the Civil Rights Act of 1964.

More Than Bows and Arrows. Producer/Distributor: Camera One, Seattle, WA. Website: www.camera-one.com.

The contributions that Native Americans have made to American culture are highlighted in this fifty-three-minute program.

Multicultural Peoples of North America. Producer: Library Video. Distributor: Social Studies School Service, Culver City, CA. Website: www.socialstudies.com.

This series of fifteen thirty-minute videotapes is based on the Chelsea House series of books The Peoples of North America. Titles are *African Americans, The Amish, Arab Americans, Central Americans, Chinese Americans, German Americans, Greek Americans, Irish Americans, Italian Americans, Japanese Americans, Jewish Americans, Korean Americans, Mexican Americans, Polish Americans,* and *Puerto Ricans.* Each videotape is thirty minutes long.

A Place at the Table: Struggles for Equality in America. Producer/Distributor: Teaching Tolerance, 400 Washington Avenue, Montgomery, AL 36104. Website: http://www .tolerance.org/index.jsp.

Eight students from different ethnic and gender groups share their perspectives on the historical and ongoing struggles their groups have experienced as they sought freedom and equality. Each student and group wants to realize the American dream and to have a place at the table.

Power, Politics, and Latinos. Producer: National Latin Communication Center, Los Angeles. Distributor: PBS Video, Alexandria, VA. Website: www.pbs.org.

The political participation of Latinos is the subject of this fifty-six-minute program, with emphasis on the 1992 election.

Preserving the Past to Ensure the Future. Distributor: Anti-Defamation League, New York. Website: www.adl.org.

This powerful fifteen-minute video deals with the 1.5 million children who were victims of the Holocaust.

Refugee Like Me. Distributor: Insight Media, 2162 Broadway, New York, NY 10024. Website: http://www.insight-media.com/IMHome.htm.

In this fifty-minute DVD, a group of refugees describe why they risked leaving their home nations to settle in faraway lands.

The Road to Freedom. Distributor: California Newsreel, San Francisco. Website: www .newsreel.org.

In this fifty-eight-minute videotape, the historical events that culminated in the landmark *Brown* v. *Board of Education* Supreme Court decision are described.

Roll of Thunder, Hear My Cry. Distributor: Macmillan/McGraw-Hill School Publishing, New York. Website: www.mmhschool.com.

This is a forty-six-minute dramatization of the powerful novel by Mildred Taylor, which chronicles events in the life of the Logan family, who lived in Mississippi in the 1930s.

Sacred Spirit: The Lakota Sioux, Past and Present. Distributor: Films for the Humanities and Sciences, Princeton, NJ. Website: www.films.com.

Oglala Lakota Sioux living on and off the Pine Ridge reservation share their perspectives on the history and present-day realities of their people.

The Shadow of Hate: A History of Intolerance in America. Producer/Distributor: Teaching Tolerance, Montgomery, AL. Website: www.tolerance.org/index.jsp.

This forty-minute program uses historical footage, photographs, and voices of individuals who participated in historical events to depict the intolerance directed against various ethnic, cultural, and minority groups in American society. This teaching package consists of the video, a 128-page text, *Us and Them,* and a teacher's guide.

Slaying the Dragon. Producer: CrossCurrent Media, San Francisco. Website: www.naatanet .org.

Hollywood and television images of Asian American women are described in this sixty-minute videotape.

Tales from Arab Detroit. (1995). Producer: Joan Mandell. Distributor: New Day Films, Hohokus, NJ. Website: www.newday.com.

In the context of a visit to Detroit by a famous old Egyptian singer and storyteller, this forty-five-minute video asks three generations of Arab Americans, both immigrants and their American-born children, the question: What does it mean to be Arab in America in these times? The video shows clearly the importance of the family in the lives and consciousness of Arab Americans.

Teens Talk Race Relations. Distributor: Anti-Defamation League, New York. Website: www .adl.org.

Several aspects of race relations are presented through dramatic situations in this twenty-five-minute videotape.

Them and Us: Cultural Awareness. Distributor: Insight Media, 2162 Broadway, New York, NY 10024. Website: http://www.insight-media.com/IMHome.htm.

This twenty-five-minute DVD focuses how people develop unwarranted assumptions about those outside their groups and then construct and perpetuate stereotypes about them.

A Time for Justice: America's Civil Rights Movement. Producer/Distributor: Teaching Tolerance, Montgomery, AL. Website: www.tolerance.org/index.jsp.

This thirty-eight-minute program describes the civil rights movement with the use of actual historical footage and the voices of people who participated in it. This teaching package consists of the videotape, a book, *Free at Last,* and a teacher's guide.

Unfinished Business: The Japanese Internment Cases. Distributor: CrossCurrent Media, San Francisco. Website: www.naatanet.org.

The stories of three Japanese American men who resisted the military orders to be interned are told in this sixty-minute videotape.

Voices in Exile: The L.A. Eight. (1989). Distributor: New Day Films, 22D Hollywood Avenue, Hohokus, NJ 07423. Phone: 888-367-9154. Fax: 201-652-1973. E-mail:tncndy@aol.com. Website: www.newday.com.

In this thirty-minute video, Joan Mandell and Laura Hayes chronicle the first year of the court case known as the L.A. Eight. It includes interviews with the FBI and Immigration and Naturalization Service officials as well as with the eight accused and their counsel. The voice-over is by Casey Kasem, the radio disc jockey.

A Weave of Time: The Story of a Navajo Family, 1838–1986. Distributor: Direct Cinema, Los Angeles. Website: www.directcinema.com.

This sixty-minute documentary describes four generations of a Navajo family.

THE CARTER G. WOODSON
AWARD BOOKS

The Carter G. Woodson Award is presented each year by the National Council for the Social Studies in honor of the distinguished African American historian and educator who wrote books for adults and young people, founded and edited the *Journal of Negro History,* and contributed in many significant ways to interracial understanding. The award is designed to "encourage the writing, publishing, and dissemination of outstanding social science books for young readers that treat topics related to ethnic minorities and race relations sensitively and accurately."

A complete list of the Carter G. Woodson Book Award winners for the years 1974 to 2006 is available online at http://www.socialstudies.org/awards/woodson//. In this appendix, we include the recipients of the Woodson Award for 2006, 2005, and 2004.

2006

Elementary-Level Award Winner

Let Them Play by Margot Theis Raven, illustrated by Chris Ellison (Sleeping Bear Press)

Elementary-Level Honor Book

Roberto Clemente: Pride of the Pittsburgh Pirates by Jonah Winter, illustrated by Raul Colon (Atheneum Books for Young Readers)

Middle-Level Award Winner

Cesar Chavez: A Voice for Farmworkers by Barbara Cruz (Enslow Publishers)

Middle-Level Honor Book

Roberto Clemente: Baseball's Humanitarian Hero by Heron Marquez (Carolrhoda Books)

Secondary-Level Award Winner

No Easy Answers: Bayard Rustin and the Civil Rights Movement by Calvin Craig Miller (Morgan Reynolds Publishing)

Secondary-Level Honor Book

Uh Huh! The Story of Ray Charles by John Duggleby (Morgan Reynolds Publishing)

2005

Elementary-Level Award Winner

Jim Thorpe's Bright Path by Joseph Bruchac, illustrated by S. D. Nelson (Lee and Low Books)

Elementary-Level Honor Book

Alec's Primer by Mildred Pitts Walter, illustrated by Larry Johnson (Vermont Folklife Center)

Middle-Level Award Winner

The Voice That Challenged a Nation: Marian Anderson and the Struggle for Equal Rights by Russell Freedman (Clarion Books)

Middle-Level Honor Book

The Power of One: Daisy Bates and the Little Rock Nine by Judith Bloom Fradin and Dennis Brindell Fradin (Clarion Books)

Secondary-Level Award Winner

The Civil Rights Act of 1964 edited by Robert H. Mayer (Greenhaven Press, an imprint of Thomson Gale)

Secondary-Level Honor Book

Alvin Ailey: Celebrating African-American Culture in Dance by Barbara C. Cruz (Enslow Publishers)

2004

Elementary-Level Award Winner

Sacagawea by Louise Erdrich, illustrated by Julie Buffalohead (Carolrhoda Books)

Elementary-Level Honor Book

Harvesting Hope: The Story of Cesar Chavez by Kathleen Krull, illustrated by Yuyi Morales (Harcourt)

Middle-Level Award Winner

In America's Shadow by Kimberly Komatsu and Kaleigh Komatsu, foreword by Kevin Starr, essay by Mitchell T. Maki (Thomas George Books)

Middle-Level Honor Book

Sojourner Truth: From Slave to Activist for Freedom by Mary G. Butler (Rosen Publishing Group)

Secondary-Level Award Winner

Early Black Reformers by James Tackach (Greenhaven Press)

Secondary-Level Honor Book

Gwendolyn Brooks: Poet from Chicago by Martha E. Rhynes (Morgan Reynolds Publishing)

TWENTY CLASSIC AND LANDMARK BOOKS IN ETHNIC LITERATURE

Adamic, L. (1932). *Laughing in the Jungle: The Autobiography of an Immigrant in America.* New York: Harper and Brothers. (Slavic American)

Allport, G. (1954). *The Nature of Prejudice.* Reading, MA: Addison-Wesley.

Anaya, R. A. (1972). *Bless Me, Ultima.* Berkeley, CA: Tonatiuh International. (Mexican American)

Banks, J. A., & Banks, C. A. M. (Eds.). (2004). *Handbook of Research on Multicultural Education* (2nd ed.). San Francisco: Jossey-Bass/Wiley.

Bulosan, C. (1973). *America Is in the Heart.* Seattle: University of Washington Press. (Filipino American)

Ellison, R. (1952). *Invisible Man.* New York: New American Library. (African American)

Galarza, E. (1971). *Barrio Boy.* Notre Dame, IN: University of Notre Dame Press. (Mexican American)

Haley, A. (1976). *Roots: The Saga of an American Family.* Garden City, NY: Doubleday. (African American)

Handlin, O. (1951). *The Uprooted: The Epic Story of the Great Migrations That Made the American People.* New York: Grosset and Dunlap. (European American)

Howe, I. (1976). *World of Our Fathers: The Journey of the Jews to America and the Life They Found and Made.* New York: Simon and Schuster. (Jewish American)

Kingston, M. H. (1976). *The Woman Warrior: Memories of a Girlhood among Ghosts.* New York: Vintage. (Chinese American)

Momaday, N. S. (1966). *House Made of Dawn.* New York: Signet. (American Indian)

Morrison, T. (1987). *Beloved: A Novel.* New York: Knopf. (African American)

Novak, M. (1973). *The Rise of the Unmeltable Ethnics.* New York: Macmillan. (European American)

Okada, J. (1976). *No-No Boy.* San Francisco: Combined Asian American Resources Project. (Japanese American)

Rolvaag, O. E. (1927). *Giants in the Earth: A Saga of the Prairie.* New York: Harper and Row. (Norwegian American)

Takaki, R. (1989). *Strangers from a Different Shore: A History of Asian Americans.* Boston: Little, Brown. (Asian American)

Takaki, R. (1993). *A Different Mirror: A History of Multicultural America.* Boston: Little, Brown.

Wong, J. S. (1945). *Fifth Chinese Daughter.* New York: Harper and Row. (Chinese American)

Wright, R. (1966). *Black Boy: A Record of Childhood and Youth.* New York: Harper and Row. (African American)

Index

Note: Information presented in tables and figures is denoted by t and f, respectively.